THE
WILLARD J. GRAHAM SERIES
IN ACCOUNTING

BOOKS IN
THE WILLARD J. GRAHAM SERIES IN ACCOUNTING

CONSULTING EDITOR ROBERT N. ANTHONY *Harvard University*

ANDERSON & SCHMIDT *Practical Controllership* rev. ed.
ANTHONY *Management Accounting: Text and Cases* 4th ed.
ANTHONY *Management Accounting Principles* rev. ed.
BARR & GRINAKER *Short Audit Case* rev. ed.
FREMGEN *Accounting for Managerial Analysis* rev. ed.
GORDON & SHILLINGLAW *Accounting: A Management Approach* 4th ed.
GRIFFIN, WILLIAMS, & LARSON *Advanced Accounting* rev. ed.
GRINAKER & BARR *Audit Practice Case*
GRINAKER & BARR *Auditing: The Examination of Financial Statements*
HAWKINS *Corporate Financial Reporting: Text and Cases*
HENDRIKSEN *Accounting Theory* rev. ed.
HOLMES, MAYNARD, EDWARDS, & MEIER *Elementary Accounting* 3d ed.
HOLMES & OVERMYER *Auditing: Principles and Procedure* 7th ed.
HOLMES & OVERMYER *Basic Auditing Principles* 4th ed.
KENNEDY & McMULLEN *Financial Statements: Form, Analysis, and Interpretation* 5th ed.
LADD *Contemporary Corporate Accounting and the Public*
MAURIELLO *The Irwin Federal Income Tax Course: A Comprehensive Text*
MEIGS & LARSEN *Principles of Auditing* 4th ed.
MIKESELL & HAY *Governmental Accounting* 4th ed.
MOORE & STETTLER *Accounting Systems for Management Control*
MURPHY *Advanced Public Accounting Practice*
MURPHY *Auditing and Theory: A CPA Review*
NEUNER & FRUMER *Cost Accounting: Principles and Practice* 7th ed.
NIELSEN *Cases in Auditing*
O'NEIL, FARWELL, & BOYD *Quantitative Controls for Business: An Introduction*
PATON *Corporate Profits*
PYLE & WHITE *Fundamental Accounting Principles* 6th ed.
SCHAFER *Elements of Income Tax—Individual*
SCHRADER, MALCOLM, & WILLINGHAM *Financial Accounting: An Input/Output Approach*
SHILLINGLAW *Cost Accounting: Analysis and Control* 3d ed.
SPILLER *Financial Accounting: Basic Concepts* rev. ed.
STAUBUS *Activity Costing and Input-Output Accounting*
VATTER *Accounting Measurements for Financial Reports*
WELSCH, ZLATKOVICH, & WHITE *Intermediate Accounting* 3d ed.
WILLIAMS & GRIFFIN *Management Information: A Quantitative Accent*

Accounting

A MANAGEMENT APPROACH

Accounting

A MANAGEMENT APPROACH

MYRON J. GORDON, Ph.D.
Professor of Business Administration
University of Rochester

GORDON SHILLINGLAW, Ph.D.
Professor of Accounting
Graduate School of Business
Columbia University
                    and
IMEDE Management Development Institute
Lausanne, Switzerland

Fourth Edition
1969

Richard D. Irwin, Inc., Homewood, Illinois
Irwin-Dorsey Limited, Georgetown, Ontario

Fourth Edition

First Printing, February, 1969
Second Printing, August, 1969
Third Printing, March, 1970
Fourth Printing, August, 1970
Fifth Printing, February, 1971
Sixth Printing, November, 1971
Seventh Printing, June, 1972

Library of Congress Catalog Card No. 68–30845
Printed in the United States of America

To
Betty and Barbara

PREFACE

THIS EDITION of *Accounting: A Management Approach,* like its predecessors, has been written for investors, managers, and others who want to understand and use the information that accounting provides on the affairs of a business enterprise. Our emphasis is on the *interpretation* of accounting figures rather than on the *process* of data accumulation and statement preparation, because we believe that this is the only way that the introductory accounting course should be taught. For those who will go no farther in the study of accounting than this introduction, knowledge of the accounting process is unimportant except insofar as it is necessary to an appreciation of the meaning of accounting figures. For the future accountant, an initial emphasis on process at the expense of meaning is likely to lend an aura of sanctity to existing methods that will inhibit the later search for meaning. For this reason we offer this book, without apology, as an appropriate introduction to accounting for the future accountant as well as for others.

Although some chapters have been completely rewritten and most of the others have been changed materially, the substantive content of this edition is basically the same as that of the third edition. Successful innovation does not come easily, and change for the sake of change has not been our objective. Except for some necessary updating of factual data, we have focused our efforts on achieving a more effective organization of the material and greater clarity of expression. We have given particular attention to the practice problems at the end of each chapter, discarding some, adding others, and revising many. For those many instructors who lean toward the case method of teaching, a number of cases or problems in case form have been provided.

The book is divided into three parts. Part I establishes the basic concepts and structure of accounting and provides an introduction to the mechanics of double-entry bookkeeping. The most important aspects of this material are contained in Chapters 2, 3, 4, and 5, which explain how the accountant uses the accounting process to derive financial statements from the data available to him. The next two chapters deal primarily with techniques of statement preparation and data processing, and are substantially the same as in the third edition. Part I then closes with a new chapter on the elements of financial statement analysis, designed to provide an initial understanding of how companywide financial statements are used. We regard this as a transitional chapter, a point of reference to return to from time to time during the study of the material in Part II.

Part II remains the heart of the book. As before, it is concerned primarily with the important issues in income determination, asset measurement, and the recognition of liabilities. One of the innovations of the third edition was to begin this part with an examination of the concept of economic value and its relationship to income measurement. The response to this has been overwhelmingly favorable and we have repeated it in this edition.

The remaining chapters of Part II are devoted to a study of the problems encountered by the accountant in his effort to apply the basic accounting model of Part I to the circumstances of the real world. In this, we have not taken the easy route, avoiding controversial issues by limiting ourselves to a statement of a set of rules that are or should be observed in practice. Instead, we have tried to present alternative solutions to measurement problems, together with their supporting arguments and some indication of their probable effects on the meaning of the information provided by the firm's financial statements. Whenever appropriate, we cite accepted practice and authoritative rulings, along with a brief summary of our evaluation of these positions.

Some may be surprised to find in Part II material that is often reserved for intermediate or advanced courses. This reflects our belief that no student should complete an introductory course in accounting unprepared to read the financial statements published by corporations. This has forced us to take up the accounting and economics of such topics as declining-charge depreciation, deferred income taxes, pension plans, stock options, and pooling of interests. While the treatment of these topics is not as thorough as we might like and does not absolve the future accountant from the need for further study, it does, we hope, assure that the user of financial statements will not find the terminology and accounting practices used in published statements completely foreign. In the interest of simplification, however, the discussion of dollar value LIFO and certain other topics in asset measurement has been curtailed from that of the previous edition. Similarly, the extensive treatment of new topics related to the equity side of the balance sheet which was introduced in the last edition has been shortened but not eliminated.

Part III has been reorganized significantly. The introductory chapter on managerial accounting and the chapter on product costing have been condensed into a single chapter. The chapter on the measurement and control of overhead has been simplified and reduced in scope to deal only with the former topic. These introductory chapters are followed by Chapter 19, dealing with the application of accounting data to pricing and other alternative choice problems, and Chapter 20, on capital investment decisions. The final three chapters of Part III are devoted to an introduction to internal systems of management control and periodic financial planning. Chapters 21 and 22 deal with the use of standard costs and flexible budgets in the control of factory costs. Chapter 23 is a new chapter, examining the use of such concepts as profit contribution and return on investment in comprehensive planning and reporting systems.

This book may be used in a one-semester, two-quarter, or one-year introductory course, or as the basic text in a liberal arts college course in accounting. It can also be used, as previous editions have been, in executive development programs of various lengths. If dealt with thoroughly, Parts I and II provide ample material for a full semester or even longer. Those instructors who want to take up some of the chapters from Part III in a one-semester course, however, will find it possible to pass over Chapters 6, 7, and 8 without serious loss of continuity. They will also find that many of the chapters in Part II, particularly Chapters 13, 14, and 15, begin with fundamental and comparatively simple topics and progress to more difficult material. To save time, the final sections of these chapters can be treated less thoroughly or passed over entirely without loss of continuity. Finally, if the length of the course prevents complete coverage of Part III, Chapters 20, 22, and 23 can be omitted without sacrificing the basic objective of providing the student with a management-oriented introduction to cost accounting.

The inclusion of an appendix containing solutions to selected practice problems from most of the chapters has proven to be highly useful and is retained in this edition. The purpose is twofold: (1) to permit the student to test his comprehension of the text material before starting on the problems assigned by the instructor; and (2) to provide the student with material that he can use independently to increase his facility in problem solving. We have not included solutions to give the student a model for solving every problem in the book, however, because we feel that the experience of coping with unfamiliar problem formats is more conducive to learning than routine memorization of a standardized solution format.

Much of whatever merit this book may have can be attributed to those who have taught us, criticized our work, and worked with us over the years. Our foremost intellectual debt is to coauthors of previous editions—Ronald H. Robnett, John Beckett, and particularly Thomas M. Hill—to the late Willard Graham, formerly the consulting editor of the Irwin Series in Accounting, and to Frank P. Smith, now with the public accounting firm of Lybrand, Ross Bros. & Montgomery. Numerous colleagues at Columbia, M.I.T., Rochester and other institutions have helped us materially with their comments. The list is not exhausted by mentioning George Benston, John Burton, William Cooper, Dennis Gordon, Philip Meyers, Russell Taussig, Zenon Zannetos, and Stephen Zeff. The critical comments of Carl Bastable and Carl Nelson have been particularly helpful. In addition, Charles Smith has materially reduced the number of errors in the problems and solutions. It goes without saying, however, that any defects in the final product are ours, not theirs.

This edition was written with one author in Rochester, New York, and the other in Lausanne, Switzerland. Communication between us might well have broken down if it were not for the diligence and extraordinary competence of Jean Dinse.

Finally, we should like to express our gratitude to our colleagues for their permission to use or adapt a number of their pet problems, and to the IMEDE management development institute in Lausanne, Switzerland, for its permission to reproduce a number of cases from its collection. Whether the figures are stated in dollars, in lire, or in francs, the accounting problems are basically the same, and we'd like to think that the presence of these cases in this edition will make this a little more obvious.

January, 1969   Myron J. Gordon
                                                  Gordon Shillinglaw

TABLE OF CONTENTS

xiii

PART II. MEASUREMENT OF CAPITAL AND INCOME

APPENDIXES

INDEX

Part I

Accounting Concepts and Methods

Chapter 1

ACCOUNTING AND
BUSINESS ENTERPRISE

ACCOUNTING MAY BE VIEWED broadly as a systematic means of writing the economic history of an organization. Its purpose is to provide information that can be drawn upon by those responsible for decisions affecting the organization's future. This history is written mostly in quantitative terms. It consists partly of files of data, partly of reports summarizing various portions of these data, and partly of the plans established by management to guide its operations.

This view of accounting applies to all kinds of organizations, including governments, fraternal societies, and educational institutions, but our main focus will be on privately owned business enterprises. The management of a business enterprise is the principal consumer of accounting information relating to that enterprise, but it is not the sole consumer. Investors, suppliers, government, labor unions, and others also make extensive use of information drawn from the accounts of business firms. The purpose of this chapter is to examine the background against which today's business accounting takes place.

THE DEVELOPMENT OF ACCOUNTING

Modern business accounting did not develop overnight, the product of a sudden flash of genius to meet a long-felt need. It is the result of a long and gradual process of evolution. This evolutionary process was most rapid during two periods which saw dramatic changes in the nature of the business enterprise: (1) the Renaissance, and (2) the emergence of the business corporation. The influences of the events of both of these periods deserve a brief review.

Influence of the Renaissance

The dominant instrument of economic activity during the middle ages was the feudal manor. For the feudal lord, war and conquest were the means of accumulating productive wealth, which consisted largely of land and serfs. The primary use of the output of the feudal manor was consumption—that the productivity of the manor might be increased and used to expand the wealth of the manor was hardly recognized. The major concerns of the feudal lord were military power, status, and ostentatious consumption. The economic management of the manor was left to subordinates, and its operation was routine, tradition-bound, and almost static.

For the medieval merchant, by comparison, wealth was an instrument for the accumulation of wealth. He engaged in a great variety of transactions, the nature and terms of which changed from one period to the next. All possible ventures were considered, the only criteria in deciding whether to undertake a particular venture being the possible profit it would bring and the degree of risk it would entail. Credit was not an instrument for living beyond one's means or a condition for surviving a crisis, an evil that might ultimately destroy the organization. For the merchant, obtaining and extending credit were useful means of accumulating wealth.[1]

The embryonic accounting systems of the Renaissance served primarily as a means of organizing the merchants' detailed records of such things as the amounts owed by and to various persons, the payment and collection of bills, and the nature, quality, location, and cost of merchandise. It was in another sense, however, that the new systems made their greatest contribution. They were used to yield a set of reports or *financial statements* which told the merchant how much he had invested in his various enterprises and how much profit or loss these enterprises had realized. Thus the accounting system tied in very well with the new system of economic organization in which profit was the goal and capital the means to a profit.[2]

The accounting systems that were developed during this period were based on a new method of record keeping known as double-entry bookkeeping. The fundamental elements of this bookkeeping

---

[1] See R. H. Tawney, *Religion and the Rise of Capitalism* (New York: Harcourt, Brace & World, 1926); and Robert L. Heilbroner, *The Making of Economic Society* (New York: Prentice-Hall, Inc., 1962).

[2] Some economic historians have assigned a great deal of importance to the development of bookkeeping and financial statements as an instrument in the rise of capitalism. For instance, Werner Sombart wrote, "One can scarcely conceive of capitalism without double-entry bookkeeping: they are related as are form and content. It is difficult to decide, however, whether in double-entry bookkeeping capitalism provided itself with a tool to make it more effective, or whether capitalism derives from the 'spirit' of double-entry bookkeeping." W. Sombart, "Der Moderne Kapitalismus," as quoted in A. C. Littleton and B. S. Yamey, *Studies in the History of Accounting* (Homewood, Ill.: Richard D. Irwin, Inc.. 1956), p. 4.

method were developed by the merchants of Genoa, Venice, and the other Italian trading cities during the 13th and 14th centuries.[3] The first textbook on the subject was written by Luca Pacioli in 1494 as part of a treatise on mathematics. The advent of printing as a means of disseminating information and the rise of business enterprises elsewhere in Europe led to the further development of double-entry bookkeeping and popularization of its use during the next two centuries.

Accounting and bookkeeping are two separate topics, as we shall see, and today's business accounting systems could conceivably be based on bookkeeping methods other than the double-entry method. Double-entry bookkeeping has proven so useful, however, that only the smallest firms fail to use it, and we shall describe its essentials in the next two chapters.

Influence of the Corporation

The modern business firm is a far cry from the merchant firms of the Renaissance. For one thing, most business today is conducted by corporations rather than by one-man firms ("individual proprietorships") or partnerships. The rapid spread of the corporation in the United States in the period between the Civil War and World War I was accompanied and made possible by a vast growth in the number of persons with ownership interests in large-scale enterprise. Most of these stockholders had no direct knowledge of the affairs of the corporations they owned, and had no way of obtaining information except through the companies' periodic financial statements. Similarly, the London bankers who arranged long-term loans to finance the growth of American railroads and other enterprises had to rely on these financial statements for information on the apparent safety of the loans they were buying, holding, and recommending to their clients.

The accountant, therefore, found himself with the responsibility of reporting not only to management but also to a large anonymous public, for whom his reports were a primary source of information on the corporation. This led to a dichotomy that was then relatively new to accounting but is now well established, the dichotomy between *enterprise accounting* and *managerial accounting*. The modern business accounting system now has to provide two main kinds of economic information: (1) information relating to the business as a

---

[3] R. deRoover, "The Development of Accounting Prior to Luca Pacioli According to the Account Books of Medieval Merchants," in Littleton and Yamey, *op. cit.*

whole, mainly intended for the use of government bodies, investors, and others outside the company's management group; and (2) information concerning individual portions or segments of the business and their relationship to the whole, mainly directed to the firm's managers. The former of these is the domain of enterprise accounting or *financial accounting*, as it is more commonly called. The business segment, in contrast, is the primary focus of *managerial accounting*.

ENTERPRISE ACCOUNTING

Enterprise accounting was the first to feel the impact of the growth of the corporation and the separation of ownership and control. This impact took two forms: (1) the development of a consistent set of accounting principles; and (2) the establishment of a strong independent accounting profession. This brief introduction to enterprise accounting will focus on three questions:

1. The nature of accounting principles.
2. The role of the public accountant.
3. The influence of government.

The Nature of Accounting Principles

Although many accounting data are generated routinely once the system has been established, it is not always obvious what the facts are or how they should be reflected in the financial statements. Contrary to popular belief, the amounts shown in accounting reports are not obtained by adding columns of numbers that are self-evident to anyone with a modicum of training. Like any other type of history, the transactions of a firm are subject to conflicting interpretations.

For example, assume that on January 1 a firm acquired 100,000 pounds of copper at a cost of 30 cents a pound. By February 1, the price of copper has gone up to 40 cents a pound. Has the company made a profit of $10,000 during January? Should the inventory of copper be reported to the public at $30,000 or $40,000? If the copper is sold in February for $45,000, did the firm make a profit of $5,000 or $15,000 in February?

Many of the data appearing in a firm's accounts and financial statements present *measurement problems* like the one just described. Ideally, the accounting profession should have a set of universal measurement principles that would permit every accountant to produce identical measurements from a given set of data. This ideal is unfortunately unattainable. No accountant can give an answer that is both precise and correct to the question of how much of the cost of an automobile is attributable to each mile it is driven. This requires the exercise of judgment within the limits imposed by general accounting principles.

It would be premature at this point to try to spell out the principles that enterprise accounting must follow. It would be equally premature for us to raise questions as to whether some of these principles should be changed or dropped or new ones added. We shall come back to both of these questions in later chapters. Broadly stated, however, the principal considerations governing the form and content of financial statements designed for public consumption have been: (1) verifiability, (2) objectivity, (3) consistency from period to period, and (4) comparability between firms.

Verifiability has been defined as "that attribute of information which allows qualified individuals working independently of one another to develop essentially similar measures or conclusions from an examination of the same evidence, data, or records."[4] *Objectivity*, on the other hand, means freedom from bias; while *consistency* requires the use of the same measurement principles, year after year.

The importance of verifiability, objectivity, and consistency stems from the previously noted requirement for reliable information. In representing investor interests, the accountant has been understandably concerned with protection against misleading or biased financial statements. Tax auditors, public utility commissions, and other government agents have been similarly motivated, although their definitions of bias are based in part on legislative, judicial, or regulatory rulings. This concern has manifested itself in two ways: first, data not directly traceable to actual historical events have been refused admission, insofar as possible; second, where estimate or judgment has been unavoidable, consistency of method from period to period has been demanded.

Comparability in reports is extremely important to investors since the results of their investment and disinvestment decisions depend heavily on the validity of comparisons between firms. It would be inaccurate to say that the public accountant has been as concerned on

---

[4] American Accounting Association Committee to Prepare a Statement of Basic Accounting Theory, *A Statement of Basic Accounting Theory* (Evanston, Ill.: American Accounting Association, 1966), p. 10. This committee report also suggests that the standard of *relevance* to the users' needs should take precedence over all others. While it is difficult to disagree with this suggestion, what relevance means for enterprise financial statements is more difficult to establish. Further consideration of this point must be deferred to later chapters.

this score as with the other two criteria, but it is indisputable that his efforts to establish universal guiding measurement principles have resulted in a much higher degree of comparability in the United States than would otherwise have prevailed.

The Role of the Public Accountant

Agreement on basic principles would be of no avail if there were no way of assuring that they were followed faithfully in the preparation of corporate financial statements. In other words, no matter how competent and honest are the company accountants who oversee the accounting system and prepare the financial statements, the investor needs an independent representative, deriving his income from not one but many sources and thus not unduly beholden to any one, who will certify that:

1. The figures representing the firm's financial status and performance are complete and are measured on the basis of the agreed-upon measurement principles; and
2. The company has provided adequate safeguards to protect its assets from fraud or embezzlement.

The public accounting profession has developed to meet these needs.[5] The importance of integrity and professional standards of conduct was well stated by one of the great figures in the development of public accounting in this country, George O. May:

The work of the financial accountant involves the assumption of responsibility to persons other than the immediate client in matters which require the exercise of judgment in the selection and application of appropriate rules or principles and the adherence thereto, if need be in the face of opposition from the client. It is clearly of a professional character. It gives the independent accountant that just ground for pride in his work which is essential to the establishment of a profession on a high ethical level.[6]

The importance of the public accountant is evidenced by the fact that practically all corporate bylaws and extended-loan contracts require periodic *audits* of the corporation's accounts by an independent certified public accountant. Auditing has been defined as "an explora-

---

[5] For a history of the development of public accounting in the United States, see James Don Edwards, *History of Public Accounting in the United States* (East Lansing, Mich.: Michigan State University Press, 1960).

[6] George O. May, *Financial Accounting* (New York: The Macmillan Co., 1943), p. 64. Public accountancy exhibits the usual characteristics of a profession in that admission, or "certification," is controlled by experience and examination requirements (in this case established by state laws), and in that accepted standards of professional conduct exist. The United States organization in this field is the American Institute of Certified Public Accountants.

tory, critical review by a public accountant of the underlying internal controls and accounting records of a business enterprise or other economic unit, precedent to the expression by him of an opinion of the propriety of its financial statements."[7]

Thus the public accountant carries out the audit both by comparing the company's measurement methods and procedures with the agreed-upon valuation principles and by testing to see whether the methods have been followed consistently. To make these tests, he must examine and test the company's system of *internal control*, defined as "the plan of organization and all of the coordinate methods and measures adopted within a business to safeguard its assets, check the accuracy and reliability of its accounting data, promote operational efficiency, and encourage adherence to prescribed managerial policies."[8] This review enables him to decide how much reliance he can place on the internal audit procedures and how much he must do himself. The auditor seldom reviews all transactions or counts all assets; instead, he uses partial samples, and the more confidence he has in the internal control system the smaller the sample he feels called upon to take.

Upon completion of the audit, the public accountant issues a letter (known as an *opinion*) which the corporation publishes as part of its financial statements. A typical opinion reads:

> To the Board of Directors and Shareholders
> of_____Corporation
> In our opinion, the accompanying statements present fairly the financial position of_____Corporation at December 31, 19xx, and the results of their operations for the year, in conformity with generally accepted accounting principles applied on a basis consistent with that of the preceding year. Our examination of these statements was made in accordance with generally accepted auditing standards, and accordingly included such tests of the accounting records and such other auditing procedures as we considered neessary in the circumstances.

If the auditor takes exception to any of the accounting or internal control practices followed by the corporation, he will qualify his opinion or refuse to issue one until the condition is corrected.

Another benefit that corporations receive from their auditors is management advice on a wide variety of subjects. The public ac-

---

[7] Eric L. Kohler, *A Dictionary for Accountants* (New York: Prentice-Hall, Inc., 1957), pp. 44-45.

[8] Committee on Auditing Procedure, American Institute of (Certified Public) Accountants, *Internal Control* (New York: AICPA, 1949), p. 6.

countant typically has a good training in business administration, a wide experience gained from auditing many companies in a variety of industries, and a comprehensive knowledge of the company's operations gained through the audit. He therefore can make numerous suggestions on the organization and operation of the company and on questions of financial policy which are profitable to the company. It should not be forgotten, however, that the audit is the auditors' prime function. In protecting the integrity of corporate financial statements, the auditor performs a function that is fundamental to the functioning of a modern capitalistic economy.

The Influence of Government

No introduction to the nature and purpose of accounting would be complete without some reference to the effects of governmental action. These effects have been relatively minor for some firms, all-inclusive in others.

Basically, the influence of government comes from two sources. First, regulatory bodies, such as the Interstate Commerce Commission, the Federal Power Commission, and their state counterparts, have influenced accounting methods and in many cases have completely specified the accounting systems to be used in the industries under their regulations. Various other government agencies, in particular the Securities and Exchange Commission, have been empowered by law to impose special reporting requirements on business firms, and have by this means exercised some influence on accounting method.

The greatest impact, however, has undoubtedly resulted from the levying of taxes upon personal and corporate incomes. By imposing a rigorous reporting requirement in the form of the tax return, income tax law has necessitated in many cases the establishment of formal accounting records where none previously existed. Furthermore, the taxing authorities have relied to a certain extent on the accounting profession to provide consistent, universally applicable definitions of business income, with the consequence that accounting standards have been made more precise than they would have been in the absence of the income tax. In the last analysis, however, if the government is to tax business income, the government must define it, and the definition of business income for tax purposes is probably more rigid than the definitions adopted by the accounting profession, although not necessarily more logical or reasonable.[9]

---

[9] The most influential tax authority from this point of view is of course the federal government. The federal agency responsible for administering the income tax laws is the Internal Revenue Service, a subdivision of the Treasury Department.

Although the fact that a company must treat an item in a certain way for tax purposes does not necessarily mean that it must adopt the same method for public financial reporting, there is a tendency to make these published reports conform to the tax rules. As we shall see, numerous areas exist in which two or more accounting methods appear equally reasonable but yield significantly different net income figures. In such cases, the taxpayer's desire to minimize his tax burden will certainly influence his choice of measurement technique. In some cases, what is actually regarded as an otherwise less desirable method may be employed for this reason. Thus the fact of income taxation can and does become a partial determinant of apparent enterprise performance. As we proceed, however, we shall emphasize those methods that reflect "good accounting," regardless of whether these methods represent the most favorable treatment for tax purposes.

A MANAGEMENT APPROACH TO ACCOUNTING

In all but the very small company, accounting is performed not by public accountants but by full-time employees, working under the direction of the company controller, the chief accounting officer. While the controller and his staff work closely with the firm's public accountants in preparing the financial statements that are destined for external consumption, their primary orientation is to serve management. For this reason, both the accountant and the manager whom he is to serve need to know what accounting can do—in other words, they need to take a *management approach* to accounting.

Accounting's Role in Management Planning and Control

The managerial processes which concern accounting most directly are those which center on *planning* for the future and *controlling* current operations. Accounting's contribution to these processes is the province of *managerial accounting*. An integral part of the company's management information system, managerial accounting serves management in several ways. First, it serves as a vital *source of data* for management planning. The accounts and document files are a repository of a vast quantity of details about the past progress of the enterprise, without which forecasts of the future can scarcely be made.

Second, it provides a cadre of *trained personnel* to assist management in the analysis of alternatives and in the preparation of plans. This analysis is not exclusively or necessarily even predominantly an accounting function, but attempting to plan without at least some participation by knowledgeable accounting personnel is a hazardous undertaking in most cases. In fact, the controller is an active and influential member of the top-management group in many companies, but he becomes so because of his personal qualities and the relevance of his experience. The title of controller does not necessarily carry with it direct control responsibilities except within the accounting organization.

Third, managerial accounting provides a *means of communicating* management plans upward, downward, and outward through the organization. At early stages in planning, this means identifying the feasibility and consistency of the various segments of the plan. At later stages it keeps all parties informed of the plans that have been agreed upon and their roles in these plans.

Fourth, it supplies *feedback reports* for both attention-getting and scorecard-keeping purposes. This is often the most visible contribution of managerial accounting within the firm and perhaps for this reason gets the most attention.

Finally, managerial accounting has a role to play in the *interpretation of results*. Response to feedback data typically requires identification of the likely cause or causes of departures from plan and location of the responsibility for follow-up action. Within certain limits, this too can be an accounting function.

Principles of Management Accounting

The basic accounting records that are used to provide data for external financial reporting are also employed to serve management's information needs. In combining and reporting these data to management, however, the accountant can relax one of the main constraints imposed for public financial reporting, the *verifiability* constraint.

The need for verifiability in external reporting arises because the outsider needs assurance that the accountant is objective. He cannot obtain that assurance by a personal review of the accountant's measurement methods. Therefore, he must insist on a fairly high standard of verifiability. In contrast, management can converse directly with the accountant. Data that are *relevant* to management's purposes, although not adequately verifiable for external reporting, are to be preferred to more verifiable but less relevant data. For example, salesmen's impressions of what customers would have purchased had adequate stocks of merchandise been available are statistics that are rightfully rejected by the accountant for public reporting but may very well be useful to management.

The principle of relevance is thus undoubtedly the first principle of management accounting. This principle also requires that data be *flexible* because different management tasks require different data combinations. The cost that is relevant to a decision to accept one additional order, for example, may be very different from the average cost of handling all orders.

Finally, management accounting requires *timeliness*. Short-term fluctuations are of greater interest to management than to most outside investors. The faster information is received, the faster it can be acted upon. In case of conflict, therefore, this need for speed often overrides the requirement of accuracy that is so important in public accounting. To help him make a decision, a manager may have to choose between waiting two weeks for substantially error-free data or using data immediately available but subject to a 5 percent maximum error. If his decision is not sensitive to the 5 percent error, the manager is likely to sacrifice accuracy for speed.

None of this means that the accountant can ignore the precept of objectivity in management accounting. Bias has no legitimate place anywhere in the accounting structure. Furthermore, the manager, no less than the outsider, needs the protection and assurance afforded by a thoroughgoing system of internal control. Being nearer the source of information, however, the manager is in a better position to gauge quality, and hence is able to make constructive use of data that are not sufficiently verifiable to be accepted by the public accountant.

Management's Interest in Enterprise Accounting

Although management accounting is generally concerned with data and financial statements relating to portions of the enterprise, this does not mean that management has no interest in financial statements prepared for the enterprise as a whole. On the contrary, the basis on which enterprise financial statements are prepared is important to management no less than to the owners of the enterprise or to lenders and other "outsiders." For one thing, the image which the enterprise presents to those outside the management is fashioned in large part by the financial statements. The company's executives cannot be indifferent to how their actions are to be presented to the owners.

On this count alone the manager should have some knowledge of the concepts underlying financial statements, but the reasons for including enterprise financial statements in a management approach to accounting are much broader. Every major management decision and many minor ones can only be made intelligently with knowledge of the past performance and current status of the firm as a whole and an evaluation of what they imply for the firm's future.

For example, one of management's most important decisions is the recommendation as to the percentage of earnings to be paid out to the owners. To make this decision, management should know how earnings were measured, at least in broad outline. Under certain conditions, the earnings figure that is computed on the basis of the measurement principles that have been agreed upon for public reporting will not be relevant to this "payout" decision. The manager should be able to recognize such situations, while the accountant, for his part, must be able to provide alternative earnings estimates on different basis when they are needed.

An understanding of enterprise financial statements is also a necessary prerequisite to any analysis of such matters as proposals to acquire or merge with other companies, to expand into new markets, or to withdraw from old ones. In fact, the accounting system can be regarded as a model of the firm, and a manager who understands this model can visualize his decisions as accounting transactions and evaluate their consequence for the financial statements and welfare of the company. This understanding must encompass the measurement principles, however, because a manager who has learned to account for transactions under a specified set of rules without any understanding of their implications and alternatives soon finds this to be useless knowledge that is soon forgotten.

By the same token, an accountant who merely accounts for the transactions of a firm under a specified set of rules is not qualified to serve on a management team. He only confirms the classic, if outmoded, characterization of accountants as wizened old men with green eyeshades who spend their lives copying figures from one book into another. Accountants do little or none of the actual recording of a firm's history. That is the function of bookkeeping, and the rules under which accounting history is written permit the delegation of this task to clerks and to an increasing extent to giant electronic computers. The accountant, on the other hand, designs the system and deals with the nonroutine items, the transactions that cannot be handled without the exercise of judgment. Furthermore, as a member of the management team, his analysis and interpretation of financial statements and other accounting data contribute to an understanding of the past and the prediction of the future.

Limitations of Accounting Data

As might be expected, the discussion in this chapter has taken a positive view of the value of accounting to management. It cannot be ignored, however, that accounting data are often regarded with a good deal of skepticism. To some extent this attitude stems from a failure of the accountant to communicate the meaning of his figures, but probably even more important is a tendency on the part of the management to expect more from the accounting data than they can possibly yield. No manager can ever hope to get all the information he needs to be certain that he is selecting the best course of action available to him, and from this standpoint accounting data are only approximations, subject to errors of varying degree.

The accounting system may provide, for example, a statement showing the profitability of each of the firm's products. For this purpose, the cost of operating a warehouse may be distributed among the products stored there. Unfortunately, the portion of warehousing cost that pertains strictly to any one product is almost never precisely measurable, and the accountant must settle for an approximation.

Perhaps more frustrating to the users of accounting data is that no one set of figures is relevant for all purposes. The purchase price of a delivery truck is highly relevant to the purchase decision. Once the purchase is made, it may still be relevant for a decision on insurance coverage or for use in the company's published financial statements, but it is completely irrelevant to the question of whether the truck should be used to deliver a particular shipment to a particular customer. An understanding of the multiplicity of the uses of accounting data and of their varying requirements can go far toward creating a constructive attitude toward accounting.

Finally, it must be recognized that investors and managers must make decisions even though the correctness of these decisions will depend on what happens in the uncertain future. Accounting data can be developed, classified, and interpreted to provide a basis for an informed analysis of a problem and a wise decision. The accountant may even participate in the analysis and in the decision. However, no accounting data and no accountant can predict with certainty the profit that will be generated in the distant future by a decision such as one to invest a million dollars in a new product.

SUMMARY

In this chapter we have attempted to describe the nature of accounting, to throw some light on the forces which have influenced its development, and to indicate the main purposes it now serves.

Accounting emerges as a special form of history devoted to describing capital and capital flows within the analytical framework of double-entry bookkeeping. The demands for accounting services have changed with changes in the form of business organization and with changes in government-business relations, and the accountant may at times find that his responsibility to provide information to management conflicts with the requirements of public reporting. Both purposes, however, have a common emphasis on performance evaluation and forecasting. The differences are largely of degree, and given patient attention, they can be reconciled.

In the remaining chapters of Part I, we shall undertake to explain, largely through illustration, the general form and characteristics of accounting method. In Part II, we shall consider the presently accepted practices of external financial accounting, examining in some detail the major problems of valuation and income determination from the standpoint of the business enterprise as a whole. Finally, in Part III, we shall turn our attention to the uses of accounting as an aid to management in allocating enterprise resources and in maintaining operational control. This does not imply that the management's call for information is or should be in any way subordinate to the needs of outside investors and others. The arrangement is one of convenience rather than of priority.

QUESTIONS AND PROBLEMS

1. When a company applies for a bank loan, what information will the bank probably require? What is the company accountant's part in providing this information? What is the independent public accountant's part?

2. The public accountant is engaged by the board of directors of the company whose statements he is to audit, and paid from company funds. How can this practice be reconciled with the public accountant's responsibilities to the investing public, to government, and to other interested parties?

3. What contributions can the independent public accountant make to the design of accounting systems? In what ways does he have an advantage over the company's own accountants? What advantages does the company accountant have?

4. The annual audit of a corporation's financial statements is performed largely to satisfy certain needs of outside investors. In what ways can it also be of service to management?

5. In conducting its first annual audit of the Lazy-Baby Nursery School at the end of June, the accounting firm of Hupp and Adam made the following discoveries:

(1) No lists of the office, playground, and classroom equipment owned by the school had been made.

(2) There was no record of which parents had paid their tuition for the previous year, but the director said that she knew which ones had not paid.

(3) The total amounts paid by the school for frozen orange juice during the year averaged 50 cents per child per school day, although the children were only given 4 ounces of juice a day.

(4) Several bills from suppliers were long overdue, having slipped down behind the director's desk.

(5) The balance in the school's bank account at the time of the audit was less than the total of bills payable plus the summer salaries of the director and her secretary.

(6) The school's board of overseers had met only once during the year, for tea at the director's apartment.

(7) A tentative budget for the coming year showed estimated cash receipts equal to estimated cash expenditures of $35,000. No further details were provided.

What recommendations should Hupp and Adam make to the board of overseers?

6. George Johnson invested $10,000 of his own money in a small service business and borrowed another $5,000 from a bank, also for business use. At the end of his first year of operations, he found that there was $17,000 in the enterprise's bank account. He owed his suppliers $3,000 and had not repaid the bank loan. His business assets other than cash were negligible. During the year he had paid himself a salary of $6,000.

a) What conclusions would you draw about his first year's operations?

b) For what decisions would this information be used? What additional information would the decision makers be likely to call for in making these decisions?

c) What problems do you foresee if Mr. Johnson's only business record is his checkbook?

7. Stanley Throckmorton, who sells popcorn at public events, has no capital invested in his business other than the cash which he keeps in his "business" wallet and a pushcart which he bought five years ago for $200. This pushcart contains a corn popping machine, storage space for materials (unpopped corn, butter, and salt), and a compartment in which the popped corn can be kept warm until a customer buys it.

One morning, Mr. Throckmorton left home with $100 in cash in his business wallet. Contemplating an unusually busy day, he bought materials (corn, butter, and salt) costing $120. Although he usually paid cash for his purchases, this was an exceptionally large one for him. Being a regular customer of his supplier, he was permitted to charge $50 of the total amount and pay cash for the rest.

He then attended a baseball game where he sold three quarters of his purchases for $135, all in cash. At the end of the day, he returned home with his unsold stock, planning to replenish his inventory, pay his bill, and obtain fuel for his corn popper on the following morning. (He normally bought fuel on alternate business days at a cost of about $4. A purchase of this size was enough for two days' operation of the corn popper.)

a) How would you measure the results of Mr. Throckmorton's operations for this day? Quantify your answer as much as possible, and list the items, if any, which you found difficult to quantify.

b) Why should Mr. Throckmorton be interested in a measure of his operating results, defined as in (a)? How might knowledge of operating results affect his business actions?

c) What other information might Mr. Throckmorton want to be able to get from his accounting records?

8. Angus MacTavish scratched his head in bewilderment. "I can't figure it out," he said. "I've been running this business for almost a year and I have more customers by far than I had expected when I started. I have had to hire a new bookkeeper just to get out the bills to my customers and to record their payments when they come in. Yet here I am, just before Christmas, and I don't have enough cash in the bank to pay for that new coat I promised to buy my wife if the business did well. I wonder what has gone wrong."

Mr. MacTavish went into business for himself on January 1, 19x1. He took $30,000 from his savings, rented a store, bought a stock of merchandise from a wholesaler, hired a shop assistant, and opened his doors for business. The store proved to be in an excellent location, and Mr. Mac-Tavish quickly earned a reputation of being an honest merchant with good-quality merchandise and favorable prices. As the year wore on, his store became more and more crowded with customers and he had to add an extra clerk to handle the business.

During the year, he bought one additional display cabinet to display his stock of a new line of products that a manufacturer's representative offered to him. Other than this, he didn't recall any major purchases of furniture or equipment. It seemed to him, however, that the better his business became, the less cash he had in the bank.

Mr. MacTavish was confident that his December business would bring in enough cash so that he needn't worry about not being able to meet the payroll at the end of December, but even so he would have a good deal less cash in the bank at the end of the year than he had when he started in business. This disturbed him because as he put it, "I have sunk everything I have into this business, given up a good steady job with a strong company and have worked day and night to make a go of it. If it's not going to pay off, I'd like to know it soon so that I can sell out and go back to work with someone else. I've made a lot of sacrifices this past year to go into business for myself, and I'd like to know whether it was all worthwhile."

This statement was made by Mr. MacTavish to Mr. Thomas Carr, a local public accountant to whom he had turned for advice. Mr. Carr replied that the first thing that he would have to do would be to try to draw up a set of financial statements for the MacTavish store that would summarize the results of the first year's operations to date.

a) To what extent does the decline in Mr. MacTavish's cash balance indicate the success or failure of his business operations during this period? What other explanations can you offer for this change? How would you measure the degree of success achieved by the store during its first year?

b) If you were Mr. MacTavish, what kinds of information would you need before you could decide whether to stay in business or to sell out? How much of this information would you expect Mr. Carr to be able to supply?

c) Assuming that Mr. MacTavish decides to stay in business and decides that he needs a bank loan to provide him with additional cash, what kinds of information do you think that the banker would want to to have before approving the loan? Would this necessarily be the same as the information needed by Mr. Carr?

9. "We can't do business if you don't give me any more to go on than that," said Claude Montrone. After 15 years on the marketing staff of a large manufacturer of office supplies and equipment, Mr. Montrone was thinking of going into business for himself. A small inheritance, added to the accumulated savings of the past 15 years, gave him approximately $70,000 to invest. His older brother had indicated that he would be willing to invest up to $15,000 if he felt that the business venture was sound. Mr. Montrone also hoped to borrow from his bank additional amounts as needed. These amounts would be repaid during the first five years of the new venture. The manager of his bank had said that the bank would be happy to consider a loan application, but of course the actual granting of the loan would depend on the bank's appraisal of the ability of the business to generate enough funds to pay back the loan plus interest.

The statement quoted at the beginning of this case was directed to Paul Alain, owner of a store in Nutley, New Jersey. Mr. Alain owned several enterprises, and as he approached retirement age he found it increasingly difficult to do an adequate management job in each one. Therefore, he had decided to sell his most important business, the Alain Stationery Store, and he was offering to sell the store's assets for $100,000. The buyer would also have to accept the obligation to pay the amounts owed to the store's suppliers (accounts payable), amounting to about $10,000.

Mr. Montrone thought that he might be able to persuade Mr. Alain to spread some of the purchase price over a five-year period, but he doubted that Mr. Alain would come down in his price as a result of bargaining. The purchaser would receive a five-year renewable lease on the store itself, tne goods in inventory, and the amount owed to the store by some of its customers. If he bought the store, Mr. Montrone would have Mr. Alain's list of customers, and he saw no reason why he would not be able to keep the two store clerks who had been working in the store for more than five years.

Mr. Montrone had inspected the store and had toured the area in and around Nutley to get some idea of the location of his customers and potential customers, and the quality of the competition. He was generally familiar with the competitive situation in the area and felt that he could develop a considerable amount of business with small and medium-sized commercial and industrial companies in the area. Mr. Alain gave him the names of several of his larger customers but was unwilling to show Mr. Montrone any details on his business with these customers.

The only data that Mr. Montrone had were the following, all supplied to him by Mr. Alain:

Year	Sales to Customers	Salaries and Dividends Paid to Paul Alain
1958	105,000	15,000
1959	100,000	15,000
1960	110,000	15,000
1961	130,000	16,000
1962	125,000	17,000
1963	120,000	12,000
1964	130,000	18,000
1965	140,000	18,000
1966	135,000	20,000
1967	150,000	20,000

a) What additional information would Mr. Montrone want to have before deciding whether to buy this business? How much of this information would you expect to find in the accounting records of Alain Stationers, Inc.?

b) If you were Mr. Montrone's banker, what information would you want to have to assist you in evaluating a loan request from Mr. Montrone? Would this information be any different from the information that Mr. Montrone would want for the purpose of deciding whether to buy the business?

c) To what extent would you expect accounting data to have entered into Mr. Alain's decision to sell the store and to set the price at $100,000? What kind of data should be looked for in making these decisions?

d) If you were Mr. Montrone, what services would you expect an independent accountant—that is, an accountant not in Mr. Alain's employ—to render in connection with this acquisition?

Chapter 2

BASIC ELEMENTS OF
ACCOUNTING METHOD

BUSINESS ENTERPRISES ARE OF MANY TYPES—engaged in a wide variety of activities. Some are *trading* enterprises, devoted to buying and selling merchandise. These include wholesalers, retailers, industrial supply houses, and so forth. Some firms exist solely to provide *services*. Barber shops, warehouses, banks, and public accounting firms are in this category. Finally, there are *manufacturing* enterprises which purchase materials and change their form in some way before offering them for sale.

While each of these three types of business has its own peculiar accounting problems, the basic concepts and elements of accounting method apply to all. The purpose of this chapter is to examine and illustrate these fundamentals.

FUNDAMENTAL CONCEPTS

From the accountant's viewpoint, a business enterprise may be defined as *a collection of assets subject to a common control and employed for profit*. One of the accountant's responsibilities, as this implies, is to measure the firm's assets and the profits which they generate.

Assets

An *asset* is any right which has value to its owner. The definition of the firm as a collection of assets implies that at any point in time the firm is in part described by a list of its assets at that time.

Examples of assets are bank deposits, the right to receive a certain sum of money from a bank (referred to by the accountant as *cash*), the amounts to be collected from customers in payment for the goods or services they have bought but not yet paid for (called *accounts receivable*), and unsold merchandise (*inventories*).

Defining the business enterprise as a collection of assets subject to a common control requires two things: (1) only the assets of this particular business should be accounted for, and (2) all of the controlled assets should be included. A list of the combined assets of General Motors and General Electric would be of no significance to the owners of these two companies, their creditors, their managements, or anyone else. A General Motors report that omitted the assets of the Chevrolet division would be similarly meaningless.

Liabilities and Owners' Equity

The firm's assets are financed from two sources: its *owners* and its *creditors*. A creditor is someone from whom the company has acquired assets or services for which the company is legally obligated to make payment or provide services in the future. The amount of assets financed by the company's creditors is the measure of its *liabilities* or *creditors' equity*.

Typical liabilities are the amounts owed to other companies ("suppliers") for goods or services provided to the firm in advance of payment (*accounts payable*), amounts borrowed from banks and others for relatively short periods of time (*notes payable*), and amounts borrowed for long periods of time (*bonds payable* or *long-term debt*).

The amounts contributed to the enterprise by the owners are the *owners' equity*, *ownership equity*, or *proprietorship*.[1] Owners are distinguished from creditors in that the firm is under no legal obligation to repay the amounts invested in the firm by the owners. The owners, in other words, have a *residual* interest in the firm. If the firm is ever liquidated—that is, if it goes out of business and its assets are all distributed among the owners and creditors—the owners are legally entitled to all the assets that are left after the creditors' claims have been satisfied in full. This may be either more or less than the owners have invested in the firm.

Creditors, on the other hand, can initiate legal action immediately if the company fails to make timely payment of any amount due them

---

[1] The owners' equity is sometimes referred to as the *net worth*, but only under highly unusual circumstances would it equal the value or worth of the owners' investment—that is, the amount that they could realize through liquidation. To avoid confusion, the term should not be used.

under the terms of the agreement under which they have lent assets to the firm. In some cases, the firm's owners can also become creditors by lending money or services to the company, but at this stage it is simpler to think of owners and creditors as two separate classes of investors.

The Accounting Equation

A careful examination of these definitions will reveal something very important: the terms "assets" and "liabilities and owners' equity" merely represent two ways of looking at the same set of resources. Looking at the firm's resources from one point of view, we see them as assets—valuable rights owned by the firm. When these same resources are reclassified according to their source, however, we call them liabilities and owners' equity or, more simply, the "equities."

This two-sidedness of accounting measurement is expressed formally in the *accounting equation:*

$$\text{TOTAL ASSETS} = \text{TOTAL LIABILITIES} + \text{OWNERS' EQUITY}.$$

The total of a firm's assets *must* equal the total of its equities because these two totals merely measure two aspects of a single set of resources.

Measurement of Assets and Equities

The accountant cannot tell anyone how large the firm's assets and equities are until he has selected a basis for measuring them. Although the accountant's records will include physical descriptions of many assets, as well as lists of the names of owners and creditors, his basic measurements are expressed in monetary terms—dollars in the United States, francs in France, and so forth. That is, a firm's *balance sheet* or *statement of financial position* is ordinarily stated in monetary terms, as in Exhibit 2–1. This statement is intended to describe the firm's financial status (i.e., its resources, measured in monetary units) at a specific point in time. It consists of a list of the assets and a list of the equities. The asset and equity totals are of course equal.

Having decided on the unit of measurement, the accountant must choose a basis for determining the monetary amounts to be assigned to each asset and each equity. One possibility is to list each asset at the amount that could be obtained by selling it, each liability at the amount that would have to be paid to liquidate the debt now, and the owners' equity at the difference between these two totals. This might be called the *liquidation basis* of measurement. To illustrate, if

Exhibit 2–1

A COMPANY
Balance Sheet
As of Some Date

ASSETS		EQUITIES	
Cash........................	$ 20,000	*Liabilities:*	
Amounts due from customers....	30,000	Amounts owed to suppliers....$ 25,000	
Inventories....................	50,000	Amount owed to bank........ 40,000	
Equipment...................	80,000	Total Liabilities.........$ 65,000	
		Owners' equity.................115,000	
Total Assets.........$180,000		Total Equities.........$180,000	

the market value of a firm's assets is $134,000 and if $58,000 would be required to pay off the creditors right now, the owners' equity is $134,000 − $58,000 = $76,000.

Another possible basis of measurement is the *historical basis.* Here, the equities are measured at the amounts invested to date by the various classes of creditors and owners, and the asset measurements show where these amounts have been invested. For assets such as inventories and equipment, this means measurement at *historical cost,* and the historical basis of measurement is sometimes referred to as the *historical cost basis.*

The time is not yet ripe for any meaningful discussion of the relative merits of these two approaches. For various reasons, the modern accounting structure for an active enterprise uses the historical bases of measurement. These reasons, as well as arguments for other basis, will be examined in Chapter 9 and elsewhere in Part II. The accounting structure introduced in this chapter, however, is a historical measurement system.

Income

The definition of a business enterprise as a collection of assets *employed for profit* implies that profit measurement is an important accounting activity. The profit figure is used by the firm's owners in such matters as deciding how much to pay themselves for the firm's use of their capital. It is also used widely by persons outside the firm's management as a measure of the productivity of the capital invested in the enterprise—partly as a measure of the effectiveness of management and partly as an aid in forecasting future productivity. As a committee of the American Accounting Association reported, "The past earnings of the firm are considered to be the most important single item of information relevant to the prediction of future earnings."[2]

The accountant's measure of the profit of the enterprise as a whole is its *net income*, also referred to as *income, earnings,* or *net profit*. Net income is measured by the difference between the amount of assets obtained by providing goods or services to outside customers and the amount of assets given up or consumed in the process.

What does the net income figure mean? By analogy with a widely accepted concept of personal income, a firm's net income might be expected to indicate the maximum amount that the owners could take out of the firm and consume during a period and still be as well off at the end of the period as at the beginning.[3] The question that must be examined in the chapters that follow is how close to this meaning the accounting measure of income is likely to come.

TRANSACTIONS ANALYSIS

The procedures used by accountants to measure the firm's assets, equities, and income call for the analysis of each *transaction* that takes place during the period—that is, each action or event in which the firm participates directly and which affects the assets or equities. To illustrate this approach, let us see how it would be applied to the transactions arising from the organization and operation of a small retail business, The Erskine Appliance Store.

Initial Transactions

In June of 19x0, the sales manager of the Ajax Manufacturing Company offered Mr. Charles Erskine the exclusive dealership rights in his community for the Ajax line of refrigerators, radios, and other electrical appliances. Mr. Erskine, a salesman for a wholesale distributor of a competing line of appliances, decided that he had a good chance of succeeding; and so he resigned his job and began to organize his own business, The Erskine Appliance Store. He found office, storage, and display space in a good location that could be rented for $400 a month and secondhand furniture and equipment that he could

[2] American Accounting Association Committee to Prepare a Statement of Basic Accounting Theory, *A Statement of Basic Accounting Theory* (Evanston, Ill.: American Accounting Association, 1966), pp. 23–24.

[3] The underlying definition can be found in J. R. Hicks, *Value and Capital* (London: Oxford University Press, 1939), p. 172. Further examination of this concept can be found in our Chapter 9 and also in Robert K. Jaedicke and Robert T. Sprouse, *Accounting Flows: Income, Funds, and Cash* (Englewood Cliffs, N.J.: Prentice-Hall, Inc., 1965), chap. ii.

buy for only $3,000. This latter figure seemed to him a bargain price, much less than the equipment was worth.

On June 30, Mr. Erskine in a sense formalized his decision to go into business by depositing $10,000 in a checking account for The Erskine Appliance Store. While he understood that the separate bank account had no legal significance, since the law made no distinction between his personal assets and liabilities and those of his business, he nonetheless felt it was wise to differentiate between his business and family affairs. He planned to "draw" $150 a week from the business (slightly less than he had earned as a salesman) to provide minimum support for his family. If the venture proved profitable during the first full year, he expected to increase his withdrawals.

Immediately after opening the new bank account, Mr. Erskine signed the Ajax franchise agreement and took delivery on merchandise for which he agreed to pay $4,000. He also purchased the furniture and equipment mentioned above and took a two-year lease (starting July 1) on the store space, paying the rent for three months in advance. Thus, by July first, the new enterprise had been organized and four transactions had been completed.

Investment, Purchase, and Payment Transactions

Mr. Erskine's initial investment of $10,000 illustrates an investment transaction. The transaction provided the firm with $10,000 in cash and simultaneously created an owners' equity of the same amount. An analysis of the event may be written as follows:

(1)

Asset Increase	*Accompanied*	*Owners' Equity Increase*
Cash.....................$10,000	*by*	Erskine, Proprietor.........$10,000

This recording indicates quite exactly the nature of the divorcement between Mr. Erskine and The Erskine Appliance Store. The store had the $10,000; Mr. Erskine had an equity in the business in the amount of $10,000. To record one without the other would paint only half of the picture.

In the second transaction, the firm acquired an asset, merchandise, costing $4,000. Since the supplier extended credit for a period of 30 days, a liability of this amount was also created:

(2)

Asset Increase	*Accompanied*	*Liability Increase*
Inventory..................$4,000	*by*	Accounts Payable...........$4,000

Note that this transaction involved both a purchase by The Erskine Appliance Store and a short-term investment in that firm by the Ajax company. Purchases made on a credit basis are an important source of capital for most business concerns. Note also that the inventory asset was measured at its *cost*, not the amount for which it could be sold. The measurement basis, in other words, was purely historical.

Unlike the inventory, the equipment was purchased for cash. In other words, one asset was exchanged for another:

(3)

Asset Increase	*Accompanied*	*Asset Decrease*
Equipment.................$3,000	*by*	Cash.....................$3,000

In the fourth transaction, the firm acquired for $1,200 the right to use building space for three months. Since such a right is clearly a "thing of value owned by a business" and hence an asset, the transaction would be analyzed as follows:

(4)

Asset Increase	*Accompanied*	*Asset Decrease*
Prepaid Rent..............$1,200	*by*	Cash.....................$1,200

Again one asset has been exchanged for another with no change in the equities, and the total assets remain unchanged at $14,000. These assets were supplied partly by Mr. Erskine ($10,000) and partly by the merchandise supplier ($4,000). The accounting equation is still in balance.

The Use of Accounts

The analysis of the four above transactions illustrates the use of a fundamental bookkeeping device, the *account*. An account is simply a place in which to record particular kinds of effects of the firm's transactions. For example, the account "Cash" is used to accumulate the effects on the company's cash position of all cash receipt and cash payment transactions. The "balance" in an account on any date is the difference between the increases in that account and the decreases that have been recorded since some specified date.

In the example, the Cash account would show the following figures prior to July 1:

	Cash			
Date	Description	Increase	Decrease	Balance
June 30	Investment by owner	10,000		10,000
" 30	Equipment purchase		3,000	7,000
" 30	Prepayment of rent		1,200	5,800

The balance in this account shows the difference between the receipts and payments of cash since the formation of the company.

The list of the accounts to be used in a particular firm is known as its *chart of accounts*, and the file of accounts which it represents is known as the *ledger*. The chart of accounts may be extremely detailed or highly compressed, depending on the nature of the business, the needs of its management, and the requirements of law.

The use of accounts is governed by one restriction—the accounting equation must always remain balanced. This means that the accounting analysis of each transaction must be balanced—that is, a change in one account must be accompanied by a change in one or more other accounts such that the total of the balances in the asset accounts remains equal to the total of the balances in the liability and owners' equity accounts.

These specifications are met by the table in Exhibit 2–2, which represents the ledger of The Erskine Appliance Store after the first four transactions were recorded. Notice particularly that the accounting equation remained balanced after each transaction was recorded.

Exhibit 2–2

THE ERSKINE APPLIANCE STORE
Ledger Accounts
As of June 30, 19x0

	Cash	+	Inventory	+	Equipment	+	Prepaid Rent	=	Accounts Payable	+	Erskine, Proprietor
(1)	+ $10,000										+ $10,000
(2)			+ $4,000						+ $4,000		
(3)	− 3,000				+ $3,000						
(4)	− 1,200						+ $1,200				
Bal.	$ 5,800 +		$4,000 +		$3,000 +		$1,200 =		$4,000 +		$10,000

INCOME MEASUREMENT

Mr. Erskine went into the appliance business for the purpose of making money—that is, to make a profit from the operation of the store. Now it is time to turn to transactions which the accountant analyzes to measure the profit or loss earned by the business during a particular period.

Revenue and Expense

The accountant uses the term *income* or *net income* to refer to the increase in owners' equity that results from business operations. Income, in turn, is defined as the difference between revenue and expense:

> *Revenue* is the gross inflow of assets (and gross increase in owners' equity) arising from the firm's performance of productive services for outside customers or clients.

> *Expense* is the outflow of assets (and decrease in owner's equity) consumed in the production of revenue.

When Mr. Erskine purchased merchandise for his store, he recorded the cost of this merchandise in an inventory account, as an asset. Neither revenue nor expense was recognized at that time. Instead, revenues and expenses were to be recognized when the merchandise was sold.[4]

Mr. Erskine's first sale was of a refrigerator which he delivered to a customer in exchange for $300 in cash. This aspect of the transaction can be analyzed as follows:

Asset Increase	*Accompanied*	*Owners' Equity Increase*
Cash......................$300	*by*	Erskine, Proprietor..........$300

This $300 was the store's revenue from the sale of the refrigerator.

The sale transaction had another aspect, however. To get the revenue, Mr. Erskine had to give up a refrigerator which had cost him $200. In other words, by selling the refrigerator, Mr. Erskine was able to obtain $300 in assets by giving up assets which had cost him only $200. The net effect of the transaction, therefore, was a $100 contribution to income. To complete the analysis of this transaction, we must recognize the cost of the refrigerator as an expense:

Owners' Equity Decrease	*Accompanied*	*Asset Decrease*
Erskine, Proprietor..........$200	*by*	Inventory..................$200

Notice the distinction between the terms cost and expense. *Cost* represents the resources sacrificed to attain a particular objective. It arises from an *expenditure*, which is the act of acquiring goods or services; cost is the measure of the *amount* of the expenditure. *Expense*, on the other hand, is measured by the cost of the resources consumed in the production of revenue. It is thus a special category of cost.

Measurement of Periodic Income

Very few expenses can be identified uniquely with any one revenue transaction. For example, the month's rent on the store is an

---

[4] Under other circumstances, revenue might be recognized either earlier or later than the date of the sale. These alternatives will be examined in Chapter 5.

expense applicable to all the month's revenues, but the amount applicable to any one sale can only be measured on some arbitrary basis.

In view of this difficulty, it is best to settle for *partial* profit information on any single sale or any small group of sales and to determine net income only for all the sales of a specified period of time. The accountant, in other words, has to decide which costs are to be charged against the sales of a particular time period. This is not always an easy task, but it is more feasible than the measurement of the net income on individual sales because many costs are more readily traced to periods of time than to individual sales.

Revenue and Expense Accounts

Up to now, only one owners' equity account has been used. If our only purpose were to identify the total owners' equity at the end of the period, revenues and expenses could be entered directly in this account. For example, the following analysis recognizes that the month's wages of a clerk employed to assist Mr. Erskine were an expense of the month:

Owners' Equity Decrease	*Accompanied*	*Liability Increase*
Erskine, Proprietor..........$340	*by*	Wages Payable...............$340

This would make it possible to measure the change in the owners' equity between the beginning and the end of the period. However, the owners' equity also changes as a consequence of other types of transactions, in particular the investment and withdrawal of funds by the owner. Furthermore, the sales revenue for the month, the expenses in total, and the amount of each type of expense would not be known, since transactions analysis in the form illustrated above establishes only the *net* effect of the month's transactions on the owners' equity. Because revenue and expense information is of considerable interest in the management of a firm, accounting for transactions should preserve this information.

The desired information on revenue, expense, and other events which change the owners' equity is generally provided by using many owners' equity accounts instead of just one. These accounts are of two kinds: (1) permanent or balance sheet accounts, and (2) temporary accounts that are used to accumulate various kinds of changes in the permanent accounts between balance sheet dates.

The permanent owners' equity account on the balance sheet is the starting point, representing the owners' equity in the assets as of the balance sheet date.[5] Thus, on July 1, the account was:

Erskine, Proprietor

Subtractions	Additions	Balance
		7/1 10,000

To keep operating results separate from the effects of additional investment or disinvestment by the owners, a second account might now be introduced. This account, which might bear some title such as Current Year's Earnings, would reflect the effects on the owners' equity of the firm's operations from day to day during the year. Anything that led to an increase in owners' equity from this source (revenues) would lead to an addition to this account; any event relating to operations that decreased owners' equity (that is, an expense) would be subtracted:

Current Year's Earnings

Expenses (−)	Revenues (+)	Balance
		7/1 0

At the end of the year, the balance in this temporary account, representing the net income for the year, could be transferred to the permanent owners' equity account.

This is fine as far as it goes, but it does not go far enough. The amount of net income could be determined directly from this account, but a number of other important factors could not be determined. For example, what is the ratio of the amounts paid to salesmen to sales? Is this ratio reasonable? Is it rising or falling? What has happened to sales volume? Is it rising or falling?

To provide answers to such questions, the typical accounting system provides for a further breakdown of the Current Year's Earnings account into separate expense and revenue accounts.

---

[5] The Erskine Appliance Store has only one such account, but corporations and partnerships have at least two and usually more.

Expense			Revenue		
Date		Amount	Date		Amount

Expense			Revenue		
Date		Amount	Date		Amount

The chart of accounts might provide separate accounts to record the revenues from individual product lines or individual groups of customers. Expense accounts might be supplied for each product line or for such classifications as salaries of employees, heating, and electricity.

Because these accounts are used to accumulate the data from which the income statement for a particular period will be prepared, they must start the period (usually a year) with a zero balance. This means that after the net income for the period has been computed, the balances in these temporary accounts should be transferred to a permanent owners' equity account so that they present a clean slate for the start of the next period. This transfer is accomplished by means of what is called a *closing entry*, to be discussed in Chapter 3.

Analysis of Operating Transactions

The transactions of The Erskine Appliance Store for its first month of operation will illustrate the ideas set forth in the preceding sections. To reduce detail, like transactions will be summarized—all events in each such group will be recorded as if they were but one. The amounts shown include the refrigerator sale previously discussed.

1. *Sales for the month totaled $4,465, of which $940 were for cash and $3,525 were on credit.*[6] The analysis shows the following:

Asset Increase		Accompanied	Owners' Equity Increase	
Cash.....................$ 940		by	Sales Revenue.............$4,465	
Accounts Receivable........ 3,525				

2. *The total cost of merchandise sold was $3,210.* The expense account used to accumulate this type of data is usually known as the Cost of Goods Sold or, more simply, Cost of Sales:

---

[6] The terms "on credit" and "on account" are used interchangeably to mean that payment for goods or services purchased or sold is to be made at some date later than the date of the delivery of the goods or the performance of the service.

Owners' Equity Decrease	Accompanied	Asset Decrease
Cost of Goods Sold........$3,210	by	Inventory.................$3,210

Because these goods have been used to produce the revenues recorded in item 1, they are no longer an asset of the company; a corresponding amount must be treated as expense so that it can be offset later against the balance in the revenue account in the calculation of the net income.

3. *Merchandise was purchased on credit at a total cost of $2,150.*

Asset Increase	Accompanied	Liability Increase
Inventory.................$2,150	by	Accounts Payable..........$2,150

No owners' equity accounts were affected by this set of transactions. Acquisition of the assets was financed temporarily by an increase in a liability.

4. *A clerk earned wages of $340 for the month.* Some people find it helpful to think of this sort of transaction in two stages: first, the acquisition of valuable services (an asset); and second, the consumption of those services in the creation of revenue (an expense). In other words, all costs may be thought of as proceeding from asset to expense. It is often more convenient, however, to record these as a single transaction:

Owners' Equity Decrease	Accompanied	Liability Increase
Wages Expense..............$340	by	Wages Payable..............$340

5. *Electricity, telephone, and other miscellaneous operating costs of the month amounted to $300.* Since these costs related to current operations, they must be regarded as having been consumed in the creation of revenues—in other words, treated as expense:

Owners' Equity Decrease	Accompanied	Liability Increase
Miscellaneous Expense.......$300	by	Accounts Payable............$300

Notice that in classifying these costs as expense we do not know whether any cash payments were made during the month. The services were consumed in creating July's revenues, and this is all we need to know. The timing of the cash payments should have no effect on the timing of expense recognition.

6. *Collections from customers on credit sales* (see transaction 1) *totaled $840.* These were pure exchange-of-assets transactions (cash increased and receivables decreased) and had no effect on the revenue and expense accounts. The analysis is:

Asset Increase	Accompanied	Asset Decrease
Cash.....................$840	by	Accounts Receivable.........$840

7. *Payments to creditors* (to pay off some of the liabilities arising from transactions, 3, 4, and 5 or included in the beginning-of-month balance in Accounts Payable) *totaled $4,525.* Here, assets were surrendered to liquidate liabilities, as follows:

Liability Decreases	*Accompanied*	*Asset Decrease*
Accounts Payable...........$4,185	*by*	Cash.....................$4,525
Wages Payable............. 340		

8. *Mr. Erskine withdrew $600 for his personal use.* This reduced both the assets and the owners' equity by $600:

Owners' Equity Decrease	*Accompanied*	*Asset Decrease*
Erskine, Withdrawals........$600	*by*	Cash.......................$600

Mr. Erskine was in doubt whether to regard the reduction in owners' equity as a salary expense or as a partial repayment of his initial investment in the business (a "disinvestment"). He decided to ask his accountant about this at the end of the month. Meanwhile, he recorded it in a separate account.

End-of-Period Entries

All of the above entries were or could be derived from data contained in various documents that were prepared or received by The Erskine Appliance Store as a matter of routine. Data for the entry to record the purchase of merchandise, for example, came from the bills or *invoices* received from the store's suppliers.

Not all the facts relevant to the preparation of periodic financial statements were covered by these documents, however, and one other entry is necessary in this case to reflect the omitted items:

9. *Portions of the assets prepaid rent and equipment were consumed during the period.* Since the rental payment of $1,200 had covered a period of three months in advance from July 1, one third of this amount, or $400, should be transferred to expense in July. The life of the equipment is more uncertain, but at the time of purchase Mr. Erskine estimated that it would have a useful life of 5 years (60 months). Therefore, one sixtieth of its $3,000 cost may be considered a cost of producing revenue in July. Accordingly, $50 of *depreciation* must be subtracted from the balance of the Equipment account and added to expense, in this instance the Miscellaneous Expense account.

Owners' Equity Decreases	*Accompanied*	*Asset Decreases*
Rent Expense...............$400	*by*	Prepaid Rent................$400
Miscellaneous Expense....... 50		Equipment.................. 50

The process of transferring these costs from asset accounts to expense accounts is known as *cost amortization.*

Exhibit 2–3

THE ERSKINE APPLIANCE STORE
Ledger as of July 31, 19x0

ASSETS | LIABILITIES AND OWNERS' EQUITY

Cash

Bal. 7/1	5,800
(1)	+ 940
(6)	+ 840
(7)	−4,525
(8)	− 600
Bal. 7/31	2,455

Accounts Receivable

Bal. 7/1	0
(1)	+3,525
(6)	− 840
Bal. 7/31	2,685

Inventory

Bal. 7/1	4,000
(2)	−3,210
(3)	+2,150
Bal. 7/31	2,940

Prepaid Rent

Bal. 7/1	1,200
(9)	− 400
Bal. 7/31	800

Equipment

Bal. 7/1	3,000
(9)	− 50
Bal. 7/31	2,950

Accounts Payable

Bal. 7/1	4,000
(3)	+2,150
(5)	+ 300
(7)	−4,185
Bal. 7/31	2,265

Wages Payable

(4)	340
(7)	−340

Erskine, Proprietor

Bal. 7/1	10,000

Sales Revenue (+)

(1)	4,465

Cost of Goods Sold (−)

(2)	3,210

Wages Expense (−)

(4)	340

Rent Expense (−)

(9)	400

Miscellaneous Expense (−)

(5)	300
(9)	50
Bal. 7/31	350

Erskine, Withdrawals (−)

(8)	600

The Income Statement

After these nine sets of transactions have been recorded in the appropriate accounts, the ledger of The Erskine Appliance Store appears as in Exhibit 2–3. The numbers in parentheses refer to the transaction numbers above. The plus and minus signs alongside the titles of the temporary owners' equity accounts indicate whether the balances in these accounts are additions to or subtractions from the owners' equity.

The usefulness of having separate revenue and expense accounts becomes very apparent when the time comes to prepare an income statement. All that Mr. Erskine had to do was to read off the balances of the revenue and expense accounts and arrange them in some suitable order. Exhibit 2–4 illustrates one such format.

Exhibit 2–4

THE ERSKINE APPLIANCE STORE

Income Statement

For the Month Ending July 31, 19x0

Sales revenue		$4,465
Expenses:		
Cost of goods sold	$3,210	
Wage expense	340	
Rent expense	400	
Miscellaneous expense	350	4,300
Net Income		$ 165

All the expense accounts indicate decreases in owners' equity. These amounts are therefore subtracted from the revenues to find the *net* increase in owners' equity accruing from the operations of the period. This is the net income. If the expenses exceed the revenues, then the difference is a net *loss*. In this case, however, a small net income of $165 was reported for the month.

Treatment of Owners' Withdrawals

It will be noticed that Mr. Erskine's $600 withdrawal was not subtracted from revenues. Mr. Erskine wanted his accountant to show the withdrawal as an expense, arguing that he could have earned much more than $600 if he had kept his former job and that this was a very reasonable charge for his services. He reasoned that the business didn't really show a profit if it couldn't pay the salary of a manager. It should make no difference whether that manager was an employee or the owner himself. Furthermore, he argued, he had invested $10,000 in the business and he ought to be able to charge interest on this investment.

His accountant agreed that this made sense and said that he would be glad to prepare a statement reflecting these elements for Mr. Erskine's own use.[7] He pointed out, however, that the salary and interest billed to the firm by its owner were not transactions between two independent parties dealing at arm's length. Mr. Erskine, the employer, could over- or underpay Mr. Erskine, the employee, without anyone else having a say in the matter. No outsider could accept statements that were subject to possible bias and manipulation by the owner in this way.

From the owner's point of view, the pertinent practical question is how much the enterprise earns as compared with the expected return from the best available alternative use of the resources employed. In Mr. Erskine's case, for example, the question would be how much more than $165 he might have made on his old job and with $10,000 invested in some good security. A measurement on this basis for the month of July would not really answer Mr. Erskine's question, of course, because the first month's operations would undoubtedly furnish too little data for a sound evaluation of the future potential of his business, but it is a test that he might wish to apply later on.

Statement of Changes in Owners' Equity

Mr. Erskine recognized the logic of his accountant's position, but said that he would still like to have a statement showing all the changes that had taken place in his owners' equity during the month. This statement is shown in Exhibit 2–5.

It is probably obvious that a similar statement could be constructed for any balance sheet account or group of accounts. For example, a statement could show the beginning-of-year cash balance, the amounts of cash received from various sources, the amounts of cash paid out for various purposes, and the ending cash balance. The published

---

[7] The economist has use for a figure which he calls profit and which bears a family resemblance to the accountant's net income. There are a number of other differences between the two figures which will be discussed later, but one difference is that in addition to all the expenses charged against revenues by the accountant, the economist also deducts "imputed wages" for any managerial services provided by the owner-managers and "imputed interest" on the owners' invested capital. If revenues are large enough to cover these expenses as well as those recognized by the accountant, with something left over, then the residual is the profit of the enterprise.

Exhibit 2–5

THE ERSKINE APPLIANCE STORE
Statement of Changes in Owners' Equity
For the Month Ending July 31, 19x0

Owners' equity, July 1, 19x0................................	$10,000
Add: Net income for the month............................	165
	$10,165
Less: Withdrawals..	600
Owners' Equity, July 31, 19x0...........................	$ 9,565

statements of companies in France, Italy, and some other countries often provide a summary of the additions to and subtractions from *each* balance sheet account. United States companies never go this far.

The Balance Sheet

Exhibit 2–6 shows both the beginning and ending balance sheets for the month of July. The July 1 figures are a repetition of those given in Exhibit 2–2; the July 31 amounts have been drawn from Exhibit 2–3 except for the balance in the owners' equity account which came from Exhibit 2–5. It should also be noted that the income statement, a statement of *performance,* together with the statement of changes in owners' equity, constitute a connecting link between these two statements of *status.* The income and owners' equity statements summarize

Exhibit 2–6

THE ERSKINE APPLIANCE STORE
Balance Sheets
As of July 31 and July 1, 19x0

ASSETS

	July 31	July 1
Cash...	$ 2,455	$ 5,800
Accounts receivable............................	2,685	...
Inventory......................................	2,940	4,000
Prepaid rent...................................	800	1,200
Equipment......................................	2,950	3,000
Total Assets...........................	$11,830	$14,000

EQUITIES

Liabilities:		
Accounts payable............................	$ 2,265	$ 4,000
Owners' Equity:		
Erskine, proprietor.........................	9,565	10,000
Total Equities........................	$11,830	$14,000

the operating transactions that took place *during* the period, while the balance sheet shows the company's position at the *end* of the period.

MANAGEMENT USE OF FINANCIAL STATEMENTS

By the end of July, the firm's bank balance (see Exhibit 2–6) had been considerably depleted. Realizing that business would continue to be slow for the next two months, Mr. Erskine foresaw that he might enter the busy fall season with insufficient funds to carry the inventory and accounts receivable necessary to the sales volume he hoped to achieve. He estimated that an additional $5,000 would be needed to carry him through the winter and decided it would be better to approach his bank for a loan soon rather than wait until his need was so urgent as to be embarrassing. He was therefore anxious that his balance sheet present every justifiable evidence of financial strength. With this objective in mind, he was concerned that his accounts ascribed no value to what he considered his most important assets: his dealership franchise and his customer following in the trade.

His accountant agreed that these items were important and suggested that their existence be pointed out to the bank in a letter accompanying the firm's financial statement. He explained that they did not belong in the balance sheet because the basis of measurement used in accounting is *cost*, and valuable though they might be, they had cost The Erskine Appliance Store nothing. He also pointed out that although the accounts reflected the rent that had been paid, they ignored the fact that Mr. Erskine had signed a two-year lease. This contract was also an important factor, one which would be favorable if property values went up and unfavorable if they went down or if the space became unsuitable to the needs of the business. The accountant then said, however, that the accounting profession did not regard the signing of a lease as an exchange of assets that should be recognized in the accounts. Only a prepayment of rent could be recognized at that time.

Finally, he noted that Mr. Erskine had apparently intuitively accepted the cost basis of measurement in developing data for his own use. As a specific illustration, he called attention to the fact that although Erskine had believed his equipment worth more than he paid for it, he had not considered recording any amount other than the actual purchase price.

Accordingly, the balance sheet that Mr. Erskine decided to submit to the bank was the one shown in Exhibit 2–6. However, in view of the fact that the best security for later repayment of the bank's loan would be a large earnings flow, the accountant urged Mr. Erskine to supplement his balance sheet and report of earnings with a *forecast* of the future earnings which the favorable franchise and reputation would permit him to achieve.

SUMMARY

This chapter has noted the repetitive nature of business activities and has identified several major types of transactions—investment, purchase and payment, sale and receipt, cost expiration, and disinvestment. In addition, enough elementary bookkeeping has been introduced to give some notion of how these transactions can be analyzed and recorded in a firm's accounts.

The most important message of this chapter, however, concerns the basis on which business events are recognized in the accounts. Conventionally, nonmonetary assets are recorded at their *acquisition cost*, measured by their *purchase price*. This price is the result of arm's length negotiation between buyer and seller and thus presumably constitutes an *objective* and *verifiable* measure at that time of the value of the good or service acquired. In other words, if the seller is willing to accept the price, then from his point of view the item is not worth more than the price offered; similarly, the buyer's willingness to buy indicates that the item is worth at least this much to him at the time of the exchange. *Expense* is determined by measuring or estimating the amount of acquisition cost that has expired in the creation of revenue. Similarly, *revenue* is measured in terms of the *sale price* obtained by the firm for its goods or services when it later reenters the market as a seller, on the grounds that the sale price provides objective, verifiable evidence of value at that point.

As a result, *income is ordinarily recognized at the time when goods or services are provided to the firm's customers and is measured by the difference between selling price established at that time and purchase price established at the time of acquisition.* In other words, conventional practice generally ignores interim value changes in goods and services owned, and recognizes gains or losses only as these are substantiated by market reentry (i.e., sale). A further analysis of these propositions will be made in later chapters.

QUESTIONS AND PROBLEMS

1. Under what circumstances does a particular cash outlay result in an asset? An expense? Give two other possible effects of a cash outlay.

2. "All business assets eventually become expenses." Defend or criticize.

3. Explain the difference between "liabilities" and "owners' equity."

4. Why does the "accounting equation" always hold true?

5. What is an account, and what is its function?

6. What is meant by the terms "revenue" and "expense"?

7. Describe the purpose of revenue and expense accounts and their relationship to the asset, liability, and ownership accounts.

8. What is cost amortization and what is its purpose?

9. What is meant by "transaction"? Describe six different kinds of transactions.

10. Distinguish between cost and expense.

11. Why is it not possible to measure the net income on any one sale transaction?

12. Distinguish between temporary and permanent accounts.

13. State whether each of the following is true, false, or doubtful. Give reasons.

a) The total assets of a business are increased by the purchase of goods on credit.
b) Cash and proprietorship are the same.
c) The recorded total of a firm's assets occasionally may exceed the total of its liabilities and owners' equities.
d) Since long-term debt and proprietary interests are both sources of long-term capital, they may be considered as essentially identical.
e) Income is a source of capital.
f) When a firm owes taxes to a governmental body, that governmental body is, in effect, providing some of the capital used by the firm.

14. Which of the following transactions lead to the recording of an increase in the balance in some asset account? How soon would you expect each of these assets to become expense?

a) Goods purchased for resale.
b) Commission paid to salesman on sales of the month before last.

c) A new delivery truck purchased for use by the business.
d) Goods sold during month just ended.
e) Wages paid to stenographers in sales department.
f) Payment for advertising which appeared during month just ended.
g) Salary advance to salesman.

15. Merchandise costing $4,000 is sold for $5,200.

a) Analyze the effects of this transaction on the assets and equities.
b) Explain the purpose of each account change which appears in your analysis.
c) What expenses connected with this transaction are known at the time the sale takes place? What expenses are not known?
d) How and when will the profit or loss resulting from this transaction be determined?

16. For each of the following transactions indicate the effects upon the various sections of the balance sheet:

a) Receipt of cash from a customer to apply to his account.
b) Payment of cash to a creditor to apply on account.
c) Purchase of raw materials to be paid for in 60 days.
d) Borrowing of cash from a bank.
e) Investment of new funds in the business by the owners.
f) Purchase of new equipment for cash.

17. An item that is Smith's asset may be Brown's liability, or owners' equity on the books of Smith's Drug Store. For each of the following items on the balance sheet of Carter's Feed Store, indicate in which section, if any, of someone else's balance sheet it would appear:

a) Accounts receivable.
b) Merchandise inventory.
c) Cash in bank.
d) Notes receivable.
e) Prepaid insurance.
f) Investments in government securities.
g) Land.
h) Wages payable.
i) Carter, proprietor.

*18. The following items, arranged in alphabetical order, comprise the assets and equities of a small business. Organize these data in the form of a balance sheet.

---

* Solutions to problems marked with an asterisk (*) are found in Appendix B.

```
Accounts payable to creditors............................$12,300
Accounts receivable from customers.......................  6,900
Building.................................................  24,000
Cash on hand and in bank.................................  9,000
Delivery equipment.......................................  9,600
Furniture................................................  4,200
Inventory of merchandise.................................  29,100
Land.....................................................  2,500
Long-term debt...........................................  16,500
Notes payable to banks...................................  8,000
Notes receivable from customers..........................  3,900
Owners' equity...........................................  52,400
```

*19. Prepare an income statement and balance sheet from the following account balances (no owner investments or withdrawals were made during the period):

```
Accounts payable.........................................$    250
Accounts receivable......................................     300
Cash.....................................................     100
Cost of goods sold.......................................     700
Furniture................................................     600
Inventories..............................................     380
Note payable.............................................     350
Prepaid rent.............................................      40
R. A. Copake, Capital....................................To be derived
Revenue from Sales.......................................   1,000
Salaries and wages expense...............................     120
Sundry expenses..........................................      60
Taxes expense............................................      20
Taxes payable............................................       5
Wages payable............................................      50
```

20. The assets and equities of the Brandon Company on December 31 were as follows:

```
Accounts payable.........................................$13,300
Accounts receivable......................................  8,120
Buildings................................................  35,760
Cash on hand and in bank.................................  6,600
Equipment................................................  4,450
Interest payable.........................................    180
Inventory of merchandise.................................  11,200
Land.....................................................  18,000
Long-term debt...........................................  10,200
Notes payable............................................  9,000
Owners' equity...........................................To be derived
Prepaid insurance........................................  2,000
Wages payable............................................  1,770
```

a) Prepare a statement or report which will show:
   (1) The total capital of the enterprise and its distribution among the various assets.
   (2) The sources of capital classified as between creditor and ownership equities.

b) Explain the probable nature of each item and identify the kind of transaction in which it probably originated.

21. How much should be charged to expense in 19x3 as a result of each of the following events:

(1) Purchased office furniture on July 1, 19x3, $4,200; office furniture has a 12-year life in this company.
(2) Hired a salesman on October 1 at a salary of $700 a month; salaries are paid on the 15th of each month. The salesman worked at this job until January 31, 19x4, when he left the company.
(3) Sold merchandise costing $220,000.
(4) Paid a supplier $24,000 for merchandise received in 19x2.
(5) Paid $22,500 for store rental on November 1, 19x3, covering the period from October 1, 19x3, through March 31, 19x4.

22. Indicate the effects, if any, of each of the following events on the firm's asset, liability, and owners' equity accounts (assume that the accounts were completely up-to-date and accurate on the first of this month and that no other entries have been made this month). Each of these events took place this month.

(1) Perform services and bill customer for $700.
(2) Order an electric typewriter for the office, to be delivered two months from now, price $420 to be paid at delivery.
(3) Purchase and pay for a two-year supply of office stationery, price $380.
(4) Repay the $1,000 borrowed from a bank on the last day of last month, plus $5 interest.
(5) Hire a new secretary on the last day of this month, salary $400 a month.
(6) Pay a salesman $650 for services he performed last month.
(7) Pay the owner's salary for this month, $1,200 (the business is organized as an individual proprietorship).
(8) Collect cash from customer, $1,500, for services performed last year.
(9) Depreciation for this month was $360.

23. For each of the following, indicate the effects on the asset, liability, and ownership accounts of an automobile supplies store:

(1) Bought merchandise inventory for $212, on account.
(2) Sold a fuel pump to a customer for $41, cash. This fuel pump had cost $28 in a previous period.
(3) Paid a total of $660 for rental of the store for three months in advance.

(4) Bought and paid for a three-year insurance policy at a cost of $72; insurance coverage began on the day of the purchase.

(5) Collected $748 from customers who owed the company for earlier purchases of goods and services.

(6) Recognized the month's depreciation on equipment, $100.

(7) Paid the following bills by check at the end of the month:

Oil	$184
Light	70
Watchman service	20
Advertising	26

What assumptions did you have to make in order to analyze the group of transactions in (7) above?

24. The accounts of Charles Fox's automobile repair shop showed the following balances on December 31, 19x6:

Accounts payable	$ 2,210
Accounts receivable	4,100
Buildings	12,000
Cash	640
Equipment	12,130
C. Fox, cash withdrawn for personal use during 19x6	6,000
C. Fox, owner's equity	*
General expenses	3,140
Inventory of repair parts	4,250
Repair parts used during 19x6	3,560
Revenues	28,940
Wages expense	15,090
Wages payable	380

* A secretary spilled coffee on this account page and made it illegible.

a) Prepare an income statement for 19x6 and a balance sheet as of December 31, 19x6.

b) Explain why the amounts shown for wages expense and wages payable are not identical.

c) What was Mr. Fox's equity in the business on January 1, 19x6 (the beginning of the year)?

*25. Earl Holt decides to operate a hot dog stand near a football stadium during the football season. The following transactions describe the financial effects of his activities in setting up the business and operating it for one week:

(1) He deposits $300 in the Second National Bank.

(2) He rents a site, paying $45 for the right to use the location on the following three Saturdays.

(3) A tent and other equipment are purchased from a bankrupt concern for $110; a check is issued in payment.

(4) Merchandise is purchased from the Hill Wholesale Company, $305; Holt pays $100 down (by check), and promises to pay the balance on Monday after the first game.

(5) All of the merchandise is sold for cash on the first Saturday, and the total receipts, $650, are deposited in Mr. Holt's bank account.

(6) Holt decides that one third of the rent payment is applicable to the business done at the first game, and that the tent and equipment will have a cash value of $47 at the end of the third Saturday, the last game of the season. After that game Mr. Holt will go out of this business.

(7) On Monday, the balance due the Hill Wholesale Company is paid in full.

a) Prepare a set of accounts in the form shown in Exhibit 2–2 and record the above information. Be sure to indicate which accounts are assets, which are liabilities, and which are owners' equity accounts.

b) Prepare a balance sheet as of Monday night, after all the above information has been recorded.

c) Prepare an income statement for the period ending on Monday night.

*26. On January 21, 19x4, three young bachelors, Mr. Robinson, Mr. Griffiths, and Mr. Thorndike formed a partnership to operate a small bar. Each partner contributed $1,500 cash, a total of $4,500. On the day the partnership was formed, the Dingy Dive Bar was purchased for $14,500. This price included land valued at $2,000, improvements to land at $2,000, buildings at $9,500, and bar equipment at $1,000. The partnership made a down payment of $3,000 (from its $4,500 cash) and signed a note for the balance of the $14,500.

After operating the bar for one month, the partners found that despite withdrawing $200 each in cash from the business, $1,000 in cash remained; in addition, there was inventory on hand amounting to $300 and accounts receivable of $150. They still owed $11,500 on the note, and now had accounts payable of $200. They also owed $50 in wages to one of their bartenders.

a) Draw up a balance sheet for the Dingy Dive Bar as of January 21, 19x4, taking into account the above data.

b) Draw up a second balance sheet as of February 21, 19x4.

c) From the information given, what can you say of the success of the venture to date?

27. The M. Wholesale Company kept no formal books of accounts. Instead the partners made up a statement of assets and liabilities at the end of each year. For 19x8 and 19x9, these were as follows:

	December 31	
	19x8	19x9
Cash..	$ 2,000	$ 4,200
Merchandise inventory...............................	12,300	15,000
Accounts receivable..................................	7,000	5,000
Accounts payable for merchandise......................	8,000	10,100
Furniture and fixtures (net after deduction of depreciation)...	3,000	2,600

All 19x9 expenses except depreciation and the cost of goods sold were paid in cash during 19x9. A further analysis of the company's checkbook for 19x9 shows two more groups of transactions: (1) deposits of all amounts received from customers during the year, $50,000; and (2) payments for merchandise amounting to $33,000. No other receipts or payments occurred during 19x9.

For 19x9, what were the:

a) Sales revenues?

b) Purchases of merchandise?

c) Cost of merchandise sold?

d) Other expenses?

e) Net income?

f) Owners' equity (12/31/x8)?

g) Owners' equity (12/31/x9)?

28. Prepare a work sheet like the one shown in Exhibit 2–2, with eight columns, one for each of the following accounts:

Cash

Accounts receivable

Inventory

Buildings

Equipment

Accounts payable

Notes and interest payable

J. Doe, Owner

Label each of these accounts to identify it as either an asset (A), a liability (L), or an owners' equity (O.E.) account. Then record the following information in these accounts and compute an end-of-month balance for each:

January 1

(1) A cash investment of $60,000 is made in the business by the owner, Mr. John Doe.

(2) A building, $40,000, and equipment, $24,000, are purchased. Cash in the amount of $39,000 is paid for these items. The balance is owed on a note payable.

January 2–31

(3) Merchandise costing $40,000 is purchased on credit.

(4) Merchandise costing $30,000 is sold for $50,000. Of this amount, $21,000 is for cash and the balance is sold on credit.

(5) Salaries and wages total $13,500 for the month and are paid in cash.

(6) Miscellaneous expenses amount to $4,200. Of this amount, $3,300 is paid in cash; the rest will be paid in February.

(7) The depreciation for the period is $150 on the building and $200 on the equipment.

(8) Mr. Doe will have to pay interest on the note payable in the amount of $500 a month. His first payment will be due for payment in cash on April 1.

What was net income for the month?

29. James Westbridge buys and sells pipe stock in a small Midwestern town. On January 1, his ledger accounts showed the following balances:

Cash, $3,000; Receivables, $50,000; Inventories, $136,000; Store Equipment, $74,800; Prepaid Insurance, $816; Accounts Payable, $33,800; J. Westbridge, Prop., $221,516; Taxes Payable, $9,300.

During January, merchandise costing $78,800 was purchased on account. Merchandise with a cost of $82,100 was sold on account for $106,300. Tax expense applicable to the month of January was estimated to be $2,000, but no taxes were paid during January.

At the end of the month, $790 of insurance remained prepaid. Depreciation of store equipment for the month was $300. Miscellaneous expenses paid in cash amounted to $16,200. During the month, customers paid bills amounting to $125,100, and Mr. Westbridge paid $109,700 to his suppliers of merchandise.

a) Arrange the accounts listed above in three groups—assets, liabilities, and owners' equity accounts—enter the January 1 balances, and record the other information given above. Use only the eight accounts given.

b) Prepare an income statement for the month of January and a balance sheet as of January 31.

30. On December 31, George Harvey completed his first year as proprietor of a men's clothing store. The following data summarize his first year's transactions.

(1) He invested $14,000 cash in the business.

(2) In January he borrowed $6,000 cash from a bank.

(3) On December 31, he repaid $300 of the amount borrowed plus an additional $360, representing one year's interest on the amount borrowed.

(4) In January he secured a five-year lease on shop space. He made cash rental payments during the year, amounting to $100 for January and for subsequent months 8 percent of the sales made during the preceding month.

(5) He bought furniture and store equipment for $7,500 cash.

(6) He bought merchandise on credit for $28,585.

(7) During the year he sold some of the merchandise described in (6). The cost of the merchandise sold was $21,690, and he sold it for $32,200, of which $17,100 was cash and $15,100 was on

credit. (December sales included in these figures totaled $4,800.)

(8) He paid himself a "salary" of $6,000, paid $642 as wages to part-time employees, and paid $2,022 for other expenses, all in cash.

(9) He returned defective merchandise to a supplier for full credit, $881. Payment for this merchandise had not been made to the supplier.

(10) He collected $4,426 owed him by customers who had bought merchandise on credit.

(11) He decided to depreciate his furniture and equipment evenly over a five-year period. He did not believe that there would be any salvage value at the end of that time.

(12) During the year, he made payments to suppliers on account, totaling $21,520.

(13) A shoplifter stole merchandise which had cost $82.

a) Prepare a set of accounts (including revenue and expense accounts) which are divided clearly into three groups—assets, liabilities, and proprietorship—and record the above transactions. Be sure to indicate whether each account change is an increase or a decrease in the account balance.

b) Prepare an income statement for the year and a year-end balance sheet. What further information would you want to have before you could tell Mr. Harvey whether his business venture was a success from a financial viewpoint?

31. In January, Mr. Alan Bucknell opened a retail grocery store. The following list summarizes the transactions of his first year of business:

(1) Mr. Bucknell invested $25,000 in cash.

(2) He bought a store building and equipment for $9,000, paying $8,000 cash and borrowing the remaining $1,000 from a bank.

(3) He bought on account merchandise costing $22,125.

(4) He sold merchandise which had cost him $18,910 for $23,725, of which $12,550 was for cash and the balance on credit.

(5) He paid his employees' wages in cash, $4,245.

(6) He paid $1,575 cash for other expenses.

(7) He received $150 cash for rent of storage space in his store loft during the year.

(8) He suffered an uninsured loss by fire of merchandise costing $1,000 and equipment which had cost him $520.

(9) He paid $19,750 of his accounts payable, $17,250 with cash and $2,500 with notes payable.

(10) His customers paid him $10,750 of the amounts they owed him.

(11) At the end of the year he owed his employees $50 for wages.

(12) During the year he withdrew for his own use $1,200 in cash and merchandise which had cost $525.

(13) Bills for expenses incurred in December but unpaid on December 31 amounted to $110.

(14) The depreciation of building and equipment during the period was estimated to be $200.

a) Establish a set of accounts (including revenue and expense accounts) in three categories—assets, liabilities, and proprietorship—and record the effects of these transactions. For each entry, be sure to indicate whether the change is plus or minus.

b) Prepare an income statement for the year and a balance sheet as of December 31.

Chapter 3

FURTHER ANALYSIS OF
BUSINESS TRANSACTIONS

THE PRIMARY PURPOSE of a technical language is to make communication more efficient. For the most part, the previous chapter used nontechnical language to describe the basic concepts of accounting measurement. This served to keep the number of side issues to a minimum, but at the cost of some efficiency of expression. To continue in this vein would be like doing arithmetic calculations by hand even though an electric desk calculator was available, just to prove that it could still be done. If accounting language has been developed for good reason, then it is costly to fail to take advantage of it. The purpose of this chapter is to introduce more of the basic vocabulary used by accountants and to demonstrate its usefulness in the analysis of an additional set of transactions.

FORM AND TERMINOLOGY

Most of the basic terms that must be introduced at this time relate to the processes of elementary bookkeeping. They pertain mostly to the structure of the accounts and to the means of getting accounting data into these accounts.

The Nature of T-Accounts

The account may take any one of a number of forms, depending on the kind of data processing equipment used and on the preferences of the accounting system designer. The accounts in the preceding chapter used a simple kind of plus-and-minus notation. This is typical of systems in which account balances are stored in the memory units of electronic computers. The computer is instructed or programmed to take the account balance from its memory location, add or subtract the change, and then return the new balance to memory, wiping out the old balance. This procedure is dictated by the scarcity of memory locations and in practice is perfectly satisfactory. To learn accounting, however, it is useful to keep a complete record of changes in account balances in problems and illustrations. Therefore, throughout this book we shall use a form of account that is simple but complete in all the essentials, the so-called *"skeleton account"* or *"T-account"* illustrated below:

Account Title

Amounts of changes in one direction	Amounts of changes in the opposite direction

The Cash account of The Erskine Appliance Store, reflecting the July transactions discussed in Chapter 2, would appear as follows in T-account form:

Cash

Balance, July 1................5,800	Transaction 7.................4,525
Transaction 1................. 940	Transaction 8................. 600
Transaction 6................. 840	5,125
7,580	
Bal., July 31..........2,455	

The T-account format is simpler than would normally be found in practice, but it shows all the data necessary for an understanding of accounting: dates, amounts, and some kind of reference that permits finding the source of the data.

Use of T-Accounts

In the above illustration it will be noted that additions or "plus changes" in the Cash account have been entered on the left-hand side of the T; minus changes appear on the right. This convention may be easier to remember if the balance sheet is thought of as a large T-account, in which positive asset balances appear on the left and positive equity balances appear on the right. An increase in the firm's assets, therefore, will increase the total on the left; a decrease will be reflected in a reduction in the total on the left-hand side of the large T. Conversely, anything that increases equities increases the total on the right-hand side of the large T and vice versa. From this it is a short step to create small T's on each side of the large one, in which positive asset balances appear on the left of their respective T-accounts and positive equity balances show up on the right:

| ASSETS (+) | | | | EQUITIES (+) | | | |
Cash		Inventory		Accounts Payable		Erskine, Proprietor	
Balance (+)	(−)	Balance (+)	(−)	(−)	Balance (+)	(−)	Balance (+)

This being the case, anything that increases the balance in an asset account should be entered on the left; anything that decreases the balance of an asset account should be entered on the right. Periodically the amounts on each side can be totaled and subtracted from each other to form the new balance. Just the reverse holds true for the equities—an increase is entered on the right, a decrease on the left.

These conventional rules governing the use of T-accounts may be summarized as follows:

1. An *increase* in an *asset* is entered on the *left* side of the T, as is the balance in the asset account.
2. A *decrease* in an *asset* is entered on the *right* side of the T.
3. An *increase* in an *equity* is entered on the *right* side of the T, as is the balance in the equity account.
4. A *decrease* in an *equity* is entered on the left side of the T.

Debit and Credit

Just as it is not precise to use the terms plus and minus without also specifying the kind of account, so is it also a bit cumbersome to use the terms left side and right side repeatedly. Furthermore, as we have seen, accounts may be constructed so as to have neither a left side nor a right side. A more concise and general notation has had to be found. The accountant says:

Debit for an entry on the *left* side, meaning by this an increase in an asset *or* a decrease in an equity; and

Credit for an entry on the *right* side, meaning by this an increase in an equity *or* a decrease in an asset.[1]

Thus, increase in cash is the event that is recorded by the debit to Cash. Similarly, to credit Cash means to record a decrease in the company's cash balance.

All this can be summarized in schematic terms very simply, as in the following diagram:

Asset		Liability		Owners' Equity	
+ Dr.	− Cr.	− Dr.	+ Cr.	− Dr.	+ Cr.

[1] The abbreviations for these two terms are *Dr.* and *Cr.*, respectively.

In practice, of course, a company would have many accounts in each of these three categories, rather than just one as in the diagram above. The owners' equity accounts, for example, would include at least one account to show the owners' equity at the beginning of the period, plus one or more revenue accounts and several expense accounts:

Owners' Equity

−		+	
Cost of Goods Sold		**Erskine, Proprietor**	
Dr.	Cr.	Dr.	Cr.
Costs of goods sold during the period			Beginning balance.......xxx
Other Expenses		**Revenue from Sales**	
Dr.	Cr.	Dr.	Cr.
Other expenses of the period			Sales revenues of the period

The expense account is the first example of an account that normally shows a debit balance but is not an asset. The reason for this, of course, is that the expense account is a negative component of the ownership equity section of the chart of accounts. The *revenue* accounts accumulate the *increases* in owners' equity resulting from the operating events of the period; the *expense* accounts accumulate the *decreases*. Because equity decreases are recorded by debiting owners' equity accounts, expense accounts have debit balances.

The General Journal

The format that was used to represent the analysis of transactions in Chapter 2 can now be replaced by a more compact form of notation. For example, the purchase of merchandise inventory for $300 in cash can be recorded as follows:

Accounts	*Debit*	*Credit*
Merchandise Inventory...................................300		
Cash...		300
To record purchase of inventory.		

In this form, *debits* are invariably written first; *credits* are written underneath, with both the account titles and amounts *indented to the right*.

This is the way that transactions would be recorded in a simple *general journal*. The journal is a book, file of papers, reel of magnetic tape, or another medium in which the accounting analysis of each transaction is recorded *in its entirety*. The record of a transaction in the journal is known as a *journal entry*.

Data enter the accounting system by means of documents, which are analyzed to determine what accounts are affected and how. In some systems, the results of these analyses are first recorded in the journal, which is a chronological record of the transactions represented by the documents, and are then transferred or *posted* to the *ledger*. The ledger differs from the journal in that it is a classified record of the effects of transactions on the assets and equities of the firm. In the ledger, the individual transaction no longer appears as a complete entity; instead, its component parts are scattered among the accounts. The sequence of these data flows is shown on the following diagram:

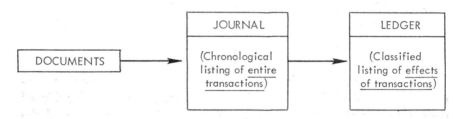

Because it provides the first point at which the accounting description is recorded, the journal is also referred to as the *book of original entry*. It should be noted, however, that some businesses will dispense with the journal completely or may keep a document file in place of a journal. Others will have several journals, each one for a specific class of transactions. These arrangements will be discussed in Chapter 7. For the moment, however, it is assumed that there is only one journal, the general journal, and that all transactions are recorded in it. For convenience, the two-column form in which we shall list transactions (the debit first, then the credit indented to the right) will be referred to as the general journal form.

FORMS OF BUSINESS ORGANIZATION

The account terminology and techniques presented above probably can best be understood with the aid of an example. Because this example will also introduce some of the accounts required by the corporate form of organization, some preliminary observations on the differences between the corporation and other legal forms of business organization are desirable.

Proprietorship Characteristics

In terms of the number of business units, the most prevalent form of business organization in the United States is the individual proprietorship. In this, its simplest form, the business unit consists of a collection of resources contributed or borrowed by a single individual and devoted to some economically productive activity. This individual proprietorship is a "natural" (common law) form of organization in that it may be assumed by anyone at will. No official permission need be obtained; from a legal point of view the activities of the business unit are regarded as simply one portion of the activities of the proprietor.

Because the individual proprietorship is established simply by a one-sided action of the proprietor, the law recognizes no distinction between the proprietor's business and his private affairs.[2] His entire fortune is vulnerable to claims arising out of his business activities. Conversely, his business resources are subject to claims arising out of his personal activities. This is known as the *unlimited liability* feature of the proprietorship form of organization. If Smith buys candy from Jones on credit for sale in his candy store and then fails to pay the bill, Jones can press his claim for payment against any of Smith's assets, whether they are used in his candy business or not.

Partnership Characteristics

Another form of organization is the *general partnership*, created by the pooling of the resources of two or more persons under a formal agreement among the partners. The general partnership arises out of the right of the individual to enter into contracts with others. The partnership agreement is such a contract and is enforceable at law.

Once again, however, the partnership has very few rights of its own—it merely represents the pooling of the rights and obligations of the individual partners. A partnership can own property in its own name, but the liability of any one partner is not limited to his investment in the business. Outsiders are not parties to the partnership agreement and therefore can press claims to the nonbusiness resources

---

[2] In certain circumstances, the individual proprietorship may file a tax return as a separate taxable entity if it meets the requirements established by law for a "tax option proprietorship." Similar treatment is available for partnerships.

of any and all of the partners for debts arising out of partnership operations.

Corporation Characteristics

In terms of the amount of economic activity carried out under its roof, the *corporation* is by far the dominant form of organization in the United States. For this reason and because the corporation tends to be the most complex form of organization and therefore to present the greatest variety of accounting problems, much of our subsequent discussion will be in terms of the corporation.[3] From the accounting standpoint, the salient features of the modern corporation are: (1) it is an artificial entity created by law and possessing no rights other than those specifically granted by its charter and the surrounding statutes; (2) the ownership interest may be subdivided almost infinitely and is evidenced by certificates representing shares of capital stock, these shares normally being transferable at the owner's pleasure; and (3) the owners are not personally liable for the obligations of the corporation.[4]

These features make it possible for the corporation to reach huge amounts of capital that are unavailable to the individual proprietorship or general partnership. Without transferability of ownership and limited liability—i.e., the right to risk only a predetermined amount of capital but still share in profits—the sources of private ownership capital would be inadequate to finance the large-scale enterprises demanded by modern technology.

Under the corporate form of organization, ownership control is exercised through a *board of directors* whose members are elected by the shareowners or *stockholders*. The members of this governing board formulate general company policy, appoint and remove the top administrative officers of the company, and carry out a number of other functions. The directors may be major shareowners, top company officers, both, or neither. Most large corporations, however, are publicly held, which means that the shares of stock are owned by a large number of individuals most of whom do not participate in

---

[3] For a clearly written and interesting discussion of the legal characteristics of partnerships and corporations, see George C. Thompson and Gerald P. Brady, *Law in a Business Environment* (Belmont, Calif.: Wadsworth Publishing Co., Inc., 1963), chaps. viii and ix.

[4] In the United States, corporate charters are granted by the several states. State incorporation laws vary considerably, and enterprises engaged in interstate operations will usually organize under whichever law is regarded as most suitable for their particular operations.

company management except through their votes in electing the board of directors.

The granting of a corporate charter typically permits the corporation to own property in its own name, to borrow or lend, and even to own shares of stock in other corporations. The life of the corporation is not dependent on the lives of its owners, directors, or executives, nor does withdrawal of one owner require liquidation of the business or reincorporation. Thus, the corporation typically has an indefinitely long life.

Formation of the Erskine Corporation

After several years, The Erskine Appliance Store was well established in the community. The store had been expanded to meet the growing needs of the business, and Mr. Erskine had reinvested a substantial percentage of the store's net income to finance this growth —that is, he had increased his investment by not withdrawing all the funds generated by profitable operations, using them instead to purchase additional inventories, furniture, and equipment. By this process he had increased his original investment of $10,000 to $35,000 by the end of 19x7, as shown in Exhibit 3–1. Total assets of the firm had grown to $55,000 by this time.

Exhibit 3–1

THE ERSKINE APPLIANCE STORE
Statement of Financial Position
As of December 31, 19x7

ASSETS		EQUITIES	
		Liabilities:	
Cash	$ 4,000	Accounts payable	$20,000
Accounts receivable	24,000		
Merchandise inventory	16,000	*Owners' Equity:*	
Furniture and equipment	11,000	Erskine, proprietor	35,000
Total Assets	$55,000	Total Equities	$55,000

On January 1, 19x8, Mr. Erskine put into effect a plan that he had been working on for some time with his accountant and his lawyer. Having decided that the *individual proprietorship* legal form of organization was no longer suited to his needs, he formed a corporation, Erskine Enterprises, Inc., and transferred to it all the assets of The Erskine Appliance Store. He received in exchange 1,000 shares of the capital stock of the new corporation. In addition, the new corporation assumed the debts shown on the final balance sheet of the unincorpo-rated store.

The new shares of stock were assigned a *paid-in value* of $35 each; that is, the owners' equity aspect of the transaction was recorded just as it would have been if Mr. Erskine had paid $35 in cash for each share of stock. This figure was obtained by dividing the amount at which Mr. Erskine's equity had been carried before the corporation was formed ($35,000) by the number of shares issued (1,000). The total recorded owners' equity was the same as before, but now it was labeled "capital stock" instead of "Erskine, proprietor."

TRANSACTIONS ANALYSIS

The remainder of this chapter is devoted to accounting for the transactions of Erskine Enterprises, Inc., for the year 19x8. This transactions analysis will not only illustrate the use of debit and credit notation and T-accounts but it will also introduce new concepts in the analysis of certain kinds of transactions.

Recording Purchase and Sale Transactions

During 19x8, Erskine Enterprises purchased merchandise on ac-count for $98,000. This required a debit to the Merchandise Inven-tory account to reflect the increase in that asset and a credit to Accounts Payable to show a corresponding increase in that category of liability:

(1)

Merchandise Inventory.....................................98,000
        Accounts Payable.....................................   98,000

(Notice again the conventional format, with the debit listed first and the credit indented to the right.)

The company also purchased a variety of other goods and services which it used in operating the store during 19x8. Expenditures for such items as telephone service, office stationery and supplies, and newspaper advertising amounted to $19,000. Because the goods and services were consumed during the year, they could not be treated as assets at year-end; instead, they had to be charged[5] to an expense ac-count, indicating a diminution of the owners' equity. (To simplify the example, one expense account is assumed to have been used by

----

[5] Debits to expense accounts are often referred to as charges. The term is also used to refer to debits to other accounts that normally carry debit balances, such as Accounts Receivable.

Erskine Enterprises for all these items, although many more accounts would probably be used in practice.) The accompanying credit was to Accounts Payable, indicating the company's liability to pay for these goods and services at a later date. The entry, then, was:

(2)

Miscellaneous Expense...............................	19,000	
Accounts Payable....................................		19,000

The company hoped, of course, that this $19,000 diminution of owners' equity would be offset by increases in owners' equity (revenues) obtained from store operations. Without revenues, however, the company's owners would have suffered an equity diminution of $19,000 in that they incurred a liability without a compensating increase in an asset or a decrease in another liability.

Cash sales during 19x8 amounted to $45,000; credit sales totaled $127,000. These transactions required debits to record the asset increases and a credit entry to record the gross increase in owners' equity resulting from product sales:

(3)

Cash...	45,000	
Accounts Receivable............................	127,000	
Sales Revenues.................................		172,000

Determining the Cost of Goods Sold

Mr. Erskine computed his cost of goods sold by the *periodic inventory method*. Under this method, no entry is made to record the cost of goods sold at the time when revenue is recorded. Instead, the cost of goods sold is determined at the end of the accounting period by counting the ending inventories and subtracting their cost from the total of beginning inventories and units received in inventory during the period. The December 31 inventory was found to be $18,000, and the cost of goods sold was calculated as follows:

Merchandise inventory, January 1........................	$ 16,000
Add: Purchases during the year..........................	98,000
Total Cost of Goods Available for Sale.................	$114,000
Less: Merchandise inventory, December 31.................	18,000
Cost of Goods Sold.....................................	$ 96,000

The entry required to transfer the cost of the goods sold from the inventory to the expense account was:

(4)

Cost of Goods Sold....................................	96,000	
Merchandise Inventory............................		96,000

This of course results in including the cost of merchandise spoiled or stolen in the cost of goods sold; information on the amount of such losses must be provided by other means if it is deemed important. Furthermore, during the year the balance in the inventory account is bound to be out of date. If the costs of goods purchased are debited to a separate Purchases account, then the balance in the inventory account remains at its January 1 level throughout the year. If purchases are debited to the Merchandise Inventory account, then the year-end balance in this account equals the total cost of the goods available for sale during the year. In either case, the balance in the Cost of Goods Sold account is zero until an adjustment is made to reflect the physical inventory count.

Wage and Salary Expense

Aside from the cost of merchandise, the largest cost incurred by Erskine Enterprises is its payroll cost. This cost for 19x8 was recognized with the following entry:

(5)

Executive Salaries	18,000	
Other Salaries and Wages	32,900	
Cash		50,900

The first two accounts in this entry are expense accounts. The executive salary was the salary paid Mr. Erskine for his services as president of the company.

The recognition of Mr. Erskine's salary as an expense of the company, and charging it to an expense account separate from other wages and salaries may come as a surprise. In Chapter 2, Mr. Erskine's accountant would not permit him to treat his withdrawals as a salary expense of the store. Nothing has changed except the legal form of organization, but this has been deemed enough of a difference to justify the different treatment. The corporation is a separate legal entity, and any salary paid by the corporation to the owners or to others for services rendered is assumed to represent a bargain agreed to by two independent parties and therefore can be treated as an expense to the corporation.

From one point of view this treatment makes sense. Because of the limited liability feature of the corporate form of organization, salaries paid to the owners are no longer available to creditors or to other owners in the event of liquidation. Thus corporate net income indicates the gross amount to be added to the owners' equity accounts on behalf of the owners *in their role as owners*. For a closely held corporation like Erskine Enterprises, however, any banker who is considering making a loan to the corporation or any informed potential shareholders will insist that owners' salaries be listed separately. If the amounts seem unreasonable, the investor with power to enforce his demands may very well insist on a reduction as a condition of his investment in the firm.

Recording Depreciation

The final item of expense to be recorded for 19x8 was depreciation on office and store furniture and equipment. Because Erskine Enterprises did not own the store building or the land on which it was situated, the furniture and equipment were the company's only *fixed assets*. (Land, buildings, and other similar assets are usually called *fixed assets, long-life assets,* or *property*.) Except for such assets as land purchased for speculation or for building construction and related uses, assets in these categories yield up their services gradually over a period of years rather than all at once, as in the case of an item of merchandise. The costs of the services yielded up each period by these *depreciable assets* must be transferred from the original asset accounts by means of a periodic depreciation charge.

In this case, $1,000 in depreciation was recorded for 19x8. The debit was to Depreciation Expense, representing a decrease in the ownership equity; and the credit was to Accumulated Depreciation, representing a decrease in an asset:

(6)

Depreciation Expense....................................1,000
    Accumulated Depreciation............................   1,000

This last account requires some explanation. The Erskine Appliance Store recorded depreciation on its equipment by debiting Depreciation Expense and crediting the equipment account. After three years, assuming that no equipment was sold, scrapped, or otherwise retired in the interim, the Furniture and Equipment account under such a scheme would reflect the following:

Furniture and Equipment

Original cost of equipment purchased	Depreciation, year 1
	Depreciation, year 2
	Depreciation, year 3

The account balance would then show that portion of original cost that had not yet been charged to expense—in other words, *unexpired cost.* The balance shown in the Depreciation Expense account for the third year would be only the cost expiring during that year, of course, because this is one of those temporary owners' equity accounts that was discussed in the previous chapter.

Although the method followed by The Erskine Appliance Store in no way violates accounting theory, it makes it impossible to identify the original cost of equipment without complete access to the company's records, and then only after a good deal of work. Because this kind of information is generally thought to be useful (and is often required by law), a more common treatment is to use a separate account in which to accumulate the figures reflecting the expired portion of original cost. This account is called *Accumulated Depreciation, Allowance for Depreciation,* or *Depreciation to Date* and is really a subdivision of the related property account:[6]

Furniture and Equipment	Accumulated Depreciation
Original cost of equipment pur- chased	Depreciation, year 1 Depreciation, year 2 Depreciation, year 3

The balances in these two accounts are offset against each other in financial reporting. For example, when Erskine Enterprises was formed, the accounts were revised and the January 1, 19x8, balance sheet could have included the following detail:

Furniture and equipment, at original cost....................$15,000
Less: Accumulated depreciation......................... 4,000
Net Furniture and Equipment............................$11,000

The net figure represents the unexpired portion of original cost and is usually referred to by such names as *book value* or *depreciated cost.*

The Accumulated Depreciation account is our first encounter with what is known as a *contra account.* In general, a contra account is used to accumulate a class of deductions from some other account, thereby providing both gross and net figures in any financial category in which such information may be deemed useful. Although the Accumulated Depreciation account normally carries a credit balance, it is neither a liability nor an owners' equity account. It is simply a deduction-from-assets account, a subdivision of the related asset ac-

---

[6] This account is still often referred to as the Reserve for Depreciation, a title which unfortunately gives the misleading idea that it represents a reserve supply of funds accumulated for the replacement of the assets. There is no reason why the firm should have idle funds equal to the balance in this account, however, and therefore the use of the term reserve in this connection should be discouraged.

count, introduced to permit the separate accumulation of some useful data. It is useful here primarily as a rough indicator of the age of the company's assets, the older the equipment the higher the ratio of accumulated depreciation to original cost. Thus, at the beginning of 19x8 Erskine Enterprises owned depreciable property that had cost $15,000 initially and had accumulated depreciation of $4,000 to that date. Hence, the assets were approximately 27 percent depreciated at that time. A reduction in this ratio from one year to the next might indicate that a modernization program is underway or that the company is expanding to provide facilities for present and future growth.

Sale of Depreciable Assets

When depreciable assets are *retired* (in most cases, this means when they are sold), their original cost and accumulated depreciation must be removed from the accounts. Such sales often lead to recognition of *capital gains or losses*. Capital gains or losses are recognized when assets other than inventories or receivables are sold at prices greater or less than their book value.[7]

For example, Erskine Enterprises sold for $80 cash an old dictating machine that Mr. Erskine had been using in his office for several years. By referring to Erskine's *property record*—a card file containing the costs, acquisition dates, and locations of each of the company's long-lived tangible properties—it was found that the dictating machine was purchased originally for $400. Depreciation of $350 had been accumulated over the years, so that the book value of the equipment at the time of retirement was $50 ($400 — $350). This means that there was a *gain* on the sale of this piece of equipment, computed as follows:

Proceeds from sale	$80
Book value of equipment sold	50
Gain on Sale	$30

In this case, the gain resulted either from an incorrect estimate of life made at the time the equipment was acquired or an error in the estimation of its ultimate salvage or resale value. From this point of view, it might be said that depreciation was overstated in the past and that prior years' earnings should be restated to reflect the correction of these errors. Unfortunately, the income statements of prior years are past history, and repeated correction of prior years' earnings

---

[7] Capital gains and losses also arise occasionally through retirement of liabilities at more or less than their book value; these are discussed in Chapter 13.

figures could be most confusing. Therefore, in conformance with common practice, the gain would be shown on Erskine Enterprises' income statement for 19x8, with no attempt to prorate a portion of it to prior years.

If this had been a sale of merchandise, of course, the gain would have been reflected in ordinary operating income. Instead, it was the sale of an asset that was acquired for use rather than resale. Such sales are highly irregular, varying widely in amount from year to year. They cannot be relied upon to indicate the company's future earning power. For this reason the effects of the sale should be kept separate from the normal operating income of the firm.

The bookkeeping entry to record a sale like this is straightforward. Because the asset was no longer owned by the company, its balances in both the asset and the contra-asset accounts had to be removed. The entry to accomplish this in this case was:

(7)

Cash..	80	
Accumulated Depreciation.................................	350	
Furniture and Equipment..............................		400
Gain on Retirement of Equipment.......................		30

In this entry, the credit of $400 removed the original cost of the item from the accounts and the debit of $350 did the same for the accumulated depreciation applicable to it. Although crediting the Furniture and Equipment account for $50 would have had the necessary effect on aggregate book value, it would not have been correct because it would have left both asset and contra-asset overstated.

Recording Cash Receipts and Disbursements

Two other important sets of transactions were recorded on the books of Erskine Enterprises during the year 19x8: cash receipts and disbursements. Some cash receipts have already been recognized in entries (3) and (7) above; the entries to record other receipts can be summarized as follows:

(8)

Cash..118,000		
Accounts Receivable.............................		118,000

This reflects the collection of cash during 19x8 from customers who purchased merchandise on credit either during 19x8 or during prior years. No owners' equity accounts were affected by this collection activity; the transactions simply represented an increase in one kind of asset and a decrease in another.

Payments were made during the year to suppliers against obligations that had previously been recorded in the accounts. Entry (9) records the decrease in the company's liabilities due to the payments to suppliers during the year:

(9)

Accounts Payable	114,100	
Cash		114,100

THE FINANCIAL STATEMENTS

The ledger of Erskine Enterprises as of December 31, 19x8, appears in Exhibit 3–2. The amounts shown in the accounts appearing in the ledger can be verified easily. First, it can be seen that the January 1, 19x8, balances in the accounts agree with the balance sheet in Exhibit 3–1. Second, each entry in the accounts is identified by a number in parentheses. This number refers to one of the transactions in the preceding pages, and the amounts shown there should be the same as those shown in Exhibit 3–2. (A useful exercise at this point is to set up a set of these accounts on a sheet of note paper and enter the opening balances and transactions data.)

The final step is to offset the debits against the credits in each account and compute the closing balances. These closing balances can then be used to derive the company's financial statements for 19x8.

Income Statement

Seven revenue and expense accounts appear in Exhibit 3–2. From them the income statement appearing in Exhibit 3–3 can be obtained.[8] This statement shows the gain on equipment retirement as an "extraordinary item," segregated from ordinary income. Neither component of income should be overlooked, but the two should not be mixed.

Closing Entry

The revenue and expense accounts used in obtaining the income statement for the year are all temporary owners' equity accounts. Before the next year's transactions can be recorded, the 19x8 balances

---

[8] Corporate income and other taxes have been assumed to be zero to avoid undue complications in this illustration. They will be given explicit recognition in the next chapter.

Exhibit 3–2

ERSKINE ENTERPRISES, INC.
Ledger Accounts and Balances
As of December 31, 19x8

Cash

Bal. 1/1	4,000	(5)	50,900
(3)	45,000	(9)	114,100
(7)	80		
(8)	118,000		
Bal. 12/31 2,080			

Sales Revenue

		(3)	172,000

Accounts Receivable

Bal. 1/1	24,000	(8)	118,000
(3)	127,000		
Bal. 12/31 33,000			

Cost of Goods Sold

(4)	96,000		

Merchandise Inventory

Bal. 1/1	16,000	(4)	96,000
(1)	98,000		
Bal. 12/31 18,000			

Executive Salaries

(5)	18,000		

Furniture and Equipment

| Bal. 1/1 | 15,000 | (7) | 400 |
| Bal. 12/31 14,600 | | | |

Other Salaries and Wages

(5)	32,900		

Accumulated Depreciation

(7)	350	Bal. 1/1	4,000
		(6)	1,000
		Bal. 12/31 4,650	

Depreciation Expense

(6)	1,000		

Accounts Payable

(9)	114,100	Bal. 1/1	20,000
		(1)	98,000
		(2)	19,000
		Bal. 12/31 22,900	

Miscellaneous Expense

(2)	19,000		

Capital Stock

		Bal. 1/1	35,000

Gain on Retirement of Equipment

		(7)	30

Exhibit 3–3

ERSKINE ENTERPRISES, INC.
Income Statement
For the Year Ending December 31, 19x8

Sales revenue..		$172,000
Less: Cost of goods sold...............................$96,000		
Executive salaries...............................	18,000	
Other salaries and wages........................	32,900	
Depreciation....................................	1,000	
Miscellaneous expense...........................	19,000	
Total Expense.............................		166,900
Income before extraordinary item......................		$ 5,100
Extraordinary item:		
Gain on retirement of equipment......................		30
Net Income..		$ 5,130

in these accounts must be removed. The entry by which this was accomplished is known as a *closing entry*. The closing entry in this case was:

(10)

Sales Revenue..	172,000	
Gain on Retirement of Equipment........................	30	
Cost of Goods Sold...............................		96,000
Executive Salaries................................		18,000
Other Salaries and Wages.........................		32,900
Depreciation Expense.............................		1,000
Miscellaneous Expense............................		19,000
Retained Earnings................................		5,130

By debiting the Sales Revenue and Gain on Retirement of Equipment accounts with $172,000 and $30, respectively, this entry exactly offset the credit balances in those accounts and thus left them with zero balances. The credits to the five expense accounts had the same effect. The difference between the sum of the debits and the sum of the credits in this case was equal to the net income for the year and was credited to the Retained Earnings account.

Retained Earnings is a permanent account in the owners' equity section of the chart of accounts. The balance in this account appears in the periodic statement of financial position, or balance sheet. It reflects the difference between the total reported earnings of the corporation since its formation and the amount of dividends paid out to stockholders during the same period. In other words, it is the amount of funds that have been earned by the corporation but which the stockholders have elected to reinvest in the business. At the date of incorporation, of course, the retained earnings to date are zero.

The Balance Sheet

The permanent accounts of Erskine Enterprises, with their balances and entries for 19x8, are shown in Exhibit 3–4. The entry

Exhibit 3–4

ERSKINE ENTERPRISES, INC.

Permanent Ledger Accounts and Balances

As of December 31, 19x8

Cash				Accounts Payable		
Bal. 1/1	4,000	(5)	50,900	(9)	114,100	Bal. 1/1	20,000
(3)	45,000	(9)	114,100			(1)	98,000
(7)	80					(2)	19,000
(8)	118,000					Bal. 12/31 22,900
Bal. 12/31 2,080						

Accounts Receivable			
Bal. 1/1	24,000	(8)	118,000
(3)	127,000		
Bal. 12/31 33,000			

Merchandise Inventory			
Bal. 1/1	16,000	(4)	96,000
(1)	98,000		
Bal. 12/31 18,000			

Furniture and Equipment				Capital Stock	
Bal. 1/1	15,000	(7)	400	Bal. 1/1	35,000
Bal. 12/31 14,600					

Accumulated Depreciation				Retained Earnings	
(7)	350	Bal. 1/1	4,000	(10)	5,130
		(6)	1,000		
		Bal. 12/31 4,650			

closing the nominal accounts has been posted to the ledger, and therefore the account balances are up-to-date and ready for the preparation of a year-end balance sheet. Mr. Erskine's accountant thought that Mr. Erskine would be interested in a comparison of the year-end and year-beginning balance sheets, and for this reason prepared the statement in the form shown in Exhibit 3–5.

Exhibit 3–5

ERSKINE ENTERPRISES, INC.
Comparative Statement of Financial Position
As of December 31, 19x7, and December 31, 19x8

ASSETS	19x7	19x8	Change
Cash..	$ 4,000	$ 2,080	$ −1,920
Accounts receivable..................................	24,000	33,000	+9,000
Merchandise inventory..............................	16,000	18,000	+2,000
Furniture and equipment...........................	$15,000	$14,600	
Less: Accumulated depreciation..................	4,000	4,650	
Furniture and equipment, net.....................	$11,000	$ 9,950	−1,050
Total Assets...........................	$55,000	$63,030	$+8,030

EQUITIES			
Liabilities:			
Accounts payable..................................	$20,000	$22,900	$+2,900
Total Liabilities............................	$20,000	$22,900	
Owners' Equity:			
Capital stock.....................................	$35,000	$35,000	....
Retained earnings................................	.....	5,130	+5,130
Total Owners' Equity.......................	$35,000	$40,130	
Total Equities...........................	$55,000	$63,030	$+8,030

Income versus Cash Flow

Several conclusions can be drawn from the financial statements of Erskine Enterprises for 19x8. First, the $5,130 net income for the year represented a rate of return on Mr. Erskine's investment of about 14.7 percent ($5,130 divided by $35,000). In most lines of business, this would be regarded as a satisfactory ratio.

Despite this favorable income figure, however, the cash balance dipped by $1,920 between the beginning and the end of the year, almost a 50 percent reduction. Assuming that the $4,000 opening balance was not excessive in view of the amount of business to be done, the year-end balance would seem to be alarmingly low.

What is to be learned from this is that net income may be a measure of the increase in the shareholders' wealth as a result of the year's business, but it does not necessarily represent the amount that the company can afford to distribute to its owners in the form of cash dividends. The reason for this apparent paradox can be deduced from an examination of the right-hand column of Exhibit 3–5. Credit sales, included in net income for 19x8, had exceeded collections from customers during 19x8 by $9,000. This means that Erskine Enterprises had increased its financing of its customers by this amount. This created a financing problem for Erskine Enterprises. It solved this problem in part by not paying its own suppliers immediately (accounts payable increased by $2,900), but a decline in cash could not be avoided entirely.

Payment and Accounting for Dividends

Payments to a corporation's shareholders for the use of their funds are known as *dividends*. Dividends are *declared* by a formal vote of the corporation's board of directors, in this case Mr. Erskine and two members of his family.[9] Mr. Erskine received no dividends during 19x8, and he decided at the end of the year that he would like to declare a modest dividend if the corporation could afford it.

One factor that influenced the dividend decision was the amount of net income reported for 19x8, which amounted to $5,130, as we have seen. Another factor influencing the dividend decision was the availability of cash, since dividends are paid with cash.

Fortunately for Mr. Erskine and Erskine Enterprises, the year-end cash shortage was very temporary. In fact, cash collections exceeded credit sales during January, 19x9, by $4,000, and Mr. Erskine decided that a small cash dividend could be paid without impairing the company's liquidity unduly. Accordingly, the board of directors voted to declare a dividend of $1 a share, payable on February 20, on the 1,000 shares of common stock outstanding.

Like proprietor withdrawals, corporate dividends are not expenses. Instead, they are regarded as *distributions* of funds earned by corporate operations. Thus they are deducted from retained earnings and are not deducted from revenues in the calculation of net income. The entry to record the dividend declaration was:

Dividends Declared	1,000	
Dividends Payable		1,000

In this case the debit was made to a special nominal account, Dividends Declared, rather than to Retained Earnings. This was done solely for convenience, to facilitate the preparation of financial statements. Declaration of a dividend reduces the company's retained

---

[9] This describes practice in the United States. In Europe and in much of the rest of the world, dividends are declared once each year by a formal vote of the shareholders at the annual shareholders' meeting. The vote is usually on a dividend proposal formulated by the directors, however.

earnings immediately, whether the amount is debited immediately to the Retained Earnings account or to Dividends Declared. The latter is a temporary owners' equity account which must be closed to Retained Earnings at the end of the year by means of a closing entry.

The credit in this entry went to Dividends Payable, a liability account. The board's declaration of the dividend made it a formal obligation of the corporation, enforceable at law as a liability. Therefore it must be included with the liabilities, even though it is payable to the company's shareholders.

Cash and Retained Earnings

The fact that dividends are charged against Retained Earnings can be misinterpreted, and often is. As the foregoing discussion showed, dividends reduce retained earnings, but the payment requires *cash*. All that a balance in the Retained Earnings account indicates is that the company has been profitable at some time in the past; it does not indicate that funds are currently available for dividends.[10] In fact, all of the funds earned and reinvested may have been used for the purchase of property or inventories, thus becoming unavailable for other use.

SUMMARY

A dominant share of economic activity in the United States is conducted by corporations. In medium- and large-scale enterprise the corporation is ubiquitous. One objective of this chapter has been to introduce the main ownership equity accounts used by corporations. These differ slightly in form from those of unincorporated enterprise, but the overall purpose and structure remain the same.

The main task in this chapter, however, has been to introduce the basic debit-and-credit notation that the accountant uses for efficient communication, and to use this notation in the analysis of another "accounting cycle," slightly more complex than the one studied in the previous chapter.

The illustrative figures were chosen in such a way as to emphasize the difference between the concepts of income and cash flow. Income is a measure of the current productivity of the owners' investment in

---

[10] Retained earnings are still often referred to as *earned surplus*, but these words convey an erroneous implication that the balance somehow represents an excess of funds that can be drawn off by the shareholders or others at any time. Nothing could be further from the truth in most instances, and the term should be avoided.

the enterprise, but immediate internal demands for cash may be so strong that the current income figure may be a very poor approximation of the amount of funds available for distribution to the shareholders.

QUESTIONS AND PROBLEMS

1. Distinguish between disbursement and expense.

2. Is the Dividends Declared account an asset, a liability, or an owners' equity account? Explain.

3. How much cash would you be likely to find in the Earned Surplus account? In Retained Earnings?

4. Explain the nature and function of a contra account. Illustrate.

5. Explain the distinction between paid-in capital and retained earnings.

6. Why do expense accounts usually have debit balances?

7. "Net income arises because the company receives more assets from its operations than it has to use to obtain them." If this is so, why are the income measurement accounts part of owners' equity instead of among the assets.

8. Is the Allowance for Depreciation account an asset, liability, or owners' equity account? Explain.

9. Why is the salary of the owner-manager of a corporation considered an expense while the salary of the owner-manager of an individual proprietorship is regarded as a distribution of net income or withdrawal of capital?

10. Indicate whether each of the following would result in an entry to the left- or right-hand side of a T-account.

a) Liability increase.
b) Asset decrease.
c) Expense increase.
d) Ownership equity decrease.
e) Revenue increase.

11. The XYZ Company balance sheet on January 1, 19x1, listed assets of $1,000,000, liabilities of $100,000, and capital stock for which the company had received $300,000.

During the year, $140,000 was received from the sale of additional capital stock, and dividends of $40,000 were declared and paid. The balance sheet on December 31, 19x1, showed assets of $1,500,000 and liabilities of $350,000.

Calculate the following (label all your calculations):

a) Retained earnings, January 1, 19x1.
b) Retained earnings, December 31, 19x1.
c) Net income for the year 19x1.

12. A business had total ownership equity at the end of a year amounting to $500,000. Present the proprietorship section of a balance sheet under the following alternatives:

a) The business is a corporation. The shareholders have paid the corporation $290,000 for their shares of capital stock.
b) The business is a two-man partnership of G. White and S. Smith. Originally each had invested $200,000 cash and had shared equally in profits of $200,000. However, White had withdrawn 50 percent more than Smith (for personal use) and neither had made additional investments.

13. The following appeared on the financial statements of a corporation:

Sales..	$100,000
Expenses other than cost of goods sold....................	30,000
Net income...	5,000
Cost of purchases..	80,000
Ending inventory...	30,000

What was the beginning inventory?

*14. The XYZ Company uses the periodic inventory method to account for its merchandise inventories. The inventory was $150,000 on January 1 and $126,000 on December 31, by physical count. Purchases during the year amounted to $386,000. During the year a minor fire in the company's stockroom damaged merchandise costing $18,000. This merchandise was sold to a junk dealer on October 18 for $1,200.

Compute the cost of goods sold to regular trade customers.

*15. The Alpha Company bought a truck on January 1, 19x7, for $4,000. It was decided to charge depreciation on the basis of a five-year life and salvage value of $800 at the end of five years, equal amounts to be charged as depreciation expense for each of the five years. The truck

---

* Solutions to problems marked with an asterisk (*) are found in Appendix B.

was placed in service immediately and used for three years, at the end of which time it was sold for $1,100 cash.

Prepare journal entries to record:

a) The purchase of the truck.
b) Depreciation for 19x7.
c) Sale of the truck.

16. After all transactions for the year had been recorded, the following balances were found in the owners' equity accounts of a small corporation (the sequence of the accounts in the list below is alphabetical and has no other significance):

	Debit	Credit
Capital stock		20,000
Cost of goods sold	70,000	
Dividends declared	6,000	
Other expenses	21,000	
Retained earnings		1,000
Sales revenue		100,000

a) What does the $6,000 figure opposite "dividends declared" mean? Were these dividends paid in cash during the year?
b) What does the $1,000 figure opposite "retained earnings" mean?
c) What balance would you show opposite "retained earnings" on the year-end balance sheet?

17. Balance sheet information:

	1/1/xx	12/31/xx
Equipment	$800,000	$900,000
Allowance for depreciation	130,000	160,000

Income statement information:

Depreciation on equipment, $80,000.
Loss on sale of equipment, $ 5,000.

Other information:

Expenditures for the purchase of new equipment, $157,000.

What were the proceeds from the sale of equipment?

18. The Sturdy Shoe Company operates a chain of retail shoe stores. The company does no manufacturing, but it buys all its shoes from a large producer who brands them with the Sturdy name. The cost of shoes purchased is debited at the time of purchase to the Inventory account.

The company's December 31 account balances (adjusted except for periodic inventory) appear below. The final inventory is $268,921. Prepare a balance sheet and a report of earnings for the year.

Cash..$	20,119	
Accounts receivable.............................	232,684	
Inventory......................................	1,058,888	
Prepaid rent and insurance.......................	22,156	
Furniture and equipment.........................	116,621	
Trucks...	51,460	
Accounts payable................................		$ 66,980
Notes payable..................................		100,000
Allowance for depreciation.......................		48,918
Common stock..................................		300,000
Retained earnings...............................		128,189
Sales..		1,428,160
Administrative expenses..........................	64,892	
Selling expenses................................	215,782	
Rent expense...................................	181,603	
Other operating expenses.........................	107,215	
Other revenues.................................		13,387
Interest expense................................	14,214	
	$2,085,634	$2,085,634

19. The bookkeeper for the Auld Sod Company recorded the following events:

(1) Purchased on credit a three-year policy from Casualty Insurers, Inc., for $732.
(2) Purchased office supplies for $99. Payment was made in cash.
(3) Paid cash, $167, for bunting, banners, displays, and refreshments provided for guests entertained two days earlier.
(4) Sold linens on credit to Talbot Textile Company for $850. The linens had cost $650.

The entries he made are shown below:

(1) Insurance Expense..	732	
Accounts Payable...		732
(2) Office Supplies..	99	
Accounts Payable...		99
(3) Advertising Expense...	167	
Inventories..		167
(4) Accounts Receivable...	850	
Inventories..		850

For each of the above entries that was made incorrectly, indicate the correct entry and your reasons for believing that the bookkeeper's entry was made incorrectly.

20. On January 2, 19x1, Company X bought an electric typewriter for office use, paying $540 in cash. The company expected to sell this typewriter for $90 after using it for six years. Depreciation was to be charged in equal amounts each year.

a) Assuming that all journal entries for the year have been made correctly but that no closing entries have been made:

(1) What balance would you expect to find in the Allowance for Depreciation account as of December 31, 19x3?

(2) What balance would you expect to find in the Depreciation Expense account as of December 31, 19x3?

(3) What was the "book value" of the typewriter as of December 31, 19x3?

b) What entry would be required on December 31, 19x6, if the typewriter were sold on that date for $90, cash?

c) What entry would be required on December 31, 19x4, if the typewriter were sold on that date for $80, cash?

21. Explain the most probable meaning of each number shown in the following T-accounts (opening balances and other entries have been omitted from these T-accounts):

Accounts Receivable				Merchandise Inventory			
....	...	....	...	....	...	....	...
....	...	....	...	....	...	....	...
....	...	....	...	....	...	....	...
June 6	712	July 17	1,019	April 28	297	March 15	990

Store Equipment				Allowance for Depreciation			
....	...	....	...	....	...	....	...
....	...	....	...	....	...	....	...
....	...	....	...	....	...	....	...
March 12	3,241	Nov. 29	2,062	Nov. 29	1,445	Dec. 31	865

*22. Analyze the following transactions and prepare journal entries to record their effects on the company's accounts. Use revenue and expense accounts. The business is organized as a corporation.

(1) The company purchases merchandise for $5,000; the supplier accepts, as payment for this purchase, the company's written promise (its *note*) to pay this amount next month.

(2) The company receives $4,000 from customers to pay for goods purchased by them during the previous month.

(3) The company pays accounts payable of $6,000.

(4) The company pays salaries of $1,000 earned by employees in the current month.

(5) The company borrows $50,000 on a long-term note.

(6) The company sells merchandise on account for $8,000; the cost of this merchandise, purchased in a previous period, was $6,000.

(7) The company purchased a piece of land at a cost of $7,000, cash.

(8) The board of directors declared a dividend of $3,000, which the company paid in cash to its shareholders.

(9) Office stationery costing $60 was purchased on credit for current use.

(10) Someone stole $100 in cash from the company. The loss is fully covered by insurance, but nothing has yet been received from the insurance company.

*23. Prepare journal entries in debit and credit form for each of the following transactions. For each debit and each credit, indicate (1) whether it represents an increase or a decrease in assets, liabilities, or ownership; and (2) whether the amount would appear in full on the income statement for the currrent year. The business is organized as a corporation. These transactions are completely independent of each other and do not represent all the year's transactions of this company.

(1) Purchase of merchandise on account, $450.

(2) Payment to supplier for goods received and recorded in previous month, $884.

(3) Issue of additional shares of capital to Mr. T. O. Pitt, principal stockholder, in exchange for $8,500 cash.

(4) Receipt of $10,000 cash as a loan from a bank.

(5) Payment of $1,000 salary to Mr. Pitt.

(6) Sale of merchandise on credit: sale price $1,200, cost $920.

(7) Store clerks' wages earned but not yet paid, $2,800.

(8) Receipt of bill for electricity used in store and office, $87.

(9) Collection of $1,106 on accounts receivable.

(10) Expiration of prepaid rent on store, $500.

24. Prepare journal entries in debit and credit form for each of the following transactions. For each debit and each credit, indicate (a) whether it represents an increase or a decrease in assets, liabilities, or ownership, and (b) whether the amount would appear in full on the income statement for the current year. The business is organized as an individual proprietorship. These transactions are completely independent of each other and do not represent all the year's transactions of this company.

(1) Purchase of merchandise on extended-payment contract, $2,100; one third of price paid at time of purchase, the remainder to be paid in installments after the first of next year.

(2) Payment of $15,000 to suppliers on account.

(3) A three-year insurance policy was taken out last year, and the three-year premium of $1,800 was paid in cash at that time. Record the amount applicable to the current year.

(4) Sale of merchandise, $8,300 for cash and $13,700 on account; cost of merchandise sold, $16,400.

(5) Purchase of land and building, $12,000 for the land and $40,000 for the building; $30,000 was paid in cash and the remainder in the form of a 20-year mortgage payable.
(6) Collection of $18,300 on customers' accounts.
(7) Use of office supplies, $800; these supplies had been placed in Office Supplies Inventory at time of purchase.
(8) Depreciation on delivery equipment, $1,550.
(9) Payment of employee salaries for current period, $700.
(10) Withdrawal of $560 cash by Mr. N. R. Gee, owner.

25. Prepare journal entries in debit and credit form for each of the following transactions. For each debit and each credit, indicate (a) whether it represents an increase or a decrease in assets, liabilities, or ownership; and (b) whether the amount would appear in full on the income statement for the current month. The business is organized as a corporation. The company prepares a separate income statement for each month's operations. These transactions are completely independent of each other and do not represent all the month's transactions of this company.

(1) Purchase of office equipment for cash, $4,700.
(2) Receipt of bill from plumbing contractor for repairs performed this month, $225.
(3) Sale of merchandise on account, $22,400; cost of this merchandise was $16,700.
(4) Issued 100 shares of the company's capital stock for $5,000 cash.
(5) Hired clerk to start work the first of next month, salary $360 a month.
(6) Collected $26,200 from customers on account.
(7) Borrowed $1,000 cash from bank.
(8) Ordered carload of bagged charcoal for sale to customers, $24,000.
(9) Recorded $1,400 depreciation and $2,200 expiration of prepaid rent.
(10) Paid $1,500 salary to Mr. N. A. Woods, owner of 75 percent of the corporation's capital stock.
(11) Received and paid bills, as follows:
       For new delivery truck, $2,600.
       For insurance policy to be effective the first of next month, $220.
       For this month's telephone service, $85.

26. The Handyman Tool Shop is an unincorporated retailer of home hardware supplies. The shop's balance sheet as of August 31, 19x1, is shown below:

HANDYMAN TOOL SHOP
BALANCE SHEET
AS OF AUGUST 31, 19x1

ASSETS		EQUITIES	
		Liabilities:	
Cash.................	$ 2,510	Accounts payable.............	$ 5,180
Accounts receivable.....	3,060	Salaries payable...............	140
Merchandise inventory...	7,200	Total Liabilities..........	$ 5,320
Equipment............$22,140		*Owner's Equity:*	
Less: Depreciation to			
date............... 7,120	15,020	T. Square, proprietor.......... 22,470	
Total Assets.....	$27,790	Total Equities..........	$27,790

The store's transactions for the month of September are summarized in the items below:

(1) Sold merchandise at an aggregate sales value of $11,700. Of this amount, $2,700 was for cash and $9,000 on credit. The cost of the merchandise sold was $6,700.

(2) Purchased merchandise from suppliers on account at a cost of $4,630.

(3) Made cash payments for the following:

September store rental..	$ 500
Purchase of secondhand delivery truck.........................	1,800
Salaries (See note below)....................................	1,480
Miscellaneous expenses for September..........................	700

(4) Paid $5,300 to suppliers of merchandise.

(5) September depreciation on equipment amounted to $160.

(6) Mr. Square, owner of the shop, invested an additional $2,000 of his own funds in the business.

(7) Collected $3,500 from customers.

NOTE: Since salaries are paid on a weekly basis, the cash *disbursed* during a month for salaries seldom equals the amount of salary *earned* by employees during the month. Thus, $140 of the cash salary payment made during the month was to pay off the liability that existed at the end of August. Mr. Square himself received no salary for working in the store.

a) Analyze each transaction, using journal entries in debit and credit form.

b) Enter in T-accounts the September 1 balances given above, set up revenue and expense accounts plus any others required by your analysis in (*a*), and post your analyses of the transactions to these T-accounts.

c) Prepare an income statement for the month of September and a balance sheet as of September 30. (Ignore income taxes.)

27. The balance sheet of the Freemont Hardware Store as of March 31, 19xx, was as show below:

FREEMONT HARDWARE STORE, INC.

BALANCE SHEET

AS OF MARCH 31, 19xx

ASSETS			EQUITIES	
			Liabilities:	
Cash		$11,000	Accounts payable	$15,800
Accounts receivable		14,100	Notes payable	3,000
Merchandise inventory		21,700	Long-term debt	12,000
Building	$30,000		Total Liabilities	$30,800
Equipment	10,800			
Total	$40,800		*Shareholders' equity:*	
Less: Depreciation to			Capital stock	$30,000
date	9,000	31,800	Retained earnings	17,800
			Total shareholders' equity	$47,800
Total Assets		$78,600	Total Equities	$78,600

The following items summarize the company's transactions for the month of April:

(1) Purchased merchandise on account from suppliers at a total cost of $13,500.

(2) Purchased on account an electric warehouse truck at a cost of $800.

(3) Sold on account for $18,200 merchandise costing $10,500.

(4) Collected $15,000 on accounts receivable.

(5) Paid $17,200 on accounts payable.

(6) Depreciation charges were:

Office and warehouse equipment	$70
Automotive equipment	80
Building	50

(7) On April 1, a two-year general coverage insurance policy was purchased for $120 cash.

(8) On April 1, paid rent of $660 for the use of additional storage space for six months, beginning April 1, 19xx.

(9) Made other cash payments for the following:

Salaries of employees	$2,800
Miscellaneous operating expenses for April	1,140
Interest for April on notes payable and long-term debt	75

(10) The board of directors declared a dividend in the amount of $500, to be paid to shareholders in cash on May 15.

a) Analyze each transaction, using journal entries in debit and credit form.

b) Enter in T-accounts the April 1 balances given above, set up revenue and expense accounts plus any others required by your analysis in (*a*), and post your analyses of the transactions to these T-accounts.

c) Prepare an income statement for the month of April and a balance sheet as of April 30. (Ignore income taxes.)

28. The Greeley School, a private preparatory day school for boys, accepted its first students and held its first classes in September, 19x1. The school was founded by Jonathan Greeley, the former senior tutor of a large eastern preparatory school.

Mr. Greeley was anxious to try out a new system of instruction and had persuaded a group of wealthy businessmen to supply most of the capital he needed to finance the new venture. He intended to operate the school for profit, partly to demonstrate that it could be done, and partly because this seemed to him the best basis on which to attract the required capital.

As expected, enrollment was below capacity during the first year, but by May, 19x2, applications for September enrollment were so numerous that Mr. Greeley believed that his classes would be filled during the second year.

His backers were impressed by the file of admission applications and were pleased by the competence that Mr. Greeley seemed to have shown in administering the school, but they were anxious to find out how much money the school had lost during its initial year of operations. As one of the shareholders said, "The enrollment figures are impressive, but so are those at the university, and they have to tap us alumni every year just to meet the payroll. I don't expect we'll show a profit at Greeley this year, but if the loss is much larger than we had expected we ought to think seriously of closing up shop or selling our shares for whatever we can get for them."

The school started its formal existence on July 1, 19x1, with the issuance of a corporate charter. The following transactions took place during its first 12 months:

(1) Two hundred shares of capital stock were issued on July 1, 19x1, for $30,000, cash.

(2) At the same time, the shareholders deposited an additional $10,000 in the corporation's bank account, receiving in exchange notes payable in this amount.

(3) A two-year lease was signed, giving the school the right to use a large mansion and its grounds from July 1, 19x1, to June 30, 19x3. The monthly rental was $2,000. An initial cash payment of $6,000 was made on July 1, 19x1, and cash payments of $2,000 each were made on the first of each succeeding month, through June 1, 19x2.

(4) A set of classroom blackboards was purchased on credit for $3,600. Other private schools in the area estimated that on the average, blackboards could be used for 12 years before replacement became necessary.

(5) Classroom furniture costing $9,000 was purchased from the Tower Seating Company, which accepted a down payment of $4,000 in cash and a note payable for the balance. Classroom furniture was expected to have an eight-year life, on the average.

(6) Equipment of various kinds, with an expected average life of five years, was purchased for $7,000, cash.

(7) Students' tuition and other fees amounted to $78,000. Of this amount, $6,000 had not yet been collected by June 30, 19x2, but Mr. Greeley was confident that this amount would be received before the new school year began in September.

(8) Salaries were paid in cash:
Teaching staff, $54,000.
Office staff, $11,000.

(9) On June 15, 19x2, two parents paid tuition for the 19x2–x3 school year, amounting to $3,400.

(10) Various school supplies were bought on credit for $4,100. Of these, $200 were still in the school's storeroom, unused, on June 30, 19x2.

(11) Utility bills and other miscellaneous operating costs applicable to the year ending June 30, 19x2, were paid in cash, $3,800.

(12) Payments amounting to $4,500 were made on account to suppliers of items referred to in items 4 and 10 above.

(13) The holders of the school's notes were paid interest of $900. In addition, the Tower Seating Company was paid $1,500 of the amount borrowed (item 5, above).

a) Prepare a list of account titles that you think would be useful for recording these transactions, including revenue and expense accounts and an allowance for depreciation account. Then analyze the above transactions in debit and credit form. For each debit and each credit, indicate (1) whether the effect is to increase or to decrease an asset (A), a liability (L), or the shareholders' equity (O.E.); and (2) whether the amount would appear in full on the income statement for the current year. For example:

```
Cash...................................................................xxx
    Capital Stock......................................................xxx
    (Increase A; increase O.E.; no effect on current income.)
```

Do not forget to record depreciation for the year.

b) Post these amounts to T-accounts.

c) Prepare an income statement for the year and a balance sheet as of June 30, 19x2.

d) Upon seeing your figures, Mr. Greeley objected to the depreciation charge. "We just can't afford to write off any of those costs this year," he said. "Next year our tuition will be up, and we can start recovering depreciation." Do you agree with Mr. Greeley, or do you have a different concept of depreciation? Defend your position.

e) If you were a shareholder, how would you use the financial statements in your evaluation of the financial success or failure of this new enterprise? Assuming that your decision to retain your shares or sell them would be based on your forecast of future financial statements, would the financial statements of a period already in the past be of any relevance to you?

Chapter 4

ACCRUAL ACCOUNTING AND
MANUFACTURING OPERATIONS

JUST AS MOLIERE'S BOURGEOIS GENTLEMAN was delighted to learn that he had been talking prose all of his life, it may be a pleasure to discover that while we were learning the rules for accounting for transactions in the two preceding chapters, we were actually practicing accrual accounting. However, to insure that the nature of this accomplishment can be fully understood, this chapter will contrast accrual accounting with its alternative, cash basis accounting, and will then examine the application of accrual accounting to manufacturing operations and to the calculation of interest expense and payroll costs.

CASH BASIS VERSUS ACCRUAL BASIS ACCOUNTING

The accrual basis of accounting, or more simply accrual accounting, is practically universal among medium and large business firms, but individuals in their personal accounting and many small businessmen use the *cash basis*. Cash basis income is defined as cash operating *receipts* minus cash operating *disbursements*. In other words, sales revenue is recognized when cash is received, not when services are performed or goods are delivered; with few exceptions, expenses are measured by the cash disbursements made during the period.

A Simple Example

To illustrate, Mr. John Appleby has a small management consulting business that he operates under the name of Appleby Associates. He bills his clients on the first of each month for work performed during the previous month. He makes no entry in his revenue account, however, until he receives payment from the client. Occasionally, Mr. Appleby assigns one of his employees to a task that will take several months to complete. He must pay the employee's salary each month, but he does not bill the client until the assignment is finished. If Mr. Appleby is accounting on a cash basis, he will report the salary as an expense at the time it is paid, even though no revenue is recorded at that time.

For example, Mr. Appleby agreed on January 2 to carry out an assignment for the Jones Company. On January 22 he purchased $1,000 of materials for use on this assignment. He paid for the materials on February 9, but he did not actually start to work on the assignment until March 5. The project was completed on March 28, and the Jones Company was billed for the contract price of $12,000 on that date. Salaries of employees who worked on the assignment

Exhibit 4–1

APPLEBY ASSOCIATES: TIMING OF EVENTS

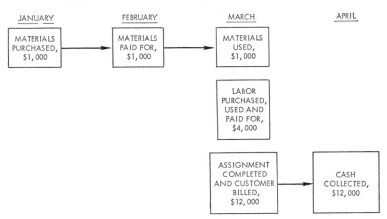

during March amounted to $4,000, and this amount was actually paid on March 31. This series of transactions is summarized in Exhibit 4–1.

Because it prepared its financial statements on a cash basis, Appleby Associates recognized expenses of $1,000 in February and $4,000 in March, and revenue of $12,000 in April.[1] In other words, if these had been the only transactions of Appleby Associates during these four

---

[1] A firm may be said to be on a cash basis even though it does not charge merchandise costs to expense until the goods are sold and even though equipment costs are capitalized subject to later depreciation. This is a hybrid system, partway between a full cash basis and a full accrual basis. The departures from a strict cash basis are designed to increase the accuracy of financial statements with respect to those items for which the cash basis is most likely to be misleading. An unmodified cash basis report of income is exceedingly rare in business, mainly because businessmen have found it unworkable (and also because the Internal Revenue Service will not accept it for income tax purposes).

months, the firm would have reported neither profit nor loss in January, losses of $1,000 and $4,000 in February and March, and net income of $12,000 in April.

This patently absurd result is avoided by accrual basis accounting. In fact, it is just this type of situation that led to the development of accrual accounting in the first place. Thus, expense is recognized not when a disbursement is made but when a cost expires or is consumed in the creation of revenues. As a general rule, revenue is recognized at the time services are performed or goods are delivered to customers, not when cash is received. In the example, Appleby Associates would have noted the existence of an asset, materials inventory, at the end of January and a different asset, accounts receivable, at the end of March. Both the revenue and the expense would have been recognized in March, so that the income reported for the four months would have been zero, zero, $7,000, and zero.

Matching Revenue and Expense

The problem of income determination under accrual accounting can be described as a problem in *revenue-expense matching*. The accountant's task is to recognize as expense all the costs applicable to the revenues recognized during a given period, regardless of when cash receipts and disbursements occurred.

This process can be illustrated adequately only with a slightly more complicated example than the Appleby Associates transactions. Marsden-Brown, Inc., is an engineering firm specializing in the design and installation of industrial and commercial lighting systems. In period 1, this company entered into a contract for the design and installation of a new lighting system in the Granco Department Store. The system was to be designed in period 1, installed in period 2, and modified, if necessary, in period 3. The contract price was $200,000, payable in three installments:

Immediately	$ 40,000
Upon completion of the installation	80,000
At end of modification period	80,000
Total	$200,000

During period 1, the following events relating to this contract took place:

(1) Design work was completed at a cost of $30,000: $29,000 in salaries and materials costs, all paid in cash during period 1, plus $1,000 in depreciation on design equipment.

(2) Down payment was received from customer, $40,000.

Two journal entries are sufficient to summarize these transactions. The first records the receipt of the advance payment from the customer:

```
Cash..........................................40,000
    Liability for Advance Payments....................          40,000
```

The second entry summarizes all of the design costs applicable to this contract:

```
Granco Contract—Costs to Date.......................30,000
    Cash.........................................          29,000
    Allowance for Depreciation.........................          1,000
```

Neither revenue nor expense was recognized in period 1; instead, the amount received from the customer was carried as a liability and the costs incurred were carried forward to period 2 as an asset. Costs amounted to $30,000 in period 1, but disbursements (payments of cash) totaled only $29,000.

In period 2, the system was installed at a further cost of $125,000: $100,000 paid in cash during period 2, $22,000 to be paid in cash during period 3, and $3,000 in depreciation charges on installation equipment. The entry to record these facts is:

```
Granco Contract—Costs to Date.......................125,000
    Cash.........................................          100,000
    Accounts Payable...............................          22,000
    Allowance for Depreciation.......................          3,000
```

Once again, disbursements were less than current operating costs— $100,000 against $125,000—and expense has not yet been determined.

Upon completion of the installation in period 2, the job was accepted by the customer and Marsden-Brown recognized the full contract price as revenue of period 2. The customer paid the agreed-upon $80,000 second installment, which left $80,000 to be recorded as a receivable. The entry is:

```
Cash..........................................80,000
Accounts Receivable...................................80,000
Liability for Advance Payments........................40,000
    Sales Revenue....................................          200,000
```

At this point, it became necessary to recognize as expense the costs already incurred in the design and installation of the system. The entry is:

```
Design and Installation Expenses........................155,000
    Granco Contract—Costs to Date..................          155,000
```

This entry serves to close out the contract cost account and transfer the balance to expense.

One more expense remains to be recognized in period 2. The job was accepted by Granco Department Store subject to a contract provision that during a three-month trial period Marsden-Brown would make without charge any modifications demanded by Granco, up to a maximum of 5 percent of the contract price. This means that the cost of obtaining the $200,000 revenues is greater than the $155,000 incurred during the first two periods. If the full contract price is recognized as revenue in period 2, an accurate measure of income can be achieved only if an estimate of the eventual cost of system modifications is recognized as an expense in that period. The amount is uncertain, but an unbiased estimate is a better measure of expense than the alternative, which is to charge nothing to expense in period 2 but wait until actual system modification costs are known in period 3.

Marsden-Brown's experience on other projects in the past had shown that their customers were very likely to use the full allowance for modifications. At 5 percent of $200,000, this would total $10,000, and the entry to record this is:

System Modification Expense...........................10,000
    Liability for Contract Guarantee......................   10,000

Accrual Accounting: Summary

The treatment accorded to the various items in the above transactions is summarized in the following diagram:

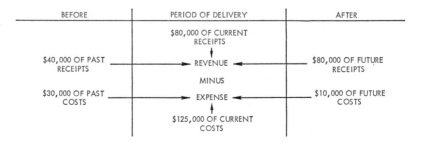

Notice that under accrual accounting revenue and expense recognition has nothing to do with the question of when cash is received or paid out. All the revenue from this contract was recognized in period 2 even though some cash was received in period 1 and some would not be received until period 3. Similarly, expense in period 2 included operating costs of all three periods, some of which (depreciation) even reflected cash disbursements made in periods prior to period 1. This is the essence of accrual accounting: costs are incurred to obtain revenues, and adequate expense-revenue matching requires charging the cost to expense in the period in which the revenue is said to be earned.

The cash basis is satisfactory only when substantially the same results are secured as under the accrual basis. This condition may be satisfied in a small service business with few inventories and little equipment. It may also be satisfied if sales and purchases of all kinds are roughly constant from period to period and if the time lags before collection and payment are also either very short or highly stable. In the more general case, however, the cash basis is patently misleading because cash flows do not coincide closely with the performance of services or supplying of goods to customers. In fact, the distorting effects of expensing cash payments for equipment are so great that equipment costs are usually recorded as assets and amortized over a period of years, even when the accounts are kept otherwise on a cash basis.

MANUFACTURING COSTS: ASSET VERSUS EXPENSE

The difference between cash basis and accrual basis accounting is perhaps most pronounced in firms that manufacture products in one period for delivery to customers in some later period. Whereas the retailer or wholesaler increases the value of merchandise by performing useful transport and storage functions, the manufacturer also adds value by using labor and machinery to convert purchased materials into new asset forms. Costs of this kind of activity are referred to as *manufacturing costs* or *conversion costs.*

Cost Flows in Trading Enterprises

The retailer or wholesaler typically purchases merchandise and stores it on his premises prior to sale. He also incurs other costs for items that are not consumed immediately in the creation of revenues, notably store and delivery equipment. The cost flows are very simple, as shown in Exhibit 4–2.

The analogy in this exhibit is with a stream of water, part of which is diverted to storage areas while the remainder flows downstream unhindered and out of sight. In this case the original flow is shown as costs incurred, entering the diagram at the upper left. Some of these

Exhibit 4–2

COST FLOWS IN TRADING ENTERPRISES

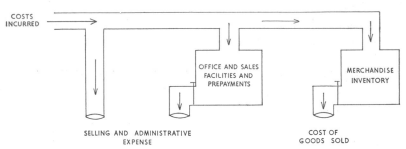

costs, such as store clerks' salaries and electricity costs, go downstream immediately in the form of selling and administrative expense charges against current revenues. These are the costs of selling the products and administering the company. The rest continue to flow along diversion channels until they reach storage reservoirs marked office and sales facilities and prepayments, and merchandise inventory, respectively.

As time passes and merchandise is sold, the reservoir outflow valves are opened and portions of the costs of sales facilities, prepayments, and merchandise inventory flow to the income statement as expense. The inventory accounts in this kind of situation typically include only the purchase price of the merchandise plus the costs necessary to transport them to the company's place of business. The latter are generally referred to as freight-in costs.

Manufacturing Cost Flows

In manufacturing, a much wider variety of costs must be incurred before the product is ready for sale, and many of these costs must be passed through the inventory accounts on their way to the income statement. The cost flows in manufacturing enterprises are pictured in Exhibit 4–3. Again the analogy with the flowing stream and reservoir is pertinent, but there are more reservoirs and some costs may flow through as many as three reservoirs (accounts) before they finally flow into the income statement. As the diagram shows, costs of selling and distributing the product and of administering the company flow in the same channels as in Exhibit 4–2. Instead of a single merchandise inventory reservoir, however, there is a small inverted pyramid of reservoirs. Some manufacturing costs are incurred for the purchase and construction of manufacturing plant, others to acquire invento-

Exhibit 4–3

COST FLOWS IN MANUFACTURING ENTERPRISES

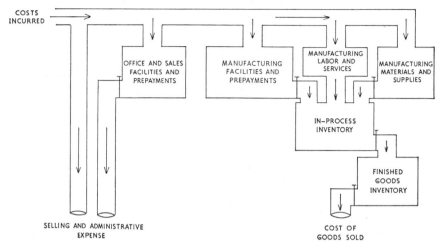

ries of materials and supplies that are to be used in the manufacturing process, and others to acquire the labor which processes the material.

The production operation begins with the transfer of materials from inventory to production departments within the factory. These materials are now in process. As men work with these materials to change their shape or combine them with other materials, other costs begin to flow down the pipelines into the in-process inventory reservoir. Then, as products take their finished form, another outflow valve is opened and the goods and their associated costs flow into finished goods inventory.

Finished goods inventory is treated in just the same way as merchandise inventory in a trading enterprise. As goods are sold, the costs finally flow out of the balance sheet and into the income statement as cost of goods sold. In the meantime, however, costs have flowed through three separate balance sheet stages instead of the one used for a trading firm. It is this greater complexity of the physical flows of resources that places heavier demands on the accounting system in manufacturing.

MANUFACTURING COSTS: TRANSACTIONS ANALYSIS

During 19x9 Erskine Enterprises, Inc., decided to expand its operations to include some minor manufacturing work. For some time the store had been selling radio tuners, amplifiers, and other components of high-fidelity radios and phonographs. For some customers, the company had provided cabinets in which the customers could install these components, but the quality of the work done by the local cabinet shop from which the cabinets were bought had been uneven and delivery dates uncertain. Mr. Erskine, the company's president, was convinced that a substantial profit could be made from the sale of cabinets, but only if he could keep the manufacturing process under his own control.

Facilities Transactions

Accordingly, on July 1, 19x9, Erskine Enterprises rented space in an adjoining building, purchased a secondhand set of cabinet-making tools and equipment, and hired a skilled cabinetmaker. The rental on the factory space amounted to $2,400 a year, payable in advance. The entry made to record this on July 1, 19x9, showed the acquisition of one asset, prepaid rent, in exchange for another, cash:

(1)

Prepaid Rent...2,400
    Cash...   2,400

The tools and equipment were purchased on account, as shown in the following entry:

(2)

Furniture and Equipment................................5,000
    Accounts Payable....................................   5,000

To simplify the presentation, the asset account used in this case is the same one used for office and store equipment in the previous chapter. (Separate accounts normally would be used in practice.) Each piece of equipment had a separate section of the company's property records, however, so that the equipment costs could be classified into the three categories of office, store, and factory equipment whenever that became necessary.

Recording Materials Purchases

During 19x9, Erskine Enterprises purchased lumber and other materials for use in the cabinet shop, as the factory was called. These items were referred to as "materials" rather than as merchandise, the latter term being reserved for products ready for sale to outside customers.

These materials were purchased on credit at a total cost of $11,000.

Because the Merchandise Inventory account was already serving as a summary account for so many different kinds of merchandise, and because of the distinction between materials and merchandise mentioned above, Mr. Erskine's accountant felt that it would be better to set up a separate inventory account to reflect the shop materials inventories. The entries recording the year's purchases of these materials showed increases in both assets and liabilities:

(3)

Materials Inventory.....................................11,000
    Accounts Payable.................................   11,000

Recording Materials Issues

When production materials are *issued*—that is, when they are taken from the materials stock room and delivered to factory operating personnel—they are merely transferred from one asset category to another. If the company wishes to recognize this transfer in the accounts, the entry takes the following form (the cost of materials issued during 19x9 totaled $7,000):

(4)

Work in Process Inventory...............................7,000
    Materials Inventory..............................   7,000

This entry could have been made at the end of the year, using the periodic inventory method described in Chapter 3. In this case, however, Mr. Erskine decided that he could not wait until the end of the year to gauge his materials consumption. Therefore, he had his accountant set up a *perpetual inventory system* by which he could have all transfers from materials inventory recorded at the time they occurred.

The perpetual inventory records required by a system of this kind show the physical quantity of *each kind* of materials on hand at all times—the balance is kept up-to-date continuously by recording both receipts and issues as they occur. If the dollar inventory accounts are to be maintained on the perpetual inventory plan, then the inventory records must also show the dollar amounts of receipts, issues, and inventory balances. The balances are verified at least once each year by taking a physical count of the materials on hand. Any discrepancies between the book value of the inventory and the cost of the actual quantity on hand on the inventory date is taken to the income statement as an adjustment to the cost of goods sold.

The main disadvantage of the perpetual inventory system is its added clerical cost, but this would be minor in the Erskine cabinet shop. The advantages are: (1) it provides an independent check on the materials lost through pilferage and waste; (2) it allows the preparation of periodic financial statements quarterly or more often without the burden of taking a physical count each time; (3) it provides a measure of the dollar investment in inventory at all times; and (4) it provides the information on the quantity of each item in stock so that management can keep its inventories at desired levels.

Recording Factory Payrolls

Payroll costs for factory employees are recorded just as for office and store employees, with one difference: the cost is charged to a factory cost account such as Work in Process Inventory rather than to an expense account. Shop labor is used to create an asset, in this case work in process, and the costs of such labor do not become expense until the revenues from cabinet sales appear on the income statement.

During the second half of 19x9 (the first six months of shop operations), wages and salaries in the Erskine cabinet shop amounted to $10,000. The employees did not receive this full amount in cash, however, because Erskine Enterprises was obliged to withhold $1,800 of the employees' gross pay for payroll and income taxes levied on the employees, to be paid to government tax collectors on the employees' behalf. The entry recording the increase in assets and the increases in liabilities was:

(5)

Work in Process Inventory	10,000	
Wages and Salaries Payable		8,200
Taxes Payable		1,800

Most large companies also make deductions for such items as hospital insurance premiums, savings bond purchases, union dues, and pension plan contributions; but Erskine Enterprises makes only the deductions required by law.

Payroll Taxes

The tax deductions from employees' gross pay are taxes on the employee, not on the employer. In addition, the employer is subject to certain taxes based on the size of his payrolls. For example, an employer whose employees are subject to F.I.C.A. taxes is required to match the deductions made from his employees' payrolls for this purpose.[2] Of the $1,800 in tax deductions recorded above, $500 repre-

---

[2] F.I.C.A. stands for Federal Insurance Contributions Act; the tax is popularly referred to as the social security tax, although it is actually only one of a number of taxes supporting the system of social security benefits.

sented F.I.C.A. taxes.[3] This means that Erskine Enterprises had to pay
$1,000 to the federal government, just twice the amount deducted
from employees' paychecks. Thus the cost of labor was actually
greater than the total gross pay, and the excess, totaling $500, must
also be charged to factory cost accounts:

(6)

Work in Process Inventory.....................................500
    Taxes Payable...   500

Most employers are also required to pay unemployment compensation taxes and workmen's compensation insurance premiums, and
many firms have pension plans, health plans, or other programs which
require additional payments by the employer to separate funds. All of
these additional charges are known as fringe benefits. Although these
were assumed to be zero for Erskine Enterprises, to avoid cluttering
the example, benefit ratios of 20 to 25 percent of gross payroll are not
at all uncommon. In such cases the employees' gross pay seriously
understates the true cost of the resources used.

Recording Depreciation

Depreciation is another example of a cost that is ordinarily treated
as a current expense when it relates to facilities used for administrative
or marketing activities but is treated as an asset when it relates to
manufacturing facilities. Once again, the argument is that the asset has
merely been converted from one form to another—the services formerly embodied in a machine have now been embodied in the goods
manufactured during the period. Thus factory depreciation does not
become an expense until revenues from the goods to which it has been
charged have been recognized on the income statement.

Depreciation on shop facilities in the Erskine cabinet shop during
the second half of 19x9 amounted to $400, and the entry had the fol-
lowing effect:

(7)

Work in Process Inventory....................................400
    Accumulated Depreciation...............................   400

Depreciation for the year on office and store equipment was still taken
directly to the income statement as expense and does not enter into
this illustration.

---

[3] The specific withholding rate on this and other payroll taxes depends on a
number of factors and varies from time to time. To keep the illustrations simple in
this book, an arbitrary rate of 5 percent of gross payrolls will be used.

Other Factory Costs

Factory utilities and other miscellaneous shop costs not recorded in any of the entries above amounted to $3,100 during 19x9. The following entry summarizes all of these transactions:

(8)

Work in Process Inventory.............................3,100
    Accounts Payable....................................   3,100

Finally, six months' rent on the cabinet shop itself had to be charged to shop operations. Rent of $2,400 was paid on July 1, 19x9 (entry [1] above), covering the next 12 months. Six months' rent therefore had to be transferred to factory cost accounts for the last six months of 19x9:

(9)

Work in Process Inventory.............................1,200
    Prepaid Rent.......................................   1,200

Once again, only the *form* of the asset was changed; the asset total remained the same after this transaction was recorded as it had been before.

Recording the Cost of Goods Finished and Sold

Charging the various costs incurred in the manufacture of the cabinets to the Work in Process Inventory account resulted in the following:

Work in Process Inventory

(4) Materials	7,000
(5) Wages	10,000
(6) F.I.C.A. (employer)	500
(7) Depreciation	400
(8) Miscellaneous	3,100
(9) Rent	1,200
	22,200

The cabinet shop had no work in process on July 1, 19x9, and thus all the costs in this account related to work initiated during 19x9. As cabinets were finished during the latter half of the year, their cost was determined and the amounts were credited to Work in Process Inventory and debited to another asset account called Finished Cabinets Inventory.[4] The shop records showed that cabinets with a total fac-

---

[4] For the cabinets, Mr. Erskine used a variation on the perpetual inventory method appropriate to manufacturing activity known as a *job cost system*. A detailed description of how this kind of system operates will be presented in Chapter 17.

tory cost of $18,300 had been completed and transferred to the merchandise stock room for sale to customers. The remaining $3,900 in shop costs was assigned to the cabinets still in process at the end of 19x9. The entry that transferred the costs of work completed during the second half of 19x9 was:

(10)

Finished Cabinets Inventory...............................18,300
    Work in Process Inventory...........................   18,300

The debit could have been made instead to Merchandise Inventory (cabinets *are* merchandise, after all), but Mr. Erskine wished to keep the cabinet line separate in the accounts until he could decide whether to keep the shop in operation.

Of the cabinets produced, those sold had a manufacturing cost of $14,000. This was accounted for by entry (11):

(11)

Cost of Cabinets Sold...................................14,000
    Finished Cabinets Inventory.........................   14,000

This flow of manufacturing costs through the accounts is diagrammed in Exhibit 4–4. Inventories may be found at all stages—unprocessed, partly processed, and finished.

These cost flows can also be summarized in tabular form, as in the *manufacturing cost statement* in Exhibit 4–5. This shows that of the $22,200 in costs actually charged to factory operations during 19x9, only $14,000 was transferred to expense on the income statement. The remaining $8,200 was divided between the Work in Process Inventory and Finished Goods Inventory accounts. In addition, materials inventories showed a year-end balance of $4,000, factory equipment

Exhibit 4–4

MANUFACTURING COST FLOWS

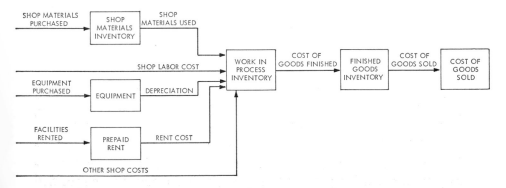

Exhibit 4–5

ERSKINE ENTERPRISES, INC.

Statement of Manufacturing Costs and Cost of Goods Sold
for the Six Months Ending December 31, 19x9

```
Materials cost:
   Materials purchased..........................................$11,000
      Less: Materials on hand, December 31.........................  4,000
         Cost of materials used...................................$ 7,000
Labor costs..............................................   10,000
Depreciation.............................................      400
Rent on factory..........................................    1,200
Other factory costs......................................    3,600
      Total Factory Cost...................................$22,200
Less: Work in process inventory, December 31, 19x9...............   3,900
         Cost of goods finished...................................$18,300
Less: Finished cabinets inventory, December 31, 19x9..............   4,300
Cost of Goods Sold.......................................$14,000
```

had a book value of $4,600, and rent prepayments amounted to $1,200 at the end of the year.

This completes the so-called *manufacturing cost cycle*, which consists of the purchasing of materials, processing them into finished goods, and selling them to customers. Payment, sale, and collection transactions are not part of the manufacturing cost cycle and for this reason have not been included in the illustration.

END-OF-PERIOD ACCRUALS

Accrual accounting has one more facet that needs to be mentioned at this point. The periodic financial statements need to reflect all of the expenditures made during the period, but some of these expenditures will very likely be unaccompanied by any specific transactions documents (invoices, checks, etc.). These must be recorded at the end of the period by means of an entry known as an accrual (whence the name, accrual accounting). It reflects a liability that will not be payable until sometime after the end of the period.

Accruing Interest Expense

Perhaps the clearest illustration of the accrual is the end-of-period recognition of interest on notes payable. For many business concerns, an important source of capital, particularly to finance seasonal peaks of activity, is short-term borrowing from commercial banks. The instrument most commonly used for this purpose is called a *promissory note*, and it is a promise to pay a specified amount on a specified date, known as the *maturity date.* The amount borrowed is termed the *proceeds;* the amount paid for the use of the proceeds is called *interest;* and the amount to be repaid to the lender on the maturity date is known as the *maturity value.*

For example, on November 15, 19x8, a company known as the Condor Company obtained a loan of $120,000 from a local bank, giving in exchange a 60-day, 6 percent promissory note. The period of 60 days is described as the *life* or *term* of the loan, and the 6 percent figure is known as the *interest rate.* Unless some other period is explicitly specified, interest rates are always stated as *annual* rates, regardless of the term of the loan.

It is accepted financial practice to compute interest on short-term loans on the basis of a 360-day year. In other words, a 60-day note would require interest at 60/360, or $\frac{1}{6}$ of the annual rate. The Condor Company, in other words, agreed to pay $120,000 plus interest of $1,200 ($\frac{1}{6} \times 6$ percent $\times$ $120,000) on January 14, 19x9, which was exactly 60 days from the date of the loan.[4] The following entry was made at the time the loan was obtained:

```
Cash...........................................120,000
    Notes Payable...............................        120,000
```

In the normal bookkeeping routine the next transaction to be recognized would be the repayment of the loan, and no entry would be made until that date. In order to measure expenses and income for 19x8 accurately, however, the Condor Company's accountants made the following entry to accrue interest expense up to December 31, 19x8:

```
Interest Expense...............................920
    Interest Payable...........................        920
```

This amount represented the portion of the total interest applicable to the 46-day period in 19x8 (15 days in November and 31 days in December) that the note was in force. Thus 46/60 of the $1,200 interest cost was a 19x8 expense.

The final entry is to record the payment of the note and accrued interest. The entry made by the Condor Company on January 14, 19x9, was:

---

[4] The maturity date is computed on the basis of actual elapsed days, not on the basis of the 360-day year. In computing the maturity date, the day the loan is made is not counted. Thus a loan made on November 15 gives rise to interest for 15 days during November, starting with November 16. Debts maturing on a day on which the banks are closed are payable on the next banking day. In this case, the term of the loan covered 15 days in November, 31 days in December, and the remaining 14 days in January, for a maturity date of January 14, 19x9.

Interest Expense................................	280	
Interest Payable................................	920	
Notes Payable................................	120,000	
Cash..		121,200

This entry recognizes an expense of $280, liability reductions of $120,920, and an asset reduction of $121,200. Of the $1,200 total interest cost, $920 was taken to expense in 19x8 and $280 was charged against 19x9.

The terms under which loans are made vary widely. Many loans, for example, require the borrower to *discount* his note. When a note is discounted, the borrower receives the face amount of the loan *less* the interest and pays the face amount at maturity. No purpose would be served by repeating the illustration with a discounted note, however, because the same principles apply in accruing the interest expense.

Accruing Salaries Payable

A second kind of accrual is the accrual of salaries payable. Salaries are often paid weekly, and the end of the accounting period sometimes does not coincide with the end of the payroll period. This means that the salaries earned by employees on the days between the last payroll date and the end of the accounting period must be recorded by an accrual entry.

For example, suppose that the Condor Company had a weekly payroll of $10,000 and that the last payroll period of 19x8 ended on Tuesday, December 28. Employees would thus have earned salaries for three days in 19x8 (December 29, 30, and 31), but these would not be entered on the books in the normal bookkeeping routine until 19x9. If Condor was working a five-day week, then three fifths of the first 19x9 payroll should be charged to 19x8 expense. This can be accomplished by the following entry in the 19x8 ledger:

Salary Expense..................................	6,000	
Salaries Payable................................		6,000

A similar adjustment should be made for payroll taxes and other fringe benefits, if they are material.

SUMMARY

This chapter has contrasted the cash and accrual bases of accounting and has introduced a new category of transactions—manufacturing or conversion transactions—to give some idea as to the full complexity of accrual basis accounting.

A strict cash basis means that revenues are measured by the amount of cash received from customers during the accounting period; expenses of the current period are the cash payments to suppliers for goods or services, regardless of whether the goods or services are consumed this period, last period, or the next. In fact, a strict cash basis recognizes no assets other than cash and no liabilities other than those arising from a direct transfer of cash to the firm (e.g., a bank loan).

Except in the limiting case in which cash and accrual accounting produce substantially identical results, accrual basis accounting is presumed to provide more accurate statements of the firm's income and financial position, year in and year out, than cash basis accounting, and for this reason is the dominant method of enterprise financial accounting. Under accrual accounting, a cost is *capitalized* (added to an asset account) if it can reasonably be expected to contribute directly or indirectly to *future* revenues. A cost is *expensed* if it has contributed to the *current* year's revenues or if the service for which it was incurred has been used during the current period in the creation of revenue. Costs that expire with no offsetting benefit—including those that actually expired in prior years but have only been recognized as expiring now—are known as *losses* rather than as expenses. The question of when revenue is to be recognized is the subject of Chapter 5.

Manufacturing costs provide an excellent illustration of the application of the accrual concept. The costs of manufacturing follow the flow of the goods themselves, from raw materials inventory to work in process to finished goods and finally to goods sold. The costs of the goods at all of these stages except the last are regarded as costs of assets and thus rest appropriately in the inventory section of the balance sheet. Only when the goods are sold do these costs become expenses as the cost of goods sold. Costs of administering the company and of selling and distributing its products, of course, are taken directly to expense, just as in a wholesaling or retailing concern.

In concentrating attention on the essence of manufacturing activity, most of the practical problems of determining the unit cost of individual manufactured products have been passed over. These problems will be dealt with in Chapter 17. For the moment, it is sufficient to understand that accounting views manufacturing as a process of adding the costs of manufacturing labor and other manufacturing services to the cost of purchased materials, and that no income arises until revenues from the final product are recognized.

QUESTIONS AND PROBLEMS

1. Why is accrual accounting regarded as more accurate than cash basis accounting? Indicate the meaning of "accuracy" in this connection.

2. What is an "accrual"? When and why is it necessary?

3. Under what circumstances would accrual accounting yield the same net income figure as the strict cash basis of accounting?

4. Distinguish between and explain the nature of each of the following:

a) Interest expense.
b) Accrued interest payable.
c) Prepaid interest.
d) Interest income.
e) Interest receivable.

5. What is meant by "revenue-expense matching"? Is it a feature of cash basis accounting?

6. "Depreciation of factory equipment is an asset, not an expense." Do you agree or disagree with this statement? Give your reasons.

7. How does the practice of recording estimated costs under contract guarantees in the manner described for Marsden-Brown, Inc., in this chapter affect the guarantor's income statements and balance sheets?

8. What difference does it make whether factory maintenance and repair cost is considered a cost of a product or a cost of a period?

9. To what extent are the operations of Erskine Enterprises' cabinet shop similar to those of Marsden-Brown, Inc.? How, if at all, do they differ?

10. Explain how the problems of accounting for manufacturing activities differ from those encountered in connection with trading activities. How are they similar?

11. Company X is a "growth company"—that is, its sales, earnings, and capital resources show a sharp upward trend from year to year. Over a 10-year period, would it make any difference whether Company X's accounting was on a strict cash basis or an accrual basis? Explain.

12. Even when a businessman computes income on a "cash basis," he typically does not classify all cash receipts as revenue or all cash disbursements as expense. Furthermore, he may have some expenses that are not represented by current cash outlays. Give examples of these departures from a strict cash basis.

13. Corporations which sell products which carry guarantees against defective parts, and so forth are now required for tax purposes to report the entire sale price of the products as revenue of the period in which the products are sold. What is wrong with this treatment as far as income measurement is concerned? Under what conditions would this treatment be satisfactory?

14. Merrill Productions, Inc., has just produced a new Broadway musical which has been acclaimed by theater critics and audiences alike. Orders for tickets for the next six months' performances are now being filled at the box office. The company prepares financial statements only once a year, after the close of its "fiscal year," which begins on July 1 and ends on the following June 30.

a) Prepare a journal entry to record the sale on October 28 of two $6.60 tickets for the evening performance on the following February 25.

b) Would you record this sale any differently if the accounting period were one month instead of one year? Explain.

c) If the procedure that you used in your answer to (*a*) is followed for *all* ticket sales, what kind of an entry would have to be made on June 30 each year? How would you obtain the data necessary to make this entry?

15. The Deeping Company employed approximately 2,000 workers. The payroll was accumulated on a weekly basis. The amount due each employee for his day's work was entered daily in the payroll book. At the end of the week these daily amounts were added and the resulting total for each employee constituted his wages. At the time of payment, the total payroll was posted to the company's accounts as wage expense.

The company's fiscal year ended November 30. One year, this date fell on Wednesday, midway between paydays. In closing his books and making up statements for the year, the bookkeeper included among the operating expenses the total amount of wages shown in the accounts as having been paid. On examining the books later, the company's auditor remarked that in his opinion the statements drawn up therefrom were inaccurate in that the amount of wages applicable to the period between November 26, the last previous payday, and November 30, the end of the fiscal year, had not been included in the figures shown on the statements. The bookkeeper replied that since a similar condition had existed at the end of the previous fiscal year, any errors involved—if they did exist—would offset each other. What was more, he did not agree that the accounting was incorrect, since the cash had not yet been paid out. Payroll expense, he said, was incurred with the payment of cash.

Discuss this matter with reference both to the company's balance sheet and income statement.

*16. On February 1, the Ready Service Company's balance sheet showed accrued wages payable of $300. The gross wages shown on the four weekly payrolls paid during February, covering wages up to and including February 25, totaled $4,200. Employee wages for the period February 26 to February 28 amounted to $500.

a) What was the total wages expense for the month of February?
b) What was the correct balance in Accrued Wages Payable as of the close of business on February 28?

17. The Farnsworth Company has two salesmen, Green and Harris. Green is on a salary of $8,000 a year and gets a 1½ percent commission on the sales for which he is responsible. Harris's annual salary is $7,000 plus 2 percent commission. Commissions and salaries are recorded in separate accounts.

Last year, Green achieved sales of $200,000, while Harris sold $150,000. Income taxes witheld amounted to 20 percent of total salaries and commissions, and the F.I.C.A. tax was 8 percent, half levied directly on the company and half to be deducted from employee wages. In addition, the company had to pay unemployment taxes of 3 percent of the first $3,000 earned by each man.

Prepare a summary entry or entries to record the payroll costs and liabilities for the year, recording first the accrual of the payrolls and related costs and then recording the payments of cash.

18. Which of the following costs of the current month represent expenses of the current month under accrual basis accounting?

a) Depreciation on office equipment.
b) Production superintendent's salary.
c) Raw materials purchased for the factory.
d) Factory labor on work shipped to customers this month.
e) Depreciation on factory machinery.
f) Materials used this month to package finished products.

---

* Solutions to problems marked with an asterisk (*) are found in Appendix B.

g) Cartons used this month to ship products to customers.
h) Sales brochures purchased for use during the next six months.
i) Wages of raw materials stockroom clerk.
j) Wages of shipping department manager.
k) Freight charge on materials received.
l) Freight charge on materials shipped.
m) Factory labor used to build new storage cabinets in sales room.
n) Factory labor used to repair office water cooler.
o) Factory labor used to repair factory water cooler.
p) Outside contractor's fee for repairing factory machine.

19. The Northumberland Company is a distributor of textiles in southern New England. Salaries and wages are paid by the month. Operating expenses are broken down by departments. Record the following data for March in journal form:

Department	Cash Payments to Employees	Income Tax Withheld	F.I.C.A. Tax Withheld	Insurance Premiums Withheld	F.I.C.A. Taxes on the Company	Unemployment Taxes on the Company
Office..........	$ 7,740	$1,500	$ 500	$260	$ 500	$ 300
Sales...........	14,988	3,500	1,000	512	1,000	600
Warehouse.....	10,016	1,200	600	184	600	360
Total......	$32,744	$6,200	$2,100	$956	$2,100	$1,260

*20. On September 15, Calhoun borrowed $6,000 from the bank, promising to pay the bank $6,000 plus accrued interest at 6 percent 60 days from the date of the note. On November 14 he paid the accrued interest and renewed the note for an additional 30 days. At the second maturity, on December 14, Calhoun paid $4,000 in cash and gave a new 30-day, 6 percent note for the remaining amount due. This last note was paid in full when due.

Journalize the entries for these transactions on Calhoun's books. Include an accruing entry for December 31, Calhoun's balance sheet date. Date all entries.

21. The Peterson Company borrowed $30,000 from a bank on January 21, giving in exchange a 90-day, 6 percent note.

a) Prepare an entry to record the borrowing.
b) Prepare whatever entry this transaction would make necessary on January 31 if the Peterson Company wishes to prepare a set of accrual basis financial statements as of the close of business on that date.
c) What entry would be necessary on January 31 if the Peterson Com-

pany prepares financial statements quarterly instead of monthly, the first quarter of the year ending on March 31? What entry would be made on February 28? On March 31?

22. The Albatross Corporation is engaged in the manufacture and sale of plastic water toys. Its inventory accounts showed the following balances as of January 1:

Raw materials.....................	$10,000
Work in process..................	40,000
Finished goods...................	20,000

During the first six months of the year, the following costs were incurred:

Factory raw materials purchased......	$90,000
Factory labor.....................	40,000
Factory depreciation...............	7,000
Factory utilities and other costs.......	13,000
Salesmen's salaries..................	5,000
Office salaries....................	8,000
Other selling and office costs..........	4,000

As of June 30, the inventory accounts showed the following balances:

Raw materials.....................	$16,000
Work in process..................	50,000
Finished goods...................	10,000

Prepare a statement showing (a) the cost of goods finished during this period, and (b) the cost of goods sold.

*23. The Buildmore Company had the following inventories on September 1:

Raw materials.....................	$20,000
Work in process..................	30,000
Finished goods...................	12,000

During the month of September: the cost of raw materials purchased was $60,000; labor cost incurred was $80,000; and other costs applicable to production totaled $30,000.

On September 30 inventories were:

Raw materials.....................	$25,000
Work in process..................	20,000
Finished goods...................	20,000

Show all journal entries necessary to record the above data.

24. Prepare debit and credit analyses of the following set of related transactions of the Goodhue Chemical Company.

(1) Ordered from a supplier 30 55-gallon drums of chemicals at $65 a drum. Of this price, $5 applied to the drum, which was returnable when empty.

(2) Received 27 of the drums ordered above.

(3) Paid freight charges of $108 for delivery of the 27 drums.
(4) Returned two drums of chemicals to the supplier for full credit as defective merchandise.
(5) Paid the bill due to the supplier after deducting the amount paid for incoming freight charges on the two defective drums.
(6) Bought 5,500 empty quart tins which cost a total of $285, delivered and labeled.
(7) Paid five temporary employees $15 each per day for two days' work to fill the tins with chemicals and put them on the shelves.
(8) Sold 4,500 quarts of chemicals on account at $0.48 each.
(9) Collected $1,450 from customers.
(10) Returned 24 empty drums to the supplier. The remaining drum had been lost from the pile at the rear of the store.

25. The Central Department Store purchased a large quantity of unfinished and unassembled wooden kitchen cabinets at a bankruptcy sale with the intention of retailing these units "as is" at a very low price. The management soon discovered, however, that the units were too complicated for the average householder to assemble without great difficulty. The company then decided to assemble and finish the cabinets and offer them at a price sufficiently above that originally intended to cover the costs of these operations. The following transactions took place:

(1) Purchase of 2,100 unassembled units for cash at $6 each.
(2) Sale of 100 unassembled units on credit at a unit price of $10.
(3) Payment of one month's wages to employees for assembling and finishing the remaining 2,000 units: four carpenters at $500 each and six painters at $450 each.
(4) Payment of one month's wages to two regularly employed warehouse men who acted as material handlers, $360 each. Because this activity occurred during a slack period, this actually entailed no extra cost to the company. For the same reason, adequate work space was available in the company's warehouse.
(5) Purchase of paint and other supplies on credit, $900. When the operation was finished, supplies estimated to have cost $60 remained on hand. These could all be used in the company's normal maintenance operations.

a) Analyze these transactions in debit and credit form.
b) In line with the company's original objective of increasing the retail price just enough to cover assembly and finishing costs, what would you set as the new selling price? Support your conclusion.
c) Using the sales price you have decided upon in (b) above, record the sale of 200 finished units.

*26. The Illumino Corporation manufactures lighting fixtures. On the first of April, the company had on hand raw materials which had cost

$17,200, finished fixtures costing $34,000, and partially completed fixtures on which $23,400 in raw materials and other costs had already been incurred.

During April, additional materials costing $35,000 were purchased, and materials costing $48,400 were put into process. April factory labor costs were $26,000, and other manufacturing costs totaled $15,600. At the end of April, incomplete fixtures on hand represented $2,200 in materials, $1,400 in labor applied, and $800 of other costs. Finished fixtures costing $97,000 were shipped to customers during the month.

Prepare journal entries for the month of April.

27. The Peerless Cloak Company manufactures silk-lined evening cloaks. The company filed a claim with its insurance company under its burglary insurance policy stating that on the night of September 10 its workroom had been burglared. Compensation was claimed for the loss of 400 cloaks ($12,000) and 1,000 yards of silk ($3,500). An insurance claims adjuster analyzed the firm's books, which produced the following information for the period from January 1 to September 10:

(1) Inventories of cloaks, cloth, and silk had amounted to $211,200 on January 1.
(2) Purchases were: cloth, 38,000 yards at $2 a yard, and silk, 11,000 yards at $3.50 a yard.
(3) 6,000 cloaks were manufactured, consuming 39,500 yards of cloth and 10,000 yards of silk.
(4) 9,000 cloaks were sold.
(5) Manufacturing cost, all cost elements other than materials, totaled $42,000.
(6) Materials and manufacturing costs per unit were approximately the same as during the previous year.

The insurance adjuster supervised a physical count of the inventories on hand on September 11 and approved the following figures:

> 3,000 cloaks, $78,000.
> 13,000 yards of cloth, $26,000.
> 6,000 yards of silk, $21,000.

The insurance policy provides for compensation equal to the cost of any items stolen. If you were the claims adjuster, how much of the company's claim would you approve for payment? (Suggestion: as one step in your analysis, you will need to compute the unit cost of the cloaks manufactured.)

28. The Poirot Company completed the following transactions during September:

(1) Materials and supplies purchased on account and received during September, $34,000.

(2) Materials and supplies issued to factory production departments, $36,000.

(3) Wage and salary costs, paid in cash:

>Factory labor............................$20,000
>Selling and administrative salaries.............   4,000

(4) Depreciation for September:

>Factory machinery...........................$500
>Administrative office equipment.................   300

(5) Sundry manufacturing costs, paid in cash, $8,000.

(6) Miscellaneous selling and administrative expenses incurred and paid in cash, $3,800.

(7) Products completed and transferred to finished goods inventories, $62,000.

(8) Sales on account, $78,000.

(9) The balance in the Finished Goods Inventory account was $1,000 greater on September 30 than on Steptember 1, after all appropriate entries for September were recorded.

(10) Cash dividends declared and paid, $20,000.

a) Prepare journal entries to record each of the foregoing items, using only the following accounts (Note: some of these accounts had opening balances on September 1, but these do not enter into the solution of the problem and have been omitted):

Cash	Accounts payable
Accounts receivable	Wages and salaries payable
Materials and supplies inventory	Sales
Work in process	Cost of goods sold
Finished goods inventory	Selling and administrative
Machinery and equipment	expense
Depreciation to date—	Dividends declared
Machinery and equipment	

b) Compute net income for the month of September (show and label your calculations).

29. On February 1, the Paltry Corporation's accounts showed the following balances (all accounts not shown had zero balances):

>| | | |
>|---|---|---|
>| Cash.. | 4,200 | |
>| Accounts receivable......................... | 8,000 | |
>| Raw materials............................... | 3,500 | |
>| Work in process............................. | 5,000 | |
>| Finished goods.............................. | 6,200 | |
>| Prepaid insurance........................... | 1,000 | |
>| Plant and equipment......................... | 62,000 | |
>| Allowance for depreciation................... | | 22,000 |
>| Accounts payable............................ | | 13,900 |
>| Taxes payable............................... | | 4,000 |
>| Capital stock............................... | | 20,000 |
>| Retained earnings........................... | | 30,000 |

The following transactions took place during February:

(1) Purchased raw materials on account, $42,000.

(2) Issued raw materials to factory for use on month's production, $38,500.

(3) Sold merchandise: for cash, $10,000; on credit, $90,000.

(4) Collected $83,000 on accounts receivable.

(5) Paid rent on office equipment for February, March, and April, $900.

(6) Purchased factory equipment on account, $9,000.

(7) Purchased office furniture on account, $1,000.

(8) Paid employees' wages: factory, $20,000; office and sales force, $8,000 (payroll taxes are to be ignored in this problem).

(9) Paid suppliers on account, $35,000.

(10) Recognized depreciation for February: factory, $300; office, $100.

(11) Paid salesmen and executives: for travel and entertainment expenses during month, $2,000; as advances against March expenses, $1,050.

(12) Property taxes for the month were $850 on the factory and $150 on the office (income taxes are to be ignored in this problem). Property taxes are paid in cash once each year, on September 30.

(13) Paid bills for miscellaneous factory costs, $25,200; miscellaneous office and sales costs, $15,000.

(14) On February 18, borrowed $15,000 from a local bank, giving in exchange a promissory note for this amount. The terms of the loan required the Paltry Corporation to repay the amount borrowed, plus interest at an annual rate of 6 percent, at the end of 60 days.

(15) Sold a piece of factory equipment for $500 cash; its original cost was $3,000 and it had accumulated depreciation of $2,100 at the date of sale.

(16) Noted expiration of insurance premiums: on office, $50; on factory, $250.

(17) Finished and transferred to warehouse goods costing $68,000.

(18) Declared cash dividend to shareholders, $2,000, payable on March 15.

(19) Counted inventories on February 28; cost of finished goods on hand was $5,800.

a) Prepare journal entries to record all of the above information.

b) Enter the February 1 account balances in T-accounts and post the journal entries to these accounts (note: you may find it helpful to post each entry as soon as you journalize it).

c) Prepare an income statement for February and a balance sheet as of February 28.

*30. The interior decorating firm of Marjoram, Inc., designs office lay-outs and decoration, purchases office furniture and decorating materials, and supervises the decoration of the offices, construction of partitions, and installation of furniture and equipment.

Marjoram, Inc., bills the client for the full price of the job when the job is completed. Unforeseen problems always arise after the offices are occupied, however; and Marjoram is called upon to deal with these problems at no extra charge. The costs of this corrective work typically average 3 percent of the amounts billed.

The following transactions took place during June:

(1) Purchased decorating materials, supplies, and office furniture for use on jobs in progress, $100,000.

(2) Prepared payrolls, as follows:

	Gross Pay	Federal Income Tax Withheld	Amounts Subject to 10 Percent F.I.C.A. Tax*	Amounts Subject to 3 Percent Unemploy-ment Tax†
Current projects...........	$30,000	$4,000	$20,000	$14,000
Corrective work..........	1,000	150	800	600
Sales and administrative....	13,000	1,300	4,000	2,800
Total...............	$44,000	$5,450	$24,800	$17,400

* One half levied on employer, one half on employee.
† Levied entirely on employer.

(3) Miscellaneous costs charged to current projects (credit Accounts Payable), $4,200.

(4) General sales and administrative expenses for the month, $5,000 (credit Accounts Payable).

(5) Work completed for clients during the month:

Client	Amounts Billed to Clients	Costs Incurred		
		Materials and Furniture	Professional Salaries	Other Costs*
State Insurance Co......	$ 54,200	$30,000	$10,000	$1,200
Chasem & Dodgem.....	7,600	5,000	1,000	100
Franklin Bros..........	26,000	15,000	4,500	500
Jordan Realtors........	1,940	1,000	400	40
Morgan Mfg. Co.......	34,660	20,000	6,000	660
Total............	$124,400	$71,000	$21,900	$2,500

* Includes the employer's share of payroll taxes.

(6) Cash received from clients, $118,300.

(7) Cash payments made:

Accounts payable, $125,000.
Salaries payable, $37,310.
Employee income taxes withheld, $5,100.
F.I.C.A. Taxes, $2,100.
Unemployment taxes, $650.

(8) On June 15, Marjoram, Inc. borrowed $50,000, giving the lender a 6 percent, 90-day, note.

a) Prepare journal entries for June, reflecting all of the foregoing information in accrual-basis accounts.

b) Prepare an income statement for June.

31. Mr. A. P. Allen and Mr. N. T. Baker organized the Alba Corporation on January 1, 19x2, for the purpose of establishing a business as wholesalers of technical books. The company's fiscal year was to coincide with the calendar year—that is, the annual financial statements were to be prepared on the basis of transactions through December 31 of each year. The following transactions took place in the first two years of operations:

19x2

(1) Allen and Baker were each issued 1,000 shares of capital stock at a price of $10 per share, paid in cash.

(2) A loft was rented on February 1 for storing inventories and for office space. Annual rental of $3,600 was fully paid on this date.

(3) On February 1, two trucks were purchased for $9,600 cash.

(4) During the year, books were bought on account at a total cost of $150,000.

(5) Payments to publishers from whom books were bought totaled $140,000 during the year.

(6) Allen and Baker commenced work for the corporation on February 1, at monthly salaries of $1,200 each for their services as president and vice president, respectively. On February 15, the company hired two truck drivers at a monthly salary of $640 each, a loftman at $420 per month, and a secretary-bookkeeper at $400 per month. They began work immediately. Payday was on the last of each month, covering time worked during the month. F.I.C.A. taxes were calculated at the rate of 8 percent of the gross payroll—half of this was deducted from employees' gross pay and the other half was paid by the employer. Unemployment taxes, levied entirely on the employer, amounted to 2 per cent of the gross payroll. Payroll taxes were remitted on the same day payrolls were paid. (You may have to round some figures off to nearest dollar.)

(7) Gasoline, oil, and other operating costs amounted to $8,500 during the year; these costs were paid in cash as they were incurred.

(8) Sales for the year totaled $226,000; collections totaled $210,000.

(9) Periodic inventory at December 31 showed books on hand with a total cost of $4,660.

(10) Estimated life of the trucks was five years. No salvage value was anticipated.

19x3

(1) A year's rental was paid in advance on February 1.

(2) Books were bought on account for a total cost of $206,000.

(3) Payments to publishers from whom books were bought totaled $191,000.

(4) Payrolls were prepared; monthly salaries and payroll tax rates were unchanged from 19x2.

(5) Sales totaled $255,000; collections totaled $260,000.

(6) Periodic inventory at December 31 showed books in stock with a total cost of $19,320.

(7) Gasoline, oil, and other operating costs totaling $810 per month were paid in cash.

a) Journalize all transactions as they would appear on accrual basis books.

b) Journalize all transactions as they would appear on books kept according to a strict cash basis.

c) Prepare a balance sheet as of December 31 each year and an income statement each year, both by the cash basis and by the accrual basis.

d) Note the differences between the financial statements prepared on these two bases and comment on their significance in financial reporting.

32. On May 1, the Deppe Company's accounts had the following balances (all accounts not listed had zero balances):

Cash	25,600	
Accounts receivable	11,800	
Materials and supplies	7,200	
Work in process	6,500	
Finished goods	12,900	
Prepaid insurance	1,200	
Plant and equipment	156,000	
Accumulated depreciation		76,000
Accounts payable		15,400
Taxes payable		9,800
Capital stock		80,000
Retained earnings		40,000

The following transactions took place during May:

(1) Materials and supplies purchased on account, $30,300.

(2) Wages and salaries earned by employees during month: factory labor, $29,700; factory supervision, $4,900; sales and office salaries, $23,400. Taxes on these payrolls were as follows: em-

ployee incomes taxes withheld, $6,200; F.I.C.A. tax withheld from employees, 5 percent of gross payroll; F.I.C.A. tax levied on employer, equal to amount deducted from employees for this tax; unemployment taxes, levied on employer, 2 percent of gross payroll. (Note: Cash payments occasioned by employee payrolls and payroll taxes are described in item [9] below.)

(3) Materials put into production, $18,800.
(4) Equipment purchased on contract, $10,000.
(5) Goods sold on account for $110,000.
(6) Supplies used: factory, $3,200; office, $2,700.
(7) Collections from customers, $106,000.
(8) Sale of capital stock for cash, $10,000.
(9) Payments made:
   To materials suppliers, on account, $32,500.
   To equipment manufacturer, on contract (see [4] above), $2,500.
   To employees, $47,740.
   Payroll taxes and withholdings, $9,800.
   Office rental for May, $2,300.
   Repairs of factory equipment, $600.
   Electricity and other utilities for May: factory, $3,600; office, $500.
   Other costs for May: factory, $4,600; office, $13,100.
(10) Equipment sold, $300 cash (original cost, $5,000; book value, $800).
(11) Dividends declared, $3,000, to be paid on June 15.
(12) Insurance premiums expired: factory, $200; office, $100.
(13) Depreciation: factory, $4,000; office, $800.
(14) Bills received during May but unpaid as of May 31:
   For May newspaper advertising, $300.
   For taxes on factory, May 1 through October 31, $1,200.
(15) Cost of goods finished, $64,200.
(16) Finished goods on hand, May 31, $11,800.

a) Prepare journal entries to record all of the above information in accrual basis accounts. You will need to open accounts in addition to those listed at the beginning of this problem.

b) Set up T-accounts, enter the May 1 account balances, and post your journal entries to these accounts.

c) Prepare an income statement for May and a balance sheet as of May 31. Ignore any income taxes that might be levied on the Deppe Company's income for the month.

33. In January, 19x3, two brothers, Davy and George Jones, went into business for themselves by purchasing a gasoline service station together

with an adjoining parcel of land. They did not incorporate but instead formed a partnership in which they shared equally. They financed the purchase in part from their own funds, borrowing the rest from a local bank on a mortgage loan.

During the year 19x3, the brothers kept no formal accounts, but they did make all payments by check. Shortly after the end of the year, they employed an accountant to help them determine their financial position and their income or loss for the year. With their help, the accountant put together the following information:

CASH TRANSACTIONS

Cash received (as shown in bank statements and checkbook):

Date	Source	Amount
Jan. 15	Initial deposit ($30,000 from each brother)	$ 60,000
Jan. 31	From bank (mortgage loan)	30,000
June 1	Sale of land	6,020
Various	Collections from customers	62,590
	Total Receipts	$158,610

Cash paid out (as shown in checkbook):

Date	Purpose	Amount
Jan. 18	Annual insurance premium (policy effective February 1, 19x3)	$ 360
Jan. 31	Purchase of station	74,625
June 1	Property taxes	1,500
Aug. 1	Mortgage payment (principal and interest)	1,900
Sept. 1	Equipment for garage	5,400
Oct. 1	Partial payment on garage construction	12,000
Various	Water	220
Various	Electricity	240
Various	Payroll	29,700*
Various	Purchases of merchandise (gasoline, oil, parts, grease, tires, etc.)	30,400
	Total Payments	$156,345

* Includes salaries of $600 a month for each of the Jones brothers, beginning February 1, 19x3.

Cash balance, December, 31, 19x3, $2,265.

PURCHASE OF PROPERTY

The purchase price of the station was $75,000. The Jones brothers and the accountant estimated that a reasonable breakdown of the price was as follows:

Building (including tanks and concrete parking area)	$35,000
Land (40,000 square feet)	25,000
Equipment (pump, tools, rack, air compressors, etc.)	14,000
Inventory (primarily oil, grease, and gasoline)	1,000
Total	$75,000
Less: Property taxes, November 1, 19x2, to February 1, 19x3	375
Net Amount Paid	$74,625

Local property taxes were due for payment each year on June 1, covering the local "tax year" period from the preceding November 1 to the following November 1. They were levied as a percentage of the property's "assessed valuation." The station building was assessed for tax purposes at $30,000, the 10,000 square feet of land occupied by the station was assessed at $12,000 as "improved land," and the remaining land was assessed as "unimproved land" at $8,000, for a total of $50,000. The tax rate was 3 percent of the assessed valuation.

Because the Jones brothers would pay the next tax bill in full, including the taxes for the first three months of the tax year before the property was theirs, the seller agreed to deduct one quarter of the annual taxes ($375) from the amount to be paid to him at the time of the sale.

MORTGAGE LOAN

The amount borrowed on the mortgage loan was payable to the bank in 30 equal semiannual installments, together with interest on the balance of the loan outstanding at the beginning of the semiannual period. The interest rate was 6 percent a year. The first payment was made to the bank on August 1, 19x3, as indicated above.

SALE OF LAND

On June 1, 19x3, the Jones brothers completed negotiations for the sale of a portion of their "unimproved" land to James Bailey, who planned to erect a roadside snack bar on the site. The amount of land sold was 6,000 square feet, and the selling price was $6,000, plus $20 to compensate the Jones brothers for taxes they had paid on this land for the period June 1–November 1. In their initial appraisal of the land, the Jones brothers and their accountant had assigned the same cost per square foot to all the land purchased, even though the tax assessment differentiated between improved and unimproved land.

NEW GARAGE BUILDING

On July 1, 19x3, new construction began on a concrete block garage building. The work was completed and the building put into use on October 1, 19x3. The total contract price was $18,000, and the contractor accepted in payment $12,000 cash and a $6,000, four-month, 5 percent note dated October 1, 19x3. Property taxes on the garage would be $480 a year, starting October 1, 19x3. The first payment of tax on the garage would be made on June 1, 19x4.

INVENTORY

On December 4, 19x3, George Jones discovered that a leak had developed in one of their gasoline storage tanks. The total gasoline loss was estimated at 1,000 gallons, cost $150. The brothers repaired the leak themselves on the following day. The final inventory (gasoline, oil, parts, grease, etc.) as taken by the Jones brothers on December 31, 19x3, was valued on a cost basis at $2,100.

MISCELLANEOUS

At the year-end, there were no accounts receivable outstanding, nor were there any liabilities other than accrued property taxes and those arising out of the note and the mortgage. Depreciation rates were estimated as follows:

Item	Annual Rate
Station building	5 percent of cost
Garage	4 percent of cost
Equipment	10 percent of cost

To simplify the records, depreciation on the station and station equipment was to be taken for an entire year; no depreciation was to be charged on the garage and garage equipment during the first year.

a) Prepare an income statement for the 12 months ending December 31, 19x3, and a statement of changes in owners' equity for the year. Ignore income taxes.

b) Prepare a balance sheet as of December 31, 19x3.

Chapter 5

THE RECOGNITION OF REVENUE AND EXPENSE

The essence of accrual accounting is the matching of revenue and expense. The timing of *revenue* recognition thus governs the timing of *expense* recognition. For this reason, it can be a highly important determinant of reported net income.

An economist would argue that each of the productive activities of the firm adds value in some measure to the goods or merchandise purchased. On these grounds, a portion of the ultimate sale price ought to be recognized as revenue as each of these activities is performed. The difficulty is that the ultimate sale price is the joint product of all activities and it is impossible to say with certainty how much is attributable to any one activity. *For this reason, the accountant selects one event as the signal for revenue recognition and ignores the others. His problem is to decide which one to select.*

The examples in the previous chapters assumed that revenues would be recognized as goods were delivered or services provided. In fact, at least five distinct events can be found in the operating cycle, any one of which might under certain circumstances be taken as the signal that revenues have been earned. They are:

1. Acquisition of resources.
2. Receipt of customer orders.
3. Production.
4. Delivery of goods or performance of services.
5. Collection of cash.

The purpose of this chapter is to discuss the relative merits of these various possibilities and to examine some of the problems encountered in putting them into use.

Criteria for Revenue Recognition

Different bases of revenue recognition are used in practice, depending on the specific circumstances in which operations take place. For

120

public reporting, revenues are generally recognized at the first point in the operating cycle at which all of the following conditions are satisfied:

1. The principal revenue-producing service has been performed.
2. Any costs that are necessary to create the revenue but have not yet been incurred are either negligible or can be predicted with an acceptably high degree of accuracy.
3. The amount ultimately collectible in cash or its equivalent can be estimated objectively with an adequately small range of error.

The argument for the second and third of these criteria is that recognition of revenue and expense before these conditions are met would introduce too great an element of subjectivity into the income statement.[1]

In applying these criteria to specific situations, the accountant most often concludes that revenues should be recognized at the time of delivery of goods or performance of services. For this reason, we shall examine this possibility first, and then turn to a brief examination of the four alternatives listed above. The chapter will then conclude with a study of some of the problems that are encountered in handling sales discounts, returns, and allowances.

REVENUE RECOGNITION AT TIME OF DELIVERY

Although cash is often received before the performance of service or the shipment of goods, the more common case is the *credit sale* in which shipment or service precedes collection. In most such cases, it is deemed proper to recognize revenue at the time the service is performed or the goods are shipped.[2]

Reasons for Prevalence of Delivery Basis

The justification of the shipment or delivery basis is simple. In most cases, it is the first point in the cycle at which all three criteria are met. The seller's economic role has been performed for the most part when the goods are delivered or the services provided, and in most cases the

---

[1] It can be argued that the accountant's usual standard of verifiability is too rigid and that less precise evidence should be accepted. How far the standard could be relaxed without impairing the credibility of the statements is not clear.

[2] This is often referred to as recognition *at the time of sale*, but this begs the question because a sale may be said to take place at any one of several points in the cycle. The salesman, for example, believes that he has made a sale when he books an order from a customer. For reasons cited in the next section, the accountant chooses not to recognize the sale when the order is received.

amount of cash ultimately to be collected is predictable with a high degree of accuracy.

At the time of delivery, of course, it is not certain that the customers' promises will result in the receipt of an equal amount of cash. In most lines of business, however, the likelihood of collection is very high. Defaults or credit losses and customer rebates are *small* relative to total credit sales and are *predictable* with a high degree of accuracy. Consequently, because it is possible to make due allowance for the probability of future noncollections, it is generally agreed that in most cases the delivery basis meets the tests for revenue recognition.

The entry to record sales on the delivery basis of revenue recognition is the one with which we became familiar in previous chapters:

```
Accounts Receivable.........................................xxx
    Revenue from Sales.......................................        xxx
```

One relatively minor problem encountered in implementing this rule is how to identify the time of delivery. It is normally resolved by identifying the delivery with the point at which the goods sold leave the seller's hands. If transport of the goods is done by common carrier rather than by the seller's own delivery vehicles, delivery is assumed to be accomplished at the time the goods are delivered to the common carrier and revenue is recognized at that time.

Revenue Adjustment for Credit Losses

Given the rule of revenue and expense recognition at the time of delivery, and given also the fact that a large portion of all sales (almost 100 percent outside of retailing and personal service) are made on a deferred payment basis, the major problem of implementing the sales recognition convention is to adjust the face value of the Sales and Accounts Receivable accounts for expected *credit losses*.

The dollar amount that customers promise to pay in exchange for goods and services generally exceeds, by some amount, the dollar amount which will eventually be received. One of several reasons for this is that some customers will be unable to fulfill their promises in full when the time comes. Therefore, both revenues and assets will be overstated unless some adjustment is made.

One such adjustment method is to estimate ultimate credit losses by applying a predetermined loss percentage to the *volume of credit sales*. At the time of delivery, it is not known which specific customers will not meet their obligations in full (if that were known, the seller would not make delivery). From past experience, however, the *aggregate amount* of these defaults can be predicted with a great deal of accuracy, accuracy being a prerequisite for the recognition of revenue at the point of delivery. If experience indicates that a percentage, r, of all credit sales, S, will produce accounts that will ultimately prove uncollectible (also referred to as *bad debts*), the adjusting entry might take the following form:

Revenue from Sales	....	rS
Accounts Receivable	....	rS

The first half of this entry serves to reduce *gross* sales to the appropriate *net* sales figure—that is, the amount of cash that the company will ultimately receive as a direct result of the period's sales. Assuming annual sales of $1 million and estimated credit losses of 1 percent, for example, the sales section of the income statement would appear as follows:

Gross sales	$1,000,000
Less: Provision for uncollectible accounts	10,000
Net Sales	$ 990,000

Similarly, the credit to Accounts Receivable reduces the book value of this asset to the amount expected to be collected.

Credit Losses: The Use of Contra Accounts

Although the entry above reflects correctly the changes in assets and equities, the entry is more likely to take the following form:

Credit Losses	....	rS
Allowance for Uncollectible Accounts	....	rS

Credit Losses is a deduction-from-sales *contra* account, while Allowance for Uncollectible Accounts is a deduction-from-assets *contra* account.

The reason for using the Credit Losses account (sometimes called Loss from Bad Debts or even Bad Debt Expense) is to reserve the Revenue from Sales account for gross sales data, figures which are usually needed for a variety of reasons.[3] The Allowance for Uncollectible Accounts account, sometimes called Allowance for Bad Debts, serves a similar purpose. Accounts Receivable is an example of

---

[3] Estimated credit losses are often shown as an expense rather than as a determinant of net sales. If expenses are expired costs, this is incorrect. A better treatment would be to determine net sales as in the illustration above but to separate the cost of goods or services provided to nonpaying customers from the figure for cost of goods sold. The reported net income would be unaffected by this refinement, but the income statement would be slightly more informative.

a *control account*, which is a running summary of a number of subsidiary accounts for the firm's individual customers. In other words, at any moment in time the balance in Accounts Receivable should equal the sum of the balances in each of the many customer accounts. In view of the fact that at the time of sale it is not known which customers' accounts will eventually prove uncollectible, the subsidiary accounts cannot be credited for the bad debt allowance at this time. Consequently, crediting Accounts Receivable directly would destroy the equality between the balances in the control and subsidiary accounts. This problem is solved by crediting a contra account, Allowance for Uncollectible Accounts.

To illustrate, let us assume credit sales of $1,000,000, collections of $800,000 during the period, and an anticipated credit loss ratio of 1 percent. The entries would be:

```
Accounts Receivable..............................1,000,000
     Revenue from Sales...........................          1,000,000
     To record credit sales for the period.


Cash.......................................... 800,000
     Accounts Receivable..........................          800,000
     To record collections during the period.


Credit Losses.................................. 10,000
     Allowance for Uncollectible Accounts............          10,000
     To record estimated uncollectibles from period's sales.
```

The balance sheet would then show the following amounts:

```
Accounts receivable....................................$200,000
     Less: Allowance for uncollectible accounts...............  10,000
     Net Accounts Receivable...............................$190,000
```

The net figure shows the amount expected to be collected from the accounts outstanding as of the end of the period.

Write-off of Uncollectible Accounts

Here, the contra account mechanism serves a new purpose in that it permits suspending the accounts receivable credit until more specific information is available. When it is decided that a particular receivable is in fact uncollectible, the subsidiary account is removed from the file of current receivables and an equal amount is eliminated from both the control and contra accounts. For example, suppose that Henry Jones, whose obligation in the amount of $2,000 is included in the balance of accounts receivable, is totally bankrupt, with no assets available to satisfy the claims of his trade creditors. The entry to record this fact is:

```
Allowance for Uncollectible Accounts.....................2,000
    Accounts Receivable.................................         2,000
```

It should be noted that *this entry has no effect on the assets or reported net income of the firm.* Crediting Accounts Receivable and debiting Allowance for Uncollectible Accounts reduces both accounts and leaves the *net* amount of accounts receivable and all other accounts unchanged. The balance sheet presentation now would be:

```
Accounts receivable......................................$198,000
    Less: Allowance for uncollectible accounts..............    8,000
Net Accounts Receivable..............................$190,000
```

This notation has simply identified the *specific* account for which a *general* provision was made at the time of the sale. The revenue deduction was recognized earlier—both revenue and receivables were recorded at their net values at the time of revenue recognition.

Recovery of Accounts Previously Written off

Accounts written off as uncollectible are not necessarily forgotten, nor do efforts at collection necessarily cease at the time of the write-off. The accounts are often simply transferred to an overdue file for future reference. If collection is made at a later time, the account is removed from the overdue file and the collection is recorded. One way to record the collection in this case is by means of the following entry (recording the fact that Henry Jones, whose account was written off earlier, is now willing and able to pay off his former creditors):

```
Cash.......................................................2,000
    Recovery of Overdue Accounts........................         2,000
```

The Recovery of Overdue Accounts account, sometimes called Bad Debts Recovered, is most simply and commonly treated as revenue of the period in which the collection is made. However, if the original provision for credit losses was based on the percentage of credit sales that would *never* be collected, the amount recovered should be credited to the Allowance for Uncollectible Accounts.

The Recovery of Overdue Accounts account serves to identify the results of one of the activities of a firm's credit department. Recoveries of this sort are often the fruit of special and perhaps expensive collection efforts, and the recovery account provides information that may be useful in gauging the effectiveness of such efforts.

Aging of Receivables

An alternative approach to bad debt estimation is through examination of the *age of outstanding receivables*. The technique of aging the accounts consists of classifying the individual customer balances by age groups and evaluating each of these in light of the proposition that the older the claim, the less likely it is to be collected. Thus, loss experience rates are applied to the amounts in each age category to arrive at an estimate of the total dollar amount of uncollectible claims. The required end-of-period entry is whatever amount is necessary to bring the balance in the contra account up to or down to the indicated level.

For example, assume that the balance in the contra account on December 31 is $8,000 before the end-of-period entry is made and that the receivables are distributed as follows:

(1) Age	(2) Amount	(3) Estimated Percentage Uncollectible	(4) Estimated Amount Uncollectible (2) × (3)
0–30 days.............	$100,000	0.2%	$ 200
31–60 days.............	50,000	1.0	500
61–90 days.............	30,000	3.0	900
91 days and older......	18,000	25.0	4,500
Total.............	$198,000		$6,100

The balance in the contra account, therefore, should be $6,100, or $1,900 less than it is. The entry to correct the overstatement of the balance is:

Allowance for Uncollectible Accounts.......................1,900
    Credit Losses..   1,900

This entry reflects the fact that credit loss experience during the period just ended was more favorable than the normal experience upon which the initial 1 percent provision was based. The balance in the Credit Losses account is now $8,000 less $1,900, or $6,100. This represents the combined effect of the estimated credit losses of this period and a correction in the estimate for a prior period or periods.

In most cases the error in identifying the entire adjustment with the sales of the current period will be immaterial.

Whereas the method described earlier yields a periodic charge proportional to credit sales volume, the aging approach is likely to be more responsive to current changes in business conditions. Use of the first procedure in connection with interim statements and of the second as an annual check upon the cumulative results of the first is fairly common. It should be noted that the aging process serves also to indicate which customer accounts have gone unpaid beyond the cash discount period and by simple calculation yields the dollar amount of cash discounts available to customers at the period end.

Managerial Implications of Credit Losses

The mechanics of accounting for bad debts are of interest for the purpose of understanding both financial statements and the detailed data underlying the receivables account. However, of more importance to the firm is the relationship of bad debts to credit policy. The character of the credit loss problem varies considerably from industry to industry and company to company. For example, a manufacturer selling industrial goods to a few large companies will in general bear less credit risk than a wholesaler selling to many small retailers. Even so, the seller has some leeway in deciding how much credit risk he will bear. Careful advance credit investigation of customers and extension of credit only to firms with the higher credit ratings will reduce the risk borne by any seller, but it will also reduce sales volume and increase the costs of credit investigation.

Consequently, in deciding whether to sell on credit and if so on what terms and to what customers, management must forecast the sales volumes, costs, and credit losses associated with each prospective credit policy. In choosing between liberal and stringent credit policies, sales volume, on the one hand, and credit losses and investigatory costs, on the other, are normally traded off. Different companies in the same line of business will find different answers to this problem.

The key accounting problem in connection with this managerial interest in credit policy is not the method of recognizing credit losses in the financial accounts but rather the means employed for estimating the amount of these losses. Although treatment of this subject is beyond the scope of an introductory text, recent work by Cyert and others suggests that the techniques of statistical inference may be employed to get more effective estimates of loss rates on receivables in various age brackets directly from the firm's past accounting data.[4] The next step is to develop from these data estimates of the changes in credit losses consequent on changes in credit policy, which is the question relevant to the business decision that must be made.

ALTERNATIVES TO THE DELIVERY BASIS

An overwhelming percentage of firms using the accrual basis of accounting recognize revenues and related product expenses at the time of delivery. It is often incorrectly inferred from this that the delivery basis for revenue recognition is the general rule, use of other bases being exceptions to the rule. A rule with a series of *ad hoc* exceptions is no rule at all but simply a convenience. The rule is provided by the three recognition criteria established earlier in this chapter.

The popularity of the delivery basis undoubtedly can be attributed in large part to its success in satisfying these criteria, but another part may very well stem from its convenience—that is, revenues are recognized as a bookkeeping by-product of the preparation of customer invoices. The delivery basis should not be used when some other recognition basis meets the criteria better. Four possible alternatives need to be examined briefly:

1. Recognition at time of sales orders.
2. Recognition at time of production.
3. Recognition at time of collection.
4. Recognition at time of purchase.

Recognition at Time of Sales Orders

One possible point for revenue recognition is the point at which the sales order is received. The order is a highly significant event in the operating cycle. Most companies which experience significant lags between the date of the order and the date of the shipment will record orders received so that the amount of orders on hand for future delivery (the backlog) can be reported periodically to management. In these circumstances the performance of the sales force probably should be judged more on the basis of orders received than on goods shipped.

---

[4] See R. M. Cyert, H. J. Davidson, and G. L. Thompson, "Estimation of the Allowance for Doubtful Accounts by Markov Chains," *Management Science*, April, 1962, pp. 287–303; and R. M. Trueblood and R. M. Cyert, *Sampling Techniques in Accounting* (Englewood Cliffs, N.J.: Prentice-Hall, Inc., 1957).

Order and backlog information is sometimes also reported to creditors and stockholders to guide them in their appraisals of the company's future prospects, but revenues and receivables are never recognized in externally published reports on the basis of orders received during the period. The reason is simply that the criteria for revenue recognition are not met at the time the order is received—the goods have not yet been produced, the costs of producing them are not adequately predictable, or order cancellations are frequent and variable.

The recognition criteria would be met at the time the order is received if (*a*) the goods ordered are in stock when the order is received, so that (*b*) all significant costs have already been incurred, provided that (*c*) the number of order cancellations is highly predictable. These conditions are likely to hold only when the interval between order receipt and shipment is so short that the distinction is of no practical importance. In these cases, convenience can govern the choice and convenience dictates that revenue be recognized as a by-product of the preparation of the normal shipping and billing documents.

Recognition at Time of Production

As stated earlier, no unambiguous way exists of dividing the income created by the firm's activities between the manufacturing and selling functions. Various formulas have been suggested—for example, in proportion to investment in production and sales facilities, or in proportion to total payroll in each of these functional areas—but the fact is that *both* production and marketing are necessary to the creation of income and it is impossible to give a nonarbitrary answer to the question of how much is attributable to each.

The case for the production basis is perhaps best illustrated by a firm that devotes its entire attention to manufacturing in one accounting period, building up inventories but making no sales. In the next period it does no manufacturing but sells the entire inventory that had been built up in the first period. The typical accounting practice would allocate all the revenues to the second period; that is, it is tactily assumed that any value in excess of cost is created by the company's selling efforts rather than by production. The question is whether revenue recognition on a delivery basis under these circumstances provides a satisfactory measure of enterprise performance during either of these two periods of time.

Most accountants probably would agree that recognition of the entire amount of income in the period in which delivery is made introduces an arbitrary element into the financial statements. Nevertheless, they would argue that in most instances revenue cannot be recognized at the time of production because two key conditions have not been met: (*a*) not all the significant value-adding services have been performed by then; and (*b*) the amount of cash ultimately collectible is too uncertain at that point.

If these objections can be overcome, then no fundamental barrier arises to recognizing revenue on the principle that income arises through changing the form, time, or place of an asset rather than through its exchange.[5] In fact, the production basis is used when no significant amount of services is required subsequent to production, when the amount of ultimate collection is reasonably certain, and when the timing of deliveries is more volatile than the timing of production. Application of this method is most common in the refining of gold and other products which have a guaranteed market at a fixed price, and in shipbuilding or other industries where the production cycle is very long and production is initiated only on receipt of a firm order at a specific price.

Implementation of the Production Basis. Recognition of revenue on a production basis is not common, and the procedure and accounts employed vary considerably among those firms that employ it. The illustration that follows is therefore designed only to provide some understanding of the process.

In mid-19x1, Marsden Brown, the engineering firm referred to in the preceding chapter, obtained a contract to install the lighting for the Arkwright County Sports Arena, a job that was to take six months. The contract price was $200,000, and the estimated total cost was $160,000. Work began on October 18, 19x1, and the actual costs charged to the job prior to December 31, 19x1, amounted to $80,000. The entry to record these costs would be:

Work in Process..80,000
    Wages Payable, etc................................   80,000

At the end of December, progress on the contract was reviewed and the job was found to be 45 percent completed. Production basis

---

[5] A rule of this kind is applied in national income accounting, although in that case the value created by adding to unsold inventories is assumed to be *equal* to cost. None of the profit that will be recognized in the accounting records of private firms in later accounting periods is included in national income of the current period.

accounting in this case would require the recognition of revenue of $90,000 for 19x1 (45 percent of the $200,000 contract price). The entry to record this would be:

Due from Customers.....................................90,000
    Revenue from Work Performed.....................   90,000

The Due from Customers account is an asset account, representing amounts earned by production to date but not yet billed. When the customer is billed, the amounts are transferred to the Accounts Receivable account.[6]

Because revenue was recognized in 19x1 for the work done on the contract during that year, the cost of doing this work had to be treated as expense of that year. This would require the following transfer of cost from the asset category to expense:

Construction Costs Applicable to Current Revenues..........80,000
    Work in Process—Contra.........................   80,000

The Construction Costs Applicable to Current Revenues account is an expense account, the counterpart of the Cost of Goods Sold account in a shipment basis company. The Work in Process—Contra account would be deducted from the balance in the Work in Process account on the December 31, 19x1, balance sheet. A contra account would be credited instead of the Work in Process account itself so that the latter could serve as a control account for the contracts in process at any given time. Upon completion of the contract, the contra account balance would be closed out against the inventory account.

Under this approach, the contract would be carried on the December 31, 19x1, balance sheet as a receivable in the amount of $90,000 instead of as an inventory, at cost. If the job were to be completed in 19x2, the revenue for that year would be the full contract price ($200,000) minus the $90,000 recognized in 19x1—that is, $110,000.

This approach has substantial managerial significance. It shows management at an early date that earnings on this contract are accru-

---

[6] The method illustrated here is a simplified version of the method in common use, referred to as the *percentage-of-completion* method. In practice, earnings may be recognized more conservatively than in this illustration, at amounts that are less than proportional to estimated progress toward completion of the job.

Furthermore, most contracts provide for partial progress payments from the buyer that are less than the sales value of the work done to date. Thus the contract might call for a payment of 85 percent of sales value, with the remaining 15 percent being held out until final completion of the contract and acceptance of the work. Thus, the amount receivable is partly a current item and partly deferred.

ing at a rate of only 12½ percent of cost instead of the anticipated 25 percent. If management is given this information at this early date, the company may be able to take action that will prevent excessive costs on the remainder of the job. The progress percentage and amount of future collections for the work done may or may not be predictable with enough accuracy to permit inclusion of this information in the company's published financial statements, but it can and should be reported to management. The same information presumably would be significant to the outside investor, but management's verifiability requirements are less stringent than those imposed for external reporting.

Recognition at Time of Collection

The third alternative to the shipment basis of revenue and expense recognition is recognition at the time of collection of cash from the customer. Notice that *this is not the same as cash basis accounting*. In cash basis accounting, expense is measured by the cash disbursements made during the period. In accrual basis accounting, on the other hand, the timing of expense recognition is independent of the timing of cash disbursement. When revenue is recognized at the time of collection under accrual accounting, the expense recognized at this time will undoubtedly reflect some past and future disbursements as well as current-period cash outlays.

In most commercial situations revenue recognition need not be deferred until the time of collection because the revenue recognition criteria are met earlier. This is the position of the Accounting Principles Board of the American Institute of Certified Public Accountants:

The Board recognizes that these are exceptional cases where receivables are collectible over an extended priod of time and, because of the terms of the transactions or other conditions, there is no reasonable basis for estimating the degree of collectibility. When such circumstances exist, and as long as they exist, . . . the installment method . . . may be used . . . . Otherwise, the installment method is not acceptable.[7]

In those rare circumstances in which the installment method is appropriate, the entries need to be designed to show as period revenue the sum of installments received during the period. The costs of the merchandise sold on installment contracts are carried in inventory

---

[7] *APB Opinion No. 10: Omnibus Opinion—1966* (New York: AICPA, 1966), paragraph 12.

accounts and are transferred to expense (cost of goods sold or, more accurately, cost of receipts from sales) in proportion to the amount of the receipts. Thus, in effect, the receivables are listed at cost rather than at the amount actually owed by the customer.[8]

The use of the installment method is now restricted mainly to the computation of taxable income. By deferring income recognition until the period of collection, federal income taxes can also be deferred. Hence, the retailer need not finance his tax payments from other sources but can pay them out of the proceeds of his collection efforts. In small retail enterprises with extremely limited access to outside capital, this may be an extremely valuable feature.

As a means of measuring the performance and status of the firm, however, this method appears unduly conservative, with reported performance lagging behind actual operating performance by an interval roughly equal to the length of the average installment period. If the rate of deliveries either increases or decreases sharply or if the terms of sale are altered appreciably, it will be some months before such changes exert a material influence on the reported operating results. For this reason, when credit losses can be predicted with reasonable accuracy, the installment basis should be rejected in favor of delivery basis recognition of revenue.

Recognition at Time of Purchase

Thus far, situations in which each of three recognition bases might be used have been noted—production, delivery, and collection. The one potential basis that has not been discussed—purchase of resources—is never used for revenue recognition in the ordinary sense because the prevalence of unperformed services at the time of acquisition and the uncertainty as to ultimate receipts violate two of the principal criteria for revenue recognition.

If this argument is accepted, then the importance to the company and to its investors of successful purchase activity cannot be reflected in the company's financial statements unless the criteria for revenue recognition are altered drastically. In a later chapter, a technique will be examined by which income can be computed at the time of resource acquisition, a computation that has relevance for internal decision making but is too subjective in most cases for public reporting.

---

[8] The entries here are of specialized interest and little purpose would be served at this point by discussing them. For a description of this method, see Rufus Wixon (ed.), *Accountants' Handbook* (4th ed.; New York: Ronald Press, 1957), sec. 11.

DISCOUNTS, RETURNS, AND ALLOWANCES

Two basic problems arise in revenue recognition: *when* to recognize revenues and *how much* to recognize at that time. Discussion of the second problem has dealt thus far with estimation of credit losses. The remainder of this chapter will be devoted to a brief examination of other sources of discrepancy between gross sale price and the net amount realized from a sale, with a parting glance at the comparable discrepancy between gross and net purchase price.

Cash Discounts on Sales

In many industries or lines of trade, a *cash discount* is offered to the customer as an incentive for prompt payment. Its effect, of course, is to reduce the price charged to customers who pay promptly. *The issue in accounting is whether the amount of the cash discount should be deducted from gross revenues* (a) *at the time of revenue recognition or* (b) *at the time of collection.*

Clearly, the figure that is really significant to the seller is the amount of cash that he is going to be able to realize from the sale. The problem is that he does not know at the time of sale whether the customer will avail himself of the discount and therefore he is uncertain at that time as to the eventual *net realization.*

To illustrate, on October 3 the Denton Company, a grocery wholesaler, shipped to the Converse Market several cases of groceries. The gross prices listed for these items on the invoice sent to the Converse market added up to $400. The customer was allowed 30 days in which to pay but was offered a 2 percent discount for payment within 10 days. These credit terms are customarily expressed by the notation, 2/10, n/30, which is read as, two ten, net thirty. At the time of shipment, the transaction was recorded as follows:

```
Accounts Receivable........................................400
    Sales Revenue........................................          400
```

The effect of this entry was to establish a record of the claim against the customer and to recognize revenue for the period by an amount equal to the quantity sold times the gross price or invoice price per unit. This is known as the *gross price method* of recording sales.

The Converse Market paid its bill within the 10-day discount period, and the cash receipt of $392 ($400 minus 2 percent of $400) was recorded:

```
Cash........................................................392
Sales Discounts.............................................  8
    Accounts Receivable....................................          400
```

Had the customer failed to pay his bill during the discount period, the entry to record his payment when it came in later would have been:

Cash..400
    Accounts Receivable.. 400

This method of recording cash discounts is to some extent inconsistent with the logic of the cash discount. It is quite clear that the price of the merchandise is really the net price, not the gross price. The seller *expects* his customers to take the discount, and he tries to assure this by making it very expensive for them not to do so. In the present case, even if the Converse Market does not take advantage of the discount, it has only 20 additional days in which to pay the full price before the invoice becomes overdue and the buyer's credit rating is impaired. Thus, Converse Market would in effect pay $8 for the use of $392 for one eighteenth of a year, which is equivalent to an annual interest charge of 36.7 percent. Hence, only the careless or financially embarrassed firm will fail to pay within the discount period. The Denton Company therefore expects that almost all sales will be made to customers who will take advantage of the discount and sets the gross price accordingly.

Following this line of reasoning, the amount reported as sales revenue should be the net price. In other words, the Sales Discounts account is a deduction-from-sales contra account:

Gross sales...............................xxx
Less: Sales discounts......................xxx
Net Sales.................................xxx

Although the Denton Company benefits from the reduction in the amount of capital required to carry receivables when the average collection period is shortened, probably the main reason for granting cash discounts is competitive pressure, reinforced by the strength of tradition in the trade.[9]

---

[9] For example, the Denton Company's annual sales amount to about $6 million. With a collection period of 30 days, or one twelfth of a year, the company would have an average investment in receivables of $500,000 ($6,000,000 divided by 12). With a collection period of 10 days, the average is reduced to $166,667, or one third of its former amount. Thus $333,333 ($500,000 minus $166,667) is released for productive investment elsewhere. If the company can invest funds to yield a return of, say, 20 percent, then this $333,333 will earn $66,667 per year, which is only a little more than half of the $120,000 that a 2 percent discount on $6 million sales would take. Most companies would find it difficult to find investments that would yield enough to justify granting a 2 percent discount just to obtain investable funds. The real explanation must lie elsewhere.

Defects in the Gross Price Method

Use of the gross price method creates some minor difficulties, such as how to report discounts forfeited during the period by slow-paying customers or discounts still applicable to gross receivables outstanding at the end of the period. For example, that portion of a customer's payment which represents discounts forfeited by late payment is in reality a form of interest rather than merchandising revenue and therefore should be separated from merchandising revenues in the income statement.

These problems could be avoided by recording sales revenue at the net price:

```
Accounts Receivable.........................................392
    Revenue from Sales......................................          392
```

Amounts collected in excess of this amount could then be credited to a separate revenue account. The net price method is seldom used, however, because the gross price method is typically more convenient to use. (The gross amount is already shown on the customer's invoice; net price would require a special calculation.) In any event, the effect of the choice on the financial statements is ordinarily immaterial.

Cash Discounts versus Trade and Quantity Discounts

The cash discount should not be confused with either quantity or trade discounts, which are devices for quoting different prices to different customers on the basis of the size of the customer's order or the services he performs. For example, a manufacturer may offer 5 percent off the catalog or list price for orders larger than a certain size, or 20 percent off to wholesalers for their services in carrying inventories of the product and contacting retailers.

All discounts have the effect of reducing the net price to be paid by the customer. The trade and quantity discounts differ from the cash discount in that they are not granted conditionally. Once the customer qualifies for the discount by virtue of his trade or the size of his order, he does not lose the discount by failure to meet some other requirement. If he is also entitled to a cash discount, however, and if he fails to pay for the merchandise within the cash discount period, then he forfeits his right to the discount. To state this another way, the cash discount is granted as an inducement for subsequent action, whereas the trade and quantity discounts are in reality a means of quoting different prices to different classes of customers. Sales subject to trade or quantity discount are almost always recorded at the gross price owed to the seller, *after* deducting trade or quantity discount but before deducting any cash discount applicable.

Sales Returns and Allowances

Whether sales are recorded at gross price or net price, a procedure must be devised to record revenue adjustments stemming from the *return* of merchandise by customers or from *allowances* or rebates granted to customers because goods were lost or received in damaged condition.

As an illustration, the Denton Company made a sale to Moore & Sons in the amount of $1,000. The entry recording the sale was:

Accounts Receivable	1,000	
Revenue from Sales		1,000

Upon receipt of the shipment, Moore & Sons notified the Denton Company that several cases of canned goods were being returned because they were not of the brand ordered. Furthermore, one carton of groceries, with a gross price of $10, had been broken in transit and the merchandise was salable only at a discount, as damaged goods. Moore & Sons offered to keep the damaged merchandise and thereby save Denton the expense of the return shipment, but only if Denton would allow a credit of $6 as compensation for the damages. In the expectation that this request would be granted, Moore & Sons forwarded their check in the amount of $729, computed as follows:

Gross price per invoice		$1,000
Less: Returns at gross		250
Corrected invoice at gross		$ 750
Less: 2% cash discount	$15	
Allowance for damage[10]	6	21
Net Amount Paid		$ 729

When the Denton Company received the check, the traffic manager approved the $6 claim and the collection was recorded as follows:

Cash	729	
Sales Discounts	15	
Sales Allowances	6	
Accounts Receivable—Moore & Sons		750

---

[10] It should be made clear in each case whether the damages are computed on the basis of gross price or net price. In this illustration a net price basis was used—that is, the customer was allowed to take the full discount on the order. The difference is unlikely to be significant.

A claim for $6 was then lodged against the transport company through which the merchandise had been shipped.

The Moore & Sons account still showed a debit balance of $250 after this entry had been recorded, because the returned merchandise had not yet been received. On receipt of the goods, a *credit memorandum* for $250 was issued to the customer, and his account was cleared by the following entry:

```
Sales Returns.....................................................250
    Accounts Receivable.......................................        250
```

Two new accounts have been set up in this illustration, both of them deduction-from-sales contra accounts. Although the return and allowance could have been viewed as forms of sale cancellation, recorded by debits to Sales Revenue, this would have led to a loss of information significant to management. Both returns and allowances are evidence that some kind of mistake has occurred. Costs incurred for handling and transportation, instead of producing revenue, have led only to additional costs for rehandling, not to mention the intangible cost of possible customer ill will. The use of the contra accounts provides a cumulative record of the magnitude of mistakes of these kinds.

Purchases Discounts, Returns, and Allowances

One firm's sale is another firm's (or individual's) purchase. Hence, the sales discounts, returns, and allowances discussed above have their exact analogies in connection with purchases. The same reasons of clerical convenience and management information lead to the use of the gross price method in accounting for purchase discounts. To illustrate, a purchase of merchandise for $10,000 less 2 percent for payment in 10 days is accounted for as follows. At time of purchase, the Inventory account is charged with the *gross price* of the merchandise:

```
Inventory.........................................................10,000
    Accounts Payable.........................................        10,000
```

At time of payment, if within 10 days, the difference between the gross amount due and the net amount paid is credited to a Purchase Discounts account.

```
Accounts Payable.................................................10,000
    Cash.........................................................        9,800
    Purchase Discounts.......................................        200
```

The effect of the discount is to reduce the cost of the merchandise. For periodic financial reporting, therefore, the balance in the Purchase Discounts account should be deducted from the costs of the goods purchased. If all of these goods have been sold prior to the end of the period, then the entire amount of the discounts should be deducted from the cost of goods sold. If all the merchandise is still in inventory, on the other hand, then the purchase discounts should be deducted from the balance in the inventory account to arrive at the net cost of the inventories.

The *return* of merchandise or an *allowance* on merchandise purchased is accounted for quite simply. For example, if merchandise costing $2,000 is returned to the supplier, the entry is:

```
Accounts Payable.......................................2,000
    Inventory...........................................        2,000
```

An allowance on merchandise purchased would be handled in exactly the same way. Management is unlikely to need separate data on total purchase returns or purchase allowances, and the credits can be made directly to the Inventory account.

SUMMARY

The timing of revenue recognition has an important bearing on the year-to-year operating results of the firm as well as on the balance sheet valuation of inventories and receivables. Costs associated with a given segment of revenue are carried as inventories until the revenues are recognized, at which time they are transferred to expense (cost of goods sold).

In most companies, revenues are *recognized* at the time of delivery of goods or at the time of performance of an intangible service for an outside customer or client. The justification for this rule is that this is the first point in the operating cycle at which the revenue is both *earned* and *quantifiable* with a sufficient degree of accuracy. Under certain circumstances, revenues may be recognized prior to delivery if they are both earned and quantifiable earlier, or they may be deferred to a later point if quantification is subject to too great a degree of uncertainty at the time of delivery.

In any case, the amount to be shown as revenue in any period is the amount ultimately collectible in cash from the sales of that period. Thus, if revenue is recognized prior to the receipt of cash, estimated credit losses and discounts taken by customers must be deducted from gross revenues in computing net income.

The underlying objective is to present in the financial statements an accurate picture of current status and the results of current operations. The detailed rules stem from this objective and must be tested against it. If the results of operations are best reflected in terms of the volume and efficiency of production, then this should be the basis of revenue recognition, regardless of whether the products are at that time actually sold, in some narrow technical sense of that term. The general consensus, however, is that the proof of the pudding is in the selling, evidenced by the shipment of goods, and that the results of operations should be measured accordingly.

QUESTIONS AND PROBLEMS

1. What income measurement problems are raised by revenue recognition at the time of delivery of goods to customers, and what solutions has the accountant devised to deal with these problems?

2. Under what circumstances, if any, would you favor recognition of a gain on the acquisition of an asset?

3. Discuss the problem of defining the "time of sale."

4. Explain the nature and the purpose of the account Allowance for Uncollectible Accounts. When would this account be debited? Credited? What other accounts would be affected by each of these entries?

5. What is meant by "aging the accounts"? What is the purpose?

6. A company uses the gross price method in recording both purchases and sales.
a) What possible objections can you see to this practice as pertains to *purchases?*
b) What kind of adjustment, if any, will this practice make necessary at the time of statement preparation?

7. In deciding from which supplier to purchase materials, how would you define "materials cost"? Would this have any bearing on your choice between the net price and gross price methods of recording purchases? Explain.

8. Why are quantity and cash discounts often recorded differently? Are there any fundamental differences in the nature of the two types of discounts that provide a conceptual basis for this differentiation in bookkeeping treatment? Should they be handled any differently in annual financial reporting? Explain.

9. Does the recording of credit losses on the basis of estimates reflect extreme conservatism? Explain.

10. Reported credit losses are based on the price due from the customer. The real loss to the seller, however, is the cost of the merchandise plus any related handling and selling costs. How can existing practice be justified in the face of this fact?

11. On what consistent basis can the following three practices in revenue recognition be justified? In other words, state the recognition principle that might be used to justify all three; also state the conditions that must be met if the practice is not to violate the principle.

a) Recognition at time of shipment by a wholesaler in grocery products.
b) Recognition at time of production by a highway contractor.
c) Recognition at time of collection by a retail installment seller of household appliances.

12. An economist would argue that income is created or earned by a wide variety of the firm's activities (e.g., production, sale, delivery, etc.), yet the accountant in the typical case selects one of these activities to signal the time at which all revenues are to be recognized.

a) Assuming that the economist's view is correct, under what circumstances would the accountant's method lead to an undistorted measure of periodic income?
b) What are the obstacles to a practical implementation of the economist's concept?

13. Twenty Companies, Inc., contracted to build the Wild Horse Canyon Dam on a "cost plus adjustable fee" basis. The dam was expected to cost $130,000,000, and the construction to continue over a four-year period. The contractor was to receive periodic reimbursements for outlays made, but payment of the fee was to be deferred until the dam was completed.

Should the contractor recognize any earnings at interim dates before completing the dam? Give reasons for your answer.

14. The balance sheet of a shipbuilding company shows among the current assets the following:

Contracts in process (Note A)..............$5,352,494.74

Note A to the balance sheet reads as follows:

Note A—The balance sheet amount for contracts in process is the accumulated cost plus or minus the portion (based on percentage of completion) of estimated final gross profit or estimated final loss, less billings (exclusive of collections against future costs); except, that unless (*a*) progress thereon has reached a point, generally, of not less than 50 percent of completion, and (*b*) experience is deemed sufficient to establish estimates as reasonably indicative of final results, no recognition has been taken of possible profit on work which, though substantially advanced, had not reached such a stage of completion. Accumulated billings on contracts, in respect of which no net profit has been taken up into income by reason of such policy, amounted to $21,605,440.00. All estimates of final contract profits or losses as of the close of any period are subject to revision as contracts progress toward completion. The amount of gross profit, or loss, taken up in any accounting period in respect of any contract is the amount accrued to the date of closing of such period less the total of amounts taken up in prior periods.

Explain briefly the asset and income measurement policy implied in this explanation. How does the policy differ from that usually followed by retailers or manufacturers?

15. The practice of selling goods on account usually results in some losses from inability to collect in full from every customer. These uncollectible amounts may be reflected in the accounts as it becomes apparent that specific accounts receivable are uncollectible or, alternatively, at some earlier time on the basis of estimates.

a) Illustrate by means of sample journal entries the kinds of recordings which would be made under each alternative accounting treatment. Indicate the nature of the event or events which would give rise to each of your illustrative entries.
b) Explain and compare the potential effects of each method on the apparent financial status and earnings performance of the firm.

16. Company A establishes its monthly allowance for credit losses by applying a predetermined rate to monthly credit sales. At the end of each year, the total credit loss recorded in this way is adjusted by aging the accounts receivable on the books.

a) Using XXX's instead of dollar amounts, show the monthly journal entry for credit losses.
b) Explain the function of each account used in (*a*).
c) Show similarly the entry to write off an uncollectible account.
d) Assuming that the year-end aging of accounts receivable indicates that the estimated monthly rate has been *too high*, show in the same manner any necessary entry to restore a proper balance to the account.

*****17.** The Ryan Company has found from experience that approximately 1 percent of its sales on credit eventually prove to be uncollectible, even after recoveries of previously written off amounts are deducted from gross write-offs. During June, the credit sales were $100,000; one

---

* Solutions to problems marked with an asterisk (*) are found in Appendix B.

customer who owed $400 was declared legally bankrupt, with no assets to offset his liabilities; another former customer whose account for $150 had been written off as uncollectible three years earlier sent in a check for the full amount of his account.

Prepare journal entries to record these events.

*18. The following is a summary of the "aging" schedule for accounts receivable of Billerica Trading Company as of the end of the fiscal year:

Total	0–30 Days	31–45 Days	46–60 Days	Over 60 Days
$348,788	$283,615	$52,110	$12,552	$511

According to past experience, bills over 60 days old were likely to be completely uncollectible, those in the third category about 4 percent uncollectible, those in the second category about 1 percent uncollectible, and those in the first category about 0.2 percent uncollectible.

At this time, the Allowance for Uncollectible Accounts has a balance of $1,816. What adjustment, if any, should be made?

19. The Flintop Company was organized and commenced business on January 1. During the year it delivered products to customers at an aggregate sales value of $200,000. Although the company had no prior experience as to the collectibility of its receivables, it decided to charge 1½ percent of sales to Credit Losses until more accurate information could be obtained.

a) Prepare a journal entry to record the estimated credit losses for the year.
b) On December 1, the Elk Products Company, one of Flintop's customers, was declared bankrupt, with no assets to satisfy creditors' claims. At that time Elk Products owed Flintop $440. Prepare the necessary entry.
c) On December 31, an analysis of accounts receivable showed the following:

Age of Accounts	Amount Receivable
0–30 days	$30,000
31–60 days	10,000
61–120 days	5,000
More than 120 days	2,000

The company's auditors suggested that the following percentages be used to compute the amounts that would probably prove uncollectible: 0–30 days, ¼ of 1 percent; 31–60 days, 1 percent; 61–120 days, 10 percent; more than 120 days, 50 percent. Prepare a journal entry to implement this suggestion.

*20. On January 18 the Sanford Plumbers Supply Corporation purchased six laundry tubs on credit from the Stone Manufacturing Company at $27 each. The tubs arrived on January 25 and were immediately re-shipped, in the original crates, to the Lowe Plumbing Company at a price of $36 each.

The following day, Lowe Plumbing notified Sanford Plumbers Supply that three of the tubs were defective. Sanford agreed to allow Lowe to deduct $6 a tub, or a total of $18, from the amount payable to Sanford. Sanford then contacted the Stone Manufacturing Company, which agreed to deduct the same amount from the amount due from Sanford.

Prepare journal entries to record each of these events on the books of the Sanford Plumbers Supply Corporation.

21. A company prepares a set of interim financial statements each month and an annual financial report once a year. Its fiscal year ends on December 31. On November 30, after all entries for the month had been made, the following balances were found in the accounts relating to credit sales and accounts receivable:

	Debit	Credit
Accounts receivable.	500,000	
Allowance for uncollectible accounts.		15,000
Credit losses.	12,800	
Recovery of overdue accounts.		300
Revenues from credit sales.		2,560,000

Bookkeeping entries during the first 11 months of the year had been based on the assumption that credit losses would average 0.5 percent of credit sales.

During December, credit sales totaled $250,000, specific accounts receivable in the amount of $1,700 were recognized as uncollectible, and $1,000 of accounts previously written off as uncollectible were collected. Collections of other accounts receivable during the month totaled $270,000. At the end of the year an aging of the accounts receivable indicated that $11,000 of these accounts would eventually prove uncollectible.

Recoveries of overdue accounts in this company are treated as miscellaneous income of the period in which recovery is made—no attempt being made to adjust the credit loss figure to reflect these recoveries.

a) Explain briefly what each of the five November 30 account balances represents.

b) Present the journal entries that give effect to the December transactions.

c) What are the balances in each of the above five accounts as of December 31 prior to the year-end aging of the accounts receivable?

d) Was the company's credit loss experience for the year normal, high, or low? If high or low, by how much?

e) Show the accounts receivable section of the December 31 sheet, in good form and with the correct account balances.

22. The Bartoli Company buys some of its merchandise subject to discounts for prompt payment. Merchandise inventories on March 31 had cost $75,000 less cash discounts of $900, and accounts payable on that date amounted to $40,000 at gross prices, against which cash discounts of $500 were still applicable.

During April, the company bought merchandise on account at a gross price of $50,000, subject to a 2 percent discount for prompt payment. A portion of the month's purchases, with a gross price of $1,500, was returned to suppliers for credit.

During the month the company paid all of its April 1 accounts payable plus $15,000 of the April purchases (measured at gross prices). The company took all available cash discounts on the April purchases, but lost $100 of the discounts available to it on the April 1 accounts payable because it failed to pay some of these accounts within the discount period. All discounts on the rest of the April purchases would be taken early in May.

The gross price of the merchandise inventory on hand on April 30 was $45,000. All of this inventory can be assumed to have consisted of goods purchased during April.

a) If you were the sales manager of the Bartoli Company and were interested in measuring the profitability of the month's sales, what figure representing the cost of goods sold would you use? Show your calculations and explain your reasoning.

b) At what amount should accounts payable be listed on the April 30 balance sheet?

c) What was actually paid on accounts payable during the month?

23. The Herklion Company purchased a large quantity of used industrial equipment and shipped it to a foreign country for use in the government's industrialization program. Herklion paid $800,000 for the equipment and an additional $30,000 to transport it to the foreign country.

By the time the equipment arrived at its destination, the customer government had no foreign exchange to pay for it. Instead, it offered to give Herklion $100 of its own 7 percent bonds for every $95 due on the shipment of equipment. At that time, these bonds had a market value of $91 for every $100 of bonds.

Herklion accepted the offer and received $1,000,000 in bonds which it kept for two years and then sold at a price of $90 for every $100 of bonds. During this two-year period, the foreign government paid interest promptly and regularly on these bonds at the prescribed interest rate of 7 percent a year.

a) Did the contractor make a profit or a loss on the equipment transaction? When and how much?

b) How, if at all, would your answer to (*a*) have differed if the bonds had been sold immediately?

c) How, if at all, would your answer have differed if the bonds had been held until their maturity date and then collected in full?

*24. The Burfran Manufacturing Company has just been formed to produce a new product at a cost of $12 a unit, which will be paid in cash at the time of production. It will cost $6 a unit to sell the product, and this amount will be paid for at the time of shipment. The sale price is to be $25 a unit; all sales will be on credit.

The following results are expected during the first two years of the company's operations:

	Units Produced	Units Shipped	Cash Collected from Customers
First year........	100,000	70,000	$1,500,000
Second year......	80,000	90,000	1,875,000

a) State the effect on the various asset and owners' accounts of producing one unit, shipping one unit, and collecting $25, if revenue is recognized at the time of production.

b) What total income would the company report in each year if revenue were recognized at the time that cash is collected from the customer? (For this purpose, assume that general administrative expenses amount to $200,000 a year and that income taxes are zero.)

25. The Swazy Construction Company has secured a contract with the state of Iowa for the construction of 15 miles of highway at a contract price of $100,000 a mile. Payments for each mile of highway are to be made according to the following schedule:

(1) 40 percent at the time the concrete is poured.

(2) 50 percent at the time all work on that mile is completed.

(3) 10 percent when all 15 miles of highway have been completed, inspected, and approved.

At the end of the first period of operation, five miles of highway have been entirely completed and approved, concrete has been poured and approved on a second stretch of five miles, and preliminary grading has been done on the third five-mile stretch.

The job was originally estimated to cost $80,000 a mile. Costs to date have coincided with these original estimates and have totaled the following amounts: (1) on the completed stretch, $80,000 a mile; (2) on the second stretch, $64,000 a mile; and (3) on the third stretch, $10,000 a mile. It is estimated that each unfinished stretch will be completed at the costs originally estimated.

a) How much should the state of Iowa have paid Swazy during or at the end of the first period of operation under the terms of the contract? Show computations.

b) How much profit would you report for this period? Show your calculations and justify your method.

26. A farmer keeps pigs. Each year his sows give birth to piglets, which he raises for eventual sale to meat-packers. Each year he buys feed for the pigs and pays a hired man to feed them. Some years when pig prices are high, he sells more pigs than are born; in other years, he sells fewer pigs than are born, resulting in an increase in the total number and weight of his herd. Sales are always for cash and quotations of prices from hog auctions are published daily in the newspapers.

a) What basis of revenue and expense recognition would be most meaningful to the farmer in this case? Explain your reasoning.

b) Assume that feed and labor costs average $2 per pig per month. A pig born on July 1 weighs 80 pounds in December when hog prices are 30 cents a pound. It is sold the following March for $50. Using the method of revenue recognition you selected in (a) above, compute the cumulative effect of these transactions on the figures shown as total assets and total owners' equity on the December 31 and March 31 balance sheets.

27. The Pacific Company purchased, on February 12, 20 radio sets at $50 each from the Amsterdam Radio Company, terms: 2 percent, 10 days; net, 30 days. On February 14, 10 of the sets were sold to the Jones Electric Company for $60 each, terms: 2 percent, 10 days; net, 30 days.

On February 16, five sets were returned by Jones for full credit because the cabinets were scarred. The Pacific Company appraised the returned sets at $30 each, wholesale value, and the Amsterdam Company agreed to deduct the difference between the original gross price and this appraised value from the gross amount due from Pacific.

The Pacific Company paid its bill to Amsterdam immediately on receipt of this credit allowance. Jones Electric, however, failed to pay its bill to Pacific until February 28, and therefore lost the cash discount.

a) Using the gross price method for both purchases and sales, analyze these transactions in debit and credit form, first for Pacific, second for Jones Electric.

b) In what way or ways did the accounts of these two companies present an inaccurate picture of company performance during February or of its financial position as of February 28? What corrections should be made before the financial statements are prepared?

28. The Saranac Company produces a single product at a cost of $6 each, all of which is paid in cash when the unit is produced. Selling expenses of $3 a unit are paid at the time of shipment. The sale price is $10 a unit; all sales are on account. No credit losses are expected, and no costs are incurred at the time of collection.

During 19x1, the company produced 100,000 units, shipped 76,000 units, and collected $600,000 from customers. During 19x2, it produced 80,000 units, shipped 90,000 units, and collected $950,000 from customers.

a) Determine the amount of net income that would be reported for each of these two years:
  (1) If revenue and expense are recognized at the time of production.
  (2) If revenue and expense are recognized at the time of shipment.
  (3) If revenue and expense are recognized at the time of collection.
b) Would the asset total shown on the December 31, 19x2, balance sheet be affected by the choice among the three recognition bases used in (*a*)? What would be the amount of any such difference?

29. The Naive Manufacturing Company produces a product at a cost of $7.50 a unit, all of which is paid at the time of production. It costs $2 a unit to sell the product, all of which is paid at the time the product is shipped to the customer. The sale price is $10 a unit. All sales are on account. Collection costs are 2 percent of the amount collected, all paid during the period of collection. No credit losses are expected.

During the first year of operation, the company expects to produce 20,000 units, to ship 18,000 units, and to collect $170,000 from its customers.

During the second year it expects to produce 30,000 units, to ship 29,000 units, and to collect $280,000 from its customers.

a) Suppose that the company recognizes revenue (and hence income) at the time of production:
  (1) State the effect on the various assets and equities of producing one unit and incurring the related production costs.
  (2) State the effect on the various assets and equities of shipping one unit and incurring the related selling costs.
  (3) State the effect on the various assets and equities of collecting $10 and incurring the related collection costs.
  (4) What net income will be reported for the first year?
  (5) What net income will be reported for the second year?
b) Repeat the calculations called for in (*a*), but on the assumption that

the company recognizes revenue (and hence income) at the time of shipment.

c) Repeat the calculations called for in (b), but on the assumption that the company recognizes revenue (and hence income) at the time of collection.

d) Companies that recognize revenue at the time of shipment ordinarily treat collection costs as an expense of the period of collection. Using this procedure, what is the net income for each year?

e) Companies that recognize revenue at the time of collection ordinarily treat selling costs as an expense of the period in which they are incurred. Using this procedure, what is the net income for each year?

30. The Quality Timberlands Company purchased for $1 million a plot of standing timber. At that time, it expected to let the timber grow for five years and then cut it and sell it during the sixth year.

During the first three years of ownership, the company spent the following amounts for the development and care of the timberland.

Development costs (road and other)	$ 80,000
Timber care (wages, etc.)	130,000
Miscellaneous other costs	45,000

During the third year, a lumber dealer offered the company $1,700,000 for the timber. To obtain this, Quality Timberlands would have had to pay approximately $50,000 in cutting costs (for cutting the timber and dressing it for shipment).

The company discussed the offer and decided to refuse it on the grounds that the expected rate of growth of the timber during the following years would be such as to justify postponement of the sale. The specific figures presented were as follows:

	Fourth Year	Fifth Year
Expected sale value of timber	$2,000,000	$2,200,000
Expected total cost for care and other	75,000	50,000

In addition, the company expected that if the timber were cut during either of these two years, cutting costs would be approximately $50,000.

Quality Timberlands kept this stand of timber through both the fourth and fifth years. Finally, in the sixth year, the timber was cut and sold for $2,300,000. The costs incurred during the last three years were:

	Fourth Year	Fifth Year	Sixth Year
Development costs	$25,000	.....	.....
Maintenance of roads	5,000	$ 2,000	.....
Timber care and other	55,000	47,000	$75,000
Cutting costs	.....	.....	55,000

After the timber was cut, the company planted young tree seedlings at a cost of $40,000, as a conservation measure. The land was then sold back to the original owner for $40,000.

Indicate, giving reasons, what net income or loss you would recognize on this stand of timber:

a) For the first three years.
b) For the fourth year.
c) For the fifth year.
d) For the sixth year.

*31. The Hyatt Company sells slot machines to the trade. The custom in the trade is to deliver on terms providing for payment in six equal monthly installments, the first payment coming due one month after the date of shipment.

The life expectancy of a slot machine is highly uncertain, and in many cases the machines are destroyed or stolen before all payments have been made to the manufacturer. A tacit understanding is that the manufacturer shares his customers' risks to the extent that if the machine is removed from the customer's control before it is paid for, the unpaid balance of the customer's debt is canceled. The manufacturer is then entitled to re-possess the machine if he can find it.

Under these circumstances, the Hyatt Company chooses to recognize revenue at the time of cash collection. It manufacturers only one type of machine, which has a manufacturing cost of $78 and a sale price of $180. The following data relate to the month of September:

(1) On September 1, customers owed $77,100 on 700 active machines still in active service on that date.
(2) 160 machines were manufactured.
(3) 150 machines were shipped to customers.
(4) Regular monthly collections were made from the owners of 670 machines.
(5) Customers defaulted on 30 machines which had a total unpaid balance of $2,250 on September 1; 10 of these machines, with a total scrap value of $150 and a total unpaid balance of $750, were recovered and scrapped.
(6) Selling and administrative expense for the month was $10,000.

a) Prepare an income statement for Hyatt Company for the month.
b) At what amount would the September 30 balance sheet show the machines which have been shipped but not completely paid for by customers?
c) Give reasons why you agree or disagree that the collection basis for revenue recognition is appropriate in this case.

32. For a number of years, the Wagner Company deferred recognition of revenues until the time of collection on the grounds that its bad debt losses were too unpredictable to record on an estimated basis. The company was 100 percent owned by members of the Wagner family until December 30, 19x2, when a few hundred shares of stock were sold to outsiders.

To meet its responsibilities to its new stockholders, the board of directors engaged the firm of Wachum and Krey, independent public accountants, to audit the company's accounts and accounting procedures as of the end of 19x3. As a result of its investigation, Wachum and Krey became convinced that the company's revenue recognition practice was providing a misleading income statement and recommended an immediate change to a delivery basis of revenue recognition.

The staff of Wachum and Krey analyzed the Wagner Company's past experience and found that uncollectible accounts had averaged 3 percent of sales, although this had been partially offset to varying amounts by recoveries of accounts written off in years prior to the year of recovery. An aging of receivables indicated that $30,000 of the January 1, 19x3, receivables was likely to prove uncollectible.

The following information relates to the year 19x3:

(1) Amounts due from customers on January 1, $300,000; merchandise costs applicable to these receivables, $180,000.
(2) Goods shipped: price, $800,000; merchandise cost, $600,000.
(3) Collections, $900,000; merchandise costs applicable to amounts collected, $650,000.
(4) Customer defaults, $18,000; merchandise costs applicable to these amounts, $11,000; the affected merchandise could not be repossessed or otherwise recovered.
(5) One customer who had defaulted early in 19x2 and whose account had been written off at that time paid his account in full, $1,200. At the time of the default, Wagner had recognized a credit loss of $950, which was the cost of the merchandise shipped to this customer.
(6) Selling and administrative expenses, paid in cash, $182,000.
(7) Merchandise purchased on account, $630,000.
(8) Payments to suppliers of merchandise, $660,000.

a) Journalize these transactions, following the method now used by the Wagner Company, and prepare an income statement for the year on this basis.
b) Convert the Wagner Company accounts to a delivery basis of revenue recognition as of January 1, 19x3, journalize the year's transactions on this basis, and prepare an income statement.

c) Which of these two bases is likely to give management and investors a better indication of the firm's current performance?

33. The Better Bottom Boatyard was organized early in 19x0 to manufacture small, high-quality pleasure boats for weekend sailors. Mr. Eben Hartley, the proprietor of the yard, estimated that the boats would cost $21,000 each to manufacture, including his own salary as an element of manufacturing cost. Actual manufacturing costs have departed from this figure over the years, but Mr. Hartley still believes that this is a good estimate, and he has used it ever since he opened the boatyard in 19x0.

The customer was required to make a deposit of $5,000 when he placed his order, another $10,000 when the boat was placed in production, and the remainder of the $30,000 purchase price when the finished boat was delivered. A number of Mr. Hartley's acquaintances agreed to act as salesmen on a part-time basis. They received no salaries, but earned a $1,000 commission whenever they took an order. Because Mr. Hartley was short of cash, each of the salesmen agreed to wait to receive his commission until the boat was delivered.

Manufacturing costs were accumulated separately for each boat. At the end of each year, Mr. Hartley estimated for any unfinished boats the percentage of the total work that had already been done. This percentage completion was measured in terms of the ratio of the *estimated* costs for the work done to date to the total estimated cost of $21,000 for the completed boat. Thus if the work done to date on a boat should have cost $7,000 according to the estimates, Mr. Hartley would say that the boat was one-third finished, even if actual costs incurred on that boat so far amounted to $10,000.

The following events took place during the first six years of the boatyard's operations:

(1) Orders, production starts, and deliveries were:

Year	No. of Orders Received	No. of Boats Started	No. of Boats Delivered
19x0............	3	3	0
19x1............	1	1	3
19x2............	5	5	2
19x3............	2	2	4
19x4............	4	4	2
19x5............	1	1	4

As soon as each boat was completed, it was delivered to the customer.

(2) The following progress and manufacturing costs were reported during these years:

Year	Boat Number	Percent of Work Performed during Year	Manufacturing Cost Incurred during Year
19x0	A-1.......	66⅔%	$16,000
	A-2.......	50	11,000
	A-3.......	33⅓	8,200
19x1	A-1.......	33⅓	8,000
	A-2.......	50	11,000
	A-3.......	66⅔	15,000
	A-4.......	50	11,500
19x2	A-4.......	50	10,200
	A-5.......	100	23,000
	A-6.......	75	14,000
	A-7.......	50	10,000
	A-8.......	25	5,000
	A-9.......	0	....
19x3	A-6.......	25	6,000
	A-7.......	50	12,100
	A-8.......	75	14,000
	A-9.......	100	23,000
	A-10......	50	11,300
	A-11......	50	11,000
19x4	A-10......	50	8,000
	A-11......	50	10,400
	A-12......	75	15,000
	A-13......	50	11,000
	A-14......	25	5,100
	A-15......	0	....
19x5	A-12......	25	5,000
	A-13......	50	11,000
	A-14......	75	16,000
	A-15......	100	20,000
	A-16......	0	....

(3) Miscellaneous selling and administrative expenses amounted to $8,800 each year.

a) Compute net income each year if revenue is recognized on the basis of (1) orders received, (2) percentage of completion, and (3) delivery. State whatever assumptions you had to make to prepare these figures.

b) Which of these three bases would provide the income statement that you, as a nonmanagement stockholder, would find most meaningful? Explain, indicating the advantages of the basis you have selected, its shortcomings, and why you have selected it rather than one of the other two.

34. The firm of Granville Associates performs consulting services and develops new products for its clients.

For its consulting services, the company bills its clients each month for the work done and for incidental expenses incurred directly for clients during the previous month. Each bill consists of two parts, a charge for "professional services" and a charge for "expenses," such as travel, secretarial, and printing costs incurred on specific client assignments. The charge for professional services averages about 300 percent of the salaries of the consulting associates and engineering personnel assigned to consulting services work. "Expenses" are charged at cost.

Revenues from consulting services are recognized in the month in which the services are performed rather than when the bills are prepared.

For product development work, Granville Associates bills its clients in the month following the month in which individual projects are completed. Revenues are recognized in the month in which the project is completed.

Product development projects are divided into two classes, successful projects and unsuccessful projects. *Successful projects* are those which yield a product or products that the client decides to add to its product line. For these projects, Granville is entitled to a fee equal to 200 percent of the professional salaries (consulting associates and engineers) that have been charged to the project, plus 120 percent of other direct project costs. (Employer's payroll taxes are treated as "other direct project costs" in this calculation.)

On successful projects, Granville Associates is obligated to help the client with problems that will arise in putting the new product into production. This "project warranty" is expected to cost 5 percent of the amount billed the client for "professional services."

If the project is *unsuccessful*—that is, if it does not yield a commercially feasible product—Granville Associates is entitled to a "professional services" fee equal to 120 percent of all project costs.

The company makes no provision for credit losses, and no accounts have proved to be uncollectible for the past eight years.

All costs except those classified as executive and administrative are charged to some project, either product development or consulting services or project warranty work. The following events took place during April:

(1) Payrolls (all employees are paid monthly, on the last day of the month):

	Gross Pay	Federal Income Tax Withheld	State Income Tax Withheld	F.I.C.A. Tax Withheld	Health Insurance Premiums	Net Pay (Paid in Cash)
Consulting associates.	$ 40,000	$ 6,600	$ 2,400	$1,600	$ 320	$ 29,080
Engineers..........	100,000	15,000	5,000	4,000	1,600	74,400
Secretarial........	20,000	2,800	600	800	400	15,400
Executive and administrative.....	32,000	5,400	2,500	1,240	240	22,620
Total..........	$192,000	$29,800	$10,500	$7,640	$2,560	$141,500

(2) Employees' time distributions:

	Consulting Services	Product Development	Project Warranty	Executive and Administrative
Consulting associates....	60%	35%	1%	4%
Engineers..............	18	80	2	..
Secretarial..............	65	20	.	15
Executive and administrative........	..	..	.	100

(3) An unemployment tax of 2 percent of gross pay was levied on the employer. The only other payroll tax was the employer's portion of F.I.C.A. tax, equal to the amounts withheld from employee payrolls for this purpose.

(4) Other operating costs for the month, charged as follows (except for materials and supplies used, and depreciation, all credits should be to Accounts Payable):

	Consulting Services	Product Development	Project Warranty	Executive and Administrative
Materials and supplies used...	$ 500	$28,000	$ 200	$ 800
Telephone and telegraph...........	900	150	40	400
Printing, etc..........	5,800	750	...	700
Independent consultants.	5,000	2,000	500	...
Travel and entertainment..............	8,000	1,800	800	4,800
Depreciation..........	...	500	...	13,000
Other costs...........	800	7,300	...	12,300
Total............	$21,000	$40,500	$1,540	$32,000

(5) Purchased on account:
   Materials and supplies, $23,400.
   Laboratory and office equipment, $20,000.
(6) Paid in cash:
   Accounts payable, $99,300.
   Federal income taxes withheld, $32,000.
   State income taxes withheld, $11,500.
   F.I.C.A. taxes, $16,800.
   Unemployment taxes, $4,000.
(7) Completed product development projects, on which the following
   costs had been accumulated to date of completion:

	Successful Projects	Unsuccessful Projects
Salaries of consulting associates and engineers.........................	$50,000	$40,000
Other direct project costs................	17,500	18,600
Total...........................	$67,500	$58,600

(8) Collected cash from clients, $408,000.

a) Prepare journal entries to record all the transactions that took place
   during April. (Note: you will find it useful to treat product development costs in the manner prescribed in Chapter 4 for manufacturing
   costs. The treatment of project warranty costs was also described in
   Chapter 4.)
b) On the basis of these data, compute and prepare journal entries to
   record the amounts to be billed to clients in May. (Remember that
   May billings are based on April's events.) For consulting services,
   assume that the fees for "professional services" amount to 300 percent
   of the salaries of consulting associates and engineers assigned to this
   work.
c) Prepare an income statement for Granville Associates for the month
   of April.
d) Given the company's revenue recognition rules, would the balance
   sheet be different in any way if all bills were dated the last day of the
   month instead of some date during the next month? Explain.
e) Do you agree or disagree with the company's bases for revenue recognition? Give your reasons.

†35. Smith & Wells, Ltd., manufacturers a variety of machined parts

  † Copyright 1967 by l'Institut pour l'Etude des Méthodes de Direction de
l'Entreprise, (IMEDE), Lausanne, Switzerland. Reproduced by permission.

which it sells to customers in the automotive and transportation industries. About half of the company's sales are of products listed in the company's regular catalog. The remainder of the annual sales is in custom items. Sales revenues for both types of products are recognized at the time the goods are shipped to the customers.

Deliveries of catalog items, except for very large orders, are made from warehouse inventories, which are allowed to fluctuate from month to month to help stabilize production levels.

Custom items, often designed to the customer's own specifications, are manufactured only upon receipt of a firm order. Cancellations of orders on which production operations have commenced are extremely rare, and Smith & Wells, Ltd., can always recover its costs on any such cancelled orders.

During 1966 the company's sales force turned in a gratifying 20 percent increase in new orders over their 1966 level, almost all of the increase being for custom products. To meet this increased demand, the rate of production in the company's factory was increased twice during the year, once in July and once again in October. Because the production cycle for custom items averages four to six months, however, the increase in the rate of production did not lead to any marked rise in revenue.

In mid-January of 1967, Mr. T. E. S. Evans, the managing director of Smith & Wells, Ltd., received a preliminary set of financial statements for 1966 from his chief accountant, Mr. J. B. Burke. Excerpts from these statements are shown in Exhibit 1. Mr. Evans was very much concerned by the decline in reported income from the 1965 level and asked Mr. Burke for an explanation to be presented to the top management group at their January meeting.

a) Did the income reported for 1966 give a reasonably accurate measure of the operating performance of Smith & Wells, Ltd., during the year?

b) What changes, if any, would you recommend making in the company's method of income measurement? Indicate why changes are or are not necessary, using figures from Exhibit 1 to illustrate your argument.

c) Would you suggest replacing the income concept by some other measure of performance?

Exhibit 1

SMITH & WELLS, LTD.
Selected Financial Data for 1964–66
(000 Omitted)

	1964	*1965*	*1966*
Net revenue from goods shipped:			
Catalog items.....................................	xxx	£ 960	£ 970
Custom products..................................	xxx	990	1,030
Total...	xxx	£1,950	£2,000
Cost of goods shipped..............................	xxx	1,170	1,240
Selling and administrative expenses.....................	xxx	600	620
Net operating income before taxes and special charges.....	xxx	£ 180	£ 140
New orders received, net of cancellations (at sale prices):			
Catalog items.....................................	xxx	£ 980	£1,000
Custom products..................................	xxx	1,020	1,400
Total...	xxx	£2,000	£2,400
Inventories as of 31 December (at cost):			
Materials..£100		£ 100	£ 150
Work in process:			
Catalog items..................................	45	50	50
Custom products...............................	148	155	230
Finished goods (catalog items only)..................	470	500	480
Details of custom products work in process as of 31 December:			
Total contract sale prices £480		£ 500	£ 625
Estimated total production cost......................	290	300	375
% of work completed to date.......................	50%	50%	60%
Production costs incurred to date....................	148	155	230
Orders on hand but not yet put into production as of 31 December, custom products (at contract sale prices)...£810		£ 800	£1,025

xxx—Data not available.

Chapter 6

FINANCIAL STATEMENT
PREPARATION

PREVIOUS CHAPTERS HAVE DEVELOPED the basic concepts of accrual accounting in considerable detail and have applied these concepts to a number of kinds of business transactions. The purpose of this chapter is to introduce and illustrate the technical procedures that may be used at the end of each reporting period to prepare company balance sheets and income statements and to prepare the ledger accounts for the start of the next period's bookkeeping operations. It should also serve to some extent as a means of reviewing the accrual concepts developed in Chapters 2 through 5.

THE TRIAL BALANCE

Most accounting entries are initiated by the receipt or preparation of action documents such as invoices or checks. After these entries have been posted to the ledger, a *trial balance* can be drawn off. The trial balance is simply a list of the balances in the general ledger accounts, and its main purpose is to bring these balances together in a compact format. Exhibit 6–1, for example, shows the trial balance of the Avery Company, a wholesale grocery distributor, as of December 31, 19x3. Notice that this shows both balance sheet and income statement accounts, without segregation. The only aspects of an account that have any relevance at this point are the amount of its balance and whether this is a debit or a credit balance.

ADJUSTING ENTRIES

The amounts given in the trial balance are the account balances that appear after posting *all journal entries made in the normal course of bookkeeping operations during the year.* The accounts, of course, can

Exhibit 6–1

AVERY COMPANY

Preliminary Trial Balance

As of December 31, 19x3

Account	Debit	Credit
Cash	$ 161,600	$
Accounts receivable	125,800	
Notes receivable	27,000	
Allowance for uncollectible accounts		1,400
Interest receivable	x	
Merchandise inventories	4,373,900	
Prepaid insurance	3,300	
Land	53,400	
Buildings and equipment	653,700	
Allowance for depreciation		332,800
Accounts payable		98,100
Wages payable		x
Taxes payable		5,100
Advances from customers		3,700
Notes payable		100,000
Interest payable		x
Dividends payable		x
Contract service liability		x
Capital stock		500,000
Retained earnings		172,700
Sales revenue		4,593,500
Credit losses	13,900	
Contract revenue		58,000
Interest revenue		x
Cost of goods sold	x	
Warehouse expense	95,400	
Delivery expense	51,500	
Selling expense	199,300	
Office expense	109,700	
Interest expense	x	
Capital gains and losses		3,200
Income tax	x	
Dividends declared	x	
Total	$5,868,500	$5,868,500

be grouped readily into income statement items and balance sheet items, but financial statements drawn directly from the account balances at this stage would be incomplete and misleading because certain kinds of facts have not yet been reflected in the accounts.

The entries to reflect these facts in the accounts at the end of the period are known as *adjusting entries*. The need for these entries arises because of errors or omissions in the day-to-day bookkeeping routine. They are not the by-product of the routine processing of transaction documents for other purposes, as is the case with most of the ordinary entries made in the course of the daily routine. They must be originated by an accountant after a personal review of the accounts and document files.[1] They fall into six general categories:

1. Amortization of capitalized costs.
2. Accrual of unrecorded liabilities.
3. Recognition of unrecorded assets.
4. Deferral of revenues.
5. Correction of measurement errors.
6. Correction of bookkeeping errors and omissions.

Amortization of Capitalized Costs

After preparing the December 31, 19x3, trial balance, the Avery Company's accountants began the work of computing the necessary year-end adjustments. The first and most obvious of these was the series of amortizations of costs capitalized in asset accounts during 19x3 and prior years. Because cost amortization transactions are not evidenced by any document that is initially prepared to serve some other purpose (an invoice or a check, for instance), the practical and obvious time to recognize them is at the end of the period, when it is necessary to bring all of the accounts fully up-to-date for the purpose of financial reporting. It is the accountant's responsibility to see that such transactions are not overlooked. In this case, three amortization adjustments were found to be necessary:

a) Determination of cost of goods sold.
b) Amortization of prepaid insurance.
c) Depreciation on buildings and equipment.

Determination of Cost of Goods Sold. The Avery Company charges the cost of all goods purchased during the year to the Merchandise Inventories account. A periodic inventory system is in use, and therefore no entry is made during the year to transfer the cost of merchandise sold from the inventory account to an expense account. This means that the year-end balance in the Merchandise Inventories account represents the sum of two elements: (*a*) the cost of the goods still in inventory on December 31; and (*b*) the cost of goods sold or lost during the year. In this case a count of the physical inventories on hand on December 31, 19x3, revealed merchandise with a total cost of $309,500. By deduction, the cost of goods sold was:

---

[1] Moonitz and Jordan point out that many adjusting entries of the first three types can be made monthly as part of the bookkeeping routine, thereby simplifying the accountant's task at the end of the year. Maurice Moonitz and Louis H. Jordan, *Accounting: An Analysis of Its Problems* (rev. ed.; New York: Holt, Rinehart & Winston, 1963), Vol. I, p. 54.

```
Inventories and goods sold, from trial balance............$4,373,900
    Less: Inventories, from physical count................   309,500
Cost of Goods Sold................................$4,064,400
```

The entry to record this adjustment was:

(1)
```
Cost of Goods Sold................................4,064,400
    Merchandise Inventories.......................          4,064,400
```

This entry reduces the balance in the Merchandise Inventories account to its correct year-end level of $309,500 and transfers all other merchandise costs to expense.

Amortization of Prepaid Insurance. Second, a review of the insurance policy file revealed the amount of the prepaid premium on each policy and the period during which it was in force. The Avery Company had in its file on December 31, 19x3, five insurance policies, two of which had expired during the year. The file showed:

Policy No.	Policy Date	Expiration Date	Un-adjusted Balance	Premium Cost per Month	Months This Year	Premiums Expired
AB 406–721......	1/1/x0	12/31/x3	$ 492	$41	12	$ 492
CD 492–881......	4/1/x2	3/31/x3	48	16	3	48
CD 712–654......	4/1/x3	3/31/x4	240	20	9	180
PL 202–903......	1/1/x3	12/31/x5	900	25	12	300
XL 172–008......	7/1/x1	6/30/x4	1,620	90	12	1,080
Total.......			$3,300			$2,100

The amounts shown in the right-hand column of this table represent the costs of insurance coverage for 19x3. Thus they must be transferred from the Prepaid Insurance account to an expense account or accounts.

Although a single expense account might have been used, the Avery Company wished to have a separate record of the costs of its three main departments. A close study of the insurance policy revealed that $1,100 of the expiring premiums applied to warehouse facilities and operations, $600 applied to the delivery function, and the remaining $400 provided insurance coverage for the office. The adjusting entry was:

(2)
```
Warehouse Expense....................................1,100
Delivery Expense.........................................  600
Office Expense...........................................  400
    Prepaid Insurance....................................        2,100
```

This served to reduce the balance in the Prepaid Insurance account to $1,200, representing the unexpired premium on the three policies still in force on January 1, 19x4. It also recognized three categories of expense. In practice, each department would probably have a separate account for insurance expense, but to simplify the illustration we shall put all the expenses of a department in a single account.

Depreciation on Buildings and Equipment. The third cost amortization entry for the year was depreciation in the amount of $25,200. Of this, $12,900 was assigned to the warehouse, $7,900 to delivery, and $4,400 to the office. The entry was:

(3)

```
Warehouse Expense....................................12,900
Delivery Expense.....................................  7,900
Office Expense.......................................  4,400
    Allowance for Depreciation.......................              25,200
```

This served to recognize depreciation expense for the year and to reduce the end-of-year asset balance by $25,200. Once again, we have assumed that the Avery Company has only one expense account for each department. Separate depreciation expense accounts would be more realistic but would clutter the illustration with unnecessary detail.

Accrual of Unrecorded Liabilities

Accrual entries, introduced in Chapter 4, serve to recognize costs and liabilities that have not been recorded in the normal bookkeeping routine. The Avery Company had to make three of these as of the end of 19x3:

a) Interest accrual.
b) Payroll accrual.
c) Payroll tax accrual.[2]

Interest Accrual. On December 1, 19x3, the Avery Company borrowed $100,000 from a local bank, giving in exchange a 90-day, 6 percent note. This loan was shown on the year-end trial balance as "notes payable." Avery used the bank's money for 30 days during 19x3, from December 2 through December 31. The cost of using it for this period was a cost of doing business during 19x3, even though the interest payment would not have to be made until March 1, 19x4

---

[2] One additional accrual had to be made, to recognize the income tax liability arising out of the year's operations. Because the amount of this accrual was affected by some of the other adjustments, however, we must postpone discussion of it until all other adjustments of all kinds have been reviewed.

(90 days after the date of the loan). Interest on $100,000 for 30 days at 6 percent a year is:

$$30/360 \times 6\% \times \$100,000 = \$500 .$$

This amount had to be included in the 19x3 expenses and in the December 31, 19x3, liabilities. The entry to accomplish this was:

(4)

```
Interest Expense........................................500
     Interest Payable.......................................      500
```

Payroll Accrual. The second accrual entry was to accrue end-of-year wages payable. Avery's last weekly payroll period of 19x3 ended on December 28. Monday and Tuesday, December 30 and 31, were full working days, which means that some wages were *earned by employees in 19x3 but not recorded* in the accounts during 19x3. These amounts were paid as part of the first weekly wage payroll of 19x4, but only part of that payroll was really a 19x4 cost.

Hourly wage employees in the warehouse and delivery departments earned $500 and $300, respectively, on the two working days between the end of the last weekly payroll period and the end of the year. The entry to accrue these costs was:

(5)

```
Warehouse Expense......................................500
Delivery Expense.......................................300
     Wages Payable.......................................      800
```

In this kind of entry it is not necessary to classify the payroll liability into the amounts that will eventually be paid to the employees and the amounts that will be paid on their behalf to others. It is the *amount* of the liability rather than its distribution that is significant at this point.

Payroll Tax Accrual. Liability for wages, of course, also creates a liability for the employer's share of payroll taxes. Payroll taxes applicable to the wages accrued for the last two working days of 19x3 were at a combined rate of 7 percent.[3] The accrual was calculated by multiplying this rate by the figures in entry (5) above:

(6)

```
Warehouse Expense........................................35
Delivery Expense.........................................21
     Taxes Payable.......................................      56
```

---

[3] For simplicity, rates of 5 percent and 2 percent have been used to illustrate the application of F.I.C.A. and unemployment compensation taxes; the actual rates would undoubtedly differ from these.

Recognition of Unrecorded Assets

The third type of adjusting entry is to record assets that have not been recognized in the normal bookkeeping routine. The Avery Company, for example, owned notes receivable on December 31, 19x3, with a maturity value, exclusive of interest, of $27,000. Interest earned on these notes but not yet recorded amounted to $200. The adjusting entry was:

(7)

Interest Receivable..	200	
Interest Revenue..		200

This entry serves to recognize both the asset and the increase in the owners' equity. (Interest revenue is more commonly referred to as "interest income," but for the sake of clarity we prefer to reserve the word "income" for measures of the net income of the firm.)

Deferral of Revenues

Another kind of adjustment is the *deferral*. Cash is sometimes received from customers before revenue is recognized. When this happens, the end-of-period balance sheet should show a liability equal to the amount deferred.

To illustrate, some of the Avery Company's customers pay Avery to provide them with merchandising advice. These advisory services are provided under the terms of contracts which run for 12 months, the contract price being fully payable in advance. For convenience, Avery credits the full annual contract price to the Contract Revenue account at the time the customer pays. This means that the year-end balance in this account will be overstated unless the contract period always coincides with the company's fiscal year.

Data for the adjusting entry at the end of 19x3 were obtained by "aging" the contracts in force at that time, using the same technique that was applied earlier to the company's insurance policies. This showed that $5,000 of the amounts collected during 19x3 was for services to be provided in 19x4. The deferral entry was:

(8)

Contract Revenue..	5,000	
Contract Service Liability...........................		5,000

This served both to correct the overstatement in the revenue account and to recognize the company's liability to provide future services. The Contract Service Liability account is sometimes referred to as a *deferred credit to income, deferred revenue,* or *unearned income,* but it is better to avoid the words income and revenue in connection with accounts of this type because neither revenue nor income has yet been earned. Instead, the balances in such accounts represent *liabilities,* not for future payment but for future performance of a service or delivery of goods.

Notice that the form of the adjustment depends on the way in which the original transactions were recorded. If the company had elected to credit the amounts received initially to the liability account rather than to the revenue account, then the adjusting entry would have consisted of a debit to the liability account and a credit to revenue. The end result would have been the same, however—an adjusted balance of $53,000 in the Contract Revenue account and a year-end liability of $5,000.

Correction of Measurement Errors

The accountant occasionally finds adequate reason to change the dollar amount or "valuation" at which certain assets are carried on the company's books. Discussion of most such changes must be deferred to the next section of this book, but one minor example is already familiar from the previous chapter, the adjustment for anticipated credit losses.

At the end of each of the first 11 months of the year, the Avery Company charges the Credit Losses account with an amount based on a predetermined percentage of credit sales. The sum of these charges for the first 11 months of 19x3 was $13,900, the amount shown in the trial balance. At the end of December, however, the Avery Company makes a final adjustment on the basis of an aging of the outstanding accounts receivable. For 19x3, this analysis indicated that the balance in the Allowance for Uncollectible Accounts should have been $1,700 instead of the $1,400 shown in the trial balance. The adjusting entry was:

(9)

Credit Losses...300	
Allowance for Uncollectible Accounts......................	300

The amount shown as Credit Losses for 19x3 was thus $13,900 plus $300, or $14,200.

Correction of Bookkeeping Errors and Omissions

Correcting Errors. In the course of their review of the company's accounts, the auditors found two bookkeeping errors large enough to justify correction. First it was discovered that a $10,000 payment had been received in advance from a customer, covering merchandise that had not yet been delivered by the end of 19x3. When the payment was received, the credit was made to Sales Revenue rather than to Advances from Customers. To correct this error and to avoid overstating sales and understating the firm's liabilities, the following adjusting entry was made:

(10)

Sales Revenue. 10,000
    Advances from Customers.   10,000

This reduced the reported revenue figure and increased the year-end balance in the liability account by $10,000.

A second error that was located by the accountants was an error of transposition. An invoice in the amount of $9,700 had been sent to a customer in December. In recording this transaction, the bookkeeper had debited Accounts Receivable and credited Sales Revenue for $7,900, having made the common error of transposing or reversing the position of the numerals 7 and 9 in the amount shown on the invoice. The difference between the two figures was $1,800, and this amount was recorded to bring the account balances back into line:

(11)

Accounts Receivable. 1,800
    Sales Revenue.   1,800

Another kind of error that is sometimes found, although not in this illustration, is evidenced by a lack of equality in the totals of the debit and credit columns on the trial balance. Either one or more journal entries were incorrectly recorded or posted, or an error was made in the computation of account balances. No entry can correct this kind of error; the only recourse is to go back and recheck the work to find the source of the discrepancy.

Adjustments to Correct Omissions. Omissions are likely to be just as important as errors in recording and no less frequent. Two such omissions were found by the Avery Company accountants. First, it was found that $24,400 worth of merchandise ordered by the Avery Company had been shipped by the supplier on December 28. These goods were still in transit on December 31, but ownership was transferred by the supplier at the time of shipment, subject only to inspection by the Avery Company upon arrival of the goods. During the year, purchases are recorded in the Avery Company's books at the time goods are received, but at the end of the year goods in transit must take their rightful place in the balance sheet. The necessary correcting entry was:

(12)

Merchandise Inventories..............................24,400
    Accounts Payable.................................   24,400

The second omission was of the amount of dividends payable to the company's stockholders. On December 20, 19x3, the board of directors of the Avery Company at its monthly meeting had declared a dividend of $6 per share, payable to stockholders on January 15, 19x4. With 5,000 shares of stock outstanding, a liability in the amount of $30,000 had been created. Although notice of the board's action had been sent by the secretary of the corporation to the controller, it had not been reflected in the accounts before the trial balance was prepared. The adjusting entry was:

(13)

Dividends Declared....................................30,000
    Dividends Payable................................   30,000

The first half of this entry shows the reduction in owners' equity that took place when the dividend was declared. The credit to Dividends Payable recognizes the company's liability to pay $30,000 to the shareholders.

Income Tax Accrual

One more accrual remained to be made, the accrual of the income tax on the year's income. This entry had to be made last, because many of the earlier accruals affected the amount of taxable income.

To estimate its tax, the Avery Company computed revised balances in all of its income statement accounts, and from these, the before-tax earnings for the year: (1) $75,344 in ordinary income, and (2) $3,200 in capital gains. The income tax rate in 19x3 was 40 percent, applicable to both income categories.[4] At this rate, the income tax for 19x3 was $30,138 on ordinary income and $1,280 on capital gains, for a total of $31,418. The entry to record an expense and a liability in this amount was:

(14)

Income Tax..31,418
    Taxes Payable....................................   31,418

---

[4] The actual tax rate changes from time to time, and the rate for ordinary income differs from the rate applicable to capital gains. This is not a taxation text, however, and use of a single round-number rate permits us to illustrate the process of income tax accrual without having to go into lengthy explanations of taxation formulas which are likely to be obsolete almost immediately.

SUMMARIZING AND CLOSING THE ACCOUNTS

Once all the necessary adjustments have been identified, two tasks remain: (1) preparation of the financial statements for the period; and (2) preparation of the ledger accounts to receive the transactions of the next reporting period.

Statement Preparation: The Work Sheet

In preparing the financial statements, the accountant often uses a device known as a *work sheet*. The work sheet could take the form of a set of T-accounts in which the unadjusted account balances and the adjustments were entered. This form of work sheet has some advantages, but it is not compact enough for our purposes. The 10-column work sheet illustrated in Exhibit 6–2 is better on this score: all of the accounts and all of the adjustments can be shown on a single two-page exhibit, a considerable advantage once the structure of the work sheet is understood.

The first step in using the work sheet is to enter the pre-adjustment trial balance in the first two columns. More than one line should be provided for accounts in which adjustments are most likely.

The next step is to enter the adjusting entries in the next two columns. For example, the first adjustment on the 19x3 work sheet was a debit to Cost of Goods Sold and a credit to Merchandise Inventories. The debit is shown in the work sheet in the left-hand "Adjustments" column, next to the number (1) which identifies the adjustment. The credit is in the right-hand Adjustments column on the "Merchandise inventories" line.

In a sense, each line on the work sheet is like a T-account spread out horizontally rather than vertically. Any line on the work sheet can be rearranged in the familiar T-account form by placing the figures in the second pair of columns beneath those in the first pair of columns. The figures shown on the "Sales revenue" line, for example, could be rearranged as follows:

Sales Revenue

(10)	10,000	Unadj. bal.	4,593,500
		(11)	1,800
			4,595,300
		Bal.	4,585,300

Exhibit 6–2

AVERY COMPANY

Work Sheet, December 31, 19x3

Account	Trial Balance Debit	Trial Balance Credit	Adjustments Debit	Adjustments Credit
Cash....................	161,600			
Accounts receivable	125,800		(11) 1,800	
Notes receivable...........	27,000			
Allowance for uncoll'ble accts.		1,400		(9) 300
Interest receivable.........	x		(7) 200	
Merchandise inventories.....	4,373,900		(12) 24,400	(1) 4,064,400
Prepaid insurance..........	3,300			(2) 2,100
Land....................	53,400			
Buildings and equipment.....	653,700			
Allowance for depreciation...		332,800		(3) 25,200
Accounts payable..........		98,100		(12) 24,400
Wages payable............		x		(5) 800
Taxes payable.............		5,100		(6) 56 (14) 31,418
Advances from customers....		3,700		(10) 10,000
Notes payable.............		100,000		
Interest payable...........		x		(4) 500
Dividends payable.........		x		(13) 30,000
Contract service liability.....		x		(8) 5,000
Capital stock..............		500,000		
Retained earnings..........		172,700		
Sales revenue.............		4,593,500	(10) 10,000	(11) 1,800
Credit losses	13,900		(9) 300	
Contract revenue..........		58,000	(8) 5,000	
Interest revenue		x		(7) 200
Cost of goods sold.........	x		(1) 4,064,400	
Warehouse expense........	95,400		(2) 1,100 (3) 12,900 (5) 500 (6) 35	
Delivery expense..........	51,500		(2) 600 (3) 7,900 (5) 300 (6) 21	
Selling expense............	199,300			
Office expense............	109,700		(2) 400 (3) 4,400	
Interest expense..........	x		(4) 500	
Capital gains and losses......		3,200		
Income tax...............	x		(14) 31,418	
Dividends declared.........	x		(13) 30,000	
Total................	5,868,500	5,868,500	4,196,174	4,196,174
Net to retained earnings.....				
Total................				

Exhibit 6–2—Continued

Adjusted Trial Balance		Income Statement		Balance Sheet	
Debit	Credit	Debit	Credit	Debit	Credit
161,600				161,600	
127,600				127,600	
27,000				27,000	
	1,700				1,700
200				200	
333,900				333,900	
1,200				1,200	
53,400				53,400	
653,700				653,700	
	358,000				358,000
	122,500				122,500
	800				800
	36,574				36,574
	13,700				13,700
	100,000				100,000
	500				500
	30,000				30,000
	5,000				5,000
	500,000				500,000
	172,700				172,700
	4,585,300		4,585,300		
14,200		14,200			
	53,000		53,000		
	200		200		
4,064,400		4,064,400			
109,935		109,935			
60,321		60,321			
199,300		199,300			
114,500		114,500			
500		500			
	3,200		3,200		
31,418		31,418			
30,000		30,000			
5,983,174	5,983,174	4,624,574	4,641,700	1,358,600	1,341,474
		17,126			17,126
		4,641,700	4,641,700	1,358,600	1,358,600

The third pair of columns, labeled "Adjusted Trial Balance," contain the T-account balances after all adjustments have been entered. When a columnar work sheet like that in Exhibit 6–2 is used, the balance on each line can be obtained by adding the debits in the first and third columns and offsetting the total against the total of the credits shown in the second and fourth columns. This is exactly the same as the procedure followed in computing a revised balance in the T-account above.

To facilitate statement preparation, the account balances are then transferred to the final two pairs of columns—balance sheet accounts to the rightmost pair and revenue, expense, and dividend accounts to the other pair. (To save copying, the Adjusted Trial Balance columns may be eliminated and the adjusted balances entered directly into the final four columns.)

It should be noted that the amount listed for the Retained Earnings account is the balance *before* adjustment for the net income and dividends of the current year. The basis for calculating this adjustment is provided by the account balances in the operating statement columns. For this reason, neither of the last two pairs of columns is balanced until this final adjustment is made. This adjustment is shown at the bottom of the work sheet in the final two pairs of columns on the line marked, "Net to retained earnings." This is not an account title but a description of the final entry that will be made to the Retained Earnings account.

In this case, earnings for the year exceeded the amount of dividends declared by $17,126. If the arithmetic has been done correctly, a debit in this amount in the operating statement columns and a corresponding credit to the balance sheet columns will produce the desired equality. The balancing debit in the operating statement columns equals the excess of earnings over dividends declared, and thus is the amount that must be credited to Retained Earnings to bring the balance of the latter-up-to-date.

Preparation of Accounts to Receive Transactions of Next Period

Closing Entries. Once the annual financial statements have been prepared, the adjusting entries are typically entered in the journal and posted to the ledger. After this has been done, the accountant's next step is to close all temporary accounts by transferring their balances to the Retained Earnings account. This is the function of the *closing entries* that we introduced in Chapter 3.

The Avery Company uses a two-stage closing process: (1) two

entries to close the revenue and expense accounts to an Income Summary account; and (2) a second pair of entries to close the Income Summary and Dividends Declared accounts to Retained Earnings. The Income Summary account is known as a *suspense account* or *clearing account* and serves as a temporary gathering point to segregate all the items to be reflected in the income statement. The final closing entry returns it to a zero balance.

The first entry, to close the Avery Company's income statement accounts showing credit balances at the end of 19x3, was:

(15)

Sales Revenue..	4,585,300	
Contract Revenue...................................	53,000	
Interest Revenue.....................................	200	
Capital Gains and Losses..........................	3,200	
Income Summary..............................		4,641,700

Because the Sales Revenue account had a credit balance prior to closing, the debit entry had the effect of reducing this account to a zero balance, which is exactly what the closing entry is designed to do.

The closing entry for sales deductions and expenses—that is, all income statement accounts with debit balances—was:

(16)

Income Summary..................................	4,594,574	
Credit Losses..................................		14,200
Cost of Goods Sold............................		4,064,400
Warehouse Expense............................		109,935
Delivery Expense..............................		60,321
Selling Expense................................		199,300
Office Expense................................		114,500
Interest Expense..............................		500
Income Tax....................................		31,418

When these entries were posted, the Income Summary account appeared as follows:

Income Summary

(16)	4,594,574	(15)	4,641,700
		Bal. 47,126	

This account, in other words, serves to bring all of the income statement accounts together in one place. The $47,126 account balance represents the net income for the year, and the next closing entry transfers this balance to Retained Earnings:

(17)

Income Summary..47,126
        Retained Earnings..................................   47,126

Finally, the balance in the Dividends Declared account is closed into the Retained Earnings account because it shows the dividends for one year only. The account must start 19x4 with a clean slate, ready to accumulate the amount of 19x4 dividends only. The final adjusting entry was:

(18)

Retained Earnings......................................30,000
        Dividends Declared................................   30,000

Post-Closing Trial Balance. This completes the task of adjusting and closing the accounts for the year 19x3. A *post-closing* trial balance can then be taken to make sure that the accounting equation is balanced at the beginning of the new year. The post-closing trial balance of the Avery Company as of December 31, 19x3, is shown in Exhibit 6–3.

Notice that the December 31, 19x3, adjustments for the Avery Company were made as though no financial statements had been prepared since December 31, 19x2, for the simple reason that adjust-

Exhibit 6–3

AVERY COMPANY
Post-Closing Trial Balance
As of December 31, 19x3

	Debit	Credit
Cash....................................	$ 161,600	$
Accounts receivable.......................	127,600	
Notes receivable..........................	27,000	
Allowance for uncollectible accounts.........		1,700
Interest receivable........................	200	
Merchandise inventories....................	333,900	
Prepaid insurance.........................	1,200	
Land.....................................	53,400	
Buildings and equipment...................	653,700	
Allowance for depreciation.................		358,000
Accounts payable..........................		122,500
Wages payable............................		800
Taxes payable.............................		36,574
Advances from customers...................		13,700
Notes payable.............................		100,000
Interest payable...........................		500
Dividends payable......		30,000
Contract service liability...................		5,000
Capital stock.............................		500,000
Retained earnings.........................		189,826
Total............................	$1,358,600	$1,358,600

ments made in prior months had never been posted to the ledger accounts. Adjustment (3), for instance, records depreciation for the entire year, not just for the month of December. The interim statements were taken directly from work sheets, and each subsequent month's transactions were recorded without regard to the off-the-record work sheet adjustments made in previous months. Because the interim operating statements were designed to reflect operations for the year to date, the revenue and expense accounts were allowed to build up from month to month until the end of the year—that is, they were not closed out until after the final December 31, 19x3, adjustments.

Reversing Entries. Once the books have been closed, one further step sometimes needs to be taken to make them fully ready to receive 19x4 entries—the preparation and posting of *reversing entries.* The reversing entry is a bookkeeping device which can best be explained by means of an example. It will be recalled that adjusting entry (5) was prepared to recognize the labor costs applicable to the last two working days of 19x3. The entry was:

Warehouse Expense	500	
Delivery Expense	300	
Wages Payable		800

The first payroll of 19x4 was prepared as of January 4, 19x4, covering work done both in 19x3 (already recorded by the entry above) and 19x4. The simplest way to make sure that the 19x4 expense figures reflect only work done in 19x4 begins with the following reversing entry, recorded on January 1, 19x4:

Wages Payable	800	
Warehouse Expense		500
Delivery Expense		300

This entry, which is exactly the reverse of the accruing entry above, removes the liability from the books and creates *negative* (i.e., credit) balances in the expense accounts, which always start the year with zero balances.

Next, the payroll is calculated and accounted for in exactly the same manner as any other payroll. Assume that the payroll for the week ending January 4, 19x4, was $2,500, with the following breakdown:

Warehouse expense	$1,600
Delivery expense	900
Paid to workers	2,050
Taxes withheld	450

The taxes withheld were the social security tax deductions and personal income tax withholdings. The payroll is accounted for with the following entry:

```
Warehouse Expense.....................................1,600
Delivery Expense......................................  900
      Cash..............................................         2,050
      Taxes Payable.....................................          450
```

The Warehouse Expense account now shows the following:

Warehouse Expense

Payroll, Jan. 4, 19x4	1,600	Reversing entry, Jan. 1, 19x4	500

The balance in this account as of January 4, 19x4, is thus $1,100. This represents the wages earned by warehouse employees *for work done in 19x4*. The rest of the wages covered by the January 4 payroll were already charged to expense in 19x3. Thus the reversing entry has succeeded in preventing this $500 from being reported as expense in *both* years.

The reason for accomplishing this result by means of a reversing entry is that it permits clerical operations to follow a normal routine. The instructions for recording the January 4 payroll are the same instructions used for recording every other payroll of the year. Clerks and computers don't need to learn something new for this one payroll and therefore are likely to make fewer mistakes and have less difficulty in getting their work done on time.

FORMAT OF PERIODIC FINANCIAL STATEMENTS

The basic data for the Avery Company's periodic financial statements are contained in the final two columns of the work sheet. The only issue that remains is how these figures should be organized in the statements. Statements for management's use may differ in format from those prepared for public consumption, but the problem of meeting management's reporting needs will be deferred to Part III. Our concern in the rest of this chapter will be with the following statements relating to the enterprise as a whole and prepared for the use of shareholders and others outside the management group:

1. Income statement.
2. Retained earnings statement.
3. Balance sheet.

The Income Statement

Although many variations are to be found in practice, essentially only two basic formats are used for the income statement. They might be called *segmented* and *nonsegmented* forms, although the difference is really between highly and slightly segmented formats. In a nonsegmented statement, all revenue items except large, nonrecurring gains are listed first. From these are deducted all the expenses of the period, again excluding any large, nonrecurring losses. The difference between the two sums is *ordinary income* or *net earnings before special items*, or some similar title. The net income figure is then obtained by adding and subtracting extraordinary gains and losses.

A statement in this form is shown in Exhibit 6–4. Except for income taxes, the expense figures in this exhibit come directly from the adjusted account balances in Exhibit 6–2. The income tax figure was divided between the tax on ordinary income and the tax on the extraordinary item.

In practice, the expenses would ordinarily be classified somewhat differently. Instead of reporting functional totals for warehousing, delivery, selling, and office functions, the company would ordinarily divide expenses into such categories as salaries, depreciation, pur-

Exhibit 6–4

AVERY COMPANY
Income Statement
For the Year Ending December 31, 19x3

Gross merchandise sales		$4,585,300
Less: Credit losses		14,200
Net merchandise sales		$4,571,100
Contract revenues		53,000
Interest revenue		200
Total Revenue		$4,624,300
Less: Cost of merchandise sold	$4,064,400	
Warehouse expense	109,935	
Delivery expense	60,321	
Selling expense	199,300	
Office expense	114,500	
Interest expense	500	
Provision for taxes on ordinary income	30,138	
Total Deductions		4,579,094
Income before extraordinary item		$ 45,206
Extraordinary item: Gain on sale of investments	$ 3,200	
Less: Income tax on gain	1,280	
Net gain on sale of investments		1,920
Net Income		$ 47,126

chased services, and so forth. Although many companies disclose such items as research and development costs on a functional basis, the general feeling is that disclosure of functional totals would reveal relationships that should be concealed from competitors.

Segmented statements may be only slightly different from this, depending on the amount of segmentation desired. The format in Exhibit 6–5 is probably representative. In this statement, the cost of goods sold is first subtracted from ordinary revenues to obtain the *gross margin* on sales. This is particularly significant in a merchandising business because the cost of goods sold is such a large percentage of total revenue deductions. The Avery Company in 19x3, for example, had only $484,056 in operating expenses in contrast to $4,064,400 in the cost of goods sold, or only about 10 percent of the total. Success or failure of the enterprise is largely determined by its success in its buying and selling operations, so that more than usual significance is attached to the two figures that represent these operations most directly.

The statement in Exhibit 6–5 distinguishes between operating income and other income and expense on the grounds that the latter is

Exhibit 6–5

AVERY COMPANY
Income Statement
For the Year Ending December 31, 19x3

Gross merchandise sales		$4,585,300
Less: Credit losses		14,200
Net merchandise sales		$4,571,100
Cost of merchandise sold		4,064,400
Gross margin		$ 506,700
Service revenues		53,000
Operating margin		$ 559,700
Less: Operating expense:		
Warehouse expense	$109,935	
Delivery expense	60,321	
Selling expense	199,300	
Office expense	114,500	
Total Operating Expense		484,056
Operating earnings		$ 75,644
Other revenue and expense:		
Interest revenue	$ 200	
Interest expense	(500)	
Net other expense		300
Ordinary income before income taxes		$ 75,344
Provision for taxes on ordinary income		30,138
Income before extraordinary item		$ 45,206
Extraordinary item: After-tax gain on sale of investments		1,920
Net Income		$ 47,126

incidental to its main business and should not be allowed to obscure the results of operations. Interest and other financial expenses are excluded from the operating category on the grounds that they reflect the company's methods of financing rather than the basic profitability of its operations.

Retained Earnings Statement

The second financial statement, the retained earnings statement, is illustrated in Exhibit 6–6. In this typical case, the Avery Company

Exhibit 6–6

AVERY COMPANY
Statement of Changes in Retained Earnings
For the Year Ending December 31, 19x3

Retained earnings at beginning of year	$172,700
Add: Net income	47,126
	$219,826
Less: Cash dividends declared	30,000
Retained Earnings at End of Year	$189,826

was able to show only two changes in retained earnings in 19x3. The retained earnings statement is also used to report any substantial adjustments made to correct prior years' income figures for such items as errors in income tax estimates.

Balance Sheet

The third financial statement is the balance sheet or statement of financial position. The amounts in this case can be taken directly from the post-closing trial balance (Exhibit 6–3). The major question here is again one of grouping. Most companies divide their assets and liabilities into groups to permit rapid calculation of relationships that various interested parties deem significant.

The Avery Company's balance sheet as of December 31, 19x3, is shown in Exhibit 6–7. This statement includes two asset groups: one liability group, and one owners' equity group. The assets are arranged roughly in order of *liquidity*, or ease of conversion into cash. *Current assets* are "assets . . . which are reasonably expected to be realized in cash or sold or consumed during the normal operating cycle of the business".[5]

---

[5] American Institute of Certified Public Accountants, *Restatement and Revision of Accounting Research Bulletins, Accounting Research Bulletin No. 43* (New York: AICPA, 1953), p. 20.

Exhibit 6–7

AVERY COMPANY

Balance Sheet

As of December 31, 19x3

ASSETS

Current Assets:

Cash...		$161,600
Customer receivables:		
Accounts receivable............................	$127,600	
Notes receivable...............................	27,000	
Interest receivable.............................	200	
Total..	$154,800	
Less: Allowance for uncollectibles.................	1,700	
Net customer receivables.....................		153,100
Merchandise inventories.........................		333,900
Prepaid insurance................................		1,200
Total Current Assets..........................		$649,800

Property and Equipment:

Land...		53,400
Building and equipment...........................	$653,700	
Less: Depreciation to date........................	358,000	295,700
Total Assets.................................		$998,900

LIABILITIES AND OWNERS' EQUITY

Current Liabilities:

Accounts payable.................................		$122,500
Wages payable....................................		800
Taxes payable....................................		36,574
Dividends payable................................		30,000
Note payable.....................................		100,000
Interest payable..................................		500
Advances from customers..........................		13,700
Contract service liability..........................		5,000
Total Current Liabilities......................		$309,074

Owners' Equity:

Capital stock....................................	$500,000	
Retained earnings................................	189,826	
Total Owners' Equity.........................		689,826
Total Liabilities and Owners' Equity..........		$998,900

Current liabilities are those that are expected to become payable within a normal operating cycle. The current portion of long-term debt, defined as the portion that will become payable during the next 12 months, is also included in current liabilities, no matter how long or short the operating cycle may be. If the company had a mortgage loan, for example, payable in installments, any installments payable in 19x4 would be moved up to the current liabilities section of the December 31, 19x3, balance sheet; the remainder would be shown as *long-term liabilities.*

Exactly what is to be classified as a current item is a matter of judgment. On the grounds that the operating cycle is a long one, some companies, such as distillers and tobacco processors, may classify certain inventories as current even though they intend to hold these goods for aging over relatively long periods. Prepaid insurance and similar items are ordinarily classified as current assets on the grounds that they will be consumed during the next operating cycle. A division should be made between current prepayments and longer term prepayments if the long-term amounts are material.

SUMMARY

This chapter completes the explanation of the basic concepts and techniques underlying periodic companywide financial statements that was begun in Chapter 2. Although it has been concerned to a large extent with procedural techniques and devices such as the work sheet and adjusting and closing entries, its primary purpose has been to demonstrate the kinds of problems that the accountant must solve in adjusting the accounts at the end of a period so that they can be used to prepare accrual basis financial statements.

In addition to amortization entries already introduced in previous chapters, the illustration in this chapter has described entries to accrue previously unrecognized assets and liabilities, to defer revenues to subsequent periods, and to correct bookkeeping errors. The chapter has concluded with a brief discussion of the format customarily used for the income statement, balance sheet, and retained earnings statement.

QUESTIONS AND PROBLEMS

1. What is an "adjusting entry"? Give some common examples.

2. *a*) What is a "trial balance," and what purpose does it serve?
b) Explain the difference between a trial balance and a balance sheet.
c) What kinds of accounts are found on the "post-closing trial balance"?

3. Explain the function of the work sheet in preparing financial statements.

4. What is a "closing entry," and what is its purpose?

5. What is a "reversing entry"? Explain and illustrate.

6. What is the "gross margin"? What significance does it have to a stockholder?

7. If the routine bookkeeping work has been done correctly during the year, why is it necessary to make adjusting entries at the end of the year?

8. *a*) Why does the balance sheet differentiate between current and noncurrent assets?
b) How would you decide in which of these two classes to place a given asset? Is your classification rule consistent with the purpose or purposes identified in (*a*)?

9. An account payable in six months' time is listed as a current liability, while employee wages for the coming month are not shown. As the account payable is paid off, however, new accounts payable are likely to be created, and thus no cash is needed to finance the payment. Try to justify current practice in the face of this apparent paradox.

*10. Indicate in which section of the financial statements each of the following would most likely be shown: (*a*) current assets, (*b*) current liabilities, (*c*) current revenues, (*d*) current expenses, or (*e*) none of these.

Accounts Receivable
Advances to Salesmen
Sales Returns and Allowances
Allowance for Uncollectible
   Accounts
Credit Losses
Customers' Notes
Depreciation of Office Equipment
Fees Received in Advance
Goods in Transit
Income Taxes Withheld
Interest Received

Investments in Short-Term
   Government Securities
Loss on Sale of Equipment
Office Salaries
Paid-In Surplus
Petty Cash
Provision for Product Warranty
Purchases Discounts
Raw Materials
Royalties Earned
Sales Equipment

*11. From the following trial balance prepare an income statement, a balance sheet in good form, and a reconciliation of retained earnings for the James Dandy Sales Company for the year 19x3. Use an all-inclusive income statement, with extraordinary items grouped at the bottom. (No entries were made in the Retained Earnings account during the year.)

---

* Solutions to problems marked with an asterisk (*) are found in Appendix B.

	Debit	Credit
Accounts payable.........................		$ 70,000
Accounts receivable.......................$	50,000	
Accrued wages...........................		2,000
Allowance for bad debts..................		1,000
Allowance for depreciation................		62,000
Cash....................................	20,000	
Common stock..........................		20,000
Cost of goods sold......................	480,000	
Depreciation............................	21,000	
Dividends..............................	3,000	
Fire loss...............................	34,000	
Furniture and fixtures....................	200,000	
Income taxes...........................	3,000	
Insurance expired.......................	1,000	
Interest expense........................	4,000	
Inventories.............................	80,000	
Mortgage payable.......................		50,000
Notes payable..........................		30,000
Office supplies used.....................	5,000	
Other expenses.........................	9,000	
Premium on common stock................		53,000
Prepaid insurance.......................	2,000	
Refund of prior years' taxes..............		8,000
Rent expense...........................	22,000	
Retained earnings.......................		48,000
Sales...................................		700,000
Sales returns and allowances..............	14,000	
Taxes payable..........................		4,000
Wages and salaries......................	100,000	
Total.............................	$1,048,000	$1,048,000

12. The Interest Income account showed the following balances and entries during 19x3:

Interest Income

12/31/x3	Adjusting entry	50	During 19x3	From cash receipts		
12/31/x3	Closing entry	700		record		660
			12/31/x3	Adjusting entry		90
		750				750

a) How much cash was received in 19x3 for interest that will not be earned until 19x4?

b) How much interest income was shown on the income statement for 19x3?

c) How much cash was received in 19x2 for interest included as income in the 19x3 income statement?

d) How much cash does the company expect to receive in some future period for interest already shown as income in the 19x3 income statement?

13. The following figures constituted the trial balance of a large manufacturing company as of December 31, 19x4. Prepare an income statement, a balance sheet, and a reconciliation of retained earnings. (No entries were made in the Retained Earnings account during the year.)

	Debit	Credit
Accounts payable..............................		$ 206
Accounts receivable............................	$ 762	
Accumulated depreciation........................		1,109
Allowance for doubtful current accounts.............		8
Bonds payable (due May 1, 19x9)...................		192
Capital stock.................................		698
Cash.......................................	227	
Depreciation.................................	129	
Dividends declared............................	198	
Dividends payable to shareowners.................		50
Employee income taxes withheld...................		52
Equipment leased to others......................	49	
Income taxes.................................	221	
Interest expense..............................	8	
Inventories..................................	821	
Investments in capital stock of other companies........	330	
Liabilities to customers and employees...............		292
Loans to suppliers and customers, long-term..........	48	
Loans and advances to employees..................	5	
Long-term receivables, miscellaneous...............	40	
Loss on sale of factory equipment..................	26	
Materials and supplies expense....................	2,142	
Miscellaneous expenses.........................	147	
Noncurrent accounts payable.....................		82
Notes payable, short-term........................		1
Plant and equipment...........................	1,798	
Prepaid taxes and insurance......................	11	
Retained earnings.............................		1,181
Sales revenues...............................		4,941
Taxes accrued................................		225
Wages and salaries expense.......................	2,075	
Total..................................	$9,037	$9,037

14. The Crown Company's accountants believe that net income should reflect only operating revenues and expenses of the current year. The company uses the periodic inventory method, and the annual physical inventory count has already been made and reflected in the ledger.

a) What adjusting entry should be made for each of the following if the error or omission is discovered *before* the closing entries for the year have been made?

   (1) A purchase of merchandise was incorrectly debited to Furniture and Fixtures.

   (2) Cash received from a customer on account was incorrectly credited to Sales.

   (3) A payment to a vendor on account was incorrectly debited to Merchandise Inventories.

    (4) A sales invoice was not recorded; payment has not yet been received from the customer.

    (5) A telephone bill was incorrectly charged to Entertainment Expense instead of to Telephone Expense.

b) What adjusting entries should be made if the errors and omissions are discovered after the closing entries for the year have been made and the financial statements for the year have been published?

15. The Ajax Company uses a *periodic* inventory system. The following errors were found to have occurred in stating the year-end inventories during a four-year period:

    (1) The December 31, 19x1, inventory was understated by $2,000 because one crate of merchandise was overlooked during the annual physical stocktaking. The purchase of this merchandise had been recorded properly.

    (2) In costing one item in the December 31, 19x2, inventory, a clerk transposed figures, producing an inventory total that was $1,800 less than it should have been on that date.

    (3) In computing the December 31, 19x3, inventory, one lot of goods costing $785 was counted twice.

    (4) The December 31, 19x0, and December 31, 19x4, inventory figures were correctly stated.

The reported income for these four years was as follows:

19x1	$50,000
19x2	58,500
19x3	63,000
19x4	67,000

What was the correct income figure for each year and what was the error in the inventory valuation on each balance sheet?

16. The Wages Expense account showed the following balances and entries during 19x3:

Wages Expense

During 19x3	From gross payroll	99,000	1/1/x3	Reversing entry	1,000
12/31/x3	Adjusting entry	3,000	12/31/x3	Closing entry	101,000
		102,000			102,000

a) What was total wages expense for 19x3?

b) What was the amount of wages paid during 19x3?

c) What was the amount of wages paid during 19x3 but included in expense during 19x2?

d) What was the amount of wages paid during 19x2 but included in expense during 19x3?

*17. At the close of 19x9, the firm of Wright Brothers, which uses the periodic inventory method, arranged for the first time for an audit by a certified public accountant. He reviewed some of the more important figures for several years past and detected the following errors:

(1) Inventory of December 31, 19x6: Error in addition which caused an understatement of $3,000.

(2) Inventory of December 31, 19x7: Item amounting to $2,875 included twice.

(3) Inventory of December 31, 19x8: Item omitted, causing an understatement of $2,200.

(4) Inventory of December 31, 19x9: Correct.

The reported profit for the year 19x6 was $60,000; for the year 19x7, $76,000; for the year 19x8, $68,000; and for the year 19x9, $83,000.

a) What was the actual profit for each year?

b) What was the error (or errors) in each annual balance sheet?

18. You are the auditor of the Canton Company which conducts a general foundry and machine shop business. A considerable number of its products are special jobs made on order to customers' specifications. In the course of your examination early in January, 19x4, you note the following situations:

(1) The December 31 inventory totaling $95,000 includes certain machines costing $16,000 which were completed in December, 19x3. These had been manufactured to the order of the Ames Company, a reliable customer of long standing. When completed, the machines were crated and prepared for shipment. Entry was made in the ledger charging the Ames Company the billed price of $24,000. Before the goods were shipped, the Ames Company wrote accepting the machines, but requested that delivery be delayed until February 1, 19x4, because of certain plant alterations then in progress. (The company uses a periodic inventory system.)

(2) In July, 19x3, a contract was accepted from the Barrett Company for a large special machine which was to be delivered in February, 19x4. The contract price was $120,000, and cost estimates made in July, 19x3, indicated that the total cost of manufacturing the machine would be $75,000. On December 31, 19x3, $70,000 of cost had been charged to the job. This was carried in an asset account "Contracts in Process, $70,000." Detailed estimates made on December 31 showed that the job would be completed about January 15, 19x4, with the expenditure of an additional $10,000.

What adjustments, if any, should be made? Explain. Indicate the effects of these upon the balance sheet and income statement.

19. The following erroneous entries were made during October by the bookkeeper for the Columbia Lumber Mill Company. Using only the information presented in each case, prepare an entry to correct the error made. You may assume that the recorded cash balance is correct as of October 31.

a) Uncollectible accounts were estimated to amount to 0.1 percent of sales.

Loss on Uncollectible Accounts	105	
Accounts Receivable		105

b) Extra labor force built a new truck loading platform.

Wage Expense	2,351	
Cash		2,351

c) A check for $87 was accepted as full settlement of a recent $89 invoice to Windlass Industries, Inc.

Cash	87	
Accounts Receivable	2	
Windlass Industries		89

d) A three-year insurance policy on branch sales offices was purchased on October 1.

Insurance Expense	756	
Accounts Payable		756

e) Wages unpaid at the end of the month were accrued.

Wages Payable	273	
Wages Expense		273

f) After a delivery truck had been damaged in an accident and then subsequently repaired, a check for the amount of the damage suffered was received from the insurance company. Repair costs were charged early in October to the Maintenance of Vehicles account.

Cash	92	
Retained Earnings		92

g) New posture chairs were purchased for the secretarial staff.

Office Expense	228	
Accounts Payable		228

20. On January 2, 19x1, the Yates Company purchased an office building which was already fully occupied by rent-paying tenants. The price was $1,000,000, of which $300,000 was for the land and $700,000 was for the building. The former owner also transferred to the Yates Company for $1,000 the last six months' coverage under a general property insurance policy.

At the time of acquisition, the Yates Company paid $201,000 in cash and gave a note for the remaining $800,000. This note called for interest to be paid annually on December 31 at a rate of 8 percent a year. The amount borrowed would have to be repaid to the lender at the end of five years.

The bookkeeper of the Yates Company set up a single ledger account entitled "Second Street Building" in which he entered the initial purchase price and all later receipts and disbursements arising from the company's ownership of this property during 19x1. This account is reproduced below. Depreciation for 19x1 was estimated to be $25,000, but no entry had been made to record this amount.

SECOND STREET BUILDING (LEDGER ACCOUNT AS OF DECEMBER 31, 19x1)

Date	Explanation	Debit	Credit	Debit Balance
Jan. 2	Purchase price............................	1,000,000		
Jan. 2	Property insurance to June 30, 19x1.......	1,000		1,001,000
	Repairs, heat, and light..................	10,000		
Totals,	Wages of employees....................	33,600		
Jan.–	Property insurance for three years to June 30,			
Dec.	19x4.................................	6,600		
	Rent from tenants for 19x1..............		170,000	
	City taxes for 19x1....................	26,000		
Dec. 31	Interest on note........................	64,000		971,200

a) Prepare any adjusting entries that you feel are necessary to correct the company's accounts. Introduce whatever accounts are desirable to reflect properly the results of the ownership of this property.

b) What effect will the journal entries you recommend have on the company's net income for 19x1?

c) How would you decide whether this building was a profitable investment for the Yates Company? Assuming that 19x1 is typical of future years, would you say that the company had made a profitable investment?

21. The Club Company was formed to provide meals and entertainment for its members. It started its operations on January 1, 19x6. The club's board of directors wants an income statement for the first nine months of 19x6. Make journal entries to bring the books up-to-date, reflecting the following information:

(1) Beverages costing $1,000 were purchased in January, at which time an account "Beverage Expense" was debited. A count of beverages

on hand on September 30 indicated that one half of the January purchase had not been consumed as of that date.

(2) Kitchen and bar equipment was purchased on January 1. The amount of $40,000 was debited to an account, "Equipment." No depreciation was charged. It was estimated that the equipment would last for 16 years from date of purchase, with no salvage value at the end of that time.

(3) On August 31, the club borrowed $5,000 from a member. The club gave the member a note, promising to repay the $5,000 within 90 days plus interest on this note at a rate of 6 percent per year. No interest payment was made prior to September 30.

(4) The club's weekly payroll amounted to $900, of which $120 was for bar service, $60 was for the building custodian, $90 was for secretarial help, and $630 was for dining room employees. The club was open three days a week—Friday, Saturday, and Sunday. Employees were paid regularly on Saturday, each weekly paycheck covering the preceding Saturday, Sunday, and Friday. The Saturday, September 29 payroll, which was recorded correctly, covered the week that ended Friday, September 28. Employer payroll taxes of 6 percent were applicable to these payrolls.

(5) The account "Prepaid Insurance" had been debited for all insurance premiums paid. The balance in this account on September 30 was $480. Analysis showed that this represented $120 paid on January 1, 19x6, for fire insurance covering the calendar years 19x6 and 19x7, and $360 for workmen's compensation and general liability insurance covering the calendar year 19x6.

(6) On June 1, 19x6, the Club Company received $360 from employees of a neighboring store in payment for parking privileges in the club's lot. The payment covered one year's parking fees to May 31, 19x7, and was entered in an account titled "Miscellaneous Rental Income."

(7) Local property taxes on the club's building, covering the period July 1, 19x6, through June 30, 19x7, amounting to $2,400, had not been paid and were not due until November 30, 19x6.

(8) The club's cigar counter and checkroom were operated by two young college students as a concession; they paid the club $10 a week for the privilege. The last payment received covered the period up to and including Sunday, September 2.

22. In each of the following, prepare the journal entry that is necessary to adjust the accounts as of the end of the fiscal year. *Each part of this question is independent of the others.* In each case, assume that the company is engaged in wholesaling, that its fiscal year ended on December 31, 19x1, and that *the books for 19x1 have not yet been closed.* (If no entry is necessary, write "no entry.")

(1) Local property taxes covering the period October 1, 19x1, through September 30, 19x2, are expected to amount to $30,000. These will be paid in July, 19x2.

(2) Bills are received on January 10, 19x2, covering electric service for the month of December, 19x1, totaling $1,000.

(3) The perpetual inventory records indicate that the cost of merchandise on hand on December 31, 19x1, was $50,500. A physical count has revealed that the amount actually on hand originally cost $48,500.

(4) The last weekly payroll period of 19x1 ended on December 27. The next weekly payroll covered the period December 27, 19x1, through January 2, 19x2. This included three working days in 19x1 and two working days in 19x2, holidays being counted as "working days" for this purpose. The total January 2 payroll was $25,000, of which $5,000 was for office employees and $20,000 was for store employees. (Employer payroll taxes may be ignored.)

(5) In 19x0 the company purchased merchandise for inventory amounting to $10,000, but at the time of acquisition the purchase was incorrectly debited to "Office Supplies Expense." The merchandise itself was placed in the storeroom, however, and was counted properly in the annual physical inventory taken at the end of 19x0. In reviewing certain records now, just after the end of 19x1, the earlier error has been discovered.

(6) A machine that had cost $11,000 when new, was sold during 19x1 for $5,000. At the time of the sale, its "book value" was $3,000. To record the sale, a bookkeeper debited Cash and credited Other Income.

(7) The company uses the gross price method of recording sales. On December 31, 19x1, the balance in Accounts Receivable was $40,-000. The company grants a 2 percent cash discount for prompt payment, and it is expected that all of the amounts receivable on December, 19x1, will be paid during the cash discount period.

23. After all entries in the journal of the XYZ Company have been posted to the ledger accounts, the journal is destroyed by fire. The company's accountants have been able to reconstruct most of the journal entries from the basic documents, but in each of the following accounts *one* entry is still unexplained. In each case, reconstruct the complete journal entry that was *most probably* made during the year and which will account for the unexplained portion of the change in the account balance. Each problem is independent of the other problems. You should assume that the balances are correct and therefore that no correcting entries are required.

Example:

Given: Capital Stock account:

Beginning balance.............................$ 40,000
Ending balance................................ 65,000

Answer:

Cash.....................................25,000
      Capital Stock...........................   25,000

a) Retained Earnings account:

Beginning balance.............................$100,000
Ending balance................................ 95,000
Profits for year, transferred by closing............ 12,000

b) Prepaid Insurance account:

Beginning balance.............................$ 2,400
Expired during period..........................   2,600
Ending balance................................   1,900

c) Wages Payable account:

Beginning balance.............................$ 1,400
Wages paid................................... 10,500
Ending balance................................   1,100

d) Accounts Receivable account (at gross):

Beginning balance.............................$100,000
Written off as bad.............................   2,000
Cash received................................ 200,000
Discounts allowed.............................   4,000
Ending balance................................ 110,000

e) Patents account:

Ending balance................................$ 20,000
Purchased for cash............................ 10,000
Beginning balance............................. 14,500

f) Accounts Payable account

Beginning balance.............................$ 50,000
Ending balance................................ 70,000
Purchases.................................... 90,000
Returns......................................   2,000

g) Buildings account:

Beginning balance.............................$200,000
New building purchased........................ 50,000
Ending balance................................ 230,000

Building—Depreciation to Date account:

Net increase in account balance..................$ 35,000
Depreciation expense........................... 42,000
     Note: There were no cash receipts from sale of
     buildings.

b) Office Equipment account:

```
Beginning balance.............................$ 30,000
Ending balance................................   36,000
Purchased.....................................   10,000
     Note: An item was sold during the year for $2,350
     cash and a loss of $150.
```

*24. On December 31, the unadjusted trial balance of the Robant Hardware Company showed the following accounts and balances:

```
Cash......................................  56,000
Accounts receivable.......................170,000
Inventory.................................525,000
Furniture and fixtures....................200,000
Allowance for depreciation—furniture and fixtures....125,000
Prepaid insurance.........................  2,000
Prepaid rent..............................  1,000
Accounts payable..........................100,000
Capital stock.............................200,000
Retained earnings.........................106,000
Sales.....................................500,000
Wage expense..............................  20,000
Miscellaneous expenses....................  55,000
Dividends declared........................  2,000
```

The accountant wished to adjust for the following expenses which he felt were applicable to the month of December:

(1) Insurance expense, $175.
(2) Rent expense, $1,000.
(3) Depreciation expense—1 percent of gross book value of furniture and fixtures.
(4) Wages owed but not paid, $4,000.
(5) The annual physical inventory showed that goods costing $225,000 were on hand as of December 31.

a) Prepare a work sheet and record these adjustments.
b) Prepare in good form an income statement for the year and a balance sheet as of December 31.

*25. The December 31, 19x3, unadjusted trial balance of the Guyton Company is shown below:

THE GUYTON COMPANY

TRIAL BALANCE

AS OF DECEMBER 31, 19x3

	Debit	Credit
Cash..	$ 28,800	
Temporary investments........................	17,700	
Accounts receivable..........................	91,600	
Inventory of merchandise, January 1, 19x3.......	89,000	
Prepaid insurance...........................	1,900	
Other prepaid expenses.......................	1,340	
Land..	16,000	
Building and equipment.......................	45,800	
Allowance for depreciation, building, and		
equipment...............................		$ 8,100
Accounts payable............................		18,800
Mortgage on real estate......................		45,000
Capital stock................................		150,000
Retained earnings............................		53,120
Sales..		412,000
Sales discounts, returns, and allowances.........	12,000	
Interest income..............................		480
Purchases...................................	344,500	
Advertising..................................	1,200	
Salaries and wages...........................	16,400	
Miscellaneous selling expense..................	5,800	
Property taxes...............................	3,300	
Insurance expense...........................	525	
Miscellaneous general expenses................	8,435	
Interest expense.............................	3,200	
Total.................................	$687,500	$687,500

Information for adjustments:

(1)	Accrued interest payable on mortgage...................	$ 400
(2)	Insurance expired (last quarter).......................	175
(3)	Accrued wages payable...............................	240
(4)	Depreciation expense, building and equipment............	1,240
(5)	Inventory of merchandise, December 31, 19x3............	86,440
(6)	Merchandise received, December 31, 19x3, but not recorded in the accounts or included in the inventory count........	975
(7)	Cash discounts available to customers, December 31, 19x3...	890

Using a work sheet, make the adjustments necessary to reflect the above information and prepare: (*a*) a balance sheet as of December 31, 19x3; and (*b*) a report of earnings for the period ending December 31, 19x3 (incorporating a reconciliation of beginning and ending retained earnings).

26. The preliminary trial balance of the Blackstone Machine Company taken on December 31 is shown below:

BLACKSTONE MACHINE COMPANY
PRELIMINARY TRIAL BALANCE
DECEMBER 31

Debit		*Credit*	
Cash......................$	60,000	Accounts payable..........$	50,000
Accounts receivable.........	197,500	Notes payable..............	140,000
Inventories.................	370,000	Accrued payroll...........	3,000
Land......................	40,000	Accrued interest...........	2,000
Buildings..................	150,000	Accrued taxes.............	5,000
Machinery and equipment.....	400,000	Mortgage on real estate....	100,000
Dividends declared..........	36,000	Allowance for depreciation:	
Sales returns and allowances....	26,000	Buildings..............	30,000
Discounts allowed customers...	17,000	Machinery and equipment.	90,000
Cost of goods sold...........	785,000	Common stock............	600,000
Administrative expense.......	45,000	Retained earnings..........	165,000
Interest expense.............	14,000	Sales.....................	1,080,000
Selling expense.............	132,000	Interest income...........	500
		Discounts received........	7,000
Total..................$2,272,500		Total................$2,272,500	

Before the books were finally closed, the auditors' investigation disclosed the facts listed below:

(1) $1,300 should be added to the Accrued Taxes account because of an additional assessment for a prior year.

(2) Merchandise shipped back for credit by a customer on December 29 and not received on December 31 has not been recorded. This merchandise cost $1,400 and had been sold to the customer at $2,100.

(3) A purchase of $1,500 worth of equipment has been debited to Inventories.

(4) $600 interest on the company's 60-day note discounted at the bank December 1 has been debited to Discounts Allowed Customers.

(5) The Cash account in the trial balance is a control account for three subsidiary accounts: Cash on Hand, Cash in Bank, and Petty Cash. Petty Cash includes $2,600 advanced to salesmen for travel and entertainment expenses. December expense statements received from salesmen early in January amount to $1,700.

(6) Machinery costing $17,000 has been sold and the proceeds of $2,000 debited to cash and credited to Sales, no other record being made. The book value of these assets at the time of sale was $4,800.

(7) An invoice for raw materials received on December 29 has been recorded at $5,920 instead of $5,290, the bookkeeper having transposed the 9 and the 2.

(8) No provision has been made for the 2 percent discounts offered

for payments within 10 days on $100,000 of sales made subsequent to December 21.

(9) The board of directors on December 15 declared a quarterly dividend to shareholders, amounting to $12,000, payable on the following January 5. This action has not been recorded.

a) Using a work sheet, make any necessary corrections to the accounts, determine the profit for the period, and show in the final columns the balance sheet items as of December 31. (Add accounts if necessary.)

b) Prepare a balance sheet and an income statement.

c) Prepare all entries necessary to close the accounts as of the end of the year.

27. The Caron Corporation operates an appliance store and repair shop. It does not keep a perpetual inventory record but instead counts the amount of inventory on hand at the end of each quarter. The fiscal year begins each year on January 1. The company's trial balance on March 31, 19x4, was as follows:

	Debit	Credit
Cash	$ 22,372	
Accounts receivable	67,840	
Allowance for uncollectible accounts		$ 1,830
Merchandise inventory	61,180	
Prepaid insurance	2,000	
Store equipment	28,600	
Allowance for depreciation—store equipment		8,150
Office equipment	10,200	
Allowance for depreciation—office equipment		3,870
Repair equipment	20,400	
Allowance for depreciation—repair equipment		7,010
Store supplies	330	
Office supplies	1,260	
Accounts payable		49,700
Notes payable		20,000
Common stock		80,000
Retained earnings		29,840
Revenue from sale of merchandise		185,130
Repair department revenues		17,440
Purchases of merchandise	97,330	
Repair supplies purchased	800	
Salaries, store employees	40,100	
Payroll taxes, store	2,807	
Sundry store expenses	7,600	
Salaries and wages, repair employees	11,900	
Payroll taxes, repair department	833	
Sundry repair department expenses	2,030	
Salaries, office employees	18,400	
Payroll taxes, office	1,288	
Sundry office expenses	5,700	
Total	$402,970	$402,970

a) Make the adjustments necessary to reflect the following (use either a set of T-accounts or a work sheet):

(1) An inventory count at the end of March revealed the following balances: merchandise, $58,920; store supplies, $140; office supplies, $660; repair supplies, $350.

(2) The balance in Notes Payable on the trial balance represents a 90-day, 6 percent promissory note dated March 16, 19x4, and due on June 14, 19x4. Interest on this note had not yet been recorded in the accounts; it was to be paid along with the face value of the note on June 14, 19x4.

(3) Depreciation is calculated at the following rates: store equipment, 10 percent of original cost per year; office equipment, 20 percent per year; and repair equipment, 8 percent per year. No purchases or sales of equipment were made between January 1 and March 31.

(4) Wages earned during March but unpaid as of March 31 were as follows: store, $1,500; office, $600; repair department, $400. These wages were subject to employer payroll taxes totaling 7 percent.

(5) Uncollectible accounts in this company average 0.5 percent of merchandise sales.

(6) The balance in Prepaid Insurance reflects the January 1 unexpired premiums on the following three policies: (*a*) a three-year fire insurance policy expiring March 31, 19x5, three-year premium $2,160; (*b*) a one-year workmen's compensation policy, expiring December 31, 19x4, annual premium $800; and (*c*) a one-year comprehensive liability policy, expiring June 30, 19x4, annual premium $600.

(7) Dividends amounting to $1,500 were declared on March 20, payable on April 15, 19x4.

(8) Property taxes amount to $6,000 a year; taxes for the calendar year 19x4 were payable on August 1, 19x4.

b) Prepare an income statement for the three months ending March 31, 19x4. In this statement separate, insofar as possible, the results of operations of the company's sales and repair departments.

c) Prepare a balance sheet as of March 31, 19x4.

d) Which of the adjustments would probably be entered in the general journal and posted to the ledger, and which would be entered on the worksheet only?

28. The Chicago Manufacturing Company accumulates all manufacturing costs during the year in three accounts: Factory Labor, Factory

Materials, and Other Factory Costs. At the end of each month, these three accounts are closed to the Work in Process account. Thus the pre-closing balance in Work in Process is its beginning-of-month balance. A perpetual inventory is maintained for raw materials.

The trial balance as of February 29, 19x8, the end of the company's fiscal year, was as follows:

	Debit	Credit
Cash....................................	$ 10,000	
Accounts receivable......................	30,000	
Allowance for bad debts..................		$ 2,000
Raw materials...........................	12,000	
Work in process.........................	8,000	
Finished goods..........................	20,000	
Prepaid insurance.......................	1,000	
Factory labor...........................	6,000	
Factory materials.......................	8,000	
Other factory costs.....................	9,000	
Buildings, furniture, and equipment...........	200,000	
Accumulated depreciation..................		120,000
Accounts payable........................		16,000
Taxes payable...........................		9,000
Capital stock...........................		50,000
Retained earnings........................		60,000
Sales...................................		500,000
Cost of goods sold.......................	302,000	
Selling expense..........................	88,000	
Office expense...........................	63,000	
Income taxes............................	....	
Total..............................	$757,000	$757,000

The following additional information is available:

(1) The balances in Work in Process and Finished Goods reflect inventories as of February 1, 19x8; the balance in Cost of Goods Sold applies to the sales of the first 11 months of the year; and the balances in the factory cost accounts reflect February operations only. Sales and expense accounts reflect transactions for the entire year.

(2) After aging the accounts, the company's accountants decided to write off as uncollectible accounts amounting to $800; after the write-off, the correct balance in the Allowance for Bad Debts was $900. Credit losses were charged as selling expense.

(3) Depreciation for the first 11 months had been recorded previously. Depreciation for February totaled $2,000 on factory plant and equipment, $700 on sales furniture and equipment, and $500 on office furniture and equipment.

(4) Unrecorded wages payable at the end of February amounted to

$300 on factory payrolls, $200 on sales payrolls, and $400 on office payrolls.

(5) Transfers to Finished Goods during the month amounted to $27,000.

(6) The annual inventory count revealed raw materials inventories of $11,800 and finished goods inventories of $21,500.

(7) Insurance costs for February totaled $200, all classified as "office expense."

(8) In response to a letter from the accountants asking for a verification of the company's recorded liabilities, one of the company's suppliers claimed that the Chicago Manufacturing Company owed him $3,200 on February 29, not the $300 indicated in the accounts payable ledger. Investigation indicated that the supplier was correct; an employee had intercepted and destroyed an invoice amounting to $2,900 in the hope of hiding the theft of the goods from the receiving platform. The company was covered by insurance for 80 percent of any losses from theft.

(9) Dividends of $7,000 were declared on February 15, payable on March 10, 19x8.

(10) Estimated income taxes for the year amounted to $5,800. (This estimate reflects all of the above adjustments.)

a) Using a work sheet, prepare an adjusted trial balance for the Chicago Manufacturing Company as of February 29, 19x8. Complete the income statement and balance sheet columns of the work sheet.

b) Prepare an income statement for the year and a balance sheet as of February 29, 19x8, in proper form.

c) Prepare the necessary closing entries to close the books for fiscal 19x8.

29. Barclay Distributors, Inc., was organized on January 1, 19x0. During its first four years of operation, only cash receipts and cash disbursements were recorded as part of the daily bookkeeping routine. Revenues were recognized at the time of collection; purchases were recognized at the time of payment. At the end of each year, a physical count of merchandise inventories was made (all goods on hand or in transit were included in the count, regardless of whether cash payment had been made), and the cost of goods sold was determined by subtracting this amount from the sum of the January 1 merchandise inventory and the cash purchases of merchandise during the year. A depreciation charge was also computed at the end of each year. No other departures were made from a strict cash basis of accounting.

The unadjusted trial balance of this company on December 31, 19x3, showed the following items:

	Debit	Credit
Cash.............................	$ 3,100	
Merchandise......................	15,000	
Furniture and equipment..........	30,000	
Accumulated depreciation.........		$ 9,000
Notes payable....................		10,000
Common stock.....................		30,000
Retained earnings................	3,000	
Dividends declared...............	0	
Sales............................		117,000
Merchandise purchases............	66,700	
Cost of goods sold...............	0	
Wages and salaries...............	33,000	
Payroll taxes....................	2,100	
Rent.............................	6,700	
Utilities........................	1,300	
Depreciation.....................	0	
Interest expense.................	400	
Other expense....................	4,700	
Total............................	$166,000	$166,000

At the end of 19x3, Mr. Dennis Barclay, the president of the company, engaged an accounting firm to review his accounting system and to draw up financial statements for the year. The accountants' first recommendation, to adopt the accrual basis of accounting, was accepted by Mr. Barclay. Investigation by the accountants then revealed the following facts:

(1) Depreciation of 10 percent of original cost had not yet been recorded for 19x3.

(2) Merchandise on hand and in transit on December 31, 19x3, amounted to $12,700; the comparable January 1, 19x3, figure was listed on the trial balance opposite Merchandise.

(3) Amounts payable for merchandise on hand or in transit but not yet paid for totaled $6,000 on January 1, 19x3, $4,500 on December 31, 19x3.

(4) Amounts due from customers for goods shipped were $14,200 on January 1, 19x3, and $19,600 on December 31, 19x3.

(5) Accrued interest on notes payable amounted to $200 on January 1, 19x3, and $100 on December 31, 19x3.

(6) Wages earned but unpaid totaled $800 on January 1, 19x3, and $1,200 on December 31, 19x3; employer's payroll taxes averaging 6 percent were applicable to these amounts.

(7) Unpaid utilities bills were $150 on January 1, 19x3, and $175 on December 31, 19x3.

(8) Rent was paid monthly until September, when a new lease was negotiated. Rent of $4,000 for one year in advance was paid on October 1, 19x3.

(9) Two employees had expense advances of $250 each, an amount that had not changed during the year. When these sums were

originally advanced in 19x1, the debit was to Other Expense. On January 4, 19x4, the two employees submitted December, 19x3, expense statements totaling $140 and checks were drawn to restore the cash advances to the full amount.

(10) A check in the amount of $1,000, dated December 31, 19x3, and in payment for two new electric typewriters for the office, was incorrectly debited to Merchandise Purchases.

(11) The balance in the Cash account represented the company's bank balance. The accountants found that an additional $150 was in the change drawer in the cash register.

(12) An additional $3,500 in undeposited checks was found in the back of Mr. Barclay's desk on January 1, 19x4. It was Mr. Barclay's custom to let the checks accumulate for a week or so until his bookkeeper told him that the bank balance was dangerously low. Then he would send all the undeposited checks to the bank for deposit. One such deposit had been made on December 31, 19x2.

(13) A check in the amount of $136, payable to the Jones Plumbing Company for plumbing repairs and dated December 18, 19x3, was incorrectly recorded in the cashbook and ledger at $163.

a) Enter the trial balance on a work sheet, leaving extra lines for Cash, Merchandise, and Other Expense, and make whatever adjustments are necessary to bring the accounts up to date on an accrual basis as of December 31, 19x3.

b) Prepare a balance sheet in good form as of December 31, 19x3.

c) Prepare an income statement for the year 19x3. The adjustment necessary to convert the balance in Retained Earnings from the cash basis to an accrual basis as of the beginning of 19x3 should be entered directly in the Retained Earnings account. It should not be shown on the income statement for 19x3.

d) Compare the net income figure for 19x3 with the figure that would have been reported for Barclay Distributors, Inc., if the company had remained on a cash basis.

Chapter 7

PROCESSING

ACCOUNTING DATA

RECORDING ACCOUNTING DATA is a much more complicated process than the preceding chapters may have implied. The years since the end of the World War II have witnessed an unparalleled growth both in the number of business transactions and in the speed and variety of the equipment available for processing them. Consequently, the design of the working details of data processing systems requires a great deal of technical knowledge, far more than this chapter can hope to provide. Its objective is more modest: to provide an understanding of the basic elements of similarity in processing systems and of some of the ways in which a few simple problems might be solved.

GENERAL CHARACTERISTICS OF DATA PROCESSING SYSTEMS

Accounting data processing is only one kind of data processing, but it shares a number of basic elements with systems designed to process other kinds of data, such as scientific data or election data. A brief look at the characteristics of data processing systems in general is therefore a useful prelude to a discussion of accounting data processing.

Basic Elements of Data Processing Systems

Every data processing system consists of inputs, files, a processor, and output. The principal inputs are various kinds of *data*. These data may be either factual or hypothetical, depending on the purpose of the system. The processor serves to convert these data into various forms of *output*, using data and instructions previously stored in the files to effect this result.

These relationships are shown graphically in Exhibit 7–1. In processing routine financial transactions, the data inputs are generally

201

contained in documents; the information output is customarily in the form of a report or reports, although in very advanced systems it may also be in the form of direct instructions governing some element of the company's operations, the result of building a decision-making routine into the processor. There are also output documents, such as bank checks or invoices. Processing is the connection between inputs and outputs. It consists primarily of *classifying* the data, *sorting* them, *reading* them into the processing unit, *performing arithmetic* operations, *updating* files of data, and *preparing output* reports and documents.

For example, in a bank the incoming checks (the documents) must

Exhibit 7–1

BASIC ELEMENTS OF A DATA PROCESSING SYSTEM

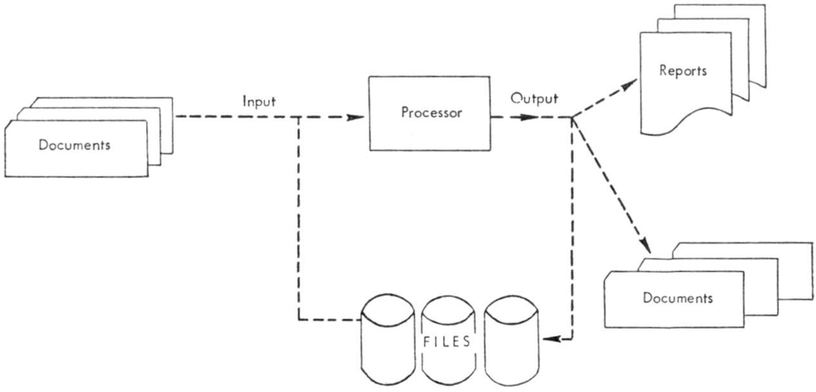

first be classified by depositor account number, sorted on this basis, and read into the processor where they are merged with the day's deposits for each account. New account balances must then be prepared, and the results summarized to show the total of the day's transactions and the new balances in all accounts (files). Reports issued periodically to depositors and to various executives of the bank provide each with information useful for the decisions he has to make.

The sequence need not always be the same—sorting, for example, may be the second, third, or fourth step—but most processing programs will include all six steps at some time. Nor is it necessary that the processor be an electronic computer; a clerk with pencil and piece of paper performs the same function, and he may be able to do some of the preliminary steps more quickly than the auxiliary units of an electronic system, thus offsetting the computer's speed in performing arithmetic operations.

Characteristics of Business Data Processing

Business data processing creates some difficult problems for the manufacturers of equipment and the designers of systems. Whereas in scientific work, relatively long and complex mathematical operations must be performed, business data processing is characterized by:

1. Large quantities of input data.
2. Extensive data files.
3. Large quantities of output documents and reports.
4. Few and simple computational operations.

For example, payroll preparation requires the extraction of basic data from each employee's attendance and work records, from records showing the number of dependents he claims for tax purposes and the other deductions he has authorized, and from tables of withholding tax rates, and so forth. The only computations required are simple arithmetic to find gross pay, deductions, and net pay for each employee. Output then consists of (1) a paycheck for each man, (2) account entries, and (3) updating of the files of employee earnings and deductions to date.

These characteristics place a premium on systems that can handle input and output rapidly; speed of arithmetic operations is important but is far less crucial than it is for scientific work. If documents can be fed into a computer at a rate of only 200 per minute, for example, it is of little relevance that the internal processor is capable of performing the arithmetic operations at a rate of 10,000 documents a minute. Consequently, progress in equipment design from a business data processing point of view is measured to a large extent in terms of the speed of input and output devices.

Business data processing also requires a large filing capacity easily accessible to the processor. A file drawer of accounts receivable cards, for example, might be located at the desk of the accounts receivable clerk. In processing either a credit sale or a collection, the clerk would remove the card from the file and make the appropriate entry, either by hand or on some kind of bookkeeping machine. Her access time to any single account would be relatively short.

The greater the storage requirements, the more space is needed and the more difficult it is to secure rapid access to all parts of the file simultaneously. One clerk can no longer handle the entire job, and means must be provided for the larger processing task. A large department store with 50,000 accounts receivable, for example, might find it more economical to store accounts receivable data on reels of magnetic tape which could be connected to an electronic computer for updating. The continuing increase in the quantities of data contained in the files places increasing emphasis on cheap, compact storage capacity, readily accessible to the processor. Increasing capacity and accessibility of data storage units, therefore, is a second dimension of progress in equipment design for business data processing purposes.

PROCESSING ROUTINE COMMERCIAL TRANSACTIONS

The largest single set of inputs to any financial information system must almost inevitably be provided by the multitude of routine commercial transactions, such as purchases and sales, payments and collections. It is not possible in these few pages to describe an actual data processing system of any complexity. Instead, the illustration that follows is intended to highlight some of the concepts underlying all or most data processing systems. To avoid obscuring this fundamental objective, discussion of the details of how computers or any other kinds of equipment work will be kept to a minimum.

The Chart of Accounts

The Graham Company is a regional distributor of industrial supplies. The data processing equipment it uses is relatively simple and inexpensive, in line with the small size of its business. All systems entail some combination of people and equipment, but in the Graham Company very little equipment is used.

The first step in describing the company's system is to examine its chart of accounts. The adoption of a chart of accounts or the alteration of an existing chart reflects crystallization of a policy decision as to the types of data to be collected and the manner in which such data are to be classified.

Data from a given transaction can be classified in many ways. For example, the revenue from the sale of merchandise might be identified as to the type of product, the department in which the sale took place, the salesman, and the type of customer. Some companies may make none of these classifications; others may make even more. The problem in each case is to try to anticipate the demands for data that will be made in the future and to design the chart of accounts to meet these demands. The problem is important. For example, if sales revenues are not classified by geographical region when they are recorded initially, a regional breakdown can be obtained later only at considerable cost.

The structure and content of the chart of accounts thus depend to a great extent on the kinds of information management and others will want to obtain. It is not surprising, therefore, that even relatively similar companies will have quite different charts of accounts. Most charts of accounts, nevertheless, have two kinds of classification in common: (1) classification by nature of the element, and (2) classification by organization unit.

As to the first of these, it is common practice to group all the asset accounts together, followed by liability, ownership, revenue, and expense accounts, in that order. Thus a representative list of accounts might be as follows:

Account Numbers	Kind of Accounts
100–199	Assets
200–299	Liabilities
300–399	Ownership
400–499	Revenues
500–599	Cost of goods sold
600–699	Selling expenses
700–799	Administrative expenses
800–899	Financial expenses
900–999	Noncurrent income

The numbering system used and the amount of detail provided in each category vary considerably, but it is from some such base that the account structure is built.

The second element common to most charts of accounts is organizational breakdown of manufacturing costs, revenues, and expenses. Most companies are organized in a network of subdivisions that might be referred to as departments. Each element of cost or revenue or expense can be traced to one or more of these departments, and the account structure generally reflects this basis of classification. A broad grouping might be:

Department Numbers	Kind of Department
10–29	Marketing
30–79	Manufacturing
80–89	Accounting
90–99	Administration

Thus the salary of a man in the marketing research department might be assigned to account 601 (salary expense), department 22 (marketing research); and the full coding would be 601–22. The larger the organization and the more kinds of data desired, the longer and more complicated this account identification will be.

Probably the most important purpose of organizational classification is in providing routine internal control reports. The responsibilities of various people within the business organization require that they be currently informed of the impact of financial events upon those business activities over which they have jurisdiction. This requires classification of costs and revenues by responsibility, and responsibility typically can be expressed in organizational terms.

The Graham Company's chart of accounts, reproduced in Exhibit 7–2, is very simple. Product revenues are divided into only two categories, direct sales and dealer sales, while expenses are divided among only three general organization units (head office, eastern region, and western region). Of course, even though the management of the Graham Company is very close to the day-to-day operations of the business, and thus has less need for the kind of impersonal financial information that stems from the accounting system, the accounts in Exhibit 7–2 are not sufficiently detailed to provide management with essential information. This shortcoming is remedied by subdividing many of the accounts to provide additional detail. For the moment, these additional refinements are ignored in order to concentrate more fully on other aspects of the company's system.

Multicolumn Journals: Purchases

Once the account structure has been established, the accountant's next task is to decide how each class of transactions is to be read into the accounting system. One of the most important classes of transactions in the Graham Company is the purchase of merchandise, equipment, and supplies. As indicated previously, the first place at which such a transaction would enter the accounting system would be in the journal, or chronological record of transactions. Until now it has been assumed that all transactions, regardless of type, are recorded in only one journal. Thus in chronological sequence might be found a purchase, a sale, a payment, another sale, etc.

A moment's reflection will indicate that even in the smallest companies this procedure would be unnecessarily tedious and expensive. For each transaction at least two account titles would have to be written out in full in the journal. Then each dollar figure would have to be posted to an appropriate ledger account. Thus, every number would

Exhibit 7–2

GRAHAM COMPANY
Chart of Accounts

Acct. No.	*Account Title*
100	Cash
101	Petty Cash
110	Notes and Interest Receivable
111	Accounts Receivable
112	Allowance for Uncollectible Accounts
120	Merchandise Inventories
150	Prepaid Insurance
170	Land, Buildings, and Equipment
171	Allowance for Depreciation
200	Accounts Payable
210	Salaries and Wages Payable
220	Payroll Taxes Payable
221	Other Taxes Payable
230	Notes and Interest Payable
300	Capital Stock
310	Retained Earnings
320	Dividends Declared
400	Direct Sales
401	Direct Sales Returns and Allowances
410	Dealer Sales
411	Dealer Sales Returns and Allowances
450	Interest Income
470	Other Income
500	Cost of Goods Sold
510	Head Office Salaries and Wages
511	Other Head Office Expenses
520	Eastern Region Salaries and Wages
521	Other Eastern Region Expenses
530	Western Region Salaries and Wages
531	Other Western Region Expenses
550	Interest Expense
560	Income Taxes

have to be recorded twice. If 100 different purchases of merchandise were recorded during a given week, 100 separate entries of the following form would be necessary, identical in all respects except amount and vendor name:

Merchandise Inventories....................................xxx
    Accounts Payable—Vendor X............................   xxx

One way to cut down on the amount of clerical work involved would be to add extra columns to the journal. For example, the journal might show the following column headings:

Date	Explanation	Debit			Credit		
		120 Merchandise Inventories	Other Debits		200 Accounts Payable	Other Credits	
			Acct.	Amount		Acct.	Amount

This is known as a *multicolumn journal* and has two main advantages over the two-column journal: (1) the merchandise inventory and accounts payable account titles do not have to be written out each time a transaction affects those accounts; and (2) the effort of posting debits to Merchandise Inventories and credits to Accounts Payable may be reduced by posting only the column totals instead of each item. Thus if 15 purchases of merchandise are listed on a single page of the journal, only one number needs to be posted to the Merchandise Inventories account instead of 15.

These advantages are important, but a single multicolumn journal is seldom sufficient except for very small enterprises with relatively few accounts. To reap the benefits from the multicolumn journal, a separate column must be made for each account that is encountered frequently, which typically would require too many columns for efficient use.

Special Journals: The Purchases Journal

The Graham Company goes one step farther and uses what is known as a *special journal* to record purchases. This journal, generally known as the purchases journal or voucher register, is shown in Exhibit 7–3. Because most purchases are either of merchandise or of supplies for the warehouse, office, or sales force, special columns have been established for debits to the four accounts designed to receive these costs. Debits to any other accounts must be recorded in the two rightmost columns of the journal and posted individually. For example, office equipment costing $737 was included in the January 3 purchase from the ABC Company (Voucher No. 1002). Because equipment purchases are relatively infrequent in the Graham Company, no separate column is provided for them. The charge to account No. 170—Land, Buildings, and Equipment—was therefore recorded in the right-hand pair of columns.

Exhibit 7–3

GRAHAM COMPANY: PURCHASES JOURNAL

Date	Voucher No.	Name of Supplier	Credit 200 Accts. Payable	Debit 120 Merch. Inventories	511 Head Office Expense	521 Eastern Region Expense	531 Western Region Expense	Other Accounts No.	Amt.
1/3	1001	Jones, Inc.	300	300					
1/3	1002	ABC Co.	867	130				170	737
1/4	1003	Ulm Bros.	242		141	23	78		
								Individual amounts posted	
			Only column totals posted						

As the exhibit shows, each purchase is assigned a "voucher number." The Graham Company's *voucher system* requires that a voucher be issued for each purchase of outside goods and services except small cash purchases which are handled by simpler means, as described later in this chapter. The purpose of this voucher is to notify the company's treasurer that the vendor's charges are legitimate, and no payment can be made unless a voucher has been issued. The purpose of this restriction is to provide an opportunity for a member of the controller's staff to answer such questions as: Was the purchase approved by someone authorized to do so? Were the goods received? Have the amounts been transcribed correctly?

In the case of services which are provided on a regular basis, such as telephone service, the requisition procedure can be bypassed, but the controller still has the obligation to examine the invoices and determine whether the charges are correct.[1]

The sequence of events in processing a purchase transaction may be summarized briefly:

---

[1] For more information on voucher systems, see Arthur W. Holmes, *Auditing: Principles and Procedures* (Homewood, Ill.: Richard D. Irwin, Inc., 1964), especially chaps. iv and v.

1. An executive (e.g., the warehouse manager) prepares a *requisition* or request for the item.
2. The requisition is *approved* by the appropriate senior executive (for purchase of equipment at the Graham Company, presidential approval is required).
3. The purchasing agent places a *purchase order* with a supplier.
4. The supplier ships the order and sends an *invoice* or bill and a shipping notice or *bill of lading*.
5. Upon arrival, the goods are inspected for quantity and condition. Any shortages or defects are noted on the bill of lading which is then forwarded to the accounting department as a *receiving report*.
6. In the accounting department the invoice and receiving report are matched; a *purchase voucher* is issued, recorded in the *purchases journal*, and filed in the purchase voucher file.

It should be noted that the form of the journal illustrated in Exhibit 7–3 is designed to accommodate a complete transaction on each line. Journals such as this are commonly prepared on a bookkeeping machine which is essentially a typewriter combined with several adding machine registers used to accumulate column totals. With the aid of carbon paper, individual postings may be made to account cards and to record the amounts owed to individual suppliers simultaneously with production of the journal record. In fact, in modern practice the journal is often more accurately described as a by-product of these other operations.

Specialization in Data Processing

The above procedure is a good example of what is known as *off-line processing*. In off-line processing, transactions are normally grouped or sorted in some fashion before processing so that the sequence of processing is different from the sequence in which the transactions enter the system. For example, the purchase transactions are pulled out of the random flow of transactions and processed as a group. After this kind of initial sorting, the input documents may undergo a second sorting into batches, each batch being homogeneous with respect to some characteristic.

For example, employee attendance cards for the week may be sorted first according to the department to which the employee is assigned so that the cards for all employees in a given department can be processed as a single batch. In other cases, the batching may be more random in nature. Thus, customer orders may be allowed to accumulate until 30 or 40 are on the supervisor's desk, at which point they will be gathered together as a batch. Batching permits a form of control over the data in that some key total may be determined when the batch is made up, such as the total number of hours or total number of dollars. This control then serves at later stages of processing as a partial check against loss or misreading of a document.

At the other extreme is *on-line processing* or *real-time processing*. It calls for processing each transaction as soon as it occurs and in the same sequence, with no intermediate batching or sorting. Such a system would permit each transaction to be put into some kind of transmitting device as it takes place and fed into a centralized computer which would identify the accounts affected, make the necessary entries, and issue instructions for the printing of any output documents required. The most familiar examples of on-line processing are in stock market transactions reporting, airline reservations accounting, and air defense warning systems; in such systems, delays may occur if the lines of communication to the processor are busy, in which case transactions must wait in line until the communication lines are cleared. For example, when trading is heavy on the stock exchange, the ticker may fall several minutes behind because the speed of the processor is inadequate to handle all of the incoming data.

The major advantage of on-line processing is its ability to keep the master files current. In certain business situations, a delay cannot be tolerated; the files must be kept up-to-date continuously. On-line processing is the best means of achieving this goal, provided of course that satisfactory equipment is available. For example, an airline reservation system has to be so organized that the availability of passenger space on any flight can be determined at any time. Interrogations of the files may come from one or many locations, and the system must provide answers to the interrogations. Therefore, as soon as a reservation is made, the master file must be corrected so that the next interrogation will not receive a misleading answer.

The main disadvantage of on-line processing, of course, is that more complex and costly equipment is required, equipment that will be at least partially idle most of the time. Because all transactions enter the processing system in a random mix, the central processor must have access to the complete files at all times. This need for rapid access means in effect that the files must be stored within or linked to the central processor in ways that will reduce the search time necessary to locate any given bit of data. Such large-scale, random-access storage is expensive.

Most accounting transactions are currently handled by off-line techniques. Bank checks are handled in batches. Payrolls are divided into groups, each group being handled as a separate payroll. Sales slips are also processed in batches. Batching permits a division of labor among the available personnel so that the work load is evenly distributed. The amount of idle time at any processing stage is reduced because the entire system does not have to be scaled to fit the speed of the slowest processing operation. For example, equipment to convert data into a form that is acceptable to electronic computers normally operates at a much slower speed than the computer itself. Similarly, the equipment used to convert the computer output into visible documents is also slower than the computer. Therefore, if these slow operations are performed off line, the central computer need be tied up only for computations. Data input can be stored temporarily on magnetic or paper tape and information output can be accumulated on magnetic tape for later printing on off-line printers. While the input and output operations are being performed, the computer is free to process other kinds of data.

Subsidiary Ledgers

Up to now, Accounts Payable has been assumed to be the one account that is credited when a purchase is made. While this may be true, some kind of supplementary record of the amounts owed to individual suppliers is also generally desirable. This record may take the form of a file of cards, one for each vendor, or a file of unpaid invoices, or perhaps a reel of magnetic tape containing the same kinds of information. Such a supplementary record is known as a *subsidiary ledger* to distinguish it from the *general ledger* which is the one reflected in the chart of accounts in Exhibit 7–2 above.

The main purpose of the subsidiary ledger is to permit the accumulation of a considerable amount of detail on some aspects of the company's operations without unduly expanding the main file of accounts, or general ledger. The physical separation of the supplementary record and the general ledger facilitates posting to the subsidiary accounts. The clerical force can make entries in the accounts payable records, for example, without tying up the general ledger for long periods of time.

Any account that is supported by additional classified data is known as a *control account*. The balance in the control account at any time should be the same as the sum of the balances in the related subsidiary accounts. The Graham Company has a number of control accounts in its general ledger. These accounts, together with the

Exhibit 7–4

GRAHAM COMPANY

General Ledger Control Accounts
and Subsidiary Ledgers

Acct. No.	Control Account Title	Subsidiary Ledger
110	Notes and Interest Receivable	Notes Receivable File
111	Accounts Receivable	Customers Ledger
120	Merchandise Inventories	Stock Records*
150	Prepaid Insurance	Insurance Policy File
170	Land, Buildings, and Equipment	Property Records
171	Allowance for Depreciation	Property Records
200	Accounts Payable	Purchase Voucher File
210	Salaries and Wages Payable	Employee Pay Records
220	Payroll Taxes Payable	Employee Pay Records
221	Other Taxes Payable	Tax Voucher File
230	Notes and Interest Payable	Notes Payable File
300	Capital Stock	Stockholders Register †

* Kept in physical quantities only.

† Maintained by the bank acting as the company's agent for recording transfers of stock ownership and for payment of dividends.

associated subsidiary ledger in each case, are shown in Exhibit 7–4. In the course of this chapter, several of these subsidiary ledgers will be discussed, but at the moment the only concern is with purchases and thus with the records underlying the merchandise inventory and accounts payable accounts.

In some instances, the merchandise inventory records do not constitute a subsidiary ledger because they are kept in physical quantities only. This is a minor quibble, however, in that the stock records perform the same general kind of function as a subsidiary ledger except that they do not permit a cross-check on dollar account balances. The physical quantity records are maintained at the warehouse and are used primarily as a means of keeping track of quantities on hand and on order, thus serving to alert the warehouse manager when it is time to reorder specific items of merchandise.

The balance in the Graham Company's Accounts Payable account, on the other hand, is supported by the purchase voucher file. Each vendor invoice is treated as a separate payable, and thus the file of unpaid vouchers can serve as the subsidiary ledger supporting the control account, Accounts Payable.

Cash Disbursements: The Check Register

Once purchases have been duly recorded, the only step remaining is to pay the supplier and record this payment in the accounts. The purchase voucher provides authority for payment, and each day all invoices due for payment that day are withdrawn from the purchase voucher file and delivered to the treasurer. Attached to each voucher is an unsigned *check* that was prepared at the time the purchase voucher was made out and bearing the same identifying number as the voucher. This check is then signed by the treasurer. The check is recorded in the *check register* or *cash disbursements journal*, illustrated in Exhibit 7–5, and then mailed to the supplier along with a copy of the invoice.

Exhibit 7–5

GRAHAM COMPANY

Check Register

Date	Check No.	Payee	Credit	Debit				
			100 Cash	200 Accts. Payable	210 Salaries and Wages Payable	Other Accounts		
						No.	Amt.
1/3	8946	Ace Stores	680.03	680.03			
1/3	1004	1st National Bank	1400.00			220	1,400.00
			Only column totals posted			Individual amounts posted	

The check register is very similar in form to the purchases journal, except for differences in column headings. Again special columns are prepared only for those accounts that are affected by large numbers of cash transactions. In many small companies, the check register and its companion, the *cash receipts journal*, may constitute the only books of original entry used in the routine recording of transactions. Accrual entries are made infrequently, perhaps no more often than once a year, if at all. In most business firms of any size, however, other journals will be necessary, and two of these will be examined shortly.

It should be emphasized again that the main purpose of most of the documents involved in the purchase-payment sequence of transactions was not to provide for accounting entries. Instead, they were designed to communicate action information (how much to order, how much to pay, etc.). Their use as sources of input data for the bookkeeping records is a bonus, obtainable at little or no extra cost.

Processing Payrolls

The Graham Company's system for handling its payrolls is tailored to the fact that a substantial amount of data must be recorded for each transaction. Although a number of alternatives exist, Graham has decided to use *punched card equipment*.

The basic feature of a punched card system is the transfer of data from the original document to a punched card in a form that can be read directly by a data processing machine. Data on the original document are transcribed onto a card by punching a series of holes representing numerals or alphabetic characters. Some of the data are transcribed in the form in which they appear on the original document (dollar amounts, customer name, and so forth) and some are first restated in terms of some code designator (account number, product number, class of customer, and so on). By reading the position of the holes and by identifying the column in which they appear, the processing machines are able to interpret the data correctly.

The card punching machine has a typewriter-like keyboard, but instead of printing letters or numerals on the card it punches holes. A separate vertical space or column must be reserved for each character, and the width of the card determines how many different letters or numbers can be punched, the most common number being 80. The position of the hole or holes punched in any one column indicates the letter or number that has been entered in that column. Once it has been reproduced in machinable form, the original document is no longer of any use except as an evidentiary record of the transaction.

In the Graham Company, a payroll data card is maintained for each employee. This card shows the employee's name, department, rate of pay, number of dependents, and other facts needed for payroll preparation, plus a cumulative record of gross pay and withholdings to date for the current calendar year. At the end of each period, attendance cards or *clock cards* for all hourly employees are collected from the time clocks, showing the number of hours worked during the period. These data are coded and punched into a separate set of cards. All the basic data are now ready for payroll preparation.

The input data described above are now processed by machines. The processing sequence is as follows:

1. Each set of cards is *sorted* alphabetically.
2. The two sets of cards are then *collated* (matched) so that each employee's attendance or performance card is paired with his pay record card.
3. The collated cards are then fed into the processing machine which *computes* automatically gross pay, tax and other withholdings, net pay, and employer's payroll tax liabilities.
4. The computed amounts are then *accumulated* in a series of adding machine registers inside the processor, one for each of the accounts affected. Thus gross pay is accumulated in accounts 510, 520, and 530, while a parallel set of debits is made to accounts 511, 521, and 531 for the employer's share of payroll taxes. The credits are made to accounts 210 and 220 (including both employee and employer payroll tax contributions).

The exact means by which the processor performs the computations depends on the design of the equipment and the way it has been instructed or *programmed* to do the job. Programming a payroll is generally quite simple, in contrast to many business and scientific applications of electronic computers for which highly sophisticated programs are necessary.

Payroll preparation is characterized by a large number and variety of output documents. These may be produced immediately as each set of computations is completed, or the results of the computations may be stored temporarily on magnetic tape and printed later. The Graham Company's equipment is designed for batch processing, in which the input cards for one employee are read in and processed before the next pair of cards is introduced. The output for each employee is printed while the next pair of cards is being read in.

The Graham Company's payroll processing system has three basic kinds of output:

1. A *paycheck* for each employee, complete except for signature, with an attached stub showing gross pay, deductions, and net pay.
2. A new set of *pay record cards* with corrected cumulative amounts.
3. A *payroll journal*, showing all pertinent amounts, one line for each employee. The column totals provide the basis for entries in the ledger accounts. An example of a payroll journal is shown in Exhibit 7–6.

The completed payroll journal for a given pay period serves as the supporting voucher for all paychecks. All paychecks are numbered sequentially, and the total only is entered in one line of the check register as a debit to Salaries and Wages Payable and a credit to Cash.

Exhibit 7–6

GRAHAM COMPANY

Payroll Journal

Date	Name of Employee	Debit						Credit	
		510	511	520	521	530	531	210	220
4/26	Adams, A. P.	80.00	5.30					66.40	18.90
4/26	Allen, D. G.			100.00	6.63			83.80	22.83
4/26	Andrews, R.	120.00	7.95					96.50	31.45
4/26	Arturo, P. X.					90.00	5.96	80.10	15.86
4/26	Bates, E. K.					160.00	10.60	130.40	40.20
4/26	.	.	.	.	.	.	.	.	.
4/26	.	.	.	.	.	.	.	.	.
4/26	.	.	.	.	.	.	.	.	.

Processing Sales Transactions

Since the Graham Company's procedures for recording sales and cash receipts do not introduce any new concepts, they can be covered quickly. The principal documents associated with sales transactions in this firm are the *sales order* prepared by the salesman, the *shipping document* prepared by the warehouse, the *invoice*, and the customer's *check*. The copies made of these documents and the disposition of each is depicted, with minor simplification, in Exhibit 7–7. Solid lines represent action communications; broken lines information communications. Copy 3 of the sales order goes to the office as a basis for follow up on the warehouse response to the original. Copy 2 of the invoice is kept by the salesman as evidence of the commission due him on the sale.

The office copies of the sales order and shipping document together constitute the *sales voucher*, that is, the authority for preparing the invoice and recording the transaction. Since customers often pay more than one invoice with a single check, the sales vouchers and invoice copies are filed by customer. This file is the customers ledger. If an inquiry is received as to the balance of a customer's account, the answer is readily found by summing the totals of the vouchers contained in his folder.

Exhibit 7–7

GRAHAM COMPANY

Sales Document Flows

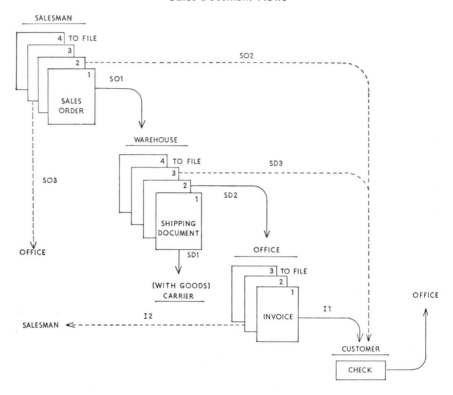

The information given on each sales voucher is transferred to a punched card, thus making available data coded for machine reading. Any or all of the following outputs can then be produced:

1. Itemized invoices ready for mailing.
2. Sales by salesmen, and hence statistics for performance analysis; and in conjunction with the pay record cards, the sales payroll.
3. Sales by inventory classes to reveal trends.
4. Sales by customer further classified by (a) geographical area and (b) order size (this information is deemed useful in evaluating and directing sales efforts).

Once a month the sales cards are fed into a tabulating machine which then prints a *sales journal*. The sales journal is very simple, with columns for invoice number, debits to account 112-Accounts Receivable, and credits to accounts 400-Direct Sales and 410-Dealer Sales.

The column totals are printed automatically at the end of the card run and are posted from there to the ledger.

The cards are then sorted by salesmen and run through the tabulating machine again. This time, however, only the total sales for each salesman are shown on the printed sheet; the amounts of the individual sales are accumulated inside the tabulating machine but are not printed. In this same tabulator run, the Graham Company's management obtains the third kind of output listed above, the amount of sales in each of the company's six main product lines.

These two card runs are made routinely each month. Sales analyses by customer group, order size, and other characteristics are performed less frequently, but having the data in coded form permits such analyses to be performed quickly and on short notice.

The point of primary interest is that *the same raw data can be classified in a number of different ways in order to extract their total information content.* Note, too, that not all of these analyses need be built into the formal account structure, nor must they be carried out routinely each month.

Recording Cash Receipts

By far the greatest number of cash receipts in the Graham Company are collections from customers on accounts receivable. Thus, the *cash receipts journal,* which is illustrated in Exhibit 7–8, has only two special columns.

Exhibit 7–8

GRAHAM COMPANY

Cash Receipts Journal

Date	Ref. No.	Payer	Debit 100 Cash	Credit 111 Accts. Receivable	Credit Other Accounts No.	Credit Other Accounts Amt.
1/1/xx	12–211	A. O. Aneen	550	550		
1/1/xx	N-27	Renton's Market	808		110	808
1/1/xx	12–212	T. H Count	300	300		

The General Journal

Each of the five special journals used by the Graham Company to record common kinds of transactions has now been discussed:

1. Purchases journal.
2. Check register.
3. Payroll journal.
4. Sales journal.
5. Cash receipts journal.

The transactions that occur too infrequently to justify the establishment of a special journal will continue to be recorded in the general journal. In the Graham Company, periodic depreciation, property retirements, and other transactions not involving purchases, sales, or the payment or receipt of cash are recorded in the general journal. These constitute a relatively minor proportion of Graham's

Exhibit 7–9

ACCOUNTING RECORDS AND DATA FLOWS

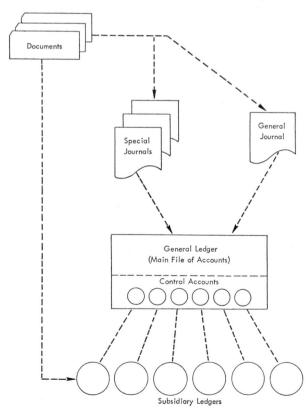

transactions, and it would actually be more costly to set up special journals than to continue to provide for them in the general journal.

To summarize, the accounting data flows in the Graham Company follow the streams indicated in Exhibit 7–9. Documents of various sorts provide the basic data not only for journalization but also for direct entries to some of the subsidiary ledgers. The general ledger includes a number of control accounts which serve to tie the subsidiary ledgers into the overall account structure and at the same time provide one check on the posting of data from documents to the subsidiary ledger accounts.

OTHER DIMENSIONS OF ACCOUNTING DATA PROCESSING SYSTEMS

The procedures described above are essentially means of carrying out the physical task of converting given inputs into desired data or document outputs. The criteria for success are much the same as in any other production process: degree of adherence to scheduled completion dates and cost effectiveness.

A similar set of criteria applies to the data files: speed of access and cost, plus the added consideration of the adaptability of the data to the many different kinds of uses to which they can be put. "Trade-offs" between these criteria are inevitable; and finding the proper balance among cost, speed, and adaptability is no easy matter.

This situation is further complicated by the need for the system to meet other constraints, and brief mention of three of these is necessary before this chapter can be brought to a close:

1. The system must provide for an adequate system of safeguards against loss of assets through fraud or carelessness.
2. The system must be so constructed as to permit an independent verification that transactions have been recorded properly.
3. The system should provide some way of handling small cash disbursement transactions at low cost and minimal delay.

While these three constraints may not be of equal importance, all of them deserve at least brief discussion here.

Internal Control

One of the main constraints imposed on any data processing system is that it provides reasonable protection against the loss of assets through fraud or carelessness. Each item of equipment purchased, for example, is typically assigned an identifying number. The *property records*, which consist of an inventory of these items, will show such details as the date purchased, original cost, dates and costs of alterations or major overhauls, and where the equipment is located. Part of this is to provide data for financial reporting or managerial decisions, but much of it is designed primarily to make sure that the company can keep track of what it owns.

Similarly, purchase orders, checks, and customer invoice forms are often numbered serially to guard against loss or unauthorized use. Totals shown on cash register tapes are checked against the amount of cash actually received. Internal audits are conducted periodically, primarily to insure that prescribed procedures are being followed, partly to discover procedures that need to be improved, and partly to prevent or detect asset losses.

The procedures illustrated above also contain internal control features, centering primarily on the division of responsibility for initiating and approving transactions. For example, the Graham Company's order clerk prepares a purchase order for the purchase of merchandise and supplies, but he does this only after receiving a purchase requisition signed by someone authorized to initiate purchases. After the goods are received, a different person, the controller, approves payment of the vendor's invoice by signing a voucher. Finally, the actual payment of cash is made by a third person, the treasurer.

This division of labor is occasioned largely by the need for different kinds of specialized skills, but also in part by the need for protecting the firm's assets. The functions of accounting and cash disbursement are divided between the controller and the treasurer primarily for the latter reason. This division is not a matter of trusting the executives but of following the first principle of internal control, which requires that significant transactions be reviewed by more than one person. Thus, embezzlement becomes more difficult and a means of preventing costly and misleading errors is also provided.

Design of the internal control system is a problem in resource allocation no less than any other financial decision. The amount of *redundancy*, or duplication of paper work, that is built into a system depends on the size of the risk it is designed to insure against. The smaller the risk, the smaller the amount that should be spent to reduce it. Absolute protection is unobtainable in any case, and management has to learn to accept a certain amount of petty theft because it would cost more to prevent it than it would cost to replace the stolen items.

The Audit Trail

Even in the light of the need for internal checks and balances, some of the procedures that have been described may have seemed wasteful and unnecessarily costly. Many accounting systems do include unnecessarily costly procedures. Much of what seems to be duplication of bookkeeping effort often does have a purpose, however, which is to leave a trail that someone else (the auditor) can retrace if he wishes to verify the legitimacy of the transactions and the accuracy of the classification and recording of the effects of the transactions. The trail is a means of locating numerical errors revealed in summarization and of preserving the raw data if later demands for information reports require reclassification on some new basis.

In some cases, the chronological record (the journal) may be dispensed with entirely, although so doing poses some problems for the auditor who is concerned with retracing the trail left by individual transactions. Furthermore, in the present state of the art, this kind of direct posting of individual transactions is rarely economical in processing accounting data.

The problem of tracing accounting transactions can be especially difficult in data processing systems that rely heavily on electronic equipment. Here the data are typically stored in a form illegible to an auditor—as magnetized spots on a tape, for example. To reconstruct a series of transactions in such a case is often quite difficult, and the accounting profession has had to devise auditing techniques to cope with this difficulty.

Petty Cash: Imprest Funds

The final constraint that we shall discuss is of a different order. Processing all cash payment transactions through the stages of purchase voucher and check preparation is seldom feasible. It is convenient to transfer small amounts of cash to *petty cash funds* (technically known as imprest funds) in the hands of supervisory employees, so that small items such as local taxi fare or C.O.D. charges can be paid quickly and with a minimum of red tape. The transfer is recorded initially by a very simple entry in the check register:[2]

101	Petty Cash..100	
100	Cash...	100

[2] This entry and most of the others in this and later chapters would of course appear in columnar form in the various special journals, but the general journal form of notation is used in text presentation for clarity and brevity.

The fund custodian or cashier then cashes the check and the fund is in operation. As disbursements are made from the fund, the custodian collects receipts from those to whom payments are made. When the cash balance in the fund gets low, the custodian takes these receipts to the accounting department where a purchase voucher is prepared and a check is issued. For example, if the custodian turns in 12 receipts for postage, taxi fare, and supplies totaling $43, the entry in the purchases journal might show the following:

    511   Other Head Office Expenses..............................43
    200   Accounts Payable..................................   43

The entry in the check register to record the issuance of the check to replenish the petty cash fund would be:

    200   Accounts Payable......................................43
    100   Cash..   43

Only one entry appears in the purchases journal instead of 12, a substantial saving in clerical effort. The credit in the check register is to Cash, not to Petty Cash, because the accounting records recognize no outlays from petty cash; only disbursements from the company's bank accounts give rise to journal entries. Thus, no entry to petty cash is made unless the amount of the fund is increased or decreased.

SUMMARY

Any accounting system must provide for the orderly and economical preparation of the data and document outputs demanded of the system. Procedures vary widely, depending on what kinds of outputs are desired and what kinds of equipment are available. Although modern electronic equipment has brought the day closer when each transaction can be posted directly to the affected accounts as soon as it occurs, the time-honored techniques of specialization of files and processing channels to carry out the accounting task are still necessary.

Specialized files, known generally as subsidiary ledgers, serve to keep a mass of data in accessible form, physically separated from other portions of the company's files. Specialized processing channels take the form of single-function clerical personnel, recording the transactions in special journals. This facilitates processing and reduces the subsequent labor of recording the effects of transactions in ledger accounts. Some equipment may also be specialized in this way (e.g., a machine that is used solely for preparing customer invoices), but the economies of joint use of the larger data processing machines are normally too great to be ignored.

The system described in this chapter should not be regarded as a model or even as typical, largely because practice varies too much for anything to be typical. The reader should concentrate on the underlying concepts, which are fundamental.

QUESTIONS AND PROBLEMS

1. What are the nature and function of a chart of accounts?

2. Explain the nature and purposes of subsidiary ledgers. Illustrate.

3. What is a control account? Give some common examples.

4. What is a voucher system? What is its main purpose?

5. In preparing a balance sheet for a company, is it necessary to know the individual balances of accounts in the accounts receivable ledger? The accounts payable ledger? Explain.

6. Explain how there may be two debits of $1 each for one credit of $1 without disturbing the fundamental balance of accounts.

7. Discuss the relationship of the bookkeeping system to the organizational structure of the business firm.

8. Discuss the functions of basic documents.

9. What purpose is served by having more than one debit and/or credit column in a journal?

10. The agreement of the balances of a control account and its subsidiary ledger proves the accuracy of the latter. Do you agree? Explain.

11. What is batching and why is it used?

12. Distinguish between off-line and real-time processing. Why is most accounting done by off-line techniques?

13. Electronic computers may be described in terms of their input speed, number of calculations performed per minute, data storage capacity, and so forth. Improvement in any one of these characteristics is usually obtainable only at higher cost. Therefore, different computers stress different characteristics, depending on the market they are intended to reach. If you were designing an electronic computer solely for use in processing accounting data, what characteristics do you think you would stress? Explain.

14. If you were designing the data proessing system of a small type-writer repair shop and wished to have as few journals as feasible, what journals would you probably have? Explain.

15. *a*) Describe the steps which might be involved in effecting a pur-chase of raw materials in a large manufacturing enterprise, indicating the nature and probable uses of any written documents that might be employed.
b) Repeat (*a*) for a small retailing enterprise such as a drugstore.

16. What officer in a corporation is particularly concerned with the information contained in each of the several accounts listed below:

> Cash in Bank
> Advertising Expense
> Medical Expense
> Sales—District No. 10
> Sales—Product A
> Purchases Discounts Lost

17. *a*) Describe the various steps which might be involved in effecting a sale in a firm manufacturing textile machinery, indicating the nature and probable uses of any written documents that might be employed.
b) Do the same for a department store, indicating any likely differences in the treatment accorded cash and credit sales.

18. You visit a local hardware store to buy a screwdriver. You select the one you want, pay for it, take it in your hand, and leave. You cross the street to the five-and-ten and select a small picture frame and some screws. Here the clerk asks you to give her the merchandise you have selected and the money in payment for it. She rings up the sale and places the goods in a paper bag which she then returns to you with the change, if any. A cash register receipt is in the bag. Why the formality in the lat-ter case? What differences in internal control are indicated?

19. What business documents might attest to the occurrence of the following events?
a) A purchase of supplies on credit.
b) Receipt of cash from a credit customer.
c) Sale of merchandise to a customer on credit.
d) Sale of merchandise to a customer for cash.

20. Late one afternoon the president of Elliot Industries, Inc., learned of the necessity for making a quick business trip to a city some distance away. He promptly asked the cashier for an advance of $200 for expenses. What documents would be required? What entries would be made? When? How does the cashier reimburse his cash fund? What check is there on the cashier?

21. Describe the documents which might support the bookkeeping record of a purchase of:

a) Office supplies by an office supply company.
b) Professional legal advice by a truck line.
c) Production machinery by a manufacturing company.
d) The services of handbill distributors by a grocery store manager.

22. *a*) Indicate the possible bases for classification of a department store's sales and the purpose of each.
b) Do the same for a manufacturer of machine tools.

*23. The sales journal of the Bemis Basket Company shows in parallel columns the amount of sales billed to customers and the cost of the particular merchandise sold. The column totals for the month of October were: sales, $50,000; cost of goods sold, $39,000.

a) To what ledger accounts should amounts be posted from this journal?
b) Which, if any, of these accounts are likely to be control accounts?

24. Shown below is a special journal:

| Date | Received from | Debit | | | Credit | | | | |
| | | Cash | Cash Dis- counts | Accounts Receivable | | Sales | Miscel- laneous | | |
				No.	Amount		No.	Amount
	Totals brought forward	26,605.50	285.70	√	16,785.20	267.35	√	9,838.65
26	Seneca Shops	3,234.00	66.00	11–2	3,300.00			
28	City National Bank	3,000.00					44	3,000.00
29	Towle Tool Company	850.00		11–7	850.00			
30	Cash sale	12.40				12.40		
31	Collection of note receivable	502.31					68	2.31
							23	500.00
	Total	34,204.21	351.70		20,935.20	279.75		13,340.96
		(1)	(63)		(11)	(61)		√

---

* Solutions to problems marked with an asterisk (*) are found in Appendix B.

a) What kind of a journal is this?
b) What postings are made from each column?
c) What control accounts are represented here?

25. Shown below is a special journal:

Date of In- voice	Name	Terms	Inv. No.	Credit Accounts Payable No.	Credit Accounts Payable Amount	Debit Mer- chandise Inventory	Debit Expense Ledger No.	Debit Expense Ledger Amount	Debit Miscel- laneous No.	Debit Miscel- laneous Amount
	Total brought forward....			✓	23,851.92	22,830.52	✓	713.50	✓	307.90
24	G. E. West Mfg. Co......	2/10, n/60	114	41–3	2,688.15	2,688.15				
28	Dunne Insurance Co......	Net 30	115	41–9	240.00				26	240.00
26	Hamler Electric Co.......	2/10, n/60	116	41–1	1,192.70	1,192.70				
31	Edison Co..............	Net	117	41–7	42.10		94	42.10		
	Total.................				28,014.87 (41)	26,711.37 (71)		755.60 (80)		547.90 ✓

a) What kind of a journal is this?
b) What postings are made from each column?
c) What control accounts are represented here?

*26. The manager of the Arlington branch store of the Wherewithal Company of America has been given a "petty cash fund" of $300 to pay small bills which are incurred at his store. In March, he spent $215 and mailed vouchers (receipts) for the following payments to the area office for reimbursement:

> Extra help on three Saturdays........................$116
> Miscellaneous drayage and cartage................... 32
> Rubbish removal..................................... 26
> Taxi fares to bank—daily deposits................... 19
> Advertising at local charity ball..................... 10
> Night watchman service............................   8
> Postage...   4
>   Total....................................$215

a) What records must be maintained in the store in connection with this fund?
b) By what entry was the fund originally set up on the books by the area office?
c) What entry is made by the area office bookkeeper when the vouchers are received from the Arlington store manager?

27. The cashier of the Willoughby Company has been custodian of a small petty cash fund ever since the company was first organized. This arrangement proved adequate for some time, but shortly after the company opened its new uptown branch office it became apparent that something would have to be done to cover small cash expenditures at the branch more conveniently.

Accordingly, a new petty cash fund was established and placed in the custody of the receptionist at the uptown branch. She was directed to prepare receipts in duplicate for each payment made. Any cash received at the branch was to be similarly receipted, but was to be remitted directly to the main office. No such funds were to be used for direct replenishment of the branch petty cash fund.

Prepare journal entries to record any of the following events that should be entered in the main office books (if no entry is required, write "no entry"):

(1) Fund established by check payable to receptionist, $100.

(2) Delivery charge on advertising materials, paid from fund, $3.50.

(3) Branch manager reimbursed from fund for theater tickets purchased for entertainment of customer, $17.60.

(4) Cash received from a customer for C.O.D. shipment, $43.12; cash collected by branch and forwarded to head office.

(5) Branch janitor reimbursed from fund for cost of a new broom, $2.50.

(6) Dry cleaner paid from fund for cleaning curtains in branch office, $33.50.

(7) Receipts for above expenditures delivered by branch receptionist to head office; check issued to replenish fund.

(8) Customer paid from fund, refund for returned merchandise, $27.50.

(9) Branch manager's request for a larger fund is granted and a check payable to the receptionist is issued, $50.

(10) A retiring branch salesman returns to branch receptionist the unused portion of his expense advance, $47.65, plus travel expense statements totaling $102.35 covering the balance of the amount advanced to him; receptionist forwards cash and receipts to main office.

(11) Postage stamps purchased from fund at branch, $30.

(12) Fund replenished.

28. The Antrax Corporation is a retailer of electrical appliances and parts. It maintains a cashbook (for cash receipts and disbursements), a voucher register, a payroll register, and a general journal. A voucher system similar to the one described in this chapter is in force.

a) Which of the following events would give rise to an entry in the voucher register? What internal evidence would you have for each event (e.g., invoice, purchase order, etc.)?

Sept. 1 Ordered and received television sets from TV Wholesalers, Inc....... $2,500
      1 Received notice from Begg Realty to pay September store rental....... 250
      2 T. Buran submitted travel expense statement for August............ 150
      2 Ordered television tubes from ABC Electronics................... 300
      6 Received invoice and shipment of refrigerators from Home
          Appliances, Inc.. 1,000
      6 Received monthly telephone bill from Central Telephone and
          and Telegraph Company.................................. 115
      8 Received and paid cash for stationery from Pacific Stationers........ 100
      9 Received invoice for washing machines from Williams Company;
          machines have not yet arrived............................... 1,500
     12 Ordered radio tubes from Electric Parts, Inc.................... 175
     12 Received invoice covering shipment of television antennas from Jones
          Radio Supply, Inc.; shipment received in good condition........... 350
     14 Received statement from Billett Oil Company, gas and oil for de-
          livery truck.. 50
     15 Ordered and received carbon paper and typewriter ribbons from Argus
          Office Supplies.. 60
     16 Received invoice from ABC Electronics, covering order of September 2   300
     16 Received invoice from Peters Company covering delivery today of
          typewriter to be used in office............................... 160
     19 Received monthly electricity bill from Union Edison.............. 140
     21 Received bill for advertising space, Morning News............... 200
     23 Received shipment from ABC Electronics, invoice of September 16.... 300
     28 Purchased on account radio parts from Jones Radio Supply; shipment
          received in good condition................................. 220
     30 Paid salesmen's salaries for September......................... 1,100

b) Set up a voucher register for the Antrax Corporation and record the
entries indicated in (*a*) above. Place a check mark opposite each figure
to be posted to the general ledger. You should have the following
columns:

Date
Vendor
Voucher Number
Credit: Vouchers Payable
Debits: Appliances Inventory
         Parts Inventory
         Office Supplies Expense
         Other Debits (two columns: Account Title and Amount)

29. The Halsey Typewriter Company sells and services typewriters.
Typewriter sales are on terms of net 30 days. Service is done on contract
or on order. Customers are billed monthly for contract services; all other
service is on a cash basis.

The company has two salesmen, one clerk-bookkeeper-typist, and four
repair men. Payroll deductions are made for F.I.C.A. taxes, federal income
taxes, state income taxes, Blue Cross premiums, and pension contributions.

The company makes frequent purchases of typewriters and of repair
supplies. These purchases are recorded in the cash disbursements journal

at the time of payment. No recording is made at the time the invoices or goods are received.

The company maintains a perpetual inventory of its typewriters. The cost of each typewriter in stock is recorded on a stock card and is transferred to the cost of goods sold at the time of shipment to the customer. No other inventory accounts are maintained.

Indicate what column headings you think would be necessary for:

a) The sales journal.
b) The payroll register.
c) The cash disbursements journal.
d) The cash receipts journal.

*30. The principal accounting records of the Mercantile Company consist of a general ledger, a customers' ledger, and the following books of original entry: cash receipts book (CR), cash disbursements book (CD), voucher register (VR), sales journal (S), and general journal (J).

Record in two-column journal form the transactions described below as they would appear in the special journals, and for each entry, indicate the journal in which it would be made. (These transactions all occurred during December.)

Example:
Transaction: Cash purchase of merchandise, $500.
Entries:

VR	Merchandise Inventory	500	
	Vouchers Payable		500
CD	Vouchers Payable	500	
	Cash		500

Transactions:

(1) Sale on account to John Jones, Inc., $1,000. A cash discount of 2 percent is offered for payment within 10 days.
(2) Purchase of new delivery truck from the Speedy Motor Company for $2,700. Terms: net amount due in 30 days. Estimated life of the truck is 1½ years; estimated scrap value, $900.
(3) Cash sale to the Rainbow Corporation, $750.
(4) Payment received within discount period from John Jones, Inc., for purchase of transaction (1).
(5) Payment of $180 made to the *Texas Bugle* for a series of nine advertisements in successive Sunday editions starting December 2 and continuing to January 27. No previous recording has been made relative to this transaction.
(6) One month's depreciation on delivery truck purchased in transaction (2) is recorded.

(7) Salesmen and office employees are paid weekly. Last payment was made on Saturday, December 29, for the week ending that date. Employees work a full six-day week. Weekly salaries total $1,500 for salesmen and $1,200 for office personnel. Adjustments for wages and salaries are made prior to closing the books for the year. (Ignore withholdings, etc.)

31. Early in June, Morris Slade entered the retail coal business under the name of the Slade Coal Company. The principal accounting records of the company consist of a general ledger, a customers' ledger, and the following books of original entry: cash receipts book (CR), cash disbursements book (CD), voucher register (VR), sales journal (S), and general journal (J).

Record in two-column journal form the transactions described below as they would appear in the specialized journals, and for each entry indicate the specialized journal in which it would be made. (See Question 30 above for sample entry.)

Date	Transaction Number	Transaction	Amount
June 10	1	Mr. Slade invested cash......................	$3,500
	2	Rent was paid for June......................	50
12	3	Coal was bought on account from the Atlantic Coal Company...........................	300
	4	Office furniture was purchased for cash..........	250
13	5	Sold coal on account to M. Musgrave...........	45
14	6	Bought coal on account from the Devon Coal Company.................................	375
15	7	Cash sales of coal............................	150
	8	Sales on account to:	
		K. Muran..............................	75
		L. Travers.............................	100
16	9	Sold additional coal on account to M. Musgrave..	65
17	10	Received cash in settlement of account of L. Travers..............................	100
17	11	Cash sales..................................	325
	12	Paid clerk's salary...........................	15
19	13	Received 60-day note from M. Musgrave in settlement of account..........................	110
20	14	Sold additional coal to K. Muran...............	80
22	15	Paid Atlantic Coal Company..................	300
23	16	Sales to A. Burton on account.................	90
24	17	Received payment from K. Muran on account....	60
	18	Paid clerk's salary...........................	15
26	19	Sale to S. Atkins on account...................	155
30	20	Paid office expenses..........................	30

32. The Fuller Linen and Uniform Company offers three types of services: (1) uniform rentals; (2) linen rentals; and (3) laundering of customer-owned linens and uniforms.

Rented uniforms and linen are delivered to and picked up from customers daily, semiweekly, or weekly, depending on the terms of the individual contract. Soiled linens and uniforms are returned to the company's plant, washed, inspected for damage, mended when necessary and feasible, and ironed. Extra linens and uniforms are kept on hand to meet peak demands. Customer-owned linens and uniforms are processed in the same way, except that no inventories are kept on hand.

Most customers are billed monthly, although some of the laundry business is on a cash basis. Customers are not billed all at one time but instead are divided into three separate groups for billing on the 1st, 11th, and 21st of each month. This serves to spread the clerical work load more evenly. When the bills are prepared, entries are made in the sales journal. Duplicate copies of the bills outstanding constitute the receivables ledger. Cash sales are recorded directly in the cash receipts journal, not in the sales journal.

The costs of operating the laundry are accumulated in a variety of accounts: Wages and Salaries, Materials and Supplies Used, and a number of less frequently used accounts. The costs of administering the company and supervising the field sales force (the route drivers) are accumulated in the Administrative Salaries account and several others.

The company leases a fleet of trucks from Truck Rentals, Inc. Truck operating costs are charged to a number of accounts: Truck Rentals; Drivers' Wages; Gas, Oil, and Lubrication Expense; and several other accounts which are affected less frequently. Truck rentals are paid quarterly.

The company makes frequent purchases of uniforms and linens, materials and supplies for the laundry, and gasoline and oil for the delivery trucks. These purchases are recorded in the voucher register on the basis of vendor invoices. Inventory accounts are maintained only for linens and uniforms and for materials and supplies on hand.

Payrolls are recorded in the payroll register, with credits to Net Wages Payable, F.I.C.A. Tax Payable, Federal Income Tax Withholdings Payable, and Blue Cross Premiums Payable. Payroll disbursements are then recorded in the cash disbursements journal.

Based on the foregoing information, design (a) a cash receipts journal, (b) a cash disbursements journal, (c) a sales journal, (d) a payroll journal, and (e) a voucher register. It is not necessary to draw up the actual forms; a listing of the column headings for each journal is sufficient.

33. The General Paper Supply Company commenced business on September 1, 19x4. The accountant for the company established the following chart of accounts. Not all of the accounts will be necessary to account for the transactions listed below, and it may be necessary to open new accounts. Assign an appropriate number to all new accounts.

Code	Account Title	Code	Account Title
100	Cash	420	Social Security Taxes Payable
110	Marketable Securities	425	Withholding Taxes Payable
120	Accounts Receivable	600	I. Fand, Owner
130	Allowance for Bad Debts	700	Sales Revenue
200	Inventory	720	Sales Returns and Allowances
220	Prepaid Expenses	730	Interest Income
300	Land	800	Cost of Goods Sold
310	Building	821	Sales Salaries
320	Allowance for Depreciation	830	Store Supplies Expense
330	Office Furniture and Fixtures	841	Office Salaries
340	Allowance for Depreciation	850	Telephone Expense
400	Accounts Payable	851	Heat, Light, and Power
410	Notes Payable		

Certain of the transactions for the month follow:

Sept. 1 Mr. Fand, the owner, invested in the business $140,000 in cash, as well as land and a building that he had acquired. The land cost $25,000 and the building cost $130,000. The building was subject to a $90,000, 5 percent, 20-year mortgage with interest payable quarterly.

1 Office furniture and fixtures costing $9,400 were acquired from the City Office Supply Company; terms, 1/10, n/30.

1 Warehouse equipment costing $18,700 was acquired from Steel Shelving Company; terms, 2/10, n/30.

2 Merchandise costing $19,000 was purchased from Wandthe and Company; terms, 2/10, n/30.

3 Warehouse supplies costing $650 and office supplies costing $400 were purchased for Merchants Supply Company; terms, n/30.

4 Sold merchandise to M. Rows for $3,750; terms, 2/10, n/30.

5 Sold merchandise for cash, $450.

6 Purchased merchandise from D. Nerwin for $8,750; terms, 1/10, n/30.

6 Acquired and paid $490 for a two-year insurance policy on the premises and its contents, effective September 1, 19x4.

8 Paid delivery charges on merchandise purchased from D. Nerwin, $80.

9 Paid $280 for a mailing advertising the company.

9 Returned merchandise costing $680 to Wandthe and Company.

9 Paid City Office Supply Company.

10 Gave M. Rows a credit of $250 on merchandise returned.

10 Paid Steel Shelving Company.

11 Paid the telephone company $30 for phone installation and $60 for an ad in the yellow pages to cover a six-month period.

Sept. 12 Sold merchandise to Bowle and Sons for $1,800; terms, 2/10, n/30.

12 Paid Wandthe and Company.

13 Sold merchandise to Krieger Company for $1,250; terms, 2/10, n/30.

15 Prepared semimonthly payrolls and paid amounts due to employees:

> Sales salaries $950
> Office salaries........................... 300
> Warehouse salaries....................... 600
>
> Deductions:
> Federal income tax...................... 150
> Social security taxes.................... 62

16 Paid Merchants Supply Company.

16 Paid D. Nerwin.

16 Received payment from M. Rows with the discount taken.

17 Received payment from Bowle and Sons.

18 Sold merchandise 2/10, n/30 to:

> M. Fried.............................$ 850
> W. Topper........................... 1,970

19 Obtained an allowance of $800 on the merchandise purchased from D. Nerwin.

20 Purchased $7,500 in merchandise from D. Nerwin.

22 Cash sales, $2,450.

22 Sold merchandise to M. Bales for $2,150.

23 Purchased a delivery truck for $2,800, paying $800 down and signing a 6 percent, 180-day note for the balance.

26 Received bill for $125 for delivery service from Delivery, Inc.

27 Paid electric bill for first 21 days of month, $36.

30 Prepared semimonthly payrolls and paid amounts due to employees:

> Sales salaries......................$950
> Office salaries..................... 300
> Warehouse salaries................ 600
> Administrative salaries............ 800
>
> Deductions:
> Federal income tax............... 250
> Social security taxes............. 78

a) Set up the following:

(1) Two-column general journal.

(2) Three-column sales journal.

(3) One-column purchases journal.

(4) Three-column cash receipts journal.

(5) Five-column cash disbursements journal.

(6) Accounts receivable ledger.

(7) Accounts payable ledger.

(8) General ledger.

b) Journalize the above transactions in the appropriate journals and post the figures to the ledgers.

c) Compute the September 30 balances in all ledger accounts.

d) What other entries would have to be made before financial statements for the month could be prepared and in which journal or journals might they be recorded? Explain.

34. The Crandall Hardware Company operates a large retail hardware store. Its special journals have the following column headings:

Sales journal: Date

Accounts Receivable, Dr.

Sales, Cr.

Voucher register: Date

Voucher Number

Vendor's Name

Accounts Payable, Cr.

Wages and Salaries Payable, Cr.

Payroll Taxes Payable, Cr.

Merchandise Inventories, Dr.

Wages and Salaries Expense, Dr.

Other Accounts, Dr. (Account Title, Amount)

Cash receipts journal: Date

Name of Payer

Cash, Dr.

Sales, Cr.

Accounts Receivable, Cr.

Other Accounts, Cr. (Account Title, Amount)

Cash disbursements journal: Date

Check Number

Voucher Number

Payee

Cash, Cr.

Purchases Discounts, Cr.

Accounts Payable, Dr.

Wages and Salaries Payable, Dr.

Other Accounts (Account Title, Amount)

On February 1, the accounts receivable and accounts payable subsidiary ledgers showed the following balances:

Accounts Receivable

Joseph Borman..........................$	86
Brown Manufacturing Company...........	348
Corson Playschool.....................	12
Jones Brothers........................	763
King's Service Station....................	44
Robert Mason..........................	15
Charles Nelson........................	50
Frank Peters..........................	70
Thompson Enterprises..................	188
Val-U Supermarket.....................	25
Total...........................$	1,601

Accounts Payable

Ajax Hardware Suppliers.................$	1,742
Edison Electric Company................	108
Franklin Paint Company.................	350
Grant Stationers.......................	45
Harkness Delivery Service..............	250
Peerless Electric Supply................	6,050
Roberts Manufacturing Company..........	2,200
Sunline Products, Inc....................	550
Trabert Distributors....................	4,810
Warren Sales Corporation...............	1,843
Total...........................$	17,948

Cash sales are journalized daily from cash register tapes. Credit sales are recorded weekly in the sales journal; postings to the accounts receivable ledger accounts are made directly from the individual sales slips.

Purchases are recorded at gross price. No cash disbursement is made without an approved voucher. Postings to the accounts payable ledger are made directly from the vouchers, which also provide the information necessary for completion of the voucher register.

All payments are made by check. A single voucher is prepared for each payroll, but a separate check is issued to each employee. A single entry is made in the voucher register to record each payroll, leaving all supporting detail on the payroll work sheets which are filed separately. Separate vouchers are prepared for payment of payroll taxes.

The first voucher issued in February was number 1076; the first check was number 3625.

The following transactions took place during the month of February:

Feb. 1 Purchased merchandise from Cranmore Distributors, $850; terms, 2/10, n/30.

1 Paid the following vouchers (starred items (*) are subject to 2 percent cash discount):

Voucher No.	Payee	Amount
1038	Edison Electric Company.........$	108
1029	Franklin Paint Company..........	350*
1030	Peerless Electric Supply..........	3,800*
1033	Roberts Manufacturing Company..	2,200*
1040	Trabert Distributors.............	4,810

Feb.   1 Cash sales, $1,000.
       2 Received payment of amounts due from Joseph Borman and
         Thompson Enterprises.
       2 Cash sales, $1,462.
       3 Purchased merchandise from Ajax Hardware Suppliers, $418;
         terms, n/30.
       3 Paid Ajax Hardware Suppliers, $763, Voucher No. 1018.
       3 Paid Sunline Products, account balance less 2 percent dis-
         count, Voucher No. 1041.
       3 Cash sales, $765.
       4 Received bill from State Telephone Company, $186.
       4 Purchased merchandise from Galbraith Manufacturing
         Company, $1,800; terms, 3/10, n/30.
       4 Cash sales, $1,440.
       5 Received payment of amounts due from Brown Manufactur-
         ing Company, Corson Playschool, Robert Mason, and Val-U
         Supermarket.
       5 Prepared and paid weekly payroll for eight employees: gross
         payroll, $825, less tax withholdings of $125.
         Purchased merchandise from Corbin Brush Company, $400;
         terms, 2/10, n/30.
         Paid amount due to Warren Sales Corporation, Voucher No.
         1045.
       5 Borrowed $5,000 on 30-day note from First National Bank.
       5 Cash sales, $1,341.
       6 Cash sales, $3,108.
       6 Credit sales for the week: Joseph Borman, $45; Brown
         Manufacturing Company, $80; Johnson Brothers, $165;
         Santos & Son, $75.
       8 Paid Ajax Hardware Suppliers, $979, Voucher No. 1046.
       8 Purchased merchandise from Trabert Distributors, $1,463;
         terms, n/30.
       8 Received payment of amount due from King's Service Station.
       8 Cash sales, $814.
       9 Paid Internal Revenue Service for January payroll taxes and
         withholdings, $1,260.
       9 Received $40 from Eben Tallman for month's rental of
         desk space in rear of store.
       9 Cash sales, $1,145.
      10 Purchased merchandise from Ajax Hardware Suppliers,
         $5,200; terms, n/30.
      10 Paid Peerless Electric Supply, $2,250 less 2 percent cash dis-
         count, Voucher No. 1070.
      10 Cash sales, $846.

Feb.   11 Paid Cranmore Distributors (purchase of February 1).
       11 Received payment from Frank Peters.
       11 Cash sales, $1,221.
       12 Weekly payroll, nine employees, $900, less tax withholdings of $135.
       12 Purchased office supplies from Grant Stationers, $362.
       12 Cash sales, $1,809.
       13 Paid Brown & Altman for preparing tax return, $1,650 (treat as current expense).
       13 Credit sales for the week: Brown Manufacturing Company, $450; King's Service Station, $10; Robert Mason, $25; Thompson Enterprises, $600; Helen's Beauty Shop, $85; Alvin and Bronson, $475.
       13 Cash sales, $1,560.
       15 Paid Corbin Brush Company (purchase of February 5).
       15 Cash sales, $540.
       16 Blizzard; store closed.
       17 Received bill from Brown & Son, plumbers, for repair of frozen water pipes, $32.
       17 Received $50 from Daniel Green, a clerk in the store, in repayment of loan.
       17 Cash sales, $1,111.
       18 Paid Grant Stationers and Harkness Delivery Service amounts due at beginning of month, Vouchers Nos. 1071 and 1072.
       18 Purchased merchandise from Warren Sales Corporation, $6,040; terms, n/30.
       18 Cash sales, $1,200.
       19 Weekly payroll, eight employees, $800, less tax withholdings of $120.
       19 Received bill from the Morning News for classified advertising, $80.
       19 Cash sales, $1,380.
       20 Cash sales, $1,995.
       22 Store closed, holiday.
       23 Paid State Telephone Company bill of February 4.
       23 Cash sales, $840.
       24 Increased amount in petty cash fund by drawing check on regular checking account, $50.
       24 Cash sales, $1,230.
       25 Purchased merchandise from Peerless Electric Supply, $3,700; terms, 2/10, n/30.
       25 Cash sales, $943.
       26 Weekly payroll, eight employees, $850, less tax withholdings of $130.

Feb.   26 Monthly payroll, five employees, $3,200, less tax withholdings of $500.
       26 Paid Morning News bill of February 19.
       26 Cash sales, $2,106.
       27 Received notification from attorneys that Jones Brothers have just filed bankruptcy papers; no assets are available to satisfy the claims of trade creditors (the company uses an Allowance for Bad Debts account).
       27 Credit sales for week: Brown Manufacturing Company, $126; Frank Peters, $15; Thompson Enterprises, $145.
       27 Cash sales, $1,656.

a) Prepare columnar accounting paper to serve as journals, using the column headings given at the beginning of this problem.
b) Prepare subsidiary accounts receivable and accounts payable ledgers, with a separate account for each vendor and each credit customer, and enter the opening balances (you may save space by putting three or four accounts on each page).
c) Enter each of the above transactions in the appropriate journal and make the necessary postings to the subsidiary accounts receivable and accounts payable ledgers.
d) List the amounts that would be posted directly to the general ledger from each of the special journals at the end of the month.

Chapter 8

INTRODUCTION TO
FINANCIAL STATEMENT ANALYSIS

THE KNOWLEDGE OF ACCOUNTING gained from study of the previous chapters is of interest to managers not as an end in itself but as a necessary step toward using financial statements for decision making. The effective analysis of financial statements for decision-making purposes requires an understanding of the accounting measurement rules to be discussed in Part II. The purpose of the present chapter is more limited: to introduce the basic concepts and methods of financial statement analysis and thereby provide a bridge between the preceding chapters and those which follow.

OBJECTIVES OF FINANCIAL STATEMENT ANALYSIS

Financial statement analysis embraces the methods by which management, investors, and others interested in the affairs of a corporation obtain information from financial statements as a basis for the decisions they make in regard to the corporation. Present and prospective stockholders need to decide whether to buy or sell the company's stock and whether to vote their shares for or against the company's management. Creditors are concerned with whether to extend or renew credit. The great variety of decisions that management makes in the administration of a company commonly requires detailed information on a part of the enterprise. However, those decisions which center on the fortunes of the company as a whole, such as dividend and financing decisions, require the analysis of financial statements. Furthermore, management is concerned with financial statements because investor attitudes toward a company are influenced in large measure by these statements.

It should be recognized at the outset that all the parties referred to above are interested in the future profits of a company. The interest

241

of stockholders is obvious, since the price of a company's stock is largely determined by the company's expected future profits. Creditors are also interested in future profits since the ability of a company to pay the interest and principal on its debts depends primarily on whether or not it is profitable. The dilemma, however, is that future profits are *uncertain*—nobody can know with certainty a firm's future profits. In particular, the analysis of financial statements which provide past profits and related data cannot reveal future profits.

Nonetheless, the analysis of financial statements can be of considerable value in arriving at judgments on the following questions of interest to investors: What is the best estimate of a company's future profits? What is the uncertainty or variability of future profits? What is the ability of a company to sustain losses for a period of time without becoming *insolvent* (unable to pay its debts) in the near future and in the long run?

ILLUSTRATIVE STATEMENTS

The financial statements of a hypothetical company, the Alpha Company, will be employed to illustrate the analysis of financial statements. The use of a real company's statements would raise questions of valuation and terminology for which no adequate foundation has yet been laid. Exhibit 8–1 presents the Alpha Company's balance sheets as of the end of 19x1 and 19x2. Exhibit 8–2 shows the company's income statement for 19x2.

One feature of these statements needs explanation. Although previous chapters have mentioned only one class of capital stock, the Alpha Company has two—preferred stock and common stock. In many respects they are similar. Both represent ownership equities in the business, and neither preferred nor common dividends are deducted in calculating net income. However, from the viewpoint of the common stockholder, preferred stock is more like debt than stock. Preferred stockholders have a *prior* and a *fixed* claim to dividends and to assets in liquidation. In Alpha's case the preferred dividend is limited to 5 percent of the so-called *par value* of the shares, or 50 cents a share.

The preferred shares are shown on the December 31, 19x2, balance sheet at their par value of $7,000, or $10 a share. The common stock also has a par value, in this case $10,000, or $5 a share. The amounts of assets received by the Alpha Company for shares of its stock, however, exceeded their par value by $12,600. By convention, this amount

Exhibit 8–1

ALPHA COMPANY
Balance Sheet
As of December 31, 19x1, and 19x2

ASSETS

	19x2	19x1
Current Assets:		
Cash....................................	$ 2,600	$ 4,300
Receivables.............................	19,800	17,100
Inventories.............................	35,900	28,700
Total Current Assets...................	$58,300	$50,100
Long-Term Assets:		
Buildings and equipment....................	$49,100	$42,900
Less: Accumulated depreciation.............	19,400	18,100
Net buildings and equipment.............	$29,700	$24,800
Land...................................	1,400	1,900
Total Assets.......................	$89,400	$76,800

EQUITIES

	19x2	19x1
Current Liabilities:		
Accounts payable..........................	$ 6,600	$ 4,800
Notes payable............................	15,500	6,200
Federal income taxes......................	2,100	2,200
Total Current Liabilities................	$24,200	$13,200
Long-term debt............................	11,700	17,400
Total Liabilities.....................	$35,900	$30,600
Shareholders' equity:		
5% preferred stock, 700 shares................	$ 7,000	$ 7,000
Common stock, par value $5 a share...........	10,000	9,000
Capital in excess of par value...............	12,600	9,900
Retained earnings.........................	23,900	20,300
Total Shareholders' Equity...............	$53,500	$46,200
Total Equities.....................	$89,400	$76,800

is usually shown separately from the par value. The dividend rate on common stock is not fixed in advance but decreases and increases with the ebb and flow of the company's fortunes. Further discussion of these points is to be found in Chapter 14.

MEASURES OF PROFITABILITY

An investor becomes and remains a stockholder in a company because he believes that dividends and capital gains (increase in the price of the stock) will compare favorably with the rate of return he can earn on alternative investments of comparable risk. The most important determinant of the future dividends and capital gains on a share is the corporation's future earnings, and the first source of data

Exhibit 8–2

ALPHA COMPANY

Income Statement

For the Year Ending December 31, 19x2

Sales revenue.............................		$105,200
Expenses:		
Cost of products sold (except depreciation).....$57,700		
Depreciation.............................	2,500	
Research and development..................	5,600	
Selling and administration..................	27,400	93,200
Income before interest and taxes...............		$ 12,000
Interest expense...........................		1,400
Income before taxes........................		$ 10,600
Income taxes.............................		4,850
Net income..............................		$ 5,750
Dividends on preferred stock................		350
Income available for common stockholders.......		$ 5,400
Dividends on common stock................		1,800
Income Retained and Reinvested in the Business...		$ 3,600

for use in forecasting future earnings is the corporation's past earnings record. Three ratios used widely as measures of the company's past earnings record are earnings per share of common stock, return on common equity, and return on total assets.

Earnings per Common Share

The most widely used measure of financial performance is net after-tax earnings per common share. Dividends to which holders of any preferred stock are entitled must be subtracted from net income to get earnings applicable to the common stock. For the Alpha Company the 19x2 calculation is:

$$\frac{\text{Income} - \text{Preferred Dividends}}{\text{No. of Common Shares}} = \frac{\$5,750 - \$350}{2,000} = \$2.70 \text{ per share .}$$

Earnings per share figures are used to compare one year's earnings with those of prior years. They are also combined with other figures, such as market price per share, to reveal relationships that the analyst wishes to examine.

The earnings component of the earnings per share figure must be examined carefully. The major questions of interpretation will be discussed in Part II, but one observation can be made now. Earnings per share reflects not only the firm's ordinary income but also income from capital gains and losses and from other nonoperating causes. For this reason, it is common practice to quote the earnings per share figure both before and after "extraordinary items" such as flood losses or gains realized on the sale of investments. Ideally, even the ordinary income component should be subdivided to provide a more adequate base for forecasting future earnings, and more and more information is being provided by United States corporations for this purpose. Income statements themselves, however, seldom show separately the results of portions of the company's operations.

Return on Common Equity

Income per share or in total is large or small in relation to the capital invested in order to obtain that income. The amounts invested by the common shareholders are measured in the financial statements by the *book value* of the shares, in this case the sum of the par value of the common stock, capital in excess of par value, and retained earnings. At the end of 19x2 this amounted to $46,500, or $23.25 a share.[1] Using these figures, the rate of return on common equity for the year was:

$$\frac{\text{Earnings per Share}}{\text{Book Value per Share}} = \frac{\$2.70}{\$23.25} = 11.6 \text{ percent .}$$

In reaching a judgment as to whether this represents good or bad performance, a number of questions must be answered. For example, how does this figure compare with the return of other firms in the industry and in industry in general? Is this company's rate of return holding steady, going up, or declining? How wide are the year-to-year fluctuations in rate of return?

It will be recalled that the investor's primary interest is in Alpha's earnings and rate of return in the future. From that point of view, the 19x2 figures might be biased. For example, the company's sales force may be engaged in heavy promotional activities on new products. Sales revenues from these activities will not be recognized until some time in the future, but the salesmen's salaries and travel costs show up among the current year's expenses. Similarly, if equipment replacement prices have been rising rapidly, current depreciation charges are likely to be much lower than they will be in the future when the present equipment is replaced. Considerations of this sort will be discussed in Part II.

---

[1] Earnings may be related to the investment at the beginning of the year, the investment at the end of the year, or an average of the two. We have used year-end investment because it is generally the most convenient.

Return on Assets and the Leverage Effect

A corporation's return on its common equity is a consequence of two factors: (1) its return on assets, and (2) the extent to which *leverage* is employed by the company. Return on assets is defined as the ratio of earnings before interest to total assets. Leverage is the percentage of total assets that is supplied by creditors and preferred shareholders.[2]

For example, if a company has $100 in assets on which it earns $11 a year before interest on its debts, its before-tax return on assets will be 11 percent. The reason for using earnings before interest and dividends as the numerator in this ratio is that the denominator represents all assets, not just those supplied by the shareholders. To be comparable, the earnings figure should show all earnings before distributions either to creditors (interest) or shareholders (dividends).

By using leverage, the company may be able to earn a rate of return on total assets that is less than that achieved by other companies but still achieve a higher return on common equity. Suppose, for example, that the company has obtained 40 percent of its capital ($40) by borrowing at an interest rate of 5 percent ($2 a year). The return on equity will be:

$$\frac{\text{Earnings} - \text{Interest}}{\text{Total Assets} - \text{Debt}} = \frac{\$11 - \$2}{\$100 - \$40} = 15 \text{ percent .}$$

This is *successful* leverage because the 5 percent borrowing rate of interest is less than the overall earnings rate on total capital (11 percent). The common shareholders, in other words, gain the full 11 percent on their own investment plus more than half (11 percent − 5 percent = 6 percent) of the return on the assets financed by creditors and preferred shareholders.

After-Tax Return on Assets

Return on equity is almost always an after-tax figure. To be fully comparable, therefore, the return on assets figure should also be stated on an after-tax basis. At first glance, this might seem to be simply a matter of subtracting the year's income taxes from earnings before interest and taxes. Unfortunately, this cannot be done because interest

---

[2] Leverage can also be defined as the ratio of *long-term* debt and preferred stock to the book value of the common stock, or as the ratio of *interest-bearing* debt and preferred stock to common equity. The definition above is appropriate when the comparison is to be made between return on total assets and return on the common shareholders' equity in those assets, as it is here.

is deductible in computing the income tax on the year's earnings. This amount of the gross earnings is shielded from the tax man's bite. The appropriate after-tax figure is the income that would have been reported if the same amount of capital had been provided by the owners alone. This will provide a true bench mark for use in evaluating the net effect of leverage.

Turning back to the Alpha Company's figures, earnings before interest and taxes was $12,000. Dividing this by the $89,400 total assets at the end of the year gives a before-tax rate of return of 13.4 percent. To convert this to an after-tax basis, the $12,000 should be multiplied by the actual tax rates that would be applied to this amount of income. The outsider seldom has access to this information, but he can compute the ratio of current taxes to income before taxes. In this case this ratio was:

$$\frac{\text{Income Taxes}}{\text{Income before Income Taxes}} = \frac{\$4,850}{\$10,600} = 45.7 \text{ percent} \,.$$

This ratio will be inaccurate if different amounts of income are taxed at different rates, but the analyst can usually assume that it is not too far from the truth.

Multiplying this rate (45.7 percent) by the Alpha Company's earnings before interest and taxes ($12,000) indicates that the tax bill would have been $5,484 in the absence of debt financing. The after-tax income would then have been $12,000 − $5,484 = $6,516. The after-tax return on assets, therefore, was:

$$\frac{\text{Adjusted After-Tax Income}}{\text{Total Assets}} = \frac{\$6,516}{\$89,400} = 7.3 \text{ percent} \,.$$

This is the return Alpha would have earned on the common equity if no debt or preferred financing had been employed. The use of debt and preferred stock, in other words, raised Alpha's return on its common equity from 7.3 percent to 11.6 percent. This is shown in the following table:

	Before Tax	After Tax
Return on assets..................	13.4%	7.3%
Return on common equity...........	22.0	11.6

Profit Margin Ratios

It is often useful to recognize that a corporation's return on assets is a consequence of its asset turnover and its profit margin on sales. The higher the ratio of sales to assets and the higher the ratio of profit to sales, the higher the rate of return on assets. These statements can be stated in the form of the following equation:

$$\text{Return on Assets} = \text{Asset Turnover} \times \text{Profit Margin}$$

$$= \frac{\text{Sales}}{\text{Assets}} \times \frac{\text{Income}}{\text{Sales}}$$

Profit margins, or *percentage-of-sales* ratios, are widely used in profitability analysis, mainly to identify trends or intercompany differences. Probably the most commonly computed profit margin ratio is the ratio of net income to gross revenues. For consistency, the profit figure should be the same one used for return on investment comparisons. In other words, if return on investment is computed on the basis of total assets, then the income figure should be before interest but after taxes, the tax figure being adjusted to eliminate the tax effect of interest deductibility, as described above. On this basis, Alpha's profit margin for 19x2 was:

$$\frac{\text{Adjusted Net Income}}{\text{Sales Revenue}} = \frac{\$6,516}{\$105,200} = 6.2 \text{ percent} .$$

Other profit margin ratios often used by analysts are the ratio of operating expenses to operating revenues (the *operating ratio*), the ratio of the cost of goods sold to gross sales, and the ratio of research and development expense to gross sales.

Asset Turnover Ratios

The main difficulty with any and all of these profit ratios is that differences in margin on sales do not indicate differences in economic efficiency. Businesses such as grocery chains and meat-packing companies operate with exceptionally narrow margins on sales and rely on a large sales volume to cover operating expenses and yield a satisfactory return on investment. Others, such as high-fashion women's specialty shops and yacht manufacturers, take the opposite tack and operate with low volume and high markups.

The solution to this problem is to supplement the profit margin ratios with asset turnover ratios. The principal turnover ratio is the ratio of total sales to total assets. Using year-end total assets as the base, this ratio for Alpha in 19x2 was:

$$\frac{\text{Sales Revenue}}{\text{Total Assets}} = \frac{\$105,200}{\$89,400} = 1.18 .$$

In other words, $1 of assets was required to support every $1.18 of sales.

Once again, the main use of this kind of ratio is to identify ways in which the company is departing from its own previous operating pattern or from that of its competitors. Turnover and percentage-of-sales ratios must be examined together, in parallel—the significance of a change in one can be appraised only if movements in the other are known.

SOURCES AND USES OF FUNDS

As we indicated earlier, the manner in which a company obtains the funds used to acquire its assets has a considerable influence on its profitability. We shall see shortly that it also influences financial position, the ability to sustain losses without becoming insolvent. The uses a company makes of its funds—that is, the types of assets it acquires—also have a considerable influence on profitability and financial position. Hence, analysis of the company's sources and uses of funds is an important ingredient of financial statement analysis.

Analysis of the Funds Structure

To the layman, funds and money are synonymous terms. This is so because funds are means of acquiring assets and paying bills, and it is clear that money is eminently usable for these purposes. However, let us go one step farther and ask what are a company's sources and uses of funds. It is clear that creditors and stockholders are sources of funds for a company, and that the various assets, including money in the bank, are uses of funds. Accordingly, the balance sheet as of some date is a statement of the firm's net sources and uses of funds up to that date, and the first kind of analysis of the sources and uses of funds is a study of the *structure* of the firm's assets and of its liabilities and owners' equities.

Equity Structure. The order in which the sources of funds are listed in the balance sheet corresponds to two important characteristics: the interest cost of obtaining the funds and the risk they bring with them. Current liabilities are an attractive source of funds because the interest cost of this capital is low. However, since they fall due in a relatively short period, the risk cost is high. They may fall due for payment just when the company finds itself temporarily short of cash. Long-term debt, in contrast, typically carries a higher interest rate but poses a smaller immediate threat of insolvency. Furthermore, the company can ordinarily pick a convenient time to refinance long-term debt before it falls due, thereby minimizing the likelihood that it will fall due during a period of losses and inability to raise funds.

Finally, funds obtained from shareholders through the sale of stock or retention of earnings carry no risk of insolvency. The company has no contractual obligations to make payments on specified dates, even to the preferred shareholders. In return for removing this risk from the corporation, the stockholders expect a higher yield on their investment than that earned by the company's creditors. This desired yield can and should be considered a cost of stockholder capital.

The Alpha Company increased its short-term debt ratio (current liabilities divided by total liabilities and ownership) from 17.2 percent at the end of 19x1 to 27.1 percent a year later. Other things being equal, this represents an increase in risk.

Debt/Equity Ratio. The most widely quoted equity structure ratio is the debt/equity ratio. In its most common form, it is the ratio of a company's long-term debt to the total of its long-term debt and owners' equity. For Alpha at the end of 19x2, this ratio was:

$$\frac{\text{Long-Term Debt}}{\text{Total Equities}} = \frac{\$11,700}{\$11,700 + \$7,000 + \$46,500} = 17.9 \text{ percent}.$$

This ratio is used as a measure of risk. Because only the near-term debt retirement and interest requirements constitute an immediate danger to the company's solvency, this ratio applies more to long-term than to short-term risks.

A great many factors enter into the determination of the risk associated with a given debt/equity ratio. The average level and volatility of the firm's earnings, the size of its liquid asset reserves, the rate of price inflation in the economy as a whole, and the debt's maturity structure all have their effect. Consequently, it is unwise to specify a figure that may be used as an evaluation standard without first examining the firm and its environment. Even more important, different companies can use different methods of asset measurement, even within the same industry, and the analyst must try to identify these differences before comparing debt/equity ratios of different companies. These differences are the subject of Part II.

Asset Structure. The way in which the firm's funds have been used is also significant. Once again, management has a balancing problem—to balance short-term, low-risk, low-yield uses against long-term, high-risk, high-yield uses of funds. While it is true that most of a company's earnings are the *joint* product of all of its operating investments as a group, an asset structure that is weighted heavily toward short-term uses of funds will ordinarily earn a lower return on total assets than a firm with a heavy commitment to fixed assets. Money in the bank enjoys little or no rate of return, but it is very liquid—that is, it can be taken out of the bank and put to another use at a moment's notice with no sacrifice in value. Plant and equipment, on the other hand, have very little liquidity. The funds invested in these assets are recovered only slowly, as the assets are used in operations. The sale of such assets in a short period of time to obtain liquid funds would typically take place at a substantial loss.

Ratios of cash to total assets, or of liquid assets to total assets can give some indication of asset structure. Both the absolute level of the asset structure ratios and their changes from period to period are significant in this respect. The Alpha Company had 34.8 percent of its assets in long-term assets at the end of 19x2, virtually unchanged from a year earlier. The analyst can compare this figure with those of comparable companies.

Funds Flow Analysis

Analysis of the balance sheet structure at a given point in time can tell a good deal about the company's management of its sources and uses of funds. Analysis of *changes* in structure may be even more revealing, however; and this is the domain of *funds flow analysis*. By examining the changes in balance sheet items between balance sheet dates, one may determine the source of the funds obtained and the ways in which these funds were used during this *limited time period*.

Funds flow analysis is of such importance that an entire chapter is devoted to it later in the book (Chapter 16). The basic idea can be seen, however, by examining the statement of balance sheet changes shown in Exhibit 8–3. This is simply a list of balance sheet changes, taken directly from Exhibit 8–1 by subtracting the figures in one column from those in the other. The rules by which these changes were organized in the statement given in Exhibit 8–3 are simplicity itself:

1. An increase in an asset is a *use* of funds.
2. A decrease in a liability or owners' equity account is a *use* of funds.
3. An increase in a liabilty or owners' equity account is a *source* of funds.
4. A decrease in an asset is a *source* of funds.

It is interesting to note that only 38 percent of Alpha's funds requirements were obtained from long-term sources (sale of stock, earnings retention, and sale of land), while 51 percent of the funds

Exhibit 8–3

ALPHA COMPANY

Statement of Sources and Uses of Funds
For the Year Ending December 31, 19x2

Sources of funds:

From decrease in cash	$ 1,700
From decrease in land	500
From increase in accounts payable	1,800
From increase in notes payable	9,300
From increase in common stock and capital in excess of par value	3,700
From increase in retained earnings	3,600
Total Sources of Funds	$20,600

Uses of funds:

To increase receivables	$ 2,700
To increase inventories	7,200
To increase building and equipment	4,900
To decrease income taxes payable	100
To decrease long-term debt	5,700
Total Uses of Funds	$20,600

were put to long-term uses (debt retirement and investment in plant and equipment).

Strictly speaking, Exhibit 8–3 is not a flow of funds statement. Instead, it is something simpler, often referred to as a "where got, where gone" statement. For example, land is shown as having produced a $500 funds inflow. In fact, the land may have been sold for more or less than this amount. If it had been sold for, say, $1,100, the $600 gain on the sale would have been included in the $3,600 net increase in retained earnings. If that is the case, the flow of funds from the sale of land is understated in Exhibit 8–3, while the net flow of funds from the year's operating earnings is overstated.

A more sophisticated and informative means of deriving funds flow statements will be taken up in Chapter 16. There we shall also make some observations on forecasting sources and uses of funds for one to five years in the future, a vital tool for management's use in planning an optimum financing and investing program. It should be noted, however, that funds flow analysis complements rather than substitutes for profitability analysis. It is designed to throw light on management's financing and investing activities before they have had a chance to affect earnings significantly.

MEASURES OF SHORT-TERM DEBT-PAYING ABILITY

Since future earnings are uncertain, a concern of management and investors alike is the company's ability to sustain losses without being forced to liquidate or undergo a financial reorganization—in other words, its ability to remain solvent. Management's main method of analysis designed to answer this question is its *cash budget,* summarizing the results of its operating and financial plans for the coming period. Outsiders, too, may attempt to prepare rough forecasts of the company's cash flows for the immediate future, but in general they lack the necessary information and must fall back upon analysis of the historical financial statements.

The funds flow statements discussed in the previous section are probably the most valuable single basis for judging short-term bill-paying ability, but other techniques are also available. The remainder of this chapter will be concerned with a number of ratios derived from financial statement information that are widely used for this purpose.

Coverage Ratios

One measure of a company's short-term vulnerability to fluctuations in earnings is the coverage ratio or *times-charges-earned ratio.* In its simplest form, the coverage ratio is the ratio of earnings before taxes and interest to annual interest charges. Although preferred dividend requirements cannot be an immediate cause of insolvency, they can be a source of financial embarrassment. For this reason, they are usually combined with the interest charge element in the coverage ratio formula. On this basis, the Alpha ratio for 19x2 was:

$$\frac{\text{Earnings before Interest and Taxes}}{\text{Interest} + \text{Preferred Dividends}} = \frac{\$12,000}{\$1,750} = 6.8 \; .$$

In other words, the company's earnings could shrink to one sixth of their 19x2 size and still be adequate to cover the interest and preferred dividend requirements.[3]

This ratio has one important advantage over all the ratios discussed previously—it is derived entirely from *flow* information. The funds for interest and dividend payments must come in the final analysis from the funds generated by the firm's operations. Most balance sheet resources are ordinarily required to support day-to-day operations and can be used to meet the company's pressing obligations only at a sacrifice of business efficiency.

---

[3] Preferred dividends are not deductible from revenues in computing taxable income. Therefore, the amount entered in the coverage ratio formula ought to be the *pre-tax* amounts necessary to provide for preferred dividends. This added refinement can be left for more advanced texts on the grounds that it will be important only if the coverage ratio is very low.

This argument actually can be carried a good deal farther. A better coverage ratio would be the ratio of cash generated by operations, before deducting fixed charges, to the total of *all* of the company's fixed cash obligations during the same period—property rentals and scheduled debt repayments as well as interest and dividends. An argument can even be made for including management salaries and other cash operating expenses that would not shrink automatically in the face of a massive reduction in company sales.

These questions will be examined further in Chapter 16, dealing with funds statement preparation, and Chapter 19, which includes a brief discussion of a technique known as *break-even analysis*. In any case, however, the coverage ratio must be examined in conjunction with some measure of volatility—that is, the amplitude of fluctuations in annual earnings or operating cash flows before taxes and interest. Presumably, the higher the earnings volatility, the higher should be the coverage ratio.

Current Ratio

The most popular indicator of near-term liquidity is the current ratio, the ratio of current assets to current liabilities. Looking back at Exhibit 8–2 we see that the Alpha Corporation current ratio at the end of 19x2 was:

$$\frac{\text{Current Assets}}{\text{Current Liabilities}} = \frac{\$58,300}{\$24,200} = 2.41 \ .$$

At one time it was widely believed that a manufacturing company should have a current ratio of at least 2 to 1 to protect the firm's short-term creditors in the event of insolvency. It was reasoned that if the firm were to go out of business, it might not be possible to sell off the current assets at their book value, but a current ratio of 2 to 1 would leave enough money to pay off the short-term creditors. It is now recognized that when a firm starts down the road toward bankruptcy, the current ratio falls below 2 to 1 regardless of what it was originally, and by the time creditors can take possession of the assets for liquidation, what remains has very little market value.

The best guarantee of a short-term loan or trade credit is a short-term excess of operating receipts over operating outlays. However, when a short-term downturn in business conditions takes place, a good current ratio provides a secondary line of defense insofar as current assets can be reduced to meet obligations due to operating losses and a shrinkage of short-term credit. It is likely that a firm with a low current ratio cannot obtain funds by reducing inventory or customer credit without severely impairing its ability to obtain and fill customer orders.

Whether Alpha's current ratio of 2.41 represents an adequate margin of safety depends on the variability of cash flows, operating liquidity of the current assets—that is, the ability of the company to reduce these assets without impairing operating performance—and the extent to which the firm's short-term debt is likely to be presented for payment on short notice. Information on questions such as these may be obtained by analysis of various operating ratios and by other means such as the determination of how inventory is valued on the company's books. Finally, it should be noted that the trend and variability over time is as important for this and other ratios as the most recent figure.

Quick Ratio

One defect of the current ratio is that it conveys no information on the *composition* of the current assets. Clearly, a dollar of cash or even of accounts receivable is more readily made available to meet obligations than a dollar of most kinds of inventory. A measure designed to overcome this defect is the *acid test* or quick ratio. This is the ratio of cash, short-term marketable securities, and receivables to current liabilities. This ratio for Alpha was as follows at the end of 19x2:

$$\frac{\text{Quick Assets}}{\text{Current Liabilities}} = \frac{\$22,400}{\$24,200} = 0.93 \ .$$

This represented a sharp decline from the previous year's value of $21,400 ÷ $13,200 = 1.62, reflecting the large increase in inventory and notes payable. This shift might be regarded as a cause for some concern.

It should be recognized that high current and quick ratios are desirable in that they provide high liquidity and a strong short-term financial position. They are undesirable, however, insofar as they reflect unprofitable uses of funds and reduced utilization of low-cost, short-term credit.

Receivables Turnover

One final set of ratios remains to be considered here: receivables and inventory turnover ratios. The accounts receivable turnover ratio is the ratio of annual sales to accounts receivable. Based on 19x2 year-end receivables balances, this ratio for Alpha was:

$$\frac{\text{Sales Revenues}}{\text{Receivables}} = \frac{\$105,200}{\$19,800} = 5.3 \ .$$

What this says is that the receivables "turned over" 5.3 times during the year.

A related and perhaps more easily understood statistic is the *collection period*—the number of days' sales in accounts receivable. On the basis of a 360-day year, $105,200 ÷ 360 = $291.60 is the average daily sales. Dividing the accounts receivable balance by this figure produces $19,800 ÷ $291.60 = 68, the number of days' sales in accounts receivable.

These ratios are regarded as indicators of (1) the liquidity of the receivables, (2) the quality of the receivables, and (3) management's credit-granting policies. A low turnover ratio—that is, a long collection period—means that in the normal course of business receivables can be turned into cash only slowly. A collection period that is long relative to the normal credit period in the industry indicates either that the firm is using a liberal credit policy to stimulate sales or that the receivables are of low quality, with many customers failing to pay their bills on time. If Alpha's terms of sale call for payment within 30 days, for example, its collection period would be regarded as quite long.

These two ratios do not give the same results that an aging of receivables would give, of course. If this company has selected its fiscal year in such a way that its receivables are considerably lower at year-end than at other times during the year, the average age of the receivables outstanding may be considerably greater than the collection period. Furthermore, if many sales are cash sales, the actual collection period on credit sales may be considerably greater than the calculation indicates. For these reasons, the emphasis again must be less on the absolute size of the ratio than on trends and intercompany comparisons.

A high turnover of receivables may not always be the most efficient policy for a firm. It may be the consequence of a tight credit policy and a vigorous collection program that unduly restricts the volume of sales. A loosening of credit standards will often increase receivables by a larger percentage than the increase in sales, but the increase in profit may be considerably higher than the company's desired rate of return on the added investment.

Inventory Turnover

Another ratio similar in purpose to the receivables turnover ratio is the inventory turnover ratio. Inventory and revenue figures are not precisely comparable: the former are on a cost basis, while the latter represent sale prices. The number of days' inventory on hand thus can be computed only if the cost of goods sold is known, in which case the ratio is cost of goods sold per day, divided by inventory. Much the same purpose can be served by sales/inventory ratios, however, and inventory turnover is often computed on this basis. Based on the year-end inventory, the 19x2 inventory turnover ratio for Alpha was:

$$\frac{\text{Sales Revenues}}{\text{Inventories}} = \frac{\$105,200}{\$35,900} = 2.9 .$$

A low ratio is indicative of slow-moving inventory, and a sign of potential danger is a ratio that is rising or higher than competitors' or both. On the other hand, a company may deliberately carry large inventories to reduce the loss of sales caused by inadequate stocks and to avail itself of economies of large purchase or production lots. Nevertheless, a rising ratio is presumptive evidence of a decline in liquidity, high carrying costs, and potential future losses from obsolescence.

Inventory turnover ratios are subject to the same defects as receivables turnover ratios. They say little about the quality of the year-end inventory mix, nor do they reflect seasonal variations in sales and inventories. Probably even more important, however, and the effects on these ratios of the inventory measurement rules used by the company. Differences among companies in this respect make the inventory ratios virtually useless for intercompany comparisons without supplementary information from the companies concerned. These measurement problems are the subject of the chapters that follow, particularly Chapter 11.

SUMMARY

Outside analysts use a company's financial statements in predicting the company's future earnings (profitability analysis) or its short-term debt-paying ability (solvency analysis).

The main index of past earnings performance is return on investment. This may be computed as a return on assets or as a return on the common stockholders' equity. The difference between these two rates is the effect of leverage, the use of capital sources other than the common shareholders. The return on investment figures can also be broken down into asset turnover and profit margin components for a more detailed analysis of trends and intercompany comparisons.

Solvency analysis focuses on comparisons of estimated cash inflows and outflows in the near future. The basic tool of this kind of analysis is the flow of funds statement. This is supplemented by examination of the relationships among various balance sheet groupings.

The validity of both kinds of analysis is conditioned not only by the comparability of past and future but also by the quality of the underlying data. The measurement rules used in preparing company financial statements have great effects on the ratios discussed in this chapter, and these effects will be the focus of the chapters that follow.

QUESTIONS AND PROBLEMS

1. An executive has to make a recommendation on the amount of the dividend to be declared by his company. How can financial statement analysis assist him?

2. Financial statements are concerned with the past. An individual who is interested in a company wants to forecast, among other things, the future profits of that company. How can financial statement analysis be useful to him?

3. Indicate how you would calculate earnings per common share when an issue of preferred stock is outstanding.

4. How does the earnings per common share differ from the return on common equity?

5. What is leverage? What effect does it have on return on common equity?

6. Company X's profit margin (net income as a percent of sales) is 2 percent, but its return on assets is 14 percent. Explain how this can be true.

7. A company's return on total assets is 4 percent. Its return on common equity is 3 percent. What do these figures indicate?

8. Company A has obtained half of its long-term capital from borrowing; Company B has no long-term debt. How would you reflect these differences in your analysis of the relative profitability of these two companies?

9. How can the financial statements of two companies of different sizes be transformed to permit a test of the hypothesis that the two companies are similar except for size?

10. A company reported net income of $10,000 for 19x1, but its cash balance at the end cf 19x1 was $5,000 less than it had been at the beginning of the year. How could this have happened?

11. A company's times-charges-earned ratio declined from 3.2 to 1.2. What conclusions could be drawn from this change?

12. A current ratio of 3.0 and a quick ratio of 1.0 give some information about the structure of the balance sheet. What information do they give?

13. What is meant by the structure of a firm's assets and equities? What purpose is analysis of this structure expected to achieve?

14. What purposes are served by a summary of the annual *changes* in the balances of balance sheet accounts? Can these purposes be served equally well by income statements?

15. Eastman Kodak Company at December 25, 1966, reported cash and marketable securities of $480,889,000 and total assets of $2,052,146,000. At December 31, 1967, it reported these amounts as $441,510,000 and $2,233,164,000. What percent of total assets did Eastman Kodak hold in the form of cash and marketable securities at each of these dates? Can you conclude from these data that the company held too little or too much cash and marketable securities at those dates? Explain.

16. A company has just sold one of its buildings at a price equal to its book value and has used the proceeds from the sale to retire long-term bonds payable. The price paid to retire the bonds was equal to the amount at which they were shown on the balance sheet. Upon selling the building, the company entered into a 20-year lease with the new owner. What effects did this series of transactions have on the following ratios:

a) Debt/equity ratio?
b) Current ratio?
c) Asset turnover ratio?

17. The Howe Company has a return on common equity of 9 percent, based on income after taxes of $4,500. Its debt/equity ratio is 50 percent, and its interest expense is $1,000. If the tax rate is 50 percent, what is the after-tax return on assets?

18. The Casey Company has a current ratio of 3.0, a quick ratio of 1.5, a receivables turnover of 6.1, and an inventory turnover of 4.5. How will each of the transactions listed below affect these ratios?

a) Purchase of merchandise for cash.
b) Purchase of merchandise on credit.
c) Sale of a marketable security at cost (i.e., at zero profit or loss).
d) Sale of merchandise for cash.

19. The 19x2 financial statements of the Axel Corporation included the following data:

Net sales..	$3,000,000
Income before interest and taxes......................	380,000
Interest expense...................................	30,000
Income tax expense................................	170,000
Net income after taxes.............................	180,000
Total assets, beginning of year.......................	1,620,000
Total assets, end of year............................	1,980,000
Common stockholders' equity, beginning of year.	1,080,000
Common stockholders' equity, end of year..............	1,320,000

a) Compute the after-tax return on common equity, the after-tax return on assets, and the before-tax profit margin on sales, using beginning-of-year balances for assets and equities.

b) Repeat these calculations, using an average of beginning-of-year and end-of-year balances for assets and equities.

c) Comment on the differences between your answers to (*a*) and (*b*). Would you have any reason for preferring one of these sets of figures over the other? Would end-of-year balance sheet figures be any better? Explain.

*20. The Barnes Company had net income after taxes of $106.0 million for 19x4, $111.3 million for 19x5, and $109.1 million for 19x6. Preferred dividends were $10.0 million in each year. The shareholders' equity section of the company's balance sheets during this period showed the following:

	12/31/x3	12/31/x4	12/31/x5	12/31/x6
Preferred stock......	$ 170,000,000	$ 170,000,000	$ 170,000,000	$ 170,000,000
Common stock, $1 par.	50,000,000	50,000,000	52,000,000	52,000,000
Additional paid-in capital............	200,000,000	200,000,000	238,000,000	238,000,000
Retained earnings.....	580,000,000	626,000,000	677,300,000	724,400,000
Total..........	$1,000,000,000	$1,046,000,000	$1,137,300,000	$1,184,400,000

a) Compute the earnings per common share in 19x4, in 19x5, and 19x6, basing your calculations on the number of shares outstanding at the end of the year.

b) Compute the book value per common share at each balance sheet date.

c) Compute the return on common equity for 19x4, for 19x5, and for 19x6. In each case, base your calculations on average common equity for the year.

*21. Below are the comparative balance sheets of the George Corporation as of December 31, 19x1, and 19x2:

---

* Solutions to problems marked with an asterisk (*) are found in Appendix B.

	19x1	19x2
ASSETS		
Current assets	$16,000	$25,000
Buildings and equipment	36,000	44,500
Accumulated depreciation	(5,000)	(8,500)
Land	3,000	5,000
Total	$50,000	$66,000
LIABILITIES AND OWNERS' EQUITY		
Current liabilities	$ 9,000	$ 6,000
Long-term debt	10,000	20,000
Capital stock	12,000	17,000
Retained earnings	19,000	23,000
Total	$50,000	$66,000

Depreciation for the year was $3,500.

Prepare a statement of balance sheet changes that will describe most clearly the company's sources and uses of funds for 19x2.

22. The Davis Company's financial statements for June, 19x2, are provided below:

BALANCE SHEETS

ASSETS	June 1	July 1	EQUITIES	June 1	July 1
Cash	$ 2,000	$ 7,000	Accounts payable	$ 3,000	$ 3,000
Accounts receivable	3,000	3,000	Capital stock	10,000	14,000
Inventory	5,000	8,000	Retained earnings	3,000	5,000
Plant and equipment (net)	6,000	4,000			
Total	$16,000	$22,000	Total	$16,000	$22,000

INCOME STATEMENT

For June, 19x2

Sales	$12,000
Cost of goods sold	$ 7,000
Depreciation expense	2,000
Other expenses	1,000
Net Income	$ 2,000

a) Prepare a statement of balance sheet changes for the month that will show, insofar as possible, (1) how much cash was collected during the month and where it came from; and (2) how much cash was spent during the month and for what purposes.

b) What was the net effect of the company's sales to its customers on its cash balance? How does this differ from net income?

23. *Fortune* magazine's list of the largest merchandising firms in the United States in 1967 showed the following data for Lucky Stores, Acme Markets, and Great Atlantic & Pacific Tea Company (A & P):

	Lucky	Acme	A & P
Rank (by sales) among merchandising firms....	26	11	2
Sales..................	$627,349,000	$1,293,765,000	$5,458,824,000
Assets................	120,363,000	274,603,000	884,001,000
Net income............	11,477,000	8,327,000	55,897,000
Shareholders' equity.....	43,554,000	163,317,000	627,366,000

a) Compute the profit margin as a percentage of sales, asset turnover, return on assets, return on equity, and debt/asset ratio for each of these three companies.

b) For return on common equity, Lucky ranked first, Acme ranked 46th, and A & P ranked 39th among the merchandising companies on Fortune's list. Basing your analysis on the financial statement data alone, prepare an explanation of the difference between the relative sales ranking and the relative return on equity ranking.

24. The manager of the Delta Company has supplied the following statistics for the Delta and Gamma Companies:

	Delta	Gamma
Sales, 19x3............................	$7,000,000	$5,000,000
Accounts receivable, December 31, 19x3....	800,000	750,000

The manager wants the answers to the questions stated below. You are expected to answer the questions if possible. If the information provided is not adequate for a satisfactory answer, you are to state the additional information you need and explain how you would use this information to answer the questions.

a) Which company has more money tied up in accounts receivable?
b) Which company has the more liquid receivables?
c) By how much will Delta's accounts receivable increase during 19x4?
d) Which company is managing its accounts receivable more efficiently?

25. Below are the income statements and balance sheets of two companies. On the basis of the available information, which do you consider to be (1) more liquid? (2) more secure? (3) more profitable? Explain your conclusions.

INCOME STATEMENT

FOR THE YEAR 19x1

	Franklin Company	Morgan Company
Sales.......................................	$8,000,000	$7,000,000
Cost of goods sold..........................	$6,000,000	$4,700,000
Selling, general, and administrative expenses........	1,200,000	1,900,000
Interest on debt............................		70,000
Income before taxes.........................	$ 800,000	$ 330,000
Income taxes...............................	390,000	160,000
Net Income.................................	$ 410,000	$ 170,000
Dividends Declared..........................	$ 100,000	$ 70,000

BALANCE SHEET

As of December 31, 19x1

ASSETS	Franklin Company	Morgan Company
Cash	$ 300,000	$ 300,000
Accounts receivable	800,000	650,000
Inventory	1,300,000	850,000
Net plant and equipment	2,100,000	1,500,000
Total	$4,500,000	$3,300,000

EQUITIES		
Accounts payable	$ 710,000	$ 400,000
Taxes payable	390,000	160,000
Long-term debt	....	1,400,000
Capital stock	2,200,000	800,000
Retained earnings	1,200,000	540,000
Total	$4,500,000	$3,300,000

26. The Alpha Company (see Exhibits 8–1 and 8–2 in the chapter) reported the following financial statements at the end of 19x3:

ALPHA COMPANY

BALANCE SHEET

As of December 31, 19x3

ASSETS

Current Assets:

Cash	$ 3,000
Receivables	20,000
Inventories	42,000
Total Current Assets	$65,000

Long-Term Assets:

Buildings and equipment	$54,000
Less: Accumulated depreciation	22,100
Net buildings and equipment	$31,900
Land	1,400
Total Assets	$98,300

LIABILITIES AND STOCKHOLDERS' EQUITY

Current Liabilities:

Accounts payable	$ 8,400
Notes payable	17,100
Federal income taxes payable	2,400
Total Current Liabilities	$27,900
Long-term debt	13,600
Total Liabilities	$41,500

Stockholders' equity:

5% preferred stock, 700 shares	7,000
Common stock, 2,000 shares	10,000
Capital in excess of par value	12,600
Retained earnings	27,200
Total Liabilities and Stockholders' Equity	$98,300

ALPHA COMPANY

INCOME STATEMENT

FOR THE YEAR ENDING DECEMBER 31, 19x3

Sales revenue.........................		$106,700
Expenses:		
Cost of products sold (except depreciation).....	$58,700	
Depreciation........................	2,700	
Research and development................	5,800	
Selling and administration..............	27,900	95,100
Income before interest and taxes..............		$ 11,600
Interest expense........................		1,500
Income before taxes.....................		$ 10,100
Income taxes..........................		4,650
Net income...........................		$ 5,450
Dividends on preferred stock..............		350
Income available for common stockholders........		$ 5,100
Dividends on common stock................		1,800
Income Retained and Reinvested in the Business...		$ 3,300

Did Alpha Company earn adequate profits in 19x3? (Hint: Decide which ratios are relevant to the question, then make the needed calculations.) Can Alpha meet its obligations promptly? Is an investment in Alpha safe?

27. The following data were taken from the 19x1 financial statements of two companies in the same industry:

	Company A	Company B
Cash............................	$ 8,000	$ 24,000
Accounts receivable................	17,000	19,200
Inventories......................	27,200	29,568
Prepaid expenses..................	2,000	4,000
Property and equipment.............	100,000	220,000
Accumulated depreciation...........	(62,400)	(57,152)
Total.......................	$ 91,800	$239,616
Current liabilities.................	$ 20,000	$ 40,000
Long-term debt—6%..............	40,000	......
Long-term debt—5%..............	.....	20,000
Stockholders' equity................	31,800	179,616
Total.......................	$ 91,800	$239,616
Sales............................	$204,000	$460,800
Cost of goods sold.................	(163,200)	(354,816)
Other expenses....................	(22,440)	(46,080)
Interest.........................	(2,400)	(1,000)
Income taxes......................	(3,990)	(14,724)
Net Income.......................	$ 11,970	$ 44,180

a) All sales are on account and there are only minor seasonal variations in sales. Compare the current debt-paying ability of the two firms. To what extent can the inventories be looked upon as a means of paying debts due in 30 days? In 60 days?

b) Compare the profitability of the two firms. What factors account for the difference? (The income tax rate is 25 percent.)

c) Compare the long-term debt-paying ability of the two firms.

28. Below are the comparative balance sheets and income statements of North Printing Company for the years 19x0 to 19x2:

COMPARATIVE BALANCE SHEETS

For the Years 19x0–x2

ASSETS	December 31, 19x0	December 31, 19x1	December 31, 19x2
Current Assets:			
Cash..................................	$ 4,000	$ 5,000	$ 2,000
Receivables, net.....................	20,000	15,000	17,000
Inventories..........................	18,000	25,000	30,000
Total Current Assets...............	$42,000	$45,000	$49,000
Net property........................	13,000	18,000	18,000
Other assets........................	1,000	2,000	3,000
Total Assets.....................	$56,000	$65,000	$70,000

LIABILITIES AND SHAREHOLDERS' EQUITY			
Current Liabilities:			
Accounts payable......................	$ 5,000	$ 6,000	$ 7,000
Notes payable (5%)....................	3,000	9,000	11,000
Other current liabilities.............	2,000	1,000	1,500
Total Current Liabilities...........	$10,000	$16,000	$19,500
Long-term debt (6%)..................	8,000	10,000	9,000
Shareholders' equity.................	38,000	39,000	41,500
Total Liabilities and Shareholders' Equity	$56,000	$65,000	$70,000

COMPARATIVE INCOME STATEMENTS

For the Years 19x0–x2

	19x0		19x1		19x2	
Sales.....................		$100,000		$105,000		$120,000
Materials..............	$35,000		$37,000		$43,000	
Labor.................	28,000		30,000		35,000	
Heat, light and power....	3,700		4,000		4,500	
Depreciation (10%).....	1,300	68,000	1,500	72,500	1,500	84,000
Gross profit..............		$ 32,000		$ 32,500		$ 36,000
Selling expenses.........$	$17,000		$17,500		$18,000	
General and administrative expenses.........	10,500	$ 27,500	11,000	28,500	12,000	30,000
Operating profit..........		4,500		4,000		6,000
Less interest expense....		700		900		1,000
Net profit before taxes.....		$ 3,800		$ 3,100		$ 5,000
Federal income taxes......		1,300		1,100		1,500
Net Income..............		$ 2,500		$ 2,000		$ 3,500

The following table was prepared by a financial analyst to help him compare various companies in the printing industry with what he considered to be the "norm" for the industry:

	19x0		19x1		19x2	
	Company	Norm	Company	Norm	Company	Norm
1. $\dfrac{\text{Current Assets}}{\text{Current Liabilities}}$		3.2		3.3		3.4
2. $\dfrac{\text{Inventory}}{\text{Net Working Capital}}$		69.4		75.0		81.0
3. $\dfrac{\text{Sales}}{\text{Inventory (at Book)}}$		5.6		5.8		6.0
4. Collection period (days)		37.0		35.0		33.0
5. $\dfrac{\text{Fixed Assets}}{\text{Owners' Equity}}$		32.0		33.1		35.0
6. $\dfrac{\text{Current Liabilities}}{\text{Owners' Equity}}$		27.6		26.9		26.3
7. $\dfrac{\text{Total Debt}}{\text{Owners' Equity}}$		49.3		49.5		52.0
8. $\dfrac{\text{Current Liabilities}}{\text{Inventory}}$		55.2		53.2		51.0
9. $\dfrac{\text{Sales}}{\text{Assets}}$		1.8		1.9		2.1
10. $\dfrac{\text{Net Income}}{\text{Sales}}$		2.5		2.6		2.8
11. $\dfrac{\text{Net Income}}{\text{Owners' Equity}}$		6.6		6.8		7.2
12. $\dfrac{\text{Operating Profit}}{\text{Total Assets}}$		7.5		7.8		8.5

a) Compute the ratios necessary to fill in the blanks in the analyst's table, using end-of-year figures for the required balance sheet items.

b) Another analyst comments that of the 12 ratios listed in the table above, only eight are of real value. The other four, he argues, contain little if any information beyond that contained in the ratios numbered 1, 3, 4, 7, 9, 10, 11, and 12. Explain why you do or do not agree with the analyst's conclusion on each of the other four ratios.

c) Prepare statements of balance sheet changes for the years 19x1 and 19x2.

d) Using whatever data seem pertinent, evaluate the profitability, liquidity, and strength of North Printing Company.

Part II

Measurement of
Capital and Income

Chapter 9

COST AND VALUE

IDEALLY, THE FIGURES shown on a balance sheet should show what the company is worth—that is, its *value*. The techniques described in the previous chapters, however, produce balance sheets which show only historical cost. The purpose of the present chapter is to examine the concept of value and the reasons for and against its use in place of historical cost as the basis of accounting measurement. This discussion will then serve as a background for the remaining chapters in this part of the book, which will explore some of the problems encountered in measuring assets, equities, and income.

THE CONCEPT OF VALUE

The value of an item to a firm or individual is the amount that the firm or individual is willing to pay for it.

Two features of this definition deserve comment. First, it is a personal definition—value is always value to somebody, and a given item may be worth more to some people than to others. A purchase-sale transaction, for example, will not take place unless the buyer values the item exchanged more highly than the seller does.

The second feature of the definition is that it is based on *expectations.* An item doesn't have value because someone has worked hard to manufacture it or has used costly materials; instead, its value arises because someone expects to be able to benefit from its use. If the item is for personal consumption, the benefit is the amount of satisfaction that its present owner or a potential buyer can derive from it. The value of an item to a business firm, in contrast, rests on the fact that the item can be sold to an outsider (bottled soft drinks, for example), utilized to produce goods that can be sold to an outsider (a bottling machine), or used to reduce the cost of the company's operations (a bookkeeping machine). In each case, the benefit to the firm is in the form of a future receipt of cash (or a smaller cash outlay, which amounts to the same thing).

Without this concept of value, a businessman would be powerless to act. The number and variety of assets a firm can acquire at the prevailing market price is nearly infinite. If the availability of an asset at its market price were the only criterion for choice, the firm would either make no purchases at all or become a dealer in a wide variety of unrelated kinds of merchandise. In either case, it would very soon be in serious financial trouble. The rational businessman presumably buys only those assets that cost less than the value of the future receipts he expects to obtain from them. Whether the purchase leads to a gain or a loss will depend on the extent to which these expectations are realized.

Timing the Expectations

Most purchases lead to a payment or outlay before the cash benefits are realized. Often this time lag is so short that it does not influence the purchase decision. Thus the pushcart vendor decides how many boxes of strawberries to buy by guessing how many he will be able to sell at a profitable price. The fact that he will have to wait a day or two to recover his outlay affects his *ability* to buy, but not his choice among the various ways in which his available capital should be invested. From his point of view, therefore, value is the expected sale price of the goods, less any costs necessary to obtain this price.

For other items, however, the time lag between purchase and sale or use is much longer. An outlay is made now to acquire assets that will swell the stream of cash receipts during some year or years in the future. This difference in timing can affect the asset-purchase decision. Given a choice between a dollar now and a dollar some time in the future, most people would prefer the present dollar. One reason is that the dollar received today can be invested to grow to more than a dollar a year from now. The man who gets a dollar now and invests it wisely will have more money a year from now than the man who waits a year for his dollar. A second reason is that the future is uncertain. Other things being equal, the longer the wait, the greater the possibility that conditions will change and that the dollar never will be received.

This being the case, the value of an item depends on *when* it is expected to yield cash receipts as well as the *amount* of these expectations.

The Concept of Interest

To ascertain the value of an item, the owner or potential owner must have some means of finding the present equivalent of the amount of future cash receipts he expects that item to yield. The theory of interest provides such a mechanism. To illustrate, if a bank will pay $1,050 one year hence in return for $1,000 now, it is paying interest at the rate of 5 percent a year. This relation can be represented mathematically with the expression:

$$F_1 = P(1 + r), \tag{1}$$

where $P =$ the present outlay or deposit in the bank, $r =$ the rate of interest, and $F_1 =$ the receipt one year later. If $P = \$1,000$ and $r = 0.05$, the receipt one year later is $1,050.

The $1,000 in this illustration is the *present equivalent* of $1,050 one year from now, assuming an interest rate of 5 percent. This figure is also referred to as the *discounted value* or *present value* of the future sum. It is the amount that the future cash receipt of $1,050 is worth today to an investor who regards 5 percent as a satisfactory return on his capital.

Continuing the example, if the $1,050 is left in the bank for another year, it will build up by the end of two years to a balance of $1,050 + (\$1,050 \times 0.05) = \$1,102.50$. Interest in this second year amounts to $52.50 and is greater than interest in the first year because the bank is now paying interest not only on the original investment but also on the interest earned during the first year.

This form of interest calculation is known as *compounding*. In this case, interest has been compounded *annually*, meaning that interest is credited to the account only once a year. It is more likely that interest will be compounded semiannually or quarterly, as in most savings banks, or even more frequently. The shorter the interest period, the sooner the interest is added to the amount on which interest is earned and the faster the amount will grow.

The mathematical formula for computing the future value of a present sum two years later is:

$$F_2 = F_1(1 + r) = P(1 + r)(1 + r) = P(1 + r)^2. \tag{2}$$

In general, it can be shown that if an amount P is put out at interest of r percent per year compounded annually, at the end of n years it will grow to:

$$F_n = P(1 + r)^n. \tag{3}$$

Exhibit 9–1

FUTURE VALUES EQUIVALENT TO PRESENT VALUE OF $1,000
(Annual Compounding at 5 Percent per Year)

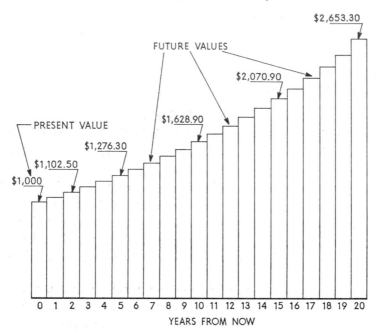

YEARS FROM NOW

The relationship between present and future values is shown graphically in Exhibit 9–1. Starting with $1,000 now, the investment will build at 5 percent to $1,050 in 1 year, $1,102.50 in 2 years, and so on, up to $2,653.30 at the end of 20 years. The longer the period and the greater the interest rate, the higher the future value will be.

Calculation of Present Value

The relationships represented in Exhibit 9–1 and equation (3) can be restated in another way. The value of an asset can be measured either by its future value (as above) or by its present value. The formula for computing present value from known or estimated future values can be found by turning equation (3) around:

$$P = F_n \times \frac{1}{(1 + r)^n}. \qquad (4)$$

If n is two years, r is 5 percent, and the asset is expected to yield a cash inflow of $1,000 two years from now, then its value today is:

$$P = \frac{\$1,000}{(1.05)^2} = \frac{\$1,000}{1.1025} = \$907.03 \ .$$

In other words, $907.03 will grow to $1,000 in two years if it is invested now at 5 percent interest, compounded annually.

Value and Decisions

As stated earlier, the quantitative basis for a purchase decision is a comparison between cost and value. To illustrate, assume that a manufacturer wants to borrow $7 million from an insurance company. In return, he offers to make a single payment of $10 million six years later to cover the amount borrowed plus interest for the six years. The insurance company has other opportunities to invest the $7 million. If it does not make the loan to the manufacturer, it will invest it elsewhere at a 4 percent rate of return. The question, therefore, is whether the loan to the manufacturer would be a more valuable asset than one of the company's regular 4 percent investments.

Equation (3) can be used to see what amount the company would receive six years from now on a 4 percent loan. In this case, $P = \$7$ million, $r = 0.04$, and $n = 6$, and equation (3) becomes:

$$F_6 = \$7,000,000 \times (1.04)^6.$$

$$= \$7,000,000 \times 1.2653 = \$8,857,000 \ .$$

This $8,857,000 is far less than the company can obtain from the manufacturer for the same $7 million investment.

Another way of analyzing this loan opportunity is to find the present value of the $10 million and compare it with the $7 million amount of the loan. Equation (4) becomes:

$$P = \frac{\$10,000,000}{(1.04)^6} = \$7,903,000 \ .$$

This shows that the insurance company would have to place $7,903,000 in one of its 4 percent opportunities in order to receive the same future benefit that it can obtain by lending the manufacturer $7 million. The $903,000 difference is the present value of the superiority of the manufacturer's loan over the company's best alternative. The comparison can be summarized in the following table:

Years from Now	Cash Receipts (+) or Outlays (−)	Present Value at 4%
0...............	−$ 7,000,000	−$7,000,000
6...............	+ 10,000,000	+ 7,903,000
Net Benefit.......		+ 903,000

The future value comparison is usually easier to understand at first, but present value is easier to deal with once the basic notion has been understood. All the remaining discussion, therefore, will focus on present value.

The Use of Interest Tables

The calculation of present values from the equations supplied earlier is time-consuming and expensive. Fortunately, the most laborious part of the calculation—the derivation of $(1 + r)^n$ for all important values of r and n—has already been done by mathematicians. The results of these calculations are available in published *interest tables* similar to those presented in Appendix A at the end of this book.

Exhibit 9–2

BRIEF TABLE OF CONVERSION FACTORS: FUTURE VALUE OF $1

(Excerpted from Appendix A, Table 1)

Periods Hence (*n*)	Interest Rate (*r*)				
	2%	2½%	3%	4%	8%
1...	1.0200	1.0250	1.0300	1.0400	1.0800
2...	1.0404	1.0506	1.0609	1.0816	1.1664
3...	1.0612	1.0769	1.0927	1.1249	1.2597
4...	1.0824	1.1038	1.1255	1.1699	1.3605
5...	1.1041	1.1314	1.1593	1.2167	1.4693
10...	1.2190	1.2801	1.3439	1.4802	2.1589

Table 1 in Appendix A presents the future value of one dollar at various interest rates and at various times in the future. To help illustrate how this table is used, a small section is reproduced in Exhibit 9–2. This table can be used, for example, to find the amount to which $50 will grow by the end of five years if it is invested in such a way as to earn 4 percent interest, interest being reinvested each year to earn at the same rate. The table is entered in the column headed 4% and on the row for the fifth period. The figure found there, 1.2167, indicates that $1 now will grow to $1.2167 by the end of five years, with annual compounding at 4 percent. Instead of $1, however, the example gives $50 so that future value is determined by multiplying 1.2167 by $50, yielding a total future value of $60.84.

If compounding is semiannual instead of annual, the procedure is to double the number of periods and halve the interest rate. For example, there are 10 6-month periods in 5 years, but money invested will only earn a half-year's interest in each 6 months, or 2 percent in the example. The multiplier from the table is now 1.2190, and the future value is 1.2190 times $50, or $60.95. This is slightly greater than the value obtained by annual compounding because interest is added six months sooner to the invested balance on which interest is earned.

Table 3 in Appendix A, which is excerpted in Exhibit 9–3, operates on the same principle. The conversion factors in Table 3 are simply the reciprocals of the factors in Table 1. To find the present value of $100 five years from now at 4 percent interest compounded annually,

Exhibit 9–3

BRIEF TABLE OF CONVERSION FACTORS:
PRESENT VALUE OF $1

(Excerpted from Appendix A, Table 3)

Periods Hence (n)	Interest Rate (r)					
	1½%	2%	2½%	3%	4%	8%
1...	0.9852	0.9804	0.9756	0.9709	0.9615	0.9259
2...	0.9707	0.9612	0.9518	0.9426	0.9246	0.8573
3...	0.9563	0.9423	0.9286	0.9151	0.8890	0.7938
4...	0.9422	0.9238	0.9060	0.8885	0.8548	0.7350
5...	0.9283	0.9057	0.8839	0.8626	0.8219	0.6806
10...	0.8617	0.8203	0.7812	0.7441	0.6756	0.4632

the number 0.8219 from the 4 percent column of Exhibit 9–3 is multiplied by $100. This says that $82.19 invested now at 4 percent will grow to $100 in five years if the interest is left on deposit and reinvested each year. For semiannual compounding, the multiplier for 10 periods at 2 percent per period, 0.8203, gives a present value of $82.03.

The Value of a Series of Cash Receipts

While some assets derive all of their value from the expectation of a single cash receipt, the value of others is based on not one but a series of future cash receipts. The value of assets of this kind is the sum of the values of the various cash flows.

For example, suppose that an investor is satisfied with nothing less than an 8 percent return on his investment. A local merchant has accepted a note from one of his customers entitling him to collect $5,000 a year from now and $10,000 at the end of the following year. The merchant is short of cash and wishes to sell the note.

If the investor were satisfied with a zero rate of return, he would be willing to pay $5,000 + $10,000 = $15,000 for this note. Because he demands an 8 percent return, however, he must *discount* each future payment to its present value—that is, deduct from the future cash receipt the amount that represents interest at 8 percent on the purchase price of the note. The calculation is:

Years from Now	Cash Receipt (+)	Multiplier from Appendix Table 3	Present Value at 8%
1..........	+$ 5,000	0.9259	$ 4,630
2..........	+ 10,000	0.8573	8,573
Total.......			$13,203

The value of this asset to this investor is thus $13,203. He should be willing to buy the note at any figure less than this.

The Value of an Annuity

The cash receipts expected from a given asset may be different each year, as in the last example, or the same. To illustrate the latter case, let us assume that a merchant has accepted a customer's note in exchange for merchandise. The note carries the customer's promise to pay $10,000 a year for five years, the first payment to be made one year from now.

One way of computing the value of this note to an investor would be to find the present value of each of the five payments and add these present values together. A faster way to find the answer is to use the *annuity* factor in Table 4 of Appendix A, a portion of which is shown in Exhibit 9–4. An annuity is simply a series of cash receipts or payments, identical in amount each period, for a specified number of periods.[1] Thus a five-year, $10,000 annuity merely means a series of five annual payments or receipts of $10,000 each. The multipliers in Table 4 are the sums of the multipliers in Table 3 (Exhibit 9–3) and can be used if the amounts in the future are the same each period. In other words, instead of multiplying $10,000 by 0.9259 and again by

---

[1] The term annuity is given a slightly different technical meaning in the field of insurance, but the basic notion is the same.

Exhibit 9–4

BRIEF TABLE OF CONVERSION FACTORS:
PRESENT VALUE OF ORDINARY ANNUITY OF $1

(Excerpted from Appendix A, Table 4)

Periods (n)	Interest Rate (r)					
	1½%	2%	2½%	3%	4%	8%
1...	0.9852	0.9804	0.9756	0.9709	0.9615	0.9259
2...	1.9559	1.9416	1.9274	1.9135	1.8861	1.7833
3...	2.9122	2.8839	2.8560	2.8286	2.7751	2.5771
4...	3.8544	3.8077	3.7620	3.7171	3.6299	3.3121
5...	4.7826	4.7135	4.6458	4.5797	4.4518	3.9927
10...	9.2222	8.9826	8.7521	8.5302	8.1109	6.7101

0.8573, 0.7938, 0.7350, and 0.6806, the analyst needs multiply it only once, by 3.9927, the sum of the five individual multipliers (corrected for an insignificant rounding error). In either case, the value of the series is $39,927.

In general mathematical terms, this result is obtained by extending equation (4). The present value of a series of future cash flows is the sum of the present values of the individual amounts:

$$P = \frac{F_1}{(1 + r)^1} + \frac{F_2}{(1 + r)^2} + \frac{F_3}{(1 + r)^3} + \cdots + \frac{F_n}{(1 + r)^n}, \qquad (5)$$

where F_1 is the amount to be paid or received at the end of one year, F_2 the amount at the end of two years, and so forth.

FINANCIAL STATEMENTS BASED ON PRESENT VALUE

The present value concept is widely used by management in evaluating the desirability of acquiring or disposing of productive assets, a use that will be discussed more thoroughly in Chapter 20. The concept could also be used to derive financial statements for the enterprise as a whole. The question here is whether the practical problems that would be encountered in doing this could be solved well enough to make such statements more useful to the investor.

Valuation of a Going Concern

The use of discounted cash flows in the valuation of a going concern can be illustrated by considering the history of the Precision Instrument Company. The corporation was formed in 1959 by four young men to market a simple but revolutionary measuring instrument invented by one of the founders, and to do further research and development work along similar lines. The corporation issued 5,000 shares of stock in exchange for $50,000 in cash and the rights to the measuring instrument.

As a means of conserving its limited capital, the company opened business in modest rented quarters equipped with a few thousand dollars' worth of "model shop" equipment that was used primarily for research and development work. Arrangements were made with established manufacturers to build instruments on order to specifications rigidly supervised by one of the young associates. Because of the peculiar scientific need fulfilled by the already developed instrument, this new company was able to show a modest profit after only two years of operation. During this period, each of the four associates was paid a small salary.

These four men proved to be an unusually well-balanced scientific, engineering, and managerial team, and it was not long before they had developed three more instruments that were very well received by both institutional research laboratories and industrial customers. By 1967, sales had grown to about $1,400,000, and the after-tax profit for the year approximated $114,000. By this time the salaries of the four associates had been raised to levels more commensurate with their contributions to the company. The corporation had also begun paying a dividend on its stock, but most earnings were reinvested, primarily in working capital and laboratory equipment. With a few exceptions, the manufacturing arrangements which had been entered into in the earlier days proved to be highly satisfactory, so the company resisted the temptation to take on the added risk and responsibility of investment in land, buildings, and production equipment.

In the spring of 1968, the R. F. Walden Corporation, a large and well-established manufacturer of precision instruments, began to explore the possibility of acquiring Precision Instrument Company. Officials of Walden had developed a healthy respect for the scientific and engineering skill of the Precision management. Sales volume for 1968 was again expected to total $1,400,000, which would yield net income of $114,000 for the year. The company's latest balance sheet, shown in Exhibit 9–5, listed the book value of the stockholders' investment at $280,000. Annual earnings therefore represented an after-tax return of slightly more than 40 percent on the book value of the capital employed. This high return was due in part to the use of other firms for manufacturing. The primary factors, however, were the in-

Exhibit 9–5

PRECISION INSTRUMENT COMPANY
Balance Sheet
As of December 31, 1967

ASSETS

Current Assets:

Cash..........................		$ 25,000
Receivables......................		160,000
Inventories......................		120,000
Current Assets................		$305,000
Equipment........................	$150,000	
Less: Depreciation to date...........	70,000	80,000
Total Assets................		$385,000

EQUITIES

Current Liabilities:

Taxes payable....................		$ 15,000
Accounts payable..................		90,000
Current Liabilities..............		$105,000
Stockholders' Equity:		
Capital stock.....................	$125,000	
Retained earnings.................	155,000	280,000
Total Equities..............		$385,000

creasing value of the company's patents and the scientific and managerial skill of the company's officers.

The management of Walden considered 12 percent after taxes a satisfactory return on investment for the type of business in which Precision was engaged. Therefore, Walden recognized that it could afford to pay more than $280,000 for Precision's assets and still earn a return in excess of 12 percent. In reviewing the Precision assets, the Walden management's investigation indicated that the $280,000 book value was reasonably close to the current replacement cost of the tangible assets. The *intangible assets*, however—patents, copyrights, customer relations, and management skill and technical knowledge—did not appear on the Precision balance sheet. The question was how much these assets were worth.

The soundest approach to an answer to this question would be to forecast the cash flows that Precision's operations would generate under Walden management during some long future period and find their present value. For example, suppose that Walden's management felt that Precision's earnings would continue to average $114,000 a year for the next 10 years, provided that equipment replacements were equal to annual depreciation charges. If Walden were to liquidate the Precision business at the end of 10 years, it would be able to recover the full value of the working capital ($305,000 — $105,000 = $200,000). It might also be able to realize something from the sale of the remaining tangible and intangible assets, but for calculation purposes let us assume that Walden's management decided to predict a zero value for these assets at that time. The anticipated cash flows, therefore, would be:

Year	Receipts
1 to 10................	$114,000 per year
10....................	$200,000

The present value of these cash flows can be calculated quite simply with the aid of figures from Appendix A. Because the $114,000 is a 10-year annuity, Table 4 is used. The multiplier for 10 equal annual receipts, discounted at Walden's desired earnings rate of 12 percent, is 5.650. The $200,000 figure, in contrast, is a single lump-sum receipt, and Table 3 must be used. The multiplier for a receipt at the end of 10 years is 0.322.

The calculation of present value can now be summarized as follows:

Year	Receipts	Multiplier	Present Value
1 to 10.........	$114,000 per year	5.650	$644,100
10............	$200,000	0.322	64,400
Total.........			$708,500

In other words, under these assumptions, Walden could afford to pay no more than $708,500 for the owners' interest in Precision.

Suppose, however, that Walden's management saw no reason why the earning power of Precision's assets should decline after 10 years. In fact, it predicted that with good management the cash flow of $114,000 a year would continue indefinitely and that it could always sell its equity in Precision for at least the amount it had invested in it. The predicted cash flows are now:

Year	Receipts
1 to 10................	$114,000 per year
10....................	P

The "P" in this case represents the maximum amount to be paid for Precision. The value formula, using the interest multipliers shown above, becomes:

$$P = \$114,000 \times 5.65 + 0.322 \times P$$
$$P = \frac{\$644,100}{0.678} = \$950,000 .$$

In other words, the value of Precision Instrument Company is $950,000.

Note that this solution is based on the assumption that Precision's earnings will continue to equal cash receipts and that both will equal $114,000 a year in perpetuity. This same result can be achieved much more simply, by dividing annual cash receipts (equal to annual income) by the desired interest rate:

$$\frac{\$114,000}{0.12} = \$950,000 .$$

This process is known as the *capitalization of earnings*. Its basis is that if $950,000 is paid for an infinitely long series of payments of $114,000 each, the rate of return on the investment will be 12 percent:

$$\frac{\$114,000}{\$950,000} = 12 \text{ percent} .$$

The Present Value Balance Sheet

The balance sheet of Precision Instrument Company could be restated to reflect its present value. One way of doing this is summarized in Exhibit 9–6. In this exhibit, all tangible assets and liabilities

Exhibit 9–6

PRECISION INSTRUMENT COMPANY
Adjusted Balance Sheet
As of December 31, 1967

ASSETS

Current Assets:

Cash...........................		$ 25,000
Receivables....................		160,000
Inventories.....................		120,000
Current Assets...............		$ 305,000
Equipment.......................$150,000		
Less: Depreciation to date.......... 70,000		80,000
Goodwill........................		670,000
Total Assets...............		$1,055,000

EQUITIES

Current Liabilities:

Taxes payable....................		$ 15,000
Accounts payable................		90,000
Current Liabilities............		$ 105,000
Stockholders' Equity:		
Capital stock.....................$125,000		
Retained earnings................. 825,000		950,000
Total Equities.............		$1,055,000

have been reported on the traditional accounting basis. The difference between this measure of *net tangible assets* (tangible assets minus liabilities) and the *going concern value* of the company (the capitalized value of its future cash flows) is imputed to the intangibles. This is typically referred to as the value of the company's *goodwill*. In other words, earnings at the normal rate attributable to the tangible assets would be 12 percent of $280,000, or $33,600 a year. Thus, the remaining $80,400 of the annual earnings must be attributable to the earning power of the intangible assets. The present value of this excess earnings stream is the value of the company's goodwill.

Income Statement Based on Present Value

Each basis of valuation carries with it a related concept of income. The economic concept of income is defined as the amount an individual can spend on consumption or a corporation can pay in dividends during a period and be as well off financially at the end as at the start of the period. A corporation remains as well off if the present value of the ownership equity at the end of the period but before the declaration of dividends is equal to its present value at the start. This means that period income is the present value of the total assets less liabilities at the end of the period less the corresponding quantity at the start, plus any dividends that have been declared during the period.

To illustrate, suppose that during 1968 Precision Instrument Company developed a new device which permitted greater automation of a wide variety of chemical processes. Sales rose rapidly in 1968, and earnings in 1969 and later years were expected to amount to $144,000. Using the same capitalization rate and the same assumptions as in the previous example, the value of the enterprise at the end of 1968 would be:

$$\frac{\$144,000}{0.12} = \$1,200,000 \ .$$

This represents an increase of $250,000 over the comparable beginning-of-year figure. The shareholders are that much better off as a result of the events of 1968, and this would be recognized as income in an income statement based on present value. In addition, assume that the shareholders received dividends of $30,000 during 1968. The total increase in their well-being thus amounted to $280,000. This calculation can be summarized in the following manner:

Net assets at end of year:
    Present value of net future receipts................$1,200,000
Net assets at start of year:
    Present value of net future receipts................   950,000
Net increase in value.............................$ 250,000
Add back: Dividends declared......................   30,000
Economic Net Income before Imputed Interest........$ 280,000

Note that income defined in this way includes *all* value changes, whether realized or unrealized. In other words, under the present value basis of measurement, income is not recognized at the time of production or of sale. It is recognized at the time the asset is purchased or at the time the company recognizes a change in the future receipts the asset will produce.

This concept of income is not an easy one to digest and possibly the following situation, which is a perfect analogy, will be helpful. Mr. Johnson bought a share of stock in the Camden Corporation on January 1, 19x3 for $25. On December 31, 19x3, the corporation paid him a $1 dividend and reported that the company earned $2.50 per share. The newspaper that day reported that the price of Camden stock was $31 per share.

On a market value basis, the shareholder has gained $6 a share from the price rise plus $1 of dividend, a total of $7. The price of the share went up because the expectations of purchasers of this stock increased sharply during the year. If Mr. Johnson had sold his stock on December 31, his income would have been reported as $7, under either basis of income measurement. Of this, $6 would have been defined as a capital gain and $1 as ordinary income. Only if Mr. Johnson did not sell his stock would the two bases of income measurement differ, because traditional cost-based accounting does not recognize unrealized gains.

The Argument for the Present Value Basis of Financial Measurement

The case for the value basis in financial reporting rests mainly on the point that owners and other investors are entitled to know how much the enterprise is worth and any other figure is misleading. The accountants' unwillingness to incorporate this kind of information in enterprise financial statements can be a source of irritation to business executives and others on occasions which clearly call for value measures.

For example, it will be recalled from Chapter 2 that when Mr. Erskine wanted a bank loan he was disappointed to discover that his balance sheet did not show the value of his dealer franchise and other intangible assets. The owners of Precision Instrument Company knew that their company was worth more than the cost or book value of the assets. They might have been disturbed by the accountants' insistence on having the assets and owners' equity appear on that basis in the belief that this treatment might limit the price they would get in selling the corporation.

The same issue from a different point of view arises when stockholders are told that their corporation has ceased operations and that their stock is worthless, even though the book value of the corporation's assets (cost less accumulated depreciation) exceeds its liabilities by a large amount.[2]

Objections to Present Value Accounting

Despite these arguments, practical application of the present value basis to external financial reporting is a long way off. In fact, two obstacles are probably insurmountable:

1. The appropriate discounting rate varies from individual to individual.
2. The earnings estimates are in most cases not subject to adequate verification.

Objection: Multiplicity of Discounting Rates. The value and earnings figures developed above for Precision Instrument Company were heavily dependent on the discount rate used. This can be demonstrated by substituting various interest rates in the capitalization formula:

Interest Rate	Present Value December 31, 1967 (Based on $114,000 Annual Cash Flow)	Present Value December 31, 1968 (Based on $144,000 Annual Cash Flow)	Income for 1968 (Including $30,000 in Dividends)
6%	$1,900,000	$2,400,000	$530,000
8.....	1,425,000	1,800,000	405,000
12.....	**950,000**	**1,200,000**	**280,000**
15.....	760,000	960,000	230,000
20.....	570,000	720,000	180,000

[2] Further argument in support of present value may be found in David Solomons' "Economic and Accounting Concepts of Income," *The Accounting Review*, Vol. XXVI, No. 3 (July, 1961), pp. 374–83. For more extensive coverage, see S. S. Alexander and David Solomons, "Income Measurement in a Dynamic Economy" in W. T. Baxter and S. Davidson, *Studies in Accounting Theory* (Homewood, Ill.: Richard D. Irwin, Inc., 1962), pp. 126–200.

This would not be a fatal objection if the only problem were the difficulty of estimating the current rate of discount. After all, depreciation estimates are far from accurate in most cases, but the inaccuracy is generally regarded as far less serious than the error that would result from abandonment of the depreciation concept.

The main difficulty with the discount rate is that each investor has his own rate. Although Walden used a 12 percent rate in valuing Precision Instrument, others might have been satisfied with, say, 8 percent and thus would have been willing to pay more than Walden. This difficulty could be resolved by reporting only the company's cash flow predictions, letting the reader apply his own discount rate. This solution might work, awkward though it may seem, but it is unlikely to be put to the test unless the second objection to present value accounting can be overcome.

Objection: Subjectivity in Earnings Estimates. This second objection is that no adequate basis for independent verification of managerial forecasts of future cash flows has yet been developed. Two accountants called upon to prepare financial statements for a company could easily come up with radically different figures for the value of the company's assets and its income. Each might have a different *judgment* as to the corporation's future cash flows, and each might feel that a different discount rate should be used to obtain their present value.

This is not to say that the task of forecasting future cash receipts can be avoided. Explicitly or implicitly, both management and the outside investor must make such forecasts in arriving at investment or disinvestment decisions. They must base these decisions on their *judgment* as to the future consequences of their actions. This judgment is improved by information, by training in the various fields of business administration, and by business experience. However, no amount of training eliminates the need for judgment, and while investors will listen to the information and advice the accountant provides, they typically insist on acting on their own judgment. It is their money.

What the outsider demands of the independent accountant is an assurance that the figures presented to him are not unduly biased upward or downward at management's request. Judgment cannot be kept out of the financial statements, but the outsider has the right to expect that judgment will be impartially applied. This means that the figures shown in the financial statements should be capable of independent verification to a far larger extent than is ever likely to be possible for management's long-range cash flow forecasts.

Strength of the Cost Basis

The main justification of the cost basis, in other words, is not that it tells the investor what the company is worth but that it provides data that are as free from personal bias as the accountant can make them. As we pointed out in Chapter 1, however, *relevance* is the first principle of accounting, and the accountant's challenge is to seek ways of improving the relevance of financial statements to the problems of outside users, without sacrificing reliability. Building on this firm foundation, the individual investor then can apply his own judgment, using whatever other information is available, to derive his own estimate of the value of the corporation. In doing this, he will find the detail and year-to-year consistency of cost basis statements of considerable usefulness.

SUMMARY

The concept of present value is of broad and fundamental relevance to business management. It reflects management's profit expectations which are precisely the information needed and used for the internal evaluation of business investments. The concept also provides the basis on which outsiders can evaluate the desirability of investing in the firm.

Nevertheless, the accountant does not incorporate this valuation technique in the measurement rules he employs in preparing periodic financial statements. He does not do so, first, because of the difficulties of objective measurement and, second, because the determination of asset value is in the last analysis an ownership or management function. Each such individual must derive his own valuation from the information at hand, and for this purpose information as to what management *expects to make* on the things it *has not sold* is no substitute for information as to what management *has made* on the things it *has sold*.

It will be seen that other means more effective than double-entry bookkeeping are used to communicate management expectations, but there is no reason to believe that a detailed permanent record of such data would be either practicable or useful. However, although the accountant does not use value as his basis of valuation, he cannot be oblivious to it if he wishes to aid management and others to make decisions on the basis of the data he produces.

QUESTIONS AND PROBLEMS

1. Define "present value." What is its relationship to "future value"?

2. What figures are used in preparing an estimate of present value?

3. Formulate a rule, using the concept of present value, that you might be willing to follow when making certain kinds of decisions.

4. Explain the relationship between the present value of a single sum and the present value of an annuity. What is meant by the term "annuity" in this context?

5. Distinguish between tangible and intangible assets.

6. What is a "going concern"? What is the main source of the value of a going concern?

7. What is "economic value"? How is it determined? By whom?

8. Define the economic concept of income. What are the obstacles to its adoption by accountants for external financial reporting?

9. What is the economic definition of goodwill? Under what circumstances would you expect to see goodwill, other than in a nominal $1 amount, listed explicitly on a company's balance sheet?

10. Is is possible to define the economic value of a single asset that is part of an integrated group of assets? Illustrate your answer in terms of a pump on an oil pipeline—if the pump breaks down, the entire pipeline ceases to operate.

11. The management of the Gupta Corporation has recently been cited by a national society of industrial engineers for its efficiency in organizing and controlling the company's affairs. The aggregate market value of the company's stock, based on the current market price per share, is $10 million; book value is only $4 million. Management's own forecast of future cash flows, discounted at an interest rate that seems appropriate for a company of its size and class, is $9 million.

The board of directors of the Marshall Company has just made a cash offer of $12 million for the outstanding stock in the Gupta Corporation. What might account for the premium valuation placed by Marshall on the Gupta Corporation?

12. An annuity in arrears of one dollar at 5 percent will amount to $4.3101 in four periods. Explain how this figure is determined.

13. The present value of an annuity in arrears of one dollar at 5 percent for five periods is $4.3295. Why is this true? Explain how this amount is determined.

14. Compute the present value of each of the following, using the interest tables in Appendix A:

a) $10,000 to be received 10 years from now. Interest is compounded annually at 10 percent.

b) $10,000 to be received at the end of each of the next 10 years. Interest is compounded annually at 8 percent.

c) $5,000 to be received at the end of each of the next five years, plus $15,000 to be received at the end of each of the five years after that. Interest is compounded annually at 10 percent.

d) $15,000 to be received at the end of each of the next five years, plus $5,000 to be received at the end of each of the five years after that. Interest is compounded annually at 10 percent.

15. For each of the situations in Problem 14, compute future value as of 10 years from now.

* 16. The Future Company has just borrowed $1 million. Interest on this amount will be paid to the lender each year for 10 years. In addition, the $1 million will have to be repaid to the lender at the end of 10 years. How much will the Future Company have to deposit in the bank at the end of each of the next 10 years to enable it to repay the $1 million at the end of the 10 years if the bank compounds interest annually at a rate of 5 percent. An identical amount is to be deposited each year.

* 17. If you are willing to accept all investment proposals that are expected to yield an annual return of 12 percent or more (before income taxes) and reject all others, which of the following proposals would you accept? Show your calculations.

a) Outlay: $35,000 on January 1, 1969.
     Receipt: $100,00 on January 1, 1979.
b) Outlays: $80,000 on January 1, 1969.
              20,000 on January 1, 1974.
   Receipts: $10,000 on each January 1, 1970 through 1975.
              20,000 on each January 1, 1976 through 1985.

---

* Solutions to problems marked with an asterisk (*) are found in Appendix B.

c) Outlays: $20,000 on each January 1, 1969 through 1979.
   Receipts: $250,000 on January 1, 1981.

18. A house can be bought for $21,000, payable in cash immediately. Alternatively, the seller will accept a series of cash payments, starting with $10,000 immediately and then $2,000 at the end of each of the next seven years.

a) If a buyer can always invest his money at 8 percent, compounded annually, which of these alternatives should he prefer?
b) Assuming that the seller can invest his money at 6 percent, what is the series of payments worth to him?

19. A man leases a store for three years. He pays rent of $2,000 each year and sublets it to someone else for $3,000 a year, both payable yearly in advance. If he invests the difference at 6 percent, how much will he have gained by the end of the third year?

20. Mr. Provident is 30 years old. He desires to have at 50 a savings fund of $100,000. He expects to earn 6 percent compounded annually on what he saves. How much must he set aside out of his earnings at the end of each year for the 20 years to accumulate his $100,000?

21. A owns some real estate which is leased to B for $20,000 a year. The lease has 10 years still to run. C offers to sublease from B for $60,000 a year. B offers, instead, to transfer his lease to C for a lump-sum payment of $320,000, in which case C would have to pay A the contract rental of $20,000 a year.

Would C be wise to accept B's counteroffer quickly if C can borrow the necessary funds at 5 percent, or should C try to persuade B to sublet to him for $60,000 a year? Compute the difference between the two propositions in dollars from C's standpoint. Assume that all payments are made in advance.

22. John Hastings has just received a tax-paid inheritance of $100,000. He has decided to use part of the inheritance to purchase an annuity from an insurance company. Under the terms of the annuity contract, the insurance company will pay Mr. Hastings $15,000 a year for 10 years. The first of these payments will be made seven years from now.

In computing the amount to charge for such an annuity, the insurance company uses an interest rate of 6 percent, compounded annually. How much of his inheritance will Mr. Hastings have left to spend after paying for the annuity?

23. Thomas Peterson is an investor who expects to earn at least 8 percent a year on his investments. He estimates that an investment in a new mine will bring him $10,000 in cash at the end of each of the next 15 years. At the end of that time, the mine will be worthless.

a) How much is the mine worth to Mr. Peterson?
b) How much would the mine be worth to Mr. Peterson if it were to produce $10,000 a year for 25 years? For 40 years? For 50 years?
c) Prepare a diagram with "values" on the vertical scale and the number of years on the horizontal scale. Enter your answers to (*a*) and (*b*) on this diagram. From the diagram, try to estimate how much the mine would be worth if it were to be productive at the present rate for 100 years. What other method or methods could you have used to calculate this figure?

24. John Hancock has plans to retire at the age of 60 and wishes to provide an income of $15,000 per year until he is 75 years old. He plans to do his saving for his old age during the 15 years prior to reaching the age of 50, leaving the resulting fund to accumulate for the next 10 years. Assuming that his savings will earn 4 percent annually, how much must he deposit at the beginning of each year starting on his 35th birthday?

25. Mr. William Lazere wished to arrange for the college education of his three children. He estimated that he would need the following amounts:

> August 31, 1970................$3,000
> August 31, 1971................ 6,000
> August 31, 1972................ 9,000
> August 31, 1973................ 9,000
> August 31, 1974................ 6,000
> August 31, 1975................ 3,000

On September 1, 1963, he asked the representative of an insurance company to draw up an endowment policy that would provide these amounts. The insurance representative said that his company compounded interest annually at 4 percent.

a) What is the amount of the *annuity* that Mr. Lazere had to pay each September 1 from 1963 to 1974, inclusive, to obtain the funds needed for his children's education? Show your calculations.
b) Recompute your answer to (*a*) on the basis of a 5 percent interest rate.

26. The Villard Corporation wants to hire Mr. Harris as a vice president. Mr. Harris asks for a salary of $28,000 a year during his active service and $10,000 a year after retirement. He is 45 years old and is expected to serve for 20 years.

Up-to-date mortality tables indicate that a man in Mr. Harris' position has an expected remaining life of 34 years—in other words, he will live until he reaches the age of 79. This means that he would be expected to receive retirement pay for 14 full years.

The money needed for Mr. Harris' pension would be invested by a pension fund at 5 percent per annum, compounded semiannually. The company would give the pension fund the necessary sum in equal installments (an annuity) at the end of each six-month period of Mr. Harris' active service. These pension contributions would cease on the day of Mr. Harris' retirement.

The board of directors is willing to pay up to the equivalent of $32,000 per year of active service for this position. Will the company hire Mr. Harris? (Assume that all payments to Mr. Harris are made twice a year, at the end of each six-month period. Show all your calculations.)

27. The Loralee Corporation's sole asset is a 100 percent stock ownership of the New York, Chicago, and Pacific Railway Company. The latter's only asset is 200 miles of mainline railroad track which it has leased on a 99-year lease to the Pennsylvania and Chesapeake Railroad at a semiannual rental of $50,000. This lease still has 25 years to run, and the P. & C. is one of the strongest railway companies in the country.

The book value of the ownership equity in the New York, Chicago, and Pacific on its own books is $1,200,000. The Loralee Corporation carries its investment on its books at an original cost of $900,000. Loralee Corporation stockholders are satisfied with a 12 percent before-tax return on their investment. Loralee stock is now selling at $800,000.

a) What is the value of the Loralee Corporation's goodwill if it is assumed that cash flows after the end of 25 years will be zero?

b) What is the value of the goodwill if it is assumed that the annual rental will remain at its present level forever?

c) Should the stockholders keep or sell their Loralee stock? State any assumptions you have made and show all your computations.

* **28.** William Appersham operates a ferry service across Deepwater Bay. A bridge is now being built across the bay. When it is completed two years from now, Mr. Appersham will close the ferry service and retire to his plantation in the Virgin Islands. He expects the following cash flows from the ferry operation:

Year	Cash Receipts	Cash Disbursements	Net Cash Receipts
1............	$300,000	$200,000	$100,000
2............	350,000	220,000	130,000

At the end of each year he will withdraw the year's net cash receipts and invest them in highway bonds where they will earn interest at an annual rate of 6 percent, compounded annually. In addition, at the end of year 2 he will be able to withdraw the $50,000 that he now has to maintain as a working cash fund to keep his ferry service going.

The sale value of his ferry boats two years from now will be virtually zero.

a) What is the present value of the ferry service to Mr. Appersham now?
b) Assuming that all forecasts are correct, what will be the present value of the assets of the ferry service a year from now, before Mr. Appersham withdraws the net cash receipts of the first year's operations?
c) Compute the net income of the ferry service for the first year on a present value basis, assuming that all forecasts are correct.
d) Compute the ferry service's income for the second year on a present value basis, again assuming that all forecasts are correct.

29. The city of Hicksville has decided to sponsor an international exposition promoting the values of rural living. The exposition will operate for a period of four years. The city will provide a site for the exposition in Bucolic Park, rent-free.

Turning to experts, the city has asked the International Corporation for Expositions (ICE) to construct the buildings and to operate the exposition. ICE has prepared the following estimates of operating cash receipts and cash disbursements:

Year	Receipts	Disbursements
1...........	$2,000,000	$1,300,000
2...........	3,000,000	1,500,000
3...........	2,000,000	800,000
4...........	1,300,000	300,000

Construction costs, all to be paid at the beginning of year 1, are estimated to be $4,000,000. An additional investment of $300,000 will be necessary at that time to provide a working cash fund; the need for this will continue throughout the four-year period. The exposition buildings will be sold to the city at the end of year 4 for $1,000,000.

ICE has enough confidence in the predictions to participate in the venture if it will earn a return of 10 percent before income taxes. If it decides to do so, it will form a subsidiary, the Hicksville Exposition Corporation. This subsidiary will issue common stock to ICE for $1,000 and will borrow the remaining $4,299,000 from ICE, giving noninterest bearing notes as evidence of its indebtedness. The subsidiary will repay the notes as rapidly as possible, keeping only a cash balance of $300,000.

ICE assumes in all of its calculations that all cash receipts and disbursements take place at the end of the year.

The subsidiary will be liquidated at the end of year 4, and its remaining cash assets will be paid back to ICE at that time.

a) Assuming that ICE agrees to undertake this project and that all the forecasts are correct, compute the subsidiary's income for each year if assets are measured by the present value approach. Ignore income taxes.

b) If the historical cost approach is used instead of present value, what will be the income for each year? Historical cost depreciation will be the same for each of the four years. Ignore income taxes.

30. On January 1, 1968, the Vista Hotel opened its doors. The hotel had just been completed at a cost of $6 million, and it had an expected life of 30 years. The hotel had been built by the Vista Realty Corporation on land acquired on a 30-year, nonrenewable lease at a rental of $75,000 per year. Vista Realty, in turn, leased the hotel on a 30-year lease to the Vista Operating Company, which was to operate the hotel and pay all operating expenses. The annual rental to be paid by Vista Operating to Vista Realty was to be 40 percent of the hotel's revenue with a minimum rental of $400,000 per year.

Realty's management estimated that the hotel would gross an annual revenue of $1,800,000. It was not ordinarily willing to undertake projects of this kind unless the anticipated rate of return on investment was at least 10 percent before income taxes.

In 1968, the Hotel earned revenue of $1,600,000. Toward the end of 1968, the city began building an auditorium and related facilities for conventions, indoor sports, and so forth. The management of Vista Realty believed that this would increase annual hotel revenue to about $2,000,000 a year starting in 1970. The projection for 1969 remained at $1,800,000.

a) Assuming that the hotel is the sole asset of Vista Realty and that its entire cost was financed by stockholder investment, present a balance sheet as of January 1, 1968, under (1) the historical cost basis of valuation, and (2) the present value basis of valuation.

b) Mr. Jones, a wealthy investor, has the opportunity to buy a 10 percent interest in Vista Realty on December 31, 1968, and he asks you to advise him what is the most he should be willing to pay for the stock if he requires a 10 percent return on his investment.

c) Present financial statements as of December 31, 1968, under the two bases of valuation. (Ignore income taxes.)

31. In June, 1967, Franchise Golf, Inc., was formed and announced that it would put on a golf tournament each year for the next 20 years.

The prizes would be: 1st place, $75,000; 2d place, $50,000; and 3d place, $25,000. Only five players would compete in each tournament and they were to be selected as follows: Franchise Golf, Inc., would sell five franchises. The owner of each franchise would select one player for each tournament. The owner would pay his player an agreed salary. Each year the player's contract would come up for renewal. The player's salary was to be negotiable, but if the owner's maximum offer were less than the player's salary for the previous year, the player would be free to reject the offer and sign up with another owner if he could find one to offer him a higher price. If the offer were equal to or higher than the player's salary for the previous year, however, the player could refuse to renew the contract but could not sign up with another owner for the next two years.

Gene Hogan, a wealthy retired golf professional, believed that he could obtain a golfer for $15,000 a tournament who had as good a chance to win as any other entry. Hogan and three members of the Rolling Hills Golf Club formed the R. H. Corporation and bought a franchise from Franchise Golf, Inc., for $100,000. They contracted with Gary Palmer, a promising young golfer, to play in the first tournament for $15,000, and he won first place in the first playing of the tournament in June, 1968.

By the end of the year, Palmer's victory and his performance in other tournaments established him as one of the top two players in the country, and it appeared likely that he would keep this position for at least five years. The managers of the R. H. Corporation believed that young Palmer would be likely to place either first or second in 60 percent of the tournaments, and place third in another 10 percent. With this in mind, they decided to raise his salary to $20,000 per tournament, a figure that was acceptable to young Palmer.

a) What would have been a fair price for Hogan to pay for a franchise as of January 1, 1968, if he wanted a 10 percent return on his investment?

b) Prepare a balance sheet and income statement for the R. H. Corporation for the year ending December 31, 1968, using historical cost as the basis of valuation.

c) A stockholder who owned a 25 percent interest in R. H. Corporation wanted to sell out on December 31, 1968. Recommend a fair price for his equity.

d) Prepare a balance sheet as of January 1, 1968, and financial statements as of December 31, 1968, for the R. H. Corporation, using present value as a basis of valuation.

Chapter 10

ACQUISITION COST:
ASSET VERSUS EXPENSE

No SERIOUS CHALLENGE has been offered to the practice of recording asset acquisitions at their purchase cost. The relevance of these figures to managerial and external uses comes more and more into question as the date of acquisition fades farther and farther into the past, but at the time of acquisition historical cost is probably the best available measure of the economic sacrifice made by the firm to acquire the asset.

Although the use of actual cost as the basis for recording assets at the time of acquisition is generally accepted, implementation of the rule poses questions on which there is considerable difference of opinion. The purpose of this chapter is to examine three of these questions in some depth: (1) How should an asset's purchase cost be measured? (2) How should intangible assets be accounted for? (3) What methods should be used when outlay cost cannot be determined?

THE MEASUREMENT OF COST: BASIC PRINCIPLES

All costs are incurred to obtain something. This something may be a physical object, a property right, or a service. The purpose of expenditures on each and all of these is to create income, either by producing revenues in excess of the cost (revenue-producing expenditures) or by reducing other costs (cost-saving expenditure). Finally, the expenditure may be designed to increase income in the current period, in some single future period, or in a number of periods.

These distinctions are reflected in the definitions of asset and expense: (1) any acquisition cost or portion thereof which is incurred for and consumed in obtaining the *current period's income* is an *expense;* and (2) any acquisition cost or portion thereof which is incurred for and will be consumed to obtain *income in one or more future periods* is an *asset*.

Application of these definitions to current expenditures requires the solution of two problems. The first problem is to decide which object each cost should be identified with. The second is to decide whether the object of the expenditure is the creation of an asset or the creation of current income.

Identification of Costs with Objects

In deciding whether to acquire an asset, management must estimate all the costs that must be incurred before the asset can be put to its intended productive use. If management makes the acquisition, this is presumptive evidence that an increase in income is expected. Accordingly, in determining the acquisition cost of an asset, a reasonable guiding principle is that *all outlays necessary to render an asset suitable for its intended use should be treated as elements of the asset's cost.*

The problem of identifying acquisition costs is probably demonstrated most effectively by means of an example. In the belief that such action would result in a substantial saving in labor costs, the Camden Company decided to install a conveyor system to transport materials, work in process, and finished products between work stations in its two-story plant. The following outlays were direct consequences of this decision:

1. Price of conveyor components.................................$26,500
2. Freight charges on conveyor components........................   800
3. Installation of conveyor...................................... 3,600
4. Compensation for injuries to an employee of the contractor engaged for conveyor installation.. 10,000
5. Alterations to building to accommodate conveyor................ 4,200
6. Payments to factory employees during period of shutdown for conveyor installation:
   a) For rearranging machines................................... 1,600
   b) For idle time.. 1,200
7. Training of one employee in conveyor maintenance...............   300

Except for the $10,000 payment resulting from failure of the contractor to carry compensation insurance, all costs actually incurred, including that of employee idle time, were approximately as had been anticipated in planning the project. In other words, the cost estimate made in deciding whether the outlay would be profitable included all the items but 4 above.

When the base rule is applied to these basic facts, it is clear that every one of these items except the compensation for uninsured injuries (item 4) is an "outlay necessary to render the asset suitable for its intended use," and hence is properly *capitalized* (i.e., treated as part of the cost of the firm's assets). It is equally apparent that item 4 is not a necessary cost of acquisition but rather a loss properly chargeable to the period in which it was incurred. Had ordinary caution been exercised, the Camden Company would have either engaged an insured contractor or itself secured the requisite coverage at a nominal charge. In either case, the insurance premium would have been part of the reasonably necessary cost of the asset and therefore capitalizable.

Unfortunately, the issue cannot rest at this point. Despite the appealing simplicity of this solution, a number of considerations, both practical and theoretical, often lead the accountant to charge some of these items immediately to expense. These considerations will be examined next.

Maintenance versus Betterments

Items 5 and 6a present an extremely subtle set of conceptual problems. On the one hand, they were made necessary by the installation of the conveyor and therefore should be considered as part of its cost. From a different point of view, however, it can be argued that these costs were incurred not "to render the asset suitable" in the sense of our rule but *to preserve the previously existing suitability* of other assets under changed operating conditions. This latter rationale leads to the conclusion that the items in question are in the nature of current (though possibly extraordinary) maintenance costs rather than additions to the cost of the assets to which they relate.

The problem, in other words, is to distinguish between *betterments,* connoting some form of progressive change, and *maintenance,* meaning the prevention or retardation of retrogressive change. Whereas costs of the former are subject to capitalization, those of the latter are properly chargeable to current operations.

A unique conceptual solution to this problem exists, although application of this solution requires the exercise of judgment by the accountant. The *total productive capacity* of a plant asset, or any complex of assets, is a joint function of the output per unit of time and the length of time over which satisfactory output is achieved (economic life), both of which factors are in turn more or less dependent upon the level of maintenance provided. At the time of acquisition, therefore, there is an *expected life-time capacity* reflecting an *intended maintenance policy.* This fact provides a basis for the following rules governing the treatment of subsequent outlays: (1) any cost incurred *to obtain the service initially expected is a maintenance cost;*

and (2) any cost *incurred to increase lifetime productive capacity by raising the output rate or by extending the economic life or by reducing operating cost is a capitalizable betterment.*

Application of these rules is most difficult in cases like the Camden Company's conveyor installation. In this case, several physically different assets were readily identifiable. Costs necessary to acquire one of these (the conveyor) were expended to effect physical changes in others (the building and the other machinery). This physical identifiability has nothing to do with the issue, however. The rearrangement and building alteration costs were costs of the conveyor system. If the other assets had given up their income-producing potential more rapidly than was originally anticipated, due to the lack of adequate conveyor facilities, then part of the cost of those assets should have been written off currently as a loss, *regardless of whether the conveyor system was purchased.* If the other assets could have achieved their anticipated productive life without the conveyor, no such write-off would have been necessary. In either case, items 5 and 6a should be shown in the accounts as part of the cost of the conveyor.

Mainenance versus Replacement

A closely related question is the distinction between replacement and maintenance. Replacement of an entire asset requires removal of any unexpired portion of original cost and the capitalization of the costs of the replacement. The cost of replacing a part of an asset, however, is usually treated as maintenance expense unless it is expected to increase the asset's service expectancy materially.

The definition, in other words, depends on what has been chosen as the unit of account. For example, the cost of new tires for a company truck might be treated either as maintenance or as a replacement. If the unit of account is the truck and if the estimated productive life of the truck was based on the assumption that the tires would be replaced periodically, then the expenditure on new tires is a maintenance cost. If, instead, the tires are retained as a unit of account in their own right so that the cost of the original tires was capitalized and depreciated separately from the truck, then this cost must now be removed from the accounts and the cost of the new tires substituted in their place. If the unit of account is made small enough, even a grease job or an oil change can be treated as a replacement, and no room will be left for the concept of maintenance.

THE MEASUREMENT OF COST: PRAGMATIC CRITERIA

In practice, the facts are often less clear-cut than a textbook description may make them appear. Consequently, the company's accountants have a good deal of latitude in applying the general measurement principle stated above. In exercising his judgment on these questions, he is influenced by a number of pragmatic considerations, most of which generally lead to an earlier recognition of expense than the basic principle would suggest.

Bookkeeping Convenience

Among the least impressive but by no means least important of such influences is that of bookkeeping convenience. Although the Camden Company did in fact isolate the cost of equipment rearrangement by its own work force, the firm's accounting system might have been so organized that this portion of factory payroll costs could not be readily distinguished. This is often the case when equipment installation, remodeling, and the like are accomplished by regular employees. Under these conditions, a management may understandably adopt the view that it is more interested in making money than in measuring precisely how much money it has made. Where the cost to be isolated is relatively small and the cost of isolating it relatively large, this argument is quite persuasive.

Tax Advantage

A more compelling and entirely rational cause for expensing costs which might otherwise be capitalized is the tax advantage to be gained thereby. So long as a firm has current taxable income, increasing the amount of current expense will have the effect of reducing current tax payments. Transferring cost to expense currently rather than deferring it to future periods generally will inflate future taxable income, but this fact is a deterrent only when an increase in the tax rate is expected.[1] The dollar surely saved this year is unquestionably worth more than the dollar that may be saved in some future year.

Since taxable income is not necessarily the same as reported income, a cost may be capitalized for public reporting while being expensed

---

[1] In some instances, the tax effect is magnified by the practice of levying local property taxes on the basis of stated book values. Under such conditions, higher asset valuations may result in both higher income taxes and higher property taxes.

for tax purposes. However, the taxpayer has a very understandable tendency to buttress the case for current tax deductibility of border-line items by expensing them for both purposes. Thus, tax matters do undoubtedly exert an influence on accounting policy.

The Principle of Conservatism

One more influence on accounting practice deserves mention. When a legitimate question exists as to whether a cost ought to be capitalized or expensed and the decision will have no impact on tax treatment, the general tendency is to invoke the principle of conservatism in support of a decision to expense the item.

For example, the employee training cost shown as item 7 in the example above was incurred to obtain a future benefit. Although the trained employees can leave the company whenever they wish, taking their skill with them, the initial training cost is like the priming of a pump—once the water is flowing, very little effort is required to keep it flowing. An argument could be made, in other words, for depreciating the initial training cost over the expected useful life of the conveyor system. Most practicing accountants would invoke the notion of conservatism, however, and charge the entire cost to expense, either immediately or over some short future period.

The major consequences of the principle of conservatism are (1) the understatement of asset values and owners' equity, (2) the understatement of current income, and (3) the overstatement of future income, other things being equal. Probably the main reason for the widespread acceptance of the principle of conservatism in the face of these obvious defects is psychological. Large fluctuations in earnings create great expectations on the part of the stockholders one year and bitter disappointment with the management the next year. Application of the principle of conservatism tends to limit this. In good years earnings are reduced, and in bad years earnings are raised, since large expenditures that benefit future years and may be expensed currently tend to be made in years when income is otherwise high.

The principle of conservatism may also have some impact on the management. Conservative accounting practice may lead management to believe that its assets and income are smaller than they actually are, and as a consequence management may pay smaller dividends, undertake fewer investments, or both. Insofar as this strengthens the financial position of the company and reduces the likelihood of ruin at some future date, some may consider it more than worth the foregone profit and growth opportunities. On the other hand, excessive conservatism may cause the decline of a firm through stagnation.

Understatement of assets and income may also cause a stockholder to make incorrect decisions, either because he believes the firm is less profitable than it in fact is or because he overcompensates for the downward bias he knows is in the data. More recently it has been noted that asset understatement may depress stock prices and make it easier for a "raider" to gain voting control of the company.[2]

Consistency and Disclosure

Probably the most serious problem posed by conservatism is that no objective basis can establish how much conservatism is enough. The most conservative action that the Camden Company accountants could have taken was expense every outlay involved in the acquisition of the conveyor system. Between this and the other extreme of capitalizing every outlay but item 4, different accountants might reach different decisions. Furthermore, the decision reached by any one accountant might depend in part on his unconscious reaction to the environmental conditions of the moment.

To avoid the abuse of the principle of conservatism, the accounting profession requires a firm to be *consistent* from year to year in its treatment of specific types of cost, or to give full *disclosure* to any change in practice from one year to the next. For example, once a firm decides to expense employee training costs, it must do so consistently, year in and year out, regardless of current conditions. This requirement is based on the proposition that a bias consistently followed impairs the usefulness of information less seriously than a bias that depends on what management wants the stockholders to believe.

As one might imagine, consistency is not an unmixed blessing. For example, partly because the amount is not *material* (i.e., not large enough to be significant), a company may decide to expense the cost of alterations to equipment and find this accounting practice to be satisfactory for a number of years. Sooner or later, however, it may come to a year in which the cost is large because of a large-scale plant modernization effort. Under these circumstances, the firm's accountants may well insist that this cost should be capitalized and amortized

---

[2] One study identified a number of instances in which this was true, but it was unable to find a measurable relationship between asset understatement and the likelihood of a take-over bid. See Russell A. Taussig and Samuel L. Hayes, III, "Cash Take-Overs and Accounting Valuations," *The Accounting Review*, January, 1968, pp. 68–74.

over the expected remaining life of the equipment. This departure from consistent reporting is justified by the materiality of the amount. The corporation, however, must disclose in its published financial statements the departure from previous practice and its quantitative implications.

These concepts of consistency and disclosure will be discussed on other occasions. Disclosure is the more fundamental and raises the more difficult issues. One of the basic tenets of public accounting is that the published financial statements must provide adequate disclosure of the firm's financial performance and position, and many issues in accounting arise from differences of opinion as to what constitutes adequate disclosure.[3]

INTANGIBLE ASSETS

Perhaps the most important reason for expensing items that might in theory be capitalized is neither convenience nor tax deferral nor conservatism, but the difficulty of identifying the cost with specific foreseeable future benefits. This difficulty is most pronounced in connection with the so-called "intangible" assets such as those which arise from sales promotion and research and development expenditures. A further problem with these intangible assets is that after they come into existence, it is practically impossible to identify the asset with specific purchase transactions. In view of the increasing importance of expenditures that lead to intangible assets, some discussion of the major categories is desirable.

Sales Promotion Expenditures

While the bulk of advertising is directed to current sales, a significant portion is designed to enhance the general reputation of the firm and its products. Costs in this latter category, plus numerous others less easily identified but likewise aimed at building goodwill, are at least partially applicable to *future* revenues. Nevertheless, it is almost universal practice to expense all selling and promotional costs as incurred. A number of factors contribute to this practice in addition to the pragmatic considerations of convenience, conservatism, and tax minimization.

First, it is difficult to distinguish between the current and probable

---

[3] For a provocative discussion of the subject, see Charles T. Horngren, "Disclosure: What Next?" *The Accounting Review*, Vol. XXX, No. 1 (January, 1958), pp. 84–92.

future effects of advertising and related costs. While the salesman confidently expects that some of today's efforts will produce subsequent orders, he has no clear idea as to when these will materialize. Second, even where current efforts are directed specifically to the future with every prospect of beneficial results, it may be impossible to establish the periods in which benefits will be realized. Consequently, it will be impossible to establish a valid basis for systematic cost amortization. Finally, it can often be persuasively argued that insofar as such costs are incurred at a reasonably uniform rate over time, consistent expensing probably yields no significant error in reported income after the first period or so.

To a greater or lesser degree, these same considerations apply to all the numerous other cost elements vaguely described as intangibles. By and large, such costs are in fact capitalized only on occasions of rather substantial and specifically defined outlays. A trademark acquired from another firm will often appear in the purchaser's accounts at a substantial figure, its purchase cost, while equally important brand names internally developed over time are carried on the books at zero valuation. Furthermore, even for purchased intangibles, the rule rather than the exception is to write off the purchase cost over an arbitrarily short period, and the residues of these often appear on balance sheets in such form as:

Trademarks and goodwill.........................$1.00[4]

Research and Development

Turning to the increasingly important area of *research and development* costs, it is generally clear that whatever benefits may result from current outlays will accrue in *future* periods. The case for their capitalization is thus stronger than it was for advertising. *All* of the intended benefits are future benefits; therefore, expensing will lead to a greater distortion of reported income than will expensing of advertising outlays, most of which have current as well as future benefits. Furthermore, research and development activities ordinarily can be curtailed without immediate adverse profit effects, albeit with considerable risk of damage to the long-run competitive position of the firm. If the costs are expensed, management may be tempted to change research appropriations annually to secure the level of current income it wants to show the stockholders. If the costs are capitalized,

---

[4] The intended implication is the probably valid one that this item is an important component of the firm's capital. It is uncertain, however, how the lay reader of the financial statement may interpret this single dollar amount nestled among the millions.

on the other hand, profits are not currently increased by curtailing research, and the function is thus shielded to some extent from the impact of short-term business recessions. Stability in the level of expenditure is probably necessary to the maintenance of successful research programs in many types of business.

The major objection to capitalizing research and development is that at the time an expenditure is made, management is generally most uncertain as to what future periods, if any, will be benefited. It is quite possible that the knowledge obtained on the particular project will prove worthless to the firm. The principle of conservatism therefore argues that all outlays be expensed at the time they are made. On these grounds, despite the clear evidence that a firm undertakes research and development because the benefits from the work in the aggregate are expected to justify the costs, research and development costs are generally expensed immediately.

The argument is sometimes made that the appropriate focal center of research costing is the patent and that acquisition of a patent right somehow is evidence of the existence of a tangible asset.[5] Therefore, the costs of developing the patented idea or device should be capitalized, whereas outlays that do not lead to a patentable advance should be expensed. Actually, patent rights are often immaterial. Although the legal protection they afford may be valuable, the patent itself by no means establishes the economic worth of an idea. Many patents prove worthless, while innumerable unpatentable developments are extremely productive.

One possible procedure for capitalizing research and development cost is to capitalize the total outlay each period, regardless of the nature of the work done or the apparent probability of future success, and then charge the cost against income over an arbitrary period of time, say the following 10 years. The validity of any such life assignment is admittedly open to question, but it is likely that any reasonable rule with respect to life will produce better results than treating the entire outlay as an expense of the current period.

Accounting for research and development expenditures for internal management use should be guided by entirely different considerations. Management needs to keep track of costs for each project, regardless of the period in which the expenditure is made. These

---

[5] A patent provides for exclusive control by the inventor for 17 years, after which the patented idea enters the public domain unless replaced by a new patent representing a demonstrable improvement over the original. A trademark is usually protected by registration, and the registrant retains exclusive rights until abandoning its use.

costs can be compared with the rate of progress of the research to assist management in judging whether to keep on with the project. Also, when the project is completed it is sometimes useful to compare cost and benefits as a guide in evaluating subsequent research proposals.

Oil Exploration and Drilling Costs

Brief mention should be made of one other type of intangible asset, the value to an oil company of any rights it possesses in underground oil deposits. Once again it is cost rather than value that enters the accounting records, but the accounting treatment of the costs involved in the search for oil may prove to be an indication of future developments in the accounting for research and development. When a development well is sunk in the search for oil, the probability that oil will be found is typically quite small. Consequently, when a wildcatter or a small firm sinks a well, the cost is written off as a loss if a dry hole is the outcome. However, with the present state of knowledge, the major oil producers, which operate on a sufficiently large scale, can predict with fair accuracy the ratio of dry holes to productive wells. In other words, in the aggregate they can be reasonably certain that their exploration and development expenditures will discover oil. Consequently, with expanding knowledge and scale of activities, some companies have adopted the practice of capitalizing so-called "intangible drilling costs" subject to amortization over subsequent crude oil production.

ACQUISITION COST APPROXIMATIONS

Even if the measurement criteria described above are clearly understood and fully accepted, measurement of the acquisition cost of an asset is not always simple. Four problems deserve brief comment here:

1. Allocation of joint acquisition cost.
2. Noncash acquisitions.
3. Acquisition by issue of stock.
4. Purchase in advance of use.

Allocation of Joint Acquisition Cost

It frequently happens that two or more assets are acquired at a single purchase price. If the life expectancies of the individual assets are approximately the same, any division of the *joint cost* will result in about the same periodic charges to expense, and the problem is limited to that of classification. If the life expectancies differ, however, the cost division will affect annual amortization charges. Where land and buildings are purchased together, for example, or where land is purchased and prepared for building construction, that portion of the total cost allocated to the land will not be subject to depreciation.

The method generally used for joint cost allocation is the *relative market value* method. This presumes that the anticipated value of the individual assets to the purchaser, and therefore the amounts that he was willing to pay for the various assets, is proportional to the prices they would have commanded if purchased separately. For example, if an independent appraiser says that comparable land could have been bought on the market for $1 million and a comparable building would have cost $4 million, then 20 percent of the total purchase price will be assigned to the land and 80 percent to the building.

This method should not be applied when a group of assets is acquired to obtain one of them. For example, a company may buy an old loft building together with the land on which it is located, intending to raze the building and erect a new one. In this case, the entire purchase price clearly relates to the land. The building is unwanted by the purchaser, and thus any portion of the joint acquisition cost that reflects the capitalization of the future earning power of the building in its former use is really part of the cost of the land. It is for this reason that land acquisition costs in urban slum clearance or redevelopment projects are often almost prohibitively high.

Joint cost problems are encountered in a wide variety of situations, and the accountant must learn to recognize them. One particularly difficult kind of joint cost problem arises when one company buys a package including intangible as well as tangible assets. In Chapter 9 we saw that the value of a company's "goodwill" is the difference between the separate values of the tangible assets and the combined value of the whole. When a company buys goodwill as part of a joint purchase, the cost of the goodwill is the difference between the total package price and the total of the price that the company would have paid to obtain the tangible assets. These figures ordinarily can be approximated by independent appraisers.

Noncash Acquisitions

While acquisition cost is normally derived from prices paid, such value determinants sometimes are either nonexistent or of dubious validity. For example, a company often pays for assets with shares of its own stock or with nonmonetary assets. In all these cases, the general approach to the valuation problem is through the *imputation of acquisition costs on the basis of currently prevailing market prices*. The accountant's task is to obtain as good an estimate of the fair market value of the assets acquired as the available data will permit.

When assets are acquired *in exchange for nonmonetary assets*—that is, when payment is made "in kind"—the transaction is really both a purchase and a sale. One possibility is to use the book value of the goods given up as the measure of the cost of the new assets obtained. This treatment eliminates any gain or loss on the exchange, implying that it is predominantly a purchase. It assumes that the goods given up could not have been sold at a more advantageous price. It also assumes that the goods were currently worth an amount equal to their book value.

The alternative is to measure cost on the basis of the fair market value of either the goods received or the goods given up. This implies domination of the sale element and results in recognition of a gain or loss.[6]

If the market prices truly represent what independent purchasers and sellers would pay or demand for the assets exchanged, the market value approach is clearly superior. Book values get out of date very rapidly and may be far from the current sacrifice made to acquire the new assets. Market price of the goods given up can be taken as the measure of current sacrifice if it can be assumed that the buying company could get this much from some other source.

Acquisition by Issue of Stock

A somewhat similar problem is raised when an asset is paid for with shares of the *firm's own capital stock*. Once again the cost of the asset can be measured by the current market value of the goods or services received. If the going market prices cannot be identified, however— for example, for a patent right—a substitute must be found. One possibility is to cost the property acquired on the basis of the market value of the shares issued. If neither of these figures can be obtained, then appraisal figures must be used.

It is also of some interest that many large corporations seek acquisi-

---

[6] An authoritative publication of the AICPA states, "In the case of noncash acquisitions . . . cost may be considered as being either the fair value of the consideration given or the fair value of the property or right acquired, whichever is the more clearly evident." American Institute of Certified Public Accountants, *Accounting Research and Terminology Bulletins* (final ed.; New York: AICPA, 1961), p. 38.

tion cost substitutes for the purpose of pricing goods transferred between operating divisions. The object of *transfer pricing* at an approximation of market value is to develop realistic measures of divisional profitability, that is, to evaluate the performance of these subentities as though they were independent enterprises. For public reporting, however, inventories of goods that include any element of intracompany profit must be restated at cost.

Purchase in Advance of Use

Land, plant, or inventory may sometimes be acquired well in advance of their intended use. Under such conditions, the purchaser will presumably anticipate in his offering price any *carrying charges* (storage, property taxes, etc.) likely to be incurred prior to employment of the asset. That is, the purchaser believes that he would have a higher total cost if he were to defer the purchase until he is ready to use the asset. Consequently, carrying charges during the expected holding period are necessary costs of acquisition and should be included in the cost of the asset.

These costs are often expensed for reasons such as conservatism or lack of materiality, but in some situations the case for capitalization is too strong to be ignored. For example, property taxes incurred during the construction period are often added to the cost of buildings if the construction period is long. Similarly, outlays for fire protection and taxes on stands of growing timber are commonly capitalized as acquisition costs of the new growth. In a sense, these situations are similar to manufacturing in that the costs incurred are necessary to the increase in the value of the asset. On the other hand, if the carrying costs are greater than the value increment, they should not be capitalized in full but should be recognized at least in part as losses of the current period. Such losses are occasioned by unexpected delays in construction. This treatment is similar to that afforded to the injury compensation payment (item 4) in the Camden Company illustration, and it is justified by the same line of reasoning.

SUMMARY

The use of historical cost as the basis of asset measurement at the time of acquisition raises a number of difficult questions. Some of these are questions of fact—e.g., was a particular expenditure necessary to obtain the services of the asset? Others result from uncertainty —e.g., will the expenditure lead to a commensurate future benefit?

Still others are definitional—e.g., did the expenditure increase the firm's total productive capacity or merely prevent it from deteriorating? All are alike, however, in that they require the exercise of accounting judgment. Even for questions of fact, the facts may be either too costly or impossible to determine.

In exercising his judgment in borderline areas, the accountant is influenced by considerations of clerical convenience, tax minimization, and conservatism, all of which typically lead to earlier charges to expense than a strict application of the all-inclusive historical cost principle would indicate.

The resulting damage to the informational value of financial statements is not as great as one might first imagine mainly because the accountant insists that a measurement practice must be followed consistently from year to year. For instance, if the company elects to expense research and development expenditures as they are made, it must do so consistently, year after year. Reported income will not be distorted if the expenditure is stable from year to year, and even if expenditures fluctuate, consistency will lead to financial statements that are more reliable than those that would result if management were free to change its asset measurement practices at will, depending on its needs of the moment.

QUESTIONS AND PROBLEMS

1. List and explain the reasons why in borderline cases a business firm may prefer to treat acquisition costs as expenses rather than assets.

2. Discuss the importance of consistency in differentiating between asset and expense.

3. Explain the distinction between "maintenance" and "betterments" and discuss the forms which the latter may take.

4. Discuss the relationship between maintenance policy and the productive capacity of plant assets.

5. What is meant by the "unit of account" for purposes of cost capitalization? Explain how selection of the unit of account bears upon the accounting distinction between "maintenance" and "replacement."

6. State briefly the various circumstances under which appraisal valuations of assets might logically be entered in a company's accounts.

7. The World Wide Oil Company capitalizes its exploration and development well expenditures and expenses them over a 10-year period. The Combination Oil Company expenses these expenditures in the year of the outlay. Discuss the relative merits of the two methods of accounting for these costs.

8. After a long study, the Ace Hauling Company decided that substantial savings could be obtained by replacing its present fleet of three trucks with two larger vehicles. This would necessitate enlarging the door openings in the company's garage, purchasing new overhead doors, and strengthening the garage floor to permit it to support the heavier trucks. Should costs of these items be capitalized or expensed? If you decide to capitalize any of these costs, indicate whether you would capitalize it as part of the cost of the trucks or of the garage or of some other asset. Give your reasons.

9. The Coyle Construction Company paid $21,000 for a house and lot. The house was then torn down at an additional cost of $500 so that Coyle could begin to construct a gasoline service station on the site. At the time of the acquisition, an appraisal of the property placed the value of the land at $18,000 and the value of the house at $9,000.

How would you record the purchase of the house and lot and the subsequent demolition of the house?

10. A farmer buys a tractor for $1,200, pays $100 to get it shipped to his farm, spends $100 painting it red so it will be uniform with his other machinery, fills the tank with gas at a cost of $10, and spends $50 training his slow-witted son to operate it. What should be the debit balance in the Tractor account?

11. The Sussex Sign Company bought a new truck at a price of $3,200 and detailed one of its employees to letter the company's name and address on the sides. The worker was paid $2.50 per hour plus payroll taxes of 10 percent. He worked four hours on the job.

The company took out a year's liability and collision insurance at a cost of $287. To provide adequate protection against theft, it had a new overhead door installed on the garage at a cost of $140.

The company's old truck, which could have been sold to a used car and truck dealer for $200, was accepted by the truck sales agency at a trade-in value of $350.

What was the cost of the new truck?

*12. As a result of a new building ordinance, the Marble Movie Palace was forced to spend $8,000 to install additional fire escapes on the build-

---

* Solutions to problems marked with an asterisk (*) are found in Appendix B.

ing that it occupied and to rearrange the seats in the auditorium at a cost of $2,000. The building was leased from a local realty group, and the lease still had 10 years to run.

What effect should each of these expenditures have on the end-of-year balance sheet and on the income statement for the year? Assume that the expenditures were made just prior to the end of the year.

*13. In 1942 the Experimental Company bought 21,600 shares of Respirator, Inc., common stock at a price of $15 a share. On January 1, 1967, this stock was given to Ordway, Inc., in exchange for an office building. The appraised value of the building on that date was $2 million, while the stock was being traded on the market at a price of $105 a share.

The Experimental Company capitalized the new asset (building) at the original cost of the old asset (stock). Do you agree with this treatment? What further information, if any, would you like to have before reaching a final decision on this question?

*14. Six heavy stamping machines were purchased on account by an automobile manufacturer in Detroit at a price of $16,250 each. When they arrived at their destination, the purchaser paid freight charges of $4,200 and handling fees of $1,000. Four employees whose wages totaled $12 an hour worked four 40-hour weeks setting up and testing the machines. Special wiring and other materials applicable to the new machines cost $610.

Show the entries to record these transactions on the purchaser's books.

15. The Wonson Shoe Manufacturing Company had built a new factory on the bank of a river. On the opposite bank were the homes of a large group of wage earners, most of whom were employed by a textile mill. The Wonson Shoe Company wished to tap this potential labor supply, and for several years had attempted to induce the city council to appropriate funds for a bridge adjacent to its property. In this it was, however, unsuccessful. As a last resort, the directors voted to contribute $300,000 toward the cost of the bridge if the city would appropriate any additional amount necessary. This offer of the company was accepted, and the bridge was built.

Should the contribution of $300,000 have been capitalized or charged immediately as a current expense? Give your reasons.

16. A stockholder in an oil company has noted that the company's annual report lists the following items among its assets:

Leasing and exploration costs.................$28,984,826
Incomplete construction...................... 62,812,187

The stockholder says, "From what I know of the oil business, exploration costs are the expenses of a bunch of geologists and prospectors who ride around in the mountains on burros looking for signs of oil. Is that what they call an asset? And how about incomplete construction? That represents costs of items not yet productive, some of which may be partly drilled wells. Lots of wells which are drilled prove to be dry holes. These dry holes will actually be liabilities, it seems to me."

Explain to the stockholder the probable reasons for the company's treatment of these items. Do you agree with the treatment? Explain.

17. A two-story structure which extended across the rear of a business building was torn down, and a 12-story building was erected in its place. The construction of the new building made it necessary to close the rear windows on several floors of the adjoining structure. It also necessitated a rearrangement of partitions and hallways at a cost of approximately $35,000.

When the owner of the building in which these alterations were made filed his income tax return, he deducted the $35,000 expenditure from his revenues for the year. Objections were taken to this procedure by the tax officials on the ground that the cost incurred in making alterations of this sort represented a capital charge and was therefore not properly treated as a deduction from revenue. The owner disagreed with the tax officials, contending that the alterations did not add to the life or to the value of the building in any way but merely kept the property in a condition to be rented.

Was the cost of alterations properly a charge to capital or a charge against revenue? Support your conclusions.

18. The Congealed Products Company has agreed to purchase the plant, equipment, trade names, and all other assets of the Frozen Assets Company. The physical assets to be acquired are listed on the books of the Frozen Assets Company at an original cost of $2,000,000, less an Allowance for Depreciation of $1,200,000. Patents, trademarks, and goodwill are shown on the Frozen Assets balance sheet at a nominal value of $1. The agreed purchase price is 100,000 shares of Congealed Products common stock. Because all shares now outstanding are held by one family, Congealed Products stock has no public market.

a) Discuss briefly the problems that would be encountered by Congealed Products in accounting for this purchase.

b) Recommend a solution to these problems and indicate, using assumed numbers if necessary, the accounting entry that should be made on the books of the Congealed Products Company.

19. How would you classify (asset or expense) each of the following costs at the time of its incurrence? Give reasons.

a) An outlay of $60,000 by a manufacturer of earth-moving equipment for research aimed at the elimination of certain undesirable operating characteristics in a standard model power shovel. Successful results are achieved in the same accounting period in which the research is authorized.

b) The costs to a chemical company of operating a research laboratory, the primary functions of which are the development of new products and the improvement of processes for the manufacture of established products. Costs average about $300,000 a year.

c) A grant of $200,000 to an engineering school by an airplane manufacturer for basic research in light plane design. All results of such research are to be generally disseminated.

d) Outlays of $1,000,000 incurred by an automotive company in retooling its plant to manufacture a new model passenger car.

e) Expenditures of $25,000 by a mail-order company for preparing and printing a new catalog for the coming year.

f) Expenditures of $30,000 for "institutional" advertising by a manufacturer of optical instruments. These costs are incurred during a year in which the company's entire output is going to the armed services, and are made solely for the purpose of keeping the company's name before the public in contemplation of future civilian sales.

g) Expenditures of $800,000 by a large oil company for exploration of a new territory. These costs include test borings and so forth. The results indicate that development of the area would not be commercially feasible.

20. The Park Wells Company has just purchased all the assets of the Crawford Corporation, giving in exchange government bonds which were purchased two years ago for $1 million. The market price of these bonds was $970,000 on the day when Park Wells purchased the Crawford assets.

On the date of the purchase by Park Wells, Crawford's books showed current assets of $300,000 and plant and equipment with a book value of $200,000. No other assets were listed on the Crawford Corporation's books.

An appraiser hired by Park Wells estimated that the replacement cost of the current assets on the purchase date was $350,000. The replacement cost of the plant and equipment, less an allowance for depreciation, was $400,000.

a) Should the Park Wells Company have recognized $1,000,000, $970,000, or some other figure as the total cost of the Crawford assets?

b) How should this total amount have been allocated among the various assets acquired? Prepare a journal entry reflecting your allocation and give your reasons for your choice.

21. In order to obtain a new factory site, the Mosk Manufacturing Company purchased a 12-acre tract of wasteland, paying $13,000 to the former owners. Expenses for searching titles and for drawing and recording deeds amounted to $300. Grading cost $2,800. As only six acres were required for its own factory, it considered two offers for six acres: (1) $12,000 for the north half, and (2) $8,000 for the south half. It accepted the offer of $8,000 for the south half and received a certified check in payment.

a) At what value should the remaining land be carried on the next balance sheet?

b) What profit, if any, was realized?

*22. The Tower Company makes machinery for sale to manufacturers. It maintains an experimental department for the development of new machines and improved models of its products. Experimental work on a projected machine was initiated in 19x5. Expenditures in that year totaled $4,346, but the results were largely negative. In 19x6, additional expenditures amounted to $18,625 and resulted in a practicable design. Legal and other fees in connection with the filing of patent applications were $1,327. Patents were issued in 19x7. In that same year, production of the new machine on a commercial scale was begun and special dies, jigs, and so forth were purchased at a cost of $2,852.

Prepare summary journal entries to record the above outlays.

23. The Curwood Manufacturing Company entered into a lease agreement with the owner of a machine shop whereby the company was to occupy the shop for a period of 10 years at an annual rental of $25,000. Five years later, the company sought and obtained a downward adjustment of its annual rental. Upon the receipt of $50,000, the lessor agreed to cancel the old lease and to execute a new contract for a 10-year period at an annual rental of $15,000.

When the new lease had been drawn up and signed and the $50,000 paid, Curwood's executives disagreed as to the nature of the transaction and the entries to be made on the books of the company. The following bases were considered:

(1) The $50,000 should be charged directly to the retained earnings account as a nonrecurring item.

(2) The $50,000 was paid in settlement of the canceled lease and should be allocated over the remaining five years which the old lease would otherwise have run.

(3) The $50,000 constituted part of the cost of the new lease and should be spread over its 10-year term.

(4) The total amount paid and to be paid for the use of the building was in the nature of rent; therefore, the entire amount of $325,000 should be reallocated in equal amounts of $21,700 over the entire 15-year period covering both the old and new leases.

Which of the bases discussed, or what other if none of these is satisfactory, would best describe this transaction? Explain.

24. The Caldbec Stationery Store has just purchased a large photo-copying machine and a manual typewriter. The photocopying machine will be used to print copies of documents, manuscripts, and other items for Caldbec customers. The typewriter has been placed on sale in the store. The following data relate to these two acquisitions:

	Copier	Typewriter
Invoice price..........................	$5,000	$100
Discount taken........................	2%	2%
Freight cost..........................	$ 200	$ 4
Insurance in transit...................	20	1
Cost of installation and testing:		
Materials.........................	175	xxx
Labor of company employees..........	250	xxx
Bill from electrician for power		
connections......................	75	xxx

a) Ignoring depreciation, at what amount does accounting theory require the machine to be shown on the company's year-end balance sheet?

b) Assuming that the typewriter is still unsold at the end of the year, at what amount does accounting theory require it to be shown on the company's year-end balance sheet? (Note: The cost to replace the item at the end of the year is higher than its original cost.)

c) Are the underlying principles the same in each case or different? Explain briefly.

d) In accounting practice, at what amounts might you expect these assets to be shown? Explain your reasons for any differences between these amounts and those given in answer to parts (*a*) and (*b*) above.

25. The managers of Enesco, Inc. planned to erect a new store and secured purchase options for 60 days on two lots. For the option on Lot A they paid $1,800, and for the option on Lot B, $2,400. After studying traffic densities, they decided to purchase Lot B. The company opened a single Real Estate account, to which were posted the following:

Debits:

Option on Lot A................................$	1,800
Option on Lot B...............................	2,400
Payment of balance on Lot B......................	40,000
Title insurance......................................	700
Assessment for street improvement.................	1,200
Recording fee for deed............................	50
Cost of razing old building on Lot B................	3,000
Erection of new building.........................	100,000

Credits:

Sale of salvaged materials from old building...........$	2,000
Refund on street improvement assessment............	150

The salvage value of material obtained from the old building and used in the erection of the new building was $2,500. The depreciated value of the old building, as shown by the books of the company from which the purchase was made, was $12,000. The old building was razed immediately after the purchase.

a) What should be shown as the cost of the land (Lot B)?
b) What should be shown as the original cost of the new building?
c) Prepare a journal entry or entries to reassign the balance in the Real Estate account to the Land account, the Buildings account, and such other accounts as you find necessary.

26. *The New York Times* carried the following report in its financial section:

"This week Guild Films, Inc., a major distributor of motion picture films to television stations, will reveal the existence of $6,500,000 to $7,000,000 of previously unreported assets in the form of rights to TV spot time. The value of this time is nearly as great as Guild's total assets as listed in its last annual report.

"The company built up its valuable bank of time by bartering exhibition rights to its film library for spots. It has cited "competitive reasons" and the difficulty of assigning a definite value to unsold future time spots as the reasons why it has not listed these rights as balance sheet assets.

"Television spot time is the twenty-second to sixty-second intervals during and between programs that are commonly sold as advertising space. Under the barter system the lease price of a motion picture film is paid for by the broadcasting station with a contract for a certain number of time spots instead of cash. This spot time can then be sold to advertising agencies or directly to companies for commercial use. It can also be bartered again for other assets."

a) Should Guild Films have listed these "spot time rights" on its balance sheet? State reasons for your answer.
b) Assuming that the company had decided to list these rights as balance sheet assets, how should their balance sheet valuation have been determined?
c) Does the signing of a contract bartering film rentals for future spot time rights constitute satisfactory evidence for the immediate recognition of sales revenue on the income statement, or should this be deferred until the rights are used or sold? State your reasons.

27. Pamela and John Batsford purchased a house from Paul Kitchener and took title to the property on May 15. Mr. Batsford drew the following checks at that time:

To Central Savings Bank	$ 7,907.06
To Paul Kitchener	19,938.41
To Crowder Realty	1,050.00
To Household Title Insurance Company	930.00
To David Walworth	341.12
Total	$30,166.59

The check to the Central Savings Bank was to pay off the amount due on Mr. Kitchener's mortgage loan from the bank. The amount of the payment was computed as follows:

Balance of loan	$8,448.00
Accrued interest, May 1–5	21.12
Total	$8,469.12
Less: Balance in tax escrow account*	562.06
Net Payment	$7,907.06

* The tax escrow account was set up to accumulate the amounts deposited in the bank by Mr. Kitchener for payment of property taxes when due.

The amount of the check to Paul Kitchener was computed from the following figures:

Contract price		$31,000.00
Property taxes, May 15–December 31*		630.00
Fuel oil in furnace storage tank		14.86
Power lawn mower		35.00
Metal screens and storm windows		342.73
Total		$32,022.59
Less: Down payment, paid previously	$3,100.00	
Payment made to Central Savings Bank	7,907.06	
Sale commission to Crowder Realty†	1,050.00	
Allowance for property transfer taxes‡	27.12	12,084.18
Net Payment		$19,938.41

* Taxes paid in advance on January 1 by Mr. Kitchener, covering property taxes for the entire calendar year.
† The sales commission is an obligation of Mr. Kitchener, paid on his behalf by Mr. and Mrs. Batsford.
‡ Property transfer taxes are an obligation of Mr. Kitchener, paid on his behalf by Mr. and Mrs. Batsford.

Household Title Insurance Company insured Mr. and Mrs. Batsford's title to the property for a lump sum of $930.00. This insurance coverage remains in force as long as the Batsfords retain title to the property, without payment of additional premiums.

Mr. Walworth, the Batsfords' lawyer, submitted the following statement:

Fee for services rendered in connection with purchase	$310.00
Property transfer taxes	27.12
Recording of deed	4.00
Total	$341.12

What costs should have been capitalized as part of the cost of house and land? Explain.

28. The Beckman Company late in 1967 requested bids from several equipment manufacturers on the construction of a unique piece of special-purpose equipment to be used in the Beckman factory to replace an outmoded piece of equipment then in use. Several bids were received, the lowest in the amount of $55,000. The management of the Beckman Company felt that this was excessive. Instead, the machine was manufactured in the company's own machine shop which was then operating at substantially less than full capacity.

The machine was built during the early months of 1968 and placed in service on July 1, 1968. The costs of manufacturing the machine were first accumulated in a factory cost sheet, as follows:

Raw materials used in construction of new machine	$ 8,000
Direct labor used in construction of new machine	20,000
Amount paid to Ace Machinery Service Company for installation of new machine	1,000
Cost of dismantling old machine	800
Cost of labor and materials on trial runs of new machine	2,000
Cost of machine tools for new machine	6,000
Savings in construction costs	17,700
Less: Cash proceeds from sale of old machine	(500)
Total Cost of Machine	$55,000

Upon completion of the trial runs, the machine was placed in service and the costs were transferred to the company's equipment account by means of the following entry:

Equipment	55,000	
Work in Process		55,000

The following additional information is available:

(1) Factory costs other than labor and materials averaged 80 percent of direct labor cost during the first six months of 1968.

(2) Freight charges on the materials used in construction of the machine amounted to $250. This amount was debited to the Freight-In account.

(3) Cash discounts on the materials used in construction amounted to $50. This amount was credited to Purchases Discounts.

(4) Savings in construction costs were computed on the basis of the difference between the lowest outside bid and the net costs charged to the job during construction. These savings were credited to the account, Gain on Construction of Equipment.

(5) Products produced during the trial runs were scrapped; scrap value was negligible.

At what amount should the new machine have been capitalized in the equipment account on July 1, 1968? Show the details.

29. The general ledger of Enter-tane, Inc., a corporation engaged in the development and production of television programs for commercial sponsorship, contains the following accounts before amortization at the end of the current year:

Account	Balance (Debit)
Sealing Wax and Kings	$51,000
The Messenger	36,000
The Desperado	17,500
Shin Bone	8,000
Studio Rearrangement	5,000

An examination of contracts and records has revealed the following information:

(1) The balances in the first two accounts represent the total cost of completed programs that were televised during the accounting period just ended. Under the terms of an existing contract, Sealing Wax and Kings will be rerun during the next accounting period at a fee equal to 50 percent of the fee for the first televising of the program. The contract for the first run produced $300,000 of revenue. The contract with the sponsor of The Messenger provides that he may at his option rerun the program during the next season at a fee of 75 percent of the fee on the first televising of the program.

(2) The balance in The Desperado account is the cost of a new program which has just been completed and is being considered by several companies for commercial sponsorship.

(3) The balance in the Shin Bone account represents the cost of a partially completed program for a projected series that has been abandoned.

(4) The balance of the Studio Rearrangement account consists of payments made to a firm of engineers which prepared a report recommending a more efficient utilization of existing studio space and equipment.

a) State the general principle or principles by which accountants guide themselves in deciding how much of the balances in the first four accounts should be shown as assets on the company's year-end balance sheet.

b) Applying this principle or principles, how would you report each of these first four accounts in the year-end financial statements? Explain.

c) In what way, if at all, does the Studio Rearrangement account differ from the first four? How would you report this account in the company's financial statements for the period?

30. The Realty Corporation owns a large number of buildings which it rents to commercial and residential tenants. In January, 1968, it bought a building for conversion into quarters suitable for use by a foreign legation. The purchase price of the building was $80,000 and of the land, $90,000.

Extensive remodeling and interior decorating was begun immediately to adapt the building to its intended use. The following outlays were made during the period January through June, 1968:

(1) Interior painting and decorating...............................$ 40,000
(2) Structural alterations including replacement of plumbing fixtures at a
    cost of $12,000, and landscaping at $8,000..................... 62,000
(3) Replacement and renewal of electric wiring.................... 10,000
(4) Removal of fourth story....................................... 50,000
(5) Payment of hospital and medical expenses of passerby injured by fall-
    ing brick..   2,000
(6) Architect's fees, building permits, etc....................... 16,000
        Total..$180,000

In addition, property taxes accrued for the period January 1 through June 30 amounted to $3,000.

Late in June, the company was notified that it was being sued for $45,000 for the personal injuries and mental anguish suffered by the passerby who was hit by the falling brick (item 5 above). The suit was scheduled for trial in February, 1969. At the time the remodeling work was done, the Realty Corporation had elected to be its own insurer in matters pertaining to public liability, and therefore it was not insured either for the medical expenses or the amount of any payment that might result from the lawsuit. The premium that an insurance company would have charged for liability coverage during the period of remodeling was $1,250.

The building was ready for occupancy on July 1, 1968, and a 10-year lease, running from July 1, 1968, to June 30, 1978, was signed with a foreign government.

Indicate how these facts should have been reflected in the company's accounts as of July 1, 1968. How much should have been capitalized and under what account titles? How much should have been charged to expense for the first half of 1968? Give your reasons for your treatment of each item.

Chapter 11

LONG-LIVED ASSETS:
DEPRECIATION AND BOOK VALUE

THE TASK OF ASSET MEASUREMENT is only begun with the decision to capitalize a cost. The next question is how the asset should be measured in the balance sheets and on the income statements of subsequent periods. This is mainly a question of deciding how to amortize the costs of various assets.

Certain forms of prepayment, such as the cost of land, may be regarded as infinitely long-lived and hence not subject to amortization. Others, such as insurance premiums, have contractually defined life spans that when given the reasonable assumption of uniform benefits over time provide an obvious basis for systematic amortization—equal amounts to each time period.

Industrial and commercial plant (i.e., buildings, equipment, etc.) offers a more challenging problem. The employment of an asset in this class does not result in its physical consumption. The asset survives the productive process in which it is employed, but because of physical deterioration and obsolescence it is eventually retired. Unfortunately, although a plant asset's life is to some extent controllable through maintenance, the vagaries of obsolescence do not allow its accurate prediction. Further, little or no apparent relation exists between the evidences of physical deterioration and the economic consumption of the asset over its life. Under these conditions, the plan under which the asset is depreciated is necessarily based as much if not more on logical argument with respect to the nature and purpose of depreciation than on factual observation.

This chapter is concerned with the question of how individual accounting periods should be charged for the services of assets in this last category—that is, depreciation charges—and how the assets should be represented on the balance sheet. This question has a long history of lively controversy for two reasons. First, because factual observation does not determine in any precise way the annual depreciation charge for an asset, considerable variation in the charge is possible. Second, the expenditure or sacrifice by a company in connection with a depreciable asset arises out of the purchase decision and not the depreciation decision. Therefore, in contrast with labor or materials expenses, depreciation expense can never be identified uniquely with any given time period. These characteristics of depreciation would make the consideration of how it should be determined practically meaningless without the careful examination of the objectives to be served.

OBJECTIVES OF DEPRECIATION

The main argument for computing periodic depreciation charges must be that this will improve the quality of income information and thereby produce better decisions. Although government bodies, labor unions, and others use company financial statements in decision making, the main emphasis is on decisions by shareholders (and others who look at the firm from the view point of *investors*) and on decisions by *management*.

Influence on Investor Decisions

Most discussion of depreciation policy focuses on its impact on financial reporting to the investing public. Without depreciation charges, it is argued, the investor might be misled into thinking that the company is more profitable than it actually is. This might lead him to invest his money imprudently. Alternatively, he might overcompensate for an error he knows is there but cannot quantify. This might lead him away from a profitable investment. In other words, the quality of investor decisions is assumed to depend significantly on the accuracy with which expense figures represent resource consumption.

It follows, therefore, that depreciation, like other expenses, should measure the consumption of productive resources during a given period of time. The technical accounting term to reflect this idea is "expiration of service potential." In this view, an asset represents a bundle of services that can be used in the future. The depreciation of an asset during a period should reflect the share of the asset's total service potential that has expired during that period. Similarly, the net balance in the asset account at any point in time should reflect the unexpired portion of the asset's service potential. Regardless of the difficulty of realizing this objective, it is the only valid basis for choice among alternative depreciation methods. This criterion, therefore, will be the guide in discussing the process of depreciation and the methods of its measurement.

Influence on Management Decisions

Management's interest in the historical net income figure, and therefore in the depreciation charge, is much more diffused. For our immediate purposes, three kinds of management problems need to be discussed briefly:

1. How large a dividend should be declared?
2. Which segments of the business deserve more than their share of management attention?
3. Which segments of the business should be expanded and which should be contracted?

Dividend Decisions. Although most firms distribute dividends that are much smaller than reported income, the income figure is a datum that cannot be ignored. A decision to declare dividends in excess of income is a decision to reduce the size of the firm, a partial liquidation. Without an income figure, a corporation's board of directors cannot know how large a dividend could be declared without shrinking the company.

For this purpose, as with investor decisions, the objective of the depreciation charge should be to indicate how much of the service potential of the assets has expired during the period. Unless an equivalent amount of the gross revenues is retained in the business and used to provide additional capacity, a partial liquidation will occur.[1]

Allocation of Management's Attention. The income concept is used within the firm, for individual portions of the firm's activities as well as for the firm as a whole. If one segment's revenues are not covering its expenses by an adequate margin, management should investigate to see what is wrong and what, if anything, can be done to redress the balance.

Once again, the appropriate measure of depreciation is the amount by which the productive capacity of depreciating assets was consumed as a result of each of the company's activities. The only new

---

[1] The term "capacity" is often used to refer to the maximum physical output obtainable from a given set of physical facilities during a specified period of time. Our usage here is slightly different, referring to the total economic service obtainable from the asset during its expected lifetime. This definition will be examined more fully later in the chapter.

problem is how to allocate the depreciation charge among the various segments, but this is a problem that we need not try to resolve at this time.

Expansion-Contraction Decisions. Each proposal to invest additional funds in a given activity needs to be judged on the basis of its *anticipated* results. In some cases, the most profitable investment opportunities within the firm are in activities with the poorest earnings records. Management cannot be indifferent, however, to the overall profitability of its investment in various areas. If an activity's rate of return on investment is low and fails to improve, management is likely to reduce its relative role in the company's overall plans for the future. It may even decide to investigate the desirability of discontinuing the activity entirely. An activity which has demonstrated high earning power, on the other hand, will bulk large in management's strategic plans for the future. Ultimately, funds should be transferred from activities with low rates of return on investment to activities promising higher yields. Here again, it would seem that depreciation should represent the portion of the assets' capacity that has been consumed during the period.

Nonobjectives of Depreciation

The objectives of depreciation are *information* objectives. A mistake that is often made is to impute to them a power of *action* that they cannot possess.

For example, some writers have stated that the purpose of depreciation is to recapture from revenues a sufficient amount of money to provide for replacement of the assets' capacity. This has not been our argument at all. Funds for replacement depend on the existence of a surplus of funds inflows over funds outflows. In other words, except for the tax effects to be discussed later, replacement funds depend on how the asset is *used*, not on how it is depreciated. No amount of depreciation will provide funds for replacement if the company cannot meet its current cash operating costs from its current revenues.

Another possible misunderstanding is very similar. Some have argued that the purpose of depreciation is to deduct from revenues an amount sufficient to recover the original investment (i.e., acquisition cost). Once again, the problem is that cost recovery depends on effective use of the asset rather than on depreciation policy. If the initial investment decision was sound and if assets have been managed effectively, the original cost will be recovered with enough funds left over to provide an adequate return on investment. Depreciation has nothing to do with this—again except insofar as it affects the company's taxes.

What depreciation does in this respect is to make stockholders and directors aware of capital consumption. This leads to smaller dividends and a retention of funds in the business. Although this is the effect, it is not the reason for depreciation. Directors may choose to declare dividends in excess of current income or, in the more usual case, to retain and reinvest portions of the annual income. Depreciation in itself neither generates nor retains funds in the business.

Depreciation and Taxes

The amount charged as depreciation for tax purposes shields the same amount of revenues from income taxation. It is thus an important element in determining annual cash flows. Although income tax regulations start from an accounting concept of income (and depreciation), they quickly acquire an overlay of adjustments and allowances designed to further specific public objectives. For example, for tax purposes a firm may be able to charge immediately to expense a large portion of an asset's cost. By reducing taxable income and thereby reducing the firm's current tax payments, the government hopes to encourage more purchases of this kind of asset.

Management is expected to take advantage of tax provisions like these, but this does not mean that the depreciation shown in the annual report to shareholders should be the figure taken from the tax return. In fact, the income statement of a firm in which reported income before taxes is the same as the taxable income figure shown on the year's income tax return is more likely to be misleading than one which follows the principles outlined in this chapter. *None of the discussion here, in other words, refers to depreciation for tax purposes.*

DEPRECIATION METHODS

Defining depreciation as the portion of an asset's lifetime service potential consumed during a period merely states the problem. A variety of solutions radically different in their consequences have been advanced as being consistent with this objective. Hence, to arrive at a basis for choice among these alternatives, it is advisable to first consider the causes of depreciation.

The Causes of Depreciation

Plant assets have finite lives because of *physical deterioration* and *obsolescence*. The former arises through asset use, the passage of time, and accidental damage. Regardless of the cause of physical deterioration, its consequence is a decline in the quantity or quality or a rise in the unit cost of the output that may be obtained through use of the asset. For many assets, of course, the effects of wear and age may be offset by maintenance expenditures. By this means, periodic service capacity may even be held reasonably constant for some portion of the asset's life. At some point, however, the maintenance expenditure needed to accomplish this begins increasing; eventually, it becomes prohibitively large. The economical level of maintenance expenditures is also influenced by the threat of obsolescence.

In a dynamic economy, obsolescence is frequently more important than wear and age in impairing and eventually terminating the useful lives of plant and equipment. Improvements in technology, changes in consumer taste, and population shifts result in products and methods of production that are superior (more economical, useful, or attractive) than those available from existing plant and equipment.

Obsolescence may be evolutionary, like wear, or revolutionary, like physical damage. In either case, however, the asset loses the ability to create value. This is the real nature of the process of depreciation. Changes in the physical characteristics of an asset, shifts in consumer demand, the discovery of new production methods, and so forth, are merely different causes of this one fundamental process.

For example, the Stengel Electric Company recently purchased a McGraw carton-making machine to do the cutting, scoring, and printing necessary to convert rolls of corrugated board into carton blanks. The machine cost $36,000, delivered and installed in the Stengel factory. The cost of operating this machine, not including depreciation, was expected to amount to approximately $45,000 a year, and the machine was expected to be useful for 12 years.

If the McGraw machine had not been bought, the company's best alternative would have been to continue purchasing the cartons from outsiders at a cost of $55,000 a year. Before deducting depreciation, the cash savings were therefore expected to amount to $10,000 a year ($55,000 minus $45,000), or $120,000 during the 12-year period. The machine's salvage value at the end of 12 years was expected to be negligible; thus the amount to be depreciated was the full purchase cost of $36,000.

Exhibit 11–1

ECONOMIC CHARACTERISTICS OF A
UNIFORMLY PRODUCTIVE ASSET

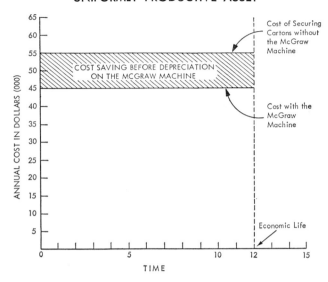

How much of the $36,000 should be charged to each of the 12 years? Examination of the year-by-year distribution of the $120,000 profit before depreciation may help answer this question. For example, Exhibit 11–1 provides a graphic representation of the distribution assumed by the plant manager. The upper line represents the value of the output of the carton machine. The lower line represents the costs exclusive of depreciation of obtaining the same output with the McGraw machine. Both of these lines are horizontal for 12 years and then terminate. This implies that the McGraw machine will function perfectly until it suddenly falls apart or suffers some other calamity which renders it useless. Although this projection of the asset's economic service and life may seem strange, it may be the most accurate possible and it may even be an approximation of reality.

On the other hand, a number of considerations argue that the annual value of the machine's output should fall as it gets older. First, as the machine ages, maintenance costs, idle machine time, and scrap losses should increase. Secondly, with the passage of time, improvements in the design of carton machinery can be expected to take place. Carton manufacturers will acquire these improved machines and offer cartons to Stengel at lower prices—the consequence being a decline in the value of the output. Third, a change in merchandising methods may require that each carton have three-color printing on silver foil paper as the outside cover, or a packing material as good as corrugated board but half its cost may be developed. In either event, the value of the machine's output would fall below its operating costs exclusive of depreciation. The machine would become worthless, and it would be sold for its scrap value.

A revolutionary event such as those just described may not take place for 20 years or it may take place in the next year or two. The probable operating savings in any given year will be less than the annual cash savings computed for the machine because there is a

Exhibit 11–2

ECONOMIC CHARACTERISTICS OF A TYPICAL DEPRECIABLE ASSET

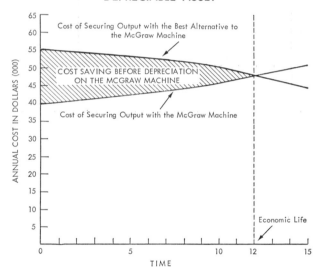

statistical probability that one of these revolutionary events will take place. Thus the gross savings must be multiplied by a probability factor to find the expected savings for the year. Other things being equal, the longer a machine is owned the longer it will have been exposed to the risk of obsolescence and the greater will be the chance that an obsolescence-causing event will have taken place. This means that the probability-weighted estimated savings will be smaller in the later years of the equipment than in its early years.

All of these considerations suggest that Exhibit 11–2 presents a more realistic representation than Exhibit 11–1 of the gain to be had from purchasing the McGraw machine. The costs of obtaining the cartons with the machine increase over time, while the costs *under the best alternative* decrease as the machine gets older. At some point the two curves will cross, and at this point it no longer pays to continue using the machine.[2] Its economic life comes to an end. The only circumstance that might cause the operating savings to increase and not diminish is excess capacity and the expectation that demand for the utilization of the machine's output will increase for a number of years. The operating saving might then be expected to rise for a few periods before it starts falling.

Annual Determination of Depreciation

One possible approach to the depreciation problem is to estimate at the end of each period the portion of an asset's lifetime service potential that has expired during the period. In view of our discussion of obsolescence and changing economic conditions, the charge determined in this way would fluctuate violently from one year to the next.

To illustrate, assume that a company has a machine for which it paid $10,000 two years ago. In the third year of the asset's life a change in economic conditions radically reduces the net income before depreciation generated by the machine. If three fourths of the service potential existing at the start of the year expired during the third year, it would follow that the depreciation charge should be $6,000 and the remaining asset value should be reduced to $2,000.

This illustration should bring to mind the discussion in Chapter 9 of economic value versus historical cost as a basis for asset measurement. Notwithstanding the apparent merits of calculating depreciation in the manner described, the objections raised in Chapter 9 to asset revaluation and income determination on the basis of economic value apply to the present situation.

Before taking up alternative depreciation plans, another approach to the annual determination of the depreciation charges should be noted. Quite often the amount that can be obtained from the liquidation of an asset can be determined objectively, and it has been advocated that liquidation value should be used as the basis of asset measurement and depreciation.[3] Liquidation value is correct for asset retention or disposal decisions. Assume that due to the specialized na-

---

[2] In Exhibit 11–2, the initial level of savings, the life, and the total savings over the life differ from those in Exhibit 11–1, but economic life is still 12 years. Mathematicians would describe the Exhibit 11–1 representation of the industrial engineers' calculations as a linear approximation of the situation represented by Exhibit 11–2.

[3] For some of the arguments relating to this issue, see R. J. Chambers, *Accounting, Evaluation and Economic Behavior* (Englewood Cliffs, N.J.: Prentice-Hall, Inc., 1966).

ture of the machine in the above illustration, it would bring only its scrap value of $500 if sold now or at any future time. In that event, the depreciation that results from keeping the machine instead of selling it is zero, not the $1,000 that the company will record in the ledger if the machine is kept in service. If revenues from use of the machine exceed the machine's operating expenses other than depreciation by as little as, say, $100, keeping it will be profitable.

However, a highly specialized asset may have a negligible liquidation value the moment it is acquired even if it is expected to be very profitable. Consequently liquidation value has been rejected as a basis for asset measurement and depreciation accounting in the going concern.[4]

Uniform-Charge Methods of Depreciation

Two methods of charging depreciation may be considered appropriate for the uniformly productive asset: straight-line depreciation and production-unit depreciation. If the asset's life depends on how much it is used, the production-unit method should be used. Under this method, the annual charge is: the number of units of output (pounds, gallons, or machine-hours) multiplied by the unit depreciation rate. This rate is calculated as follows:

$$\frac{\text{Original Cost} - \text{Estimated Salvage Value}}{\text{Lifetime Production Capacity (Units of Output)}}.$$

If the factors that bring life to an end are a function of the passage of time rather than of asset use, then the charge should be the same amount each year, and the divisor in the rate formula becomes the number of years of expected life rather than lifetime production capacity.

Of these two methods, the straight-line method has been far more widely used—in large measure because obsolescence is more often the dominating factor in asset retirement than physical deterioration. The production-unit method has been used most widely in recording *depletion* of such natural resources as mineral deposits, in which useful life ordinarily terminates with the exhaustion of the deposits.

Some firms have adopted a combination of the two methods, in which a basic periodic charge is supplemented in times of abnormally

---

[4] For a brief elaboration on this point, see W. T. Baxter, "Accounting Values: Sale Price versus Replacement Cost," *Journal of Accounting Research*, Vol. II (Autumn, 1967), pp. 208–14.

high activity. For example, if the overall rate of output increases to 110 percent of what is considered normal, the total period charge is correspondingly increased to compensate for such intensive utilization, and hence unusual wear on plant facilities.

Declining-Charge Depreciation Methods

Another group of depreciation methods leads to a periodic depreciation charge that declines over an asset's expected life. Methods of this type are appropriate if (1) the receipts are expected to decline as the asset gets older; and (2) it is believed that the allocation of depreciation should be related to the pattern of the asset's expected receipts.[5]

The method that would best accomplish the desired result under these assumptions would be to base each year's depreciation on that year's proportionate share of the estimated total net cash receipts during the asset's lifetime. For example, if the first year's savings for the McGraw carton machine were $12,000 and the 12-year total were $120,000, then one tenth of the total depreciable cost, or $3,600, would be charged as depreciation for the first year.

Unfortunately, this kind of a solution would be expensive to administer and would also imply a more precise knowledge of the year-to-year pattern of cash flows than is likely to obtain in practice. For these reasons, declining-charge depreciation is usually derived from some simple formula. The resultant depreciation pattern is to some extent arbitrary, but it may conform more closely than straight-line methods to the expected pattern of cash receipts. Though not perfect, it is likely to be an improvement over straight-line methods when applied to assets similar to the one represented in Exhibit 11–2.

Two such formulas are reflected in the *sum-of-the-years' digits* and *declining-balance* methods. The sum-of-digits method is used as follows. Let n be the asset's life. Each year from 1 to n is represented by a digit, 1, 2, 3, . . . , n. The fractions of the asset's cost charged as depreciation in the years 1, 2, 3, . . ., n are the digits in reverse order divided by their sum. If $n = 5$, the sum of the digits is $1 + 2 + 3 + 4 + 5 = 15$ and the depreciation rates for the five years are 5/15, 4/15, 3/15, 2/15, and 1/15, in that order.

The diminishing-balance method involves the application of a fixed

---

[5] For concise expression, the annual value of an asset's services will be referred to as its annual cash *receipts*.

percentage to the *book value* of the asset at the beginning of the period rather than to the original cost.[6]

The three methods—straight line, sum of digits, and declining balance—are illustrated in Exhibit 11–3 for an asset with a cost of $6,000, a life of five years, and a salvage value of approximately $800. The diminishing-balance rate that satisfies these conditions is 33⅓ percent.

Notwithstanding the logical merits of a depreciation method under which the charge declines over time,[7] few firms used such methods prior to 1954. In that year, Congress responded to a mounting wave of

Exhibit 11–3

COMPARISON OF STRAIGHT-LINE AND ACCELERATED DEPRECIATION METHODS*

Periods	Straight Line		Diminishing Balance		Sum-of-the-Years' Digits	
	Beginning Balance	Period Charge	Beginning Balance	Period Charge	Beginning Balance	Period Charge
Year 1	$6,000	$1,040	$6,000	$2,000	$6,000	$1,733
Year 2	4,960	1,040	4,000	1,333	4,267	1,387
Year 3	3,920	1,040	2,667	889	2,880	1,040
Year 4	2,880	1,040	1,778	593	1,840	693
Year 5	1,840	1,040	1,185	395	1,147	347
Balance	800		790		800	
Total Amortized ..		$5,200		$5,210		$5,200

* Asset cost is $6,000, has a life of five years, and a salvage value of $800.

criticism of the existing law with respect to depreciation by liberalizing the basis on which declining-balance methods were permissible for tax purposes. The critics argued first that actual asset lives were in fact shorter than those prescribed by the Bureau of Internal Revenue. The

---

[6] In theory, the appropriate rate is obtained by the formula $r = 1 - \sqrt[n]{S/C}$, where r is the desired rate, n the number of periods of expected asset life, S the expected salvage value, and C the acquisition cost. A positive salvage value must be assumed because an amount cannot be reduced to zero by successive applications of a fixed rate. Note, however, that minor changes in S will have greatly exaggerated effects on r, and hence will yield large differences in the depreciation charges for the early years. Consequently, practical application of the method generally requires selection of a reasonable rate, with the result that the salvage value becomes an arbitrary residual figure.

[7] For a further discussion of the subject, see Robert L. Dixon, "Decreasing Charge Depreciation—A Search for Logic," *Accounting Review*, October, 1960.

consequence of any such bias was that depreciation was smaller and income taxes were higher during the actual life of an asset, and companies were thus forced to prepay taxes in some measure. Second, it was argued that liberalizing depreciation allowances would stimulate business investment and the country's prosperity by increasing the profitability of investment and the funds available to firm for investment.

Neither of these arguments leads logically to any specific depreciation formula, but the 1954 revision of the federal tax code authorized the use of the declining-balance method with rates as high as twice the normal straight-line rate (the reciprocal of the life estimate that has been accepted for income tax purposes). This variant of the diminishing-balance method is known as the *double-rate, declining-balance* method, and is applicable for tax purposes to any asset acquired in new condition since 1954. For the asset illustrated in Exhibit 11–3, the depreciation charge would thus be $2 \times 20\% \times \$6,000$, or $\$2,400$ the first year, $2 \times 20\% \times (\$6,000 - \$2,400)$, or $\$1,440$ the second year, and so on. The amount depreciated during the five years would total $\$5,533$, leaving an undepreciated balance of $\$467$ at the time of asset retirement. The difference between this amount and the salvage recovered by sale of the machine would be subject to taxation at that time.

Annuity Method Depreciation

Other patterns of lifetime service benefits are of course possible, but the only other depreciation method that needs discussion here does not pretend to parallel the benefit pattern. This is the so-called *annuity method*, under which the depreciation charge is designed to produce a constant reported return on reported investment throughout the asset's life.

For example, assuming that the McGraw machine was expected to yield cash savings of $\$10,000$ a year for 12 years, the implicit rate of return is 26.05 percent.[8] During the first year, the $\$36,000$ invested in the machine should earn $\$36,000$ times 26.05 percent, or $\$9,378$. The year's cash savings were expected to be $\$10,000$, leaving $\$622$ for the year's depreciation. The book value of the machine at the beginning of the second year would thus be $\$36,000$ minus $\$622$, or $\$35,378$.

---

[8] This is the rate of interest at which the present value of the future savings is equal to the initial outlay of $\$36,000$. Calculation of this rate of return will be discussed in Chapter 20.

The second year's income is 26.05 percent of this, or $9,215, leaving $785 for depreciation.

The complete depreciation table is shown in Exhibit 11–4. Each year's income represents a return of 26.05 percent on the book value at the beginning of the year. Income declines from year to year, while the amount recorded as depreciation increases.

This method of depreciation is implicit in the methods many companies use to evaluate investment proposals, but its use for financial reporting is rare if not nonexistent. Nevertheless, a number of ac-

Exhibit 11–4

ANNUITY METHOD DEPRECIATION CHARGES

(1) Year	(2) Book Value, Beginning of Year	(3) Income for Year (2) × 26.05%	(4) Depreciation for Year $10,000 − (3)
1............	$36,000	$ 9,378	$ 622
2............	35,378	9,215	785
3............	34,593	9,011	989
4............	33,604	8,753	1,247
5............	32,357	8,429	1,571
6............	30,786	8,020	1,980
7............	28,806	7,504	2,496
8............	26,310	6,854	3,146
9............	23,164	6,034	3,966
10............	19,198	5,001	4,999
11............	14,199	3,698	6,302
12............	7,897	2,103*	7,897*
Total......		$84,000	$36,000

* Adjusted by $46 to allow for rounding error in the 26.05 percent figure.

counting theorists maintain that it is the only correct method. Boiled down to its bare bones, the argument is that any other method will distort the return on investment ratios.

For example, if the cash flows are constant from year to year and straight-line depreciation is used, depreciation would be $3,000 a year and net income would be $7,000. This would indicate a rate of return of $7,000/$36,000 = 19.4 percent in the first year. In the 12th year when the book value of the machine would be down to $3,000, the indicated return on investment would be $7,000/$3,000 = 233.3 percent.

To do justice to this argument would lengthen an already lengthy chapter intolerably. We remain convinced, however, that current operating costs should represent the current consumption of productive services. The increased relevance of the operating cost and income figures in our opinion justifies paying the price of some distortion in the return on investment ratio.[9]

Group Depreciation

The statement that the expected life of an asset, say a truck, is six years means that the *average* truck will last six years. Some trucks will, in fact, be retired in their first year, and some will remain in use 10 years or longer. This is the *normal* expectation. It may, therefore, be considered incorrect to assign a life of six years to *each* truck and to recognize a gain or loss on retirement for an individual truck that has a life of more or less than six years.

On this reasoning, and for other reasons to be noted shortly, many companies use *group depreciation* for many of their assets instead of the *item depreciation* that has been implicit in all the previous discussion. Under group depreciation, all items with generally similar average life expectancies are grouped together in a single asset category. One summary account is established for each group, and the original cost of all assets in the group is charged to this account. Depreciation is charged for the group in total and not item by item, and may be either straight line or declining balance. The depreciation rate is based on expected average service life for the group, and this rate is multiplied by the depreciable amount to determine the depreciation charge for the year.

Up to now, nothing has been introduced to distinguish group depreciation from item depreciation. The only really unique feature of the group method is that *each unit retired is assumed to be fully depreciated down to the actual proceeds from the sale of the unit.* Thus, no gain or loss is recorded on any item retired in the normal course of events.

To illustrate, assume that a company purchases 100 identical machines on January 1 at a cost of $1,000 each. On the basis of the company's past experience, these 100 machines are expected to follow the mortality pattern shown in the first two columns of Exhibit 11–5.

---

[9] For further discussion see Hector Anton, "Depreciation Cost Allocations and Investment Decisions," *Accounting Research*, April, 1956; and Harold Bierman, "Depreciable Assets—Timing of Expense Recognition," *Accounting Review*, October, 1961.

Exhibit 11–5

GROUP METHOD DEPRECIATION FOR A GROUP
OF 100 IDENTICAL ASSETS COSTING $1,000 EACH

(1) Years after Acquisition	(2) No. of Items Retired during Year	(3) Average Age of Items Retired during Year	(4) Total Life of Items Retired during Year (2) × (3)	(5) Number of Machines in Use during Year	(6) Group Method Depreciation for Year (5) × $200
1.........	3	1	3	100	$ 20,000
2.........	9	2	18	97	19,400
3.........	15	3	45	88	17,600
4.........	25	4	100	73	14,600
5.........	14	5	70	48	9,600
6.........	10	6	60	34	6,800
7.........	8	7	56	24	4,800
8.........	6	8	48	16	3,200
9.........	4	9	36	10	2,000
10.........	3	10	30	6	1,200
11.........	2	11	22	3	600
12.........	1	12	12	1	200
Total....	100		500	500	$100,000

Although the average life expectancy for these machines is five years,[10] 34 of these machines will still be in service at the beginning of the 6th year, and all machines will not be retired until year 12.

To simplify the calculations, depreciation is assumed to be by the straight-line method, with estimated salvage value of zero. It is also assumed, again for simplicity, that retirements always take place at the end of the year.

The average life expectancy is used as the basis for depreciation charges both in group depreciation and in item depreciation. The straight-line rate for a five-year life is 20 percent, or $200 per machine. Under either method, the first year's depreciation would be 20 percent of $100,000, or $20,000. The difference between the two methods lies in the treatment of the machines retired during the year. Under item depreciation, the accountant would record a $2,400 loss on retirement (original cost of $3,000, less a year's depreciation, 20 percent of $3,000, or $600). Under the group method, in contrast, it is assumed that $3,000 of the first year's depreciation for the group

[10] The calculation of average service life is summarized in column (4). The three machines retired during the first year are assumed to have "lived" approximately one year each, or three years in total. The entire group of 100 machines is expected to live a total of 500 machine-years, an average of 5 years per machine. This is the actuarially determined expected average service life of all the assets in this group.

applied to the items retired. In other words, book value is assumed to be equal to the sale value of the property retired, in this case zero. The entry would be:

```
Allowance for Depreciation.............................3,000
    Machines........................................        3,000
```

No gain or loss would be recognized as a result of the retirements because *they were entirely expected.*

If the actual mortality experience is as shown in column 2 of Exhibit 11–5 and if salvage value at retirement is always zero, group depreciation charges will be as shown in column 6. These figures are obtained by multiplying the original cost of the machines still in

Exhibit 11–6

DEPRECIATION CHARGES AND RETIREMENT LOSSES
UNDER ITEM METHOD OF DEPRECIATION

(1) Year	(2) Number of Items Retired during Year	(3) End-of-Year Book Value per Machine	(4) Loss on Retirement (2) × (3)	(5) Depreciation (from Exhibit 11–5)	(6) Total Charges (4) + (5)
1...........	3	$800	$ 2,400	$20,000	$ 22,400
2...........	9	600	5,400	19,400	24,800
3...........	15	400	6,000	17,600	23,600
4...........	25	200	5,000	14,600	19,600
5...........	14	0	0	9,600	9,600
Total.....	66		$18,800	$81,200	$100,000

service at the beginning of the year by 20 percent (or by multiplying the number of active machines by $200, which amounts to the same thing).

Notice that group depreciation charges are made as long as the assets are in service, provided that the original mortality estimates were correct. Under item depreciation, in contrast, charges would be made only for the first five years, as in Exhibit 11–6. Depreciation charges (column 5 of this exhibit) are the same for these five years as under group depreciation. In addition, however, a retirement loss is recognized on each machine retired during this period. Because salvage value is zero, the retirement loss is the book value of the machines retired. At the end of 5 years, the assets are fully depreciated, even though 34 of them are still in service.

The figures will be different if salvage values are present, of course, but the approach is the same. Suppose, for example, that the deprecia-

tion rate of 20 percent was based on a four-year estimated life and
$200 salvage value per machine. Suppose further that the three ma-
chines retired in the first year were sold for a total price of $350.
Unless the evidence was strong that this represented an abnormally
high mortality rate, group depreciation would recognize no gain or
loss on the retirements. The entry would be:

```
Cash.................................................... 350
Allowance for Depreciation...............................2,650
    Machines.........................................        3,000
```

Salvage on these three machines was below expectations, but this
might be offset by above-average recoveries in the future. The depreciation rate would not be changed until more evidence was accumulated that the original forecasts were wrong.

DEPRECIATION ADJUSTMENTS

Unless something interferes, the depreciation schedule established
at the time an asset is acquired will be used each year to compute the
annual depreciation charge. Later on, one or more of three kinds of
events may interfere with this orderly progression and lead to a
change in the depreciation schedule:

1. The company undertakes a *major overhaul* or reconditioning of
   the asset to extend its total lifetime service potential.
2. The original estimate of total *lifetime service potential* proves to
   have been too high.
3. The company finds reason to change its estimate of the *length of
   the period* during which the asset will remain useful.

The Effect of Major Overhauls

As we noted in Chapter 10, any depreciation schedule carries with
it an implicit maintenance policy. For example, achieving an asset's
anticipated life may require one or more major overhauls. In other
cases, the estimated life may assume no major overhaul at all. In either
circumstance, an unanticipated major reconditioning may extend the
asset's total lifetime service potential. When it does this, its cost should
be capitalized and the depreciation schedule recalculated.

Eighteen years ago, for example, the Puhlan Waite Railway purchased a group of freight cars and began depreciating their cost by the
item method at a straight-line rate of 5 percent a year. Ten of these
cars were still in service until a few months ago, when they were

reconditioned at a cost of $62,000. Their combined book value prior to reconditioning was:

Original cost	$100,000
Less: Accumulated depreciation	90,000
Undepreciated Cost	$ 10,000

This was approximately equal to their salvage value at that date.

The original depreciation rate in this case was based on an assumed life of 20 years, with zero salvage value. The reconditioning is expected to extend the life to 10 years from the date of the reconditioning. Salvage value is expected to be negligible at the end of that time.

It should be clear from this description that this expenditure is a *betterment*, as that term was defined in Chapter 10, and should be capitalized. One possibility would be to charge the $62,000 to the Freight Cars account without any further adjustment. This would be appropriate if the purpose of the expenditure was to provide the cars with characteristics they had never possessed. In this instance, however, the reconditioning consisted mainly of *replacing* various component parts. The original cost of these parts, therefore, should be removed from the Freight Cars account (and from the allowance for depreciation), to be replaced by the cost of reconditioning the cars.

In practice, the accountant usually cannot identify clearly the original cost of replaced parts. His solution is to charge the expenditure to the accumulated depreciation account:

Allowance for Depreciation—Freight Cars	62,000	
Accounts Payable, etc.		62,000

This increases the book value of the asset by $62,000 without including both the original cost and the replacement cost in the Freight Cars account. The overhaul is thus seen as a partial restoration of the service potential that expired in previous years, and the $72,000 book value is depreciated over the 10-year remaining life.

Revision of Service Estimates

Depreciation adjustments may also be necessary even if no major overhaul or change in maintenance policy is made. It is common practice to write down the book value of an asset if it becomes clear that the present value of the asset's remaining service potential has fallen materially below its book value. The adjustment takes the following form:

Write-down of Fixed Assets................................xxx
    Allowance for Depreciation.............................   xxx

The write-down is ordinarily included in the income statement as a charge against current revenues. If the amount is material, it will appear separately as an extraordinary loss. After this has been done, depreciation for subsequent periods should then be recomputed so as to amortize the remaining depreciable cost over the remaining life.

Revision of Life Estimates

Adjustments to reflect the discovery of the errors of the third kind —revisions of estimated economic life—might take either of two forms. The first alternative is to spread the remaining book value on the date of the discovery over the remaining life. For example, suppose that an asset's book value is $150,000 and that the remaining life estimate has been shortened from five years to three, with no salvage value. Under straight-line depreciation, the annual depreciation charge would be raised from $30,000 to $50,000 a year.

The second alternative is to readjust the entire lifetime depreciation schedule retroactively. For example, suppose that the asset cost $300,000 originally and has been depreciated by the straight-line method on the basis of a 10-year life and no salvage, or $30,000 a year. After five years, when the book value is $150,000, the life estimate is reduced from 10 to 8 years. On this basis, depreciation should have been $300,000 divided by eight, or $37,500 a year. Recomputing depreciation on this basis for the first seven years yields a corrected book value of $112,500. To reach this level, the asset would be written down by $37,500 ($150,000 — $112,500).

Write-down of Fixed Assets...........................37,500
    Allowance for Depreciation........................   37,500

Depreciation for the remaining three years would then be $37,500 a year. The write-down would be treated as a correction of prior periods' income and would be charged against Retained Earnings. Similarly, a write-up would increase the asset's book value and lead to smaller depreciation charges each year in the future.

The main argument for the first of these alternatives is that retroactive correction of the income statements of prior periods will be confusing, and in the case of write-ups, nonconservative. The argument for the second alternative is that the operating cost for any period should reflect the best estimate of resource consumption available at that time. In other words, it has the advantage of producing more accurate depreciation charges during the remaining years of life.

Further discussion of this question must be deferred to more advanced texts, but the position of the American Institute of Certified Public Accountants is worth mentioning. An opinion of the Institute's Accounting Principles Board states that ". . . changes in the estimated remaining lives of fixed assets . . . should be considered prospective in nature and not prior period adjustments."[11] This would seem to sanction the first alternative and require that the asset be neither written up nor written down to reflect a revision of the remaining life estimate. In practice, however, downward revisions in life estimates often lead to write-downs charged against ordinary operating revenues of the period in which the write-down takes place.

HISTORICAL VERSUS CURRENT COST

The discussion thus far has dealt with the *time pattern* of depreciation charges rather than with the dollar amounts. Measurement of service potentials, expired and unexpired alike, in terms of historical cost has probably been assumed by the reader without question. However, an alternative that has considerable theoretical merit and has had some influence on practice is *current cost*.

Shortcomings of Historical Cost

The justification for deducting depreciation from revenues is that the resulting income figures will have relevance to certain kinds of management and investor decisions. As time goes by, however, the price paid for an asset is less and less likely to be an adequate measure of the current cost of equivalent services. The income statement becomes a mixture of revenues measured in terms of the current value of assets received in exchange for the company's goods and services, expenses measured in terms of the current prices of goods and services used, and other expenses measured in terms of prices that prevailed in various periods in the past.

When prices change, expense charges based on previously existing prices no longer have the same meaning. For example, a company's income statement shows the following:

Revenues...........................		$100
Less:		
Depreciation.....................	$ 8	
Other expenses..................	80	88
Net Income.......................		$ 12

---

[11] "Opinion No. 9, Reporting the Results of Operations" (New York: AICPA, 1966), published in *The Journal of Accountancy*, February, 1967, pp. 55–66.

Investigation reveals that the amount of capacity represented by the depreciation charge would now cost three times as much at today's prices as it did originally. Depreciation in current terms is thus $24 instead of $8. This means that the revenues are inadequate to cover the current costs of providing capacity. Instead of a net income of $12 that could be distributed to shareholders without reducing the firm's capacity, the firm actually has a $4 loss.

Furthermore, the historical cost margin provides a poorer basis for forecasting future income than the current cost margin. As assets are replaced, historical cost depreciation will rise. An investor who bases his share purchase decision on an assumption that current income margins will continue is likely to be very disappointed. A man who is used to paying 35 cents a gallon for gasoline is bound to misunderstand a transport cost figure that is based on a 15-cent price.

Computation of Current Cost

The procedure for implementing the current cost basis with respect to long-life assets involves: (1) periodic revaluation of such assets at some reasonable approximation of their current replacement costs (presumably through the use of price indexes); and (2) periodic amortization of these new amounts by whatever depreciation method is deemed appropriate. The use of current cost in financial statements is discussed further in the next chapter.[12]

Application of this concept has been restricted mainly to countries which have experienced extreme inflation. Probably the most careful and painstaking application to public financial reporting has been made by several large Dutch companies, notably the huge Philips group, but this has had little impact on practice in the United States.[13]

SUMMARY

Reporting annual depreciation charges and the book value of depreciated assets serves no purpose unless these figures affect decisions. The accounting model presumes that income and asset figures will influence investors' decisions to buy or sell shares in the company and a wide variety of managerial decisions as well.

---

[12] A more detailed explanation of how current cost might be implemented is contained in Myron J. Gordon, "The Valuation of Accounts at Current Cost," *The Accounting Review*, July, 1953, pp. 373–84.

[13] The Philips method is described by A. Goudeket, "An Application of Replacement Value Theory," *The Journal of Accountancy*, July, 1960, pp. 37–47.

For these purposes the accounting model requires estimates of the amount of an asset's service potential that is consumed during each period and the amount that remains at the end of the period. Because patterns of depreciation are difficult to identify, the accountant has generally used some simple formula as an approximation. The most widely used formulas are straight-line (uniform annual amounts) and declining-charge methods (smaller amounts in each succeeding year). Another method, the annuity method, has considerable theoretical support but little practical application. In any case, if large enough asset groups can be identified, depreciation ought to be based on the life of the group as a whole rather than on the lives of individual items in the group.

Although these formulas are always applied in the United States to the assets' original cost, many authorities believe that they should be applied instead to estimates of current replacement cost. This last possibility will be taken up again in the next chapter, after a review of inventory accounting permits us to take a comprehensive view of the impact of price level changes on the measurement of assets of all kinds.

QUESTIONS AND PROBLEMS

1. Why is the depreciation expense for any one year more difficult to calculate than insurance expense? Can depreciation be measured by factual observation?

2. What is meant by "service potential?" Why is it important in discussions of depreciation policy?

3. Is depreciation purely a concept related to public financial reporting or does it have managerial significance as well?

4. To what extent, if at all, is the objective of depreciation to provide funds for the replacement of depreciating plant and equipment?

5. What are the causes of depreciation? To what extent can they be controlled by management?

6. What is meant by the "economic life" of a depreciating asset? When does it come to an end?

7. What relevance, if any, does liquidation value have to the determination of the annual depreciation charge?

8. Company X depreciates its equipment on a straight-line basis, while Company Y uses a declining-charge method. Are the depreciation charges of these two companies necessarily noncomparable?

9. Should the depreciation shown on the firm's published income statement always be identical to that shown on its income tax return?

10. How does group depreciation differ from item depreciation? Under what circumstances would group depreciation be preferable to item depreciation?

11. State the argument for basing depreciation on current replacement cost rather than original cost. If current cost depreciation is used, is it likely that the lifetime total of these charges will equal the asset's replacement cost at the time of replacement?

12. The Pilot Company has just purchased a piece of equipment. This equipment is expected to produce approximately the same number of units of product each year until it is retired, and the company sees no reason why the prices of the products sold will either increase or decrease during the machine's lifetime. Operating and repair costs per year are expected to increase each year, however, and economic life is expected to come to an end seven years from now when the cost savings from a new machine will be adequate to justify replacement.

What method would you use to calculate annual depreciation charges on this machine? State your reasons.

13. The controller of Miller Enterprises, Inc., proposes that in view of rising prices of equipment, depreciation charges should be based on replacement cost. He suggests the use of the following journal entry:

Depreciation X
    Allowance for Depreciation . . . . Y
    Reserve for Replacement . . . . Z

where X is the depreciation charge based on replacement cost and Y is the regular depreciation charge based on acquisition cost.

a) What is the effect of the proposed method on reported profit during and after a period of rising equipment prices?
b) Where would the Reserve for Replacement appear on the company's statements? How would you interpret it?

14. A company purchased a large piece of equipment 15 years ago at a cost of $300,000. At that time it was estimated that the economic life of the equipment would be 20 years and that its ultimate scrap value would be $30,000.

Assuming that the company uses straight-line depreciation, study the following events and state whether each one necessitates a revision of the original depreciation rate, with reasons for your answer.

a) Due to recent price increases, the present replacement cost of the same type of equipment is $500,000.
b) For the same reason as in (a), end-of-life scrap value is now estimated at $50,000.
c) The company could sell the equipment now at a sale price of $100,000.
d) At the end of the last year, a major breakdown impaired the efficiency of this equipment. After a thorough overhaul, the equipment now has a productive capacity of 9,000 units per month instead of the initial capacity of 10,000 units per month. The company still expects to use the equipment for 5 more years, retiring it when it is 20 years old.

*15. A company has been using an annual depreciation rate of 20 percent of original cost for a certain type of office equipment. Now, after several years of experience, a study of actual equipment mortality rates indicates that the rate should have been based on a life of six years and an end-of-life resale value of 16 percent of original cost. The original cost of the equipment now on hand was $200,000, and its average age is two years. Straight-line depreciation by the item method has been used.

a) Compute the amount by which depreciation to date is overstated or understated.
b) Present the journal entry that would be necessary to adjust the book value of the equipment to its correct level.

* 16. The Votrun Corporation bought several pieces of equipment in 19x0 at a total price of $100,000. The estimated average service life of this equipment was 10 years, with an expected average salvage value of 10 percent of original cost. Acquisitions and retirements each year were assumed to take place on January 1. The following pieces of equipment were retired during the first three years:

Year	Original Cost of Equipment Retired	Actual Salvage Recovered
19x0.................	$ 0	$ 0
19x1.................	5,000	1,000
19x2.................	10,000	3,000

Give the entries to record depreciation and retirements for each of the three years:

---

* Solutions to problems marked with an asterisk (*) are found in Appendix B.

a) Using group method, straight-line depreciation.

b) Using group method, double-rate, declining-balance depreciation.

17. Cadabra, Inc., uses the group method of depreciation on its fleet of delivery trucks. All trucks are placed in a single group; thus trucks purchased in 1969 are added to the same group that contains trucks purchased in 1968 and earlier years.

The group was first established in 1966. For simplicity, it is assumed that truck purchases and retirements take place on January 1 of each year. The following data are available:

Year	Purchases		Retirements		
	No. of Trucks	Original Cost per Truck	No. of Trucks	Original Cost per Truck	Salvage per Truck
1966.............	10	$3,000	.	. . . .	. . . .
1967.............	8	3,100	1	$3,000	$1,000
1968.............	4	3,200	2	3,000	800

a) Prepare journal entries to record acquisitions, retirements, and depreciation for each of the three years:

(1) Using a straight-line depreciation rate of 20 percent a year.

(2) Using double-rate, declining-balance depreciation.

b) Do you think that the group method in this case is likely to produce more accurate depreciation figures? Explain.

18. In January, 1966, a storekeeper purchased a used delivery truck for $1,000. Before putting the vehicle into service, $140 was spent for painting and decorating the body, and $260 for a complete engine overhaul. Four new tires were bought for $100. The storekeeper expected to keep the truck in service for three years, at the end of which time he anticipated it would have a trade-in value of $300.

Gasoline, oil, and similar items were charged to expense as procured. In January, 1967, a new battery ($20) and miscellaneous repairs ($90) were purchased. Straight-line depreciation was used.

Four new tires were bought for $110 in January, 1968, and the body was repainted at a cost of $175. Miscellaneous repairs were made at a cost of $150.

A new truck costing $3,400 was bought in January, 1969. The trade-in allowance on the old vehicle was $430.

a) All of the above purchases were paid for in cash. Show journal entries to record:

(1) The purchase of the used truck;

(2) The purchase of the various other items detailed above;

(3) Depreciation expense for 1966, 1967, and 1968, using straight-line depreciation.

(4) The retirement of the truck and the purchase of the new one.

b) Show the accounts for Truck and Allowance for Depreciation as they appeared on December 31, 1968.

*19. In January, 1949, Abercrombie Mills, Inc., placed in service a new paper machine costing $50,000. Its estimated useful life was 20 years.

In December, 1952, certain improvements were added to this machine at a cost of $6,000. Twelve years later, in the fall of 1964, the machine was thoroughly overhauled and rebuilt at a cost of $12,000. It was estimated that the overhaul would extend the machine's useful life by five years, or until the end of 1973. Depreciation charges for 1964 were unaffected by the overhaul.

a) Show the journal entry required to record the improvements added in December, 1952.

b) Compute depreciation for 1953 on a straight-line basis.

c) Show the journal entry required to record the overhauling of the machine in the fall of 1964.

d) Compute depreciation for 1965 on a straight-line basis.

20. In 19x1, Company Alpha bought 10 identical machines at a price of $10,000 each. These were thereafter depreciated on a *group basis* at a straight-line rate of 10 percent a year. In 19x4, four other machines of this same type were acquired at a price of $12,000 each, and were thereafter included in the same group with the other 10 for depreciation purposes. At the end of 19x8, two of the original machines were sold for $2,000 each. For convenience in computing depreciation, all purchases were assumed to take place as of the beginning of the year.

a) Compute the depreciation charge for the year 19x2.

b) Compute the depreciation charge for the year 19x5.

c) Prepare a journal entry to record the retirement and sale of two machines in 19x8.

d) Compute the depreciation charge for the year 19x9.

21. On January 1, 19x1, the Lubberdink Company purchased a machine for $56,910. The machine was expected to produce cash savings at the rate of $15,000 a year for a period of five years and to have a salvage value of $5,000 at the end of that time.

a) Compute annual depreciation by the straight-line method. For each year, compute the ratio of the machine's earnings after depreciation to its book value as of January 1 of that year.

b) Recompute annual depreciation by the annuity method such that the annual rate of return on the machine's January 1 book value is 12 percent each year.

c) Is the rate of 12 percent an appropriate one to use in this case? Could the annuity method have been applied with a rate such as 15 percent? Support your conclusion with appropriate calculations.

22. A barge costing $64,000 estimated to have a 20-year life and a zero salvage value was acquired in January, 19x2. It proved too small to be profitable, and five years later, in 19x7, was lengthened at a cost of $18,000. The annual repairs, while fluctuating somewhat, averaged $1,800 per year. At the end of 15 years (in January, 19x7), the barge was throughly overhauled and reconditioned at a cost of $24,000, and this action was expected to extend its life to 10 years from date of reconditioning (i.e., to 25 years from date of original acquisition). Early in its 22d year, the barge was lost in a storm, and $15,000 insurance was collected. Depreciation was by the straight-line method.

a) Show journal entries to record:
    (1) The annual depreciation for the first year.
    (2) The cost of lengthening the barge.
    (3) The annual depreciation for the sixth year.
    (4) The cost of reconditioning the barge.
    (5) The annual depreciation for the 16th year.
    (6) The loss of the barge and the collection of the insurance.
b) Show the balance of the Barge asset account and the balance of the corresponding Allowance for Depreciation account at the end of 21 years.

23. The Prometheus Bindery installed a new binding machine to take the place of an old machine which had become obsolete. The cost of the new machine was to be depreciated by the double-rate, declining-balance method. Data relating to the old and new machines as of January 1, 19x1, the replacement date, were:

Old Machine:

Original cost	$19,000
Scrap value	5,000
Accumulated depreciation	12,000

New Machine:

Invoice price	30,000
Installation cost	1,600
Cash discount	600
Estimated scrap value	3,100
Estimated economic life	12½ years

At the end of the year 19x1, while the plant was temporarily closed for stock taking, a conveyor attachment was built onto the machine at a total cost of $2,700. After the books had been closed and the statements prepared for the year 19x1, the management decided, on the basis of the plant engineer's recommendation, that the depreciation on this machine should have been computed (and should be computed in the future) on a *production basis*, using a *machine-hour rate*. The following additional data are available as of January 1, 19x2:

Estimated total life of machine from date of installation,
January 1, 19x1.................................. 30,000 machine-hours
Production time for the year 19x1..................... 3,000 "   "
New estimated scrap value of machine, including the
conveyor......................................$ 3,370

a) Prepare journal entries to record the retirement of the old machine and the installation of the new machine on January 1, 19x1.

b) Compute the depreciation on the new machine for the year 19x1.

c) Prepare journal entries to record:
   (1) The installation of the conveyor on January 1, 19x2.
   (2) The correction of the accounts when the machine-hour rate of depreciation was established on January 1, 19x2.

d) Compute the depreciation charge for 19x2. The machine operated 2,700 machine-hours during the year.

24. The Acme Company owns a large quantity of pumps and pumping equipment in various company locations. Although this equipment includes many different kinds and sizes of items, they are all expected to have approximately the same average service life, 10 years. End-of-life salvage value is assumed to be negligible. All equipment in this category is depreciated on a group basis, using a single group to include all items.

On December 31, 19x1, the balances in the property accounts were:

Pumping equipment......................................$150,000
Allowance for depreciation—pumping equipment............ (75,000)

Acquisitions and retirements subsequent to this date were as follows (for ease of computation, assume that all acquisitions and retirements took place on January 1):

Year	Acquisitions at Cost	Retirements	
		Original Cost	Net Salvage
19x2.................	$10,000	$10,000	$1,000
19x3.................	25,000	15,000	3,000
19x4.................	.....	10,000	....
19x5.................	20,000	8,000	1,000
19x6.................	25,000	30,000	4,000
19x7.................	35,000	20,000	Insurance
19x8.................	20,000	45,000	2,000

All retirements were of equipment on hand on December 31, 19x1, except for the 19x7 retirement. In 19x7, equipment that was purchased in

19x5 for $20,000 was completely destroyed by fire. The insurance recovery on the equipment destroyed in 19x7 amounted to $12,000.

a) Prepare journal entries to record acquisitions and retirements, compute straight-line depreciation for each year, and compute the December 31, 19x8, balances in the two property accounts.

b) Do this again on the assumption that the Acme Company depreciates each item separately rather than as part of a group, again at a 10 percent rate. Assume for simplicity that each item in the December 31, 19x1, property records was five years old (i.e., that accumulated depreciation was one half of original cost for each item as well as for the group as a whole). Also assume that each year's acquisition consisted of a single item.

c) Which of these two methods gives (1) a more representative picture of annual income during the period, and (2) a more representative balance sheet as of December 31, 19x8? State your reasons.

25. Faced with a substantial increase in the replacement cost of its plant and equipment, the United States Steel Corporation attempted to reflect current replacement costs in its depreciation charges for 1947. The method failed to gain wide support within the accounting profession and United States Steel returned to the historical cost basis in 1948. The following notes were appended to the company's financial statements for 1947, 1948, and 1949:

1947 Annual Report: "Wear and exhaustion of facilities of $114,045,483 includes $87,745,483 based on original cost of such facilities and $26,300,000 added to cover replacement cost. The added amount is 30 percent of provisions based on original cost, and is a step toward stating wear and exhaustion in an amount which will recover in current dollars of diminished buying power the same purchasing power as the original expenditure. Because it is necessary to recover the purchasing power of sums originally invested in tools so that they may be replaced as they wear out, this added amount is carried as a reserve for replacement of properties. The 30 percent was determined partly through experienced cost increases and partly through study of construction cost index numbers. Although it is materially less than the experienced cost increase in replacing worn out facilities, it was deemed appropriate in view of the newness of the application of this principle to the costing of wear and exhaustion."

1948 Annual Report: "A method of accelerated depreciation on cost was adopted in 1948 . . . and was made retroactive to January 1, 1947. Wear and exhaustion of facilities in 1948 includes accelerated depreciation of $55,335,444 including a deficiency of $2,675,094 in the amount of $26,300,000 reported in 1947 as depreciation added to cover replacement cost. Such accelerated depreciation is not presently deductible for federal income tax purposes.

"The accelerated depreciation is applicable to the cost of postwar facilities in the first few years of their lives, when the economic usefulness is greatest. The amount thereof is related to the excess of current operating rate over U.S. Steel's long-term peacetime average rate of 70 percent of capacity. The annual accelerated amount is 10 percent of the cost of facilities in the year in which the expenditures are made and 10 percent in the succeeding year, except that this amount is reduced ratably as the operating rate may drop, no acceleration being made at 70 percent or lower operations. The accelerated depreciation is in addition to the normal depreciation on such facilities but the total depreciation over their expected lives will not exceed the cost of the facilities."

1949 Annual Report: "Wear and exhaustion of facilities includes accelerated depreciation of $22,045,743 in 1949 and $55,335,444 in 1948. Such accelerated depreciation is not presently deductible for federal income tax purposes.

"The accelerated depreciation is applicable to the cost of postwar facilities in the first few years of their lives, when the economic usefulness is greatest. The amount thereof is related to the excess of current operating rate over U.S. Steel's long-term peacetime average rate of about 70 percent of capacity. The annual accelerated amount is 10 percent in the succeeding year, except that this amount is reduced ratably as the operating rate may drop, no acceleration being made at 70 percent or lower operations. The accelerated depreciation is in addition to the normal depreciation on such facilities, but the total depreciation over their expected lives will not exceed the cost of the facilities.

The following comment appeared in the corporation's quarterly report for the *fourth quarter* of 1949:

"Because of strikes, United States Steel's production of steel ingots and castings during the fourth quarter of 1949 averaged only 46.6 percent of rated capacity. The operating rate for the entire year of 1949 averaged 82.5 percent of rated capacity. It will be recalled that the corporation's operating rate during the first half of 1949 averaged slightly in excess of 100 percent of rated capacity.

"Shipments of steel products by United States Steel in the fourth quarter of 1949 amounted to 2,662,209 net tons, as compared with shipments of 4,781,000 net tons in the third quarter. Shipments for the year 1949 amounted to 18,211,893 net tons, compared with 20,655,491 net tons in 1948.

"Income of the corporation for the fourth quarter of 1949, before declaration of dividends, was reported on January 31, 1950, as amounting to $32,735,397. Income for the year 1949 was then reported as $165,958,806, or a return of 7.2 percent on sales, as compared with income for 1948 of $129,627,845, or a return of 5.2 percent on sales, all before declaration of dividends.

"The income for the fourth quarter would have been $6,700,000 but for certain adjustments in accounts because of the steel strike. These adjustments resulting from the effect of the strike on the 1949 operating rate and on inventories, increased the income for the fourth quarter by $26,000,000."

a) Would you have supported U.S. Steel in its attempt to introduce the new depreciation method in 1947?

b) Was the new depreciation policy adopted in 1948 designed to meet the same objectives as the policy adopted in 1947 and abandoned in the following year? Explain your reasoning.

c) Contrast the 1948 depreciation method with diminishing-charge methods. Do both of these kinds of methods follow from the same accounting principle or are they fundamentally different?

d) If you had been one of the company's accountants in 1948, would you have favored or opposed the new method? Explain.

e) Explain how the steel strike in the fourth quarter of 1949 led to an increase in the company's fourth-quarter earnings. Should this be possible?

26. The 1961 Annual Report of the United States Steel Corporation included the following comment:

"The $326.8 million of property expenditures compares with recorded wear and exhaustion of $210.5 million for the year. This latter amount was inadequate to recover the buying power originally expended for facilities used up during the year. The resulting deficiency is primarily due to inflation in the cost of new facilities while depreciation under existing tax laws continues to be based on the original cost of facilities purchased many years ago."

The following note appeared among the notes to the financial statements in this report:

"For a number of years, U.S. Steel has followed the policy of reflecting accelerated depreciation on the cost of new facilities in the first few years of their lives when the economic usefulness is greatest. As permitted under the Internal Revenue Code the declining balance method of depreciation is being applied to the cost of certain facilities; and the cost of certain other facilities is covered by Certificates of Necessity under the Defense Production Act of 1950 and is being written off at the rate of 20 per cent per year. The effect thereof is to charge to income a greater portion of their cost in the earlier years of life and, therefore, follows the principle of accelerated depreciation.

"The amount included in wear and exhaustion for the cost of facilities not covered by the declining balance method of depreciation or Certificates of Necessity is for the most part related to U.S. Steel's rate of operations."

a) In what respects did U.S. Steel's depreciation policy change between 1948 and 1961 (see Problem 25 above)?

b) Comment on the impact of the tax law on the company's depreciation policy for public reporting to stockholders.

27. †The Alexander Cargo Service was started in 1957 to carry freight from a coastal seaport in the United States to several inland locations. By the beginning of 1966, the company had three small cargo vessels capable of operating in the small river which flowed into the port. These vessels had been acquired at various times at low prices and the company had been able to expand gradually over the years and operate profitably carrying low-value bulk cargoes almost exclusively.

Late in 1965, Mr. Hugo Alexander, the president of the company, saw an opportunity to expand his business by taking containerized freight from ocean-going vessels and delivering these by ship to the company's inland delivery points. A survey of the market convinced Mr. Alexander that most of this freight did not demand high-speed road transport and that the low cost of his water-borne cargo service would permit him to attract enough business to justify the purchase of an additional vessel.

Accordingly, early in January, 1966, the company purchased a vessel which had originally been a naval landing ship but which had been converted some years earlier for use as a coastal cargo carrier. The earlier conversion had added a set of deck cargo compartments which the Alexander Cargo Service would have to remove. Otherwise the ship could not pass under some of the bridges along its shipping routes. The bridge and pilot house would have to be rebuilt for the same reason. The ship also was in need of fairly substantial outlays for new deck machinery, overhaul of the engines and painting, but the purchase price was low enough that Mr. Alexander felt that he had found the vessel he needed to inaugurate his new container-carrying service.

During the first six months of 1966 the work of converting the ship was performed and the new ship was placed in service on July 1, 1966. The cost incurred by Alexander Cargo Service during the first six months of 1966 was as follows:

---

† Copyright 1967 by l'Institut pour l'Etude des Méthodes de Direction de l'Entreprise (IMEDE), Lausanne, Switzerland. Published by permission.

(1)	Purchase price of ship	$ 40,000
(2)	Remove deck cargo compartment	15,000*
(3)	Lower bridge and pilot house	17,000*
(4)	Engine overhaul	16,000†
(5)	New deck machinery	12,000
(6)	Painting deck and hull	10,000*
	Total	$110,000

* Treated entirely as current expense for tax purposes.
† Of this amount, $8,000 is to be treated as current expense for tax purposes.

The public accountant who prepares the annual tax returns for Alexander Cargo Service has ascertained that a life of 20 years has been accepted by the income tax authorities for similar vessels and for deck and engineroom machinery in the past. For tax purposes, depreciation can only be by the straight-line method but no estimated salvage value need be entered into the depreciation calculations for tax purposes.

Mr. Alexander could not agree that the estimated life of this new vessel would be as long as 20 years. He had seen so many changes in the transportation pattern in his area just since he started in business that he felt that a 10-year life would be much more likely. From experience that he had had in buying and selling second-hand ships, he also concluded that he could sell the ship for at least $10,000 at the end of 10 years even if economic conditions did not permit its use for containerized service locally after that time.

By the time the ship went into service on July 1, 1966, it was clear to Mr. Alexander that his original estimates were sound, at least for the first few years of the new ship's life. Contracts had been signed with several shippers. Bookings for space on the new vessel continued near capacity throughout the first six months of its operation. Mr. Alexander felt that he might gradually lose some of this business from year to year as the pattern of local cargo operation changed, but he saw no reason why he could not continue to operate the vessel for at least 10 years before the volume of business declined so far that he would find it necessary to take the new vessel out of service and sell it.

Sales revenues of the Alexander Cargo Service amounted to $1,000,000 in 1966, and were expected to reach $1,200,000 in 1967. Net income, before taxes and before deducting any of the cost items listed above, amounted to $50,000 in 1966 and was expected to total $100,000 in 1967. The book value of all assets other than this new vessel totaled $250,000 and was expected to remain constant at this level. The income tax rate was 40 percent of taxable income.

The company had in the past sometimes used the tax basis for capitalizing and depreciating costs when this seemed to fit the facts of the case. At other times it felt justified in using some basis other than the tax basis for the financial statements that it issued to its shareholders and to its bank creditors and which its management also used. Capitalizing a cost for financial reporting purposes did not prevent the company from deducting this cost as an expense on its current tax return if the tax regulations made it deductible.

For its published statements, the Alexander Cargo Service used only straight-line depreciation or the double-rate, declining-balance method.

a) In your opinion, how much of the $110,000 listed above should be capitalized as part of the cost of an asset on the books of the Alexander Cargo Service?

b) How much of the cost should be shown as an expense on the income statement for 1966? For 1967?

c) How important are these decisions on cost capitalization and expense recognition? Try to support your answer by giving figures from the case.

Chapter 12

INVENTORY COSTING
AND PRICE LEVEL CHANGES

IN EARLIER CHAPTERS, costs were transferred without question from one inventory account to another and from inventory to cost of goods sold. Inventory measurement is not without problems, however. This chapter will examine some of these problems and then move on to the broader question of accounting in an inflationary environment.

STATEMENT OF THE PROBLEM

At least initially, it is useful to look on inventory measurement and cost of goods sold determination as a problem in distinguishing between the items sold or otherwise consumed during a period and the items remaining on hand at the end of the period. The issue is illustrated in Exhibit 12–1. It is assumed that a firm starts the year with an inventory of 250,000 units, purchases 2,500,000 units, and has 750,000 units remaining on hand at the end of the year. The cost of the opening inventory, $40,000, has been given by whatever procedure was used in determining the prior year's closing inventory, and the cost of each purchase is given by the actual outlay involved.

It will be recalled that given the closing inventory, the cost of goods is determined by the formula,

Cost of Goods Sold = Beginning Inventory + Purchases −
Closing Inventory

The problem arises because this equation contains two unknown elements: the cost of goods sold and the closing inventory. These two figures are thus interdependent. The cost of goods sold will depend on which units are assumed to remain on hand at the end of the period. Similarly, the measure of the ending inventory will depend on which units are assumed to have been sold during the period.

356

Exhibit 12–1

INVENTORY MEASUREMENT AND THE COST OF GOODS SOLD

The goods on hand at the beginning of a period:
250,000 units at $0.16.............................. $ 40,000

Plus the goods purchased during that period:
500,000 units at $0.18.............................$ 90,000
500,000 units at   0.20............................. 100,000
500,000 units at   0.22............................. 110,000
500,000 units at   0.24............................. 120,000
500,000 units at   0.26............................. 130,000   550,000

Equals the goods available for sale:
2,750,000 units with a total cost of................. $590,000

This quantity, less the goods sold during the period:
2,000,000 units at ? cents..........................   ?

Equals the goods on hand at the end of the period:
750,000 units at ? cents............................   ?

For example, if the closing inventory is assumed to consist of the *last* units purchased, the inventory figures will be:

500,000 units at $0.26 = $130,000
250,000 units at $0.24 =   60,000
Total............ $190,000

Under this assumption, the cost of goods sold is $590,000 — $190,000 = $400,000.

Alternatively, if the closing inventory is assumed to consist of the *first* units purchased, the inventory figures will be:

250,000 units at $0.16 = $ 40,000
500,000 units at $0.18 =   90,000
Total............$130,000

The cost of goods sold now becomes $590,000 — $130,000 = $460,000.

Since neither the revenues nor the other expenses of the period are affected by which alternative is chosen, the entire difference between these two cost of goods sold figures, $400,000 and $460,000, a difference of $60,000, will be reflected in the period's net income. It should be apparent that whenever (1) merchandise cost is a large fraction of sales price, and (2) merchandise purchase prices have changed, the inventory pricing practice used will have a very large influence on the income figure reported.[1]

TRADITIONAL METHODS OF INVENTORY COSTING

An obvious solution to the foregoing problem is to charge Cost of Goods Sold with the acquisition costs of those specific units actually sold, thus leaving in Merchandise Inventory the acquisition costs of those specific units actually remaining on hand. Where each unit or lot is readily distinguished from all others, this practice, termed *specific lot costing*, is commonly used, and it strikes most people as a reasonable and natural procedure. If a used-car dealer sold a 1968 Ford convertible, he would be expected to debit Cost of Goods Sold with the price paid for that particular vehicle, not with the price of the Buick that happened to be either his earliest or latest acquisition.

In many cases, however, units or lots are physically indistinguishable one from another. Unless some other business purpose requires separate identification, the cost of doing so solely for accounting reasons may well be prohibitive. Moreover, where selection from among such items is a matter of indifference to the customer, specific lot costing has the inherent disadvantage of permitting management to influence reported profits simply by selection of the particular units to be shipped, that is, low cost units to raise current net income and vice versa. In such cases, accountants have customarily used either the *first-in, first-out* method or the *moving average* method.

The First-In, First-Out (FIFO) Method

Many accountants believe that costs should flow through the balance sheet to the income statement in the same sequence followed by the goods themselves as they flow out of the stock room and into customers' hands. One plausible flow-of-goods assumption is the first-in, first-out assumption.

The protection of goods against deterioration will in many cases make it advisable to move stock more or less on a first-in, first-out basis. Therefore, an assumption that costs flow in this manner is often quite realistic.

The inventory costing method based on this premise, commonly identified by the letters FIFO, is widely used both for internal book-

---

[1] Although this illustration relates to a firm engaged in trading activities only, the same considerations apply to manufacturing firms' inventories of raw material, finished goods, and even work in process.

keeping and for periodic financial reporting. It necessarily results in measuring the ending inventory in terms of the purchase prices most recently paid. In other words, it is assumed that the first units received are the first to be sold and that the last units received are still in inventory at the end of the period. In our example, the cost of goods still in inventory at the end of the period is:

500,000 units at $0.26	......	$130,000	
250,000 units at 0.24	......	60,000	
FIFO Inventory Cost	......	$190,000	

The remaining $400,000 is the FIFO cost of goods sold during the period.

The Moving Average Method

The bookkeeping required to maintain perpetual FIFO inventory cost records is somewhat cumbersome. For this reason, many firms use what is described as the moving average method of inventory costing.[2]

As illustrated in Exhibit 12–2, the moving average procedure is to

Exhibit 12–2

THE MOVING AVERAGE METHOD

On hand, January 1	250,000 at $0.16	=	$ 40,000	
Purchased, January 4	500,000 at 0.18	=	90,000	
New inventory total	750,000 at 0.173	=	$130,000	
Issued, January 8	400,000 at 0.173	=	69,200	
Leaving on hand	350,000 at 0.173	=	$ 60,800	
Purchased, January 10	500,000 at 0.20	=	100,000	
New Inventory Total	850,000 at 0.189	=	$160,800	

add the cost of each new acquisition to the total cost of the inventory previously on hand, to calculate an average unit price by dividing this total by the number of units now on hand, and to price all issues prior to the next purchase at the resulting figure. Thus, the inventory is always carried at a single "moving average" price, which simplifies the bookkeeping and to some extent smooths out purchase price fluctuations.[3]

---

[2] The physical flow of goods may in some cases actually conform to the pattern implicit in this method—that is, the goods may be so handled that each issue tends to be a proportional sample from all lots then on hand.

[3] A variant of this method, used when purchases are frequent, is to recalculate the average once a month rather than after each purchase.

The smoothing effect of the averaging process is limited mainly to short-term fluctuations. Over a period as long as a year, this method typically yields a cost of goods sold approximately the same as that given by FIFO. Unless inventory turnover (the ratio of cost of goods sold to inventory) is very low, the moving average figure for the ending inventory will be weighted predominantly by the prices of the most recent purchases—the same prices that determine the FIFO measurement.

The "Cost or Market" Rule

When FIFO or moving average methods of inventory costing are used, the end-of-year inventories are typically written down whenever the year-end "market price" is less than the cost figure shown in the ledger. "Market" usually means current replacement cost, not sales value. However, "market" is sometimes taken as sales value less any costs necessary to complete and/or to sell, if this is less than current replacement cost. The amount of the write-down, if any, is sometimes determined by comparing the *total* market value of all inventories with the total inventory cost and sometimes by comparing market and cost values *for each item in the inventory*. The latter practice leads to a somewhat lower inventory figure, but otherwise the two approaches are the same.

Writing assets down when the market declines but not writing them up when the market rises is of course inconsistent. It reflects the persistence in accounting of what might be called a bankruptcy complex, largely a carryover from an earlier day when the main readers of the statements were short-term creditors who expected their loans to be repaid when short-term assets were liquidated. Business operations today, however, are more continuous, and while one batch of inventories is being liquidated, another is being acquired. Even short-term creditors recognize that their best protection is a healthy cash flow and an adequate profit margin. The emphasis, in other words, has shifted from the statics of the balance sheet to the dynamics of the income statement and funds flow statement.

The main objection to the lower of cost or market rule is that it distorts the income statement and makes year-to-year comparisons difficult. Because the write-down is buried in the cost of goods sold figure, the outside analyst cannot know how much of this figure represents an inventory write-down. Even more important, although the lower of cost or market rule sounds like an instrument of conservatism, it may have just the opposite effect on the income statement.

When prices fall, the closing inventory is written down accordingly, and the year's net income is thus conservatively stated. However, one year's closing inventory is next year's opening inventory, and the lower this is the higher are the second year's earnings. For example, when prices fall in one period only to turn up again in the next, application of the rule has the result of exaggerating the resultant fluctuation in earnings. In general, the net income effects of "cost or market" are somewhat erratic, and in this respect the rule appears to promote no obviously useful objective.

COMPARISON OF FIFO AND CURRENT COSTS

Although FIFO and similar flow-of-goods methods of inventory costing and cost of goods sold determination may at first glance appear quite reasonable, they have been subject to considerable criticism. This criticism has come from the same authorities who have criticized depreciation charges based on historical cost, and the recommended solution is the same—the substitution of current cost for historical cost.

FIFO versus Current Cost Margins

To understand the case for current costing of inventory transactions (sometimes called "next-in, first-out" or NIFO), let us consider a hypothetical case involving the manufacture of cotton cloth. Let us assume that the price of cotton is 17.5 cents a pound and that the price of cloth is 27.5 cents per pound of cotton content. Let us assume further that the price of cotton rises steadily during the next three months to 22.5 cents at the end of this first quarter-year period. The average purchase price during the quarter is therefore 20 cents a pound.[4] Applying this approach to the prices paid for cotton during the following six quarters produces the following averages:

Quarter	Average Price per Pound
1	$0.200
2	0.250
3	0.325
4	0.425
5	0.450
6	0.400
7	0.400

[4] To simplify the example, it is assumed that purchases of cotton during a quarter are made at the average of the prices prevailing at the beginning and end of each quarter.

If the acquisition of cotton, its conversion into cloth, and the sale of the cloth can be accomplished instantaneously, so that the manufacturer carries no inventory, the cotton content of the cost of goods sold in any period will be equal to the prices paid for cotton in that period. If any inventories are carried, however, the reported cost of goods sold under FIFO accounting will reflect to some extent the prices paid in previous periods.

For example, let us assume that the manufacturer's inventory turnover period is three months, that purchases and sales are constant from month to month, and that in each quarter from the second quarter onward the cotton content of the goods sold is exactly equal to the quantity of cotton purchased during that quarter.

Under the FIFO costing method, which reflects faithfully the physical flow of goods, the material content of the goods sold during a quarter is costed at the cotton prices prevailing during the previous quarter. For example, computed from the basic formula, the cost of the materials content of the goods sold during the second quarter is:

Opening inventory, 100,000 lbs. at $0.20.....................$20,000
Purchased, 100,000 lbs. at $0.25............................. 25,000
Cost of goods available......................................$45,000
Ending inventory, 100,000 lbs. at $0.25...................... 25,000
Materials Content of Cost of Goods Sold..................... $20,000

In other words, the cost of goods sold under these conditions is exactly equal to the cost of the goods in inventory at the beginning of the quarter. This exact correspondence results from the assumption that the inventory turns over once each quarter—that is, purchases and consumption are each equal to the beginning inventory.

These relationships are diagrammed in Exhibit 12–3. The thin solid line shows the purchase price of cotton, while the broken line traces the path followed by the cotton content of the FIFO cost of goods sold. This is parallel to the cotton price line but one period later.

The third line in this diagram represents the prices at which the cotton cloth is sold. This line is drawn on the assumption that cloth prices always change immediately in response to a change in cotton prices, and by an equal amount. A spread of 10 cents a pound between cloth price and current cotton price has been assumed here, but any other pattern could have been assumed without altering the argument. (Similarly, to avoid cluttering the illustration, manufacturing costs other than the cost of cotton have been assumed to be zero.)

If FIFO inventory costing is used, reported income per pound will be represented by the vertical distance between the cloth price and

Exhibit 12–3

COMPARISON OF FIFO AND CURRENT COST MARGINS

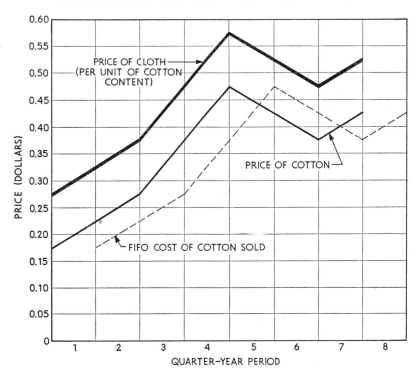

PRICE OF CLOTH
(PER UNIT OF COTTON
CONTENT)

PRICE OF COTTON

FIFO COST OF COTTON SOLD

PRICE (DOLLARS)

QUARTER–YEAR PERIOD

the FIFO cost curve. This we shall call the *historical cost margin*. By contrast, the *current cost margin* is what the reported profit would have been if the firm had been able to operate with no inventory, the spread between the cloth price and cotton price lines.

Computation of Inventory Profit or Loss

These relationships are shown in tabular form in Exhibit 12–4. The figures in the first six columns have been taken from the diagram in Exhibit 12–3. The remaining columns assume that inventories are constant at a level of 100,000 pounds of cotton and that in each quarter 100,000 pounds of cotton are purchased and an equivalent amount of cloth is sold.

The quarterly historical cost margins of column (7) are the differences between sales at the average cloth prices for the period and cost of cotton sold at the average FIFO cost, both as given in the prior columns. The current cost margins of column (8) are $10,000 in every period, since cotton and cloth prices are assumed to move together. The differences between these two sets of margins are shown in column (9) as *inventory profit or (loss)*. This is the portion of the firm's reported income that results solely from the difference between current purchase prices and the prices transferred from inventory accounts to the cost of goods sold.

The lower table in the exhibit demonstrates that these last figures are mirrored in the period-by-period changes in the amounts of the FIFO inventories. Since the amount by which the FIFO profit differs from the current cost profit is exactly equal to the write-up or write-down in the inventory, this component of a FIFO determined profit will be called an *inventory profit*.

Examination of the data contained in Exhibit 12–4 reveals that when materials prices rise, the historical cost margin is greater than the current cost margin, as in quarters 2, 3, 4, and 5. When prices fall, the opposite result occurs, as in quarter 6. The general observation is

Exhibit 12–4

**HISTORICAL VERSUS CURRENT COST MARGINS
AND EFFECTS OF PRICE CHANGES ON FIFO INVENTORIES**

(1)	(2)	(3)	(4)	(5)	(6)	(7)	(8)	(9)
				Profit Margin/Lb.		Total Profit Margin		
Period	Cost per Lb.		Selling Price per Lb.	FIFO Cost (4) − (2)	Current Cost (4) − (3)	FIFO Cost	Current Cost	Inventory Profit or (Loss)
	FIFO	Current						
1......		$0.200						
2......	$0.200	0.250	$.0350	$0.150	$0.100	$15,000	$10,000	$ 5,000
3......	0.250	0.325	0.425	0.175	0.100	17,500	10,000	7,500
4......	0.325	0.425	0.525	0.200	0.100	20,000	10,000	10,000
5......	0.425	0.450	0.550	0.125	0.100	12,500	10,000	2,500
6......	0.450	0.400	0.500	0.050	0.100	5,000	10,000	(5,000)
7......	0.400	0.400	0.500	0.100	0.100	10,000	10,000	0

FIFO INVENTORY CHANGES

Period	(10) FIFO Beginning Inventory (100,000 Lbs.)	(11) FIFO Ending Inventory (100,000 Lbs.)	(12) Change in Valuation (7) − (8)
2........	At $0.200 = $20,000	At $0.250 = $25,000	+$ 5,000
3........	At 0.250 = 25,000	At 0.325 = 32,500	+ 7,500
4........	At 0.325 = 32,500	At 0.425 = 42,500	+ 10,000
5........	At 0.425 = 42,500	At 0.450 = 45,000	+ 2,500
6........	At 0.450 = 45,000	At 0.400 = 40,000	− 5,000
7........	At 0.400 = 40,000	At 0.400 = 40,000	0

that *carrying a given physical inventory quantity under conditions of changing prices results in an inventory profit or loss equal to the increase or decrease in the book value of that quantity of inventory.*

This discussion is based on the implicit assumption that current cost is the best measure of the cost of goods sold and that the adequacy of other methods is best tested by comparison with current cost. The reasoning behind this is fairly simple. In a going concern, a certain physical inventory quantity is necessary for smooth business operations. The inventory may be depleted for short periods without harmful effects, but if inventory levels have been set rationally in the first place, units used or sold must be replaced within a fairly short period of time. Inventories are replenished at current replacement prices, and these represent the economic sacrifice that the company makes when it sells goods. If replacement prices rise from 20 cents to 30 cents, then the company will have to spend 30 cents merely to keep its inventory quantities constant. If only 20 cents is shown as the cost of goods sold, then 10 cents of the reported income of the current period must be reinvested so that the company will be as well off in physical terms at the end of the period as at the beginning. From this point of view, income is *overstated* to the extent of the price level gain component of reported income.

This distinction is reflected in columns (8) and (9) of Exhibit 12–4. The FIFO historical cost margin of column (7) has been broken down into two components: current cost margin (column [8]) and inventory profit (column [9]). Only the $10,000 current cost margin is available for distribution as dividends. The balance of the reported profit, the inventory profit, is automatically spent along with the reported cost of goods sold to replace the goods sold.

Determinants of the Size of Inventory Profits

Two main factors affect the amount and direction of the inventory profit or loss:

1. The amount and direction of the price change from one period to the next; and
2. The size of the inventory.

The faster the price change and the larger the inventory, the greater the inventory profit or loss.

It should be noted that the correlation between the inventory profit or loss and the price change during a period is reduced when the firm has a slower inventory turnover. For example, assume that the firm has a two-period inventory (200,000 pounds) and that the price of cotton changes from 30 cents to 40 cents during period 1, but then remains constant at 40 cents during period 2. Notwithstanding the fact that the price of cotton did not change in period 2, there is an inventory profit of 10 cents a pound because the 30 cents per pound inventory on hand at the start of period 1 was sold in period 2. With a one-period turnover, in contrast, the FIFO cost of goods sold in period 2 would be 40 cents a pound and the inventory profit would be zero.

Exhibit 12–5

COMPARATIVE MARGINS ASSUMING A CONSTANT MARKUP ON FIFO COST

(1)	(2)	(3)	(4)	(5)	(6)	(7)	(8)	(9)
	Cost per Lb.		Selling	Profit Margin/Lb.		Total Profit Margin		Inventory
Period	FIFO	Current	Price per Lb.	FIFO Cost (4) − (2)	Current Cost (4) − (3)	FIFO Cost	Current Cost	Profit or (Loss)
1......		$0.200						
2......	$0.200	0.250	$0.300	$0.100	$0.050	$10,000	$ 5,000	$ 5,000
3......	0.250	0.325	0.350	0.100	0.025	10,000	2,500	7,500
4......	0.325	0.425	0.425	0.100	—	10,000	—	10,000
5......	0.425	0.450	0.525	0.100	0.075	10,000	7,500	2,500
6......	0.450	0.400	0.550	0.100	0.150	10,000	15,000	(5,000)
7......	0.400	0.400	0.500	0.100	0.100	10,000	10,000	0

The *relative* importance of the inventory profit or loss depends on still a third factor, the size of the percentage margin between sales revenue and the cost of goods sold. If the margin is reduced by lowering the cloth price curve, the inventory profit or loss will represent a larger percentage of the total profit or loss.

Despite this, the *absolute* amount of the inventory profit is not affected by the size of the margin between purchase and selling prices. It doesn't matter, in other words, whether the price of the product changes with changes in replacement cost or with changes in FIFO cost or with some other factor. In Exhibit 12–4, for example, the current cost margin was assumed to be constant at 10 cents a pound. If instead a constant markup of this same amount on FIFO cost is assumed, the margin variability effects are reversed, as shown in Exhibit 12–5, but the price gains and losses are not modified in any way.

The historical cost margin in quarter 2, for example, becomes $10,000 instead of $15,000 but $5,000 of this amount is still required to finance the replacement of the goods sold at a cost of $25,000. The inventory profit or loss is the difference between the current and historical cost of goods sold. The sales revenue does not enter into its determination.

The Significance of Inventory Profits

The main argument against inventory costing methods which include inventory profits or losses in reported income is that the amount and direction of this component of income are uncertain. When prices are rising, managers generally find it easier to achieve a satisfactory historical cost marign than when prices are falling. Selling prices do not always follow the movements taken by replacement prices, of course, but it is usually easier to raise selling prices when replacement prices are going up than when they are steady or declining. But even if this is not so, movements in the current cost margin are more indicative of current conditions than movements in the historical cost margin in which one of the determinants is partially out of date. For these reasons, a segregation of the inventory profit or loss ought to be helpful to investors in their evaluation of company management or to top management in the evaluation of individual company activities.

Furthermore, the historical cost figure does not measure as well as current cost the current sacrifice made by the company when it sells or uses an item of inventory. In a period of rising replacement costs, every dollar of inventory profit must be reinvested in inventory replacement if stocks are to be maintained at the same physical level. The opposite is true when replacement prices are falling.

Finally, if dividends are based on the historical cost margin, they may exceed the current cost margin. In this case, funds must be provided from other sources merely to maintain a constant physical inventory quantity. This possibility is strengthened when income taxes are based on the historical cost margin. For example, in Exhibit 12–4, the period 3 historical cost margin was $17,500. With an income tax rate of 50 percent, $8,750 would have been paid in taxes. The sales revenue of $42,500 less the $8,750 in taxes and the $25,000 cost of goods sold leaves a net profit after taxes of $8,750. However, the cost of replacing the goods sold was $32,500, not $25,000, so that with a reported profit of $8,750 after taxes the firm only had $1,250 available to pay dividends.

THE LAST-IN, FIRST-OUT (LIFO) METHOD

In an attempt to remedy these defects, accountants in the United States tried out various alternative inventory costing methods, but it wasn't until the first decade after World War II that one of these methods came into widespread use. This is the last-in, first-out or LIFO method.

Description of the Method

For an understanding of the LIFO method, two points must always be kept in mind. First, the method does not require the physical movement of inventory on a last-in, first-out basis. The method is used only in the *costing* of inventory and goods sold. Second, each sale or issue or even a month's sales or issues are not costed in this way: *the method is applied to the year as a whole*, without regard to interim increases or decreases in inventory quantities on hand.

To illustrate, assume that Swift Oil Company adopted LIFO as of the beginning of 1959. The company is able to express its entire inventory in an equivalent number of barrels of crude oil, the product the company buys. The December 31, 1958, inventory was two million barrels; and the actual cost of this inventory at FIFO, the method of costing then in use, was $1.50 a barrel. The 2,000,000 barrels at $1.50 = $3,000,000 is called the LIFO base.

Because of the continuing prospect of increasing business activity and rising prices, purchases exceeded sales in each of the following two years. In 1959, purchases were 4,000,000 barrels at $2 and sales were 3,800,000 barrels. Under LIFO the barrels sold were all costed out at the current purchase price of $2. The excess of the purchases over the sales, 200,000 barrels at $2 = $400,000, was the 1959 *layer* or *increment*. In 1960, the layer was 300,000 barrels as $2.40 = $720,000. In 1961, business activities leveled off and purchases and sales were equal. Thus, each year's cost of goods sold from 1959 through 1961 reflected purchase prices paid in that year, and the 1961 ending inventory consisted of the LIFO base quantity, costed at 1958 prices, plus two layers, each costed at the prices prevailing in the year in which the layer was added to inventory:

1958 base................	2,000,000 bbls. at $1.50	$3,000,000
1959 layer..............	200,000 bbls. at 2.00	400,000
1960 layer..............	300,000 bbls. at 2.40	720,000
Total..............	2,500,000 bbls.	$4,120,000

Inventories fluctuated during the next few years, but on December 31, 1967, the physical quantity of inventory on hand amounted to 2,500,000 barrels, exactly the same amount that had been in stock on December 31, 1961. Under the LIFO method, this inventory was shown on the December 31, 1967, balance sheet at $4,120,000.

In 1968, purchases were held down to 4,100,000 barrels at a cost of $2.60 per barrel, even though sales increased to 4,500,000 barrels. The result was an inventory *depletion* or *liquidation* of 400,000 barrels. Under LIFO, the cost of goods sold was the cost of 1968 purchases plus the cost of 400,000 barrels from *the most recently added* inventory layers. Specifically, the 1968 cost of goods sold was:

1968 purchases............4,100,000 bbls. at $2.60	$10,660,000
1960 layer............... 300,000 bbls. at 2.40	720,000
1959 layer............... 100,000 bbls. at 2.00	200,000
Total..............4,500,000 bbls.	$11,580,000

The procedure described in the above illustration may be summarized as follows:

1. When the quantity of goods purchased during a *year* is *equal* to the quantity sold, the purchases are charged against sales and the closing inventory is the same (in price as well as in quantity) as the opening inventory.
2. When the quantity purchased is *greater* than the quantity sold, say by x units, the quantity purchased less the x units is charged against sales and the closing inventory is the opening inventory plus this increment.[5]
3. When the quantity purchased is less than the quantity sold, say by y units, sales are charged with the purchases for the year plus the cost of y units taken from inventory. The decremental y units are costed out of inventory on a last-layer-in, first-layer-out basis.

Deficiencies of the LIFO Method

Although the use of LIFO continues to expand, many accountants continue to oppose it. One basis for opposition is that LIFO is not truly a method of recording cost expirations but purely a means to avoid or postpone taxes. Some evidence does exist that LIFO is adopted or rejected largely on the basis of tax considerations.[6] To get

---

[5] Under the tax law, the increment of x units may be costed at the cost of the first purchases, the last purchases, or an average of all purchases during the year. Election from among these options must be made in the year of LIFO adoption, and the procedure elected must be followed consistently thereafter.

[6] If LIFO is used for tax purposes, then by law it must also be used for public reporting. This provision presumably reflects a widespread view in Congress that LIFO is a tax reduction device, pure and simple.

the greatest amount of cost into the income statement and leave the smallest amount on the balance sheet, thus minimizing taxable income, the proper time to adopt LIFO is when prices are at their lowest. Many would-be users of LIFO in the inflation years after World War II kept predicting that prices were at their peak and would fall later. Thus they deferred adoption of LIFO in anticipation of a price decline that never occurred. The opponents of LIFO point to this experience as evidence that LIFO is first and foremost a device for tax avoidance, and have thus opposed it.

A more fundamental reason for opposing LIFO is rejection of the basic philosophy of earnings measurement in current cost terms. Since this issue, like most others in accounting, does not hinge upon the correct interpretation of any natural law, it can be resolved only by a majority judgment as to the relative utility of the information obtained.[7]

An entirely different tack is taken by those who feel that LIFO doesn't adhere faithfully enough to the current cost concept. The major criticism on this score centers on the effect of inventory liquidations on reported income. In the Swift Oil example, inventories were reduced in 1968 by 400,000 barrels. These were included in the cost of goods sold at the prices paid for oil in 1959 and 1960, almost a decade earlier. This led to an inventory profit (current cost minus historical cost of goods sold) just as FIFO costing would have. Had Swift Oil Company been able to acquire at the prevailing cost ($2.60) the oil needed to replace fully the quantity sold during the year, no depletion would have occurred. The 1959 and 1960 prices of 400,000 barrels would not have been removed from inventory, and the cost of goods sold would have been $120,000 greater:

Cost of 1959 and 1960 layers transferred to cost of goods
    sold in 1968.......................................$ 920,000
Current cost in 1968 (400,000 bbls. × $2.60)............. 1,040,000
    Inventory Profit...................................$ 120,000

In other words, reported income included $120,000 which would not have been reported if inventories had not been reduced during the year. This inventory profit is called a *liquidation profit*. Because long

---

[7] Further discussions of the arguments for and against LIFO may be found in Maurice Moonitz, "The Case against LIFO," *Journal of Accountancy*, June, 1953; H. T. McAnly, "The Case for LIFO," *Journal of Accountancy*, June, 1953; Charles E. Johnson, "Inventory Valuation, the Accountant's Achilles Heel," *The Accounting Review*, January, 1954; and James L. Dohr, "Limitations on the Usefulness of Price Level Adjustments," *The Accounting Review*, April, 1955.

intervals can elapse between the acquisition of an inventory and its liquidation, this liquidation profit can be extremely large if any substantial inventory quantities are liquidated. *The spasmodic appearance of such price gains or losses, unless these are clearly distinguished from normal current cost margins, seriously detracts from the interperiod comparability of the operating statistics of the firm.* That such effects can be important is indicated by the fact that during World War II and for some time thereafter, special tax relief was provided with respect to gains resulting from *involuntary* LIFO inventory liquidations.[8]

Another argument is that since the majority of firms are not LIFO users and hence include inventory profits and losses in their net income figures, the LIFO elimination of these elements markedly reduces the interfirm comparability of performance data. LIFO also reduces the comparability of the inventory figure with those of firms using other methods. After LIFO has been used for a number of years, the inventory figure shown on the balance sheet becomes a meaningless conglomeration of various physical quantities measured at prices prevailing in a number of different years, some in the distant past. Since the inventory figure is so difficult to interpret, then any other quantity dependent on it—the current ratio, for example—is also less useful for either interfirm or interperiod comparisons.

Finally, the use of LIFO may lead management to make business decisions that would be regarded as unsound if it were not for tax considerations. For example, under conditions of severe and/or prolonged inflation, the tax penalty for depleting a LIFO inventory may be sufficiently great to dictate full replenishment of stocks in any given year despite prospects of lower purchase prices after the year-end. This is, however, but one of the many ways in which a tax on income reacts upon income-determining decisions, and therefore the criticism is less persuasive than those previously noted.

Possible Modifications of the LIFO Method

Most of the foregoing objections can be met at least part way by some rather simple procedural modifications. For example, recall that the Swift Oil Company data for 1968 were as follows:

---

[8] During that period, the problem was magnified by severe materials shortages occasioning numerous unavoidable liquidations and also by an excess profits tax which sharply increased the penalty for depleting stocks carried at low prewar prices. Relief took the form of a tax rebate in the period or periods of inventory replenishment.

Inventory January 1, 1968

1958 base................2,000,000 bbls. at $1.50		$ 3,000,000
1959 layer............... 200,000 bbls. at 2.00		400,000
1960 layer................ 300,000 bbls. at 2.40		720,000
Total...............2,500,000 bbls.		$ 4,120,000

Cost of Goods Sold, 1968

1968 purchases............4,100,000 bbls. at $2.60		$10,660,000
1960 layer............... 300,000 bbls. at 2.40		720,000
1959 layer............... 100,000 bbls. at 2.00		200,000
Total..............4,500,000 bbls.		$11,580,000

It would be very simple in this case to disclose on the balance sheet the inventory at its current cost—the outlay that would be needed to acquire a comparable inventory as of the date of the financial report. For the January 1, 1968, inventory, one reasonable approximation of current cost may be the last price paid by the company for oil during 1967. Assuming that this figure is $2.50 a barrel, a meaningful measure of the inventory would be 2,500,000 barrels at $2.50 = $6,250,000. If interfirm comparability is the principal objective, the ending inventory can be measured instead at the prices paid during the closing weeks or months of the year, the actual period depending on the rate of turnover. The inventory figure determined in this way would be comparable with the FIFO inventories of other firms.

If the current cost inventory is shown on the balance sheet, something must be done to adjust it to the LIFO figure. One way to handle this is as follows:

Inventory at current cost......................$6,250,000
Less: Adjustment to LIFO cost.............. 2,130,000
LIFO Cost of Inventory......................$4,120,000

The Adjustment to LIFO Cost account is another example of a deduction-from-assets contra account. If the current cost of the year-end inventory is approximately the same as FIFO cost would be, then the change in the balance in the adjustment account from one year to the next is the unrealized inventory profit or loss for that year, the amount by which the FIFO cost of goods sold would have been lower or greater than the LIFO figure for the year.

On the income statement, when purchases equal or exceed sales, LIFO shows the current cost of the goods sold, and this figure is superior to the FIFO cost of goods sold in that it contains no inventory profit.[9] However, when an inventory liquidation takes place, the

---

[9] This is not precisely accurate. The current cost margin theoretically should be computed by comparing selling price with replacement cost *at the time of each sale*.

income figure contains an inventory profit, as discussed earlier. The full disclosure of this information is accomplished by reporting the cost of goods sold at current cost and showing the amount by which the LIFO cost was below this figure as a gain on inventory liquidation. Since the average purchase price of oil in 1968 was $2.60 per barrel, the cost of goods sold at current cost was 4,500,000 barrels at $2.60 = $11,700,000, which exceeded the LIFO cost of goods sold by $120,000. Using hypothetical sales revenue data, the proposed income statement format would be:

Sales.	$12,000,000
Cost of goods sold.	11,700,000
Net operating income.	$ 300,000
Plus gain on inventory liquidation.	120,000
Net Income.	$ 420,000

Through this format the reader of the financial statement could see how much of the period's income is due to operations and how much is due to the liquidation of inventory purchased at lower prices in earlier periods.

The inventory account in the balance sheet at the end of 1968 would read as follows:

Inventory at current cost.	$5,460,000
Less: Adjustment to LIFO cost.	2,260,000
LIFO Cost of Inventory.	$3,200,000

LIFO and the Perpetual Inventory

LIFO is primarily a basis for *annual* financial reporting. Although it could be used for day-to-day inventory bookkeeping, it is not used for this purpose. A simple example may demonstrate why.

A company started the year with 10,000 tons of a certain commodity in its inventory. This was shown on its balance sheet at a LIFO cost of $10 a ton. The company sold 3,000 tons of the commodity in March and bought 3,000 tons in October, at a price of $18 a ton. No other transactions in this commodity took place during the year.

If LIFO had been used for cost bookkeeping, the account would have shown the following:

If purchases are made in March and sales in June, the reported income for the year may include some inventory profit or loss even if year-end and year-beginning quantities are equal. In most cases, however, it does no harm to include this as a component of the current cost margin.

	Quantity	Unit Cost	Total Cost
Balance, January 1...............	10,000	$10	$100,000
Cost of goods sold, March..........	3,000	10	30,000
Balance, March 31...............	7,000	10	$ 70,000
Purchased, October..............	3,000	18	54,000
Balance, December 31............	10,000		$124,000

In this case, even though the year-ending quantity was the same as the opening balance, the balance in the inventory account would have increased by $24,000. To avoid including this amount as an inventory profit in the net income figure for the year, the company would have had to make a correcting entry at the end of the year to return the inventory account balance to the $100,000 level.

In a more typical case, with many purchases and many sales during the year, some monthly financial statements would include inventory profits while others would not. To avoid this kind of confusion, companies that use LIFO for public financial reporting use some other method for cost bookkeeping, usually either the moving average method or the standard cost figures to be described in Part III.

Dollar Value LIFO

The LIFO method is designed to accomplish a particular result with respect to the measurement of period net income; no pretense is generally made that the last-in, first-out assumption reflects the physical flow of goods. Unfortunately, however, its advocates did not limit their original arguments to end purposes but attempted to strengthen their case by contending that LIFO was as reasonable as any other flow assumption with respect to fungible (i.e., interchangeable or identical) goods. This somewhat opportunistic approach resulted in confusion as to legislative intent and consequent inequities in the administration of the tax law: the method was initially allowed only when its assumed flow of goods was physically possible. Firms engaged in the processing of one or a few basic commodities such as oil, cotton, and copper were the first to adopt the method, while many firms that might otherwise have adopted it prior to World War II were restrained from doing so.

Some department stores, however, refused to give up without a battle the tax savings LIFO would provide. Such firms satisfied all the conditions under which inventory profits are a large component of income, since their inventories were large in relation to sales, the merchandise they purchased was rising in price, and merchandise costs represented a very large fraction of the department store sales dollar.

However, a department store could not follow the lead of oil, textile, and other such companies and adopt LIFO on a unit basis. Not only would the large number of items in the inventory make the bookkeeping prohibitive but the advantages of LIFO would not be realized. Although a department store inventory is quite stable in the aggregate, individual items are not. The inventory of 1962-model refrigerators, for example, is often zero by the end of 1962, certainly by the end of 1963. Thus large liquidation profits would be included in reported income each year.

To deal with this problem, the *LIFO dollar value method* was developed. Although a thorough explanation of this method is beyond the scope of this text, some understanding of the method is highly desirable. The cost-of-living index compiled by the Bureau of Labor Statistics (BLS) has become widely known. What the BLS does to compile this index is first establish a "basket of goods" that is representative of what a typical family unit buys during the year. The basket includes pork chops, electricity, television sets, and other goods and services in appropriate proportions. The BLS then prices this basket of goods periodically to determine the index. For instance, if the basket cost $7,000 on January 1, 19x1, and $7,700 on January 1, 19x2, the cost of living rose 10 percent during the year; and if the index were 120 on January 1, 19x1, it would be 132 on January 1, 19x2.

Consider now a department store that kept its inventory on a regular FIFO basis, and assume that a price index is available for a "basket of goods" that is representative of the inventory a department store carries. This price index would be used to "deflate" the inventory—that is, break down the dollar value increase (or decrease) into the portion due to the *physical* increase and the portion due to the rise in *prices*. For instance, assume that a store inventory increased from $3,000,000 to $3,750,000 over the course of a year, and the end-of-year index was 110 with 100 the index at the start of the year. The start-of-year inventory at end-of-year prices is $3,000,000 × 110 = $3,300,000. Hence, the physical increase in the inventory was only $450,000 at end-of-year prices. Under LIFO, $450,000 rather than $750,000 would be added to the inventory.

The mechanics by which a department store actually uses dollar value LIFO to calculate its inventory and cost of goods sold on LIFO need not detain us here. Manufacturing firms with inventories that contain a large number of items or are subject to periodic model changes employ variations on the same principle to separate the physical and price level changes in their inventories.[10]

PRICE LEVEL ADJUSTMENTS TO FINANCIAL STATEMENTS

The discussion of LIFO in this chapter and of declining-charge depreciation methods in the previous chapter was concerned with the most accurate and meaningful methods of measurement for financial statements. At the same time it was acknowledged that the motivation of many accountants and companies in advocating and adopting these methods of measurement was the tax advantage they provided.

Most academic accountants have acknowledged that traditional historical cost measurement rules severely impair the validity of financial statements in an economy with a fluctuating or rising price level. However, many of these academic accountants do not look with favor on LIFO and accelerated depreciation as a means of dealing with the problem. Some have advocated the substitution of current cost for historical cost as the basis of measurement, while others have gone on to recommend the comprehensive adjustment of historical cost statements for changes in the general purchasing power of the dollar. A comprehensive survey of the alternatives advanced is beyond the scope of this text, but an understanding of the issues is of the greatest importance.[11]

Current Cost Financial Statements

In this and the previous chapter the current cost concept was used to establish the limitations of historical measurement of depreciation and merchandise cost of goods sold. This discussion made evident the

[10] For an early but detailed discussion of these methods, see R. A. Hoffman, *LIFO: A Review of Its Applications in Inventory Valuation* (Chicago: Price Waterhouse & Co., 1953).

[11] Four notable landmarks in the history of the search for methods of dealing with price changes are H. W. Sweeney, *Stabilized Accounting* (New York: Harper & Bros., 1936); Ralph C. Jones, "Effect of Inflation on Capital and Profits: The Record of Nine Steel Companies," *Journal of Accountancy*, January, 1949, pp. 9–27; Perry Mason, *Price-Level Changes and Financial Statements: Basic Concepts and Methods* (Columbus, Ohio: American Accounting Association, 1956); and Edgar O. Edwards and Philip W. Bell, *The Theory and Measurement of Business Income*, (Berkeley: University of California Press, 1961). For an excellent survey and analysis of the literature on this subject through 1961, see Steven A. Zeff, "Replacement Cost: Member of the Family, Welcome Guest, or Intruder?" *The Accounting Review*, October, 1962, pp. 611–25.

implications for the income statement of adopting current or replacement cost as the basis of measurement. The net income figure would represent the income from operations in the sense that the expenses would reflect the cost of replacing the equipment and merchandise *consumed* in realizing the period's sales revenue. This income figure would exclude gains or losses due to changes in the cost of assets acquired prior to the current period.

The difficulties with current cost are much greater when we turn to the balance sheet. For the balance sheet to be meaningful, the replacement cost of inventory, plant, equipment, and similar assets should appear on the balance sheet. The rise (or fall) in the replacement cost of these assets from one period to the next is a *holding gain* (or loss).[12] Under historical cost, realized holding gains are recognized on the balance sheet and income statement whereas unrealized gains are not. Under current cost, realization is not a valid criterion for recognition.

Three alternative courses of action are possible in the treatment of holding gains. One alternative is to report but not recognize the holding gain by carrying it to a contra account as proposed on page 372 in the discussion of how to deal with the limitations of LIFO. The second alternative is to carry the holding gains or losses directly to the owners' equity. This portion of the owners' equity might be shown separately under the account title Excess of Replacement over Purchase Cost of Assets Carried Forward. The third alternative is to carry the period's holding gain or loss to the income statement with the total income (operating income and holding gain) carried to retained earnings. The tax treatment of capital gains and losses is of course independent of how they are reported in financial statements to investors. It also may be noted that the adoption of current cost causes no change in the liability accounts.[13]

Purchasing Power Adjustments

So far we have not considered the purchasing power of a company's operating income or of its assets. Once again the income statement problems are easier to handle. Assume that the firm's current

---

[12] For monetary assets such as cash and accounts receivable, the actual amounts are the replacement cost, and no capital gains or losses can take place with respect to these assets.

[13] Proposals to adopt a current-cost basis of measurement are contained in Robert T. Sprouse and Maurice Moonitz, *A Tentative Set of Broad Accounting Principles for Business Enterprises*, Accounting Research Study No. 3 (New York: AICPA, 1962); and American Accounting Association Committee on Concepts and Standards —Long-Lived Assets, "Accounting for Land, Buildings and Equipment, Supplementary Statement No. 1," *The Accounting Review*, July, 1964, pp. 693–99.

cost operating income was $100,000 in 19x1 and $120,000 in 19x2. Are the stockholders 20 percent better off by virtue of the 20 percent increase in income if the general price level has gone up by 15 percent during the same period? If interperiod comparison of wage and salary income requires adjustment for changes in the cost of living, it would seem appropriate to make the same adjustment to corporate income.

Turning to the balance sheet, an analogous problem may be said to exist. Assume that the replacement cost of a firm's assets rose from $1,000,000 to $1,300,000 over the same period with the Excess of Replacement over Purchase Cost of Assets Carried Forward rising by $130,000. Have the firm's assets really increased by 30 percent if the price level has gone up by 15 percent? Has the owners' equity really increased by $130,000 plus the operating income less the dividends? The answer would appear to be no, and deflation by some price level index would seem to be appropriate for interperiod comparison in "real" terms.[14]

SUMMARY

Inventories and the cost of goods used are generally measured in conventional income statements by one of three costing methods: FIFO, moving average, or LIFO. End-of-period inventory balances under the first two of these are reduced to a replacement cost basis by many firms if replacement cost is less than historical cost. This adjustment is known as the lower of cost or market adjustment.

All three of these methods of inventory costing have been rationalized as an implementation of the historical cost basis of measurement, but for LIFO the rationalization is quite tortured. The LIFO cost figure on the balance sheet is quite meaningless, although the cost of goods sold figure is typically a close approximation of current cost.

Many accountants believe that superiority of current cost and the departures of all three methods from current cost justify its substitution for the historical cost basis. Some would go even farther and adjust the statements to a purchasing power basis, recognizing gains and losses in the purchasing power represented by the company's assets. This chapter has attempted to examine some of the arguments relevant to these issues.

---

[14] The most recent major work on the price level problem, including a survey of accounting practice throughout the world, was prepared by the American Institute of Certified Public Accountants, *Reporting the Financial effects of Price-Level Changes*, Accounting Research Study No. 6 (New York: AICPA, 1963).

QUESTIONS AND PROBLEMS

1. Under what conditions will the choice of inventory costing method have a large impact on net income?

2. What is meant by "specific lot costing" as applied to the inventory measurement problem? For what reasons may this method be undesirable or unsuitable? When would you expect to see it used.

3. Explain in detail the nature, purpose, and effect of the "cost or market" rule. Does it represent a "conservative" accounting practice?

4. What is meant by the "inventory turnover rate"? How does the magnitude of this rate affect the magnitude of the "inventory profit or loss"?

5. What are the objectives of LIFO? How well do you feel that it meets these objectives?

6. What does the difference between the historical cost margin and the current cost margin mean? Under currently accepted accounting methods, which of these would be reported on the current year's income statement?

7. The LIFO method has been criticized on a number of grounds. List the major objections to the use of this method and indicate how, if at all, the method might be modified to meet any objection that you feel is valid.

8. How does "dollar value LIFO" differ from the basic LIFO method described in this chapter? When would you expect it to be used?

9. If prices of all goods and services are rising, what happens to the value of the company's cash balances? Should this change in value be shown on the income statement? How would you measure the change in value?

10. The balance sheet in a company's annual report described the company's inventories as follows:

Inventories—substantially all stated at cost on "last-in, first-out" basis with current replacement cost approximately $28,100,000 in excess of stated value. $53,334,933

A year earlier, the corresponding inventory figure was $56,047,919, and current replacement cost was approximately $24,200,000 in excess of stated value.

What information about the financial position and operations of the company do the figures on excess of replacement cost over stated value provide?

11. A balance sheet included the following account among the current liabilities:

Provision for replacement of basic LIFO inventories...............$650,000

This account did not appear in the previous year's balance sheet.

The balance in the inventory account at the close of each of the two years was as follows:

Most recent year...................$11,735,039
Previous year..................... 12,785,001

a) What is the meaning of the "provision" account, and what effect did it have on the reported income for the year?

b) The balance in this account went back to zero at the end of the next year. What happened?

c) Do you think that the company's method was a desirable accounting practice?

*12. The Winchester Coal Company sells and delivers stove, nut, and powder coal. One year's transactions in nut coal were:

Month	Tons Purchased	Purchase Price per Ton	Tons Sold
January 1, beginning inventory.........	1,000	$11.00	
January.............................	100	11.20	300
February............................			400
March..............................			300
April...............................	100	11.30	100
May................................			50
June................................	200	11.50	
July................................	200	11.50	
August..............................	300	11.55	50
September...........................	300	11.55	100
October.............................	300	11.60	150
November...........................	400	11.60	250
December...........................	200	11.70	300
Total........................	3,100		2,000
December 31, Ending Inventory........	1,100		

a) What is the cost of the ending inventory on the basis of—
  (1) First-in, first-out?
  (2) Last-in, first-out?

---

* Solutions to problems marked with an asterisk (*) are found in Appendix B.

b) What difference in reported earnings would be shown by the two methods?

*13. The following data are taken from the records of the Briggs Sales Company of East Greenwich, Vermont:

	Units	Unit Cost	Total Cost
Inventory—March 1...............	1,600	$10.00	$16,000
Purchase—March 5...............	800	11.00	8,800
Purchase—March 20..............	500	13.00	6,500
Purchase—March 31..............	1,400	12.00	16,800

During the month, the following number of units were sold:

March 3.........................900
March 10........................800
March 23........................700

What were the March cost of the goods sold and the March 31 inventory figures:

a) Assuming cost to be determined on a first-in, first-out basis?
b) Assuming cost to be determined on an average cost basis?
c) Assuming application of the "cost or market" rule in connection with (*a*) above?

14. The Advance Corporation began business in September, 1963. Its purchases and sales of merchandise for its first three months of operation are tabulated below:

Month	Purchases			Sales, Pounds
	Pounds	Price	Amount	
October................	17,000	$2.00	$34,000	4,000
November..............	5,000	2.30	11,500	4,500
December..............	4,000	2.50	10,000	4,800

a) At what amount should the December 31 inventory be carried on the balance sheet if the company adopts the—
   (1) First-in, first-out basis?
   (2) Last-in, first-out basis?
b) Which basis would show the larger profit for this period and by how much?

15. The following data relate to purchases and issues of a raw material used by a manufacturer:

Inventory: January 1....   30,000 lbs. at $0.30........$ 9,000
Purchases: January 20... 22,000 lbs. at 0.35........ 7,700
         February 16.. 20,000 lbs. at 0.38........ 7,600
         March 12.... 28,000 lbs. at 0.40........ 11,200
         April 5...... 25,000 lbs. at 0.34........ 8,500
         April 30..... 20,000 lbs. at 0.33........ 6,600
         May 27...... 27,000 lbs. at 0.32........ 8,640
         June 21...... 30,000 lbs. at 0.37........ 11,100
         July 18...... 24,000 lbs. at 0.41........ 9,840
         August 14.... 20,000 lbs. at 0.43........ 8,600
         September 8.. 25,000 lbs. at 0.40........ 10,000
         October 2.... 33,000 lbs. at 0.38........ 12,540
         November 1.. 28,000 lbs. at 0.39........ 10,920
         December 1.. 31,000 lbs. at 0.36........ 11,160

Issues: January 1–January 20.............20,000 lbs.
           January 21–February 16..........26,000
           February 17–March 12...........21,000
           March 13–April 5...............28,000
           April 6–April 30...............22,000
           May 1–May 27.................24,000
           May 28–June 21................22,000
           June 22–July 18................25,000
           July 19–August 14..............21,000
           August 15–September 8..........19,000
           September 9–October 2..........20,000
           October 3–November 1..........24,000
           November 2–December 1........21,000
           December 2–December 31........19,000

Determine the cost of materials used during the year and the cost of the year-ending inventory:

a) By the FIFO method.

b) By the FIFO method coupled with "cost or market," assuming the year-end market price to be 37 cents per pound.

c) By the LIFO method.

16. The Weeks Woolen Company has always used the first-in, first-out method of inventory costing. For the calendar years 1967 and 1968, its reported net income or loss before deducting income taxes was as follows:

        1967............$234,690 profit
        1968............ 60,140 loss

Early in 1969, the company's management was considering shifting to a last-in, first-out basis. Investigation revealed that the inventory figures for the three years were or would have been as follows:

	Pounds	FIFO Amount	LIFO Amount
December 31, 1966...........	500,000	$225,000	$225,000
December 31, 1967...........	475,000	403,000	210,000
December 31, 1968...........	513,000	338,000	235,000

a) Compute the net income before income taxes that the company would have reported each year if it had adopted the LIFO method of inventory costing as of January 1, 1967. Would adoption of LIFO as of that date have led to more informative income statements for the two years? Explain your reasoning.

b) By the beginning of 1969, management no longer had the option of adopting LIFO as of January 1, 1967, but it could adopt it as of January 1, 1968. Write a brief report to management, recommending for or against adoption of LIFO as of that date, giving your reasons for your recommendation.

17. The Tanlon Corporation determines its cost of goods sold as follows. The issues during a quarter are charged out at the average cost of the inventory on hand at the start of the period. At the end of the quarter, a new average is computed on the basis of the inventory remaining at the end of the quarter. Below are the transactions for 19x1 and 19x2:

Period	Units Purchased	Units Sold
Balance January 1, 19x1............	10,000 at $0.60	
Quarter I, 19x1..................	6,000 at 0.56	9,000
II......................	8,000 at 0.52	6,000
III......................	6,000 at 0.52	5,000
IV......................	4,000 at 0.48	3,000
I, 19x2..................	4,000 at 0.45	4,000
II......................	5,000 at 0.48	6,000
III......................	5,000 at 0.50	9,000
IV......................	10,000 at 0.54	6,000

a) Determine the cost of goods sold and the ending inventory for 19x1 and 19x2.

b) Compute the cost of goods sold for each year on a FIFO basis.

c) Compute the cost of goods sold for each year on a "current cost" basis. How much holding loss or gain would be included in ordinary income each year by each of the above methods?

18. The Fine Thread Company uses LIFO and counts its entire inventory in terms of equivalent pounds of cotton. On January 1, 1967, the company had the following inventory:

Base quantity.................100,000 lbs. at $0.18		$18,000
1948 layer.................... 20,000 lbs. at 0.24		4,800
1956 layer.................... 30,000 lbs. at 0.30		9,000
1960 layer.................... 20,000 lbs. at 0.32		6,400
Total.....................170,000 lbs.		$38,200

During 1967 and 1968, the company had the following transactions:

Period	Purchases	Sales
Quarter I, 1967..........	120,000 lbs. at $0.40	100,000 lbs.
II...............	60,000 lbs. at 0.42	90,000
III.............	40,000 lbs. at 0.42	80,000
IV.............	180,000 lbs. at 0.38	110,000
I, 1968..........	110,000 lbs. at 0.38	90,000
II...............	50,000 lbs. at 0.36	70,000
III.............	20,000 lbs. at 0.36	80,000
IV.............	130,000 lbs. at 0.35	110,000

a) Determine the cost of goods sold and year-end inventory for 1967 and for 1968.

b) Compute the cost of goods sold and year-end inventory for each year on a "current cost" basis.

c) Show how you might present both LIFO and current cost figures in the company's annual reports for the two years. In what respects, if any, would your method of presentation improve the quality of the information given to the shareholders?

19. In 1968, the Copper Corporation annual report contained the following information:

Income Statement

Sales..		$160,000
Cost of goods sold............................$128,000		
Selling, general, and administrative expense...........	26,000	154,000
Income from operation...........................		$ 6,000
Other income....................................		1,500
Net income......................................		$ 7,500
Taxes on income.................................		3,000
Income after Taxes..............................		$ 4,500

From the balance sheet:

	1968	1967
Inventory—copper.............................$50,300		$56,000
Other materials and supplies.................... 12,000		13,000

A note to the financial statement states that the copper content of the firm's entire inventory is valued at LIFO. The firm's inventory in pounds declined from 350,000 pounds at the end of 1967 to 320,000 pounds at the end of 1968. The quantity liquidated had a LIFO cost of $0.19 per pound. Finally, the price of copper was $0.22 at the end of 1967 and $0.25 at the end of 1968.

a) How much of the company's profit for 1968 was due to inventory liquidation?

b) Present the data reported above in a form that communicates more effectively the company's status and performance.

*20. The Franklin Steel Warehouse Company uses a periodic inventory system and states year-end inventory quantities on a LIFO basis. Annual increments to the LIFO inventories are placed in inventory at the *average of all purchase prices paid during the year.* Physical inventory figures are:

> December 31, 1957.................15,000 tons
> December 31, 1958.................20,000
> December 31, 1959................. 5,000

The company adopted LIFO on January 1, 1958, and its 15,000-ton inventory was priced at $125 per ton on that date, a total of $1,875,000. The company purchased 100,000 tons during 1958 at an average price of $130 per ton. The last 20,000 tons purchased during December, 1958, cost $135 per ton.

Purchases during 1959 totaled 90,000 tons at an average cost of $140 a ton. (The last 5,000 tons purchased during 1959 also cost $140 per ton.) Stocks were depleted by a steel strike, and the company expected to re-build its inventories to 15,000 tons as soon as steel became available again in 1960.

a) Provide the figures necessary to complete the following table, show-ing inventories and cost of goods sold on both a FIFO and a LIFO basis:

	Inventory Value		Cost of Goods Sold	
	FIFO	*LIFO*	*FIFO*	*LIFO*
January 1, 1958	$1,875,000	$1,875,000		
			1958 _____	_____
December 31, 1959	_____	_____		
			1959 _____	_____
December 31, 1958	_____	_____		

b) Assuming that 15,000 tons is the normal inventory quantity and that the company intended to rebuild its inventories to this level as soon as possible, what was the effect of the "involuntary liquidation" of inven-tory on reported profit for 1959? (Remember that the company was on LIFO.)

c) Assuming that inventories were increased to 15,000 tons by the end of 1960, with 1960 purchases at an average cost of $145 per ton, what was the net effect of the 1959 involuntary liquidation on LIFO inven-tory cost as of December 31, 1960?

21. The Alpha Company and the Omega Company are both engaged in the smelting and refining of copper. The following inventory data were taken from the annual reports of these two companies for the year ending December 31, 1968:

	December 31, 1967	December 31, 1968
Alpha Company inventories (last-in, first-out).....$32,825,000		$26,450,000
Omega Company inventories		
(first-in, first-out, lower of cost or market)......$77,140,000		$63,750,000

The income statements for the two companies for the year ending December 31, 1968, were as follows:

	Alpha	Omega
Sales............................	$95,000,000	$215,000,000
Cost of goods sold...............	$74,300,000	$180,000,000
Depreciation....................	3,700,000	9,000,000
Other expenses..................	9,000,000	20,000,000
Total Expenses...............	$87,000,000	$209,000,000
Net income before taxes..........	$ 8,000,000	$ 6,000,000
Income taxes....................	4,000,000	3,000,000
Income after Taxes..............	$ 4,000,000	$ 3,000,000

a) Assuming that the market prices of copper and of unsmelted ores were approximately the same at the end of 1968 as they were at the end of 1967, how would the companies' inventory valuation methods influence your interpretation of the companies' financial statements for the year 1968?

b) How would your answer to (a) differ if prices in December, 1968 were lower than in December, 1967?

22. Purchase and sales transactions for the Carson Merchandising Company were:

	Units Purchased	Units Sold
19x1:		
1st quarter..............	100,000 at $1.00/unit	40,000 at $1.20/unit
2d quarter..............	100,000 at $1.02/unit	60,000 at $1.22/unit
3d quarter.............	50,000 at $1.04/unit	75,000 at $1.24/unit
4th quarter.............	50,000 at $1.06/unit	75,000 at $1.26/unit
19x2:		
1st quarter.............	90,000 at $1.08/unit	60,000 at $1.28/unit
2d quarter.............	80,000 at $1.06/unit	70,000 at $1.27/unit
3d quarter.............	70,000 at $1.08/unit	100,000 at $1.29/unit
4th quarter.............	60,000 at $1.10/unit	100,000 at $1.30/unit
19x3:		
1st quarter.............	75,000 at $1.12/unit	(Data not available)

All purchases were made on the first day of the quarter. Sales were evenly distributed within each quarter and price changes for purchases, both up and down, occurred gradually within each quarter—e.g., the average replacement cost during the first quarter of 19x1 was $1.01.

The company had no inventories on January 1, 19x1. The company elected to cost increments to its LIFO inventories at the first prices paid during the year.

Expenses other than cost of goods sold were:

$$19x1...................\$51,000$$
$$19x2................... 65,400$$

a) Compute net income for each year, using the FIFO method of inventory costing.

b) Compute net income for each year on a LIFO basis.

c) How much inventory profit (holding gain) was included in income each year if FIFO was used?

d) How much inventory profit was included in each year if LIFO was used?

23. The Rainbow Manufacturing Company uses two basic raw materials. As of January 1, 19x0, when the company abandoned FIFO costing and adopted the LIFO method of costing its raw material inventories, its stock records showed the following:

	Quantity on Hand (Units)	Average Unit Cost	FIFO Inventory Cost
Material A......	60,000	$ 5.00	$300,000
Material B.......	20,000	12.00	240,000
Total.......			$540,000

During the four succeeding years, annual purchases and issues were as follows:

Year	Material A			Material B		
	Quantity Purchased	Average Unit Cost	Quantity Issued	Quantity Purchased	Average Unit Cost	Quantity Issued
19x0..	700,000 units	$6.00	670,000 units	220,000	$11.00	210,000
19x1..	740,000	7.00	730,000	250,000	10.00	240,000
19x2..	720,000	8.00	780,000	280,000	9.00	240,000
19x3..	855,000	7.00	790,000	300,000	10.00	320,000

The company elected to cost increments to its LIFO inventories at the *average* unit prices paid during the year.

Treating materials A and B separately, compute:

a) The LIFO inventory cost as of the end of each year 19x0 through 19x3; and

b) The LIFO cost of raw materials used during each of these years.

24. The quantities of work in process and finished goods inventories maintained by the Rainbow Manufacturing Company (see Question 23 above) are very small, and it may therefore be assumed that the raw materials content of the cost of goods sold for any year is approximately equal to the cost of raw materials issued.

a) Using the data given in Question 23 above, compute for materials A and B separately the approximate amounts of price gain or loss on raw materials inventories eliminated through use of the LIFO method:

(1) For the period January 1, 19x0, to December 31, 19x1.

(2) For the period January 1, 19x0, to December 31, 19x3.

b) Compute the profit effects of the inventory liquidations which occurred in 19x2 and 19x3.

25. The Rainbow Manufacturing Company (see Questions 23 and 24 above) depleted its inventory of material A in 19x2 in anticipation of a price decline. As can be seen from the data given in Question 23, the price did fall in 19x3, and the company then built its inventory back up to a level somewhat above that of January 1, 19x2.

Assuming that the company is in the 55 percent corporate income tax bracket, evaluate the profitability of this purchasing decision.

26. Nutco, Inc., is a distributor of heating oils and petroleum products. Its inventories are costed on a LIFO basis. As of January 1, 1967, its inventory of No. 2 heating oil was as follows:

	Gallons	Price	Amount
Base quantity........	1,000,000	$0.08	$80,000
1947 layer..........	100,000	0.09	9,000
1952 layer..........	50,000	0.10	5,000
Total..........	1,150,000		$94,000

During 1967, the company purchased 4 million gallons of No. 2 heating oil at an average price of $0.12 per gallon. During December, 1967, a shortage of heating oil developed and the purchase price rose to $0.13. Even at this price, however, the company was unable to obtain a sufficient quantity of No. 2 heating oil to maintain its inventories at their January 1 level, and the December 31, 1967, inventory of No. 2 heating oil consisted of 800,000 gallons.

a) Compute the cost of No. 2 heating oil sold during 1967, as shown on the company's financial statements.

b) Compute the price level gain or loss on No. 2 heating oil that was included as part of the ordinary reported income for Nutco, Inc., for the year 1967. (You should assume that with proper planning of purchases, enough inventory could have been purchased at the average price paid during the year to avoid the inventory liquidation.)

c) The average price paid for No. 2 heating oil in 1968 was $0.125 per gallon. The physical inventory of this product as of December 31, 1968, was 1,150,000 gallons. Compute the LIFO inventory valuation as of December 31, 1968. Total purchases of No. 2 heating oil amounted to 8 million gallons during 1968.

d) How much of the company's reported earnings for the years 1967 and 1968 did the company have to reinvest merely to restore inventory quantities to their January 1, 1967 levels? (Ignore income tax effects.)

e) It has been said that LIFO leads to a reported income that approximates more closely than FIFO the amount of assets that could be distributed to stockholders without impairing real capital. Under what circumstances is this likely to be true? Under what circumstances would this increase in the "accuracy" of reported income be reduced or eliminated? (You may wish to illustrate your answer with figures from the preceding parts of this problem.)

27. Upon its formation on January 1, the Nuovo Company bought inventories at a cost of $2,000 and equipment at a cost of $4,000. The balance sheet at that point was as follows:

ASSETS		LIABILITIES AND OWNERS' EQUITY	
Cash	$1,000	Liabilities	$1,500
Inventory	2,000	Capital stock	5,500
Equipment	4,000	Retained earnings	0
Total	$7,000	Total	$7,000

On that date, of course, the figures for inventory and equipment represented not only original cost but current cost as well. (The Nuovo Company operated in a country which had no income taxes. Its monetary unit was the dollar.)

The income statement for the first year of operations was computed both on a conventional historical cost basis and on a replacement cost basis, using *average* replacement costs for the year. This produced the following figures:

	Historical Cost Basis	Replacement Cost Basis
Sales	$6,000	$6,000
Cost of goods sold	$4,100	$4,400
Depreciation	600	612
Other expenses	900	900
Net Income	$ 400	$ 88

The year-end balance sheet was also stated on an historical cost basis and on a replacement cost basis, using *year-end* replacement prices to restate Inventory and Equipment account balances. The figures were:

	Historical Cost Basis		Replacement Cost Basis	
ASSETS				
Cash		$2,100		$2,100
Inventory		2,300		2,400
Equipment	$4,000		$4,160	
Less: Allowance for depreciation	600		624	
Equipment, net		3,400		3,536
Total Assets		$7,800		$8,036
LIABILITIES AND OWNERS' EQUITY				
Liabilities		$1,900		$1,900
Common stock		5,500		5,500
Retained earnings		400		88
Accumulated holding gains		...		548
Total Liabilities and Owners' Equity		$7,800		$8,036

The "accumulated holding gains" figure in the right-hand column was obtained as a residual by subtracting the sum of the liabilities, capital stock, and retained earnings from the adjusted asset total.

Further investigation revealed that the general price level on December 31 had reached 110 percent of the January 1 level. The average for the year was 105 percent of the January 1 figure.

After examining these figures, the company's purchasing agent commented that although operating income on a replacement cost basis was not satisfactory, the holding gains experienced during the period were very gratifying. The marketing vice president, on the other hand, rejected the replacement cost figures, saying that he had done his job selling the company's products at a good margin over their cost. No bookkeeper was going to take that away from him.

The treasurer took a different tack. As he put it, the holding gain wasn't a real gain because the purchasing power of the dollar had fallen during the year. Working quickly on the back of an envelope, he produced the following calculation:

(1) Assets, January 1 .... $7,000
(2) Liabilities, January 1 1,500
(3) Net assets, January 1 ([1] − [2]) $5,500
(4) Purchasing power index, December 31 .... 110%
(5) Adjusted net assets, January 1, at end-of-year
     prices ([3] × [4]) $6,050
(6) Adjusted net assets, December 31 (from balance sheet) 5,900
(7) Loss in Purchasing Power during the Year ([5] − [6]) $ 150

a) Whose side would you take in this argument? Prepare a short statement that you might use to try to convince the others that you were right?

b) If accounting reports had been stated in units of stable purchasing power, would this company have reported a profit or a loss on its ordinary operations (exclusive of holding gains and losses)? Explain.

c) What changes in management policies would you recommend for the future if events during the next several years seem likely to follow the pattern set this year?

d) What is the explanation of the gap between the treasurer's income figure and income on a replacement cost basis? Do you agree with the treasurer's method of computing a purchasing power loss?

28. "We'd be foolish to buy now," the Carthage Company's purchasing agent said. "The price can't be any higher next spring than it is now and I expect it to be much lower. We can make $7,000 by keeping our inventory down to 80,000 pounds until the new crop comes in next year."

"You forget," the company's controller replied, "that if we don't replace these inventories before the end of the year we'll lose our favorable

LIFO base. Not only that, but if you aim at an 80,000-pound inventory you'll be buying in uneconomically small lots. You'll probably have to pay premiums on rush orders, too."

The Carthage Company is a large wholesale distributor of food products. One of these products is made from citrus fruits. The annual price is determined largely by the size of the winter crop in Florida. A very severe winter in 1967–68 caused heavy damage to the Florida citrus crop. The price went up to $0.32 a pound in the spring of 1968 and remained at this level throughout the year.

In 1962, the company had adopted the LIFO method of inventory costing for all its products, both for tax purposes and for financial reporting. The balance in the company's inventory account as of January 1, 1962, became the LIFO base quantity. For this product, the company had 100,000 pounds in inventory on January 1, 1962, at an inventory cost of $0.20 a pound, a total of $20,000. Increments to inventories in subsequent years were priced at beginning-of-year prices.

The following table shows purchases and inventory data for this product for the first six years of operation under LIFO:

Year	End-of-Year Inventory (Thousands of Pounds)	Beginning-of-Year Purchase Price per Pound	Cost of Units Purchased (Thousands of Dollars)
1962........	100	$0.20	$ 60
1963........	110	0.22	74
1964........	150	0.23	92
1965........	180	0.24	96
1966........	130	0.30	88
1967........	200	0.26	112

The purchasing agent's recommendation was to maintain inventories of this product at approximately 80,000 pounds until the new crop was processed in the spring of 1969. An average crop in 1969 would lead to a price of about $0.26 a pound.

The controller opposed this and recommended that inventories be rebuilt to 200,000 pounds by the end of 1968, at a purchase price of about 32 cents a pound. He estimated that if this were not done, the lower inventory levels would increase purchasing and handling costs by $2,000 in 1968 and $400 in 1969.

Both executives were agreed that an inventory of 200,000 pounds of this product represented an optimum inventory level. If his proposal were to be accepted, the purchasing agent planned to rebuild inventories to this level as soon as the 1969 crop was processed.

The income tax rate in both years was 55 percent of taxable income.

a) Show the LIFO cost of goods sold and end-of-year inventory for each year, 1962–67.

b) How successful was LIFO in keeping "inventory profits and losses" out of the Carthage Company's income statements during this period?

c) By how much would 1968 reported income before taxes have been increased or decreased if the purchasing agent's proposal had been accepted?

d) Assuming that all purchases are paid for immediately in cash, would the purchasing agent's proposal or the controller's alternative have led to a larger cash balance after inventories were replenished in 1969? What would have been the amount of the difference? Ignore interest costs.

e) Should the purchasing agent's proposal have been accepted? Would your conclusion be different if the company's inventory had been on FIFO? How, if at all, does the inventory costing method influence decisions of this kind?

29. Since 1954, the annual reports of the Indiana Telephone Company have included adjustments for price level changes. The 1966 report showed conventional statements and adjusted statements in separate columns. The excerpts below have been condensed from this report (all figures except earnings per common share are in thousands of dollars):

INCOME STATEMENT

	Column A Historical Cost		Column B Historical Cost Restated for Changes in Purchasing Power of the Dollar	
	1966	1965	1966	1965
Operating revenues..................	$6,254	$5,593	$6,254	$5,593
Operating expenses: Depreciation: To cover historical cost...........	$1,039	$ 926	$1,039	$ 926
To recover cost of inflation........	—	—	194	191
Total Depreciation...........	$1,039	$ 926	$1,233	$1,117
Other operating expenses...........	4,094	3,765	4,094	3,765
Total Operating Expenses.....	$5,133	$4,691	$5,327	$4,882
Operating income...................	$1,121	$ 902	$ 927	$ 711
Income deductions (interest, etc.).......	363	264	363	264
Net Income........................	$ 758	$ 638	$ 564	$ 447
Earnings per Common Share...........	$3.13	$2.67	$2.26	$1.79

STATEMENT OF ASSETS
DECEMBER 31, 1966

	Column A Historical Cost	Column B Historical Cost Restated
Telephone plant, at original cost........	$21,909	$25,473
Less: Accumulated depreciation......	6,051	7,549
	$15,858	$17,924
Working capital....................	490	490
Other assets........................	713	712
Total Investment...............	$17,061	$19,126

COMMON SHAREHOLDERS' INTEREST
DECEMBER 31, 1966

	Column A Historical Cost	Column B Historical Cost Restated
Effect of inflation to date:		
Applicable to earnings since January 1, 1954	$	$1,792
Applicable to future earnings...........	....	2,066
Earned surplus.......................	2,217	425
Other elements of shareholders' interest.....	3,162	3,162
Total Common Shareholders' Interest...	$5,379	$7,445

Note 1 to Financial Statements:

In the accompanying financial statements, costs measured by the dollars disbursed at the time of the expenditure are shown in Column A—Historical Cost. In Column B—Historical Cost Restated for Change in Purchasing Power of Dollar, these dollars of cost have been restated in terms of the price level at December 31, 1965, and 1966, as measured by the Gross National Product Implicit Price Deflator, to recognize the inflation experienced to the date of these statements. The effect of inflation on these dollars of cost has been redetermined each year since 1954 in order to recognize the constantly changing price levels.

Since 1954, the corporation has presented such supplemental financial statements recognizing the effect of the change in the purchasing power of the dollar on the cost of telephone plant and on depreciation expense in the annual report to shareholders in the same basic manner. This accounting has the approval of Arthur Andersen & Co., the corporation's independent public accountants, as set forth in their opinion included herewith.

Dollars are a means of expressing purchasing power at the time of their use. Conversion or restatement of dollars of differing purchasing power to the purchasing power of the dollar at the date of conversion results in all the dollars being treated as mathematical likes for the purpose of significant data. The resulting financial statements recognize the change in price levels between the periods of expenditure of funds and the periods of use of property. Accordingly, the earnings, results of operations, assets, and other data available for use by management and other readers of financial statements provide important information and comparisons not otherwise available.

No one would attempt to add, subtract, multiply, or divide marks, dollars, and pounds. The failure to change the title of the monetary unit may be partially responsible for this violation of mathematical principle. This is important for it conceals the fact that mathematical unlikes are being used and therefore unfortunate results are produced by generally accepted accounting methods. This should help explain why we are talking about income and expenses in terms of current dollars.

Auditor's Opinion (Final Paragraph):

In our opinion, however, the accompanying financial statements shown under Column B more fairly present the financial position of the corporation and the results of its operations since appropriate recognition has been given to variations in the purchasing power of the dollar, as explained in [the notes] to the financial statements.

a) Are these statements expressed in units of common purchasing power? How do they differ, if at all, from "current cost" statements?
b) How much "extra" depreciation did Indiana Telephone Company charge against revenues during the period 1954–66 inclusive?
c) What does the amount of $2,066,000 "applicable to future earnings" represent? Why is it included in the "Common Shareholders' Interest?" Do you think it should be reported in some other section of the balance sheet instead of in the shareholders' equity?
d) Do you agree with the auditors that the column B figures "more fairly" present the company's financial situation? Explain your reasoning. Would you suggest any changes in the company's methods of income measurement?

Chapter 13

LIABILITIES

A COMPANY'S CAPITAL STRUCTURE has great significance to management and to outsiders alike. As we saw in Chapter 8, the amount and composition of the liabilities can have a great influence on the profitability of the shareholder's investment and on the risks associated with the enterprise. This chapter will examine the problems encountered in measuring various kinds of liabilities and will discuss their managerial implications.

CURRENT LIABILITIES

Current liabilities include accrued wages and taxes payable, accounts payable to trade creditors, notes payable to banks, and a number of others. To avoid repetition, only four of these will be examined briefly: trade accounts payable, notes payable, deferred performance liabilities, and short-term accrued liabilities.

Trade Accounts Payable

Accounts payable arise because the company defers payment for goods and services purchased. The debtor pays no interest on accounts payable balances, and this provides management with a strong incentive to obtain as much capital as possible from this source. In extreme cases, the merchant or manufacturer may be able to shift to his suppliers the entire burden of financing inventories and receivables by deferring payment until he has sold the merchandise and collected from his customers.

This form of financing can be quite expensive if it entails giving up discounts that are available for prompt payment (see Chapter 5), and usually only small, poorly financed companies will use trade credit to this extent. Most companies, however, try to make their payments to trade creditors as close to the end of the normal credit period as possible.

As with other forms of short-term credit, the risk cost of this form of financing is relatively high. The period required to collect from customers is likely to fluctuate, and if a period of slow collections happens to coincide with a period of heavy cash requirements elsewhere, the demands of trade creditors can become extremely embarrassing. Many receivables can be pledged or sold as a means of obtaining ready cash, but this too is likely to be expensive.

Notes Payable

Short-term notes payable arise mainly from two sources: (1) giving a promissory note to a trade creditor as a means of deferring payment until after the end of the normal trade credit period; and (2) borrowing from commercial banks. Both types of notes ordinarily have an interest cost, and both have a relatively high risk cost because they allow only a few weeks or months for payment.

Short-term bank loans have traditionally been used to meet seasonal fluctuations in the capital required by inventories and receivables. The alternative is to maintain enough long-term financing so that funds are idle during slack periods. Balance sheet evidence of the use of the latter method is found in heavy short-term securities investments during a portion of the year.

Some firms use this form of financing on a more or less permanent basis, partly because of its lower interest cost and partly because the amount of borrowing from short-term sources often can be adjusted to meet immediate needs more quickly and more simply than long-term borrowing.

Deferred Performance Liabilities

A third major type of short-term liability arises from the receipt of cash or its equivalent from customers as *advance payment* for services to be performed in the future. Liabilities of this type are often referred to as *deferred credits to income* or *unearned income*. These terms do not make it absolutely clear that these are liabilities, not ownership equities, however; and for this reason the term *deferred performance liabilities* is preferable. They differ from accounts or notes payable in that they are ordinarily liquidated by the delivery of merchandise rather than the payment of cash, but they are contractual obligations to outsiders and thus should be recognized in the accounts.

One example of the deferred performance liability is a magazine publisher's liability to deliver forthcoming issues to subscribers who have paid in advance. A more difficult example is the obligation of an appliance manufacturer to provide free service to his customers during a specified warranty period. In other words, a portion of the appliance sale price applies to costs that have not yet been incurred. At the time of sale, the estimated future warranty costs should be debited to current expense and credited to a liability account, Liability for Warranty Costs. This type of liability differs from the liability for unfilled magazine subscriptions only in the degree of certainty as to the amount of the obligation. Warranty costs are uncertain as to amount and timing and ordinarily must be estimated on the basis of past experience, but they are nonetheless obligations that the company must meet.

Short-Term Accrued Liabilities

A fourth category of current liabilities, accrued liabilities, arises because certain payment dates do not coincide with the end of the accounting period. This category includes such items as accrued wages, accrued interest, accrued taxes, and accrued vacation pay. Of these, only the latter two are likely to be material in amount, and both of these are seasonal in nature. Vacation rights, for example, are ordinarily earned throughout the year and are used primarily during the summer months. If the fiscal year ends on December 31, the company should show a vacation accrual on its year-end balance sheet unless unused rights are cancelled at year-end.

Management's control over these items is severely circumscribed. Tax payments ordinarily must be made on specified dates, and in some cases payment even has to be made in advance. On vacation pay, the most that management could do would be to encourage employees to postpone their vacations to a later date. This is a particularly unreliable source of funds, however, and most companies actually go to the opposite extreme and insist that vacations be taken within a certain period.

LONG-TERM BORROWING

Most large corporations in the United States obtain large quantities of quasi-permanent capital from long-term lenders. As we saw in Chapter 8, debt financing permits the shareholders to benefit from the *leverage* effect of using low-cost funds to finance high-yield operations. It also allows the firm to grow larger than it could if it had to rely on shareholder capital alone.

Bonds and Bond Values

When a corporation or other entity wishes to borrow from a large number of lenders, it is not feasible to negotiate a separate loan contract with each. Under these circumstances, a single loan contract is signed by the borrower and a representative of the lenders. The contract is known as an *indenture* and the lender's representative is the *trustee*. Each lender is given one or more certificates, called *bonds*, representing his share of the overall loan contract.

Each bond specifies the amounts to be paid the owner of the bond and the times at which the payments are to be made. The final payment, the amount to be paid on the maturity date (the date on which the contract expires if all its provisions have been met), is called the *maturity value* or *face value* of the bond. Interim interest payments are customarily made semiannually, but they are normally expressed as an annual percentage of the face value. This percentage is called the *coupon rate* or *face rate* of interest. Thus a $1,000, 6 percent, 20-year bond represents an agreement to pay $1,000 at the end of 20 years plus $30 (one half of 6 percent of $1,000) at the end of each half-year for 20 years.

The value of this bond to an investor depends on the *yield to maturity* that he could earn on other bonds of comparable risk that are now available on the market. Yield to maturity is the rate of interest the investor can earn if he purchases a bond at a given price, holds it until the maturity date, and then collects the face value from the lender.

For example, suppose that other comparable bonds now yield 7 percent if held to maturity. If the investor buys this 6 percent bond, he becomes entitled to two things: (1) a stream of 40 semiannual payments of $30 each; and (2) a payment of $1,000 40 periods hence. The present value of these cash flows can be determined by multiplying them by discount factors taken from Tables 3 and 4 in Appendix A. The factors are taken from the 3½ percent columns of the two tables (half of the 7 percent annual rate). The calculation is:

Period	Amount	Discount Factor	Present Value
1 to 40..........	$30/period	21.3551	$640.65
40.............	$1,000	0.2526	252.60
Total.......			$893.25

The value of this 6 percent bond today is thus $893.25 to an investor whose comparable alternative is a bond yielding 7 percent interest. The $106.75 difference between this amount and the $1,000 maturity value serves to bring the yield on the bond up from 6 percent to 7 percent.

The Use of Bond Value Tables

If investors had to go through the previous calculations every time they considered buying or selling a bond, much time would be wasted unnecessarily. To avoid this, special tables have been prepared for the financial community, based on the kind of calculations just illustrated. A partial set of such tables is included in Appendix A (Tables 5 through 11). The present value of a 20-year, 6 percent bond in a market in which the prevailing yield is 7 percent may be found in Table 11 (the table for a coupon rate of 6 percent) by locating the column for bonds with 20 years to maturity and the row for the 7 percent yield rate. The figure is 89.32, which means that the market price will be $893.20 for each $1,000 of face value. Except for an insignificant rounding error, this is the same figure we obtained using Tables 3 and 4.

The value of the bond will approach face value as it gets closer to maturity, other things being equal. For example, if the 6 percent bond is still outstanding five years later (15 years before maturity), and the market yield rate is still 7 percent at that time, Table 11 indicates that the bond will have a value of $908. If interest rates fall in the meanwhile, however, so that newly issued bonds of comparable risk are being sold to yield 5 percent, then the value of this 6 percent bond with 15 years to go to maturity will have climbed to $1,104.70. This figure is derived from the 110.47 factor listed in the 15-year column, 5 percent row of Table 11.

Conversely, given the market price of the bond, its yield to maturity can be determined and compared with the rate of return obtained elsewhere. For example, if the bond has 10 years to maturity and is selling for $1,015, its yield is 5.8 percent. This can be determined from the 10-year column of Table 11.

Issuing Corporate Bonds

The issuing corporation of course views the bonds from the other side. For example, suppose that late in 1961 the Reading Company decided to issue $1 million of 4½ percent, 20-year debenture bonds. By the time the bonds were issued on January 1, 1962, the going market rate of interest had gone up to 5 percent. Therefore, the bonds had to be sold at a *discount* (i.e., the sale price or proceeds was less than face value). The total amount received from the sale was $937,243. The purchasers needed the $62,757 discount from face value to compensate them for accepting annual interest payments of $45,000 (coupon rate times face value) instead of $50,000 (market rate times face value) for the life of the bonds. If the coupon rate had exceeded the market rate, on the other hand, the investor would have been willing to pay a *premium* for the right to the higher annual interest payments.

The general rule in accounting for equities is to record for each source of funds *the amount that the investor has invested in the corporation*. Accordingly, the company's accountants first thought of recording the issue of the bonds on the Reading Company's books as follows:

Cash..937,243
    Bonds Payable.................................   937,243

Although this entry would have been correct, the controller decided to conform to the more usual practice of recording the face value of the bonds and the discount or premium in two separate accounts, as follows:

Cash..937,243
Discount on Bonds............................. 62,757
    Bonds Payable.................................   1,000,000

Some consider this treatment more informative, and in any event it produces the same balance sheet valuation as the first method. The bond and discount would have appeared on a January 1, 1962, balance sheet as:

Bonds payable (face value)............................$1,000,000
    Less: Discount on bonds............................   62,757
Bonds Payable (Book Value)...................... $ 937,243

For some reason, many firms choose to carry bond discount on the asset side of the balance sheet, including it with other items in a miscellaneous category labeled *deferred charges*. The only asset derived from the borrowing transaction, however, was the $937,243 in cash, and no other amount should be added to the assets.

Periodic Interest Expense

If the Reading Company's bonds were to remain outstanding until the January 1, 1982, maturity date, the bondholders would receive the

$1 million face value plus $900,000 in coupon interest payments ($22,500 every 6 months for 20 years). The difference between this lifetime total of $1,900,000 and the $937,243 proceeds of the issue ($962,757) represents the price paid by the corporation for the use of the bondholders' money, or *interest expense*. The $62,757 discount is just as much a component of interest expense as the semiannual payment—after all, the company's alternative was to sell the bonds at a higher coupon rate and higher semiannual payments—and the problem is to decide how much of the $962,757 interest to charge to expense each period.

One approach is to amortize the discount in equal installments, in this case one fortieth of $62,757 each 6-month period for 40 periods, or approximately $1,569. Using this method, the entry for the first period's interest would have been:

Interest Expense	24,069	
Cash		22,500
Discount on Bonds		1,569

Although this treatment of bond discount is common, another method of determining periodic interest expense, the *effective interest method*, is more accurate. Obtaining $937,243 in return for a promise to pay $22,500 semiannually for 20 years plus $1 million at the end of that time is equivalent to paying interest at a rate of 5 percent a year. This figure can be derived from Table 8 of Appendix A. At a price of $93.72 per $100 of face value, a 20-year, 4½ percent bond provides a yield to maturity or effective interest rate of 5 percent. Applying this rate to the amount borrowed indicates the interest cost for the first period. The first period is only six months long, however, and therefore only half of the effective rate is used to compute the first six months' interest, which was 2½ percent of $937,243, or $23,431. Only $22,500 was actually paid out at that time, so the entry was:

Interest Expense	23,431	
Cash		22,500
Discount on Bonds		931

This entry says, in effect, that the interest *earned* by the bondholders during the period was $931 *more* than the amount *paid* to them, with the result that the company's liability increased accordingly. In other words, the amount invested in the company by the bondholders actually increased because they had agreed in advance to receive in cash less than the full 2½ percent earned. This invested sum or *principal* thus became $938,174 ($937,243 + $931), or approximately

$93.82 per $100 of face value. This corresponds to the figure given in Table 8 of Appendix A for a 4½ percent coupon rate, a 5 percent yield rate, and 19½ years to maturity.

Similarly, the interest cost during the second six-month period was 2½ percent times the amount actually at work during that period—the principal at the beginning of that specific period, $938,174. Interest expense was thus $23,454, which requires amortization of $954 of the bond discount. Interest expense was slightly greater during the second six months than during the first because more money was at work and the liability was greater during the second period. The interest *rate* charged to expense was the same, however.

Interest expense and bond discount amortization were calculated in similar fashion for the other 38 6-month periods. These calculations were summarized in a table, a portion of which is shown in Exhibit 13–1. Note that the principal at the end of 5, 10, 19, and 19½ years (i.e., with 15, 10, 1, and ½ years to maturity) corresponds in each case to the pertinent Appendix A, Table 8 values.

Had these bonds sold for more than their face value (i.e., at a premium), the interest expense would have been less than the coupon

Exhibit 13–1

LIABILITY AND INTEREST EXPENSE

4½ Percent, 20-Year, $1,000,000 Bond Yielding 5 Percent

(1) Beginning of Period Date	(2) Beginning Liability per (6)	(3)* Period Interest Expense	(4)† Period Coupon Payment	(5) Liability Increase (3) − (4)	(6) Ending Liability (2) + (5)
January 1, 1962............	$937,243	$23,431	$22,500	$ 931	$ 938,174
July 1, 1962..............	938,174	23,454	22,500	954	939,128
January 1, 1963..........	939,128	23,478	22,500	978	940,106
July 1, 1963..............	940,106	23,503	22,500	1,003	941,109
January 1, 1964..........	941,109	23,528	22,500	1,028	942,137
July 1, 1964..............	942,137	23,553	22,500	1,053	943,190
January 1, 1965..........	943,190	23,580	22,500	1,080	944,270
July 1, 1965..............	944,270	23,607	22,500	1,107	945,377
January 1, 1966..........	945,377	23,634	22,500	1,134	946,511
July 1, 1966..............	946,511	23,663	22,500	1,163	947,674
January 1, 1967..........	947,674‡	23,692	22,500	1,192	948,866
.... January 1, 1972..........	... 961,027‡	... 24,024	... 22,500	... 1,504	 962,533
.... January 1, 1981..........	... 995,181‡	... 24,880	... 22,500	... 2,380	 997,561
July 1, 1981..............	997,561‡	24,939	22,500	2,439	1,000,000

* (0.05/2) × (principal per column [2]).
† (0.045/2) × ($1 million face value).
‡ See Table 8 of Appendix A.

payment in each period. For example, had they sold for $1,068,400 to yield 4 percent (see Appendix A, Table 8), the first interest expense recording would have been:

```
Interest Expense......................................21,368
Premium on Bonds................................... 1,132
    Cash.........................................            22,500
```

This entry indicates that the interest *earned* by the bondholders would have been $1,132 *less* than the amount *paid* to them, with the result that the coupon payment would have been in part a return of principal, serving to reduce the company's liability.

Retirement of Long-Term Debt

When the corporation buys its bonds back from the bondholders, the bonds are said to be *retired*. Bonds are sometimes retired at maturity, but other arrangements are also common. For one thing, bond issues are often very large, and it may be more convenient to retire them gradually rather than all at once. Furthermore, a company may not need all of the borrowed funds continuously until the maturity date or may have an opportunity to obtain substitute financing on more favorable terms prior to that date. For these reasons, most bond issues provide the issuing corporation with opportunities for early retirement.

One possibility is to let the bonds be *convertible* into shares of common stock. Such issues are often more properly regarded as indirect means of selling stock than as borrowing transactions, and in some cases the entire issue has been converted within a few years of the date of issue.

Another possibility is to provide for gradual retirement by making the issue subject to *serial redemption*—that is, by staggering the due dates of the component securities. Thus an issue of $100 million of serial bonds may provide for $10 million to mature each year for 10 years, the first maturity coming 10 years after the date of original issue. Serial bonds are usually offered at a range of prices, set to provide higher yields for the longer maturities. Each separate series is treated as a separate issue, using the accounting method described earlier.

Another device for orderly debt retirement is the *sinking fund*. Each year the corporation sets aside a certain amount of cash for the sinking fund, and this is then used to purchase company bonds. Bond indentures often provide that the corporation or the trustees of the sinking fund have the right to require the holders of some bonds to sell their bonds back to the corporation or to the trustees prior to the maturity date. Such bonds are said to be *callable* for sinking fund purposes. If the market price of the bonds is less than the price at which the bonds can be called (their *call price*), the corporation or trustees will ordinarily buy bonds on the market. Otherwise, enough bonds will be called at the call price to use up the funds available. The call price is either equal to or slightly higher than the maturity value of the bonds.

For example, because of a general tightening of the bond market, the market yield on the Reading Company's 4½ percent bonds had been forced up to 6 percent and the market price of the bonds on January 1, 1967, was $85.30. (This price can be verified from the 15-year column, 6 percent row of Table 8 in Appendix A.) It might have seemed profitable to buy bonds at this price. A purchase of $100,000 bonds at $85,300 would have led to a reported gain of $9,467, computed as follows:

Maturity value	$100,000
Less: Unamortized bond discount (from Exhibit 13–1)	5,233
Book value	$ 94,767
Purchase price	85,300
Gain on Retirement	$ 9,467

The entry to record this purchase would have been as follows:

Bonds Payable	100,000	
Discount on Bonds		5,233
Cash		85,300
Gain on Bond Retirement		9,467

This gain might have been more apparent than real, however. If the Reading Company had need of funds, it would have had to obtain them at a cost of at least 6 percent, the current rate of bond interest. In such a case, the gain on retirement would have disappeared entirely.

These market prices, it should be emphasized, have no effect on the company's accounts unless the firm engages in some market transaction. The company continues to amortize bond discount (or bond premium) on the basis of the original yield rate, as in Exhibit 13–1, on the grounds that this represents the cost of the financing.

Bond Refunding

For most large corporations, debt is a more or less permanent component of the capital structure. Far from wishing to reduce its indebtedness, the corporation seeks to maintain or increase it. When one bond issue matures, it is succeeded by another. Replacing one bond issue with another is known as *refunding*, and callability permits the corporation to refund prior to maturity if conditions seem right. The borrowing corporation can take advantage of declines in money rates by calling the old higher yield bonds, replacing them with bonds at the new lower rates.

To protect the bondholder, the bond contract usually specifies that an amount greater than the face value of the bond will be paid in the event of premature retirement. This call price normally varies with the age of the debt, approaching the face value at maturity or at some earlier date.

To illustrate, suppose that borrowing conditions have improved considerably by 1971 and that an insurance company offers the Reading Company a $1,000,000 loan at 3½ percent for 10 years. The treasurer recommends that this offer be accepted as of January 1, 1972, and that the proceeds be used toward retirement of the outstanding 4½ percent bonds. The call price in effect on January 1, 1972, is $107 per $100 of face value, and the book value is $961,027 (Exhibit 13–1 and Appendix A, Table 8). The entry to record the proposed refunding would therefore be as follows:

Bonds Payable....................................	1,000,000	
Loss on Bond Retirement..........................	108,973	
Discount on Bonds............................		38,973
Cash..		1,070,000

Several points are worth mentioning. First, the amount to be paid to the bondholders is $1,070,000, based on the call price. The face value loses any significance when the bond does not go to maturity. Second, the unamortized balance of $38,973 ($1,000,000 less $961,-027) in the Discount on Bonds account is closed out along with the bonds payable. Finally, the amount by which the call price exceeds the book amount of the liability is $108,973, which is the loss on retirement.

This loss is in some respects analogous to a loss on plant retirement. Just as the actual service life and salvage value of a machine may differ from those assumed in computing depreciation charges, so may the actual term and liquidation price of a debt differ from those assumed in computing interest charges. Had a term of 10 years and a maturity payment of $1,070,000 been foreseen, the yield rate on these bonds would have been slightly more than 5½ percent. The loss may therefore be viewed as correcting the reported operating results to date for the effects of these unforeseen changes.[1]

Refunding Decisions

Because the immediate consequence of refunding in this case would be a substantial reported loss, the reasons for the treasurer's recommendations may not be readily apparent. The benefit comes from a reduction of future interest *payments*. Since the semiannual bond coupon payments are $22,500 and the semiannual note interest payments are $17,500 (one half of 3½ percent of $1,000,000), there is a future reduction in cash payments to creditors of $5,000 per 6-month period for 20 periods (10 years). The analysis by which the treasurer was persuaded that the refunding of the issue is a profitable course of action is beyond the scope of this chapter, but the general approach will be examined in Chapter 20.

CURRENT PROBLEMS IN LIABILITY ACCOUNTING

The liabilities of a modern corporation are considerably more varied and arise in many more ways than those of an earlier era. Three items that can be and sometimes are placed in this category will be considered in the pages that follow:

1. Deferred income taxes.
2. Pensions.
3. Leases.

Liability for Deferred Income Taxes

One of the newer types of liabilities that has provoked considerable debate arises from the recent developments in depreciation discussed in Chapter 11. It will be recalled that with asset lives unchanged, sum-of-the-years' digits and declining-balance depreciation result in a higher depreciation charge in an asset's early years and a lower charge in its later years than straight-line depreciation. The consequent reduction in taxes during the early years, though offset by an increase in

---

[1] While losses on plant retirements are invariably recognized in the period of retirement, losses on debt retirements by refunding are in practice sometimes spread over a number of subsequent periods. For further discussion of this departure from the general realization convention, see American Institute of Certified Public Accountants, *Accounting Research and Terminology Bulletins* (final ed.; New York: AICPA, 1961), pp. 129-33.

the later years, represents a net gain in the present value of the firm's future cash flows. Consequently, when these methods were made permissible for tax purposes, business firms with taxable income had an economic incentive to adopt them.

Some corporations believed that the new methods reflected the true pattern of depreciation of their assets, and thus also adopted them in reports to their stockholders. Many corporations, however, looked on these methods as merely an instrument for reducing or deferring taxes and were reluctant to adopt the method for their stockholder statements. Doing so would misrepresent their expenses and income, it was believed.

To illustrate, let us assume that a corporation that has been using straight-line depreciation has income before depreciation and taxes of $100,000 a year. Its depreciable property has an original cost of $300,000 and an expected life of 10 years. The company buys new equipment at a cost of $30,000, replacing old equipment with the same original cost and life. In other words, if it continues to use straight-line depreciation, its depreciation charge for the year will remain at $30,000, and its net income will be as follows:

Income before depreciation	$100,000
Reported depreciation expense	30,000
Reported income before tax	$ 70,000
Income tax	28,000
Net Income	$ 42,000

(To simplify the calculation, the income tax rate is assumed to be 40 percent. The actual rate is likely to be higher.)

If the company adopts the double-rate, declining-balance method, however, depreciation on this new equipment becomes $2 \times 10\% \times \$30,000 = \$6,000$, as opposed to the $3,000 straight-line figure.[2] The depreciation charge for tax purposes is thus raised to $33,000, and the income tax currently payable is reduced to $26,800.

This company now has a choice. It can report depreciation on its published income statement on either a straight-line or a declining-balance basis, depending on which method seems to represent more faithfully the decline in the assets' service potential. If decline in service potential is best approximated by declining-balance depreciation, the solution is simple: report depreciation on a declining-balance

---

[2] Depreciation on the other $270,000 in old assets remains on a straight-line basis. Conversion to declining-balance basis is not possible for these assets.

basis; report tax expense as the amount called for by the tax return for the year.

Income before depreciation	$100,000
Reported depreciation	33,000
Reported income before tax	$ 67,000
Income tax	26,800
Net Income	$ 40,200

A problem arises only when the decline in service potential is best measured by some depreciation method other than the method used on the current year's income tax return. For example, if straight-line depreciation represents the service decline, then reported depreciation for the year should be $30,000 and income before taxes should be $70,000. The normal income tax on this amount of income is $28,000, and this is the amount that should be reported on the income statement as current tax expense. Although only $26,800 need to be paid now, because of the liberal features of the tax law, the remaining $1,200 presumably will have to be paid in some future year when declining-balance depreciation falls below the straight-line rate. In this view, the tax has been *deferred*, not avoided.

The reported income calculations under these various alternatives are summarized in Exhibit 13–2. Notice that the net income figures shown in column (1) and (4) are identical. This reflects the view that

Exhibit 13–2

EFFECTS OF DECLINING-CHARGE DEPRECIATION ON AFTER-TAX REPORTED INCOME

	(1) Straight-Line Depreciation Used for Tax and Reporting	(2) Declining-Balance Depreciation Used for Tax and Reporting	(3) Declining-Balance Depreciation Used for Tax; Straight-Line Used for Reporting — Reported Tax Is the Amount Currently Due	(4) Declining-Balance Depreciation Used for Tax; Straight-Line Used for Reporting — Reported Tax Includes Deferred Tax
Income before depreciation	$100,000	$100,000	$100,000	$100,000
Reported depreciation	30,000	33,000	30,000	30,000
Income before tax	$ 70,000	$ 67,000	$ 70,000	$ 70,000
Income tax	28,000	26,800	26,800	28,000
Net Income	$ 42,000	$ 40,200	$ 43,200	$ 42,000

if straight-line depreciation is the correct depreciation, it should be used in computing the year's tax expense, no matter when the taxes are payable. The payment date is not relevant to the determination of any other expense and thus should not enter into the calculation of tax expense.[3]

The entry to record the income tax expense for the year under these assumptions is:

```
Income Tax Expense.....................................28,000
    Accrued Taxes Payable.............................          26,800
    Liability for Deferred Income Tax.................           1,200
```

If in some future year the normalized tax expense is, say, $40,000, and the amount currently due is, say, $40,500, the entry for that year will be:

```
Income Tax Expense.....................................40,000
Liability for Deferred Income Tax......................    500
    Accrued Taxes Payable.............................          40,500
```

The meaning of the Liability for Deferred Income Taxes has been questioned by a number of accountants. They ask when the corporation will pay these deferred taxes. With the passage of time, as the fraction of the corporation's assets subject to declining-charge depreciation increases, the balance in the account will increase. The balance in the account will never fall as long as the net amount in the plant account does not fall. In other words, the deferred taxes will never be paid until that uncertain and distant date in the future when the corporation is liquidated. Because corporations are rarely liquidated, either column 2 or 3 is the correct procedure, the choice depending on whether declining charge depreciation is considered valid.[4]

---

[3] The position of the Accounting Principles Board of the American Institute of Certified Public Accountants is that provision for deferred income taxes should be made if tax depreciation and reported depreciation differ for this reason. *Opinion No. 1, New Depreciation Guidelines and Rules* (New York: AICPA, 1962).

[4] A lively controversy on this subject has taken place. Some of the interesting articles are Maurice Moonitz, "Income Taxes in Financial Statements," *The Accounting Review*, April, 1957, pp. 175–83; T. M. Hill, "Some Arguments against the Inter-Period Allocation of Income Taxes," *The Accounting Review*, July, 1957, pp. 357–61; Sidney Davidson, "Accelerated Depreciation and the Allocation of Income Taxes," *The Accounting Review*, April, 1958, pp. 173–80; and Robert K. Jaedicke and Carl L. Nelson, "The Allocation of Income Taxes—A Defense," *The Accounting Review*, April, 1960, pp. 278–81. An authoritative review of this literature and comprehensive analysis of this subject is contained in Homer A. Black, *Interperiod Allocation of Corporate Income Taxes*, Accounting Research Study No. 9 (New York: AICPA, 1966).

Taxes and the Investment Credit

The income tax laws have given rise to another somewhat similar situation. The United States Revenue Act of 1962 provided for an "investment credit" against income taxes due on current income. This credit was equal to 7 percent of current outlays for certain depreciable assets, subject to certain maximum limitations prescribed in the act.

For example, assume that the Trilby Company's equipment purchases for the year amounted to $1 million. Before reflecting the investment credit, its income statement was as follows:

Sales...................................		$6,180,000
Less: Cost of sales......................	$4,206,500	
Other expenses.....................	1,386,000	5,592,500
Income before taxes......................		$ 587,500
Income taxes...........................		235,000
Net Income.............................		$ 352,500

In this case, the tax credit was 7 percent of $1 million, or $70,000, and the net current income tax liability was thus reduced to $165,000. The company had no liability for the future repayment of this tax reduction.

A major split occurred in the accounting profession over the appropriate method of reporting this investment credit. In the example, if the tax credit had been reflected in the year's income, net income would have been increased by $70,000 to $422,500 (almost a 20 percent increase). In a highly controversial opinion issued in December, 1962, the Accounting Principles Board of the American Institute of Certified Public Accountants argued that this was not a valid component of current income and that therefore provision ought to be made to spread the amount of the investment credit over the life of the assets acquired.[5] The Board later reversed this opinion and recognized immediate recognition in the income statement as an acceptable alternative.[6]

The only basis on which deferral of a portion of tax incentives like the investment credit can be justified is that the cost of the assets is reduced by this amount. Since no liability exists for future repayment, it must be either an addition to shareholders' equity or a reduction in asset cost. Carrying the deferral on the right-hand side of the balance sheet, to be credited to the income of subsequent periods, is totally illogical.

---

[5] *Opinion No. 2, Accounting for the "Investment Credit"* (New York: AICPA 1963).

[6] *Opinion No. 4, Accounting for the "Investment Credit* (New York: AICPA, 1964).

Liability under Pension Plans

One of the more complex questions in the recognition and measurement of liabilities has arisen in connection with the employee pension plans which have been widely adopted during the last two decades. The nonaccounting as well as the accounting issues in these plans are quite complex, and in order to focus attention on the questions of interest, the nonaccounting issues will to the extent possible be passed over.

The number of variations in pension plans is virtually limitless, but the most important variations come in a few key elements. First, the plan may be *fully vesting, partially vesting,* or *nonvesting.* Under a fully vesting plan, the employee's rights to retirement benefits accrue periodically and cannot be revoked or withdrawn by the employer. If the employee's rights are not vested, however, he loses all his retirement credits under the plan if he leaves the company prior to retirement. Between these two extremes are a host of intermediate arrangements.

Second, the plan may be *funded* or *nonfunded.* In a fully funded plan, enough cash has been set aside to meet the expected future costs of all retirement benefits earned to date, assuming that these segregated funds are invested at the rates of interest assumed or specified in the plan. In a nonfunded plan, the employee relies on the future solvency of his employer; no cash is set aside until actual payments have to be made.

In some plans, retirement benefits are based on the employee's wages or salary during the period immediately prior to retirement; in others, the amounts depend on his actual salary since the inception of the plan or the beginning of his employment. Some plans are partially contributory; others provide that the employer will bear all costs. There are unilateral plans and negotiated plans, cancelable and noncancelable plans, plans tied to social security benefits and plans covering dependents as well as the employees themselves. In short, as stated above, so many variations exist that the discussion could quickly become lost in a sea of detail without covering more than a fraction of the possibilities.

To illustrate the accounting problems raised by the existence of pension plans, assume that the Genesee Corporation adopted a pension plan for the first time on January 1, 1964. Under this plan, the company enters into a *contract* with each *new* employee. This contract requires the company, when the employee retires at age 65, to deposit with an insurance company an amount equal to 5 percent of the employee's wages from date of employment until retirement, compounded annually at 4 percent interest. This money will be used by the insurance company to provide the employee with a pension.[7]

At the time it hires the new employee, Genesee has no pension liability to him. At the end of his first year of employment, the company's liability amounts to 5 percent of the employee's wages for the year. (Because interest is compounded annually under this agreement, the year-end liability includes no accrued interest at the end of the first year.) At the end of 1, 2, 3, . . . , n years, the company has a liability arising from the employment contract equal to 5 percent of the employee's wages for the 1, 2, 3, . . . n years plus interest on these amounts compounded at 4 percent.

Although this plan is not funded, each year Genesee should credit a pension liability account by an amount equal to 5 percent of the wage payroll for the year, plus 4 percent interest on amounts accrued previously. The entry is:

Pension Expense. xxx
    Liability for Pensions.   xxx

When payment is made to the insurance company at the time of the employee's retirement, the insurance company takes over the obligation and the entry is:

Liability for Pensions. xxx
    Cash.   xxx

The discussion thus far has been limited to pension accruals for employees hired after the adoption of the pension plan on January 1, 1964. The company also entered into pension contracts with all employees in active service on that date. These contracts provided that the amount to be paid to the insurance company at retirement would equal 5 percent of wages, compounded annually at 4 percent, from the *date of employment*, not from the date of the contracts. Thus, on

---

[7] Two very common options are (*a*) annuity payments for a fixed number of years, and (*b*) annuity payments for life. In the latter case, the insurance company must consult actuarial tables to find the remaining life expectancy of the retiring employee. For example, if the employee is expected to live for 13 years after retirement, the company's lump sum payment to the insurance company on the retirement date is $18,000, and the insurance company accrues interest at 4 percent, the annual payment to the pensioner will be approximately $1,800 (derived from Table 4 of Appendix A), assuming one payment a year rather than the more usual monthly sums. Under this type of option, if the pensioner lives longer than 13 years, the insurance company will lose; if he dies earlier, the insurance company will gain. Most such options, incidentally, provide for some death benefit for death prior to a specified age, but this is obtained only by accepting a somewhat lower annuity.

January 1, 1964, Genesee had a substantial *liability for past service benefits* that had never been reflected in the company's financial statements.

The main accounting issue with respect to pension plans is whether the liability for past service benefits should be recognized immediately or gradually over time. On the one hand, the liability comes into existence at the time the pension plan is adopted. On the other hand, the company assumed this obligation in the expectation that future production costs would be reduced through lower employee turnover, greater company loyalty, and so forth.

The position of the Accounting Principles Board of the American Institute of Certified Public Accountants is ambivalent. In an opinion issued in 1966, it stated that "the entire cost of benefit payments ultimately to be made should be charged against income subsequent to the adoption or amendment of a plan and that no portion of such cost should be charged directly against retained earnings."[8] Unfortunately, the Board could not agree on a common definition of the "benefit payments ultimately to be made." It authorized companies either to accrue the liability for prior service benefits over a 10-year period, or to make no such accruals at all, apparently on the rather curious grounds that these payments will never be made as long as the company remains a going concern. It specifically disapproved faster recognition of the liability.

We remain convinced, however, that no matter what method is used for expense recognition, the balance sheet should reflect the present value of the company's pension commitments, determined actuarially without distinguishing between vested and nonvested rights. Perhaps the best way to accomplish this is to show on the balance sheet the full amount of the estimated liability, with a contra account deduction showing that portion that has not yet been charged to expense. This position is taken with the knowledge that few plans are based on contracts with individual employees and that if the company is sold or liquidated or if it runs into financial difficulties, many of these pension rights will vanish or be severely curtailed. Nevertheless, the company has a moral obligation to honor the commitments, and in the going concern the presumption is that these obligations will indeed be honored.[9]

---

[8] *Opinion No. 8, Accounting for the Cost of Pension Plans* (New York: AICPA, 1966).

[9] For a broader discussion of these matters, see Ernest L. Hicks, *Accounting for the Cost of Pension Plans,* Accounting Research Study No. 8 (New York: AICPA, 1965).

Leases in Financial Statements

Prior to World War II, leasing was limited for the most part to residential property and to space in general-purpose commercial buildings for offices, retailing, and light manufacturing. Furthermore, these leases were short term, a lease that ran for five years or more being quite rare. Accordingly, the signing of a lease was looked on by the accountant as an *agreement* to buy the *use* of property. No transaction was recognized as a consequence of this event. The use of the property, the payment of rent, or the prepayment of rent were the events which gave rise to the recognition of a transaction.

Since the end of World War II, the *sale-leaseback* and other types of leasing arrangements have become increasingly popular as a means of acquiring the use of land, buildings, and equipment by chain stores, department stores, and companies in many other industries. The essential characteristics of this type of leasing arrangement are provided by the following illustration. To serve its southeastern market, the Trevett Company has decided to build a new manufacturing plant in a small town about 50 miles from Atlanta, Georgia. The cost of the land and buildings is $1 million, and it is estimated that the facility will be used for 30 to 40 years. The company does not have the liquid assets needed to finance the investment. Its financial position is strong but a firm of investment bankers has advised Trevett against trying to float a bond issue until additional ownership capital has been obtained. Trevett's present owners are unwilling to increase their commitment in the firm and are equally unwilling to endanger their operating control by broadening the ownership base to include new outside owners.

With the conventional avenues to new financing thus closed off, Trevett has explored the feasibility of financing by means of leasing and has decided to enter into a sale-leaseback agreement with the Globe-Wide Insurance Company. This agreement provides that Trevett will have the plant built to its own specifications, after which the insurance company will buy the land and building at Trevett's cost ($1 million) and lease it back to Trevett on a 30-year lease. Trevett will make an $86,187 annual rental payment to Globe-Wide and will also pay property taxes, insurance, maintenance, and all other operating costs. All that Globe-Wide will do each year is collect the rent. At the end of the initial 30-year lease term, Trevett can either vacate the property or buy it by meeting the best offer received by Globe-Wide at that time.

A sale-leaseback of this type differs from purchase financed by borrowing in that the lease entitles Trevett to the use of the property for a specified period of time, but it does not convey any title to the rights to any residual values at the end of the lease period. If conventional debt financing had been available at an effective interest rate of 6 percent, and if the estimated market value of the property at the end of 30 years is $300,000, the two alternatives might be described as follows:

Purchase: Pay $60,000 a year for 30 years and $1 million at the end of the 30 years.

Sale-Leaseback: Pay $86,187 a year for 30 years and about $300,000 at the end of the 30 years if the continued use of the property is desired.

In other words, the choice of lease financing requires Trevett to pay $86,187 a year, or $26,187 more than if it had borrowed the money in a more conventional manner. However, if it leases, it will have to pay out $700,000 less 30 years from now.

It should require no calculation of present values to see that the postwar growth in leasing has not occurred because lease debt is cheaper than conventional debt.[10] Its main advantages over other forms of borrowing lie in its adaptability to a wide variety of specific circumstances and to its availability when conventional borrowing is either not feasible or impossible.[11] When used within limits, however, leasing is often a considerably cheaper source of funds than additional ownership investment. The cost of the Trevett Company's lease is approximately 8 percent before taxes and slightly more than 4 percent after taxes, which is much less than the usual stockholder expects as a return on his money.[12] Leasing, therefore, affords the stockholder the

---

[10] Leasing involves paying out more in the near future and less in the distant future, and over the life of the lease $85,610 more is paid than would have to be paid under conventional financing. A comparable but smaller disadvantage obtains after income tax effects are considered. Of course, some firms have obtained lease arrangements more attractive financially than conventional borrowing, but the above figures are quite representative.

[11] The United States Post Office Department has contracted with private investors to build local post offices for long-term lease to the federal government. Since it is unlikely that the private investor can obtain funds more cheaply than the government, the reason must be sought elsewhere, in the reluctance of Congress to appropriate funds for post office construction. For a review of the many advantages and disadvantages of leasing, see Albert H. Cohen, *Long-Term Leases: Problems of Taxation, Finance, and Accounting* (Ann Arbor: Bureau of Business Research, School of Business Administration, University of Michigan, 1954); and D. R. Gant, "Illusion in Lease Financing," *Harvard Business Review*, March–April, 1959, pp. 121–42.

[12] These calculations can be reproduced using Tables 3 and 4 in Appendix A and the following additional information. Of the $1 million original cost, $160,000 was the

same kind of leverage that was described earlier in the case of long-term bonds.

The concern here is not with the desirability of lease financing, difficult though it is to keep away from that topic. The main interest is in the representation of the lease on the company's published financial statements. If the plant were financed by conventional borrowing, the Trevett balance sheet would report an increase in fixed assets and in long-term debt. Investors considering the purchase of the company's stock would note the greater risk caused by the increased leverage. Furthermore, they would also include the $1 million cost of the plant in its asset base in calculating return on investment. By contrast, under the sale-leaseback arrangement no recognized accounting transaction takes place and the corporation's balance sheet is unaffected by the acquisition of the plant. In short, Trevett's debt/equity ratio and return on investment ratio both appear to be materially stronger under the sale-leaseback arrangement.

The word "appear" is used advisedly, because the sale-leaseback involves no less of a debt burden than the long-term borrowing. If anything, the burden is heavier because the fixed annual payments include the amortization of the principal as well as the interest on the loan. It is also true that with a 30-year commitment to the plant, it is a part of the capital employed by the company. Perhaps the most convincing evidence in support of the thesis that obligations under long-term leases are no different from debt is the fact that many banks, insurance companies, and other large lenders consider them as such. These financial institutions require applicants for loans or lease credits to submit financial statements which include the property and the obligations under existing lease contracts.

Many accountants have expressed concern with the present nonrecognition of lease contracts in financial statements. They advocate that the lessee's rights to use the property and the corresponding liability for future rental payments be shown in both the asset and liability sections of the company's published balance sheets. This balance sheet recognition is known as *lease capitalization*. Leases can be capitalized in much the same manner as any other liability, at the present value of the future obligatory payments under the lease, discounted at a rate equal to the cost of the specific lease. This is the principle implicit in the effective interest method of amortizing bond

---

cost of the land, the remainder being depreciated at a straight-line rate of 2½ percent of depreciable cost per year. The income tax rate is 50 percent and the building is expected to be useful for 40 years, after which the land and building can be sold for $160,000. The calculation is somewhat unusual, and it may be better to carry it out after studying Chapter 20.

premium and discount described earlier in this chapter, and is consistent with our method of handling other liabilities.

Few practicing accountants approve of lease capitalization, and the Accounting Principles Board has specifically refused to recommend it.[13] The ultimate test, of course, is whether lease capitalization will assist investors in making investment decisions. The presumption is that it will, insofar as it forces the investor to discard the illusion that leases do not represent debts. The empirical data on this question are not very convincing in either direction, and it might be very useful to give lease capitalization a trial.[14]

SUMMARY

In this chapter, consideration has turned from the *forms* capital takes once it has been injected into the enterprise to an examination of one of the major *sources* of capital, borrowed money. Although current liabilities are typically larger in amount than long-term debt, concentration has been on the latter, partly because management has greater discretion over the use of long-term debt financing and partly because the authors find it more interesting. This chapter has strayed somewhat farther from accounting than others, largely because the interesting questions in connection with long-term debt are questions of finance rather than of accounting.

Nevertheless, an attempt has been made to outline a consistent procedure whereby any long-term financial obligation can be capitalized, which has then been applied to three different types of liabilities —long-term bonds, employee pension obligations, and financing leases. In the authors' opinion, all three of these deserve balance sheet recognition; at present only the first is fully capitalized.

QUESTIONS AND PROBLEMS

1. What is a deferred performance liability? How does it differ from other liabilities? How would you measure it for balance sheet presentation?

2. Why are future interest payments under a long-term liability not shown as separate liabilities on the balance sheet?

---

[13] *Opinion No. 5, Reporting of Leases on Financial Statements of Lessee* (New York: AICPA, 1964)

[14] For further discussion of the merits and mechanics of lease capitalization, see John H. Myers, *Reporting of Leases in Financial Statements*, Accounting Research Study No. 4 (New York: AICPA, 1962); and Gordon Shillinglaw, "Long-Term Leases," in Morton Backer (ed.), *Modern Accounting Theory* (Englewod Cliffs: Prentice-Hall, Inc., 1966), chap. xvii.

3. Explain the difference between the coupon rate and the yield to maturity on a bond. Under what conditions will the two rates be equal?

4. What is the nature and purpose of a call premium on a bond?

5. Justify the use of the effective interest method of amortizing discount or premium on bonds.

6. How does a "liability for deferred income tax" arise? Should it be shown on the company's balance sheet?

7. With respect to pension liabilities, how is the problem of funding different from the problems of measuring corporate income?

8. Corporations that sell products which carry warranties against defective parts and defective workmanship are now required for tax purposes to recognize warranty expense when repairs are made rather than when the products are sold. Under what circumstances, if any, would this treatment be satisfactory for income reporting to shareholders?

9. What are the similarities between a five-year lease and a five-year bond? What are the differences? Do you think the differences are great enough to warrant the exclusion of leases from the lessee's balance sheet?

10. A 4½ percent bond due 12 years hence is selling to yield 4¼ percent.

a) What does this statement mean?
b) Is the selling price greater than, equal to, or less than the face value? Explain.

11. Concerning a sinking fund:

a) What is it?
b) What journal entry should a company make to record its contributions to the sinking fund?
c) How do a company's contributions to the sinking fund affect the company's reported income for the period during which the contributions are made?

12. The Weiner Corporation has a noncontributory employee pension plan under which employees receive a pension on retirement at age 65 that is based on the employees' length of service and employment income prior to retirement. The current service cost of the plan for this year is 4 percent of the payroll, or $820,000. The company's contributions under the plan on the behalf of an employee "vest" with him after 10 years' service. That is, if he leaves the company's employment after 10 years' service but before he reaches the age of 65, he receives a pension at 65 on the basis of the contribution on his behalf up to the termination of his employment.

The vice president for marketing, who is upset with the company's lack of funds for long-term market development, discovers that of the above $820,000 about $300,000 is on behalf of employees with less than 10 years' service. He argues that many of these employees will leave before they have 10 years' service, and the company should charge only $520,000 pension expense. The controller disagrees and argues that the full $820,000 is an expense for the current year. Comment.

*13. The Crowder Lunch sells coupon books good for $10 in meals for $9. On January 1, books in the hands of patrons contained unused coupons with a face amount of $300. During January, 100 coupon books were sold. Cash receipts for meals exclusive of coupons were $1,200, and coupons with a face value of $1,050 were received in payment for meals.

a) How large could the total expenses have been and yet permit the Crowder Lunch to make a net profit of $100 for the month of January?
b) How, if at all, would the above facts affect the right-hand side of the January 31 balance sheet?

*14. How much would you pay for a 10-year bond that has a face value of $100 and a coupon rate of 5 percent if you want a yield of 4 percent and interest is paid semiannually? Show your calculations. (Do not use bond yield tables except to check the accuracy of your answer.)

15. What is the maximum price which you would pay for a $1,000, 5 percent bond maturing eight years hence if you required an annual return of at least 8 percent on your investment? Coupon payments are made twice a year. (Do not use the bond yield tables.) Show your calculations.

*16. A deed of trust provides that all income from the trust fund shall be paid to the beneficiary during her lifetime, but that the principal shall be held intact and paid to a remainderman on the death of the beneficiary. The trustee buys for $1,039.90 a $1,000, 5 percent bond maturing in ten years.

a) Assuming that the bond is held to maturity, how much should the trustee pay to the beneficiary over the 10-year period?
b) What is the yield on this bond?

---

* Solutions to problems marked with an asterisk (*) are found in Appendix B.

17. Howell Company borrows $2,000,000 to be repaid with respect to interest and principal by means of 10 annual payments of $271,740 each. The payments are to be in arrears. What is the interest rate on the loan? Prepare journal entries to record the payments in the first and second years.

18. The Bell Company borrows $100,000 with the understanding that it will pay the interest and principal on the loan in five equal annual payments, the first payment to be a year from the date the money is borrowed.

a) If the interest rate is 8 percent, what will be the amount of each annual payment?
b) Present a schedule showing the interest and the principal components of each of the five payments, assuming an 8 percent interest rate.
c) Prepare journal entries to record the loan and the payment at the end of the first year.

*19. The Mountain Electric Company sells a million-dollar issue of 3½ percent bonds on a 4 percent basis.

a) What does this mean?
b) The price is $1,086,900 or $913,100. Which, and why?
c) What entry should be made at issue on the books of the Mountain Electric Company?
d) What entry should be made by the company at the first coupon payment six months later?
e) What entry should be made at the second coupon payment?
f) What is the term of this issue?

20. At the time of issue, an insurance company purchases $400,000 (face value) of 3 percent, 30-year municipal bonds at a price to yield 3.3 percent. Ten years later, it sells $100,000 (face value) of these bonds for $97,000.

a) What is the insurance company's total interest income on these bonds for the first year of ownership?
b) What is the gain or loss on the sale 10 years after purchase?
c) What is the total interest income for the 11th year of ownership?

21. Robert Peters purchased for $1,020 a 20-year, 4½ percent bond issued by the Jasper Corporation. Attached to this bond was a warrant, entitling its owner to purchase 10 shares of Jasper Corporation common stock at a price of $40 per share at any time during the next 10 years.

The market price of Jasper Corporation common stock at the time of purchase of the bond was $30. The market yield to maturity on bonds of comparable quality was 4.8 percent at that time.

a) How much of the $1,020 purchase price of the bond was actually a payment for the warrant?

b) Assuming that Mr. Peters expects a 20 percent return before taxes on any speculative investment and that he exercises the warrant five years after he purchased the bond, what is the lowest market price of the common stock at that time that would justify the price he paid for the warrant? (Assume semiannual compounding.)

22. A firm needs an additional machine and determines that it can acquire the use of a particular machine in two ways. The machine will have a useful life of 15 years and no salvage value at the end of its life.

(1) It can purchase the machine for $92,442, paying $10,000 in cash on the date of purchase and promising to pay the remainder and 8 percent interest in 14 equal annual payments of $10,000 per year starting one year after the date of purchase.

(2) It can lease the machine for 15 years, paying an annual rent of $10,000 at the beginning of each year.

The president can see no difference between the two methods but wonders how the financial statements would be affected by the method selected. If the asset is purchased it will be depreciated on a straight-line basis.

a) Would the balance sheet at the date of acquisition be any different if the asset were purchased rather than leased? If so, how?

b) What would be the difference in net income before taxes for the first year? Show the calculations.

23. The Blair Company sells calculating machines at a price of $600 each. This price includes one year's free service, the cost of which is estimated as of January 1, 1964, to be $60 per year. The company also sells service contracts for subsequent years at a price of $80 per year. Revenues from service contracts are recognized monthly during the year in which the coverage is in effect.

In January, 1964, Blair sold a machine and a service contract for 1965. The total price was $680.

In March, 1964, customers owned 500 machines for which the initial guarantee was still in force. Service contracts were in force on an additional 1,000 machines. The actual cost of the service department for the month was $8,100. The company prepares financial statements monthly.

Present journal entries that will most accurately record:

a) In January, 1964: the sale of the machine and service contract.

b) In March, 1964: the service department's operations for the month.

(AICPA Adapted)

24. A company needs approximately $1,000,000 in new capital for long-term investment. Management is undecided whether to obtain the needed funds from the sale of bonds or from the sale of additional shares of common stock. Given the following information, prepare an analysis to show the earnings per share under each method of financing.

a) Number of shares of stock now outstanding: 300,000.
b) Current annual earnings after taxes: $1,200,000 ($4 per share).
c) Anticipated increase in earnings (before interest and income taxes) from investment of additional capital: $400,000.
d) The proposed bond issue would consist of 20-year, 5 percent bonds with a face value of $1,000,000, to be sold to an insurance company at their face value.
e) The proposed stock issue would consist of 82,300 shares of common stock, to be sold at a price of $12 per share.
f) The effective income tax rate is 50 percent.

*25. The Randolph Corporation is planning to expand its manufacturing plant and requires $5,000,000 of new long-term capital for this purpose. It is anticipated that the proposed expansion will increase annual net income before taxes to $2,500,000 from its present level of $1,500,000. It appears feasible to raise these funds by sale of either $4\frac{1}{2}$ percent, 20-year bonds or additional capital stock. There is no long-term debt presently outstanding, the common stock is selling at $7.50 per share, and the owners' equity accounts appear as follows:

Capital stock, 1,000,000 shares, par value $4.............$4,000,000
Premium on capital stock.............................   800,000
Retained earnings....................................   2,200,000
    Total Shareowners' Equity........................ $7,000,000

a) Analyze the effect of the proposed expansion in terms of earnings per share:
(1) Assuming borrowing.
(2) Assuming stock sale.
(Note: A 50 percent tax rate may be assumed.)
b) What other factors should be considered in reaching a decision?

26. On January 1, 1954, the Lambert Corporation purchased a mill at a cost of $10,000,000 under a "certificate of necessity." This certificate allowed Lambert to depreciate the full cost of the mill for tax purposes at a straight-line rate of 20 percent of original cost per year for five years. In its financial statements, however, Lambert depreciated the cost of the mill by the straight-line method over its estimated normal life, 20 years, and accrued the deferred income taxes.

Assume that the mill is the Lambert Corporation's only depreciable asset, that the corporation's income before depreciation and income taxes is $4,000,000 in each year, and that the income tax rate is 50 percent.

a) Derive the corporation's income after taxes in 1957 and 1963, as reported to stockholders.

b) State the balance in the Provision for Deferred Income Taxes at the close of 1954, 1956, 1959, and 1963.

*27. The Winston Corporation's income before depreciation and taxes in 1963 was $6,200,000. Its depreciation for tax purposes was $1,250,000, and the depreciation for financial statement purposes was $850,000. Derive the corporation's income after taxes, assuming a 50 percent tax rate, and present the journal entries that account for the year's depreciation and accrual of the income tax liability for the year.

28. The Winston Corporation's income before depreciation and taxes in 1990 is $10,600,000, its depreciation for tax purposes in that year is $2,400,000, and the depreciation for financial statement purposes is $3,100,000. The January 1, 1990, balance in the Provision for Deferred Income Taxes is $3,000,000. (See Problem 27.)

a) Derive the corporation's income after taxes on the assumption that the 50 percent tax rate is still in effect, and present the journal entries that account for the year's depreciation and tax accruals.

b) What adjustment should be made as of January 1, 1990, if Congress reduces the corporate income tax rate to 25 percent, the reduction to take effect on that date? What is income tax expense for 1990?

c) Derive the corporation's income after taxes for 1990 on the assumption that the tax rate is 50 percent and that income before depreciation and taxes is $2,600,000. (Assume that tax losses in any one year can be carried forward or carried back to reduce taxable income.)

d) What problems did you meet in parts (*b*) and (*c*) that might cast doubt on the practice of income tax deferral? Do you feel that income tax deferral is appropriate, despite these problems? Explain your reasoning.

29. On January 1, 19x0, the Dan Realty Company purchased a supermarket building from Nabor Stores, Inc., at a price of $462,200. Dan Realty immediately leased the store back to Nabor Stores at an annual rental of $50,000, payable in advance on January 1 of each year. The lease term was 15 years, which was also the building's expected useful life. Its expected end-of-life salvage value was zero.

a) Assuming that Nabor Stores treated the lease as an ordinary rental:

   (1) Show how, if at all, this lease would be reflected on a balance sheet prepared immediately after the lease was signed and the first payment was made.

   (2) Compute the amount of expense that would be reported on the income statement for each of the first two years of the lease.

b) Assuming that Nabor Stores treated the signing of the lease as a simultaneous *purchase* of the store and *borrowing* of the purchase price:

(1) Show how this lease would be reflected on a balance sheet prepared immediately after the lease was signed and the first payment was made.

(2) Compute the amount of expense that would be reported on the income statement for each of the first two years of the lease, assuming that depreciation was straight-line with zero salvage value.

(3) Compute the book value of the asset and of the liability at the end of each of the first two years.

c) Comment on any differences between your answers to (*a*) and (*b*). How did they arise? Could they have been eliminated?

30. On January 1, 19x3, Companies A, B, C, D, and E adopted pension plans for their employees. Benefits under the five plans were identical and were based on the employee's salary or wages and total length of service from his date of employment rather than from the date of adoption of the plan.

On January 1, 19x3, the present value at 5 percent of each corporation's future pension payments arising from its employees' past services ("past service costs") was $4,000,000. The present values on December 31, 19x3, of the future pension payments arising from its employees' services during 19x3 ("current service costs") was $1,200,000.

A retirement annuity is purchased for each employee on the date of his retirement. The total price of such annuities for employees retiring in 19x3 amounted to $280,000. All of these employees retired on December 31, 19x3.

Although benefits under the five plans were identical, the companies adopted different policies with respect to financing and accounting.

Company A decided to recognize the January 1, 19x3, liability for past service costs by a direct charge to retained earnings. This liability was not funded. On December 31 of each year, the company was to deposit with the pension plan trustee an amount equal to the current service costs for the year just ended, plus an amount equal to one year's interest on the unfunded liability as of the beginning of the year, at an interest rate of 5 percent per year. An amount equal to this deposit was to be charged as pension expense for the year.

Company B decided to fund its past service costs immediately and to charge this amount against retained earnings. The current service costs were also to be funded with the pension fund trustee at the end of each year.

Company C decided to fund both current and past service costs, but the latter were to be funded over 10 years by means of 10 equal annual payments. The first payment was made on January 1, 19x3. The amount contributed to the fund each year was also the amount charged as expense for that year.

Company D decided not to make a firm decision with respect to past service costs and funded $1,500,000 with the trustees on January 1, 19x3. This was charged to retained earnings. Current service costs were to be funded and expensed annually.

Company E decided not to fund its plan but instead to charge as current expense each year the amounts needed to purchase annuities for the employees retiring during that year.

a) How would these differences in the companies' financial and accounting policies affect their financial statements for 19x3?
b) Do the differences in the financial statements indicate real differences in the financial position and performance of the various companies or are the statements noncomparable?

31. On July 1, 1948, the Vulcan Gas Company sold a $1,000,000 issue of 4½ percent, 20-year bonds to an investment banking syndicate at a price of 98.70. The bonds were marketed to investors at an average price of 102.66.

On July 1, 1963, the company sold a new $2,000,000 issue of 4 percent, 10-year bonds at 100.82 and retired the original issue at a call price of 102.

Financial statements are prepared annually. No interest accruals are made prior to payment except on December 31 of each year. Interest expense for the first six months of the year is accrued at the time of payment of the July 1 coupon. The effective interest method is used.

Show the journal entries to record:

a) Issue of the 4½ percent bonds.
b) Accrual of interest expense as of December 31, 1948, when the company closed its books for the year.
c) Payment of the January 1, 1949, coupon.
d) Payment of the July 1, 1949, coupon.
e) Payment of the July 1, 1963, coupon. (Note that the interest expense is for the period of January 1 to June 30.)
f) Issue of the 4 percent bonds.
g) Retirement of the 4½ percent bonds.
h) Accrual of bond interest expense as of December 31, 1963.
i) Payment of the January 1, 1964, coupon.
j) Payment of the July 1, 1964, coupon.

32. On October 1, 1938, the Bellingham Western Railway sold $10,000,-000 (face value) of 4 percent, 30-year bonds at a price to yield 4.8 percent.

In October, 1948, $5,000,000 (face value) of this issue was retired by purchase on the open market at an average price of 96.00. On October 1,

1958, the Bellingham Western negotiated a 10-year loan of $5,000,000 from an insurance company at 3.7 percent and retired the remainder of the bond issue at a call price of 103. Financial statements are prepared annually. No interest accruals are made prior to payment except on December 31 of each year.

a) Prepare journal entries to record:
    (1) The bond issue of October 1, 1938.
    (2) The accrual of bond interest expense as of December 31, 1938, when the corporation closed its books for the year.
    (3) The payment of the April 1, 1939, coupon.
    (4) The October, 1948, purchase.
    (5) The retirement of October 1, 1958.
b) Compute interest expense for the year 1939.
c) Compute interest expense for the period April 1–September 30, 1958.
b) What factors should have been considered in making the decision to refund the bond issue in 1958?

33. The American Sugar Refining Company reported the following account balances in its 1961 annual report:

Among the assets:

Pension fund—Note 3	1961	1960
Cash	$ 69,482	$ 51,329
U.S. Government Bonds	3,920,240	4,796,226
Company's own preferred stock, 20,000 shares at cost	632,650	632,650
Total	$4,622,372	$5,480,205

Below long-term debt in the balance sheet:

Pension fund reserve—Note 3	$5,205,582	$6,144,409

Note 3 to the financial statements read as follows:

Note 3: *Pensions*—Pension costs charged against earnings were $1,541,611 in 1961 and $1,561,945 in 1960, after applicable income taxes. Each of these amounts included a provision of $474,800, after taxes, toward past service costs to augment amounts previously provided.

The pension fund reserves of $5,205,582 represent that portion of the past service costs of the plans which were provided in prior years and which have not been deposited with the trustees of the pension plans. Additional provisions of approximately $2,425,000 will be required from future earnings to reflect total past service costs of the pension plans. Both amounts are after applicable income taxes at current rates.

It is intended that the assets of $4,622,372, segregated for the pension fund of the company, and the pension fund reserves of $5,205,-

582 of the company and its subsidiaries, augmented by additional provisions from future earnings, will be used for funding the full past service costs of the plans over a period of years. However, the right is reserved to make the assets and reserves available for other corporate purposes at any time.

a) Does this represent adequate disclosure? What improvement, if any, would you like to see made?
b) Comment on the company's method of financing its past service benefits.
c) Assuming a 50 percent income tax rate, present journal entries which might account for the costs charged against earnings as reported in the note, the change in the net balance of the pension fund, and the change in the pension fund reserve.

34. The annual report of the Air Reduction Company for 1962 included the following:

From the income statement:

	1962	1961
Income before federal and foreign taxes on income...	$32,205,208	$29,403,632
Provision for federal and foreign taxes on income (Note G)		
Current....	8,189,995	12,909,560
Deferred....	7,661,413	2,294,995
Total....	$15,851,408	$15,204,555
Net Income for the Year....	$16,353,800	$14,199,077

From the balance sheet below long-term debt:

Deferred income taxes (Note G)....	$17,307,123	$10,141,599

Note G reads as follows:

The Revenue Act of 1962 provides for an investment credit, based on the cost of certain property additions, which reduced the company's federal income taxes for 1962 by $1,861,000. The company has provided $968,000 for the related estimated deferred income taxes which will be payable in future years, and the estimated permanent tax saving of $893,000 is reflected in net income.

In 1962, the company adopted, for income tax purposes only, revised depreciation rates under guidelines and rules established by the U.S. Treasury Department. The resulting reduction of $3,833,660 in federal income taxes for 1962 has no effect on net income since an equivalent amount has been provided for the estimated deferred income taxes which will be payable in future years.

How would the above figures have been different in the absence of (a) the investment credit, (b) the adoption of revised depreciation rates under "guidelines and rules established by the U.S. Treasury Department?" What was the advantage to the company of adopting the revised depreciation rates if they had no effect on net income?

35. The 1967 annual report of Uniroyal, Inc., included the following note:

Retirement Allowances:

The company and certain subsidiaries have retirement plans covering the great majority of their employees. Most plans provide for payment to independent trustees of amounts computed by independent actuaries, sufficient to provide for current service costs and the amortization of prior service costs over periods ranging from 24 to 40 years.

In 1967, the total cost before reduction for income taxes of the retirement plans, including health and life insurance, was $30,080,000, of which $28,716,000 was charged to operations and $1,364,000 was applied to the Reserve for Retirement Allowances.

The Reserve for Retirement Allowances was provided from income prior to the adoption of funding; the charges thereto represent a portion of the funded cost relating to past service cost. At December 31, 1967, the reserve included $3,362,000 which will be used in future years to absorb a portion of the costs relating to past service. The remainder, $2,644,000, covers certain employees ineligible under funded plans.

The actuarially computed value of vested benefits for all plans as of December 31, 1966, adjusted for the substantial increase in retirement benefits granted during the year 1967, exceeded the total of the pension fund and balance sheet accruals by approximately $275,000,000. The 1967 benefit increases were granted to nearly all active and retired employees in the United States.

The company reported total assets of $1,014,517,000 and stockholders' equity of $439,042,000 at the end of 1967. Net income for the year was $32,978,000.

a) Explain in your own words the company's methods of accounting for and reporting its retirement allowances.

b) How would balance sheet recognition of the full "actuarially computed value of vested benefits" affect the company's financial statements? How might it affect the company itself?

c) Would you recommend that the amount discussed in (*b*) be recognized on the balance sheet? Would you recommend any change in the company's accounting treatment of its pension obligations? Explain your reasons.

Chapter 14

THE SHAREHOLDERS' EQUITY

INTEREST IN THE OWNERS' EQUITY accounts centers mainly on the items that make up the annual income statement. The purpose of this chapter is to examine other kinds of transactions which affect the owners' equity accounts from time to time. Although these other transactions do not affect the reported income of the period in which they take place, they can be extremely important to management, shareholders, and others. The most significant of these are:

1. Additional issues of capital stock.
2. Retained and distributed earnings.
3. Executive stock options plans.

ADDITIONAL ISSUES OF CAPITAL STOCK

The initial source of corporate financing is the sale or issuance of capital stock. Without an adequate base of ownership capital, the corporation is unable to obtain debt financing and will even experience difficulties in obtaining short-term trade credit. Much of the ownership capital needed to finance corporate growth is supplied by the reinvestment of funds generated by periodic earnings. This source is often inadequate to support the desired rate of growth, however, and in that case the board of directors may decide to sell additional shares of common stock to obtain the needed cash.

Ownership Rights

What does the owners' equity in a company represent? The money figure on the balance sheet, like that of a creditor's equity, represents the amount that this class of investors has put into the corporation, either by purchase of stock or by reinvestment of earnings. That is, the basis of valuation is the amount invested. The similarity ends, however, when the rights enjoyed by shareowners and creditors are considered. Under most circumstances, the creditor's only right is to receive specified sums of money on specified dates in the future. By contrast, the owner has a wide range of *managerial rights*—rights to employ the company's assets as he pleases, subject to restrictions that may be imposed by law or by his contracts with his employees or creditors or others, plus residual *financial rights* in the net income and net assets of the company.

In the corporation, the managerial rights are exercised by officials appointed by the board of directors or by their appointees. The board, in turn, is elected by the stockholders. The stockholder's financial rights are not fixed in amount or specified as to date. He has the rights to the income of the enterprise, and acting through his board of directors, the right to declare and receive dividends. If earnings are low or if no dividends are declared, he cannot force the company into receivership or bankruptcy as the unsatisfied creditor can. His only recourse is to elect a new board of directors or, acting through the existing board, to change the management. If the company is liquidated, the creditor's claims must be satisfied first; the stockholder is then entitled to any residual that may remain.[1] Thus, in any given company, the stockholder assumes a greater risk than a creditor with an identical investment in the company, but has an opportunity for far greater reward. No matter how successful the company, the ordinary bondholder will receive no more than the amounts specified in his agreement with the corporation.

Preferred Stock

A company's capital stock may be divided into two or more classes, each with its own set of rights and privileges. When this is done, one class is ordinarily called preferred stock or preference stock and the other is called common stock. Each share of a given class has the same rights as any other share of that class. Thus an owner of 1,000 shares of common stock has twice as many votes as a holder of 500 common shares, twice as many dividends, and so forth.

The characteristics of preferred stock vary widely from issue to issue, but they usually entitle the holder to a fixed dividend that must be paid before any dividends can be paid on the common stock. They also have precedence over common stock in any liquidation of assets, up to a specified maximum amount per share. The dividend priority is

---

[1] Outright liquidation of the assets of a large corporation to satisfy the demands of creditors is extremely rare. Instead, the assets are transfered by agreement to a new or reorganized corporation under a reorganization plan in which both owners and creditors share in the reorganization loss. The owners' share of this loss is greater than that of the creditors.

usually *cumulative*, meaning that no distribution can be made to the common shareholders until all current and back dividends have been paid on the preferred. A preferred stock differs from a bond in that the stockholders have no legal right to insist on payment of their dividends on specified dates. Furthermore, the security has no maturity date. A corporation may omit or pass the dividend on the preferred indefinitely without being declared insolvent, although some preferred stocks provide for the transfer of corporate control to the preferred shareholders when the dividends have fallen a specified amount in arrears.

Most preferred stocks issued during the last two decades have been *convertible* into common shares at the owner's option and *callable* or subject to repurchase at the corporation's option at a specified call price. The purchaser of a convertible share purchases a more or less assured dividend as long as he continues to hold the preferred and as long as the company is able to pay preferred dividends, plus an opportunity to participate in any growth in the company's earnings by converting his preferred shares into common shares when the common dividend and market price have risen higher than the fixed preferred dividend and preferred price. Many companies have used the sale of convertible preferred stock as an indirect way of selling large quantities of common stock.

Par Value

The company's articles of incorporation specify the *par value* to be assigned to each share of a given class of stock. This par value is an arbitrary amount, equal to or less than the prices at which the corporation will sell the stock. Stock may even be issued without par value, in which case it is referred to as *no-par* stock. Stocks having no par value are often assigned a so-called "stated value," which is treated in the accounting records in the same manner as par value.

Shares of stock are typically sold at prices in excess of par value. This excess is typically credited to an account titled Premium on Capital Stock or Paid-In Capital in Excess of Par Value. The older terminology, Capital Surplus or Paid-In Surplus, has the advantage of brevity but may convey the misleading impression that the corporation has surplus liquid funds that might safely be withdrawn. For this reason, the use of these terms in financial statements is undesirable.

Preferred stock, unlike common stock, ordinarily has a par value that is fairly close to the price paid by the original stock purchaser. Any excess over par should be credited initially to a Premium on

Preferred Stock account, but the amounts are often small and the credit, if any, is to a single premium account covering both preferred and common stocks.

Share Issues and Dilution of the Equity

Shares of stock issued to different individuals or at different times have identical rights, no matter how much or how little the original shareowner paid for his stock. For this reason, the purchasers of common shares are understandably anxious to make sure that other purchasers are not allowed to purchase shares at lower prices than they themselves are paying. Any such purchase would result in *dilution of the equity* of the other owners. In other words, if a new corporation is financed initially by the sale of stock for $100,000, the investor who contributes $5,000 of this amount is entitled to a 5 percent equity in the company. If the shares are sold at $10 each, then he gets 500 shares out of the 10,000 shares issued; if 1,000 shares are issued, he gets 50 shares, and so on. Regardless of the price per share or the number of shares issued, however, if another investor is now allowed to purchase shares at a lower price per share, the equity of the original shareowners is diluted.

Unfortunately, this problem of detecting dilution of the stockholders' equity is not one of simple arithmetic, both because stock is sometimes exchanged for assets other than cash and because shares are issued at different times. To illustrate, assume that the Space Age Corporation was organized in January, 19x1, with an authorized capital stock of 200,000 shares of no-par value. The stated value of the stock was $10 a share. Initially, only 50,000 shares were issued: 40,000 for cash at $25 per share, 8,000 in exchange for a patent, and 2,000 for the services of an entrepreneur who organized the corporation.

The entrepreneur's shares in this case were issued to compensate him for expenditures he had made to obtain the corporation's charter, engrave the shares of stock, and offer them to the public, as well as for his personal services in performing these tasks. The amounts paid by the corporation for activities of this kind are called *organization costs*. Organization costs are typically shown initially as assets and are written off as expenses in a relatively short time.

The journal entry to record the issue of stock in this case was:

Cash	1,000,000	
Patent	200,000	
Organization Costs	50,000	
Capital Stock		500,000
Premium on Capital Stock		750,000

Notice that each share of stock was recorded at the price received for the shares exchanged for cash. This presumes that the deals with the patentee and the promoter were the result of arm's length bargaining in which the other stockholders agreed that the assets received from these sources were worth to the company at least as much as the $25 per share they had paid in cash for their equity in the corporation. The patentee and the promoter, for their part, were in effect agreeing that a 20 percent interest in the company was a fair price for the assets they had to offer. If these assets had in fact been worthless, the inventor and the entrepreneur who organized the corporation would have received 20 percent of the corporation's profits in return for nothing. In that case, the equity of the other stockholders would have been diluted in that each one had paid $25 for a share that was worth only $20 at that time.[2] Whether the property or services are worth the assigned value, or more or less, is a question of business judgment and economic analysis on which each investor must make his own decisions.

Dilution of the equity which arises from the issue of shares at different points in time is a somewhat different matter. If the company has been profitable in the past and seems likely to be profitable in the future, the market price of its common stock is likely to rise. Under these conditions, if the corporation decides to raise additional capital by issuing additional shares of common stock, it will probably be able to market these shares at higher prices than were obtained for earlier issues. If market prices have declined, on the other hand, the price obtained for new shares will be less than was received for older shares, plus reinvested earnings to date.

For example, assume that five years after incorporation Space Age had retained earnings of $550,000 in addition to the $1,250,000 of initial paid-in capital. The $1,800,000 total, divided by the 50,000 shares outstanding, establishes the book value or investment per share, $36. Space Age's stock was then being traded on the market at $51 per share, indicating that expected earnings were high in relation to what investors considered a normal return on investment in the net assets of a corporation in Space Age's industry.

---

[2] The justification for capitalizing organization costs is that they are necessary to produce future earnings in excess of the earnings normally to be expected from the other assets, tangible and intangible. Some organization costs may be paid for immediately in cash—e.g., legal fees—but the amounts are not likely to be significant unless shares of stock are issued to promoters for their organizational services. Excessive assignments of stock to promoters in the late 19th and early 20th centuries often led to highly inflated balance sheets, and shares of stock in such companies were said to be watered. The S.E.C. now scrutinizes very carefully each stock sale that falls within its jurisdiction to make sure that any indication of possible dilution is fully and accurately disclosed to prospective purchasers.

The company's rapid growth had placed heavy demands on its cash resources, and the board of directors decided to sell 5,000 of the authorized but unissued shares to obtain the funds it needed. Lacking experience in marketing capital stock themselves, the directors arranged to sell the 5,000 shares to an investment banking house at a price of $47 each. The banker then resold the shares to the public at approximately $50 each, keeping the $3 difference as his fee.[3] This sale was recorded in the following entry:

```
Cash.......................................... 235,000
      Capital Stock.....................................        50,000
      Premium on Capital Stock.........................       185,000
```

the excess of the sale price over the stated value was credited, as before, to the account Premium on Capital Stock. The shareholders' equity section of the balance sheet, therefore, was as shown in Exhibit 14–1.

Exhibit 14–1

SPACE AGE CORPORATION
Shareholders' Equity
As of December 31, 19x5

	Before Stock Sale		After Stock Sale	
	Total	per Share	Total	per Share
Capital stock—stated value.........	$ 500,000	$10	$ 550,000	$10
Premium on capital stock...........	750,000	15	935,000	17
Earnings retained in the business.....	550,000	11	550,000	10
Total Shareholders' Equity.....	$1,800,000	$36	$2,035,000	$37

Whether any dilution of the equity occurred in this case depends on the point of view. The old stockholders had invested $36 in the corporation for each share held, in contrast to the $47 received from the new stockholders. The book value of their investment went up from $36 to $37 as a result, and no dilution was apparent. Before the stock issue, however, each stockholder had had the option of selling his stock for $51, and by not selling had indicated his belief that the

---

[3] The prices paid for the stock may be less than the market price on the date of the sale because of the lack of enough buyers willing and ready to pay the market price. Because the investment banker typically does not sell all the shares immediately, he may also price them at slightly less than market to counteract the effects of a possible mild reduction in the market prices of stocks in general.

stock was worth at least that much. New shares were issued at only $47, and thus some dilution in terms of market value did occur.

Dilution on an historical basis is of academic interest only. What really matters is the relationship of issue price to current market price or, perhaps even more important, its relationship to the price that present shareholders think is a fair price for the stock. If the company issues shares of common stock to the general public at a time when share prices do not reflect the company's earnings prospects adequately, the existing shareholders will be injured.

For this reason, many articles of incorporation and many state incorporation statutes give the shareholders *preemptive rights*—that is, the right to purchase additional shares of stock at or below the public offering price prior to any offering to the general public.

RETAINED AND DISTRIBUTED EARNINGS

The corporation's most accessible source of investment capital is its net income. Cash dividends paid by United States corporations are typically much less than reported income, and retained earnings provide a major percentage of corporate equity financing.[4] Earnings retention of this magnitude creates several managerial and accounting problems which deserve brief discussion here.

Stock Dividends

Space Age Corporation had been extraordinarily successful during its early years of operation, and the balance in retained earnings had reached $715,000 by the end of 19x6. The demand for funds to finance the company's growth was equally strong, however, and consequently no cash dividends were declared after the second year of operations. Noting the large retained earnings balance, several stockholders were exerting pressure on the board to declare a dividend. Unfortunately, dividends are paid with cash, not with retained earnings, and Space Age was chronically short of cash. Each year the company had invested its earnings in operating assets, and at the end of 19x6 it had only $50,000 in the bank. Since $50,000 was barely adequate to meet the day-to-day operating needs for cash, the company had no money to pay dividends.

In this situation, to give partial satisfaction to the stockholders'

---

[4] For a discussion of the relationship between earnings and dividends, see John Lintner, "Distribution of Income of Corporations among Dividends, Retained Earnings, and Taxes," *American Economic Review*, May, 1956, pp. 97–113.

demands and to advise them that the retained earnings had in large measure been *permanently* reinvested in the company, the directors decided to declare a 10 percent *stock dividend*. A stock dividend consists of the distribution of additional shares of stock to the existing stockholders in proportion to their holdings. With 55,000 shares outstanding, the Space Age 10 percent dividend consisted of 5,500 shares, 1 for every 10 outstanding.

This transaction was treated as if the corporation had declared a cash dividend equal to the market value of the 5,500 shares and the stockholders had simultaneously purchased the 5,500 shares at their current market price.[5] Because the market price of the stock at the time of the stock dividend was $60, the journal entry was:

Earnings Retained in the Business	330,000	
Capital Stock		55,000
Premium on Capital Stock		275,000

The dividend reduced retained earnings, and the stock sale increased the paid-in capital by the market value of the number of shares. The owners' equity accounts before and after the stock dividend appear in Exhibit 14–2.

Exhibit 14–2

SPACE AGE CORPORATION
Shareholders' Equity
As of December 31, 19x6

	Before Stock Dividend		After Stock Dividend	
	Total	per Share	Total	per Share
Capital stock—stated value	$ 550,000	$10.00	$ 605,000	$10.00
Premium on capital stock	935,000	17.00	1,210,000	20.00
Earnings retained in the business	715,000	13.00	385,000	6.36
Total Shareholders' Equity	$2,200,000	$40.00	$2,200,000	$36.36

It should be evident that the stock dividend may properly be called a paper transaction. After the dividend, each stockholder had 11

---

[5] Valuing the stock dividend at the market price of the stock is logically inconsistent. The same future earnings must now be spread over a larger number of shares and thus market price must be lower than it would have been without the stock dividend. The main reason for valuing the additional shares at amounts greater than par value or other legal minimum is probably that this permits the capitalization of a larger portion of the retained earnings with a given increment to the number of shares outstanding.

shares which conveyed the same rights as the 10 shares he had owned previously. The total owners' equity was unaffected by the stock dividend; it was merely divided into a larger number of shares, each one representing a smaller portion of the company than formerly. After the dividend, 11 shares had the same $400 book value (11 × $36.36) that the owner's 10 shares had had before.

Although the stock dividend does not give the stockholder any new asset, the market in the stock may be slightly more active than formerly because of the increase in the number of shares outstanding. Many companies also follow the practice of paying the same cash dividend per share after the stock dividend that they had been paying previously. Furthermore, the market often interprets the declaration of a stock dividend as evidence of management's faith in the continued growth of the company. The combined effect of these and other factors often is to increase the total market value of the company's stock. In other words, although 11 shares should sell for what 10 shares would have brought previously (10 × $60 = $600), in fact they might sell for more (e.g., 11 × $56 = $616). This effect will not persist, however, if the expected growth does not materialize.

Stock Splits

A stock split is akin to a stock dividend in that each stockholder is given additional shares in proportion to the number he owns. Although the par or stated value is usually reduced to accompany a stock split, the main difference is in the number of shares distributed. Although exceptions to the rule are numerous, when an increase of more than about 20 or 25 percent in the number of shares outstanding is contemplated, the mechanism of the stock split is usually employed.[6]

Stock splits are employed to bring the price of a share down to an attractive range. Authorities on the valuation of common stocks maintain that a price range of $30 to $50 attracts the widest market and the most favorable price in relation to the share's intrinsic value.[7] Many investors refuse to consider a share that sells for a price in excess of $100, regardless of its merits. Accordingly, a corporation that retains a large fraction of its earnings and enjoys profitable operations will periodically split its stock.

---

[6] This is the dividing line recommended by the American Institute of Certified Public Accountants, *Accounting Research and Terminology Bulletins* (final ed.; New York: AICPA, 1961), pp. 52–53.

[7] See Robert W. Johnson, *Financial Management* (2d ed.; Boston: Allyn & Bacon, 1962), pp. 516–17.

For example, the market price of Space Age Corporation had risen to $90 by the end of 19x9, and the board of directors decided to declare a 2 for 1 stock split and to reduce the stated value of the stock from $10 to $5. The journal entry that gave effect to this transaction was:

Capital Stock (Stated Value $10)......................605,000
    Capital Stock (Stated Value $5)...................   605,000

Only the capital stock account was involved in the transaction, and no transfers occurred between the various ownership accounts, as shown in Exhibit 14–3.

Exhibit 14–3

SPACE AGE CORPORATION
Shareholders' Equity
As of December 31, 19x9

	Before Stock Split		After Stock Split	
	Total	per Share	Total	per Share
Capital stock—stated value.......	$ 605,000	$10	$ 605,000	$ 5
Premium on capital stock.........	1,210,000	20	1,210,000	10
Earnings retained in business......	1,089,000	18	1,089,000	9
Total Shareholders' Equity....	$2,904,000	$48	$2,904,000	$24

A few months after the stock split, the new shares were selling for $49, something more than half the price of the stock prior to the split. The reduction in the stock's price range may have been partly responsible for this increase in market value, although a larger share of the responsibility was probably attributable to circulation of rumors that the company was about to begin paying dividends.

Our need to discuss both stock dividends and stock splits in a very short space for the sake of concise illustration should not be allowed to obscure the basic importance of cash dividends. Although most young growth companies do reinvest the bulk of their earnings, seldom would they be able to retain as much as our hypothetical Space Age Corporation ($1,419,000 in nine years on a paid-in capital base of only $1,485,000). Dividends and the prospect of dividends in the near future are usually necessary to a sustained growth in market prices, and stockholders' demands for dividends usually cannot be long ignored.

Appropriations of Retained Earnings

One way to inform stockholders that large portions of retained earnings have been more or less permanently reinvested is to declare stock dividends. Another way is to appropriate segments of retained earnings for specific purposes such as debt retirements or plant expansion. Although earnings appropriations of this kind are much less common than they used to be, they still occur often enough to require discussion here.

For example, suppose that the Space Age Corporation directors decided to appropriate $200,000 for debt retirement. The entry would be:

```
Earnings Retained in the Business......................200,000
    Earnings Appropriated for Debt Retirement..........        200,000
```

This action serves simply as a memorandum to stockholders that one reason dividends will not be declared is that the company needs to accumulate funds for debt retirement. The appropriation account remains a subdivision of retained earnings and does not necessarily indicate that a corresponding amount of liquid funds is currently available for this or any other purpose. In fact, once the debt is retired, it is virtually certain that no liquid funds will remain, although the balance in the appropriation account will still remain until it is transferred back to the retained earnings account.

Whether this practice constitutes an effective means of disclosure is debatable. If the intent is to reinvest earnings permanently, it can be argued that capitalization, as by a stock dividend, is preferable. Furthermore, if *any* portions of retained earnings are appropriated in this manner, it might be argued that the *entire* amount ought to be appropriated, to indicate all of the reasons for retention. Otherwise, the stockholder may get the impression that the unappropriated balance is available for dividend distribution.

It should be emphasized that these "surplus reserves" (the older name for appropriations of retained earnings) are not properly established by charges against revenues. Revenue charges mean that an asset has been consumed, and this is not the case. The major problems arise in connection with a class of appropriations known as *contingency reserves*. For example, a company may decide to recognize that its equity in its foreign subsidiaries is subject to the risk of loss due to currency devaluation, expropriation, war, or other extraordinary event. If the risk of loss could be determined actuarially, an argument

could be made for an annual charge to expense analogous to a charge
for insurance against such losses:

Losses on Foreign Investments. xxx
    Reserve for Losses on Foreign Investments.   xxx

When and if the contingency materialized, the recording would be
similar to that for writing off an uncollectible account:

Reserve for Losses on Foreign Investments. xxx
    Foreign Investments.   xxx

Losses of this kind are not actuarially determinable, however. This
means that establishment of an appropriation for future losses on
foreign investments is a recognition of a *possibility*, not a *probability*.
The amount of current asset expirations therefore cannot be determined and thus no basis exists for an anticipatory charge against
revenues. For this reason, this kind of reserve should be created only
by charges to retained earnings; losses should not be recognized in
income until they can be determined objectively.[8]

Other Types of "Reserves"

Despite earlier admonitions against the use of the word reserve, it
was used deliberately in the last illustration to emphasize further the
danger of imprecise terminology in accounting. It is impossible to tell
from the account title in what section of the balance sheet a particular
reserve account belongs. The term reserve may be used in the titles of
three distinct types of accounts. First are the *surplus reserves* discussed above. Second are contra-assets or *valuation reserves* such as
the reserves (allowances) for depreciation and uncollectible accounts.
The related charge in these cases is a proper revenue deduction, and
the account exists only because it is desirable to show the gross as well
as the net valuation of the asset.

A corporation's year-end income tax liability is an example of a
third type of reserve, the *liability reserve*. The amount of this liability
will not be known exactly until the Internal Revenue Service makes a
final determination of what the corporation's taxable income is, and
even then further court action may occur before the issue is finally
settled. To emphasize that the year-end account balance reflects an
estimate, it is called Reserve (or Provision) for Income Taxes. The
discussion of deferred income taxes and pension liabilities in the pre-

---

[8] See also American Accounting Association Committee on Concepts and Standards, "Reserves and Retained Income, Supplementary Statement No. 1," *The Accounting Review*, April, 1951, p. 153.

vious chapter indicates that a liability reserve may be very difficult to measure, but it does represent a liability and should be shown on the balance sheet as such.

In short, if there is an objective basis for anticipating the event or for deciding how much of any resultant losses should be charged against the current year's income, then the reserve is either a liability or a contra-asset. Otherwise, it is an appropriation of retained earnings and remains a part of the owners' equity.

A fourth type of reserve is the *hidden reserve*, so-called because it does not appear on the company's balance sheet. In an economic sense, a hidden reserve is present any time that the present value of the future earnings exceeds the book value of the shareholders' equity, but the term is usually given a narrower meaning. A hidden reserve is said to be created when an asset is written down to a lower figure than a strict application of the accounting model would warrant.

The creation of hidden reserves is not sanctioned by any accounting body in the United States, but it often happens nevertheless. For example, a company which has spent large sums on advertising and other activities to establish the value of a trademark but which has charged all of these expenditures to expense is very likely to have a hidden reserve. Similarly, if straight-line depreciation is the closest approximation to the pattern of the decline in the service potential of plant and equipment but the company uses declining-balance depreciation on its published financial statements, a hidden reserve will arise. The same thing happens when price levels rise sharply without adaptation of the accounts to a current cost basis, but this kind of hidden reserve arises from the nature of the accounting model itself rather than from its misapplication. A good financial analyst will try to identify hidden reserves, no matter what their source, but this is seldom easy.

Treasury Stock

Corporations from time to time have occasion to repurchase shares of their own stock.[9] Such repurchased shares are called treasury stock.

Share repurchase may have a number of objectives. Some reacquired shares may be used for distribution to executives in bonus or stock option plans. Others may be used for distribution to shareholders as stock dividends, to employees in stock purchase plans, or to the

---

[9] Statistics on share repurchases are reviewed by Leo A. Guthart, in "More Companies Are Buying Back Their Stock," *Harvard Business Review*, March–April, 1965, pp. 40–53, 172.

company's pension funds for long-term investment. Share repurchase may also be viewed as a more profitable use of the company's funds than the available alternatives. If the company has more cash than it can invest profitably internally, stock repurchase may prevent a dilution in earnings per share.[10]

The negative aspects of these transactions should not be overlooked, however. For one thing, the purchase and sale of treasury stock in any volume can generate short-term movements in the price of the stock which might be interpreted as the use of the corporation's funds by "insiders" to influence the price of the stock to their advantage. Similar objections can be raised to the use of the corporation's funds to purchase stock to prevent voting control from being concentrated in unfriendly hands. Furthermore, the purchase of treasury shares might weaken the company's financial position and thereby impair the rights of the company's creditors, employees, and remaining stockholders.

Share repurchase is common, nevertheless, and accountants have developed two methods of accounting for such shares: the cost method and the par value method.

The Cost Method. Under the cost method, which is used in most states to record temporary reacquisitions of common shares, the treasury shares appear on the corporation's balance sheets at their purchase price, shown as a contra account in owners' equity. For example, if Space Age Corporation were to repurchase for $46,000 a total of 1,000 shares of its common stock after the stock split on December 31, 19x9, the revised December 31, 19x9, balance sheet would show the following:

Capital stock—stated value	$ 605,000	
Premium on capital stock	1,210,000	
Earnings retained in the business	1,089,000	$2,904,000
Less: Treasury stock (at cost)		(46,000)
Total Shareholders' Equity		$2,858,000

Treasury stock is a deduction from owners' equity, not an asset. Shares of stock represent portions of the owners' equity in the firm's assets. When the shares are repurchased, the assets are reduced and so is the owners' equity. To treat treasury stock as an asset would imply

---

[10] This last objective is strongly supported by Charles D. Ellis, "Repurchase Stock to Revitalize Equity," *Harvard Business Review*, July–August, 1965, pp. 119–28. A lively exchange of views on the wisdom and propriety of share repurchases is presented in the same issue under the heading, "Letters from the Thoughtful Businessman," pp. 30–40, 178.

that the company has ownership rights in itself, and this is not true. Treasury shares cannot be voted, nor do they participate in cash dividends or carry any other perquisites of ownership. The purchase of treasury shares represents a partial and perhaps temporary liquidation of the enterprise and represents a reduction in both total assets and total owners' equities. Thus, the amount paid for the stock should be deducted from the shareholders' equity. It should not be included among the assets.

Resale of treasury stock at prices different from their acquisition cost is not reported as a gain or loss on the company's income statement. The company cannot make or lose money by buying and selling a portion of itself, although the equity of the surviving shareholders can be increased or decreased by such actions. Instead, the difference should be carried to the Premium on Capital Stock account to show that the amounts received from shareholders have increased or decreased.

The Par Value Method. The par value method is used most widely in connection with the purchase and retirement of shares. Any shares purchased for retirement must be eliminated from the ownership accounts and should be accounted for as follows:

If the price paid exceeds the paid-in capital per share:
Capital Stock. . . . . (number of shares at par or stated value)
Premium on Capital Stock. . . . . (pro rata portion of account balance)
Retained Earnings. . . . . (remainder of price paid)
    Cash. . . . . (price paid)

If the price paid is less than the paid-in capital per share:
Capital Stock. . . . . (number of shares at par or stated value)
Premium on Capital Stock. . . . . (remainder of price paid)
    Cash. . . . . (price paid)

In other words, if the price exceeds the paid-in capital per share, the excess is debited to retained earnings to avoid showing a distribution of the continuing stockholders' paid-in capital to the departing stockholders. If the price is less than the paid-in capital, the paid-in capital is only reduced by the amount paid for the stock, indicating that the departing stockholders have surrendered a portion of their paid-in capital to those that remain. A credit to retained earnings would imply that some kind of gain had accrued to the corporation by virtue of the purchase, and this is inconsistent with the accountant's concept of income.

Ordinary versus Extraordinary Earnings

The events which change a company's retained earnings account fall into two categories: income and financial. "Financial" events include cash and stock dividends, treasury stock transactions, and other events discussed above which do not result directly from the company's income-producing activities. These go directly to retained earnings without passing through the income statement.

The effects of income events, on the other hand, enter the retained earnings account from various income accounts. If the company includes all the gains and losses recognized during a period in its net income for the period, the only income event to affect retained earnings will be the net income for the year. Some accountants maintain, however, that including extraordinary gains and losses in net income is misleading in that many readers of financial statements do not look behind the net income figures. They prefer to carry these extraordinary items directly to retained earnings, bypassing the income statement entirely.

The use of direct charges or credits to retained earnings poses new problems, however. The series of annual net income figures constitutes a running history of the corporation's earnings over the years. The validity of this record is impaired if any significant quantity of gains and losses is consistently excluded from the determination of net income. Because recorded losses are typically larger and more frequent than reported gains, the total reported income for any 10-year period is likely to be overstated. True, direct charges and credits to retained earnings can be disclosed in a separate statement of changes in retained earnings, but there is no reason to assume that the reader who never looks behind the net income figure will ever look into this statement either.

The plain fact is that forecasting errors are inevitable in the determination of revenues and expenses for periods shorter than the total life of the enterprise. By excluding the corrections of these errors from the income statement, the possibility of manipulation of periodic income is created. Recognition of this possibility has led to the widespread adoption of the *clean surplus rule*, which bars direct adjustments to retained earnings for gains and losses and leads to an *all-inclusive income statement*.

In the years following World War II, committees of both the American Accounting Association and the American Institute of Certified Public Accountants issued statements that recommended partial or total adherence to the clean surplus rule.[11] More recently, the Institute's Accounting Principles Board went even further, recommending that the net income ". . . should reflect all items of profit and loss recognized during the period with the sole exception of the prior period adjustments described below. *Extraordinary* items should, however, be segregated from the results of ordinary operations and shown separately in the income statement. . . ."[12]

It remains to be seen how much success will be achieved by the Board's attempt to draw a precise dividing line between extraordinary items (to be segregated from ordinary income but included in the calculation of net income for the period) and prior period adjustments (to be entered as corrections of the opening balance in retained earnings).

In any event, extraordinary items should be segregated on the income statement and a separate earnings per share figure should be given for each category of income. Prior period adjustments should also be disclosed and, in our opinion, should be stated as a total amount per share currently outstanding, even though they are not included in the current year's income. This should insure that the reader of the statements does not overlook adjustments that are material in amount.

EXECUTIVE STOCK OPTION PLANS

In a very important book published in 1933, Berle and Means,[13] examined the implications of the separation of ownership and control in the modern corporation. They noted that one argument advanced in favor of the private enterprise system is that the prospect of profit leads the owner of a company to employ his property as efficiently as possible. However, in the large publicly owned corporation, the stockholders who own the company make no business decisions, while the corporate officers who make the decisions own little or no stock.

To illustrate the consequences of this state of affairs, assume that the president of the General Products Company is presented with the opportunity to make an investment of $10 million, a large sum for his corporation. The chance that the investment will earn a large return,

---

[11] *Accounting Research and Terminology Bulletins*, final ed., p. 63; and American Accounting Association Committee on Concepts and Standards, "Accounting Corrections, Supplementary Statement No. 5," *The Accounting Review*, April, 1954, p. 186.

[12] Opinion No. 9, *Reporting the Results of Operations* (New York: AICPA, 1966); see *Journal of Accountancy*, February, 1967, p. 57.

[13] A. A. Berle and G. C. Means, *The Modern Corporation and Private Property* (New York: The Macmillan Co. 1933).

20 to 30 percent after taxes, and substantially raise the value of the stock is good. However, the investment could possibly also turn out to be a total loss. From the stockholders' viewpoint the investment may be attractive—the expected return justifies the risk. The decision may look very different from the president's chair, however. If the investment succeeds, he may get a salary increase, perhaps from $60,000 to $80,000 a year, and practically all of the increase will go to the government in income taxes. By contrast, if the investment fails, he may well be looking for another job, characterized as the man who pulled that boner over at General Products. Unless he is by temperament a gambling man, he is likely to regard this investment as highly unattractive.

Stock option plans are a major development in executive compensation designed to bridge the gap between ownership and control in the large publicly owned corporation. The following example illustrates the essential features of such a plan. The directors of the General Products Corporation initiated an executive stock option plan at the end of 19x1, with the approval of their stockholders. The corporation had five million shares of common stock outstanding at that time, and 40,000 of the authorized but unissued shares were made available to the stock option plan. In 19x2, the corporation's top four officers were given options to buy 15,000 shares at $47.50 per share, 5 percent below the market price of $50 at the time the option was granted. They could not exercise this option before two years from the date of the grant; if the option was not exercised within four years from the date of the grant, the executive's rights would lapse and the option would be canceled.[14]

If the stock were to stay at $50 per share or fall, the option would be worth little or nothing. On the other hand, if by bold and successful decisions (and some measure of good luck) the corporation were to prosper and the stock price were to rise, then the option could be extremely valuable. For example, suppose that the price of the stock is $100 per share in 19x6 and that the officers exercise their options at that time. Under the terms of this plan, they may resell the 15,000 shares shortly thereafter at about $100 per share and pocket a gain of about $787,500.[15] This gain is taxed at the modest capital gains rate of

---

[14] These plans vary somewhat in such particulars. For a discussion of the various possible terms, their motivation and consequences, see Daniel L. Sweeney, *Accounting for Stock Options* (Ann Arbor: University of Michigan, 1960).

[15] Many plans require the executives to hold shares purchased under the plan for a specified period; this merely increases the complexity of the manager's decision whether to exercise the option.

25 percent and not at the much steeper regular and surtax rates on ordinary income. A number of corporate officers have become multimillionaires through arrangements such as these.

While executive stock option plans may have provided corporate management with the incentives necessary for the dynamic functioning of the economy, they have also posed some problems for accountants. The official position of the AICPA is that if the price of the option is equal to or greater than its fair market value at the time it is granted, no accounting entry is made until the option is exercised.[16] At that time the sale of stock is recorded exactly as any other sale of stock. If the fair market value of the shares exceeds the option price at the time the option is granted, however, the excess is considered an employee compensation expense.

There is no set formula for the measurement of fair market value. Presumably an option price equal to 95 percent of the quoted market price for the stock would be regarded as equal to or greater than market value and no compensation expense would be recognized. Suppose that the option price in our example had been $40 per share, however, and that fair market value was assumed to be $47.50 at that time. In this case the element of compensation would be $7.50 a share, or $112,500 for 15,000 shares, and the journal entry would be:

```
Executive Compensation Expense......................112,500
    Capital Represented by Unexercised Stock Options.....        112,500
```

The Capital Represented by Unexercised Stock Options account is regarded as a temporary owners' equity account, representing an "investment" made by the executive by not taking all of his compensation in the form of cash. (There is no liability, nor has an asset been reduced, so it must be an addition to owners' equity.) Then two or more years later, when the stock is issued at the option price, the entry is:

```
Cash ($40 per share)................................600,000
Capital Represented by Unexercised Stock Options........112,500
    Paid-In Capital ($47.50 per share)................        712,500
```

The arguments for and against this treatment are too complex for consideration here. In addition, most executive stock option plans provide for option prices close enough to quoted market prices at the date of the grant to eliminate the compensation element, at least as

---

[16] *Accounting Research and Terminology Bulletins,* final ed., pp. 119–24; see also Rufus Wixon and Walter G. Kell (eds.), *Accountants' Handbook* (4th ed.; New York: Ronald Press Co. 1957), sec. 21, pp. 26–28.

measured above. It should be noted, however, that stock options, whether costless to the corporation or not, do have a cost to the stockholder. The reason is that the benefit to the exerciser of the option is achieved by diluting the equity of the other stockholders. They accept this dilution on the grounds that it will lead to better executive performance that will produce offsetting gains in owners' equity that would not otherwise occur. The validity of this proposition in any particular case is not always clear.

This danger of undue dilution underlies the requirements that stockholders vote their approval of stock option plans and that financial statements include details on outstanding stock options. Such disclosure is an essential means of discouraging an unscrupulous management from creating excessively generous plans to their own enrichment and the other stockholders' cost.

SUMMARY

In a private enterprise economy in which the search for profit is the private mechanism by which economic resources are directed into the channels preferred by society as a whole, the most important source of investment capital is the proprietary investor. His funds provide the cushion needed to attract borrowed capital, and in most kinds of enterprise they constitute the bulk of the invested capital. Some of this capital is supplied by equity investors who are willing to limit their returns by accepting the lower risks attached to ownership of preferred stock. Most of the equity capital, however, is supplied by the residual risk takers, the owners of common stock.

Most of the problems of accounting for the common stock equity arise in connection with the reinvestment of earnings. This may be emphasized by declaration of a stock dividend or, occasionally, by earmarking of retained earnings to indicate some specific purpose or purposes of reinvestment. If earnings reinvestment is successful, stock splits will be necessary to keep the market price of the stock within a range appropriate for trading.

Other problems arise in connection with the purchase of treasury stock or the issue of stock on stock options or in exchange for convertible bonds or preferred stock. Because executive stock options are of relatively recent vintage, the accounting procedure still needs review. In other respects, the accounting for owners' equity is relatively routine and straightforward.

QUESTIONS AND PROBLEMS

1. What does the owners' equity in a company represent? What rights do the owners have?

2. Explain the meaning of "6 percent, cumulative, convertible, callable, $100 par value preferred stock."

3. What advantages and disadvantages do the cumulative, callable, and convertible features of preferred stock confer on the company's management? On the preferred stockholders?

4. What is meant by dilution of the stockholders' equity? Give an example.

5. What are "preemptive rights"? What advantages do they offer to the stockholder? To the corporation?

6. How may a corporate stockholder benefit from the retention of corporate earnings as opposed to their distribution in the form of cash dividends?

7. Distinguish between a stock dividend and a stock split. Do they serve the same purpose or do they have different objectives?

8. What is the purpose of appropriations of retained earnings? Should direct charges against the balances in the appropriation accounts be permitted?

9. Distinguish between a "surplus reserve" and a "liability reserve." Which of these contains cash?

10. What arguments can you advance for giving corporations the right to acquire treasury stock by open-market purchases? Is this practice subject to any dangers?

11. Should the company report a gain or loss on the purchase and sale of treasury stock? Should it report a gain or loss on the purchase and retirement of shares of its own stock? Explain.

12. Distinguish between ordinary and extraordinary earnings. What is the main alternative to showing extraordinary earnings on the income statement for the year? Which alternative do you prefer, and why?

13. "Stock options provide a means of compensating the company's officers without cost to the other stockholders." Discuss.

*14. Company A's board of directors declared a stock dividend of one share of common stock for each 20 shares outstanding. Prior to the stock dividend, 20,000 shares were outstanding with a par value of $10 a share. The company's accountants decided to capitalize the stock dividend at $30 a share. Present the required journal entries.

*15. On January 4, Company B repurchases 100 shares of its $5 par common stock at a price of $30 a share. The shares are held as treasury stock. On March 18, it resells these shares at a price of $40 a share. Present entries for both dates.

*16. Company C's board of directors votes to appropriate $1,000,000 of earnings to provide for future debt retirement. At the same time it votes to transfer $800,000 in cash to the sinking fund for bond retirement. Present the related entries.

*17. Beehive Industries secures permission to issue 3,000,000 no-par shares at a stated value of $5. The stock is placed on the market at $7.50 a share, and 400,000 shares are sold at that price.

Show the entry that you would make on the books of the company.

*18. The Myrex Preparations Company appropriated $10,000 of retained earnings for the contingency of an expected lawsuit arising out of the harm suffered by one of its customers through the use of its product. The suit was settled for $11,500 in the year following the appropriation. Indicate the pertinent journal entries in the two years.

19. On January 8, 19x0, the Alpine Company started operations by issuing 100,000 shares of common stock, $10 par, at a price of $15 a share. Retained earnings of the company as of December 31, 19x3, totaled $2,000,000.

a) Prepare a journal entry to record the issuance of the stock.
b) What was the book value per share of common stock as of December 31, 19x3?

20. On January 2, 19x4, the Alpine Company (see Problem 19) repurchased 1,000 shares of its stock at the market price of $28 a share. This stock was held as treasury stock.

---

* Solutions to problems marked with an asterisk (*) are found in Appendix B.

a) How should this treasury stock have been listed on the company's June 30, 19x4, balance sheet?

b) Did the purchase of this treasury stock increase, decrease, or leave unchanged the book value per share of stock issued and outstanding?

c) Should a gain or loss be shown in the 19x4 income statement as a result of the repurchase of the stock? Why?

21. On July 1, 19x4, the company (see Problem 20) resold its treasury stock at a price of $34 a share.

a) Prepare a journal entry recording the sale.

b) Should a gain or loss be shown on the 19x4 income statement as a result of the resale of the stock? Why?

22. A balance sheet showed the following owners' equity section on December 31:

```
Stockholders' investment:
   $5 par value common stock (5,559,500 shares issued)...$27,797,500
   Other paid-in capital............................... 10,960,500
   Income invested in the business..................... 55,389,500
   Cost of shares held by the company (9,500 shares)...... (153,500)
       Total Stockholders' Investment...................$93,994,000
```

The market price of the stock on December 31 was $25 per share.

a) What was the book value per share of common stock issued and outstanding at the end of the year?

b) Give three alternative explanations as to how the "Other paid-in capital" might have been accumulated. (One phrase or sentence for each will be adequate.)

c) If the corporation decided to cancel and retire the 9,500 "shares held by the company," what journal entry should be made? Explain your choice.

23. Assume that the corporation in Problem 22 declared a 10 percent stock dividend on December 31.

a) What journal entry would the corporation make?

b) What would be the new book value per share?

c) What would be the new book value (on the corporation's books) of the shares owned by an investor who had owned 10 shares of stock prior to the stock dividend?

24. Assume that *instead of* a stock dividend, the corporation in Problem 22 declared a 2-for-1 stock split (two new shares for each old one), and changed the par value to $3 per share.

a) What journal entry would the corporation make?

b) What would be the new book value per share?

c) What would be the new book value (on the corporation's books) of the shares owned by an investor who had owned 10 shares of stock prior to the stock split?

25. The following balance sheet items were taken from an annual report of the Multnomah Corporation:

Reserve for federal income taxes	$ 120,000
Reserve to reduce inventory values to market	40,000
Reserve for possible losses on foreign investments	1,000,000
Reserve for depreciation on plant	875,000
Reserve for expansion of plant	500,000
Reserve for employees' pensions	329,000
Common stock issued	2,000,000
Bonds	1,500,000
Treasury stock (at par)	100,000
Sinking fund for retirement of bonds	800,000
Goodwill	50,000
Retained earnings	1,400,000

a) Describe the probable nature of each of the items above which are captioned "Reserve." Your description should include reference to the following points:
   (1) The probable origin of the reserve (i.e., whether it arose out of an accounting entry debiting expense or one debiting retained earnings).
   (2) The purpose and function of the reserve.
   (3) Whether the reserve is essentially an asset valuation account, a liability, or retained earnings.
b) Prepare a schedule of the corporation's *owners' equity*.

26. On December 31, 19x5, the stockholders' equity section of the Broadmoor Corporation was as follows:

Capital stock, 400,000 shares, par value $1	$ 400,000
Additional paid-in capital	3,000,000
Retained earnings	2,700,000
Total	$6,100,000

The following events took place during 19x6, in the sequence given:
   (1) A cash dividend of 50 cents a share was declared.
   (2) A stock dividend of 5 percent was declared and issued; the stock was capitalized at the market price of $40 a share.
   (3) 5,000 shares of stock were repurchased to be held as treasury stock; the cost was $42 a share.
   (4) 3,000 shares of treasury stock were sold at $45 a share.
   (5) A contingency reserve of $400,000 was set up for possible future losses on overseas investments.
   (6) 40,000 new shares of stock were issued at a price of $48 a share.
   (7) The stock was split 2 for 1 without changing the par value. The treasury shares participated in the split.
   (8) Net income for 19x6 was $900,000.

a) What was the total stockholders' equity on December 31, 19x6? Show your calculations.

b) How many shares were issued as of December 31, 19x6?

c) How many shares were outstanding as of December 31, 19x6?

d) What was the book value per share on December 31, 19x6?

e) Prepare the owners' equity section of the corporation's balance sheet on December 31, 19x6.

27. The shareholders' equity section of the Corky Company's balance sheet showed the following amounts on January 1:

Preferred stock, 10,000 shares, $100 par	$ 1,000,000
Common stock, 400,000 shares, no par, stated value $5	2,000,000
Premium on capital stock	4,000,000
Retained earnings	8,000,000
Total Shareholders' Equity	$15,000,000

The following transactions affecting the shareholders' equity took place during the year:

Jan. 1	Sale of common stock, 100,000 shares at $12 a share—proceeds received in cash.
Jan. 20	Declaration and payment of cash dividend: common stock, $0.25 a share; preferred stock, $1.50 a share.
Mar. 20	Declaration and distribution of stock dividend, one common share for each 20 common shares outstanding—to be capitalized at the stock's current market price of $18.
Apr. 20	Declaration and payment of cash dividends: $0.25 a share on common stock; $1.50 a share on preferred stock.
Apr. 28	Purchase of 2,000 shares of the company's common stock for cash, $20 per share.
June 1	Repurchase and retirement of preferred stock by cash payment of $110 a share. The stock thus reacquired was canceled, not held as treasury stock.
July 20	Declaration and payment of cash dividends on common stock outstanding, $0.25 a share.
Aug. 15	Appropriation by the board of directors of $5,000,000 of retained earnings for plant expansion.
Oct. 20	Declaration and payment of cash dividends on common stock outstanding, $0.50 a share.
Nov. 15	Sale of treasury stock, 2,000 shares at $22 a share.
Dec. 1	Stock split 2 for 1; new stated value $2.50 a share.

a) Prepare journal entries to record each of the above transactions.

b) Present the owners' equity section of the balance sheet as it would appear on December 31 after all of the above transactions were recorded. Net income for the year was $1,000,000.

28. The Speed Corporation had been expanding rapidly to take advantage of growth opportunities, and in March, 19x1, it approached the Apex Insurance Company to borrow $2,000,000. Apex replied that it was against company policy to lend money at an interest rate in excess of 6 percent, and that it could not approve a loan to Speed at a 6 percent rate due to the amount of risk that such a loan to this company would entail.

Speed then "sweetened" the loan request by offering Apex the option to purchase 40,000 shares of Speed common stock at $20 a share. The option was to expire five years from the date of the loan.

Apex accepted these conditions and granted the loan in March, 19x1. Speed's common stock was then selling at a market price of $16 a share. In February, 19x6, when Speed stock was selling at $42 a share, Apex exercised the warrants and purchased the 40,000 shares.

a) Indicate what information you would have included in a footnote to the Speed Corporation's 19x1 financial statements. Why do you think that it would have been desirable to disclose this information? What harm would failure to disclose this information have done?
b) How did the exercise of the warrants in 19x6 affect the Speed Corporation's liabilities and shareholders' equity? Did this constitute dilution of the equity?
c) Did the warrants add to the cost of the loan? If so, how might this added cost be measured or estimated?

29. The stockholders of Topper Corporation voted approval of an executive stock option plan at the annual stockholders' meeting on May 14, 19x0. The vote authorized the board of directors to grant purchase options to key executives up to a maximum of 30,000 shares of the company's previously unissued stock.

The first options were granted on September 10, 19x0. Various executives were given rights to purchase a total of 12,000 shares at $22 a share, the market price of the stock at the close of trading on that date. These options would lapse if they were not exercised within two years.

On June 1, 19x2, officers were given three-year options to buy an additional 15,000 shares at $28 a share, the market price on that date.

Options on 8,000 shares at $22 a share were exercised in November, 19x3. The company's stock was then selling at $36 a share.

In 19x4 the stockholders approved the addition of another 20,000 shares to the stock option plan. In September of that year three-year options were granted on 6,000 shares at $43 a share, the market price at that time.

Options on 4,000 shares at $22 a share and 3,000 shares at $28 a share were exercised in 19x4. The stock was selling at $40 a share at the time.

a) Prepare a footnote to be appended to the 19x0 financial statements, giving adequate disclosure of the stock option plan. The company's fiscal year ends on December 31 each year.
b) Prepare a footnote on the stock option plan for the 19x4 financial statements. Explain your reasons for disclosing each item that you have included in your footnote. Why is it important to disclose this information?
c) Did the exercise of the options in 19x3 and 19x4 constitute dilution of the equity? Explain.

d) What was the effect of all the above transactions on the stockholders' equity in Topper Corporation?

30. On February 12, 19x1, the Burgoyne Corporation issued 100,000 shares of $3.50, no-par, convertible preferred stock at an issue price of $55 a share. All shares were paid for in cash. These shares were convertible into common stock (par value, $5 a share) at a rate of 2½ shares of common stock for each share of preferred. The company's earnings increased sharply during the next two years, and during the second quarter of 19x3 all shares of preferred were converted into common shares. Other data were as follows:

	February 12, 19x1	Second Quarter, 19x3
Market prices:		
Burgoyne common stock	$ 20	$ 40
Burgoyne $3.50 preferred stock	55	110
Index of common stock prices	100	109
Book value per Burgoyne common share		
(before conversion of preferred)	28	32

a) What was the effect of the conversion on book values and earnings per common share? One million common shares were outstanding prior to the conversion. If the conversion had not taken place, the company's earnings for 19x3 would have amounted to $2 per common share.

b) Did the conversion of the preferred shares into common stock lead to a dilution of the common shareholder's equity? Explain your reasoning.

c) Prepare journal entries to record the issuance and conversion of the preferred stock.

31. An excerpt from the Weston Corporation's 19x3 income statement and its statement of retained earnings are shown below:

INCOME STATEMENT
YEAR ENDED DECEMBER 31, 19x3

Income from operations		$ 196,650
Special items:		
Gain on sale of North Division	$(160,000)	
Provision for future declines in market value of inventories	30,000	
Estimated recovery of excess costs on defense contracts completed in 19x3	(90,000)	
Elimination of reserve created in 19x1 for possible award under a damage suit	(40,000)	(260,000)
		$ 456,650
Taxes on income		120,000
Net Income		$ 336,650

STATEMENT OF RETAINED EARNINGS
YEAR ENDED DECEMBER 31, 19x3

Balance, January 1	$1,650,000
Net income for the year	336,650
Dividends declared	(140,000)
Balance, December 3	$1,846,650

Reorganize the year's income statement and retained earnings statement to whatever extent you deem desirable for accurate disclosure. Explain the changes you have made and give your reasons for deciding that no other changes are necessary.

32. A company's income statements for three successive years disclosed the following:

	19x2	19x1	19x0
Operating profit	$4,590,914	$6,784,176	$4,097,642
Other income:			
Dividends, royalties, and fees from foreign subsidiaries not consolidated	$ 421,551	$ 447,931	$ 295,872
Other dividends, royalties, and engineering fees .	352,167	227,918	167,901
Interest income	169,137	237,564	115,580
Gain on sale of patent rights	375,600	. . . . .	. . . . .
Gain on sale of property, plant, and equipment . .	156,440	35,016	56,037
Insurance proceeds in excess of fire loss and expense	. . . . .	262,678	. . . . .
Miscellaneous income (net)	57,286	34,504	20,252
Total Other Income	$1,532,181	$1,245,611	$ 655,642
Other deductions:			
Interest expense	$ 634,422	$ 513,769	$ 494,589
Expenses of idle plants	. . . . .	35,004	241,012
Plant closing and moving costs	64,135	209,333	178,271
Loss on sale of assets of closed plants	. . . . .	458,325	. . . . .
Total Other Deductions	$ 698,557	$1,216,431	$ 913,872
Income before provision for income taxes	$5,424,538	$6,813,356	$3,839,412
Provision for U.S. and Canadian income taxes (including deferred taxes of $260,950)	2,815,000	3,286,000	1,725,000
Net Income	$2,609,538	$3,527,356	$2,114,412

The balance sheet for 19x0 and 19x1 carried a Reserve for Settlement of Patent Litigation. The balance in this account was $295,210 at the end of 19x1. The suit was defended successfully, and the reserve was closed out in 19x2 by a credit to retained earnings of $259,076.

Reorganize each year's income statement to whatever extent you deem desirable for accurate disclosure. Explain the changes you have made and give your reasons for deciding that no other changes are necessary.

33. The stockholders' equity section of the balance sheets shown in the 1967 annual report of Uniroyal, Inc., was as follows (in thousands of dollars):

	December 31 1967	December 31 1966
8% noncumulative preferred stock, $100 par value:		
Authorized and issued—651,091 shares................$ 65,109	$ 65,109	
Common stock, $2.50 par value:		
Authorized—20,000,000 shares		
Issued—12,446,858 shares, 1967; 12,369,929 shares, 1966.... 31,117	30,925	
Capital surplus....................................... 48,209	46,069	
Retained earnings.................................... 300,275	287,308	
	$444,710	$429,411
Less treasury stock at cost:		
Preferred stock held for retirement—39,520 shares, 1967;		
9,000 shares, 1966...................................$ 5,368	$ 1,413	
Common stock held by subsidiary—8,602 shares at cost...... 300	300	
	$ 5,668	$ 1,713
Total Stockholders' Equity...........................$439,042	$427,698	

In addition, an item called "Reserves" was located on the right-hand side of the balance sheet, following the listing of deferred taxes but before the stockholders' equity section:

Reserves...$ 14,471 $ 15,609

The statement of retained earnings for 1967 showed the following:

Net income........................$32,978,000
Cash dividends distributed:
Preferred stock, $8 a share......... 5,125,000
Common stock, $1.20 a share....... 14,886,000

Net income for the year included $7,028,000 in "other income."

The notes and supplement to these financial statements included the following additional information:

Other Income

"Other Income included dividends from foreign and domestic affiliated companies, gain on disposition of properties, and royalties from licenses."

Reserves

"Reserves at December 31, 1967 consist of Retirement Allowances, $6,006,000; Insurance, $4,012,000; and Foreign Activities, $4,453,000."

Retirement Allowances

"The company and certain subsidiaries have retirement plans covering the great majority of their employees. Most plans provide for payment to independent trustees of amounts computed by independent actuaries, sufficient to provide for current service costs and the amortization of prior service costs over periods ranging from 24 to 40 years.

"In 1967, the total cost before reduction for income taxes of the retirement plans, including health and life insurance, was $30,080,000, of which $28,716,000 was charged to operations and $1,364,000 was applied to the Reserve for Retirement Allowances.

"The Reserve for Retirement Allowances was provided from income prior to the adoption of funding; the charges thereto represent a portion of the funded cost relating to past service cost. At December 31, 1967, the reserve included $3,362,000 which will be used in future years to absorb a portion of the costs relating to past service. The remainder, $2,644,000, covers certain employees ineligible under funded plans."

Capital Stock—Capital Surplus

During 1967, 60,950 shares of common stock were issued under employees' stock options and 15,979 additional shares were issued to employees in part payment of Bonus Plan Awards for 1966. The excess of market price (at date of grant for options and issue date for awards) over par value of these shares, $2,140,000, was credited to Capital Surplus. The company purchased in the open market 30,520 shares of its 8% non-cumulative preferred stock, for retirement, at a total cost of $3,955,000.

"In accordance with the approval by the stockholders at their annual meeting held April 18, 1967 and subsequent action by the Board of Directors on the same date, 335,000 shares of common stock were made available for bonus awards under the Management Incentive and Bonus Plans of the company. An additional 15,000 shares were made available for the issuance of stock options under the Bonus Plan.

"On January 2, 1968, 10,366 shares of common stock were issued to participants in the Bonus Plan and the Management Incentive Plan as part payment of awards for the year 1967.

"On January 10, 1968, the Board of Directors recommended that the stockholders be asked to approve, at their annual meeting on April 16, 1968, an increase of 10,000,000 shares in the authorized common stock, and a new series of 10,000,000 shares of second preferred cumulative no-par stock issuable in series and convertible into common stock as to any series at the discretion of the Board of Directors."

Stock Options

"At December 31, 1966, options with respect to 230,677 shares of common stock were held by officers and other key employees. The options generally are granted at market price and are not exercisable for certain periods after grant and expire at varying dates not less than five nor more than ten years from date of granting. During 1967, options were exercised with respect to 60,950 shares of common stock at prices ranging from $21.00 to $40.75 a share. Options expired or were cancelled for 1,776 shares and options were granted for 65,134 shares at prices ranging from $39.625 to $46.125 a share.

"At December 31, 1967, after providing for shares applicable to outstanding options, there remained 369,297 shares of common stock available for granting further options. Of these remaining shares, options were granted under the Management Incentive Plan on January 9, 1968 for 2,943 shares at $49.5625 a share and options were granted under the Stock Option Plan on January 10, 1968 for 15,000 shares at $49.50 a share."

Principles of Consolidation

". . . . Cumulative foreign exchange gains are carried in a reserve. Current losses are charged to such reserve, or, if no reserve is available, to consolidated income. . . ."

a) Insofar as possible, explain the January 1–December 31 change in each of the stockholders' equity and reserve accounts listed at the beginning of this problem.

b) Prepare a journal entry that would be appropriate at the date of retirement of the shares of preferred stock held in the treasury on December 31, 1967. Do company purchases of preferred stock result in a dilution of the equity? What are the company's probable objectives in making such purchases?

c) Describe each of the three "reserves." Do you agree with the company's method of accounting for changes in these reserve accounts?

d) Did the granting of stock options in 1967 lead to any dilution of the equity? Did the exercise of stock options during the year dilute the equity? Explain.

e) Should the company have reclassified any of the amounts shown as "Other Income" on the income statement? Why or why not?

Chapter 15

CORPORATE INVESTMENTS
IN SECURITIES

THREE BASIC TYPES of investments in securities are frequently encountered on corporate balance sheets. First are investments of funds that are temporarily in excess of current requirements. These funds are invested to earn a higher rate of return than they could earn if left on deposit in commercial banks. Second, some corporations purchase stocks of other corporations as long-term income-producing investments, with no thought of obtaining or exercising operating control. Such investments are made presumably because the income prospects are greater than those available from internal investment and also greater than the rate of return demanded by the company's stockholders. Third, a corporation acquires stock in other companies with the objective of obtaining control over them and integrating their operations with those of the owning corporation. Such investments reflect management's view that this is the most effective way to expand and diversify the firm's operations.

The purpose of this chapter is to examine the various kinds of intercorporate investment by nonfinancial corporations and to study some of the accounting problems such investments create. The chapter will then close with a brief discussion of one of the most controversial current issues: how much detail relating to the operations of individual company product lines or other activities the corporation should be required to disclose.

MARKETABLE SECURITIES

Cash temporarily in excess of current operating needs is often invested in government securities, high-grade commercial paper such as the promissory notes of other business firms, and similar credit instruments. Investments of this type are commonly carried in an account titled Marketable Securities. The primary consideration in selecting securities for this purpose is the safety and liquidity of the amount invested. The principal should be readily convertible back into cash without substantial loss; the return on the investment is secondary. Accordingly, the term *marketable securities* is ordinarily restricted to those that can be sold on short notice at relatively stable market prices.

The only accounting issue with respect to marketable securities is whether they should be carried on the balance sheet at cost or at market value. A strong case can be made for carrying these securities at market value, recognizing changes in market value as gains or losses of the period. The securities can almost always be sold at quoted market prices, so that uncertainty is not an argument for failing to recognize unrealized gains.

The most common practice, however, is to carry the securities at cost and to show parenthetically the market value of the securities. Since the difference between the two figures is typically negligible, the issue is of no great importance. However, failure of a corporation to show the market value of its marketable securities is a questionable practice.

MINORITY STOCK INTERESTS IN OTHER CORPORATIONS

Apart from marketable securities, the securities held by a corporation are typically the common stocks of other corporations. The objective in acquiring such stocks may be either to produce income for the shareholders or to control the other company, which also has an income objective. In either case, the stock is not purchased and sold in response to short-term changes in cash position.

Except for such financial institutions as mutual funds, investment companies, and insurance companies, most companies' purchases of shares of stock in other companies are for the purpose of obtaining managerial control. A block of stock that is a *minority interest* in another corporation—less than 50 percent of its stock—may be acquired as a step in the direction of obtaining a majority or all of the stock. In the interim, the minority interest may provide a voice in the management or even effective control over its affairs.

The purchase by one company of shares of stock in another is always recorded at cost. For example, suppose that the National Company buys 30,000 shares of the Local Company's common stock (a minority interest). The price paid is $30 a share, and the purchase is recorded as follows:

Investment in Local Stock............................900,000
    Cash..   900,000

Recognizing Income: Dividend Basis

The simplest and most widely used method of recognizing income on these shares is to recognize as income only National's portion of the dividends declared by Local during the period. For example, if Local earns $3.25 per share and declares a dividend of $1.50 per share, National's 30,000 shares are entitled to $45,000 in dividends and the entry on National's books will be:

Dividends Receivable (or Cash)........................45,000
    Revenue from Investments........................   45,000

The argument for this treatment is that National does not control Local, nor does it decide what Local will declare in dividends. The directors of Local may never distribute the year's retained earnings of $1.75 per share. Since National cannot use this $1.75 to pay dividends to its shareholders, it should not be part of National's income.

Recognizing Income: Equity Basis

The policy of recognizing only dividends received as income has been criticized on the grounds that the shareholders benefit from the accumulation of retained earnings over time. Evidence shows a very high correlation in the long run between increases in a corporation's retained earnings and increases in its shares' market value, earnings, and dividends.[1] It is true that the company holding the stock does not have these retained earnings at its disposal, available in cash for the payment of dividends to its stockholders, but this is not relevant. Income derived from products sold on account or exchanged for notes is not available in cash either and yet it is reported as current income without hesitation. The owning company's share of the other company's earnings retention represents no less an investment of corporate funds than the purchase of additional securities or plant and equipment. In all cases, the underlying justification is that the investment will produce future earnings at a satisfactory rate.

According to this reasoning, a corporation should treat as income the *earnings* on the stock it owns and not merely the dividends

[1] For example, see Myron J. Gordon, *The Investment, Financing, and Valuation of the Corporation* (Homewood, Ill.: Richard D. Irwin, Inc., 1962).

declared. Applying this reasoning to National's investment in Local requires the following entry:

```
Dividends Receivable (or Cash)..........................45,000
Investment in Local Stock...............................52,500
     Revenue from Investments...........................            97,500
```

In other words, National's equity in the retained earnings of the Local Company (30,000 shares at $1.75 a share) is added to the balance in National's investment account. The balance in this account at any date thus equals cost at the date of acquisition plus the subsequent retained earnings on the shares owned. This can be interpreted as the amount paid for the company's equity in the shares held, which is wholly consistent with the cost basis of valuation.

Recognizing Income: Other Bases

An argument can be made for recognizing changes in the market values of long-term investments as current income or loss if market values are highly reliable. In most cases, however, quoted prices do not necessarily indicate the amounts at which large holdings of securities actually could be sold. Market prices are also highly volatile in many cases, thus making market value calculations more difficult.

Under these circumstances, unrealized holding gains cannot be recognized as current income unless accounting is to be based on current replacement cost or liquidation value. In the absence of such a shift in the basis of accounting, however, the two methods discussed earlier are the only alternatives available.

CONTROLLING STOCK INTEREST IN OTHER CORPORATIONS

When a company owns more than 50 percent of the stock in another company, it has a controlling interest in the other company.[2] The former is commonly referred to as the *parent* company, and the controlled company is referred to as its *subsidiary*. When a controlling interest in another company exists, the rationale given earlier for treating only the dividends received as income and the acquisition cost of the stock as the investment disappears. A parent company should report as income its equity in the subsidiary's earnings, and the excess of the earnings over the dividends received will be carried to the parent's Investment in Subsidiary account.

---

[2] Although control often can be exercised with less than a majority ownership, this chapter will identify as subsidiaries only those companies in which the parent owns more than 50 percent of the voting power.

Reasons for Consolidated Statements

A parent that merely showed one figure for its investment in a subsidiary and one figure for the income on the investment would not be providing adequate information on its assets and operations. Within very broad limits, the parent company's management can use the resources of one legal entity to finance the requirements of another, and often it can allocate the given total earnings arbitrarily among them. Thus it is the *total* assets and total earnings of the parent and subsidiaries *combined* that are significant.

A parent company report showing the investment in the subsidiary and the income from it as single figures would be like a company report showing only a total asset figure and a net income figure. In fact, a parent company which is solely a *holding company*, with no direct operations of its own, would present such a report if it reported on a parent-only basis. Its only assets would be its investment in subsidiaries, and its income statement would show merely the subsidiaries' net income figures or the amount of dividends received from them.

To meet the informational needs of investors in the parent company and others, financial statements can be drawn up to present the combined assets, equities, and operating results of the group of related corporations. Known as *consolidated statements*, their objective is to reproduce the results that would have been achieved had all transactions been recorded in a single set of accounts. For example, the consolidated balance sheet will show the cash balances of the parent and its consolidated subsidiaries as a single figure, representing the sum of the cash balances of the individual companies in the consolidation. Similarly, the sales revenue figure on the consolidated income statement will show the combined sales revenues of all the consolidated companies rather than those of the parent company only.

The argument for preparing consolidated statements is that it is the entire group of companies that the investor is placing his trust in, not just the parent. The various corporations are separate *legal entities*, but common control serves to merge them into a single *economic entity*. For this economic entity, it is argued, consolidated statements portray overall performance and status more accurately than separate statements for the parent and each subsidiary. Even the minority stockholders in the various subsidiaries need consolidated statements in addition to the unconsolidated statements of their companies alone that they receive. In the final analysis, the strength of the subsidiary depends largely on the strength of the consolidated group and on the competence of the parent company management. The main interest in the consolidated statements, however, comes from investors and potential investors in the parent.

Consolidation Policy

The consolidated financial statements of nonfinancial corporations in the United States often exclude the accounts of some of its wholly owned subsidiaries from the consolidation. These nonconsolidated subsidiaries fall largely into two categories: (*a*) customer finance companies, and (*b*) foreign subsidiaries.

The financial subsidiaries are usually excluded on the ground that their operations are so different from those of the parent that to include them would produce distorted statements. For example, the General Motors Acceptance Corporation (GMAC) was organized to finance consumer purchases of General Motors cars and other products. Like banks and independent finance companies, the common equity in this subsidiary finances a very small percentage of its total assets. GMAC assets are almost exclusively the notes of the purchasers of General Motors products, and GMAC finances this extension of credit predominantly by borrowing. Since the financial structure of a financial subsidiary is so different from its parent's, consolidation would seriously distort the picture presented by the consolidated statements. Common practice, therefore, is to report the financial subsidiary's statements separately in the corporation's annual report.

In the case of foreign subsidiaries, the situation is different but the practice is about the same. Although the United States parent may own 100 percent of the subsidiary's stock, its control is subject to the laws of the foreign country in which the subsidiary is incorporated. Under normal conditions, these laws may be no more restrictive or even less so than those governing domestic subsidiaries. This is true of Canada and many of the countries in Western Europe, although even there economic nationalism is not always dormant. Situations exist, however, in which the operations of a subsidiary abroad are highly regulated, expropriation is a near possibility, or the repatriation of dividends is severely restricted or prohibited. Under these conditions, some corporations do not consider themselves in full control of the foreign subsidiary and do not include its financial statements in the consolidation. Instead, they recognize as income only the dividends received and show only the purchase price of the investment on the balance sheet.

The exclusion of foreign subsidiaries from the consolidation should be justified by the circumstances of each individual case. A general policy of excluding all foreign subsidiaries may produce misleading financial statements. Corporations with rapidly growing foreign subsidiaries will allow a large fraction of the foreign earnings to remain abroad, while other corporations may be drawing dividends in excess of earnings from their foreign subsidiaries. Hence the dividend is a very poor basis on which to report earnings of foreign subsidiaries. For instance, in its 1966 annual report Eastman Kodak showed investments in and advances to foreign subsidiaries of $70,026,000 and dividend income from these subsidiaries of $16,719,000, indicating an unusually high return on investment. However, a supplementary statement revealed that Eastman Kodak's equity in the assets of its foreign subsidiaries was $329,487,000 and not $70,026,000. Further, its equity in the foreign earnings was $48,793,000, almost thrice the dividend received.[3] If foreign subsidiaries are excluded in consolidation, the consolidated statements should be accompanied by supplementary statements for its foreign and financial subsidiaries. Whether this is done or not, the limitations of the reported earnings per share should be pointed out clearly to investors when foreign operations are significant and the earnings reinvested abroad are material.

The Consolidated Balance Sheet

To illustrate the consolidation process, let us assume that Parent Corporation has just purchased 100 percent of the common stock of Subsidiary Corporation (10,000 shares) at a total price of $400,000. Subsidiary has assets with a book value of $500,000 and liabilities of $100,000. Its owners' equity is thus $400,000, or $40 a share. In other words, the book value of Parent's equity (10,000 shares at $40 per share) is just equal to its cost ($400,000).

Consolidation in this case would be very simple. Subsidiary's $500,000 assets and $100,000 in liabilities would be substituted on the consolidated balance sheet for the $400,000 balance in the parent's investment account. The latter would be canceled out against the subsidiary's owners' equity accounts. To show both the investment

---

[3] This reporting method ended with the 1966 financial statements. In 1967 Eastman Kodak decided to consolidate its foreign subsidiaries; and the asset, sales, expenses, and income figures included the data for these as well as the domestic subsidiaries. The difference between the investment in these subsidiaries "at cost" and on a consolidated basis, $267,239,000, was credited directly to retained earnings. The company used a supplementary statement to show financial data for subsidiaries outside the United States.

and the subsidiary's net assets on the consolidated balance sheet would be double counting.

Consolidation Procedures

The technical process of consolidating the accounts of a parent and its subsidiaries is not accomplished by entries in the ledger accounts of any of the companies. Instead, it is done outside the accounts, in work sheets or their equivalent.

The most widely used work sheet format lists the accounts of parent and subsidiaries in parallel columns, with all like items (e.g., cash in bank) on a single line, followed by two columns for "eliminations." The amounts entered in the elimination columns are those amounts which should not appear on the consolidated statements. The elimination is performed by crediting the accounts having any unwanted debit balances and debiting accounts with redundant credit balances.

Exhibit 15–1 illustrates this format. Because the consolidated balance sheet should show neither the balance shown in Parent's investments account nor Subsidiary's shareholders' equity account balances, these amounts must be "eliminated" in the consolidation. The eliminating entry in this exhibit can also be expressed in conventional journal form:

Exhibit 15–1

PARENT CORPORATION AND SUBSIDIARY

Condensed Consolidated Balance Sheet Work Sheet

| | Parent | Subsidiary | Eliminations | | Consolidated |
			Debits	Credits	
ASSETS					
Investment in Subsidiary....	$ 400,000	. . . . . .		(1) 400,000	. . . . . .
Other assets......	5,000,000	$500,000			$5,500,000
Total Assets...	$5,400,000	$500,000			$5,500,000
EQUITIES					
Liabilities........	$1,000,000	$100,000			$1,100,000
Shareholders' equity:					
Parent........	4,400,000				4,400,000
Subsidiary......		400,000	(1) 400,000		. . . . . .
Total Equities..	$5,400,000	$500,000			$5,500,000

(1)

Shareholders' Equity (Subsidiary)......................400,000
    Investment in Subsidiary (Parent)...................   400,000

The net result is to produce a balance sheet representing the combined assets and equities of the economic entity—the resources of the integrated operation under the common control of the owners of the parent company. In this case the total operating assets amount to $5,500,000, not $5,400,000 as indicated by the balances in the parent company accounts alone.

BASIC CONCEPTS IN CONSOLIDATED BALANCE SHEETS

The issues and techniques in the development of consolidated financial statements are among the most complicated and difficult in the whole field of accounting, and no useful purpose is served by dealing with them in this book. However, to read consolidated statements with an adequate degree of comprehension, some study of the commonly encountered practices is necessary. This section will deal with the balance sheet and the next section with the income statement.

Minority Interests

The foregoing procedure would have to be modified slightly if Parent had purchased less than a 100 percent ownership interest in Subsidiary. For example, if Parent had purchased only 8,000 shares (an 80 percent interest) for $320,000, the equity of the minority shareholders in Subsidiary would have been 20 percent of $400,000, or $80,000. This amount cannot be canceled out against the balance in Parent's investment account.

When minority interests are present, the consolidated balance sheet continues to include *all* of the assets and liabilities of the subsidiary company and lists the minority shareholders' equity as a separate category of ownership equity. The consolidated balance sheet of Parent Corporation and its subsidiary would show the following:

ASSETS		LIABILITIES AND OWNERSHIP	
Investments in nonconsolidated subsidiaries................$	0	Liabilities....................$1,100,000	
		Minority interest in subsidiary..	80,000
Other assets................. 5,580,000		Equity of parent company shareholders.................... 4,400,000	
		Total Liabilities and	
Total Assets..........$5,580,000		Ownership..........$5,580,000	

The asset total is $80,000 greater than in Exhibit 15–1 because in this case minority shareholders have provided some of the financing which in the former case was provided entirely by the parent company shareholders. The parent company only had to use $320,000 to gain control over a corporation with net assets of $400,000.

Consolidation Goodwill

An additional complication is introduced whenever the parent company pays more or less than the book value per share for the common stock of its subsidiary. For example, suppose that Parent Corporation paid $55 a share for 8,000 shares of Subsidiary Corporation. This was $15 a share greater than the book value of these shares on Subsidiary's books at the date of acquisition.

Why might Parent have been willing to pay this premium price? One possible reason is that Subsidiary's accounting practices (e.g., LIFO) may have resulted in an understatement of the current replacement cost of certain tangible assets. Second, Subsidiary's intangible assets, reflected in the earning power of the company as a whole, may have justified a higher price than the tangible assets themselves would have commanded. Finally, Subsidiary's earning power as an integrated unit in Parent's empire may have been in excess of its independent earning power, thus justifying a premium price.

Regardless of the cause, Parent paid $440,000 for its 8,000 shares of Subsidiary's stock, and this was $120,000 more than the book value of the equity acquired (8,000 shares × $15 a share). If the accountants had been able to find objective evidence that specific tangible assets were understated on Subsidiary's books, they could have written these assets up to an appropriate level. Otherwise, the excess of cost over the book value of the underlying equity would ordinarily be treated as an amount paid for Subsidiary's intangible assets. The traditional name for this amount is *consolidation goodwill*, although modern practice leans toward some title such as "investment in subsidiary in excess of equity in tangible assets."

Notice that Parent would record the investment in Subsidiary on its own books at the full cost of $440,000. In the consolidated balance sheet, this would be replaced by the following items:

Assets:

Tangible assets.......................	$500,000
Consolidation goodwill................	120,000
Total Assets......................	$620,000

Liabilities and shareholders' equity:

Liabilities..........................	$100,000	
Minority interest.....................	80,000	
Total Liabilities and Shareholders' Equity.		$180,000

This substitution could be achieved by adding each line across the work sheet after entering the following two eliminating entries:

(1*a*)

Consolidation Goodwill.................................120,000		
Shareholders' Equity (Subsidiary)......................320,000		
Investment in Subsidiary (Parent)...................		440,000

(1*b*)

Shareholders' Equity (Subsidiary)...................... 80,000		
Minority Interest................................		80,000

Intercompany Receivables and Payables

Suppose that prior to the acquisition of stock, Parent had lent $60,000 to Subsidiary. This amount would be shown as an asset on Parent's balance sheet and as a liability on Subsidiary's. The consolidated group as a whole, however, has neither asset nor liability in this amount. The group has no claim on any party outside the group, nor does it have any obligation to make payment to anyone outside the group.

To avoid double counting, in other words, this $60,000 must be subtracted from both the assets and the liabilities. The eliminating entry in this case would be as follows:

(2)

Liabilities (Subsidiary)................................60,000		
Other Assets (Parent).............................		60,000

The final consolidation work sheet would take the form illustrated in Exhibit 15–2. This worksheet differs from the one in Exhibit 15–1 in three ways. First, Parent has only an 80 percent interest in Subsidiary instead of 100 percent. Second, the price paid exceeded the book value of the equity acquired, resulting in the recognition of consolidation goodwill. Third, the amount shown for "other assets" on Parent's balance sheet had been reduced to compensate for the higher price paid for the Subsidiary stock. Parent's asset total is the same as in Exhibit 15–1. Finally, $60,000 has been eliminated from consolidated assets and liabilities in recognition of the intercompany loan in this amount.

Negative Goodwill

A corporation's equity in a controlled subsidiary may have been purchased, of course, at a price per share *less than* the book value of the subsidiary's stock. Sometimes this means that the stock was ob-

Exhibit 15–2

PARENT CORPORATION AND SUBSIDIARY

Condensed Consolidated Balance Sheet Work Sheet

| | Parent | Subsidiary | Eliminations | | Consolidated |
			Debits	Credits	
ASSETS					
Investment in Subsidiary............	$ 440,000	......		(1a) 440,000	......
Other assets.........	4,960,000	$500,000		(2) 60,000	$5,400,000
Consolidation goodwill	....	......	(1a) 120,000		120,000
Total Assets...	$5,400,000	$500,000			$5,520,000
EQUITIES					
Liabilities..........	$1,000,000	$100,000	(2) 60,000		$1,040,000
Shareholders' equity:					
Parent............	4,400,000				4,400,000
Subsidiary........		400,000	{ (1a) 320,000 (1b) 80,000		
Minority interest...				(1b) 80,000	80,000
Total Equities..	$5,400,000	$500,000			$5,520,000

tained at a bargain price, far less than its true worth, but in general the implication must be that the subsidiary's assets are worth less than their book value. Thus, they should be written down to the value indicated by the purchase price.

Whenever sufficient supporting evidence exists, specific assets should be written down. More often, however, the depressed price of the stock is due to the poor earning power of the subsidiary as a whole rather than to any one asset or group of assets. By analogy with the earlier discussion, this should be treated as *negative goodwill*, shown on the asset side as a deduction from the total book value of the tangible assets.

For semantic reasons, the excess of subsidiary book value over parent's cost is more commonly called *consolidation surplus*, or "excess of value over cost of assets in subsidiaries consolidated," and is shown as an element of the consolidated ownership equity. The assumption is that the parent acquired assets for less than their value, which may be true in a certain sense. However, the entire structure of accounting measurement rests on the assumption that exchange price at the time of asset acquisition (acquisition cost) represents a market value consensus which is more objective than the purchaser's calculation of economic value. The purchase price of the subsidiary's stock is a far better approximation of economic value than the unamortized historical cost of the subsidiary's net assets, and therefore whenever consolidation surplus is encountered, it should be treated as a deduction from assets.

Consolidated Retained Earnings

Both companies would of course have more accounts than those shown in the previous exhibits. One pair of accounts of particular interest is the pair of retained earnings accounts. Suppose, for example, that the shareholders' equities of Parent and Subsidiary were divided as follows:

	Parent	*Subsidiary*
Common stock............	$2,000,000	$150,000
Retained earnings...........	2,400,000	250,000
Total................	$4,400,000	$400,000

The eliminating entries would have to be modified as follows:

(1a)

Common Stock (Subsidiary).............................	120,000	
Retained Earnings (Subsidiary).........................	200,000	
Consolidation Goodwill................................	120,000	
Investment in Subsidiary (Parent)....................		440,000

(1b)

Common Stock (Subsidiary)............................	30,000	
Retained Earnings (Subsidiary)........................	50,000	
Minority Interest..................................		80,000

The totals are the same as before; the change is simply in the number of equity accounts affected by the entry.

Notice that this entry completely eliminates the subsidiary's retained earnings. The consolidated retained earnings at the date of acquisition would be $2,400,000—that is, the retained earnings of Parent Corporation only. In other words, the intent is that the retained earnings figure shown on the consolidated balance sheet should represent the earnings accruing to the parent company's shareholders from operations under their control. By purchasing Subsidiary's stock, Parent bought a share of the earnings retained prior to the acquisition, but in no sense did Parent or its shareholders *earn* this amount. Thus consolidated retained earnings represents the retained earnings of the parent company plus the parent's share of any earnings retained by the subsidiary *after* the date of acquisition.

THE CONSOLIDATED INCOME STATEMENT

Income statement consolidation is based on the same principles. The income statement for the parent company alone may have a separate legal significance, but as long as the earnings of the subsidiaries are subject to the parent's control it is the total controlled earnings that parent company investors are interested in.

Technique of Consolidation

To illustrate, Exhibit 15–3 shows the separate income statements of

Exhibit 15–3

PARENT CORPORATION AND SUBSIDIARY CORPORATION

Statements of Income and Dividends for the Year

		Parent		*Subsidiary*
Revenue from sales...................		$7,500,000		$700,000
Revenue from dividends..............		28,000		......
Total Revenue...................		$7,528,000		$700,000
Cost of goods sold..................	$4,700,000		$500,000	
Other expenses.....................	1,900,000		150,000	
Total Expense...................		6,600,000		650,000
Net income........................		$ 928,000		$ 50,000
Dividends declared..................		500,000		35,000
Net Addition to Retained Earnings......		$ 428,000		$ 15,000

Parent Corporation and its subsidiary, Subsidiary Corporation, for the year following the acquisition. Neither company bought any goods or services from the other during the year. Thus all sales were to customers outside the consolidated entity, and consolidated sales revenue, cost of goods sold, and other expenses can be determined simply by adding together the figures for the two companies, without elimination of any kind.

The $28,000 shown on Parent Corporation's statement as revenue from investments is a different matter. This represents dividends received from Subsidiary, and to avoid double counting this amount must be eliminated in the consolidation.[4] The consolidated net income before providing for minority interests, therefore, was as follows:

---

[4] If Parent Corporation took up its full equity in Subsidiary's earnings as its revenue from investments, then the amount shown on its income statement would be 80 percent of $50,000, or $40,000. In that case, this is the amount that would have to be eliminated in the consolidation.

Parent Corporation income. $928,000
Subsidiary Corporation income. 50,000
   Less: Parent Corporation's share in Subsidiary Corporation's
      dividends. . . . . (28,000)
Consolidated Income before Minority Interest. $950,000

The interest of the minority shareholders in Subsidiary's income in
this case amounted to 20 percent of $50,000, or $10,000. The net
income applicable to the Parent Company shareholders was thus
$950,000 less $10,000, or $940,000. This is shown in Exhibit 15–4.

Exhibit 15–4

PARENT CORPORATION AND SUBSIDIARY

Consolidated Income Statement for the Year

Revenue from sales.		$8,200,000
Less: Cost of goods sold.	$5,200,000	
Other expenses.	2,050,000	
Total Expenses.		7,250,000
Income before minority interest.		$ 950,000
Less: Equity of minority shareholders in net income		
of Subsidiary.		10,000
Net Income.		$ 940,000
Dividends declared.		500,000
Net Addition to Retained Earnings.		$ 440,000

Intercompany Sales

The prime motive in the acquisition of another company quite
often is not merely ownership but a full or partial integration of the
operations of the two companies. For instance, a shoe manufacturer
may acquire a chain of shoe stores to assure a market for his products.
The manufacturer's trial balance, therefore, will have sales and receivables that correspond to purchases and payables in the accounts of the
chain. When the two legal entities are consolidated, these *intercompany* transactions become *intrafirm transfers*. Adding the total sales
and cost of goods sold of the two companies to obtain the consolidated sales and cost of goods sold would be like treating every transfer
of merchandise from one department to another within a company as
a sale and purchase.[5] No matter how many sales the two companies
make to each other, the parent company stockholders gain nothing

---

[5] Many companies do in fact treat internal transfers as sales for the purpose of
measuring the profit performance of each of the various divisions or departments of
the company. In preparing company-wide financial statements, however, these internal sales must be canceled out, using techniques identical to those used in preparing
consolidated statements for two or more corporations.

unless sales are made to outsiders as well. In other words, to avoid double counting, all intrafirm sales and purchases, like intrafirm receivables and payables, must be netted out.

For example, assume that a parent company sold merchandise costing $700,000 to its wholly owned subsidiary for $1,000,000. The subsidiary then sold this merchandise to outside customers for $1,200,000. The total gross margin on these sales was $500,000 ($1,200,000 less $700,000), $300,000 on the parent's books and $200,000 on the subsidiary's. The consolidated net income figure was not overstated. Total sales, however, amounted to only $1,200,000, not the $2,200,000 that would be obtained by adding the companies' sales figures together without adjustment. Similarly, the cost of goods sold was only $700,000, not $1,700,000. In this situation, an eliminating entry is required to eliminate the overstatement in both accounts:

```
Sales...........................................1,000,000
    Cost of Goods Sold...........................              1,000,000
```

A more difficult problem is posed by the shoe manufacturer's inventory on the chain's shelves. The manufacturer sold the shoes to the chain and recorded a gross margin on his own books. If the stores and the plant were part of a single corporation, however, the corporation as a whole would recognize no profit on this transaction. The shoes would be transferred to the stores at cost, and the combined manufacturing and retailing profit would be earned by the company only when the stores sold the shoes to consumers.

The interposition of a corporate frontier between these two units makes no fundamental difference in the situation. Any intrafirm profit on inventories of goods must be eliminated in consolidation.[6] For example, if the entire $1,000,000 transfer discussed earlier remained in the subsidiary's inventory at year-end, the eliminating entries would be:

```
Sales (Parent)....................................1,000,000
    Cost of Goods Sold (Parent)...................              700,000
    Inventory (Subsidiary)........................              300,000
```

---

[6] On sales made by a partly owned subsidiary to its parent, the equity of the minority stockholder in the intercorporate profit may not be eliminated. See W. A. Paton and W. A. Paton, Jr., *Corporation Accounts and Statements* (New York: The Macmillan Co., 1955), pp. 685-89. The techniques of consolidation are explored quite thoroughly in this and other advanced accounting texts such as W. B. Meigs, C. E. Johnson, and T. F. Keller, *Advanced Accounting* (New York: McGraw-Hill Book Co., Inc., 1966).

This reduces the inventory to cost and eliminates the $300,000 parent gross margin from consolidated income. If only part of the inventory had been resold, then the eliminating entry would have been somewhere between this one and the one discussed above.

POOLING OF INTERESTS

A very large fraction of acquisitions or mergers in the postwar period have been effected by means of an exchange of stock rather than a transfer of cash. In other words, Subsidiary's stockholders have exchanged their stock for newly issued shares of Parent stock.[7] In most of these cases, the market value of Parent's stock issued in the acquisition has been substantially greater than the book value of Subsidiary's assets.

Until fairly recently, such an acquisition was treated as a purchase on Parent's own books (and in reports to its stockholders). If this is done, the market price of the stock Parent issues is used as the basis of valuing the assets acquired and the excess of this amount over the cost of the assets on Subsidiary's books is debited to a Consolidation Goodwill account. Typically, this goodwill is amortized over a number of years, thus reducing reported income in each year. Further, the goodwill is not recognized as an asset for tax purposes, and thus its subsequent amortization is not recognized as a tax allowed expense. Therefore, the *full* amount of the expense is a deduction from income after taxes. If earnings are not exceptionally high otherwise, the amortization may convert an apparently favorable financial record into a picture embarrassing to management.

Through the concept of *pooling of interests*, a rationalization has been found for treating the acquisition of another corporation by means of exchange of stock on the corporation's reports in the same way as it is treated for tax purposes. It is argued that when two or more corporations pool their interests, their operations are continued in the joint enterprise and the cost of the constituent companies' assets prior to the pooling is the basis for their valuation to the continuing operation.

---

[7] The directors of the two corporations work out an exchange agreement, which is submitted to the stockholders of both corporations for approval. If both groups approve, and if the majority required by state law or corporate bylaws is achieved in the vote by Subsidiary's stockholders, the exchange is binding on all Subsidiary's stockholders. This procedure is subject to slight variation depending on state laws and tax consideration, but the underlying concept is universal.

What this means concretely is illustrated by considering the acquisition by the Amalgamated Company of 100,000 shares of Paltry Corporation stock, a 100 percent ownership interest, in exchange for 200,000 shares of Amalgamated stock. Prior to the acquisition, the ownership equity accounts of the two corporations were as follows:

	Amalgamated	Paltry
Common stock:		
Amalgamated—1,800,000 shares, $5 par......	$ 9,000,000	
Paltry—100,000 shares, $15 par............		$1,500,000
Premium on common stock..................	6,200,000	200,000
Retained earnings........................	13,600,000	1,500,000
Total Owners' Equity.................	$28,800,000	$3,200,000

At the time of the exchange, Amalgamated stock was selling at $25 per share. The 2-for-1 share exchange, therefore, indicated that the purchase price of the Paltry stock was approximately $50 per share. If this transaction had been accounted for as a *purchase*, it would have been recorded in the following entry:

Investment in Paltry..............................5,000,000	
Common Stock..............................	1,000,000
Premium on Common Stock....................	4,000,000

In consolidation, the Investment in Paltry would be replaced by:

Assets of Paltry...................................3,200,000
Consolidation Goodwill..........................1,800,000

The above assumes that Paltry has no liabilities.

Under a pooling of interests, however, the transaction would be accounted for differently in two important ways. First, the book value of Paltry's assets on Paltry's books would be the basis for valuing the stock issued by Amalgamated. Second, the increase in Amalgamated's equity accounts would be distributed between contributed capital and retained earnings in the proportions that existed on Paltry's books. The journal entry is:

Investment in Paltry..............................3,200,000	
Common Stock $5 par value....................	1,000,000
Premium on Common Stock....................	700,000
Retained Earnings............................	1,500,000

The total paid-in capital becomes $16,900,000, just equal to the combined paid-in capital of the two companies prior to the pooling ($15,200,000 + $1,700,000). Similarly, the combined retained earnings is the sum of the retained earnings of the constituent corporations. The distribution of Paltry's paid-in capital between Amalgamated's capital stock and premium is governed by the number and par value of Amalgamated shares issued in the exchange.

Some attempts have been made to define the conditions under which an acquisition may be treated as a pooling of interests and when it must be treated as a purchase.[8] These definitions are phrased in such general terms, however, that it is fair to say that unless the minority interests are material, it is at a corporation's discretion whether to treat the acquisition of another corporation as a purchase or as a pooling of interests.[9] Resolution of this question is extremely important since the balance sheet at the time of acquisition and both financial statements for a period thereafter will differ materially, depending on the method employed in accounting for the combination.

FINANCIAL REPORTING BY CONGLOMERATE COMPANIES

The merits of consolidated financial statements have become so widely recognized in the United States that advocates of reporting on a parent-company-only basis are hard to find.[10] Controversy now focuses on whether, *in addition to* consolidated statements, the so-called "conglomerate" corporation should be required to provide separate financial statements for each of the company's major lines of business.

Nature of the Conglomerate Company

A conglomerate corporation is diversified into a number of product lines which are relatively unrelated with respect to manufacturing facilities and marketing organization. The conglomerate is a recent phenomenon. Until the 1950's, mergers and acquisitions involved firms in related fields of business. For example, a shoe manufacturer might acquire another shoe manufacturer, a chain of retail shoe stores, or a leather tanner. The motive for the acquisition would be the higher profits from large-scale operations, the reduction in competi-

---

[8] Committee on Accounting Procedure, American Institute of Certified Public Accountants, Accounting Research Bulletin No. 48, *Business Combinations* (New York: AICPA, 1957).

[9] For a thorough study of this subject, as well as an account of how the original criteria for recognition of a pooling of interest situation were gradually eroded away, see Arthur R. Wyatt, *A Critical Study of Accounting for Business Combinations,* Accounting Research Study No. 5 (New York: AICPA, 1963).

[10] Not so in Western Europe, where only a minority of companies issue financial statements on a fully consolidated basis.

tion, or vertical integration. The acquisition of a firm in an unrelated line of business was frowned upon because it offered none of the above advantages and it presented difficult and costly problems of management. However, diversification can be a profitable mode of growth, and one corporation may be engaged in such diverse businesses as ocean shipping industrial chemicals, electronic equipment, and consumer food products.

Arguments for More Detailed Disclosure

The basic argument for separate financial statements for each of the major product lines or divisions of a conglomerate corporation is that investors need such information to evaluate the past properly and forecast the future. For instance, a given net income figure combines the results of profitable and unprofitable lines of business. If these are developing at different rates, the outsider will be hard-pressed to identify the component trends on which forecasts of the future need to be based.

A second argument is that diversification has specific benefits as well as costs, and that to evaluate the company's management the investor is entitled to know something about the company's efforts to diversify. As one writer suggests, "It is . . . fair to assume that investors would want to measure both flexibility achieved and its cost in terms of profits foregone in order to avoid undervaluation of their investment."[11]

Difficulties in Product-Line Reporting

Product-line reporting is opposed by some on the grounds that it would disclose information of benefit to competitors, or that disclosure of high rates of profit in certain activities would lead to regulatory pressures from the government or price pressures from customers. Most opposition, however, centers on measurement difficulties, and these must either be solved or circumvented before product-line reporting can become widespread.

Two kinds of measurement difficulties should be noted: (1) difficulties in finding an adequate classification of industries or product lines for which separate reports must be issued; and (2) difficulties in measuring assets, liabilities, and income for individual product lines. On the first of these, Mautz could find no single classification of

---

[11] Leopold Schachner, "Corporate Diversification and Financial Reporting," *The Journal of Accountancy*, April, 1967, pp. 43–50.

industries or activities that could be used as a reporting basis by all diversified companies.[12] After examining the defects of industry classification schemes used by the United States government and by individual companies, he concluded that the classification scheme must be flexible and adaptable to the specific circumstances of each diversified company.

The main problem is that no matter how the company's activities are classified, some financial data are going to be extremely difficult to identify on a divisional basis. If two divisions share a common manufacturing facility or sales organization, allocations of assets and of expenses must be made to obtain separate financial statements. If one division sells part of its output to another, similar allocation problems arise. At the very least, the divisions of a conglomerate have a common top management. As will be seen in Part III, company managements are able to solve these allocation problems for internal reporting and management control purposes. However, using such allocations in published financial statements poses problems of objectivity and verifiability that public and corporate accountants have not resolved to their complete satisfaction.

The scope of this chapter allows only a few observations on the allocation problems raised by divisional statements.[13] First, the Securities and Exchange Commission has long required companies with registered securities to segregate some of their revenues without apparent harm to the corporate well-being. Second, a number of companies have published partial or complete breakdowns of their financial statements on a product-line basis, again without obvious damage.[14] Third, it seems apparent that some form of product-line disclosure is likely to be required by the S.E.C., probably while this edition is still in print.

In all likelihood, it will sooner or later be found possible to allocate a company's financial statement data completely among the various product lines, with allocations based on a broad set of conceptual

---

[12] Robert K. Mautz, "Bases for More Detailed Reporting by Diversified Companies," *Financial Executive*, November, 1967, pp. 52–60.

[13] For an account of the difficulties to be encountered, see A. A. Sommer, Jr., "Conglomerate Disclosure: Friend or Foe?" *Journal of Accountancy*, May, 1967, pp. 61–67 (reprinted from *The Business Lawyer*, January, 1967). For a broader examination of the problems of divisional performance measurement, see David Solomons, *Divisional Performance: Measurement and Control* (New York: Financial Executives Research Foundation, 1965); and Gordon Shillinglaw, *Cost Accounting: Analysis and Control* (rev. ed.; Homewood, Ill.: Richard D. Irwin, Inc., 1967), chap. xxv and xxvi.

[14] For some evidence on these points, see Andrew Barr, "Comments on the Conglomerate Reporting Problem," *Financial Executive*, November, 1967, pp. 39–46; and "New Disclosures Noted in Annual Reports," *Financial Executive*, June, 1967, pp. 68–77.

guidelines. Footnotes to the financial statements would be employed to disclose how the guidelines were applied in the individual case, and the company's public accountants would have to certify to the accuracy of the description.

SUMMARY

Nonfinancial corporations often hold government and commercial securities as a means of earning a return on temporarily idle funds. Securities held for this purpose ordinarily earn relatively low yields but are highly liquid. Called "marketable securities," they are usually listed among the current assets on a cost basis.

The securities held for longer-term investment are mostly common stocks of other corporations. The primary motive is to produce income, and short-term marketability is seldom a consideration. When such investments constitute a majority of the voting power in the other corporation, the holder is referred to as a parent company. Its financial statements will ordinarily represent the consolidated results and position of parent and subsidiary combined. This means, for example, that instead of an "investments" figure on the balance sheet, the assets and liabilities of the subsidiary will be merged with those of the parent.

Some companies are now supplementing their consolidated financial statements by publishing information on the results of individual segments of the business, using geographical, industry, or customer-group breakdowns, as appropriate. This form of disclosure poses a number of measurement problems, but enough attention is being given to it to justify a prediction that some form of segment reporting is likely to become the general rule in the United States within a fairly short period of time.

QUESTIONS AND PROBLEMS

1. Explain the meaning of the term "accounting entity."

2. What is a consolidated financial statement, and what is it intended to reveal?

3. To whom and for what purpose are consolidated financial statements more useful than unconsolidated statements?

4. List and explain the reasons for the more common adjustments required in the preparation of consolidated financial statements.

5. Explain the probable nature and origin of balance sheet items captioned "consolidation goodwill" or "consolidation surplus."

6. How do "inventory profits on intercompany sales" arise and how are they treated in the preparation of consolidated financial statements?

7. What is a "minority interest?" How does it arise? In what part of the balance sheet does it appear?

8. How do "marketable securities" differ from "investments?" To what extent should the accounting treatment of these two items differ?

9. What is the rationale of the "pooling of interests" concept in financial statement consolidation?

10. If conglomerate companies are required to disclose separately the results of individual divisions or activities, should they also be required to prepare and publish consolidated statements? Would these two requirements be consistent with each other?

11. Company P has just acquired all of the assets of Company Q by an exchange of stock. Company Q has achieved a notable rate of growth in recent years, both in sales and in earnings, and its stock has been selling at market prices considerably in excess of its book value. The financial statements of Company P are footnoted to indicate that this acquisition was treated as a pooling of interests.

In what ways would next year's reported net income and the end-of-year balance sheet have differed if the acquisition had been treated as a purchase rather than as a pooling of interests?

12. The board of directors of a U.S. corporation is often self-perpetuating in that the voting stockholders typically elect to the board the slate of candidates proposed by the board. Often the board offers in nomination no one who is not already a member of the board. Under these circumstances a small group of men is able to control a corporation with total shareholdings of only a tiny fraction of the shares outstanding.

a) Company A owns 25 percent of the stock of Company B and its representatives constitute a majority of the board of Company B. Should consolidated financial statements be prepared for these two companies? Give reasons.

b) How, if at all, would your answer differ if Company A owned 51 percent of the stock of Company B? 75 percent? 99 percent?

13. The Merton Company paid $16,000 to its wholly owned subsidiary for certain equipment. This equipment had been carried on the subsidiary's books at its original cost of $31,000, less accumulated depreciation of $17,000.

a) At what amount would the Merton Company show this equipment on its own unconsolidated balance sheet? At what amount would it be shown on the consolidated balance sheet?

b) Show in journal form the eliminating entries, if any, that would be required to prepare consolidated financial statements immediately after this transaction.

14. On December 31, 19x1, the Pilot Company paid $92,000 in cash for an 80 percent interest in the Essex Company. The Essex balance sheet on that date showed the following balances in the shareholders' equity accounts:

Common stock	$ 40,000
Premium on common	20,000
Retained earnings	50,000
Total	$110,000

a) What was the amount of the consolidation goodwill on the date of the purchase?

b) What was the amount of the minority interest on this date?

15. On December 31, 19x5, the Ajax Company purchased 8,000 shares of the common stock of the Achilles Company from John and Alfred Achilles, the majority shareholders. The purchase price was $11 a share, paid in cash. These shares constituted 80 percent of the Achilles Company's outstanding common stock. The Achilles Company balance sheet on that date showed the following balances in its stockholders' equity accounts:

Common stock	$ 60,000
Premium on common stock	10,000
Retained earnings	50,000
Total	$120,000

The Achilles Company had only one asset, the patent rights to a hair-coloring compound, listed on the December 31, 19x5, balance sheet at $120,000. The company had no liabilities on that date.

a) Show how the assets and equities of the Achilles Company would appear on the Ajax Company's consolidated balance sheet on January 1, 19x6, immediately after the purchase.

b) What alternative accounting treatments did you consider? Give your reasons in favor of the treatment you selected.

16. The Homer Company purchased 8,000 shares of the common stock of the Cicero Corporation on December 31, 19x3. The purchase price was $12 a share, paid in cash. These shares constituted 80 percent of the Cicero Corporation's outstanding common stock. Cicero's balance sheet on that date showed the following balances in its shareholders' equity accounts:

Common stock.........................	$ 60,000
Premium on common stock.............	25,000
Retained earnings.....................	35,000
Total........................	$120,000

In 19x4 the Cicero Corporation had net income of $30,000 and paid $20,000 in dividends to its stockholders. The Homer Company's net income for the year amounted to $50,000, including dividends from Cicero. Neither company included any intercompany profit in the inventory it reported at the end of the year.

a) What was the amount of the consolidated net income for 19x4, after providing for minority interests?
b) At what amount would minority interest be shown on the December 31, 19x4, consolidated balance sheet?
c) How much of Cicero's retained earnings would be shown in consolidated retained earnings as of December 31, 19x4?

*17. Among the assets on the December 31, 19x4, balance sheet of the Wolfe Corporation was the following:

Investment in Lamb Company:
    1,000 shares at $90, bought January 1, 19x4.......$90,000

The stockholders' equity section of the balance sheet of the Lamb Company on the same date was as follows:

Capital stock, 1,000 shares..............		$100,000
Deficit, January 1, 19x4................	$20,000	
Less: Operating profit 19x4..........	15,000	
Deficit, December 31, 19x4.............		(5,000)
Total Stockholders' Equity.........		$ 95,000

a) Indicate how the above information would be reflected on a December 31, 19x4, consolidated balance sheet.
b) Show in journal form the entry to eliminate the intercompany investment that would be shown on a consolidated work sheet for 19x4.

*18. Company X purchased an 80 percent interest in Company Y on January 1, 19x2. The price was $80,000, paid in cash, and the purchase was recorded in the Investments account of Company X.

The directors of Company Y declared cash dividends in the amount of $10,000 during 19x2.

When Company X received its share of Company Y's dividends, it debited Cash and credited Dividend Income. Company X's unconsolidated reported earnings for 19x2 amounted to $55,000, including dividend income. No other transactions between Company X and Company Y took place during the year.

---

* Solutions to problems marked with an asterisk (*) are found in Appendix B.

Company X declared cash dividends of $30,000 during 19x2.

The stockholders' equity sections of the beginning and ending balance sheets of the two corporations showed the following:

	Company X		Company Y	
	1/1/62	12/31/62	1/1/62	12/31/62
Common stock...............	$100,000	$100,000	$ 30,000	$ 30,000
Premium on common stock.....	20,000	20,000	10,000	10,000
Retained earnings............	375,000	400,000	60,000	65,000
Total...................	$495,000	$520,000	$100,000	$105,000

a) What was consolidated net income for 19x2?

b) Show the stockholders' equity section of the consolidated balance sheet as of December 31, 19x2.

19. Company P owns 80 percent of the shares of Company S. It carries these shares on its balance sheet at acquisition cost—that is, the price it paid to the previous owners of the shares when it acquired them. This cost was $100,000, and at that time the balance sheet of Company S showed assets of $300,000 and liabilities of $200,000. Company S at that time had 10,000 shares outstanding with a par value of $1 each.

During 19x4, Company P sold half of its output to Company S at a total price of $100,000. The cost of these goods to Company P was $70,-000. One fifth of these goods were in Company S's inventory on December 31, 19x4. The two companies' books showed the following totals for 19x4:

	Company P	Company S
Sales......................	$240,000	$500,000
Cost of goods sold...........	140,000	300,000

a) Did company P pay for goodwill? If so, was it positive or negative goodwill? How much, if anything, did Company P pay for this goodwill? Show your computations and give *one sentence* to explain your answer.

b) Compute consolidated sales and consolidated cost of goods sold for 19x4. Show your calculations.

20. On November 30, 19x3, the Fair Deal Corporation exchanged 10,000 shares of its $5 par common stock for a 100 percent ownership in Strate & Shute, Inc. At that time, Fair Deal stock was selling at a market price of $40 per share; Strate & Shute was a family-owned corporation, and there was no market in its shares. Balance sheets drawn up for the two corporations before the acquisition transaction was consummated showed the following (in summary form):

ASSETS	Fair Deal	Strate & Shute
Assets...........................$1,000,000		$250,000

OWNERS' EQUITY		
Common Stock......................$ 200,000		$100,000
Premium on Common Stock.......... 300,000		70,000
Retained Earnings.................. 500,000		80,000
Total Owners' Equity...........$1,000,000		$250,000

Earnings for the two companies for 19x3 were:

	Fair Deal	Strate & Shute
January 1–November 30.................$120,000		$40,000
December 1–December 31........... 20,000		5,000
Total..........................$140,000		$45,000

There were no intercompany sales during the year. No dividends were declared by either company during the year. A set of consolidated financial statements was prepared at the end of 19x3. Fill in the blanks in the following table:

	If the Acquisition Were Treated—	
	As a Pooling of Interests	As a Purchase
Consolidation goodwill, December 31, 19x3...........	_____	_____
Consolidated retained earnings, December 31, 19x3...........	_____	_____
Minority interest, December 31, 19x3...........	_____	_____
Consolidated net income for the year 19x3..................	_____	_____

21. Below are the balance sheets of the Single and Multiple Product Corporations as of December 31, 19x3:

ASSETS	Single	Multiple
Assets....................................$156,000		$3,400,000

EQUITIES		
Liabilities...............................$ 50,000		$ 650,000
Capital stock, 32,000 shares................ 32,000		
Capital stock, 800,000 shares...............		800,000
Capital contributed in excess of par value...... 17,000		600,000
Retained earnings........................ 57,000		1,350,000
Total Equities.....................$156,000		$3,400,000

At the start of 19x4 Multiple exchanged 20,000 shares of stock for the 32,000 shares of Single. The market price of Multiple's stock was then $9.50 a share.

a) Prepare a post-exchange consolidated balance sheet on the assumption that the acquisition was treated as a purchase.

b) Prepare a post-exchange consolidated balance sheet on the assumption that the acquisition was treated as a pooling of interests.

22. The income statements of Single and Multiple Product Corporation (see Problem 21) for 19x4 prior to consolidation appear below:

	Single	Multiple
Sales......................................	$800,000	$10,000,000
Cost of goods sold.........................	700,000	8,700,000
Operating income..........................	$100,000	$ 1,300,000
Dividend received.........................		40,000
Total Income before Taxes.............	$100,000	$ 1,340,000

a) Present a consolidated income statement on the assumptions:
   (1) That the acquisition was treated as a purchase.
   (2) That consolidation goodwill is amortized equally over seven years.
   (3) That income was taxed at a rate of 50 percent.
b) Present a consolidated income statement for 19x4 on the assumption that the acquisition was treated as a pooling of interests. Income was taxed at a rate of 50 percent.

*23. Prepare a consolidated income statement and balance sheet from the following data relating to the Sumner Corporation and its subsidiary, the Acme Company:

BALANCE SHEETS

AS OF DECEMBER 31, 19x1

	Sumner Corporation	Acme Company
ASSETS		
Cash.....................................	$ 3,450	$ 2,400
Accounts receivable......................	6,500	4,250
Inventory................................	7,100	6,500
Investments..............................	21,000	....
Fixed assets (at net book value).............	15,500	14,850
Total Assets......................	$53,550	$28,000
EQUITIES		
Accounts payable..........................	$ 5,200	$ 1,700
Capital stock (par value $1 per share).........	35,000	20,000
Retained earnings........................	13,350	6,300
Total Equities....................	$53,550	$28,000

INCOME STATEMENTS FOR THE YEAR 19x1

	Sumner Corporation	Acme Company
Sales.....................................	$60,000	$30,000
Cost of goods sold.........................	48,000	19,800
Gross margin.............................	$12,000	$10,200
General expenses.........................	3,400	6,900
Net operating income......................	$ 8,600	$ 3,300
Other income.............................	750	....
Net income...............................	$ 9,350	$ 3,300
Dividends paid............................	5,000	1,000
Undistributed earnings for the year...........	$ 4,350	$ 2,300
Retained earnings, December 31, 19x0.........	9,000	4,000
Retained Earnings, December 31, 19x1........	$13,350	$ 6,300

NOTES:

(1) Of the total sales of the Sumner Corporation, $10,000 were to the Acme Company. The cost to Sumner of the merchandise sold to Acme was $8,000.

(2) The "other income" of $750 recorded by the Sumner Corporation represents dividends received from the Acme Company.

(3) The investments owned by the Sumner Corporation consist of 15,000 shares in the Acme Company purchased on December 31, 19x0.

(4) Of the inventory on hand in the Acme Company at December 31, 19x1, $1,000 represents materials purchased from the Sumner Corporation. The cost of the merchandise to Sumner was $800.

(5) As of December 31, 19x1, the Sumner Corporation has $700 accounts receivable from the Acme Company.

24. The Sutton Company is a wholly owned subsidiary of the Porter Company. The assets, liabilities, and stockholders' equities reported by these two companies as of December 31, 19x9, were as follows:

	Porter Company	Sutton Company
Cash	$ 250,000	$ 130,000
Marketable securities	400,000	150,000
Accounts receivable—customers	1,250,000	540,000
Allowance for doubtful accounts	(25,000)	(10,000)
Accounts receivable—subsidiary	100,000	
Inventories	1,100,000	600,000
Stock of Sutton Company (at cost)	150,000	
Advances to subsidiary	420,000	
Plant, property, and equipment (net)	1,525,000	710,000
Total Assets	$5,170,000	$2,120,000
Accounts payable—trade	$ 575,000	$ 185,000
Accounts payable—parent		90,000
Accrued liabilities	350,000	100,000
Taxes payable	525,000	275,000
Advances from parent		420,000
Capital stock	1,000,000	140,000
Retained earnings, 1/1/x9	2,420,000	835,000
Net income, 19x9	650,000	250,000
Dividends declared, 19x9	(300,000)	(175,000)
Treasury stock	(50,000)	
Total Equities	$5,170,000	$2,120,000

The two companies' income statements for 19x9 showed the following figures:

	Porter Company	Sutton Company
Net sales	$10,000,000	$4,600,000
Other income	250,000	20,000
Cost of goods sold	(6,700,000)	(3,210,000)
Selling, general, and administrative expenses	(2,400,000)	(900,000)
Income taxes for the year	(500,000)	(260,000)
Net Income	$ 650,000	$ 250,000

Further information:

(1) Porter purchased the Sutton stock in 19x1 for $150,000 in cash. As shown on Sutton's books, the book value of Porter's equity at that time was $120,000.

(2) Merchandise in transit from the Porter Company to the Sutton Company on December 31, 19x9, was recorded by Porter as a sale transaction, billed at $10,000. This transaction had not yet been recorded by Sutton.

(3) Sales by Porter to Sutton in 19x9 totaled $1,700,000, including the transaction described in item (2) above. Sutton made no sales to Porter during the year.

(4) Porter's billings for merchandise shipped by Porter to Sutton during the year but not sold by Sutton prior to December 31, 19x9, included an intercompany profit of $20,000.

a) Prepare a consolidated balance sheet as of December 31, 19x9.
b) Prepare a consolidated income statement for the year 19x9.

25. Late in 1967 the Glarus Corporation, a manufacturer of grinding wheels and other abrasive products, accepted an offer of $3 million for the assets of its plastics division. Introduced as the first step in a diversification program some 10 years earlier, the plastics division had never reported a profit and management finally decided to sell.

Opportunities for successful expansion in abrasive products seemed unattractive in 1967, and Glarus invested the proceeds from the sale of the plastics division temporarily in short-term government securities.

In January, 1968, Mr. Theodore Grumek, the company's treasurer, saw an opportunity to invest these funds profitably in the stock of the Urban Corporation, a manufacturer of office copying machines. He sold the short-term government securities for $3 million and used the proceeds to buy 100,000 shares of Urban stock from their former owners. This represented a 10 percent ownership interest in Urban. The book value per common share on Urban's books was $18 a share at that time.

Urban's earnings for 1968 amounted to $3 per common share; cash dividends of $1.20 a share were distributed to Urban's shareholders during the year.

a) As a stockholder in the Glarus Corporation, how much of the Urban Corporation's earnings for 1968 would you want Glarus Corporation to include in its reported net income for the year? Write a letter to the management, giving your reasons for your recommendation. (You may assume that income taxes would be totally unaffected by the choice. You may also assume that all of Urban's income and dividends took place after the date of Glarus's acquisition of the stock.)

b) Should Glarus prepare consolidated financial statements, including the Urban Corporation in the consolidated group?

c) Indicate the amount at which Glarus would report its investment in Urban on its December 31, 1968, balance sheet if it used the equity basis of measurement.

26. Reichhold Chemicals, Inc.'s net income for 1966 included as "other income" a $196,084 gain on the sale of investments in foreign associated companies. The company's annual report for the year showed the following balance sheet items:

	December 31, 1966	December 31, 1965
ASSETS		
Investments in and receivables from foreign associated companies (Note 1)	$4,670,276	$4,669,601
STOCKHOLDERS' EQUITY		
Excess of equity over cost of investments in foreign associated companies (Notes 1 and 6)	1,270,530	1,155,048

From Note 1:

Investments in foreign associated companies are carried at the corporation's equity therein based on underlying book values reflected on the latest available audited or unaudited balance sheets, foreign currency being converted at year-end rates of exchange. Changes in equity in the investment in each company are accounted for through the account "Excess of equity over cost of investments in foreign associated companies," except that changes in equity in the subsidiary when below cost are accounted for in the income statement. The investments in and noncurrent receivables from such companies are summarized as follows:

	Investments		Non-current Receiv-ables	Total Equity and Noncurrent Receivables
	Cost	Equity		
Subsidiary (not consolidated):				
Unlisted security	$ 975,871	$ 708,720	$387,691	$1,096,411
Associates:				
Listed securities (quoted market values $3,133,380)	728,980	2,044,169	......	2,044,169
Unlisted securities	1,538,356	1,493,696	36,000	1,529,696
	$3,243,207	$4,246,585	$423,691	$4,670,276

As investments are sold, the difference between proceeds and average cost (equity in subsidiary when below cost) is credited or charged to income. In 1966, the corporation's share of the net income of the foreign subsidiary amounted to $73,266, and there were no dividends received.

From Note 6:

Excess of Equity over Cost of Investments in Foreign Associated Companies:

```
Balance at January 1, 1966............................$1,155,048
Add: Increase in equity in investments...................  185,821
Deduct: Portion applicable to investments sold...........   70,339
Balance at December 31, 1966........................$1,270,530
```

a) Compare the company's accounting treatment of its investments in foreign associated companies with some other method it might have used. Would your alternative method have led to substantial differences in reported income and balance sheet measurements?

b) Would you recommend any changes in the Reichhold Chemicals' approach? Outline your reasoning.

27. The Radio Corporation of America reported total assets of $2,083,-796,000 at the end of 1967. It operated in a wide variety of fields, including the following:

Radio and television receivers.
Tape recorders and phonographs.
Phonograph records and tapes.
Broadcasting (National Broadcasting Company).
Publishing (Random House).
Vehicle and equipment renting (Hertz).
Computers.
Electronic components.
International communications.
Defense products.
Space research.

The company's consolidated income statements for the years 1966 and 1967 were as follows (in thousands of dollars):

	1967	*1966*
Sales and other income:		
Product sales...............................	$1,751,647	$1,692,415
Broadcasting, product services, communications, and other services.............................	1,262,427	1,186,734
Interest on short-term investments...............	1,084	6,305
Other interest, dividends, and income............	12,058	6,521
Total Sales and Other Income...............	$3,027,216	$2,891,975
Cost of operations:		
Cost of product sales.........................	$1,256,430	$1,248,645
Cost of broadcasting, product services, communications, and other services......................	811,674	775,075
Selling, general, and administrative expenses........	421,270	354,616
Depreciation...............................	150,699	140,911
Rent......................................	46,280	42,002
State, local, foreign, and miscellaneous taxes........	39,492	35,348
Interest on long-term debt......................	29,362	24,044
Total Cost of Operations.....................	$2,755,207	$2,620,641
Profit before federal taxes on income...............	$ 272,009	$ 271,334
Federal taxes on income, less investment credit........	124,500	126,875
Net Profit for Year.............................	$ 147,509	$ 144,459

Further income statement information was contained in the financial summary section of the 1967 annual report to shareholders:

Sales and other income of RCA and its consolidated subsidiaries in 1967 included (dollar amounts in thousands):

		Percent	
	Amount, 1967	1967	1966
Commercial products and services............	$1,441,091	48	47
Broadcasting, publishing, and communications..	675,179	22	22
U.S. government contracts..................	548,278	18	19
Auto rentals and related activities............	362,668	12	12
Total, Including $212,390 from Foreign Sources)........................	$3,027,216	100	100

The ratio of consolidated net profit to sales for the year 1967 was 4.9 percent. The highest ratio of net profit to sales was achieved by the broadcasting, publishing, and communications group, followed by commercial products and services, while the lowest percentage was realized on U.S. government contracts.

The annual report also contained 31 pages of text and photographs commenting on the company's products, its prospects, and its past record. The following quotations are representative, and include all significant information of a quantitative nature presented about individual product lines or groups:

"There was a decline in our government business. This resulted from changes in military spending, which shifted to tactical weaponry, and a cut in appropriations for the nation's space program. Nevertheless, we still maintain a considerable backlog of orders in government projects, and this area accounted for 18 percent of our total sales in 1967. . . .

"By 1975, we expect that RCA and the industry as a whole will have grown far beyond their present technology and business to achieve a new type of enterprise based upon information in all its forms, extending in scope and function to capabilities unattainable by our most advanced systems today. This new information industry is expected to become one of the largest in the national economy, exceeded by few in volume and by none in the extent of its penetration into the pattern of daily life. And so, while we retain our strong roots in the past, we also recognize that RCA will be engaged in the years ahead in enterprises that demand entirely new approaches and different solutions. . . .

"We are engaged in the rent a car business through The Hertz Corporation, the leading concern in the field. The company and its licensees now operate more than 130,000 automobiles and trucks in renting and leasing service through 2,900 locations in 1,800 cities throughout the world. . . . The Hertz Corporation maintained its leadership in the multibillion-dollar renting and leasing business in 1967 by setting a new all-time sales record. . . .

"In 1959, our first active commercial year in the [computer system] business, we shipped equipment with a sales value of $6.8 million. In 1967, we shipped equipment with a record sales value of $230 million. . . .

"The year brought a resurgence of our broadcast-quality tape recorder business, with delivery of approximately 300 color TV tape machines. . . .

"Our subsidiary, RCA Communications, Inc., remains the nation's leading international telegraph carrier. In 1967, the company's sales increased for the 14th successive year, and earnings also were at a record high."

a) As an RCA stockholder, would you support a proposal to require the company to disclose separately the financial results of its various major activities? Would you change in any way the company's present approach to reporting the activities of its various divisions and subsidiaries? Write a letter to the board of directors stating and supporting your views on these questions.

b) As a member of the company's board of directors, what action would you take in response to a request by a number of stockholders to include in future annual reports separate income statements and balance sheets for Hertz, Random House, National Broadcasting Company, RCA Communications, and other major company subdivisions? Explain your reasons.

Chapter 16

ANALYSIS OF FUNDS FLOWS

THE FOCUS in previous chapters has been on two financial statements: the income statement and the balance sheet. Now it is time to turn to the third kind of statement listed in Chapter 8, the *statement of the sources and uses of funds* or *funds statement*.

The funds statement, like the income statement, summarizes the effects of events occurring during a specified period such as one year. But whereas the income statement accounts for one portion of the change in *owners' equity* between two successive balance sheet dates, the funds statement explains the change in the *funds position* during the same period of time. Our purpose in this chapter is to go beyond the rudimentary approach introduced in Chapter 8 to indicate how funds flows differ from income flows and how the funds statement relates to the income statement and balance sheets.

FUNDS AND FUNDS FLOWS

John Prout is a junior executive in a large corporation. His salary is $12,000 a year and he receives dividends and interest on investments of about $1,000 a year. Last year Mr. Prout bought a house for $30,000, paying $10,000 in cash and borrowing the remaining $20,000 from a bank. During the year he received $4,000 from the estate of a great-uncle who had died during the previous year. He spent $12,500 during the year on day-to-day living expenses, including taxes. He also bought a new sports car for $5,500. At the end of the year, the balances in his bank accounts were $11,000 less than they had been at the beginning. All of this information can be summarized succinctly in a funds statement, as shown in Exhibit 16–1.

Uses of Funds Flow Data

This funds statement could serve several purposes. First, it could show Mr. Prout why his bank balance had declined so markedly

Exhibit 16–1

JOHN PROUT

Statement of the Sources and Uses of Funds
For the Year Ending December 31, 19xx

Funds received from:
Income:
Salary..$12,000
Dividends and interest.......................... 1,000 $13,000
Inheritance...   4,000
Bank loan...   20,000
Bank balances from previous years..................   11,000
Total Sources of Funds......................... $48,000

Funds used to:
Purchase house...................................... $30,000
Cover living expenses...............................   12,500
Purchase automobile.................................   5,500
Total Uses of Funds........................... $48,000

during the year. Second, by projecting a similar statement for the following year, Mr. Prout could see whether he was likely to have enough funds to pay for all the things he would like to do. He might wish to buy a boat, for example, or take a foreign vacation, or buy shares of his company's capital stock. A projected funds statement might show him that he could do these things only if another relative died or if he sold investments that he had made to provide for his children's education.

Mr. Prout's banker would also be interested in this statement, particularly if Mr. Prout were to apply for a loan to finance some of his projects for the coming year. The banker might think, for example, that the $5,500 outlay for a sports car in a year in which Mr. Prout bought a new house was evidence of a certain lack of financial discretion, particularly if in the next year Mr. Prout proposed to borrow money to finance the purchase of a new boat and a trip abroad.

In short, the purposes for which statements of the sources and applications of funds for an individual firm might be derived fall into two general groups: internal and external. The outside investor's interest in the flow of funds stems from his need to appraise the company's performance in using the funds that he has invested or might invest in the future. He is interested in the current funds-generating capacity of the normal operations of the business, and in the company's financing policy as indicated by methods of financing employed in the recent past. He wants to know what current and long-term drains on the funds are likely to occur and he needs information on how management has utilized liquid funds in the past.

Management imposes a different set of demands on the funds analysis. Funds statements are employed in establishing and reviewing cash budgets. They enter into the evaluation of alternative financing plans and into long-range forecasts of cash needs and availability. Frequently they are tied into the capital budget by indicating the estimated amounts of funds available for this purpose. These are primarily forward projections rather than historical flow-of-funds statements, but the historical analysis is used as a guide and checking device.

Definition of Funds

In the illustration above, funds were defined implicitly as *cash*. For most individuals, this is the appropriate definition and the funds statement is approximately the same as a statement of the inflows and outflows of *cash*. For most business firms, however, funds are equated with *working capital* or *circulating capital*, the excess of current assets over current liabilities. Current assets were defined earlier as those that can or will be converted into cash during a complete operating cycle of the business. Current liabilities are those that will become due for payment within this same interval. Working capital is thus equivalent to the amount of liquid funds under the company's control.

Other definitions are also possible. One measure is the sum of cash and marketable securities. Another is *net quick assets*, usually defined as cash plus marketable securities plus accounts receivable minus current liabilities. The appropriate measure to use depends in any given case on the nature of the firm's operations and the particular problem under consideration. For example, if funds are defined as cash, then borrowing on a 90-day note provides funds. This is a useful definition as long as the problem is one of planning for the payment of the note at maturity. On the other hand, although short-term funds of this sort might well be used for the temporary expansion of inventories, it obviously would be dangerous to use them for the purchase of production equipment.

If the problem is to examine the amount of funds that will be available more or less indefinitely, then either net quick assets or working capital should be adopted as the measure of funds. When funds are measured in this way, the cash received in the short-term borrowing transaction is offset by an increase in notes payable. The funds statement will show no increase in the funds available for such purposes as the purchase of equipment, which is a true picture of the situation. In general, as long as no significant changes occur in the composition of working capital, the use of a working capital definition of funds will be satisfactory and will also reduce the amount of work required for funds statement preparation.

MEASURING FUNDS FLOWS

The process of funds statement preparation can be divided into two stages: (1) measuring balance sheet changes; and (2) reclassifying these changes on the basis of additional information available from other sources. We shall examine this reclassification process under the following headings:

1. Analysis of changes in owners' equity accounts.
2. Development of a figure representing the amount of funds provided by operations.
3. Analysis of changes in fixed asset accounts.
4. Examination of the connection between depreciation and the flow of funds.
5. Treatment of capital gains.
6. Treatment of adjustments to retained earnings balances.

This section will then end with a short comment on the format of the funds statement.

Measuring Balance Sheet Changes

The first step in funds statement preparation is to tabulate the changes in individual balance sheet items that have occurred between two successive balance sheet dates. This tabulation is the "where got, where gone" statement illustrated in Chapter 8.

For example, the balance sheets of the XYZ Corporation on January 1 and December 31, 19x1, are shown in Exhibit 16–2. This balance sheet has been condensed by subtracting the current liabilities from the current assets to get a single figure identified as *working capital*, the definition of funds in this illustration.

The changes shown in the right-hand column are summarized in the "where got, where gone" statement shown in Exhibit 16–3. This kind of statement can be prepared by classifying the balance sheet changes according to the following scheme:

Sources of Funds	*Uses of Funds*
Increases in liabilities	Decreases in liabilities
Increases in owners' equity	Decreases in owners' equity
Decreases in assets	Increases in assets

Exhibit 16–2

XYZ CORPORATION

Comparative Balance Sheets
January 1 and December 31, 19x1

	January 1	December 31	Increase or (Decrease)
ASSETS			
Working capital.......................	$100,000	$112,000	$ 12,000
Plant and equipment.................	200,000	235,000	35,000
Total Assets.....................	$300,000	$347,000	$ 47,000
LIABILITIES AND OWNERS' EQUITY			
Long-term debt......................	$ 90,000	$ 80,000	$(10,000)
Shareholders' equity.................	210,000	267,000	57,000
Total Liabilities and Owners' Equity..............	$300,000	$347,000	$ 47,000

The changes listed as sources of funds are all *credit* changes—that is, they represent increases in the balances of accounts which have credit balances or decreases in accounts with debit balances. Conversely, the uses of funds are all *debit* changes. Because the balance sheet is the product of double-entry bookkeeping, it follows that the total of the debit changes will equal the total of the credit changes. In other words, total sources and uses of funds will always be identical, by definition.

Exhibit 16–3

XYZ CORPORATION

Statement of Balance Sheet Changes
For the Year Ending December 31, 19x1

Sources of funds:
   Increase in shareholders' equity.................$57,000

Uses of funds:
   Increase in plant and equipment.................$35,000
   Increase in working capital.................... 12,000
   Decrease in long-term debt..................... 10,000
      Total.................................$57,000

Changes in Owners' Equity

The simple statement which represents only the net changes in balance sheet items does not really say very much about the sources and uses of funds. The only unambiguous fact shown is that the amount of working capital on hand increased by $12,000. The other

changes were net changes, the result of offsetting the increases resulting from some transactions against the decreases resulting from others.
In many cases the individual increases and decreases that are hidden
in the overall total may be highly significant.

The $57,000 increase in the shareholders' equity is a case in point.
The detailed owners' equity accounts were as follows:

	January 1	December 31	Increase
Common stock................	$100,000	$155,000	$55,000
Retained earnings.............	110,000	112,000	2,000
Total....................	$210,000	$267,000	$57,000

Some of the additional information needed to explain the changes in
the right-hand column can be found in the statement of changes in
retained earnings:

Retained earnings, January 1................		$110,000
Add: Net income........................		40,000
		$150,000
Less: Cash dividends.....................	$18,000	
Stock dividends.....................	20,000	38,000
Retained Earnings, December 31............		$112,000

In addition, a footnote to the financial statements reveals that the
company issued new shares of its common stock during the year for
$35,000 in cash.

With this information, the $57,000 change in owners' equity can be
restated as follows:

Sources of funds:	
Net income..	$40.000
Sale of stock.......................................	35,000
Total.......................................	$75,000
Uses of funds:	
Cash dividends.....................................	18,000
Net Change..	$57,000

Notice that this summary makes no mention of the stock dividend.
The stock dividend merely represented a transfer from one ownership
equity account to another and was neither a source nor a use of funds.

Funds Provided by Operations

The current operations of the business are the most important
single source of funds. The business ordinarily depends on operating
funds flows to pay its debts, pay dividends, and replace worn-out
equipment. Most companies also use it to finance a good portion of the
assets required for growth.

The relationship between net income and the amount of funds

provided by operations is illustrated in a simple way in Exhibit 16–4. This shows the XYZ Corporation's income statement for 19x1. The upper part summarizes those items which represent current inflows or outflows of funds; the lower part shows items (in this case, only one) which do not represent current flows of funds.

Exhibit 16–4

XYZ CORPORATION

Income Statement
For the Year Ending December 31, 19x1

Sales revenue.....................................$400,000
Expenses representing current outflows of funds......... 349,000
FUNDS PROVIDED BY OPERATIONS.......................$ 51,000
    Less: Depreciation............................... 11,000
Net Income......................................$ 40,000

The amount that should appear on the funds statement as a source of funds, in other words, is $51,000. Recall, however, that in the previous section, net income of $40,000 was shown as a source of funds. Now we can see that this *understated* by $11,000 the amount of funds provided by operations. That is, if the analyst starts with net income as his *first approximation* to the amount of funds provided by operations, he must *add back* such items as depreciation:

Net income........................$40,000
Add: Depreciation.................. 11,000
Funds Provided by Operations........$51,000

Depreciation has to be added back because it represents no current outflow of funds. It is an appropriate deduction in the calculation of net income but not in the calculation of the amount of funds provided by operations.

Purchase and Sale of Fixed Assets

The depreciation adjustment to the funds statement is not difficult to fit into the earlier analysis of balance sheet changes. Recall from Exhibit 16–2 that the Plant and Equipment account balance increased from $200,000 to $235,000 during the year. If depreciation had been the only item affecting this set of accounts, the net balance would have *decreased* by $11,000. That is, to achieve the net increase of $35,000, gross increases in the account must have amounted to $46,000:

Plant and Equipment

Bal. 1/1	200,000	Depreciation for the year	11,000
???	46,000		
		Bal. 12/31	235,000
Bal. 12/31	235,000		

Without further information, the likeliest explanation of this $46,000 change is that it represented purchases of plant and equipment during the year. Fortunately, most company statements provide supplementary information on property changes, so even this figure can be checked. For example, the XYZ Corporation's annual report included the figures shown in Exhibit 16–5. The figure for additions to

Exhibit 16–5

XYZ COMPANY

Statement of Property Changes
For the Year Ending December 31, 19x1

	Gross Property	Allowance for Depreciation	Net Property
Balance, January 1	$290,000	$90,000	$200,000
Additions	50,000	11,000*	39,000
Retirements	(30,000)	(26,000)	(4,000)
Balance, December 31	$310,000	$75,000	$235,000

* Depreciation charge for year shown as expense on income statement.

gross property shows that property purchased during the year amounted to $50,000. From the retirements row we learn that property with an original cost of $30,000 and a net book value of $4,000 was retired during the year.

If no further information on these retirements is provided in the financial statements, the $4,000 can be assumed to approximate the proceeds from the sale of these assets. Gains or losses that are material in amount should be disclosed separately in the financial statements. If no separate disclosure is made, the gains and losses can be assumed to be immaterial.

Suppose, however, that the income statement included the following item:

Loss on sale of equipment....................$1,000

This would mean that the equipment was sold for $1,000 less than its book value—that is, for $3,000. In this case $3,000 would be shown on the funds statement as a source of funds. The $1,000 loss, like depreciation, would have to be *added back to net income* as a component of the funds provided by operations.

Once again, net income understates the amount of funds provided by operations because the loss of $1,000 did not represent an outflow of current funds. A similar treatment would have to be afforded such items as a write-off of a portion of goodwill against current revenues. *Any deduction from revenues which did not represent a current outflow of funds must be added back to net income in order to get a correct statement of the amount of funds provided by operations.*

The original $35,000 increase in the balance in the Plant and Equipment account can now be replaced on the funds statement by the following four items:

	Sources	Uses
Used to acquire plant and equipment................		$50,000
Obtained from sale of plant and equipment.........$ 3,000		
Added to net income in calculating the amount of funds provided by operations:		
Depreciation................................ 11,000		
Loss on sale of equipment..................... 1,000		

Funds provided by operations, in sum, can be reconstructed as follows, starting with the net income figure:

Net income....................................	$40,000
Add: Depreciation.............................	11,000
Loss on sale of plant and equipment.........	1,000
Funds Provided by Operations..................	$52,000

Depreciation Is Not a Source of Funds!

The mechanics of adding depreciation back to net income on the funds statement may lead to the hasty conclusion that depreciation is a source of funds. It must be emphasized most strongly that this is not the case. Funds, if any, come from operations. If no sales are made, then no funds are derived from operations no matter how big the annual depreciation charge. Similarly, although losses must be added back to net income to get a correct measure of the funds provided by operations, these losses are not sources of funds. Depreciation and losses allowed in the computation of taxable income do affect the amount of taxes currently payable, but even here the funds flow is reflected in the tax figure and not in the write-off or amortization of the cost.

The Treatment of Capital Gains

Capital gains need to be treated in just the opposite way from losses. For example, suppose that the annual report discloses that long-term debt with a book value of $10,000 was repurchased at a cost of $9,500 and retired. The transaction was recorded as follows:

```
Long-Term Debt......................................10,000
    Cash...........................................          9,500
    Gain on Debt Retirement........................           500
```

The $500 gain was included in net income for the period.

The $10,000 balance sheet change should now be subdivided into two parts for the funds statement:

```
Funds used to retire debt.......................$ 9,500
Amount to be subtracted from net income in
    computing funds provided by operations.........    500
        Total..................................$10,000
```

The gain must be *subtracted* from net income because it did not represent an inflow of current funds. Net income, once again, is only a first approximation to the amount of funds provided by operations. Just as nonfunds charges deducted in the income computation must be added back, *so must the amount of capital gains and other nonfunds credits be subtracted from net income in calculating funds provided by operations.* Although they are appropriately included in the calculation of net income, they are not a component of operating funds flows.

Adjustments to Retained Earnings

Adjustments representing corrections of figures for prior years are sometimes charged or credited directly to retained earnings. When this is the case, they should not be added back to or subtracted from net income in the calculation of funds provided by operations but should be treated independently.

For example, suppose that a tax refund is received in 19x1 because the company overpaid its taxes in a previous year. The amount was $800, and the credit was made directly to the retained earnings account. This doesn't have to be subtracted from net income because it was never included in net income in the first place. A separate $800 item should be shown on the funds statement as a source of funds.

Or, suppose that a bookkeeping error in calculating depreciation in a prior year was corrected in 19x1 by charging $700 directly against the Retained Earnings account. This doesn't have to be added back to net income because it was not deducted from revenue. In this case, no funds flow occurred and this transaction should not be recorded on the funds statement at all.

Format of the Funds Statement

From all this additional information, the funds statement of the XYZ Corporation for 19x1 shown in Exhibit 16–6 can now be pre-

Exhibit 16–6

XYZ CORPORATION

Statement of the Sources and Uses of Funds
For the Year Ending December 31, 19x1

Sources of funds:
  From operations:

Net income	$40,000
Add: Depreciation	11,000
Loss on sale of plant and equipment	1,000
Total	$52,000
Less: Gain on debt retirement	500
Funds provided by operations	$51,500
From sale of common stock	35,000
From sale of plant and equipment	3,000
Total Sources of Funds..	$89,500

Uses of funds:

To purchase plant and equipment	$50,000
To pay cash dividends	18,000
To retire debt	9,500
To increase working capital	12,000
Total Uses of Funds	$89,500

pared. (To avoid the necessity of correcting earlier figures, the two illustrative adjustments to retained earnings discussed in the last paragraph have not been reflected in this statement.) Notice how much more informative this is than the "where got, where gone" summary of simple balance sheet changes in Exhibit 16–3. This statement identifies funds flows, not balance sheet changes. More detail has been inserted to account for every balance sheet change except the change in working capital, and if desired, this figure can be subdivided to show any significant changes in the composition of working capital.

Even this statement represents a great amount of compression of the transactions that affected the funds reservoir during the year. Each of the items is a summary of a number of transactions affecting that item. It would be possible to break the totals down further, but increases in detail frequently confuse more than they inform. Therefore, care should be exercised to show details only insofar as the details provide additional useful information to management. As the statement now stands, each item, with the exception of net income, summarizes a group of similar effects—that is, purchases of property includes only debits to the property account that arose as a result of purchases, while nonfunds charges include only credits to the property account that arose out of offsetting debits against income. The net income figure could be broken down in similar fashion, but the importance of the net income figure and its position as a summary of the operating results of the firm for the period in question generally make this undesirable.

PREPARING THE FUNDS STATEMENT

The previous illustration was highly simplified to let the basic principles show through clearly. The funds analysis was conducted informally, more or less on the back of an envelope. In simple situations, this procedure is adequate, but in the more common practical case some kind of organized approach is generally necessary to keep the analysis under control; that is (1) to prevent errors, and (2) to discover information that might otherwise go unnoticed.

The Work Sheet Method

All formal methods of statement preparation start with a list of balance sheet changes between two dates. The method used in this chapter is to try to reproduce, in summary form, the journal entries that together produced the changes in balance sheet balances during the period being studied.[1]

In practice, these journal entries would be entered on a columnar work sheet. We shall use, instead, a set of T-accounts because these are ordinarily easier to follow at this stage. A columnar work sheet will then be introduced at the end of the chapter for purposes of summary and comparison.

Exhibit 16–7 shows in T-account form the net changes in the XYZ Corporation's balance sheet accounts during the year. This information was obtained from Exhibits 16–2 and 16–5. Our objective will be to move in a systematic manner from these T-account balances to the corporation's actual sources and uses of funds. The three additional T-accounts—Funds Provided by Operations, Other Sources of Funds, and Uses of Funds—will be used to realize that objective.

---

[1] This method has been ably presented, using more complex examples, by Robert H. Gregory and Edward L. Wallace in two articles, "Solution of Funds Statement Problem: History and Proposed New Method," *Accounting Research*, Vol. III (1952), pp. 99–132; and "Work Sheets for Funds Statement Problems," *The Accounting Review*, January, 1953, pp. 88–97.

Exhibit 16–7

XYZ CORPORATION

T-Account Work Sheet for Funds Statement Preparation
For the Year Ending December 31, 19x1

Working Capital	Long-Term Debt
Net change 12,000	Net change 10,000

Plant and Equipment	Common Stock
Net change 20,000	Net change 55,000

Allowance for Depreciation	Retained Earnings
Net change 15,000	Net change 2,000

Funds Provided by Operations	Other Sources of Funds

Uses of Funds

Reconstructing Transactions

The first item to be entered on the work sheet is the change in working capital. Because this figure is not to be subjected to further analysis, it can be accounted for by a single entry:

(1)

Working Capital...................................12,000
    Uses of Funds....................................   12,000

In other words, working capital increased by $12,000 during the year, and this represented a use of funds. The Working Capital T-account now appears as follows:

Working Capital	
Net change	12,000
(1)	12,000

The amount "below the line" just equals the amount "above the line," indicating that the change in this account has been completely accounted for.

The next account to be examined is the Common Stock account. This showed an increase of $55,000 during the year. Of this amount, $35,000 represented the proceeds from the sale of new shares of stock to outside investors. The entry that would have been made to record this is:

```
Cash.................................................35,000
    Common Stock....................................        35,000
```

The inflow of cash was a source of funds. Therefore, we can restate this entry as follows on the T-account work sheet:

(2)
```
Other Sources of Funds..............................35,000
    Common Stock....................................        35,000
```

In other words, whenever a transaction has increased or decreased the total amount of funds, the work sheet entry is identical to the entry that was made to record the transaction on the company's books, with one slight change: one of the work sheet accounts—Funds Provided by Operations, Other Sources of Funds, or Uses of Funds —is debited or credited instead of the Working Capital account.

The remaining $20,000 increase in the Common Stock account resulted from a stock dividend issued during the year. The entry to record this is:

(3)
```
Retained Earnings...................................20,000
    Common Stock....................................        20,000
```

This transaction had no effect on funds flows and therefore requires no entry in any of the funds change accounts on the work sheet. It was simply a paper transaction, transferring figures from one ownership equity account to another without changing the substance.

These two entries account for the entire change in the Common Stock account balance, so we can move on to another account, Retained Earnings. One change in this account was brought about by the $40,000 net income for the year:

(4)
```
Funds Provided by Operations.........................40,000
    Retained Earnings...............................        40,000
```

Another change was the declaration of cash dividends for the year:

(5)

Retained Earnings...18,000
    Uses of Funds.......................................   18,000

The Retained Earnings account on the work sheet now shows the following:

Retained Earnings

		Net change	2,000
(3) Stock dividend	20,000	(4) Net income	40,000
(5) Cash dividend	18,000		

The three changes recorded in this account fully explain the net change in the account balance, and thus we can once again pass on to the analysis of another account.

It will be recalled that the $10,000 reduction in long-term debt was accomplished by repurchasing bonds at a price of $9,500. The entry to record this would have been:

Long-Term Debt..10,000
    Cash..   9,500
    Gain on Debt Retirement...........................   500

The $9,500 outlay of cash was definitely a use of funds, and thus the work sheet entry is to debit Long-Term Debt and credit Uses of Funds. The appropriate treatment of the $500 gain, on the other hand, is to subtract it from the net income figure in computing the amount of funds provided by operations. Because the net income figure was debited in entry (3) to the Funds Provided by Operations work sheet account, the $500 gain should be credited to that account. The composite work sheet entry is thus:

(6)

Long-Term Debt..10,000
    Uses of Funds......................................   9,500
    Funds Provided by Operations......................   500

This leaves only the fixed asset accounts to be analyzed. The next worksheet entry records the purchase of plant and equipment during the year:

(7)

Plant and Equipment....................................50,000
    Uses of Funds......................................   50,000

The second entry records depreciation:

(8)

```
Funds Provided by Operations..........................11,000
    Allowance for Depreciation........................         11,000
```

(Remember again that the depreciation amount is placed in the Funds Provided by Operations account as an adjustment to net income—it is not a source of funds in its own right.)

Finally, the compound entry that would have been made to record the retirement and sale of plant and equipment during the year is:

```
Cash...............................................  3,000
Loss on Sale of Plant and Equipment.....................  1,000
Allowance for Depreciation............................26,000
    Plant and Equipment...............................         30,000
```

On the funds statement work sheet this would appear as:

(9)

```
Other Sources of Funds...............................  3,000
Funds Provided by Operations..........................  1,000
Allowance for Depreciation............................26,000
    Plant and Equipment...............................         30,000
```

The Completed Work Sheet

This completes the analysis. The T-account work sheet now appears as in Exhibit 16–8. Notice that for each of the original accounts the sum of the entries below the line is equal to the net change in the account balance shown in the upper part of the account. The other three accounts contain all the items that will go into the funds statement itself. The funds statement that was given earlier in Exhibit 16–6 is simply a formal presentation of the amounts shown in these three analytical accounts.

The Columnar Work Sheet

Exactly the same result can be achieved by using a columnar work sheet instead of T-accounts. Although other formats are possible, Exhibit 16–9 illustrates a six-column work sheet. The first and last pairs of columns show the beginning and ending balance sheets. The two middle columns are used to reconstruct the year's transactions. The objective is to accumulate debits and credits in each row of the middle pair of columns until the change from the beginning to the end of the year is accounted for.

Just as in the work sheet used in Chapter 6, each line on this work sheet represents a T-account. The figures are spread out horizontally instead of vertically. The two credit changes in the "Transactions" columns of the Common Stock account, for example, would appear in

Exhibit 16–8

XYZ CORPORATION

Completed Funds Statement Work Sheet
For the Year Ending December 31, 19x1

Working Capital		Long-Term Debt	
Net change 12,000		Net change 10,000	
(1) 12,000		(6) 10,000	

Plant and Equipment		Common Stock	
Net change 20,000			Net change 55,000
(7) 50,000	(9) 30,000		(2) 35,000
			(3) 20,000

Allowance for Depreciation		Retained Earnings	
Net change 15,000			Net change 2,000
(9) 26,000	(8) 11,000	(3) 20,000	(4) 40,000
		(5) 18,000	

Funds Provided by Operations		Other Sources of Funds	
(4) Income 40,000	(6) Gain on	(2) Sale of	
(8) Depre-	debt	stock 35,000	
ciation 11,000	retire-	(9) Sale of	
(9) Loss on	ment 500	equip-	
sale of		ment 3,000	
equip-			
ment 1,000			

Uses of Funds

(1) Increase working capital	12,000
(5) Dividends	18,000
(6) Debt retirement	9,500
(7) Equipment purchases	50,000

a T-account under the opening balance. The closing balance in the account would also appear in the right-hand column of the T-account as the opening balance for the next accounting period.

The items that were entered in the three funds flow accounts on the T-account work sheet are segregated in the lower portion of the columnar work sheet. The figures shown in this section can then be used directly as the basis for the funds statement.

Exhibit 16–9

XYZ CORPORATION

Columnar Funds Statement Work Sheet
For the Year Ending December 31, 19x1

	Balance, January 1		Transactions		Balance, December 31	
	Debit	Credit	Debit	Credit	Debit	Credit
Working capital.....................	100,000		(1) 12,000		112,000	
Plant and equipment.................	290,000		(7) 50,000	(9) 30,000	310,000	
Allowance for depreciation...........		90,000	(9) 26,000	(8) 11,000		75,000
Long-term debt.....................		90,000	(6) 10,000			80,000
Common stock.....................		100,000		(2) 35,000 (3) 20,000		155,000
Retained earnings..................		110,000	(3) 20,000 (5) 18,000	(4) 40,000		112,000

Funds provided by operations:
  Income........................
  Gain on debt retirement..........
  Depreciation.....................
  Loss on sale of equipment.........
			(4) 40,000
			
			(8) 11,000
			(9) 1,000
				(6) 500		

Other sources of funds:
  Sale of stock.....................
  Sale of equipment................
			(2) 35,000
			(9) 3,000			

Uses of funds:
  Increased working capital.........
  Dividends.......................
  Debt retirement.................
  Equipment purchases.............
				(1) 12,000
				(5) 18,000
				(6) 9,500
				(7) 50,000		

Total.......................	390,000	390,000	226,000	226,000	422,000	422,000

Analytical Rules

The methods described in this chapter can be applied to any set of financial statements. Although information is not always as readily available as in this simple example, a few general rules may help to keep the analysis in focus. Different rules apply to transactions in each of the following three classes:

1. Those affecting funds accounts only (in this case, current assets and current liabilities).
2. Those affecting both funds accounts and other accounts.
3. Those affecting nonfunds accounts only.

Transactions of the first type do not affect the funds position. For example, the use of cash to purchase marketable securities neither uses nor provides funds as the term has been defined in this particular case. (If funds were defined as cash, then of course the purchase of marketable securities would be a use of funds.)

Transactions of the second class should always be reflected in the funds statement. For example, when XYZ Corporation bought equipment for cash or on accounts payable during the year, the transaction led to a reduction in working capital (funds) and an increase in a nonfunds account (equipment).

Only the transactions in the third category offer any conceptual difficulty. These may or may not be included in the funds statement, depending on the analyst's interpretation of the facts. For example, a stock dividend should not appear on the funds statement, for the reasons cited earlier. If the company had acquired property in exchange for shares of the company's own stock, on the other hand, this should be treated as two transactions of the second type: a purchase of property (use of funds) and a sale of stock (source of funds).[2]

SUMMARY

Although net income is rightly regarded as the only generally valid summary measure of the results of the firm's operations, limited only by our inability to measure the future effects of current actions, it is sometimes more important to measure the flow of funds. Failure to understand the distinction between these two concepts has placed more than one inexperienced businessman in financial difficulties. Young growth companies, in particular, often find great difficulty in meeting their needs for investment funds despite satisfactory and rapidly growing reported earnings. For these and older companies as well, the amounts of available funds devoted to dividends, property additions, and debt retirement are important pieces of information for the evaluation of the firms' financial management, and for future planning by the management.

In response to these needs, accountants have developed the flow-of-funds statement, and more and more companies are including such statements as an integral part of their annual financial summaries. In this chapter, an explanation of the concept has been attempted and a model provided that the beginner can use in preparing funds statements for himself. Just which method is used to derive funds statements is of considerably less importance, however, than the concept itself and its application. The student should not become so entwined in work sheet mechanics that he loses sight of the end product he is trying to obtain.

---

[2] Vigorous support for this treatment can be found in Perry Mason, "*Cash Flow*" *Analysis and the Funds Statement,* Accounting Research Study No. 2 (New York: AICPA, 1962); for another examination of funds statements and funds flow reporting, see Leonard E. Morrissey, Jr., *Contemporary Accounting Problems* (Englewood Cliffs, N.J.: Prentice-Hall, Inc., 1963), chap. 4.

QUESTIONS AND PROBLEMS

1. Explain the nature and functions of a funds statement.

2. Describe and explain some of the important differences between revenues and expenses, on the one hand, and sources and uses of funds, on the other.

3. Explain in detail what differences may be expected in a funds statement depending on whether funds are defined as: (*a*) working capital, (*b*) net quick assets, or (*c*) cash.

4. "You can't pay your creditors with 'funds.' The only sensible solution, therefore, is to use cash as your definition of funds." For what purpose or purposes does the author of this comment probably use funds statements? Explain.

5. Why may it be reasonable to assume that there has been no gain or loss on the retirement of capital assets in the absence of statement evidence to the contrary?

6. The following comment appeared in an annual report: "Funds provided by depreciation were adequate to finance only 50 percent of our purchases of plant and equipment during the year. Earnings for the year were inadequate to finance the balance and so your company was forced to resort to borrowing." In what sense were funds provided by depreciation?

7. Explain the effect of each of the following on the company's funds position ("funds" is defined as working capital):
a) Receipt of dividends from a consolidated subsidiary.
b) Write-off of an uncollectible account against the allowance provided.
c) A stock split.
d) A stock dividend.
e) Purchase of treasury stock.
f) Write-off of goodwill against retained earnings.
g) Sale of machinery subject to group depreciation.

8. In what sense can a loss be a source of funds? Where should such losses appear in the funds statement?

9. A newspaper headline some years ago read: "Company Borrows $200 Million to Pay Income Taxes." Explain the company's action in the face of the fact that taxes are levied only on income and income typically provides funds.

10. The Tanker Corporation has financed the acquisition of a fleet of tankers which cost $10,000,000 by means of a 10-year, 6% bond issue. The bonds are to be retired by lot at the rate of 10 percent a year. The president of the company asks why depreciation must be charged on the tankers, which have an expected life of 15 years, in view of the provision for retiring the debt. The company uses the sum-of-digits method to charge depreciation.

Write a memo to the president which explains the interrelation of the operating and financial consequences of the tanker acquisition.

11. The Fine Tobacco Corporation's annual report states that due to a decline in the market price of tobacco the corporation's year-end inventory was written down from $92,000 to $87,000. This write-down was charged to a Reserve for Inventory Price Fluctuations, a subdivision or appropriation of retained earnings.

a) With cash the definition of funds, how would this transaction be reflected in the funds statement?

b) How would your answer change if funds were defined as working capital? Explain.

c) How would you change your answers to (a) and (b) if the write-down had been charged against current revenues?

*12. The Hansard Corporation annual report for 19x1 shows the following account balances:

	19x1	19x0
Investment in other companies	$ 56,000	$ 68,000
Retained earnings	135,000	114,000

A note to the statements reports that the corporation sold its 40 percent interest in the Hamburg Corporation for $47,000. There was a gain of $27,000 on the transaction, and it was credited directly to retained earnings.

What were the sources and uses of funds arising out of transactions in investments in other companies?

13. Below are certain account balances from the Placque Corporation's financial statements:

BALANCE SHEET

	19x3	19x2
Plant and equipment	$8,900	$8,500
Allowance for depreciation	3,600	3,300

INCOME STATEMENT

Depreciation expense	$ 900
Loss on retirements	400

---

* Solutions to problems marked with an asterisk (*) are found in Appendix B.

A note to the statement reports that property with an original cost of $1,300 and accumulated depreciation of $600 was sold during 19x3 for $300.

a) What sources or uses of funds were connected with transactions in plant and equipment during the year?

b) Present and explain work sheet entries to account for the changes in the Plant and Equipment account.

*14. A stockholder of the Revolving Dollar Company is alarmed when he finds from the company reports that bank deposits have remained about the same in spite of profits of $16,211,410 during the year and dividends of only $3,000,000. The facts appear as follows in the annual report:

ASSETS	December 31 This Year	December 31 Last Year
Cash..	$ 2,271,876	$ 2,309,929
Marketable securities.........................	4,000,000	3,200,000
Accounts receivable..........................	6,161,539	8,376,036
Inventories.................................	22,769,013	16,670,371
Equipment, land, fixtures, etc. (net)...........	26,725,711	22,286,333
Total Assets..........................	$61,928,139	$52,842,669

LIABILITIES		
Accounts, notes, and taxes payable.............	$ 5,324,072	$ 9,450,012
Bonds outstanding...........................	None	None
Net Assets...........................	$56,604,067	$43,392,657

Depreciation for the year amounted to $5,447,120; no capital assets were sold or scrapped.

Explain to the stockholder how all of the year's dollars were spent.

15. In May, 1968, an investor was studying the desirability of purchasing shares of Marshall Company common stock. The relationship between earnings and market price seemed reasonable and growth prospects seemed good, both for the company and for its industry. A friend suggested that the investor study the company's funds flows before deciding whether to buy the stock, and pointed out the following comparative funds statement in the company's 1967 annual report:

	1967	1966
Sources:		
Net income.........................	$ 3,500,000	$3,000,000
Depreciation........................	2,300,000	2,000,000
Sale of 5% debentures.................	......	2,500,000
Sale of 7% convertible preferred.........	1,500,000	......
Other sources (net)....................	100,000	200,000
Total Sources of Funds...............	$ 7,400,000	$7,700,000
Uses:		
Plant additions.......................	$ 4,900,000	$5,500,000
Dividends...........................	2,000,000	2,000,000
Purchase of stock in Franklin Company...	2,200,000	......
Total Uses of Funds.................	$ 9,100,000	$7,500,000
Increase (Decrease) in Working Capital....	$(1,700,000)	$ 200,000

On February 15, 1968, the board of directors voted the regular quarterly cash dividend of $500,000. On April 1, 1968, the president of the Marshall Company announced plans to sell several buildings to the Federal Leasing Company and lease them back on long-term leases. Plans to double production capacity in the next five years were announced at the same time. An announcement on the method of financing to be used was to be made shortly.

In what way, if any, would this information have helped the investor to make his decision? Would he have been more likely or less likely to buy the stock as a result of an informed analysis of this information? Support your opinion with figures drawn from the problem.

16. The Arkville Transit Company operates a network of bus lines in a small city. Last year it reported a small operating loss, and earnings are unlikely to improve in the near future. The following income statement for last year is likely to be typical of those to be prepared for the next few years:

Fares and other revenues....................		$1,000,000
Expenses:		
Salaries and wages.......................	$650,000	
Fuel and lubricants.......................	170,000	
Depreciation............................	100,000	
Tires and batteries.......................	20,000	
Repair parts............................	30,000	
Other expenses.........................	40,000	
Total Expenses.....................		1,010,000
Net Income (Loss).......................		$ (10,000)

The company's balance sheet showed the following amounts at the beginning and end of last year:

	Beginning of Year	End of Year
ASSETS		
Current assets...........................	$ 300,000	$ 290,000
Plant and equipment (net)................	940,000	920,000
Total Assets....................	$1,240,000	$1,210,000
LIABILITIES AND STOCKHOLDERS' EQUITY		
Current liabilities........................	$ 70,000	$ 150,000
Bonds payable..........................	100,000	......
Common stock..........................	260,000	260,000
Retained earnings.......................	810,000	800,000
Total Liabilities and Stockholders' Equity......................	$1,240,000	$1,210,000

Mr. John Bergson recently bought an 80 percent interest in this company for $200,000. When shown the income statement above, he replied, "Good! That's just what I'd hoped for."

Mr. Bergson is a professional investor, not given to letting sentiment or emotion affect his investment decisions. Furthermore, he has little time to devote to active participation in the management of the companies he invests in.

a) How did he probably justify his decision to invest in the Arkville Transit Company?
b) What plans does he probably have for his investment in Arkville Transit? How do these plans differ from the actions of the previous owners? Do you think that he is likely to achieve his objectives? Support your answers with figures from the problem.

*17. The following information was taken from an annual report of the Woven Hose and Rubber Company for the fiscal year ended August 31 (all figures are in thousands of dollars):

BALANCE SHEET

		August 31 This Year		August 31 Last Year
ASSETS				
Current Assets:				
Cash......................................		$ 883		$ 954
U.S. government securities.....................		1,222		1,704
Accounts receivable........................$1,504			$1,553	
Allowance for uncollectible accounts............. 119		1,385	115	1,438
Inventories....................................		1,946		2,651
Total Current Assets.....................		$5,436		$ 6,747
Long-Life Assets (at Cost):				
Land..		$ 295		$ 295
Buildings, machinery, and equipment............$6,610			$5,998	
Allowances for depreciation.................... 2,685		3,925	2,410	3,588
Prepaid expenses.............................		170		88
Total Long-Life Assets....................		$4,390		$ 3,971
Total Assets.........................		$9,826		$10,718

	August 31 This Year	August 31 Last Year
EQUITIES		
Current Liabilities:		
Accounts payable...........................	$ 505	$ 609
Accrued taxes..............................	556	896
Total Current Liabilities..................	$1,061	$ 1,505
Long-Term Liabilities:		
Mortgage..................................	1,000	1,500
Total Liabilities	$2,061	$ 3,005
Stockholders' Equity:		
Capital stock..............................	7,000	7,000
Retained earnings..........................	765	713
Total Equities........................	$9,826	$10,718

STATEMENT OF INCOME AND RETAINED EARNINGS
FOR THE YEAR ENDED AUGUST 31

Net sales...		$13,380
Less: Cost of goods sold..............................	$10,880	
Selling and administrative expenses...................	1,623	
Income taxes.................................	367	
Total Expense*.............................		12,870
Net income..		$ 510
Retained earnings, beginning of year...................		713
		$ 1,223
Less: Dividends declared..............................	$ 300	
Loss on sale of plant assets.........................	158	458
Retained Earnings, End of Year.......................		$ 765

* Includes depreciation, $350 thousands.

SCHEDULE OF CHANGES IN PLANT ASSET ACCOUNTS

	August 31 Last Year	Increase	Decrease	August 31 This Year
Cost.........................	$5,998	$894 (additions)	$282*	$6,610
Allowance for depreciation.....	2,410	350 (depreciation)	75*	2,685
Balance......................	$3,588			$3,925

* Sale of plant assets.

Prepare a statement of sources and applications of funds for the year. Funds should be defined as cash and marketable securities.

18. The Sandwich Company showed the following post-closing account balances at the end of the years 19x2 and 19x3:

	December 31, 19x2		December 31, 19x3	
	Debit	*Credit*	*Debit*	*Credit*
Current assets.........................	$400		$460	
Investments...........................	100		60	
Plant and equipment (net)..............	330		380	
Unamortized bond discount.............	5		...	
Current liabilities......................		$200		$290
Bonds payable........................		100		...
Reserve for contingencies..............		...		40
Common stock........................		200		220
Additional paid-in capital..............		50		60
Retained earnings.....................		285		290
Total...........................	$835	$835	$900	$900

The Retained Earnings account for the year 19x3 showed the following transactions:

Retained Earnings

Loss on bond retirement	10	Gain on sales of equipment	15
Stock dividend	30	Net income	130
Cash dividend	60		
Appropriation for contingencies	40		

Bonds payable were retired on January 1, 19x3. Investments with a book value of $40 were sold during the year for $57.

The declaration of a 10 percent stock dividend was recorded by transferring $20 to the Common Stock account and $10 to Additional Paid-In Capital.

Land and equipment that had a book value of $112 was sold for $127. Expenditures for additions to plant and equipment amounted to $208 during the year. Depreciation recorded for the year was $46.

Prepare a statement of the sources and applications of funds, distinguishing among (a) funds provided by operations, (b) funds provided from other sources, and (c) applications of funds. *Define "funds" as net working capital.*

19. The Traydown Corporation's financial position went from bad to worse during 1968, although net reported income showed a satisfactory increase over that of prior years. Despite the company's negotiation of a $100,000 bank loan early in 1968, the cash balance decreased to a dangerous point by the end of the year. The balance sheets showed the following:

TRAYDOWN CORPORATION

COMPARATIVE BALANCE SHEET

(Thousands of Dollars)

	December 31, 1967	December 31, 1968
ASSETS		
Current Assets:		
Cash	$ 50	$ 30
Receivables	200	220
Inventories	150	200
Total Current Assets	$400	$450
Buildings and fixtures	$300	$280
Less: Allowance for depreciation	(90)	(70)
Net Buildings and Fixtures	$210	$210
Total Assets	$610	$660
LIABILITIES AND STOCKHOLDERS' EQUITY		
Current Liabilities:		
Accounts and wages payable	$200	$180
Bank loan payable	50	150
Total Current Liabilities	$250	$330
Mortgage payable	100	90
Total Liabilities	$350	$420
Shareholders' Equity:		
Common stock (par)	$140	$130
Retained earnings	120	110
Total Stockholders' Equity	$260	$240
Total Equities	$610	$660

NOTES (All figures are in thousands of dollars):
(1) Net income for 1968 was $30.
(2) Total sales were approximately the same in 1968 as in 1967.
(3) A building with an original cost of $50 and accumulated depreciation of $30 was sold for $56, cash.
(4) Depreciation for the year was $10.
(5) Cash dividends paid were $24.
(6) One stockholder sold his common stock back to the company for $26, cash. The par value of this stock was $10, and the remaining $16 of the repurchase price was charged to retained earnings.

a) From the information provided below, prepare a statement of sources and uses of funds for 1968. Define funds as *cash*.

b) Prepare a brief report, addressed to the loan officer of the company's bank, commenting on any items in your funds statement that you think would help him reach a decision on renewing or increasing the size of his loan to the company.

c) Would working capital have been better than cash as a measure of funds in this instance? Explain your answer.

*20. From the following data, prepare a statement of the sources and applications of funds from a corporation's annual report for the year. All balance sheet figures are in thousands of dollars.

CONDENSED COMPARATIVE BALANCE SHEETS

	Last Year	This Year
Current assets	$56,746	$ 77,091
Investments in associated companies, at cost	.....	1,005
Property, plant, and equipment, at cost	31,414	49,096
Allowances for depreciation	(13,237)	(18,421)
Total Assets	$74,923	$108,771
Current liabilities	$42,536	$ 48,898
Payable to General Tile and Rubber Co.	.....	7,000
Total Liabilities	$42,536	$ 55,898
Preferred stock	1,347	1,123
Common stock, at par ($1 per share)	4,317	4,492
Capital surplus	7,179	19,551
Earned surplus	19,544	27,707
Total Equities	$74,923	$108,771

Additional information:
(1) Sale of common stock during the year, 175,000 shares.
(2) Net income for the year, $8,203,000.
(3) Preferred dividends paid, $40,000.
(4) Depreciation and amortization for the year, $5,501,000.
(5) Property, plant and equipment acquired during the year, $18,082,000.

21. The net changes in the balance sheet accounts of X Company for the year 19x0 are shown below:

	Debit	Credit
Investments...........................		$25,000
Land.....................................	$ 3,200	
Buildings.............................	35,000	
Machinery............................	6,000	
Office equipment......................		1,500
Allowance for depreciation:		
Buildings............................		2,000
Machinery............................		900
Office equipment......................	600	
Discount on bonds......................	2,000	
Bonds payable.........................		40,000
Capital stock—preferred................	10,000	
Capital stock—common.................		12,400
Premium on common stock...............		5,600
Retained earnings......................		6,800
Working capital........................	37,400	
Total............................	$94,200	$94,200

Additional information:

(1) Cash dividends of $18,000 were declared December 15, 19x0, payable January 15, 19x1. A 2 percent stock dividend on the common stock was issued March 31, 19x0, when the market value was $12.50 per share.

(2) The investments were sold for $27,500.

(3) A building which cost $45,000 and had a depreciated basis of $40,500 was sold for $50,000.

(4) The following entry was made to record an exchange of an old machine for a new one:

```
Machinery........................................13,000
Allowance for depreciation—Machinery..............5,000
     Machinery..........................................     7,000
     Cash...............................................    11,000
```

(5) A fully depreciated office machine which cost $1,500 was written off.

(6) Preferred stock of $10,000 par value was redeemed for $10,200.

(7) The company sold 1,000 shares of its common stock (par value $10) on June 15, 19x0, for $15 a share. There were 13,240 shares outstanding on December 31, 19x0.

Prepare a statement of the sources and applications of funds for the year 19x0.

(AICPA Adapted)

22. The Apex Company's financial statements for 1968 showed the following (all figures are in thousands of dollars):

BALANCE SHEETS

	December 31, 1968	December 31, 1967
ASSETS		
Current Assets:		
Cash	$ 2,133	$ 2,250
Accounts receivable, net	1,382	1,064
Inventories	1,179	936
Total Current Assets	$ 4,694	$ 4,250
Long-Term Assets:		
Land	273	198
Buildings, machinery, and equipment	6,700	6,750
Less: Allowance for depreciation	(2,270)	(2,000)
Investments in subsidiaries	3,018	3,002
Goodwill	90	100
Total Assets	$12,505	$12,300
LIABILITIES AND SHAREOWNERS' EQUITY		
Current Liabilities:		
Accounts payable	$ 1,080	$ 2,350
Taxes payable	550	650
Dividends payable	350	....
Total Current Liabilities	$ 1,980	$ 3,000
Long-Term Liabilities:		
Bonds payable	1,000	....
Bond premium	72	....
Provision for pensions	150	150
Provision for deferred income taxes	110	90
Total Liabilities	$ 3,312	$ 3,240
Shareowners' Equity:		
Common stock, at par	1,510	1,500
Premium on common stock	2,000	1,910
Appropriation for contingencies	400	300
Retained earnings	5,283	5,350
Total Liabilities and Shareowners' Equity	$12,505	$12,300

INCOME STATEMENT
FOR THE YEAR ENDED DECEMBER 31, 1968

Sales		$ 9,880
Income from unconsolidated subsidiaries		206
Total		$10,086
Less: Cost of goods sold	$ 7,484	
Selling and administrative expenses	1,843	
Amortization of goodwill	10	
Interest expense	27	
Taxes on ordinary income	354	
Total Deductions		9,718
Income before special item		$ 368
Add special item:		
Gain on sale of land, less applicable income taxes		15
Net Income		$ 383

Notes to financial statements:

(1) All the company's subsidiaries were located in the United States. Income on investments in unconsolidated subsidiaries was recognized on an equity basis.

(2) Expenses for the year included depreciation in the amount of $496 thousands. The Apex Company used the group depreciation method on almost all of its depreciable assets.

(3) The only dividend declared during the year on Apex common stock was the cash dividend declared during December and payable on January 20, 1969.

(4) Buildings, equipment, and machinery purchased in 1968 cost $246 thousands.

(5) The Apex Company issued stock during the year in exchange for land. No other common stock transactions occurred during the year.

(6) Bonds were issued on July 1, 1968, with a 6% coupon rate—interest expense therefore was for the period July 1 to December 31 only.

a) Prepare a statement of the sources and uses of funds for the year 1968. Use working capital as your definition of funds.

b) How would your statement have differed if you had defined funds as cash? In your opinion, would such a definition have led to a more informative statement in this case? Give your reasons.

23. The Mastik Company was incorporated in 1962 by two young electronics engineers, Frank Orsini and Robert Newman, to manufacture and market a new electronic relay that they had developed. The initial share capital consisted of 10,000 shares, divided equally between the two founders. Each of the men paid the company $10,000 in cash for his shares. An additional block of 2,000 shares was issued in 1964 to a friend of the two men. The issue price of these shares was $5 a share.

The company's first product was highly successful, and in 1964 operations were transferred to a larger building which the company leased for five years. Purchase of additional equipment at that time was financed by a five-year loan from an equipment finance company. This same company also granted loans for equipment purchased in subsequent years.

Mastik's sales continued to grow at a rapid rate as new products and services were introduced. Net income grew even faster, as shown in the following table:

	1965	1966	1967
Sales..	$194,000	$318,000	$390,000
Expenses:			
Wages and salaries.....................	$ 87,000	$178,000	$191,000
Materials and supplies..................	58,000	75,000	94,000
Rent....................................	12,000	12,000	12,000
Depreciation...........................	5,000	7,000	8,000
Other operating expenses (including interest)	20,000	22,000	31,000
Income taxes...........................	4,000	8,000	18,000
Total Expenses....................	$186,000	$302,000	$354,000
Net Income...........................	$ 8,000	$ 16,000	$ 36,000

In March, 1968, however, Mastik's commercial bank notified management that the company's bank balance had fallen to less than the minimum required by the bank. The bank was unwilling to extend additional credit unless the company was able to broaden its ownership base and attract more stockholder capital. The company's balance sheets for the previous four years were as follows:

	1964	1965	1966	1967
ASSETS				
Current Assets:				
Cash...........................	$18,000	$ 21,000	$ 15,000	$ 8,000
Accounts receivable................	20,000	29,000	48,000	74,000
Inventories.......................	11,000	15,000	30,000	55,000
Prepayments.....................	2,000	3,000	4,000	5,000
Total Current Assets...........	$51,000	$ 68,000	$ 97,000	$142,000
Long-Term Assets:				
Machinery and equipment.............	$50,000	$ 60,000	$ 65,000	$ 82,000
Less: Accumulated depreciation.....	(6,000)	(11,000)	(18,000)	(26,000)
Net Long-Term Assets..........	$44,000	$ 49,000	$ 47,000	$ 56,000
Total Assets.................	$95,000	$117,000	$144,000	$198,000
LIABILITIES AND STOCKHOLDERS' EQUITY				
Current Liabilities:				
Accounts payable....................	$ 3,000	$ 6,000	$ 10,000	$ 14,000
Wages and taxes payable.............	4,000	5,000	9,000	20,000
Notes payable to bank...............	2,000	7,000	12,000	20,000
Total Current Liabilities.........	$ 9,000	$ 18,000	$ 31,000	$ 54,000
Equipment loan payable...............	30,000	35,000	30,000	25,000
Notes payable to stockholders..........	4,000	4,000	7,000	12,000
Total Liabilities..............	$43,000	$ 57,000	$ 68,000	$ 91,000
Stockholders' Equity:				
Common stock.....................	$30,000	$ 30,000	$ 30,000	$ 30,000
Retained earnings...................	22,000	30,000	46,000	77,000
Total Stockholders' Equity........	$52,000	$ 60,000	$ 76,000	$107,000
Total Liabilities and Stock- holders' Equity..............	$95,000	$117,000	$144,000	$198,000

Mr. Orsini and Mr. Newman were stunned by this news. They did not understand how they had gotten into such a difficult position, since they had never reported a loss, even in their first year of operations, their customers were all good credit risks, and finished goods were always shipped soon after completion.

Prepare a report for Mr. Orsini and Mr. Newman explaining to them what had happened. Use a funds statement or statements as part of your explanation.

24. In November, 1968, Mr. Mark Spencer, the newly appointed treasurer of Calvert Products, Inc., was trying to plan for the retirement of a large bond issue that was due to mature in 1970. He had before him the 1967 income statement and year-end balance sheet, together with a forecasted income statement for 1968 and an estimated balance sheet as of December 31, 1968. These showed the following:

INCOME STATEMENTS

	1968 Estimated	1967
Revenues	$127,000,000	$132,970,000
Cost of goods sold	$ 96,200,000	$100,046,000
Selling and administrative expense	23,500,000	23,498,000
Interest expense	1,400,000	1,292,000
Total Expense (Including Depreciation of $3,560,000 in 1968 and $3,715,000 in 1967)	$121,100,000	$124,836,000
Income before taxes	$ 5,900,000	$ 8,134,000
Income taxes (including provision for deferred taxes of $505,000 in 1968 and $558,000 in 1967)	2,700,000	3,605,000
Net income	$ 3,200,000	$ 4,529,000
Cash dividends:		
Preferred stock	$ 512,000	$ 514,000
Common stock	1,488,000	1,480,000
Total Dividends	$ 2,000,000	$ 1,994,000
Added to Retained Earnings	$ 1,200,000	$ 2,535,000

BALANCE SHEETS

	December 31, 1968 Estimated	December 31, 1967
ASSETS		
Current Assets:		
Cash	$ 3,400,000	$ 3,431,000
Short-term securities	1,600,000	2,278,000
Accounts receivable (less allowance for doubtful accounts, $750,000 for 1968, $816,000 for 1967)	24,200,000	24,066,000
Inventories	30,600,000	32,884,000
Total Current Assets	$ 59,800,000	$ 62,659,000
Investments and noncurrent receivables	3,600,000	3,044,000
Property, plant, and equipment, at cost	$ 85,700,000	$ 80,804,000
Less: Accumulated depreciation	(47,600,000)	(45,430,000)
Net Property, Plant, and Equipment	$ 38,100,000	$ 35,374,000
Total Assets	$101,500,000	$101,077,000
LIABILITIES AND STOCKHOLDERS' EQUITY		
Current Liabilities:		
Accounts payable	$ 9,100,000	$ 9,077,000
Short-term borrowings	6,600,000	7,658,000
Accrued taxes	3,200,000	4,285,000
Other accrued liabilities	5,500,000	5,129,000
Total Current Liabilities	$ 24,400,000	$ 26,149,000
Long-term debt	26,100,000	26,100,000
Deferred taxes	3,660,000	3,501,000
Other noncurrent liabilities	2,100,000	1,408,000
Minority interest in subsidiaries	1,200,000	1,149,000
Total Liabilities	$ 57,460,000	$ 58,307,000

Stockholders' Equity:

Preferred stock	$ 6,511,000	$ 6,511,000
Common stock	3,155,000	3,092,000
Premium on capital stock	5,010,000	4,607,000
Retained earnings	29,931,000	28,731,000
	$ 44,607,000	$ 42,941,000
Less: Treasury stock at cost:		
Preferred stock	$ 537,000	$ 141,000
Common stock	30,000	30,000
Total Treasury Stock	$ 567,000	$ 171,000
Total Stockholders' Equity	$ 43,040,000	$ 42,770,000
Total Liabilities and Stockholders' Equity	$101,500,000	$101,077,000

Property, plant, and equipment purchased during 1968 would total approximately $6,590,000.

Due to what Mr. Spencer considered poor financial management in the past, all of the long-term debt would mature at once, in May, 1970. Mr. Spencer was aware of the advantages of debt—he figured, for example, that 1967 earnings per common share would have been reduced by 20 percent if the $26,100,000 in long-term debt had been provided instead by common shareholders at the market prices prevailing when the loan was floated. He hoped, therefore, to be able to finance the retirement of the debt by means of a new bond issue. At the same time, he was aware that the bond market was very tight, and he was afraid of the consequences of opening negotiations with potential lenders without an acceptable alternative financing plan.

a) Prepare a statement of the estimated sources and uses of funds for 1968, using whatever definition of funds you deem appropriate.

b) How could your funds statement help Mr. Spencer prepare an alternative plan or plans for debt retirement? What specific suggestions can you offer as a result of your analysis of these figures?

Part III

Accounting Data for Management Planning and Control

Chapter 17

MANAGERIAL ACCOUNTING
AND PRODUCT COSTING

MANAGEMENT'S INFORMATION needs are far from satisfied by the financial information provided to shareholders and the general public. Providing this additional information is the province of *managerial accounting*. This chapter has two purposes: (1) to outline the basic requirements of managerial accounting; and (2) to introduce one method of providing management with data on the cost of manufacturing individual products.

ACCOUNTING AND MANAGERIAL PROCESSES

Management exercises control over its operations (1) by selecting the course of action it wishes to follow (*planning* or *decision making*); (2) by issuing instructions and seeing that they are carried out (*direction* and *supervision*); and (3) adjusting its methods or its plans on the basis of analyses of the results achieved (*responsive control*).

Managerial accounting is concerned primarily with providing information to assist management in carrying out the first and third of these activities. In addition, systems designed to serve these purposes in manufacturing firms must also provide the data necessary for the costing of inventories and the measurement of the cost of goods sold for external financial reporting. The focus of the remainder of this book, however, will be on the managerial aspects of accounting data.

Data Required for Planning

Planning is the process of deciding on a course of action—of finding and choosing among the alternatives available. It takes three forms: (1) *policy formulation*—establishment of the major ground rules that determine the basic direction and shape of the enterprise, thus establishing the limits within which management has decided to confine itself; (2) *decision making*—the choice among alternative solutions to specific operating or financial problems within the prescribed policy limits; and (3) *budgeting*—the preparation of comprehensive operating and financial plans for specific intervals of time.

All three of these forms of action require choosing among alternatives. Underlying each of these choices is the *incremental principle* that data for decisions should represent the *differences* between alternative courses of action. In other words, the concept that is relevant in quantitative analysis for decision making is the concept of *incremental profit*, which is the difference in profit for the company as a whole that will result from choosing one alternative instead of another.

The incremental basis of the planning process holds true just as strongly in the preparation of periodic plans or budgets as in other decision-making activities. Plans are of necessity expressed in absolute terms—the costs to be incurred and the results to be achieved—but the process of selecting one plan instead of another is a decision process. The choice of a plan is inevitably based on comparisons, implicitly or explicitly made.

A second characteristic of planning processes is their emphasis on the future. Decisions can influence only what lies ahead, not what has gone before. Historical data are useful in decision making only insofar as they contribute to better forecasting of future results under alternative courses of action.

Data Requirements for Responsive Control

Responsive control processes require the *measurement* and *reporting* of operating results. Control reporting is tied closely to the concept of responsibility—that is, results should be reported to those executives who are responsible for achieving them. This concept is reflected in the company's organization chart. Each block in the chart represents a *responsibility center*—an organization unit headed by a single person, *answerable* to higher authority and obligated to perform certain tasks. The responsibility centers of the lowest level are known by different names in different companies, *department* being perhaps the most common.

Control reports are always *comparative*—that is, they embody or facilitate comparisons between observed performance and some reference point. In some cases the comparison may be with a prior time period; in others, the current budgetary plan provides the point of reference.

In any case, control reports should identify the *deviations* of actual performance from the planned or prior performance that is being used as the reference point. Each manager should be informed of deviations within his own area of responsibility, so that he can investigate the causes and take whatever action seems most appropriate. The identification, reporting, and analysis of deviations on this basis is the subdivision of managerial accounting known as *responsibility accounting*.

Structure of Managerial Accounting Data

Data to meet these managerial needs are ordinarily cross-classified by organization unit and by activity. Many marketing costs, for example, can be assigned to individual sales districts. Many of these same costs may also be assigned to individual product lines or individual classes of customers or both.

The design of data accumulating and reporting systems that will serve both the decision-making and the control-reporting needs of management, as well as the company's external financial reporting requirements, is a challenging and often frustrating task. Data designed to meet one objective may in some measure conflict with the data required to realize other objectives. Furthermore, system costs rise rapidly as system complexity increases. The managerial accountant must be able to estimate the costs of refinements in his systems and the extent to which management decisions would be improved by the refinement.

THE PROBLEM OF FACTORY UNIT COSTING

In view of the potential complexity of the managerial accounting system, it is difficult to decide where to begin. We have decided to start with what is probably the most widely used kind of managerial cost data—factory cost per unit of product.

Management Uses of Factory Unit Cost Data

Management uses unit cost data mainly for decision making. Is the product profitable or should it be dropped from the line? At what price should it be sold? Should it be redesigned so that it can be produced more cheaply? Should it be made on the premises or bought outside? The accountant's problem in all these cases is to develop a product costing system that will permit him to approximate incremental product cost, no matter what kind of decision is being made.

Unit cost data also play a role in responsive control processes. Product line or regional profit reports, for example, ordinarily cannot be prepared without unit cost figures. Unit costs are less useful in factory cost control because they ordinarily represent the combined results of a number of factory departments. To be useful for cost control, product cost must be reclassified on a departmental basis. One way of doing this will be discussed in Chapter 21; until then, we shall focus on the development of product costs for other purposes.

The Role of Unit Cost in Financial Accounting

Factory unit costs were originally designed for and are still used primarily by management. They also serve an important purpose in connection with external financial reporting, however. For example, a steel company converts iron ore, coal, and limestone into steel. The cost of a ton of steel in its inventory or that it has sold is the cost of these materials plus the cost of the labor and other costs required to produce the ton of steel. Therefore, to arrive at the financial statements of a manufacturing company, the accounting system must be designed to develop the unit cost of each product it produces. With that information, the cost of the inventory on hand at the close of a period and the cost of the goods sold in a period may be ascertained.

Types of Costing Systems

The methods used to measure product unit cost depend heavily on the nature of the manufacturing process and are subject to wide variation. Basically, these methods fall into two broad categories: *process costing* and *job order costing*.

Process costing is applicable when the production process turns out a single kind of product for long periods of time at a stretch (cement, flour, etc.). In this case, product cost per unit can be computed easily from the formula:

$$\text{Average Cost Unit} = \frac{\text{Total Production Costs for the Period}}{\text{Total Units of Product Manufactured}}.$$

Job order costing, in contrast, is used when the production facilities are used to produce many different kinds of products simultaneously or in rapid succession (job printing, furniture manufacture, etc.) In this case, costs must be assigned to each batch or job lot of products so that a separate unit cost figure may be calculated for each.

The simple job order costing system described in the next few pages should be viewed as an unsophisticated introduction to a much more complex subject. Later chapters will indicate how this system can be adapted to meet some of management's needs more satisfactorily.

A JOB ORDER COSTING SYSTEM

The Pyle Company, a manufacturer of men's work clothes, uses a job order costing system. For product unit costing purposes, factory costs are divided into three classes:

1. Direct materials.
2. Direct labor.
3. Factory overhead.

Unit cost on any job order is determined by assigning costs in each of these three categories to that job and dividing the total by the number of units produced.

Measuring Direct Materials Cost

The production process in the Pyle Company is initiated by a *manufacturing request* from the sales manager who has responsibility for maintaining finished goods inventories at appropriate levels. This request lists the catalog number of the product and indicates the number of units required and the desired completion date.

From the manufacturing request, the factory office prepares a *production order* containing a list of materials, complete manufacturing instructions, and a production schedule. The physical production process begins with the transfer of *direct materials* from the storeroom to a production department. Direct materials are all materials and parts that are used specifically on one particular job order. *Indirect materials* or *supplies*, on the other hand, are issued for general factory use and not for the specific benefit of any one job.

Production departments obtain materials and supplies from the storeroom by submitting *materials requisitions*. Each requisition shows the items required and the quantities of each. For direct materials, the requisition shows the job order number, while for indirect materials it shows the department number and an account number indicating how the materials were used (e.g., lubricating materials, cleaning supplies, packing materials, etc.).

Finally, if a production department finds that it has requisitioned more materials than it needs, it returns the excess to the storeroom, noting the quantity on a *returned materials card*, a form identical to the requisition but of a different color.

The Job Cost Sheet

All issues and returns of direct materials are recorded on a job cost sheet similar to the one shown in Exhibit 17–1. One of these sheets is prepared by the accounting department for each job order as soon as the production order is issued.

Exhibit 17–1

PYLE COMPANY

Job Order Cost Form

JOB COST SHEET

For_____   Job No._____
Item_____   Start_____
Stock No._____   Quantity_____   Finish_____

DIRECT LABOR			MATERIALS		COST SUMMARY		
Card No.	Hours	Amount	Req. No.	Amount	Labor	$	
		$		$	Materials	$	
					Overhead	$	
					Total	$	
					Unit Cost	$	
					Shipments		
					Date	No.	Balance

As materials are issued, the accounting department ascertains the cost of the materials issued and enters this amount in the "Materials" column of the job cost sheet. If direct materials are returned to the storeroom, their costs must be entered in this column as a deduction. Finally, when the job has been completed, the amounts shown in the "Materials" column are totaled and the sum is entered in the "Cost Summary" block on the job cost sheet, on the line marked "Materials."

Measuring Direct Labor Cost

Direct labor costs are handled in much the same way as direct materials costs. Direct labor cost is any labor cost specifically traceable to one particular job. Indirect labor is labor expended on tasks such as machine repair, lubrication, cleaning, or other tasks not related to a particular production order.

Factory workers in the Pyle Company's plant, other than supervisors and clerks, are paid weekly on the basis of the number of hours worked times an hourly rate. Factory supervisors and clerks, as well as personnel in sales and administration, are paid monthly salaries. When an hourly worker is assigned to work on a particular production order, the job number is entered on a card or *time ticket* which is stamped with the date and hour. At the end of the day or of the work to be done, whichever comes first, the time ticket is again stamped by time clock, and the time ticket is forwarded to the accounting department. (For indirect labor the time ticket will show the number of the department in which the work was done, together with a number denoting the kind of work.) The hours shown on the direct labor time tickets are then multiplied by the appropriate hourly rates and posted to the Direct Labor column on the job cost sheet.

The Nature of Factory Overhead

The job cost sheet has not yet been charged for any of the factory costs that cannot be traced specifically to that job—that is, the *indirect manufacturing costs, factory overhead*, or *factory burden*. This category includes the indirect labor and indirect materials mentioned earlier, clerical and supervisory salaries, depreciation on buildings and equipment, maintenance, repairs and taxes on property, and so forth.

Although most costs classified as overhead *cannot* be traced to individual job orders, two other groups of costs are commonly placed in this category for different reasons. For some, the reason is that tracing the cost to the job would cost more than the added accuracy would be worth. For example, the Pyle Company would find it possible but not economical to measure the amount of thread or buttons consumed on each production order. The costs of these items are therefore classified as overhead costs.

Finally, some costs are treated as overhead because it would be *unsound* to treat them as direct costs. For instance, overtime premiums paid to direct labor should not be charged to the jobs that the foreman happens to schedule during overtime hours. Instead, this portion of direct labor cost should be treated as factory overhead.

Factory Overhead: The Burden Rate

Since factory overhead represents costs incurred to obtain the production of a period, it would seem reasonable that these costs should be included as part of the cost of the products produced. Doing this poses a problem, however, since the overhead assignable to a job cannot be measured in the same way as the direct costs. The only way that overhead costs can be included in product cost is to assign them to jobs on the basis of some average rate. An average of this kind is known as a *burden rate* or *overhead costing rate*.

For example, suppose that the overhead costs for a given period total $80,000. To state this as an average, we must divide it by some measure of the total volume of production activity, such as the total number of units of products produced during the period:

$$\text{Burden Rate} = \frac{\text{Overhead Cost}}{\text{Production Volume}}.$$

Units of product output are not usually a very good measure, however, because different products vary so widely in size and complexity. Instead, a measure of production *input* is usually chosen, such as machine-hours or direct labor cost. Thus if the total direct labor cost for the period is $100,000 and the total factory overhead is $80,000, the charge to each job could be 80 percent of the direct labor cost incurred on that job.

Charging job orders with overhead on the basis of direct labor cost is common practice, but the use of *actual* total overhead and *actual* direct labor costs to arrive at the overhead rate is not common. A *predetermined* rather than an actual overhead rate is commonly used for a number of reasons, of which only one will be mentioned in this chapter. The total actual overhead cost and direct labor cost figures are not known until the end of the period. It would be very inconvenient for the Pyle Company to wait until the end of the period to apply factory overhead because all of the work of costing the job order cost sheets would have to be done at the same time. The bookkeepers' work load would be very uneven or else reports would be considerably delayed.

A predetermined burden rate is based on *estimates* of the direct labor cost and the overhead cost made at the start of the period. At the Pyle Company, each of these cost figures is estimated at the start of the year on the assumption that output for the year will be a normal or average percentage of capacity operations. In 19— the Pyle Company estimated that factory overhead at normal operating volume would be 70 percent of direct labor cost. Therefore, the overhead rate for the year beginning on July 1, 19—, was 70 percent.

Assigning Overhead Costs to Job Orders

Once the burden rate has been established, the assignment of overhead costs to individual jobs is a simple matter. In the Pyle Company, the direct labor costs shown on the job cost sheet are simply totaled and multiplied by 70 percent. The resulting amount is entered in the "Cost Summary" on the right-hand side of the job cost sheet on the line marked overhead. Thus if some job, say Job No. 3442, has been charged with $200 in direct labor cost, the job cost sheet will be charged with $140 in overhead costs.

Unit Cost

Once the job cost sheet has been completed, unit cost can be computed by dividing the total cost assigned to the job by the number of units of product manufactured. The job cost sheet is then removed from the work in process file and transferred to the finished goods inventory file. As units are sold, unit cost is multiplied by the number of units sold to obtain the cost of goods sold.

Summary of Document Flows

This sequence of events is illustrated in Exhibit 17–2 in terms of the documents used in the process. The sales department issues a manufacturing request upon receipt of a customer order for special items or when the inventory level of a stock item declines to a predetermined level known as a *reorder point*. The manufacturing department issues a production order, which the factory accountant uses to prepare a job cost sheet. A copy of the production order goes to the materials storeroom. If additional materials are required, a purchase requisition is prepared and sent to the purchasing agent who places a purchase order for the desired quantity.

As the work progresses, the production department heads draw materials from the storeroom by means of materials requisitions. Direct labor time is assigned to the job on the basis of time tickets. Finally, overhead is assigned to job orders by multiplying a predetermined burden rate by some index of the size of the job, such as total direct labor hours, as shown on the job cost sheet. Unit cost is

Exhibit 17–2

DOCUMENT FLOWS IN JOB ORDER COSTING

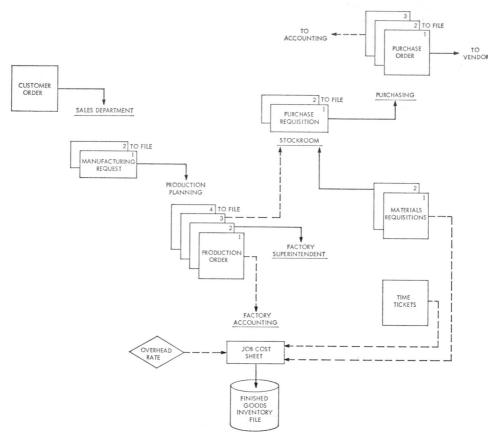

calculated, the job cost sheet is removed from the in-process file, and this ends the process of product costing.

THE FLOW OF COSTS

The requisitions, time tickets, and job cost sheets described in the preceding pages are not only the means by which unit cost figures are obtained for management and other uses. They are also the means by which the flow of costs through the manufacturing cost accounts can be organized. Although Chapter 4 described the basic cost flow pattern, the procedures described in this chapter add a few complexities that require a second examination.

Exhibit 17–3

PYLE COMPANY

Inventory and Manufacturing Cost Accounts
As of July 1, 19—

Raw material and supplies	$ 98,300
Materials in process	48,320
Labor in process	52,400
Overhead in process	36,680
Finished goods	161,700
Indirect materials	0
Indirect labor	0
Factory supervision	0
Other factory costs	0
Manufacturing overhead	0
Cost of goods sold	0

Exhibit 17–3 shows the balances in the manufacturing cost accounts as of July 1, 19—, the beginning of the Pyle Company's fiscal
year. The first five accounts in this exhibit indicate the amounts of
inventory on hand on July 1. Notice that three work in process
accounts have been supplied—Materials in Process, Labor in Process,
and Overhead in Process—instead of the one account used in Chapter
4. The reason for this is to provide a record of the amounts of each of
these cost classes assigned to inventory during each period. The remainder of the accounts are for the purpose of accumulating the costs
incurred during the period, and they therefore have zero balances at
the start of the period.

Receipt and Issue of Materials

The purchases of raw materials and supplies during the period are
recorded in entry (1) below, while entry (2) records the issuance of
materials and supplies to operating departments during the quarter, as
revealed by the materials and supplies requisitions:

(1)

Raw Material and Supplies	181,500	
Accounts Payable		181,500

(2)

Materials in Process	170,400	
Indirect Materials	21,100	
Raw Material and Supplies		191,500

The new element in this second entry is the distinction made between direct and indirect costs. The direct materials costs are charged
to Materials in Process, an inventory account, while indirect materials

and supplies are charged to Indirect Materials, a factory overhead account. Simultaneously with these entries in the ledger accounts, the detailed amounts are entered in the subsidiary *stores ledger* (file of accounts, one for each kind of materials and supplies in the stock room) and in the job cost sheet.

Raw Material and Supplies is the control account for the stores ledger, while Materials in Process is the control account for the Materials columns on the job cost sheets for jobs in process on any given date. This means that after all the bookkeeping work has been done, the balance in the Raw Material and Supplies account should agree with the total of the balances in the individual stores ledger cards and the balance in Materials in Process should equal the total of the items shown in the Materials columns of the various job cost sheets.

Labor Costs

As work is performed in the plant and time tickets are generated, the tickets are costed and classified as direct or indirect labor. This classification gives rise to the following entry:

(3)

Labor in Process.	184,700	
Indirect Labor.	45,300	
Accrued Wages.		230,000

Once again, the debits to Labor in Process represent the direct labor costs, while the charges to Indirect Labor are the overhead charges, not traceable to individual jobs. The Accrued Wages account is a liability account. (Since this illustration is concerned only with the cost side of factory transactions, no attention will be given to payroll preparation and the liquidation of payroll liabilities.)

Overhead Absorption

The process of charging jobs with factory overhead is commonly called the *application* or *absorption* of overhead. The amount of overhead absorbed is obtained by multiplying the burden rate by the production volume for the period. In this case, production volume is measured by direct labor cost, and the burden rate is 70 percent. Entry (4) summarizes the overhead charges made to job order cost sheets during the quarter for jobs *completed* during the quarter (70 percent of the direct labor cost incurred on these jobs during the quarter):

(4)

Overhead in Process...................................115,220
    Manufacturing Overhead.........................   115,220

Because the Pyle Company uses a *predetermined* burden rate, this entry can be made before the *actual* overhead costs for the quarter have been determined.

The amount recorded in entry (4) is not 70 percent of the direct labor cost for the quarter. It reflects only the amounts absorbed during the quarter on jobs *completed* during the quarter. This means that another entry must be made at the end of the quarter to record the overhead costs applicable to the jobs that are still in process at that time. In this case, the direct labor cost recorded during the quarter on these jobs amounted to $20,100 and their job cost sheets must therefore be charged with $14,070 in overhead. The summary entry is:

(5)

Overhead in Process...................................14,070
    Manufacturing Overhead.........................   14,070

Actual Overhead Costs

While overhead is being *absorbed* into work in process through entries (4) and (5), throughout the period the *actual* overhead costs are being accumulated in appropriate cost accounts. The indirect material and indirect labor costs have already been recorded in entries (2) and (3). Entries (6) and (7) below record the cost of the salaried personnel in the factory and other factory costs:

(6)

Factory Supervision....................................28,500
    Salaries Payable.................................   28,500

(7)

Other Factory Costs....................................42,900
    Accounts Payable................................   38,100
    Allowance for Depreciation......................   3,000
    Deferred Charges................................   1,800

Ordinarily a number of accounts would be used instead of the single "Other Factory Costs" account, to provide detailed data for management's use. In this respect as in others, the Pyle Company's system is unrealistic, with only four overhead accounts, but this permits us to demonstrate the concepts without expanding the bookkeeping unnecessarily.

The various overhead cost accounts are temporary accounts. Their only purpose is to preserve information in a useful form, and once this purpose has been served they can be discarded. Accordingly, at the end of the period the balances in these accounts are closed out to the Manufacturing Overhead account, as in entry (8):

(8)

Manufacturing Overhead................................137,800		
Indirect Material..................................	21,100	
Indirect labor....................................	45,300	
Factory Supervision...............................	28,500	
Other Factory Overhead...........................	42,900	

The Manufacturing Overhead account is a clearing account. The overhead charged to work in process during the period is accompanied by credits to this account, while the actual overhead costs accumulated in various cost accounts are debited to it. After this has been done, the account still has a debit balance of $8,510:

Manufacturing Overhead

(8)	137,800	(4)	115,220
		(5)	14,070
Bal. 9/30	8,510		129,290

This should come as no surprise, since it would be most unlikely that the conditions presumed by the predetermined burden rate—that is, normal costs at normal volume—would prevail in any particular short period of time.

The analysis of over- and underabsorbed overhead will be examined in the next chapter. For the present we shall look on the underabsorbed balance as an *operating loss,* on the grounds that it represents overhead costs that were incurred during the period but did not result in any production. The transfer of the balance in Manufacturing Overhead to a loss account is accomplished by entry (9):

(9)

Loss from Underabsorbed Production Costs.................8,510	
Manufacturing Overhead.............................	8,510

Cost of Goods Finished and Sold

When a job is completed, the output is transferred to the place where finished goods are stored. The accounting department has charged the job's cost sheet with the direct material and labor, and on completion the absorbed overhead is posted as described earlier. With the total cost incurred on the job posted to the job cost sheet, it is transferred from the work in process ledger to the finished goods ledger. Entry (10) summarizes the entries made in the general ledger accounts to recognize these transfers:

(10)

Finished Goods...................................	.504,200	
Materials in Process.............................		187,150
Labor in Process.................................		186,500
Overhead in Process.............................		130,550

As we noted earlier, the completed job cost sheets in the Pyle Company are used as the finished goods inventory ledger. As finished products are shipped to fill customer orders, the cost of the quantity sold is entered on each item's job cost sheet, and the amount is credited to Finished Goods and charged to Cost of Goods Sold. If the shipment covers an entire job order, as in the case of goods produced to customers' specifications, it is a simple matter to pull the job cost sheet from the file and transfer the balance to the Cost of Goods Sold account. If it is a partial shipment, on the other hand, a notation is made on the job cost sheet and the proportional amount is transferred from Finished Goods to Cost of Goods Sold. Entry (11) records the cost of all goods shipped during the quarter:

(11)

Cost of Goods Sold.................................	.437,200	
Finished Goods.................................		437,200

Transactions Summary

This process is summarized in the T-account model shown in Exhibit 17–4. Costs enter the system initially as the firm incurs liabilities for goods and services purchased. Some of these goods and services are used outside the manufacturing area and therefore do not pass through the manufacturing accounts. Others are used immediately in manufacturing and are therefore charged immediately to manufacturing cost accounts. Still others, such as purchases of raw materials and factory equipment, are entered first in other accounts and are transferred to the manufacturing cost accounts as the goods and services are used. Then, as goods are completed, the costs are transferred from the manufacturing cost accounts to the finished goods inventory account, and from there they go to the income statement as the cost of goods sold at the time when revenue is recognized.

Exhibit 17–5 presents the portion of this model most directly concerned in this illustration, with the Pyle Company's first-quarter transactions entered in. All of the company's manufacturing costs for this period are summarized here, just as they appeared in the journal

Exhibit 17-4

PYLE COMPANY

T-Account Model of the Flow of Factory Costs

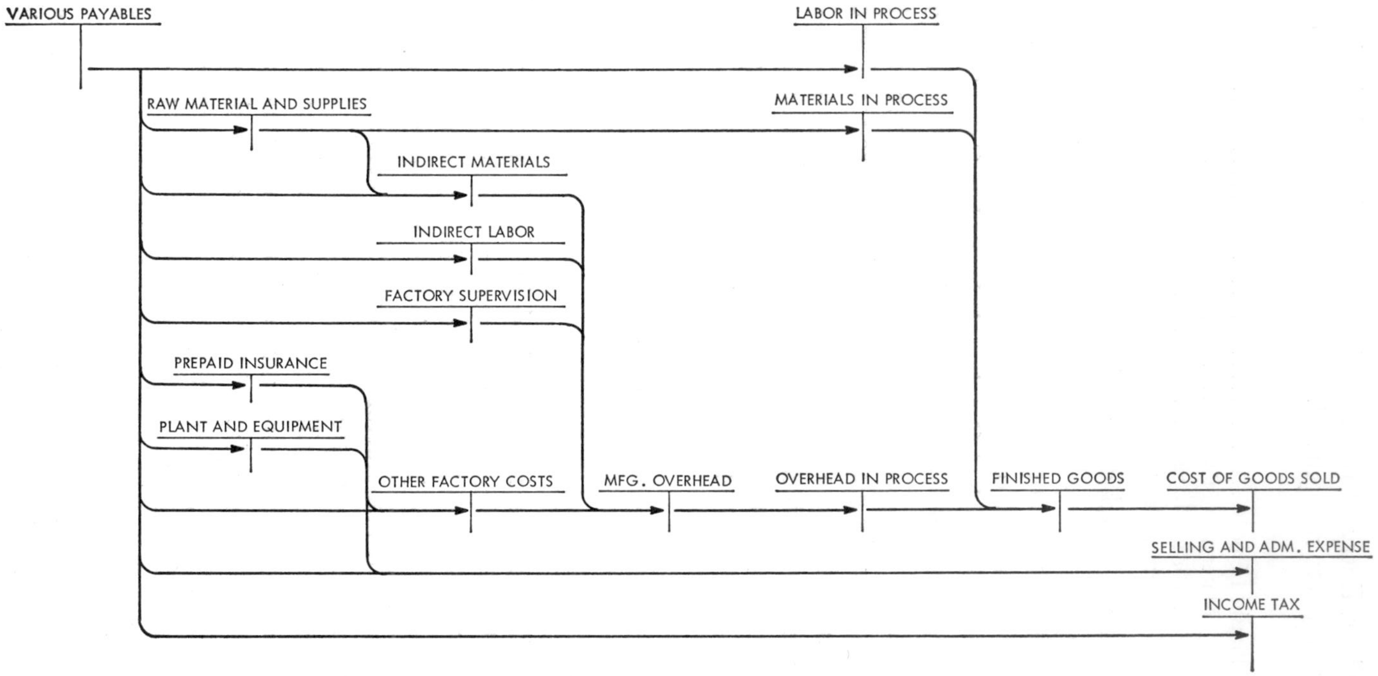

VARIOUS PAYABLES

RAW MATERIAL AND SUPPLIES

LABOR IN PROCESS

MATERIALS IN PROCESS

INDIRECT MATERIALS

INDIRECT LABOR

FACTORY SUPERVISION

PREPAID INSURANCE

PLANT AND EQUIPMENT

OTHER FACTORY COSTS

MFG. OVERHEAD

OVERHEAD IN PROCESS

FINISHED GOODS

COST OF GOODS SOLD

SELLING AND ADM. EXPENSE

INCOME TAX

Exhibit 17–5

PYLE COMPANY

Manufacturing Cost Flows
For the Three Months Ending September 30, 19—

Raw Material and Supplies

Bal. 7/1	98,300	(2)	191,500
(1)	181,500		
Bal. 9/30	88,300		

Materials in Process

Bal. 7/1	48,320	(10)	187,150
(2)	170,400		
Bal. 9/30	31,570		

Labor in Process

Bal. 7/1	52,400	(10)	186,500
(3)	184,700		
Bal. 9/30	50,600		

Manufacturing Overhead

(8)	137,800	(4)	115,220
		(5)	14,070
		(9)	8,510

Overhead in Process

Bal. 7/1	36,680	(10)	130,550
(4)	115,220		
(5)	14,070		
Bal. 9/30	35,400		

Loss from Underabsorbed Production Costs

(9)	8,510

Finished Goods

Bal. 7/1	161,700	(11)	437,200
(10)	504,200		
Bal. 9/30	228,700		

Cost of Goods Sold

(11)	437,200

entries given above. Notice that the Manufacturing Overhead account has a zero balance at the end of the quarter, as do all of the detailed factory overhead accounts (not shown in the exhibit). The manufacturing overhead accounts are temporary accounts, designed to accumulate information relating to the events of a single quarter alone. Overhead in Process and Finished Goods, on the other hand, are inventory accounts, and these still contain some of the overhead costs of the period just ended.

AN ESTIMATED COST SYSTEM

As we pointed out earlier, a great variety of alternatives are available in the design and use of a managerial accounting system; the choice among these alternatives depends on the informational needs of management. For example, the management of the Pyle Company was unhappy about the amount of clerical effort and management time consumed in costing each production order, and the controller proposed the following estimated cost system to meet management's objections to the existing system.

The Accounting Rules

Under the proposed system, the company would continue to keep a perpetual inventory of material and supplies as before, since the perpetual inventory in quantities provided information that was needed to make purchasing and production scheduling decisions. The development of cost on each production order via the job cost sheets would be eliminated, however. Instead, all requisitions for direct materials would be charged to a Direct Materials account, and direct labor would be charged to an account with that name. The labor charge would be made periodically when the payrolls were prepared. Finally, all indirect material, indirect labor, and other manufacturing overhead costs would be charged, as before, to the various manufacturing overhead accounts, but the amount of overhead absorbed during the period would not be computed.

In place of the completed job cost sheets, a set of finished goods ledger cards would be kept, one for each type of stock item. The *quantities* of goods completed or shipped would be entered on these cards, but no entry would be made in the ledger to record the *cost* of the goods produced or shipped. (For goods produced to special customer orders, a copy of the completed production order would serve as the record of quantities produced and shipped.)

At the end of the quarter, the labor and material cost per unit of product for each item of finished goods inventory would be *estimated* by production management on the basis of estimated material and labor quantities per unit of product and of unit material prices and labor wage rates during the quarter. A predetermined burden rate of 70 percent of direct labor cost would be used to determine the amount of overhead cost to be assigned to the finished goods inventory on hand at the end of the quarter.

Work in process at the end of each quarter would be determined on the assumption that the amount does not change over the course of the year. Annually a physical inventory count would establish the actual work in process. With the above data, the cost of goods sold for each quarter would be determined by deduction.

To illustrate the system, assume that it had been adopted on July 1. The trial balance of the Pyle Company would then have appeared as follows on September 30, before any adjusting entries had been made.

Raw material and supplies, September 30.	$ 88,300
Work in process, July 1.	137,400
Finished goods, July 1.	161,700
Direct labor.	184,700
Direct materials.	170,400
Manufacturing overhead.	137,800

The Work in Process and Finished Goods accounts would have had the same balances they had had at the start of the quarter, since no entry would have been made transferring the labor, material, and overhead costs into and out of work in process. The last three figures are the actual labor, material, and overhead costs incurred during the quarter.

Because the system was to presume that no change in the work in process inventory took place during the quarter, the cost of goods sold would be calculated as follows if the estimated cost of the finished goods inventory was $225,000:

Finished goods inventory, July 1.	$161,700
Add: Direct material.	170,400
Direct labor.	184,700
Manufacturing overhead.	137,800
Total Costs.	$654,600
Less: Finished goods inventory, September 30.	225,000
Cost of Goods Sold.	$429,600

The company's accounts would then be brought up to date by the following entry:

Cost of Goods Sold.	429,600	
Finished goods inventory.	63,300	
Direct Materials.		170,400
Direct Labor.		184,700
Manufacturing Overhead.		137,800

Evaluation of the Proposal

The main argument for this estimated cost system is that it could be operated at considerably less clerical cost than the Pyle Company's existing system, and would require considerably less management time. Its main disadvantage is that it would generate fewer data for management's use. Although management in any case must use *estimated* cost in pricing and other decisions, the managerial purpose of a job order costing system is to provide data on which more accurate estimates can be based. The decision to retain the actual job cost system, therefore, will depend in large measure on the extent to which unit cost figures are used in pricing and other decisions and on the extent to which these decisions are improved by the greater accuracy in the unit cost data.

Another question is whether management and outside investors would make seriously incorrect decisions as a result of errors in the inventory and cost of goods sold figures. This, in turn, will depend partly on how much less accurate these figures would be under the proposed system. To help management evaluate this point, the Pyle Company's controller prepared the comparison shown in Exhibit 17–6. In this case the two systems led to substantially the same figure

Exhibit 17–6

PYLE COMPANY

Comparative Cost Account Balances under Actual and Estimated Cost Systems As of September 30, 19—

	Actual	*Estimated*
Raw material and supplies	$ 88,300	$ 88,300
Work in process	117,590	137,400
Finished goods	228,700	225,000
Underabsorbed manufacturing overhead	8,510	. . . . . .
Cost of goods sold	437,200	429,600
Total	$880,300	$880,300

for finished goods inventory, but the assumption that work in process did not change introduced a large error into the cost of goods sold figure reported under the estimated cost system. Reported net income would have been almost $20,000 less than under the actual cost system.

An error of this size would probably prevent the Pyle Company's management from adopting the proposed system, but this does not mean that an estimated cost system should never be used. What a particular firm should do will depend largely on its circumstances. For instance, the estimated cost system would be better suited to a firm with a small, stable work in process inventory than a firm with a large, fluctuating inventory.

On the other hand, the system need not always take the same form, and it can be changed to make it more suitable in a particular situation. Rough estimates of work in process, for example, might be obtainable at a very low cost, and this might be enough to reduce the error in reported income to tolerable levels. Occasional observations of actual costs on individual operations might also be enough to give management the data it needs to make satisfactory cost estimates.

SUMMARY

Management expects the accounting system to provide a large portion of the data necessary for internal decision making, for forward planning, and for reviewing the current operating performance of various segments of the business. This is the domain of managerial accounting.

In manufacturing companies, a key component of the financial information system is the set of procedures used to estimate the unit cost of manufactured products. When products are manufactured in batches or job lots, product cost is often measured by means of job order costing. A highly simplified version of this kind of measurement system has been presented in this chapter. Job order costing is expensive, however, and simpler methods such as the estimated cost system outlined at the end of the chapter may in some cases be more suitable.

QUESTIONS AND PROBLEMS

1. For what purposes is it necessary or desirable to calculate manufacturing cost per unit of product?

2. What is the difference between a job cost system and a process cost system?

3. What basic documents are used by the Pyle Company in connection with its manufacturing operations, and what is the purpose of each?

4. Discuss the functions of the job cost sheet and explain its relation to the inventory accounts.

5. Why is the burden rate usually related to such measures of manufacturing *input* as direct labor hours rather than to some direct measure of output?

6. "The accuracy of manufacturing cost per unit of product is increased by basing the overhead portion on a predetermined burden rate rather than on the average actual overhead cost for the period." Discuss.

7. What is a "responsibility center?" What role does it play in responsibility accounting?

8. Could a file of estimated costs conceivably be more useful for decision making than a file of recent job order cost sheets? Give your reasons.

9. Prepare a diagram that will show the relationships among the three management processes of planning, direction, and responsive control. Try to indicate on your diagram how accounting data enter into these processes.

10. Think of some decision you have recently made. Prepare a list of the sequence of steps you took from the time that you recognized that a decision had to be made until the time that you reached your decision. Would this same sequence of steps be appropriate for executive decisions?

*11. The Basic Foundry prepares metal castings for specific orders, using a job order cost system. During the month of January, job No. 103 calling for 10,000 machine parts was started and completed. Information about this order is summarized as follows:

(1) Material requisitioned: 21,000 pounds at $0.66 a pound.
(2) Labor hours expended: 2,000 at $2.15 an hour.
(3) Manufacturing overhead charged to production: $4.00 a direct labor hour.
(4) Unused material returned to storeroom: 800 pounds.
(5) Castings completed: 9,800.

a) Find the unit cost of production, accurate to the nearest cent.
b) Prepare journal entries to record these transactions.

12. The Cobbett Woodworking Company manufactures chairs and other pieces of wooden furniture. Production is on a job order basis. The factory burden rate is $2 per direct labor dollar. The following data relate to job No. 876, an order for 200 wooden footstools:

(1) Lumber issued from storeroom: $49.70.
(2) Direct labor: 35 hours at $2 an hour.
(3) Footstools completed: 196 (4 footstools were rejected in final inspection, broken up and burned).
(4) Footstools sold on credit to Ye Olde Roadside Store: 10.

---

* Solutions to problems marked with an asterisk (*) are found in Appendix B.

a) Compute unit cost to the nearest tenth of a cent.

b) Prepare journal entries to record these transactions.

*13. The burden rate is $2 per direct labor hour and a job order costing system is in use.

Inventory balances on December 1 were:

Materials.....................................	$10,000
Work in process..............................	15,000
Finished goods...............................	20,000

During December, the following data were recorded:

Materials purchased...........................	$16,000
Direct materials issued........................	18,000
Direct labor, 10,000 hours......................	27,000
Manufacturing overhead (actual)................	17,000
Cost of goods finished.........................	60,000

On December 31, finished goods costing $23,000 were still on hand.

a) Prepare entries, in two-column journal form, to record the transactions of the month.

b) What was the cost of goods sold for the month?

c) What was the over- or underabsorbed overhead for the month?

d) What was the December 31 balance in the Work in Process account?

14. The records of the Gargoyle Company showed the following information relating to its manufacturing operations for the year 19x1:

Raw material inventory, January 1, 19x1.................	$ 40,000
Purchases of materials.............................	172,000
Purchases returns and allowances.....................	2,000
Raw material inventory, December 31, 19x1..............	35,000
Direct labor......................................	75,000
Indirect labor....................................	12,000
Factory supplies used..............................	15,000
Depreciation.....................................	9,000
Miscellaneous factory costs.........................	1,000
Factory overhead cost absorbed......................	40,000
Work in process inventory, January 1, 19x1.............	12,000
Work in process inventory, December 31, 19x1...........	16,000
Finished goods inventory, January 1, 19x1..............	58,000
Finished goods inventory, December 31, 19x1............	55,000

a) Set up the following six T-accounts, enter the January 1 balances, if any, and make the entries necessary to trace the flow of costs through these accounts. Do not use any other accounts.

Raw Material Inventory	Factory Overhead
Work in Process Inventory	Cost of Goods Sold
Finished Goods Inventory	Payable to Home Office

b) Compute the amount of the over- or underabsorbed overhead for 19x1.

15. The Oxford Company has a single work in process account, plus a Manufacturing Overhead account to accumulate actual factory overhead costs. A burden rate of $1.60 per machine-hour is used to charge factory overhead to individual job orders. The January 1 balance in Work in Process was $17,460 (including direct labor, direct materials, and applied factory overhead at $1.60 per machine-hour). The following data relate to operations during January:

(1) Materials and supplies purchased: $3,500.
(2) Materials and supplies issued:
    For specific job orders, $3,000.
    For general factory use, $700.
(3) Machine-hours: 10,000.
(4) Direct labor:
    On specific job orders, 6,000 hours at $2.50.
    On other factory activities, 1,000 hours at $2.20.
(5) Factory supervision: $2,000.
(6) Other factory costs: $5,800.
(7) Goods completed:
    Direct materials, $2,400.
    Direct labor, $12,000.
    Machine-hours, 9,000.

a) Prepare journal entries to record these transactions.

b) Prepare a manufacturing cost summary for the month, using the following format: actual costs for the month, plus or minus over- or underabsorbed overhead equals costs charged to product accounts; add the beginning balance in Work in Process and distribute the total between ending work in process and the cost of goods finished.

*16. Complete the missing items in each of the following unrelated problems; all information necessary for completing the problems is given.

a) Finished goods inventory, March 31 ....$ 5,000
    Cost of goods sold, January 1–March 31 65,000
    Indirect labor, January 1–March 31 5,000
    Finished goods inventory, January 1 10,000
    Direct materials used, January 1–March 31 20,000
    Work in process inventory, January 1 5,000
    Total factory payroll, January 1–March 31 35,000
    Overhead absorbed, January 1–March 31 15,000
    Work in process inventory, March 31 ....

b) Cost of goods sold, January 1–31 ....$75,000
    Overhead absorbed, January 1–31 (80% of direct labor cost) 24,000
    Finished goods inventory, January 1 10,000
    Direct materials used, January 1–31 30,000
    Work in process inventory, January 31 8,500
    Cost of goods completed 80,000
    Overhead underabsorbed 1,000
    Direct labor, January 1–31 ....
    Work in process inventory, January 1 ....

i) Net income for year..$ 4,000
   Sales.. 50,000
   Selling and administrative expense................................ 15,000
   Work in process inventory, January 1............................. 3,000
   Raw materials inventory, December 31............................ 8,000
   Overhead absorbed, January 1–December 31...................... 15,000
   Finished goods inventory, December 31........................... 10,000
   Finished goods inventory, January 1............................. 5,000
   Cost of goods completed... 34,000
   Other income and other expenses................................. 0
   Overhead incurred, January 1–December 31.......................   .....
   Underabsorbed overhead is deducted in computing net income.

17. The Broxbo Manufacturing Company uses a job order cost system. On July 1, Work in Process had a balance of $2,200, made up as follows:

Job No.	Materials	Labor	Overhead
101................	$ 620	$240	$340
102................	730	150	120
Total..............	$1,350	$390	$460

Finished Goods on this same date had a balance of $3,000, representing the cost of job No. 100.

During July, material cost, labor cost, and labor hours were:

Job No.	Material Cost	Labor Cost	Labor Hours
101.............	$ 100	$ 560	200
102.............	200	900	300
103.............	1,500	480	150
104.............	2,000	620	200
105.............	3,000	145	50
Total......	$6,800	$2,705	900

In a normal month, the factory is expected to operate at a volume of 1,000 labor hours and factory overhead is expected to amount to $3,000. Actual factory overhead cost for July was $2,950.

Job Nos. 101, 102, and 103 were completed during July and were placed in the finished goods storeroom.

Job Nos. 100, 101, and 102 were delivered to customers during July at a billed price of $12,000.

a) Enter the above information on job order cost sheets.

b) What was the total gross margin on job Nos. 100, 101, and 102?

c) What was the amount of the over- or underabsorbed overhead for the month?

d) Prepare summary journal entries to record the above information. Make the simplifying assumption that all factory labor and overhead costs were paid in cash. All materials came from the materials inventory.

e) For what purposes might management wish to use the information summarized in your answers to (*a*), (*b*), and (*c*) above? Is this information well suited to these purposes?

18. On November 30, a fire destroyed the plant and factory offices of the Swadburg Company. You are called upon to assist in the preparation of the insurance claim as to inventory values at November 30. Information you obtain is as follows:

(1) From the balance sheet at November 1 you find the beginning inventories: materials, $5,000; work in process, $15,000; finished goods, $27,500.

(2) The factory burden rate in use during November was $0.80 per dollar of direct material cost.

(3) Total sales for the month amounted to $60,000. The gross profit margin constituted 25 percent of selling price.

(4) Purchases of materials during November amounted to $30,000.

(5) The payroll records show wages accrued during November as $25,000, of which $3,000 was for indirect labor.

(6) The charges to factory overhead accounts totaled $18,000. $2,000 of this was for indirect materials and $3,000 was for indirect labor.

(7) The cost of goods completed during November was $52,000.

(8) Underabsorbed overhead amounted to $400. This amount was not deducted in the computation of the gross profit margin [item (3) above], but it had been charged against revenues for the month.

Show in T-accounts summary entries for the transactions affecting these inventory items and show the inventory of raw materials, work in process, and finished goods at November 30.

*19. The DEF Company manufactures metal parts to be sold to manufacturers of production machinery. The cost of materials requisitioned for specific job lots is charged to Work in Process. The straight-time wage costs (not including overtime premiums) of all labor traceable to specific job lots is charged to Work in Process. All other costs, including overtime premiums, are charged to a Manufacturing Overhead Cost Summary account. Manufacturing overhead costs are applied to jobs in process at a constant burden rate of $4 per direct labor hour.

During December, the following events were recorded by the DEF Company:

(1) Materials purchased: $50,000.
(2) Materials issued to production:
Direct materials, $35,000.
Indirect materials, $12,000.
(3) Direct labor hours: 10,000 (straight-time wage rate is $2 per hour).
(4) Overtime hours included in direct labor hours: 500 (a premium of $1 per hour is paid for overtime labor).
(5) All other manufacturing overhead: $30,000.
(6) Content of jobs completed and transferred to finished goods inventory:

Materials cost.............................$32,000
Direct labor hours............................ 9,000

a) Prepare journal entries to record the foregoing events.
b) Compute the amount of over- or underabsorbed overhead.
c) Assume that an additional 400 hours of direct labor time at overtime rates occurred during December but were not included in the figures given above. By how much would this change the amount of over- or underabsorbed overhead?

20. The Sandrex Company uses a job order cost accounting system. Direct labor costs are charged daily to Work in Process and credited to Accrued Wages Payable on the basis of time tickets. Direct materials costs are charged to Work in Process and credited to Materials Inventory. Factory overhead costs are charged initially to a Factory Overhead account. Overhead costs are charged to the Work in Process account by means of a predetermined burden rate of $2 per direct labor hour. The costs of goods finished are transferred from Work in Process to a Finished Goods account at the time each job is completed. A perpetual inventory system is used for both materials and finished goods.

Prepare journal entries to record the facts described below. Each of these events should be regarded as independent of the others, and it should be assumed in each case that any pertinent prior recordings have been made correctly unless it is stated otherwise. If no entry is required, explain why.

a) Goods manufactured at a cost of $8,000 are sold on credit for $14,000. Manufacture of these products was completed in the preceding accounting period. The job cost records show that the total manufacturing cost of $8,000 includes $2,000 of materials, $3,000 of direct labor, and $3,000 of overhead.
b) Factory overhead is charged to a job on which 480 direct labor hours have been recorded during this period.
c) It is discovered prior to the end of the period that an error in analyzing

a batch of timecards has resulted in treating 500 hours of direct labor at $2.50 per hour as indirect labor (i.e., the charge was made to Factory Overhead). The job on which this labor was used has been finished but not yet sold.

d) Materials costing $5,000 and supplies costing $500 are issued from the factory storeroom. Of the materials, $1,000 is for use in constructing new display cases in the salesroom. The display cases are completed and placed in use this period. The remaining materials are issued to the factory for specific job orders. Of the supplies, $100 is for the immediate use of the sales office. The remainder are for factory use.

e) Prior to the end of the period, it is discovered that $1,000 of direct materials have been charged to the wrong job. At the time this error is discovered, both jobs have been completed but not yet sold.

f) Prior to the end of the period, it is discovered that an error was made in adding up the direct labor hours on a certain job which has now been completed and sold. The dollar amount of direct labor was added correctly, but the hours were overstated by 100.

g) At the end of the period, factory wages earned but as yet unpaid amount to $3,000 for direct labor and $1,000 for indirect labor. Employer's payroll taxes on these wages are 6 percent. This company treats all payroll taxes as overhead.

21. The L. Chief Company showed inventories as follows:

	June 1	June 30
Materials and supplies........	$10,000	$8,000
Work in process.............	6,000	8,000
Finished goods..............	6,000	5,000

The following transactions were completed during the month of June:

(1) Raw materials and supplies were purchased in the amount of $24,000.

(2) Of the materials and supplies issued during the month, $3,500 were *indirect*.

(3) The payroll for the month was as follows:

	Gross Payroll	Income Tax Withheld	F.I.C.A. Tax Withheld	Paid in Cash to Employees
Direct labor—factory......	$15,000	$1,500	$540	$12,960
Indirect labor—factory.....	5,000	500	180	4,320
Sales salaries.............	3,000	300	100	2,600
Administrative salaries.....	2,000	200	60	1,740

(4) The employer's payroll taxes consisted of a matching amount for F.I.C.A. taxes, plus unemployment taxes of $500 on factory payrolls, $80 on sales payrolls, and $30 on administrative payrolls.

(5) Sundry manufacturing overhead costs were incurred and paid in cash, $9,000.

(6) Depreciation charges for the month were: factory machinery, $200; equipment in sales and administrative offices, $100.

(7) Manufacturing overhead costs were applied to work in process on the basis of $1.20 per dollar of direct labor.

(8) Miscellaneous nonmanufacturing expenses incurred and paid for in cash totaled $3,600.

(9) Sales on account totaled $90,000.

a) Show the flow of manufacturing costs through T-accounts.

b) Prepare an income statement for June. (Treat under- or overabsorbed manufacturing overhead as an addition to or deduction from cost of goods sold.)

22. The cost accounts of the Sandusky Metals Company include a single Work in Process account, to which the costs of direct materials and direct labor are charged as they are incurred, and the following accounts for manufacturing overhead: Indirect Labor, Factory Supplies, Maintenance, Rent, Depreciation, and Miscellaneous. Overhead costs are charged initially to the latter accounts, which are closed into the Manufacturing Overhead account at the end of each month. Factory overhead is applied to jobs at a burden rate of 120 percent of direct labor cost.

The September 1 balances in the various inventory accounts were as follows:

```
Materials and supplies.............................$35,000
Work in process...................................  22,400
Finished goods....................................  30,500
```

The following transactions occurred in connection with the manufacturing activities of the plant for the month of September:

(1) Materials purchased on account: $101,000.

(2) Materials requisitioned:
    For job orders, $87,000.
    Factory supplies, $3,900.

(3) Factory payrolls:
    For job orders, $34,000.
    Supervisory and other indirect labor, $9,000.

(4) Machinery repairs performed by outside contractor: $600.

(5) Rent paid for the factory building for September, October, and November: $18,000.

(6) Machinery depreciation for September: $7,500.

(7) Miscellaneous factory overhead accrued: $5,000.

(8) Jobs completed and transferred to finished goods stock room: $124,000.

(9) Finished goods inventory, September 30: $33,400.

a) Prepare T-accounts, enter the opening balances, record the transactions of the month, and compute the closing balances.

b) Prepare an itemized statement of the cost of goods manufactured and sold, leaving the over- or underabsorbed factory overhead as a deferred credit or deferred charge to operations of future months.

23. The Nesbitt Company uses a Lifo basis for costing its finished goods inventories; materials and parts are costed on a Fifo basis; and work in process is inventoried on the basis of the cost of specific job lots. Annual increments to finished goods inventories are assumed for Lifo purposes to be from the first job lots completed during the year.

One of the company's products is the Model G Hand Stapler, and on January 1, 1968, the Lifo inventory valuation of this product was:

	No. of Dozen	Cost per Dozen	Inventory Valuation
Base quantity.......	1,000	$25.20	$25,200
1962 layer.........	100	28.80	2,880
1966 layer.........	150	31.20	4,680
Total.........	1,250		$32,760

A burden rate of $2 per direct labor hour was used throughout the factory in 1968. No Model G staplers were in process on January 1, 1968.

The following transactions relating to production and sale of Model G Hand Staplers took place during 1968:

(1) Shipped 250 dozen to customers during January.

(2) Manufactured 1,000 dozen on job No. 2246 during February: direct materials, $9,800; direct labor, 6,000 hours at $2.20 per hour.

(3) Shipped 1,500 dozen to customers during March, April, May, and June.

(4) Manufactured 1,200 dozen on job No. 2873 during July: direct materials, $12,100; direct labor, 7,100 hours at $2.30 per hour.

(5) Shipped 900 dozen to customers during August, September, October, and November.

(6) Started job No. 3045 on November 21, but delays in receiving materials prevented completion of this job in 1968. This job order consisted of 1,000 dozen, with accumulated costs to December 31 of: direct materials, $10,200; direct labor, 5,900 hours at $2.30 per hour.

a) Compute total cost of Model G Hand Staplers sold for 1968 and the cost of staplers in process and in finished goods inventory on December 31, 1968.

b) The company wishes to keep perpetual inventory records on its finished goods. What problems would be encountered and how would you solve them?

c) What additional problems would be raised if materials inventories were costed on a Lifo basis?

24. The Subway Car Company manufactures railway and subway cars to customer orders. Revenues are recognized at the time finished products are shipped to customers. A predetermined burden rate of $3 per direct labor hour is used in the company's factory.

On March 1, $120,000 in materials and supplies were on hand. The company maintains no inventory of finished goods, but it had three jobs in process in its factory on March 1:

Job No.	No. of Cars	Costs Accumulated in Prior Months
6456.........	1	$ 43,000
6457.........	4	134,000
6459.........	3	27,000

The following transactions affecting manufacturing costs occurred during the month of March:

(1) A new job order, No. 6460, was placed in production.

(2) Materials, supplies, and parts in the amount of $97,000 were purchased on account.

(3) Materials, supplies, and parts were issued to production departments, as follows:

Job No. 6456	$ 2,000
Job No. 6457	20,000
Job No. 6459	35,000
Job No. 6460	5,000
General factory use	18,000

(4) Labor time tickets showed the following totals:

Job No. 6456	1,200 hours,	$ 5,000
Job No. 6457	8,000 hours,	20,000
Job No. 6459	10,000 hours,	26,000
Job No. 6460	800 hours,	3,000
Indirect labor	3,000 hours,	5,400

(5) Factory depreciation for the month, $10,000.

(6) Other factory operating costs amounted to $35,000 (credit Accounts Payable).

(7) Job No. 6456 was finished and shipped to the customer on March 18.

(8) Two cars in job No. 6457 were finished and shipped to the customer on March 28. The remaining two cars in the job were one-half completed on March 31.

a) Record the above information in appropriately titled T-accounts. Direct labor and direct materials costs are charged directly to a single Work in Process account. When incurred, all manufacturing overhead costs are charged to a Manufacturing Overhead account. Factory overhead absorbed is credited to this manufacturing overhead account.

b) Prepare a schedule showing March 31 balances in the Work in Process and Manufacturing Overhead accounts.

25. The Lasill Company manufactures several types of pumps, partly to order and partly for stock. In both cases, work is done on the basis of production orders, and costs are recorded by job. The company's balance sheet as of August 31, 19x4, and its transactions for the month of September, 19x4, are shown below.

THE LASILL COMPANY

BALANCE SHEET

As of August 31, 19x4

ASSETS

Current Assets:

Cash	$ 23,280	
Accounts receivable	31,070	
Materials and supplies	15,120	
Work in process	8,300	
Finished goods	6,730	$ 84,500

Long-Life Assets:

Machinery and equipment	$248,600	
Less: Allowance for depreciation	83,200	165,400
Total		$249,900

LIABILITIES AND SHAREHOLDERS' EQUITY

Current Liabilities:

Accounts payable	$ 27,650	
Accrued wages and salaries	1,830	$ 29,480

Shareholders' Equity

Common stock	$150,000	
Retained earnings	70,420	220,420
Total		$249,900

Transactions during September:

(1) Purchased: Materials and supplies......................$28,310
          Machine.................................. 21,000 $49,310

(2) Issued materials and supplies:
      Direct materials—job No. 17.........................$ 2,530
              No. 18........................ 7,120
              No. 19........................ 6,690
      Indirect materials................................. 4,060   20,400

(3) Accrued wages and salaries:
      Direct labor—job No. 16, 1,200 hrs....................$ 2,440
             No. 17, 3,600 hrs.................... 7,370
             No. 18, 5,600 hrs.................... 10,580
             No. 19,   800 hrs.................... 2,000
      Indirect labor and supervision.......................... 5,420
      Office salaries (administration and sales)................. 4,590   32,400

(4) Other manufacturing costs:
      Power, light, and heat..............................$ 3,830
      Repairs.. 1,160
      Sundry... 790   5,780

(5) Administrative and sales expenses incurred.................   2,770
(6) Depreciation on equipment: Plant.......................$ 2,040
                   Office...................... 120   2,160

(7) Jobs finished during month: Nos. 16–18
(8) Sales during month: job No. 15 (balance)................$ 8,350
               No. 16 (all)...................... 16,300
               No. 17 (all)..................... 18,300
               No. 18 (20 out of 50 pumps)........ 13,400   56,350

(9) Received payments from customers on account.............   47,800
(10) Paid: Accounts payable...............................$43,690
      Wages... 31,850   75,540
(11) Received loan from bank on September 30 (90-day note).....   30,000

Additional information:

(1) Payroll deductions and taxes are omitted for purposes of simplification.
(2) All costs incurred other than payrolls are in the first instance credited to Accounts Payable.
(3) Manufacturing Overhead is charged to jobs at the rate of $1.50 per direct labor hour.
(4) The opening balance of Finished Goods represents part of job order No. 15; that of Work in Process, Job No. 16 (Materials, $4,500; Direct Labor, $1,700; Overhead, $2,100).

a) Enter the above transactions in T-accounts and job order cost sheets. (Use a single T-account for all factory overhead costs.)

b) Prepare financial statements for the month. Over- or underabsorbed overhead is to be entered as a special item on the income statement.

†26. Mr. Giulio Cattani, founder and president of Tipografia Stanca, S.p.A., was worried. The company was doing more business than ever

---

† Copyright 1968 by l'Institut pour l'Etude des Méthodes de Direction de l'Entreprise (IMEDE), Lausanne, Switzerland. Published by permission.

before—sales were at an annual rate of about L.125,000,000 a year‡—but net income had decreased slightly during recent months and the ratio of income to sales had dropped sharply. Mr. Cattani wondered what had gone wrong and what he could do about it. He called in his chief (and only) accountant, Mr. Gaetano Pareto, and asked him to find out what was happening.

Tipografia Stanca was an Italian corporation, located in Milan and doing a general printing business on a customer order basis. Mr. Cattani set the price to be charged for each job. When possible, he waited until the work was done and then quoted a price equal to 140 percent of the cost of the paper stock used, plus L.2,500 for each labor hour. Straight-time wage rates in the past, adjusted for recent wage rate increases, had averaged about L.800 an hour, and this formula seemed to provide an adequate margin to cover overhead costs and provide a good profit.

Most of Tipografia Stanca's work was done on the basis of predetermined contract prices. In bidding on these jobs, Mr. Cattani applied his standard pricing formula to his own estimates of the amount of labor and paper stock the job would require. He prided himself on his ability to make these estimates, but he sometimes quoted a price that was higher or lower than the formula price, depending on his judgment of the market situation.

Stanca's production procedures were fairly simple. When a customer's order was received, it was assigned a production order number and a production order was issued. The material to be printed, known as the customer's "copy," was given to a copy editor who indicated on the copy the sizes and styles of type that should be used. The editor sometimes made changes in the copy, usually after telephoning the customer to discuss the changes.

Once the customer's material had been copy-edited, it was sent to the composing room, where it was set in type. A "proof" copy was printed by hand and returned to the copy editor, who checked the printed copy against the original. Any errors in the proof were indicated in the margin and the marked proof was sent to the customer for approval. At this point the customer might decide to make changes in the copy, and these changes, as well as corrections of type-setting errors, were made as soon as the corrected proof was returned to the composing room.

In some cases a second proof was sent to the customer for his approval, but at Tipografia Stanca most orders were sent to the pressroom as soon as the customer's corrections had been made and the second proof had been approved by the copy editor.

At this point, the order was ready for production on one of the presses

---

‡ In 1968 the Italian lira could be exchanged at the rate of approximately L.620 to the United States dollar.

in the pressroom. Printing instructions were contained in the production order, which specified the particular press to be used, the number of copies to be printed, the color, size, style, weight and finish of the "stock" or paper to be used, and similar details. Copies were then printed, bound, and packaged for delivery to the customer.

An order could take as little as one day in the copy-editing and composingroom stages or as long as several weeks. Printing, binding, and packaging seldom took more than two days except on very large production runs of multi-page booklets.

For many years the shop had had enough work to keep it busy steadily throughout the year, without serious seasonal slack. As a result, Tipografia Stanca's before-tax profit had fluctuated between 13 and 15 percent of net sales. The interim profit report for the first half of 1968 therefore came as a great shock to Mr. Cattani. Although volume was slightly greater than in the first half of 1967, profit was down to 8.8 percent of sales, an all-time low. The comparison, with all figures expressed as percentages of net sales, was as follows:

	Six Months 1968	Six Months 1967
Net sales......................	100.0%	100.0%
Production costs.................	77.6%	72.3%
Selling and administrative costs.....	13.6	13.9
Profit.........................	8.8	13.8

Mr. Pareto knew that the company's problem must be either low prices or excessive costs. Unfortunately, the cost data already available told him little about the cost/price relationship for individual jobs. Tipografia Stanca's operating costs were classified routinely into twenty categories, such as salaries, pressroom wages, production materials, depreciation, and so forth. Individual job cost sheets were not used and the cost of goods in process was estimated only once a year, at the end of the fiscal year.

Detailed data were available on only two kinds of items: paper stock issued and labor time. When stock was issued, a requisition form was filled out, showing the kind of stock issued, the quantity, the unit cost, and the production order number. Similar details were reported when unused stock was returned to the stockroom.

As for labor, each employee directly engaged in working on production orders filled in a time sheet each day, on which he recorded the time he started on a given task, the time he finished it or moved on to other work, and (in the case of time spent directly on a specific production order) the order number. His department number and pay grade were recorded on the time sheet by the payroll clerk.

Mr. Pareto's first step was to establish some overall cost relationships. Employees, for example, fell into three different pay grades, with the following regular hourly wage rates:

Pay Grade	Regular Hourly Wage Rate
1.....................L. 1,200	
2..................... 800	
3.................... 600	

These rates applied to a regular work week of 44 hours a week. For work in excess of this number of hours, employees were paid an overtime premium of 50 percent of their regular hourly wage. Overtime premiums were negligible when the work load was light, but in a normal year they averaged about 5 percent of the total amount of hourly wages computed at the regular hourly wage rate. In a normal year this was approximately L.40 per direct labor hour.

In addition to their wages, the employees also received various kinds of benefits, including vacation pay, health insurance, and old-age pensions. The cost of these benefits to Tipografia Stanca amounted to about 70 percent of the total payroll. Mr. Pareto estimated that all other shop overhead costs—that is, all copy department, composing room and pressroom costs other than direct materials, direct labor, overtime premiums, and employee benefits on direct labor payrolls—would average L.400 per direct labor hour in a normal year.

Armed with these estimates of general relationships, Mr. Pareto then proceeded to determine the costs of several recent production orders. One of these was order A-467. This was received for copy editing on Monday, October 5 and delivered to the customer on Friday, October 9. Mr. Cattani had quoted a price of L.180,000 on this job in advance, on the basis of

Exhibit 1

PARTIAL LIST OF MATERIALS REQUISITIONS

For the Week of October 5–9

Req. No.	Job No.	Amount*
4058.................	A-467	L.30,000
R162.................	A-469	(2,000)
4059.................	A-467	6,000
4060.................	A-442	600
R163.................	A-455	(900)
R164.................	A-472	(800)
4060.................	A-467	3,600
R165.................	A-465	(1,200)
4062.................	A-467	9,600
4063.................	A-471	32,000
4064.................	A-473	26,400
4065.................	A-458	2,200
R166.................	A-467	(3,300)
4066.................	A-481	17,600

(*) Amounts in parentheses are returned materials.

Exhibit 2

PARTIAL SUMMARY OF LABOR TIME SHEETS

For the Week of October 5–9

Employee No.	Pay Grade	Dept.	Job No.	Hours
14.............	2	Copy	A-463	6.6
14.............	2	Copy	A-467	1.4
15.............	1	Copy	A-467	3.3
15.............	1	Copy	—	2.7
15.............	1	Copy	A-467	8.8
18.............	3	Press	A-467	4.0
18.............	3	Press	A-472	4.6
22.............	1	Composing	A-455	3.8
22.............	1	Composing	A-467	8.4*
22.............	1	Composing	—	1.5
23.............	2	Press	A-458	3.4
23.............	2	Press	A-467	4.7
23.............	2	Press	—	1.1
23	2	Press	A-459	2.5*
24.............	2	Copy	A-470	7.4
28.............	1	Press	A-467	7.0
28.............	1	Press	A-458	1.0
31.............	3	Press	—	8.0
33.............	1	Composing	A-471	7.6
33.............	1	Composing	A-472	4.2
40.............	2	Press	A-469	3.6
40.............	2	Press	A-467	4.9
40.............	2	Press	—	0.2
43.............	1	Press	A-467	3.5
43.............	1	Press	A-481	5.8

(—) Indicates time spent on general work in the department and not on any one job.
(*) Employee No. 22 worked 6 hours of overtime during the week, none of them on job A–467, while employee No. 23 worked 8 hours of overtime, including 4.0 hours spent on job A–467.

an estimate of L.48,000 for paper stock costs and 45 direct labor hours. All requisitions and time records relating to order A-467 are included in the lists in Exhibits 1 and 2. (To save space, some of the details shown on the requisitions and time tickets have been omitted from these exhibits.)

a) Develop costing rates for use in charging labor costs to individual job orders. Also develop a burden rate for use in charging shop overhead costs to individual job orders. For this purpose overtime premiums and the cost of employee benefits accruing as a result of overtime premiums should be regarded as shop overhead.

b) Prepare a job order cost sheet for production order A-467, and enter the costs that would be assigned to this order, using the costing rates you developed in the answer to (*a*) above.

c) What conclusions might Mr. Pareto have reached on the basis of his analysis of this order? What suggestions would you make to Mr. Cattani?

d) What would be the advantages of developing product unit costs routinely for every job? Do you think that these advantages would be great enough to persuade Mr. Cattani to hire an additional clerk for this purpose at an annual cost of about L.2,000,000?

e) What method or methods other than the one used in (*a*) and (*b*) above might be used to charge overtime premiums to individual job orders? Which method would best meet Mr. Cattani's needs?

Chapter 18

FACTORY OVERHEAD

MEASUREMENT PROBLEMS

THE JOB ORDER COSTING procedures described in Chapter 17 permit a highly accurate measurement of direct labor and direct materials cost per unit, but only a very rough approximation to the amount of factory overhead costs attributable to any one unit of output. The purpose of this chapter is to examine three sets of issues relating to the development of burden rates, the means by which factory overhead cost per unit of product is determined:

1. How can differences in the relative importance of overhead costs in various factory departments be reflected in product costs?
2. How accurately does the burden rate indicate the effect of changes in production volume on total overhead cost?
3. How does the use of predetermined burden rates affect a company's reported income and balance sheet?

The first section of this chapter, on departmental overhead rates, attempts to answer the first of these questions. The second section, on the economics of overhead costs, focuses on the second question, while the two final sections center on the third issue, the relationship of burden rates to company financial statements.

DEPARTMENTAL OVERHEAD RATES

The amount of factory overhead cost assigned to a unit of a particular product is ordinarily based on *departmental* overhead rates rather than a single plantwide burden rate of the kind described in Chapter 17. Our first task, therefore, is to see why departmental rates are used and how they can be constructed.

Reasons for Departmental Overhead Rates

Plantwide burden rates are regarded as too inaccurate for management use, first because the relative importance of overhead cost is likely to vary widely from department to department, and second because products differ widely in their relative use of the various departments.[1]

The table in Exhibit 18–1 is designed to illustrate the argument for

Exhibit 18–1

LION EQUIPMENT CORPORATION

Budgeted Production Department Overhead Costs per Month
For the Year 19x1

Type of Cost	Department			Plant Total
	A	B	C	
Indirect labor	$ 7,000	$15,000	$ 6,000	$28,000
Indirect materials	3,000	8,000	2,000	13,000
Depreciation	5,000	6,000	5,000	16,000
Power	3,000	2,000	4,000	9,000
Other costs	14,000	9,000	7,000	30,000
Total	$32,000	$40,000	$24,000	$96,000
Direct labor costs	$20,000	$40,000	$12,000	$72,000
Burden rate (% of direct labor)	160%	100%	200%	133%

departmental burden rates. The upper part of this table presents the overhead costs that are traceable to each of the three production departments of the factory of the Lion Equipment Corporation, a manufacturer of industrial parts and equipment. For reasons to be examined later, the burden rates for the three producing departments in this example are all expressed as percentages of departmental direct labor cost. These burden rates are shown on the bottom line of the exhibit.

The variations from department to department are striking. The overhead costs traceable to department C are expected to average 200 percent of direct labor cost in 19x1, as against 100 percent in depart-

[1] For purposes of this discussion, a "department" is defined as a group of productive resources used for performing operations with highly similar cost/output relationships. Other equivalent terms are "production center" and "cost center."

ment B, 160 percent in department A, and an average of 133 percent in the plant as a whole. This means that product unit costs based on a single factorywide burden rate could be highly misleading.

For example, suppose that the direct labor cost of two products, X and Y, is $40 a unit. Three quarters of the labor needed to make a unit of product X is performed in department C; the rest is performed in department B. These percentages are reversed for product Y. The departmental burden rates indicate that product X has an overhead cost of $70, against $50 for product Y. These figures are shown in the following table:

	Product X		Product Y	
	Direct Labor Cost	Overhead Cost	Direct Labor Cost	Overhead Cost
Department B...........	$10	$10	$30	$30
Department C...........	30	60	10	20
Total..............	$40	$70	$40	$50

By comparison, a single factorywide burden rate of 133 percent would assign an overhead cost of $53.20 to each product. This would be far too little for X and slightly too much for Y. Under such a system, product X would appear to be a good deal more profitable relative to product Y than it actually is.

Overhead Cost Allocation

This discussion has ignored one important dimension of the Lion Equipment Corporation's factory cost structure. In addition to the three production departments shown in Exhibit 18–1, the factory has three *service* departments: factory management, building service, and equipment maintenance.

Service departments do not engage directly in production; instead, they contribute to the plant's output by providing services that facilitate the activities of the producing departments. Hence, before the output of a producing department is charged with overhead costs, the department's burden rate is ordinarily expanded to include a provision for the cost of the services provided to it by the service departments. This process is known as *cost allocation* or *cost redistribution*.

The budgeted service department costs for the Lion Equipment

Exhibit 18–2

LION EQUIPMENT CORPORATION

Budgeted Monthly Costs of Factory Service Departments
For the Year 19x1

	Factory Manage-ment	Building Service	Equipment Mainte-nance
Wages and salaries.................	$4,800	$1,000	$1,500
Supplies.........................	200	300	400
Depreciation.....................	50	1,400	100
Power...........................	...	350	150
Property taxes....................	...	700	...
Other costs......................	950	250	250
Total......................	$6,000	$4,000	$2,400

Corporation are shown in Exhibit 18–2. The accountant's objective is to find a way of allocating these costs so that the allocations will most closely approximate the amount of service department cost attributable to each of the production departments.

In this case, the company's accountants decided to base their allocations on the statistics given in Exhibit 18–3. For example, they redis-

Exhibit 18–3

LION EQUIPMENT CORPORATION

Estimates Used in Distributing Estimated Service
Department Costs for Burden Rate Determination

	Number of Employees	Floor Space Occupied (Square Feet)	Number of Equipment Maintenance Labor Hours to Be Used Each Month
Department A..................	21	12,000	225
Department B..................	27	18,000	175
Department C..................	12	10,000	200
Subtotal..................	60	40,000	600
Factory management............	8	2,000	..
Building service................	3	500	20
Equipment maintenance..........	4	2,500	..
Total..................	75	45,000	620

tributed the expected factory management costs among the three production departments in proportion to the total number of employees (direct and indirect) in those departments. This produced the following:

	(1) Number of Employees	(2) Percent of Production Employees	(3) Allocation of Factory Management Cost (2) × $6,000
Department A...............	21	35%	$2,100
Department B...............	27	45	2,700
Department C...............	12	20	1,200
Total.................	60	100%	$6,000

The justification for using the number of employees as the allocation basis was that this was judged to be the major determinant of the size of the factory management department.

Similarly, building services costs were allocated among the producing departments on the basis of relative floor space occupied:

	(1) Floor Space Occupied (Square Feet)	(2) Percent of Floor Space Occupied	(3) Allocation of Building Service Cost (2) × $4,000
Department A..............	12,000	30%	$1,200
Department B..............	18,000	45	1,800
Department C..............	10,000	25	1,000
Total................	40,000	100%	$4,000

Once again, the assumption was that the cost of providing building service was closely related to the amount of floor space occupied.

Finally, budgeted equipment maintenance costs were allocated in proportion to each department's estimated consumption of maintenance department services. The maintenance department's budgeted cost amounted to $2,400 a month. Spreading this over the 600 hours of maintenance services to be provided to the three producing departments during an average month gave a budgeted cost rate of $4 per maintenance hour. Using this rate, the budgeted allocation was:

	Estimated Number of Maintenance Hours Used	Allocation of Maintenance Service Costs at $4 per Mainte-nance Hour
Department A....................	225	$ 900
Department B....................	175	700
Department C....................	200	800
Total.....................	600	$2,400

After all these allocations were made, the estimated costs of the three producing departments were as shown in the last three columns of Exhibit 18–4. The burden rates shown at the bottom of these columns are larger than the burden rates in Exhibit 18–1 because they include provision for all factory costs, not just those that were directly traceable to the production departments. The service departments have no burden rates because no production work is done there.

Exhibit 18–4

LION EQUIPMENT CORPORATION

Factory Overhead Cost Allocation for 19x1

	Factory Manage-ment	Building Service	Equip-ment Mainte-nance	Producing Department		
				A	B	C
Indirect labor........	$4,800	$1,000	$1,500	$ 7,000	$15,000	$ 6,000
Indirect materials.....	200	300	400	3,000	8,000	2,000
Depreciation.........	50	1,400	100	5,000	6,000	5,000
Power..............	...	350	150	3,000	2,000	4,000
Property taxes.......	...	700	...	...	...	...
Other costs..........	950	250	250	14,000	9,000	7,000
Total Traceable..	$6,000	$4,000	$2,400	$32,000	$40,000	$24,000
Allocated charges: Factory manage-ment.............	(6,000)	...	...	2,100	2,700	1,200
Building service....	...	(4,000)	...	1,200	1,800	1,000
Equipment mainte-nance...........	...	...	(2,400)	900	700	800
Total Budgeted Cost..........	...	...	...	$36,200	$45,200	$27,000
Burden rate (% of direct labor........				181%	113%	225%

Alternative Allocation Methods

It is probably evident that service departments serve each other as well as the producing departments. Consequently, the distribution of budgeted service department costs only to the producing departments may be considered incorrect. One method commonly employed to overcome this difficulty is a "step-down" procedure. The costs of the department served least by the others are first distributed among all other departments, including both service and producing departments. The costs of that service department which qualifies second by this criterion are then accorded similar treatment, and so on until all service costs have been transferred to producing department budgets. The desirability of adding to the complexity of the system by this device or similar ones must be judged on the basis of the increase in the accuracy of the burden rates and the value to management of this increase.

ECONOMICS OF OVERHEAD COSTS

The overhead rates described in the preceding pages are often called *full-cost overhead rates* because their objective is a unit cost for each product that includes an equitable share of *all* manufacturing costs. Full-cost overhead rates are widely criticized on two grounds. First, many of the allocations are approximations that do not represent the amounts of service department costs that are in fact incurred for the benefit of the individual producing departments. Second, average full cost does not represent the effect on cost of variations in production volume. The first of these needs no further comment here. To examine the second, however, we need to make an elementary study of the economics of overhead costs.

The Variation of Cost with Output

The full-cost burden rate is seldom an accurate indicator of the relationship between overhead cost and production volume. Taken literally, it says that total cost will be proportional to production volume. That is, if total overhead costs are $40,000 at a production volume of 20,000 direct labor dollars ("DLD") so that the average cost per DLD is $2, then an increase in output of one DLD will increase overhead costs by $2. Unfortunately, even a crude examination of a company's actual cost experience would reveal that total overhead cost per unit of output rarely if ever varies with output in this way.

To establish the relation between some category of overhead cost and output, one might show on a chart the actual cost and actual output for a number of past periods. For example, Figure 1 in Exhibit 18–5 shows the relation between indirect material cost and volume measured by direct labor dollars. Each dot represents the cost and output for a particular month. The line drawn through the dots indicates the cost/output relationship that is suggested by the observations. It represents the overhead cost that the firm might be expected to incur at each level of output if future conditions are like the past.

The line fitted to the observations in Figure 1 is described by the equation:

$$\text{Total Cost} = C = a + bQ \,,$$

with $a = 0$, since $C = 0$ when $Q = 0$ in Figure 1. To obtain the cost per unit of output, we divide both sides of the equation by Q, and we find that $C/Q = b$. That is, the indirect material cost per unit of output is b at all levels of production volume.

Variable Costs. A cost that behaves in the way indicated by Figure 1 is called a variable cost. A variable cost is approximately constant per unit of output; that is, in total it varies proportionately with volume. The total indirect materials cost at any level of output [Q] can be estimated by multiplying Q by the average unit cost, b.

Fixed Costs. By contrast with a variable cost, a fixed cost does not vary from period to period in response to changes in the degree to which factory capacity is used. Figure 2 in Exhibit 18–5 illustrates one kind of fixed cost, depreciation charges on equipment. Again, the line that fits the observations recorded or "plotted" in Figure 2 is:

$$\text{Total Cost} = C = a + bQ \,.$$

This time, b is equal to zero and C is equal to a at all volumes of output. Depreciation, for example, may vary from one period to the next due to changes in the amount of equipment subject to depreciation, but the depreciation charge is not dependent on the rate of capacity utilization. Within the limits of factory capacity, the total depreciation cost does not vary as a result of output changes, and the cost per unit of output falls as the rate of output per period increases. At any output [Q], the cost per unit of output is a/Q.

Semivariable Costs. Cost elements that are neither variable nor fixed may be classified as semivariable. One kind of semivariable cost is represented by Figure 3 in the lower part of Exhibit 18–5. In this

Exhibit 18–5

COST/VOLUME RELATIONSHIPS

FIGURE 1
VARIABLE COST

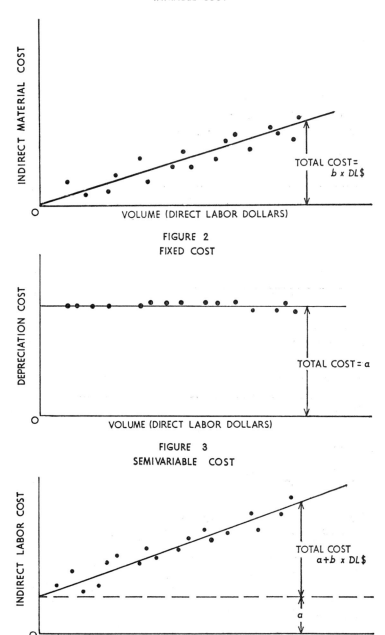

TOTAL COST=
b x DL$

INDIRECT MATERIAL COST

VOLUME (DIRECT LABOR DOLLARS)

FIGURE 2
FIXED COST

TOTAL COST= *a*

DEPRECIATION COST

VOLUME (DIRECT LABOR DOLLARS)

FIGURE 3
SEMIVARIABLE COST

TOTAL COST
a+b x DL$

a

INDIRECT LABOR COST

VOLUME (DIRECT LABOR DOLLARS)

case, indirect labor cost falls as output falls toward zero, but it does not fall proportionately with the change in output. Once again, this kind of cost can be described by the equation,

$$C = a + bQ,$$

but this time both a and b are positive. Dividing both sides by Q, therefore, we get:

$$\text{Cost per Unit} = \frac{C}{Q} = \frac{a}{Q} + b.$$

As output (Q) increases, a/Q decreases and so does average overhead cost per unit (C/Q). A cost like this can also be regarded as consisting of two parts: one for the fixed component of the cost (a) and one for the variable component (bQ).

Since each of these three categories of cost is encountered in a firm or department of a firm, overhead costs as a whole are semivariable with respect to output within the limits of existing productive capacity.

Choosing an Index of Volume

The size of the deviations of the observed data from the line of relationship (the *regression line*) drawn through them can be used in selecting the measure of output. Indirect materials cost in the example could have been plotted against the number of units of product output, the number of pounds of materials processed, the number of machine-hours used, or the number of direct labor hours worked. In each case a regression line could have been drawn through the observations. The closer the observations to the line, the higher the *correlation* between the actual cost at an output level and the cost predicted by the line. The best measure of volume is the one that gives the highest correlation.

For example, if overhead cost varies more closely with direct labor than with the weight of the factory's output, then two products that weigh the same but require different amounts of direct labor will lead to different amounts of overhead cost. In such a case, a cost/volume formula based on direct labor will be a better device for cost forecasting than a formula based on product weight.

The burden rates that were developed earlier in this chapter for each of the Lion Equipment Corporation's three producing departments used departmental direct labor cost as the index of production volume. In practice, each department might use a different index.

Machine-hours, direct labor hours, and direct labor cost are the three measures of production volume most commonly employed. Machine-hours are used when machine activity is the predominant feature of the operation. Direct labor hours are preferred when overhead apparently varies with labor usage but is independent of differences in wage rates. Direct labor cost is superior only when overhead costs are higher on jobs involving skilled labor, and/or are much influenced by changes in wage rates. When no one of these bases appears to be more accurate than any other, the one involving the least bookkeeping is preferred.

Cost and Management Policy

Fixed overhead costs and the fixed component of semivariable costs may be further classified according to the reason why the cost is fixed. Certain fixed costs are fixed as a consequence of *past* management decisions. Costs such as depreciation of equipment and rent on the building are fixed by past decisions to acquire productive facilities. For all practical purposes, the amounts of these costs cannot be reduced by a current decision that the plant is too big.

Other costs are fixed because the management's *policy* is not to change the cost in response to a change in output. For example, sometime in the past management may have decided to employ four industrial engineers to study work methods. Although the management may at any time decide to raise or lower the number of industrial engineers, its present policy is to have four, no matter what the current level of output. Accordingly, these costs may be considered as *management policy* costs.

Relevance to Product Costing

From this discussion, it should be obvious that a full-cost burden rate is very likely to overstate the cost of manufacturing another unit of product within the limits of existing capacity. If the decision is between different ways of utilizing factory capacity, product cost determined by full-costing techniques will not be a good basis for cost estimation.

In recognition of this, accountants often replace or supplement full-cost product costs with costs based on the *variable costing* principle. Under variable costing, product cost is defined as average variable factory cost. Factory fixed cost is not assigned to products at all. Instead, it is budgeted as a total amount per period.

The validity of the variable costing approach can be judged only after a further examination of the data required for managerial decisions. This will be the central theme of the next chapter. For the moment, it is enough to observe that the presence of substantial quantities of fixed costs may rob departmental burden rates of much of their supposed accuracy. A figure is not accurate if it is not relevant to its intended use. We should not become so fascinated with the full-costing mechanism that we mistake complexity for relevance.

ACCOUNTING FOR OVERHEAD ON A DEPARTMENTAL BASIS

Because product cost is determined on the basis of *predetermined* burden rates, departmentalization of *actual* overhead costs serves no product costing purpose.[2] Actual overhead costs are ordinarily classified departmentally, however, for reasons that we shall examine in Chapter 22. The absorption of overhead costs is also recorded on a departmental basis. Let us see what the accounts will look like after these entries have been made.

Recording and Allocating Overhead Costs

Recording actual factory overhead costs presents no particular difficulty. The amounts are identified by department and by cost element (indirect labor, etc.). These amounts are then debited to the departmental accounts. For example, the actual costs for April, 19x1, were recorded as in the summary entry below:

(1)

Factory Management Department.....................	6,150
Building Service Department.....................	3,810
Equipment Maintenance Department.....................	2,660
Department A—Overhead.....................	31,510
Department B—Overhead.....................	38,080
Department C—Overhead.....................	24,160
Various Accounts.....................	106,370

To simplify this illustration, only a single overhead account is used for each department instead of the many subaccounts that would be encountered in practice.

In addition, the Lion Equipment Corporation chooses to allocate service department costs to producing department accounts. The charges for factory management and building service department costs are identical to the monthly amounts *budgeted* at the beginning

---

[2] The departmentalization of actual costs during a period may provide information for developing the predetermined burden rates the firm will use during the next year or accounting period.

of the year, as given in Exhibit 18–4 above. The allocation of these costs for April was as follows:

(2)

Department A—Overhead................................	3,300	
Department B—Overhead...............................	4,500	
Department C—Overhead...............................	2,200	
Factory Management Department.....................		6,000
Building Service Department.........................		4,000

The charges for equipment maintenance, on the other hand, were computed by multiplying the estimated cost per maintenance hour ($4) by the actual number of maintenance hours used by each department during the month. For April, 19x1, the calculation was:

	Number of Maintenance Hours Used	Maintenance Charge at $4 per Maintenance Hour
Department A.............	250	$1,000
Department B.............	230	920
Department C.............	170	680
Total................	650	$2,600

The entry to record this allocation was:

(3)

Department A—Overhead................................	1,000	
Department B—Overhead...............................	920	
Department C—Overhead...............................	680	
Equipment Maintenance Department...................		2,600

This method of allocation leaves debit or credit balances in each service department account. For example, the Equipment Maintenance Department account showed the following balance at the end of April, 19x1:

Equipment Maintenance Department

Actual costs	2,660	Costs charged to producing departments	2,600
Bal. 4/30 60			

This kind of imbalance is inevitable when allocations are partially or wholly predetermined. It could be avoided by recalculating the hourly maintenance service rate each month on the basis of the actual average cost for the month. The management of the Lion Equipment Corporation, however, believes that the month-to-month variations in maintenance cost should not enter into their evaluation of the performance of the producing departments. The "charging rate" is therefore kept constant throughout the year.

Absorption of Factory Overhead

Each month, the producing department overhead accounts are credited and the work in process accounts (representing the job orders) are debited. The amount of this cost transfer is obtained by multiplying the departmental predetermined burden rates by the actual direct labor cost expended on the various job orders during the month. The total amount transferred to job orders from a given department is the amount of overhead cost *absorbed* by the work done in that department. The relevant figures for April were:

	(1) Direct Labor Cost	(2) Burden Rate (Percent of Direct Labor Cost)	(3) Amount Absorbed (1) × (2)
Department A..............	$18,000	181%	$ 32,580
Department B..............	41,000	113	46,330
Department C..............	10,000	225	22,500
Total................			$101,410

The entries to record these amounts in the job order cost sheets and in the departmental overhead accounts can be summarized as follows:

(4)
```
Overhead in Process (Various Job Cost Sheets)............101,410
    Department A—Overhead.........................        32,580
    Department B—Overhead.........................        46,330
    Department C—Overhead.........................        22,500
```

The flow of overhead costs achieved by the above entries is pictured in Exhibit 18–6. Each producing department's overhead account was charged for the costs traceable to it and also for a share of the cost of operating the service departments. These costs were then passed on to individual job orders. In each department, however, the amount absorbed was different from the total amount charged to the department during the month. This difference in the producing departments is known as the amount over- or underabsorbed. The comparable amounts in the service departments are the amounts over- or underdistributed.

The costs of departments A and C were *underabsorbed* during

Exhibit 18–6

LION EQUIPMENT CORPORATION

Factory Overhead Accounts
For the Month of April, 19x1

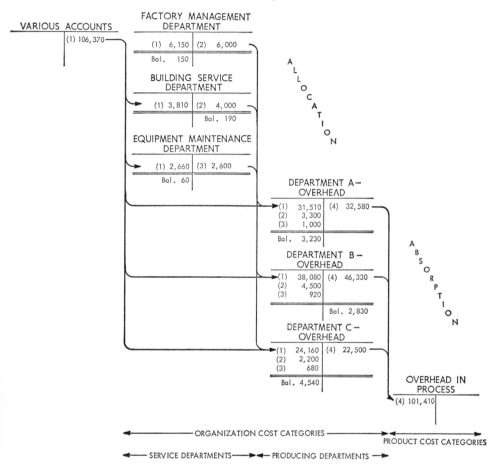

April, the actual costs being greater than the amounts carried into Overhead in Process. The overhead costs of department B, on the other hand, were *overabsorbed*, the costs charged to work in process having exceeded those charged to departmental overhead accounts by $2,830. Similarly, the costs of factory management and equipment maintenance were slightly *underdistributed*, while the cost of building service was slightly *overdistributed* during April.

OVER- AND UNDERABSORBED OVERHEAD

The balances remaining in the departmental accounts in Exhibit 18–6 are an inevitable result of the use of predetermined burden rates. In this case, actual costs for the month exceeded the amounts charged to product accounts by $4,960. This was divided among the departmental accounts in the following amounts, as shown in Exhibit 18–6:

	Underabsorbed/ Underdistributed	Overabsorbed/ Overdistributed
Department A overhead................	$3,230	
Department B overhead................		$2,830
Department C overhead................	4,540	
Factory management department........	150	
Building service department...........		190
Equipment maintenance department.....	60	
Total........................	$7,980	$3,020

Two problems need to be discussed briefly: (1) how do these balances arise; and (2) where should they be placed in periodic financial statements?

Reasons for Over- and Underabsorbed Overhead

Over- and underabsorbed overhead balances arise as a result of two phenomena:

1. Production volume during the period differs from the volume used to set the burden rate.
2. Actual costs differ from the amounts that would normally be expected at the production volume actually achieved during the period.

For example, department A's burden rate for 19x1, given in Exhibit 18–4 above, was 181 percent of direct labor cost. This was computed as follows:

$$\frac{\text{Estimated Overhead Cost at Normal Volume}}{\text{Estimated Direct Labor Cost at Normal Volume}} = \frac{\$36,200}{\$20,000} = 181 \text{ percent}.$$

Let us assume that further analysis of the $36,200 overhead cost estimate indicates that $26,200 was regarded as a fixed cost, the remaining $10,000 being a proportionately variable cost of $0.50 a direct labor dollar.

This relationship is pictured by the line BB′ in Exhibit 18–7. The

Exhibit 18–7

LION EQUIPMENT CORPORATION

Expected Variation in Actual and Absorbed
Overhead for Department A for the Year 19x1

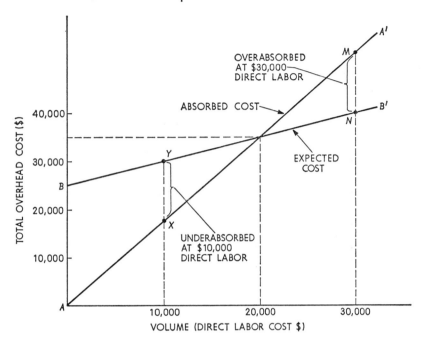

other line, *AA′*, indicates the amount of overhead cost that will be *absorbed* at different volumes by a burden rate of 181 percent of direct labor cost. For instance, at a direct labor cost of $10,000, the overhead absorbed will be $18,100 (point *X* on the chart). Line *BB′* shows, however, that the cost expected at this volume is $31,200, computed as follows:

$$\$26,\!200 + \$0.50 \times 10,\!000 = \$31,\!200 \,.$$

In other words, if volume in department A were to be only 10,000 direct labor dollars in some month, the Lion Equipment Company would *expect* to underabsorb its overhead costs by $13,100, the difference between the expected cost of $31,200 and the absorbed cost of $18,100. This is represented on the diagram by the vertical distance between points *X* and *Y*. This difference would be due to the difference between actual and normal operating volume. Accountants call it the *volume variance*.

During April, volume in department A was $18,000 direct labor dollars. The amount of overhead expected at this volume was:

$$\$26,200 + \$0.50 \times 18,000 = \$35,200 .$$

The amount absorbed was:

$$\$18,000 \times 181 \text{ percent} = \$32,580 .$$

The volume variance for April was therefore $35,200 - $32,580 = $2,620. Because volume was less than normal, this volume variance was referred to as *unfavorable*.

Actual cost in department A during April exceeded the amount absorbed by $3,230 (Exhibit 18–6). This was $610 bigger than the volume variance, showing that something other than volume had departed from normal during the month. This $610 is known as the *spending variance*, and it results from all causes other than deviations from normal volume. The analysis can be summarized quickly:

(1)	Costs charged to department.......................$35,810	
(2)	Costs expected at actual volume..................... 35,200	
	Spending variance (1) − (2).....................	$ 610
(3)	Costs absorbed by production....................... 32,580	
	Volume variance (2) − (3).....................	2,620
	Total Variance (1) − (3)....................	$3,230

Further analysis of the spending variance will be deferred to Chapter 22.

Disposition of Over- and Underabsorbed Overhead

A balance such as the $4,960 unabsorbed overhead for April might be carried to the income statement as a loss or gain for the period in which it arises. Alternatively, the amount might be carried on the month-end balance sheet, to be added to or offset against similar amounts in later months, the net balance at the end of the year being closed out to the income statement. A third possibility, intermediate between the first two, is to divide the $1,960 between the income statement and balance sheet in direct proportion to the distribution of the overhead absorbed for the period.

To illustrate this third option, suppose that 70 percent of the $101,410 overhead absorbed during April applied to the goods that were sold during the month. In this case, 70 percent of $4,960, or $3,472, would be added to the cost of goods sold, and the remaining $1,488 would then be added to the April 30 inventory balance. The adjustment would approximate the account balances that would have resulted if the predetermined burden rate had been a correct forecast of the actual overhead rate.

This last possibility implies that overhead cost per unit of inventory should be based on the actual overhead costs during a period and not the predetermined burden rate. One may refer to a burden rate that exactly absorbs the actual overhead costs during a period as the actual burden rate. However, it should not be inferred that an actual burden rate or the approximation of it for financial statement purposes described above is the "true" or "correct" burden rate. Does a bottle of soda pop produced in a summer month cost less than one produced in a winter month when volume is lower and cannot be spread over as wide a base? Does a ton of steel cost more if produced in a year of low volume than in a year of high volume? Does a ton of steel produced in a period of numerous plant breakdowns cost more than a ton produced in a period of normal efficiency?

Many accountants and managers have decided that the answer is no to all of the above questions. They argue that inventory should be measured at costs reflecting (1) a relatively long-term average level of output, and (2) a reasonably attainable level of production efficiency —that is, at *normal cost*. The cost of producing a unit of inventory does not rise because it was produced in a month or year output is low or when the plant is inefficient. The consequence is that by comparison with the actual burden rate for a period, a predetermined rate based on normal conditions is the *preferred* basis for inventory costing and cost of goods sold determination—not a poor substitute adopted for reasons of convenience.

Under the above reasoning, over- or underabsorbed overhead is a gain or loss due to volume or operating efficiency or inefficiency. If the firm's business is highly seasonal in character, the over- or underabsorbed overhead may be carried forward from one month to the next. Otherwise, it should be carried to the period's income statement as a gain or loss.

While there is little disagreement on the soundness of carrying underabsorbed burden (not due to seasonal fluctuations in output) to the income statement, some accountants are reluctant to treat overabsorbed burden in the same way. The principle of conservatism makes them reluctant to show a profit on production.

It should be noted that the previous discussion has been concerned only with the financial statement implications of over- or underabsorbed overhead. Insofar as full-cost burden rates are used for such managerial purposes as pricing, there is general agreement that pre-

determined burden rates based on normal operating conditions should
be used.

SUMMARY

Overhead costs are spread unevenly throughout a factory. Some
departments are responsible for much overhead; others require very
little. To get product costs that are sensitive to these differences,
departmental rather than factorywide burden rates are usually used.
These burden rates are prepared only for departments directly engaged in production operations, but the burden rate for any production department will usually reflect allocations of costs to be incurred
in service departments elsewhere in the factory, as well as the costs
incurred directly in the producing department itself.

Full-cost burden rates, whether departmental or factorywide, do
not indicate how overhead costs will vary with short-period changes
in volume. This kind of information can be approximated by the use
of variable costing, under which product cost is limited to variable
factory costs. The usefulness of variable costing information for decision making will be discussed in the next chapter.

Although a substantial proportion of United States manufacturers
now use variable costing for some or all of their production, full
costing continues to be required for external financial reporting. The
differences between the overhead costs incurred and the overhead
costs absorbed by production during a period are known as overhead
variances or over- or underabsorbed overhead. These amounts appear
in the accounts as a by-product of routine bookkeeping. The accountant then has the twin tasks of analyzing these variances and of disposing of them in the periodic financial statements.

In later chapters, the study of factory overhead costing will be
carried still further, but one final point should be made now. Although all of the discussion has been in terms of *factory* overhead
costs, a wide range of *nonmanufacturing* costs must also be treated as
overhead. These costs are not included in the costs of inventories, but
much of the discussion in the next few chapters applies equally to
nonmanufacturing as well as factory overhead.

QUESTIONS AND PROBLEMS

1. Why are departmental burden rates usually thought to be superior
to a single plantwide burden rate?

2. "Departmental burden rates give an illusion of accuracy that an understanding of cost behavior and overhead allocation methods would soon serve to dispel." To what extent do you agree or disagree with this statement? Explain.

3. What is the distinction between a service department and a producing department? Why are the costs of one usually transferred to the other?

4. What are the characteristics of overhead which make it difficult to reduce these costs when volume falls?

5. As output varies, how will (*a*) total cost, and (*b*) cost per unit of product vary for a variable cost? A fixed cost? A semivariable cost?

6. Suggest bases that might be appropriate for distributing the costs of the following service departments and in each case give the reasons for your choice:

(1) Plant management.
(2) Building ownership and maintenance.
(3) Receiving and storeroom.
(4) Personnel and payroll.
(5) Power plant.
(6) Machinery maintenance.
(7) Production planning.
(8) Plant safety and medical care.

7. State the argument for taking all over- and underabsorbed overhead balances to the income statement of the period in which they occur. Do you agree with this argument? Give your reasons.

8. Does the factory overhead volume variance indicate the effect on net income of a deviation of factory production volume from normal levels? Under what circumstances would you expect the volume variance to be zero or close to it?

9. How would you decide what index of volume to use for burden rate determination? Might different indexes be appropriate for the fixed and variable components of overhead cost? Explain.

10. The Roddy Machine Company distributes factory overhead by using departmental rates determined at the close of each quarter. Department Q is an automatic machine center including 20 identical automatic screw machines. Overhead in this department has always been distributed upon the basis of the average cost per machine-hour.

In the third quarter of last year, the rate for department Q was almost double that of the prior quarter, and the vice president in charge of operations claimed that an error had been made. An accountant was called to investigate and discovered that one half of the machines in the department were idle during the greater part of the quarter, which accounted for the increase in the burden rate. The vice president expressed his opinion that the cost department was confusing "cost" and "loss."

Discuss the matter and explain briefly what recommendations the accountant should have made.

11. The Baton Company manufactures precision plastic molded products for the electrical and other industries. On occasion, a batch of products does not come up to standards and is scrapped. The production manager has complained that the present practice of including the cost of the defective material in a job's costs is misleading. He argues that the labor and material cost of defective work should be charged to an overhead account and spread over all jobs through the burden rate. Discuss.

12. The Smooth Paint Company manufactures a complete line of paints under its own brand name. There is a considerable setup cost of cleaning out the mixing machines and preparing the equipment for the manufacture of a new batch. This cost is of course independent of the length of the production run, which is determined by the popularity of the paint, the size of the inventory that the company is willing to carry, and other such considerations. The company has been carrying these setup costs to an overhead account so that they are absorbed into production as part of the burden rate which is based on machine-hours. Discuss.

13. The overhead costs in department X are expected to conform to the following equation:

$$\text{Cost per Month} = \$3,300 + \$0.42 \times \text{Direct Labor Hours}.$$

Normal volume in this department is 8,250 direct labor hours a month.

a) Compute a burden rate for this department.
b) Recompute the burden rate on the basis of an operating volume of 10,000 direct labor hours. Explain the reasons for the difference between this rate and the rate developed in (*a*) above.

*14. A department's fixed costs are expected to be \$12,450 a month, and the variable costs \$1.15 per direct labor dollar. In arriving at a burden

---

* Solutions to problems marked with an asterisk (*) are found in Appendix B.

rate, it was estimated that the normal direct labor cost would be $15,000 a month.

During the month of March the actual direct labor cost was $17,600 and the actual overhead was $33,150.

Account for the department's overhead during March, using T-accounts, and develop the volume and spending variances for the month.

15. Overhead costs in one of the Bastian Corporation's factory departments are expected to total $8,000 a month plus $1.40 per direct labor hour. The estimated average level of output is 11,000 direct labor hours a month.

During the month of June the actual overhead costs were $22,100 and the actual level of activity was 9,300 direct labor hours.

a) Establish a burden rate for the department.
b) Compute the volume and spending variances for the month.
c) Using T-accounts, show how these facts would be reflected in the factory accounts.

16. A company's power department provides power to four factory departments. Power consumption is measured indirectly by the number of horsepower hours used in each department. Consumption data are shown in the following schedule:

SCHEDULE OF HORSEPOWER HOURS

	Producing Departments		Service Departments	
	A	B	X	Y
Needed at capacity production...	10,000	20,000	12,000	8,000
Used during an average month...	8,000	13,000	7,000	6,000

The cost of operating the power department was expected to total $2,000 + $0.20 per horsepower hour.

The company wishes to establish burden rates for the two producing departments, both on a full costing and on a variable costing basis. What dollar amounts of power department costs should be included in the budget of each producing and service department? Give reasons for your answer. Indicate why you either did or did not allocate power department costs to the two service departments.

17. The Robertson Company has been using a single burden rate for its entire factory. An alternative has been proposed: departmental overhead rates. You are given the following information:

(1) Three products (A, B, C) are produced in three departments (1, 2, 3).

(2) Labor hours required for each product are:

LABOR HOURS REQUIRED PER UNIT OF PRODUCT

| | Department | | | Total |
	1	2	3	
Product A........	2	1	1	4
B........	0	2	2	4
C........	2	3	3	8

(3) Products produced in a normal year: A—40,000 units; B—40,000 units; and C—10,000 units.
(4) Overhead incurred in a normal year: department 1—$400,000; department 2—$300,000; and department 3—$100,000.

Should the company use a plantwide or departmental burden rates? Why? (In either case, the burden rate would be based on direct labor hours.)

18. Department S has the following estimated monthly cost at its normal volume of 1,400 service hours:

Service labor.....................................	$4,000
Supervision......................................	700
Supplies...	300
Depreciation.....................................	1,750
Other costs......................................	250
Total.....................................	$7,000

All of these except supervision and depreciation are proportionately variable with volume. Supervision and depreciation are fixed.

Departments 1 and 2 use 200 department S hours and 300 department S hours, respectively, in a typical month. Department 1's production volume is measured in direct labor hours, with a normal volume of 10,000 direct labor hours a month. Department 2's output is measured in pounds of product, with a normal volume of 30,000 pounds a month.

A unit of product X weighs 10 pounds and requires 5 direct labor hours in department 1. How much department S cost should be included in the cost of a unit of product X on a full-cost basis and on a variable-cost basis?

*19. The Hubbard Woods Company applies manufacturing overhead to all orders by use of a departmental burden rate. The divisions of the factory for this purpose are (1) melting and pouring, (2) molding, (3) core making, and (4) cleaning and grinding. From the data shown below, prepare an overhead distribution sheet showing in detail the manufacturing overhead chargeable to each department in a full costing system.

NORMAL MANUFACTURING OVERHEAD COSTS PER MONTH

Indirect labor:
Melting and pouring.....................................$1,000
Molding..   300
Core making..   100
Cleaning and grinding...............................   300
Supplies used:
Melting and pouring.................................   50
Molding..   50
Core making..   200
Cleaning and grinding...............................   100
Taxes (machinery and equipment, $12; building, $24).........   36
Compensation insurance...............................   65
Power..   50
Heat and light.....................................   80
Depreciation—building...............................   64
Depreciation—machinery and equipment..................   60

Total..$2,455

OTHER OPERATING DATA

Department	Floor Space (Sq. Ft.)	Cost of Machinery and Equipment	Direct Labor per Month	Compensation Insurance*	Horsepower Rating
Melting and pouring......	500	$2,000	. . .	$2.00	10
Molding...............	2,000	500	$1,200	1.00	. .
Core making...........	500	1,500	500	1.00	10
Cleaning and grinding.....	1,000	2,000	1,300	1.50	30
Total.............	4,000	$6,000	$3,000	. .	50

* Rate per $100 of payroll.

*20. In calculating the machine-hour cost of the Winston engine lathe No. 14, the accountant of the Horton Machine Works considered the following data:

ESTIMATED COST OF MAINTAINING BUILDINGS

Depreciation on buildings................................$18,000
Care of grounds....................................... 1,200
Repairs and upkeep.................................... 13,730
General factory lighting...............................   470
Cleaning...   380
Heating.. 1,500
Insurance on buildings................................ 10,600
Taxes on buildings................................... 14,120

Total..$60,000

Area available for manufacturing: 75,000 square feet. Area required by Winston engine lathe No. 14, including share of aisle space: 120 square feet. Original cost of engine lathe No. 14: $4,000. Depreciation: 10 percent, straight-line.

Work reported on engine lathe No. 14 during the previous year totaled 2,080 hours. The normal running time for this lathe was computed at 2,500 hours per year. The cost of power for the factory was $0.015 per kilowatt-hour. The lathe required 20 kilowatts per hour of operation.

Other estimated charges against the Winston engine lathe No. 14 at normal volume were as follows:

```
Proportion of taxes.......................................$ 10
Proportion of insurance....................................  12
Proportion of stores and supplies..........................  38
Repairs....................................................  35
Tools and jigs used....................................... 169
Proportion of scheduling cost..............................  69
Proportion of functional foremen........................... 131
Indirect labor used.......................................  70
        Total..............................................$534
```

From the data given, compute a machine-hour rate for Winston engine lathe No. 14. Show all computations.

21. The Franklin Company's factory has a drill press department with six style A, three style B, and two style C machines. These machines have the following characteristics:

	Machine Style A	Machine Style B	Machine Style C
Cost—each machine....................	$2,000	$3,000	$4,500
Horsepower rating—each machine.........	5	10	20
Space occupied—each machine (sq. ft.)......	20	50	60
Labor rate per hour, machine operators......	$3.00	$3.60	$4.80
Normal hours operated per month—each machine..........................	170	160	150

A machine operator operates only one machine at a time; the number of direct labor hours is therefore equal to the number of machine-hours.

The normal overhead costs of the drill press department for one month are as follows:

```
Depreciation, taxes and insurance—buildings.................$ 910
Depreciation, taxes and insurance—machinery................  600
Heat and light............................................  260
Power.....................................................  545
Miscellaneous costs.......................................  300
        Total.............................................$2,615
```

a) Calculate burden rates for each machine style on both a labor cost and a machine-hour basis.

b) Job No. 2051 was run on one of the style C machines and required 15 hours of machine time. Compare the amount of overhead costs that would be assigned to this job under each of the two burden rates computed in (*a*). How would you choose between the two?

*22. The Zebra Company used an estimated overhead rate of $2.50 per direct labor hour for 19x3. At the end of 19x3, after having worked 125,000 labor hours, the company had an underabsorbed overhead of $46,750. It apportioned this in proportion to the labor hours in work in process and finished goods inventories and in cost of goods sold. The labor hours in each of these were:

Work in process.............................	15,000
Finished goods..............................	25,000
Cost of goods sold..........................	85,000
Total.................................	125,000

While auditing the records of the Zebra Company, you find:

(1) A machine costing $10,000 was charged to Manufacturing Overhead; a fixed asset record card for this machine was prepared correctly, however, and depreciation on the machine was correctly charged to Manufacturing Overhead during the year.

(2) The president's salary for July ($3,000) was incorrectly charged to Manufacturing Overhead.

(3) Job No. 389 was charged with overhead of $250 which should have been charged to Job No. 298. Both jobs have been completed and sold.

Prepare any necessary adjustments and apportion any under- or overabsorbed overhead resulting from those adjustments.

23. The following data represent the departmental direct labor hours and indirect labor cost for a factory department for the past 12 months:

Direct Labor Hours	Indirect Labor Cost
14,400..............................	$5,520
10,650..............................	4,140
14,100..............................	5,640
15,000..............................	6,600
13,650..............................	4,680
13,050..............................	5,100
13,350..............................	4,860
13,500..............................	4,740
13,500..............................	5,460
14,250..............................	4,800
13,200..............................	4,140
13,350..............................	4,800

a) Plot these data on a sheet of graph paper and draw a straight-line regression line which seems to fit the observations most closely.

b) Derive the mathematical equation that describes this line.

c) What difficulties do you foresee in trying to determine cost-volume relationships by this method? Would you use the method, despite these difficulties?

24. The assembly department of the Hyde Company uses a predetermined burden rate to absorb overhead costs. Last year the burden rate was $3 per direct labor hour. The wage rate for direct labor employees was $2.50 an hour. A total of 20,000 direct labor hours were worked in the assembly department during the year, and $62,000 was charged to the department's overhead account for overhead costs either traced or allocated to the department.

a) By how much was overhead over- or underabsorbed in the assembly department?

b) By how much would assembly overhead have been over- or underabsorbed if the following events had occurred, while everything else remained the same? (Treat each event as independent; that is, each answer should be based on the effects of that event taken separately.)

  (1) An additional 200 hours of direct labor were worked on overtime in the assembly department at a wage rate of one and one half of the regular rate. The Hyde Company adds overtime premiums (that is, the overtime bonus paid in excess of the regular wage rate) to the overhead account of the department in which the overtime is worked.

  (2) All direct labor employees received a wage increase of $0.10 an hour beginning in December. A total of 1,100 direct labor hours were worked in December.

  (3) The price of food went up during the year, adding $1,000 to the deficit incurred by the employees' cafeteria. All losses of operating the cafeteria are distributed to the producing departments on the basis of their total number of employees. The assembly department has 14 employees out of a total of 100 employees in all of the plant's producing departments.

25. From the following information, prepare an overhead cost distribution sheet and develop predetermined labor-hour burden rates for each of the Sender Company's four producing departments (machine No. 1, machine No. 2, assembly, and painting) on a full costing basis.

ESTIMATED OVERHEAD COSTS

Indirect labor and supervision:

Machine No. 1	$33,000
Machine No. 2	22,000
Assembly	11,000
Painting	7,000
Storage	44,000
Maintenance	32,700

Indirect materials and supplies:

Machine No. 1... 2,200
Machine No. 2... 1,100
Assembly... 3,300
Painting.. 3,400
Maintenance.. 2,800

Other:

Rent of factory... 96,000
Depreciation of machinery and equipment................. 44,000
Insurance and taxes on machinery and equipment.......... 2,400
Compensation insurance at $2 per $100 of labor payroll..... 19,494
Power.. 66,000
Factory office salaries.................................... 52,800
General superintendence................................... 55,000
Miscellaneous office costs................................ 21,620
Heat and light.. 72,000
Miscellaneous storage charges (insurance, etc.)........... 3,686

PROJECTED OPERATING DATA

Department	Area (Sq. Ft.)	Cost of Machinery and Equipment	Raw Materials Used	Horse-power Rating	Direct Labor Hours	Direct Labor Payroll	Number of Employees
Machine No. 1..	65,000	$220,000	$520,000	2,000	120,000	$440,000	200
Machine No. 2..	55,000	110,000	180,000	1,000	44,000	220,000	120
Assembly......	44,000	55,000		100	60,000	110,000	60
Painting.......	32,000	22,000	90,000	200	27,500	55,000	30
Storage........	22,000	11,000					28
Maintenance...	11,000	16,500					20
Office.........	11,000	5,500					22
Total.....	240,000	$440,000	$790,000	3,300	251,500	$825,000	480

[NOTE: Allocate office and general superintendence costs on the basis of direct labor hours, maintenance on the basis of machinery and equipment cost, and storage costs on the basis of materials (direct and indirect) used.]

26. The Grimes Corporation is engaged in the manufacture of metal stampings for the automotive industry. The manufacturing cycle is quite short so that the work in process inventories are small and may be ignored for this problem. A job order cost system is used in the factory. A factory-wide burden rate is established quarterly on the basis of the anticipated production volume for the ensuing three months and is used to apply manufacturing overhead costs to the company's products.

The company ends its fiscal year so as to conform to the model change period in the auto industry, since it normally has no finished goods inventory at this time. The company's cost accountant prepared the following estimates of manufacturing overhead cost:

If Production During Quarter Is—	Factory Overhead Costs Will Be—
300,000 units	$420,000
400,000 units	460,000
500,000 units	500,000
600,000 units	540,000
700,000 units	580,000

The estimated production volume for the first quarter was 400,000 units. Actual production during the first quarter totaled 380,000 units, and actual factory overhead costs totaled $456,000. At the end of the quarter 38,000 units were still in finished goods inventory, the remaining 342,000 units having been sold during the quarter.

Estimated production for the second quarter was 600,000 units, and a new burden rate was established on that basis. During the second quarter, the factory produced 620,000 units at a total factory overhead cost of $570,400. Sales during the second quarter totaled 558,000 units, the remaining production being added to inventory.

Finished goods inventory is costed on a Fifo basis during the year.

a) Compute the amount of the over-or underabsorbed overhead and the overhead spending variance for each quarter.

b) Indicate for each quarter the amount of manufacturing overhead costs that would be carried to the income statement and the amount that would remain on the end-of-quarter balance sheet:

(1) If cost variances are closed out to the income statement at the end of the quarter.

(2) If the variances are divided between balance sheet and income statement in the same proportion as the absorbed overhead for the quarter is divided between finished goods inventory and the cost of goods sold.

c) Assuming that the burden rate is constant from quarter to quarter, based on a normal quarterly production volume of 500,000 units, indicate for each quarter the amount of manufacturing overhead costs that would be carried to the income statement and the amount that would remain on the end-of-quarter balance sheet, if all cost variances are carried forward on the end-of-quarter balance sheet as deferred charges or deferred credits against the operations of subsequent quarters.

d) Compare the company's financial position and earnings performance as revealed by financial statements prepared by the three methods of variance disposal used in (b) and (c). Indicate which method you prefer and why.

27. The Langdon Company has two producing and two service departments. Estimated monthly cost and operating data for the year 19x1 are:

Cost	Department			
	Producing Able	Producing Baker	Mainte-nance	General Plant
Direct labor cost...........	$15,000	$20,000	$6,000	
Indirect labor..............	8,000	14,000	1,500	$13,900
Indirect materials..........	3,000	7,000	800	1,500
Miscellaneous costs.........	4,000	4,000	1,500	1,000
Maintenance hours.........	1,800	1,200	....	....

General plant costs are entirely fixed; it is assumed that the other three departments benefit from general plant services in proportion to their total budgeted direct labor cost.

Develop full-cost burden rates for the two producing departments, including a provision for absorption of estimated service department costs. Use direct labor cost as the index of volume in each case.

28. Analysis of the four departments in the Langdon Company (see question 27) established the following additional information:

(1) The fixed indirect labor cost in each producing department is: Able, $3,000; and Baker, $4,000.
(2) Indirect materials are completely variable in both producing departments.
(3) Miscellaneous costs are completely fixed in both producing departments.
(4) Maintenance hours required by each producing department increase by one hour for every $10 increase in direct labor cost (output) in Able department and by one hour for every $20 increase in direct labor cost in Baker department.
(5) In the maintenance department direct labor cost and indirect materials are considered variable while indirect labor and miscellaneous costs are fixed.

Prepare departmental burden rates on the variable costing principle.

29. The normal monthly operating volume for one of the Wyman Company's factory departments is 10,000 direct labor hours. Direct labor hours and indirect labor costs for the past two years were:

Month	19x1		19x2	
	Direct Labor Hours	Indirect Labor Costs	Direct Labor Hours	Indirect Labor Costs
January...............	9,000	$12,820	12,000	$18,800
February.............	8,000	11,290	10,000	14,730
March...............	6,000	12,400	11,000	17,050
April................	7,000	13,100	10,000	15,220
May.................	8,000	11,540	11,000	16,350
June.................	7,000	10,600	12,000	17,900
July.................	8,000	11,580	12,000	15,700
August..............	9,000	12,600	9,000	11,860
September...........	7,000	9,820	10,000	13,050
October.............	6,000	8,800	8,000	10,120
November...........	7,000	9,680	6,000	7,960
December...........	9,000	12,430	7,000	9,180

a) Plot these observations on a sheet of graph paper and prepare a tentative estimate of indirect labor cost at a normal operating volume of 10,000 direct labor hours a month.

b) Draw a line that seems to show most accurately the cost-volume relationship, and prepare tentative indirect labor cost allowances at operating volumes of 6,000, 7,000, 8,000, 9,000, 11,000, and 12,000 direct labor hours.

30. Further investigation reveals certain additional facts relating to the data given in question 29:

(1) A fire destroyed a machine in March, 19x1. Direct production workers were not laid off but instead were assigned to other tasks classified as indirect labor until the replacement machine was ready for operation on April 10, 19x1.

(2) Rearrangement of the department's machines on July 1, 19x2, made it possible to reduce materials handling time. The factory's industrial engineer estimates that this reduction has led to an indirect labor cost saving of approximately 20 cents per direct labor hour. The rearrangement has had no effect on the amount of overtime worked.

(3) Employees are paid a premium of 50 percent of their regular hourly wage rate for each hour of overtime work. Overtime premiums paid on direct and indirect labor have been included in the cost figures given in question 29. Analysis of payroll documents shows that overtime premiums were as follows during the two years:

Month	19x1	19x2
January..............	$520	$2,400
February............	290	930
March..............	0	1,750
April...............	0	920
May................	340	1,250
June................	100	1,800
July................	280	1,500
August.............	600	560
September...........	120	1,150
October.............	0	320
November...........	80	0
December...........	630	80

(4) Wage rates were 5 percent higher in 19x2 than in 19x1. Wage rates will remain at their 19x2 level throughout the current year.

Separate overtime premiums from other components of indirect labor cost, make any other adjustments that seem appropriate, plot the adjusted observations on graph paper, and prepare cost estimates for both components of indirect labor cost at various operating volumes.

Chapter 19

ACCOUNTING DATA FOR
EXECUTIVE DECISIONS

In all functional areas of the business enterprise, management is continuously engaged in searching out various possible courses of action and in selecting the best from among these. As one would imagine, cost and revenue data drawn from the company's accounts and related sources are widely used in the analysis of alternative opportunities. The purpose of this chapter is to examine some of the methods and problems relevant to this application of accounting information.

THE INCREMENTAL APPROACH

The basic principles governing the analysis of alternative choice situations are quite simple: first, it is assumed that the objective is to maximize profits; second, all likely courses of action (one of which is usually maintenance of the status quo) are examined to establish which one will yield the greatest increase (or sometimes the least decrease) in profits. Since profit differences depend in turn upon revenue and expense differences, the analyst's job is to determine the cost and revenue *changes* consequent upon each possible election. This emphasis explains the common use of the terms *incremental* and *marginal* to describe the technique employed.

The Profit Maximization Assumption

The objective of maximizing profit may be questioned on the grounds that managerial decisions are often based on factors other than estimates of profit differentials. More often than not, however, the reason for management's interest in these other factors is that they are assumed to have profit consequences; they are left outside the profit calculation only because they are so difficult to quantify. Insofar as possible, all consequences of a choice should be included in the quantitative analysis; these quantitative results can then be compared with the qualitative, or intangible, factors involved.

The assumption that profit maximization is a guiding principle in decision making may also be criticized on other grounds. The mind has only a limited ability to identify and make rational comparisons among alternative courses of action. A solution short of the profit-maximizing ideal may be adopted, therefore, because it meets minimum standards of profitability and appears to be the best of the alternatives that have been suggested. Thus profit maximization operates within a somewhat narrower range than a literal interpretation of the term might imply.

Finally management may deliberately reject the profit-maximizing alternative because it places different weights on the probabilities of favorable and unfavorable deviations from expected values. In this introductory material, however, a symmetrical attitude toward uncertainty will be assumed.

The Variable Profit Concept

The concepts embodied in the incremental approach are best explained by illustration. The Van Horn Company manufactures lawn mowers. Exhibit 19–1 shows the revenues and expenses reported for each of the company's six mower models for the year 1968. Noting the losses reported for the 16″ Economy and Estate models, Van

Exhibit 19–1

VAN HORN COMPANY

Sales and Expenses by Product, 1968

Item	Manual Mowers			Power Mowers			Total
	16″ Economy	16″ De Luxe	18″ De Luxe	Clipper	Sub-urban	Estate	
Sales (units)...............	30,000	65,000	15,000	20,000	10,000	5,000	
Sales revenue..............	$300,000	$910,000	$240,000	$900,000	$600,000	$350,000	$3,300,000
Manufacturing cost of goods sold....................	300,000	715,000	185,100	750,000	440,000	325,000	2,715,100
Manufacturing margin.......	.....	$195,000	$ 54,900	$150,000	$160,000	$ 25,000	$ 584,900
Selling expense..............	$ 24,000	$ 72,800	$ 19,200	$ 72,000	$ 48,000	$ 28,000	$ 264,000
Administrative expense......	15,000	45,500	12,000	45,000	30,000	17,500	165,000
Total expense..........	$ 39,000	$118,300	$ 31,200	$117,000	$ 78,000	$ 45,500	$ 429,000
Net Profit (Loss) before Tax	$(39,000)	$ 76,700	$ 23,700	$ 33,000	$ 82,000	$(20,500)	$ 155,900
Net Profit (Loss) per Unit Sold....................	$(1.30)	$1.18	$1.58	$1.65	$8.20	$(4.10)	

Horn's management raised the possibility of eliminating these two models from the product line.

Unfortunately, the cost data of Exhibit 19–1 cannot be used as they stand for reaching decisions of this sort. First, they relate to the past, not to the future. In this case, this was not a serious drawback because management predicted that the economic conditions that gave rise to the 1968 revenues and expenses would be typical of the future.

More important, data in the form required for a report such as Exhibit 19–1 represent totals, not increments. If the 16″ Economy and Estate mowers were dropped, the direct labor and materials costs used in their production would be eliminated, but the same is not true of all other manufacturing costs. The overhead charged to these two machines was arrived at by the full-costing methods described in Chapter 18. Specifically, service department overheads were distributed among the producing departments, and producing department overheads, including these reallocations, were charged to production via burden rates. Dropping these mowers would not eliminate all of the overhead charged to them. Many of the fixed costs which they were absorbing would still be incurred and would appear either as underabsorbed overhead or as increases in the costs of the remaining products.

In other words, many of the fixed costs assigned to a given model of mowers may be *sunk costs* with respect to the decision to drop the model from the line. A sunk cost is any cost that will not be affected by a choice between alternatives. It thus complements the *incremental costs*—those that *will* be affected by the choice. Once the alternatives have been defined, every cost is either sunk or incremental with respect to the choice between these alternatives.

In an attempt to overcome the limitations of the data in Exhibit 19–1, Van Horn's accountants prepared the profit summary shown in Exhibit 19–2. The profit reported for each model is not a net profit but a *variable profit*. Variable profit is defined as the difference between selling price and variable cost. For each model, it measures the contribution made to the company's fixed costs and profits by the sale of a single unit of that model.

The use of the factory cost records to establish the unit material and labor costs requires no further explanation. The variable factory overhead costs per unit were derived by applying burden rates that cover variable overheads only. These variable costs include the variable components of producing department costs and also those portions of service department costs which change with changes in producing department volume.

Exhibit 19–2

VAN HORN COMPANY

Price and Variable Unit Costs by Products

	Manual Mowers			Power Mowers		
	16" Econ- omy	16" De Luxe	18" De Luxe	Clipper	Sub- urban	Estate
Price.......................	$10.00	$14.00	$16.00	$45.00	$60.00	$70.00
Direct material...............	$ 5.00	$ 5.80	$ 6.43	$24.00	$27.50	$32.00
Direct labor..................	2.50	2.60	3.00	6.00	7.50	12.00
Variable factory overhead.......	1.50	1.55	1.75	3.50	5.00	6.00
Variable factory cost.........	$ 9.00	$ 9.95	$11.18	$33.50	$40.00	$50.00
Other variable costs...........	0.70	0.90	1.00	2.45	3.20	3.70
Total Variable Cost........	$ 9.70	$10.85	$12.18	$35.95	$43.20	$53.70
Variable Profit per unit........	$ 0.30	$ 3.15	$ 3.82	$ 9.05	$16.80	$16.30

The "other variable costs" listed in Exhibit 19–2 were calculated at 5 percent of sales (salesman's commission), plus $0.20 a unit (variable shipping and handling costs).

The data of Exhibit 19–2 can be read as follows. The figures for the Estate mower in the right-hand column show that selling an additional Estate mower increases revenue by $70. Producing the mower increases factory costs by $50 and selling it adds $3.70 to selling expense. The total variable cost is thus $53.70, and each unit sold therefore contributes $16.30 toward fixed costs and profit. Since 5,000 Estate mowers were sold in 1968, the total variable profit on this model was 5,000 × $16.30 = $81,500.

Reconciling Variable Profit with Net Profit

The reconciliation of the variable profit figures with the reported net income or loss is illustrated in Exhibit 19–3, using figures for the Estate mower. The first step is to compute the average factory cost. From Exhibit 19–1 we find that the total factory cost charged to Estate mowers in 1968 was $325,000. Dividing this by the quantity sold, 5,000 units, reveals that the *average full cost* of production was $65 a unit.

The average variable factory cost figure of $50 shown in column 2 comes from Exhibit 19–2. Subtracting this from the $65 average full

Exhibit 19–3

VAN HORN COMPANY

Reconciliation of Variable Profit with Net Loss
Reported for Estate Mower, 1968

	(1) Total Cost per Unit	(2) Variable Cost per Unit	(3) Fixed Cost per Unit (1) − (2)	(4) Total Fixed Cost Absorbed (3) × 5,000
Factory costs...............	$65.00	$50.00	$15.00	$ 75,000
Selling costs................	5.60	3.70	1.90	9,500
Administrative costs.........	3.50	...	3.50	17,500
Total Fixed Cost Absorbed.............				$102,000
Variable profit..............				81,500
Reported Net Profit (Loss) ...				$ (20,500)

cost indicates that the amount of fixed factory cost absorbed by each Estate mower was $15, shown in column 3. The total amount of fixed cost absorbed is then obtained by multiplying this $15 by the 5,000 units sold during the year—a total of $75,000. This is the figure given in column 4 of Exhibit 19–3.

The same procedure is followed for selling and administrative expenses, building the total amount of fixed cost assigned to Estate mower sales to $102,000. Subtracting this from the variable profit of $81,500 produces the $20,500 net loss reported in Exhibit 19–1.

Variable versus Incremental Profit

From the foregoing analysis, it might seem disadvantageous to drop either the Economy or the Estate mower. Instead of increasing profits by the $59,500 reported loss, such action would reduce profits by $90,500, the Estate's contribution being the above-noted $81,500 and that of the Economy 30,000 units at $0.30 = $9,000. This conclusion rests, however, on two assumptions: (1) that the sales of other products will not be affected; and (2) that the variability of costs with output shown in Exhibit 19–2 holds for reductions in output to zero.

Data of the type given in Exhibit 19–2 are sometimes described as *general-purpose* incremental costs and revenues. While they show the profit effects of fluctuations in the sales of each product over some range above and below a normal level, they may be unsatisfactory as indicators of cost and revenue behavior under conditions of extreme variations in volume. Consequently, the analyst should make every effort to determine whether or not the assumptions implicit in such figures are in fact reasonable under the special conditions relevant to the particular problem at hand.

In the present case, consultation with the sales and production people added certain new dimensions. As regards the Estate mower, the sales department forecast that if this item were dropped, many buyers would switch to the Suburban, with the result that sales of the latter would increase by an estimated 3,000 units. The production department, after careful study, reported that $27,000 of overhead costs, which were fixed so long as *any* Estate mowers were manufactured, could be eliminated if *none* were produced.

With respect to the Economy mower, it was found that certain of Van Horn's dealers regarded this item as essential to the hand mower line to convince their customers that they were competitive with chain stores and mail-order houses. It was estimated that were the Economy model eliminated, so many dealers would drop the remaining hand mowers that sales of both De Luxe models would be reduced by 10 percent. The production department's estimate of reducible fixed overhead in this case was $14,000.

In the light of this new information, the relative profitability of retaining these products can be restated as follows:

Estate Power Mower:

Variable profit on present sales of Estate mower..........		$81,500
Less: Variable profit on increased sales of Suburban mower		
(3,000 at $16.80)...............................	$50,400	
Savings in fixed overhead costs......................	27,000	77,400
Net Loss from Dropping Estate Mower...............		$ 4,100

16" Economy Manual Mower:

Variable profit on present sales of Economy mower.......	$ 9,000	
Add: Variable profit on complementary sales of De Luxe		
mowers (6,500 at $3.15 plus 1,500 at $3.82)...........	26,205	$35,205
Less: Savings in fixed overhead costs..................		14,000
Net Loss from Dropping Economy Mower.............		$21,205

While both items remain profitable on an incremental basis, this more refined analysis reverses their relative positions and reveals that what before appeared to be the better product is definitely borderline.

This illustration points up two facts generally relevant to the incremental analysis of alternative choice problems. First, because any cost factor is fixed only over a finite period of time and/or range of output, *it is essential that the data used be specific to the problem under consideration.* Decisions are based on *incremental profit* estimates. Incremental profit is not always equal to *variable profit.* Second, because certain major determinants of cost and revenue expectations may not be revealed by any data accumulated in the firm's accounts, *it is essential that all available sources of information be throughly explored.*

ACCOUNTING DATA FOR PRODUCT PRICING

One of the most common uses of accounting data is in product pricing decisions. Ideally, the pricing decision should be based on estimates of the sales volume obtainable at various prices. Comparison of the profit estimates for the various price/volume combinations would then indicate the most profitable price.

Most pricing decisions unfortunately must be made without specific estimates of the price sensitivity of sales volume. Even so, cost data are often highly relevant to the pricing decision. Two examples may serve to explain how they might be used.

Pricing Additional Business

The Wilde Company, which operates a chain of automotive and hardware supply stores, sells a power mower under its own brand name, Wilcut. Wilde's buyer has asked if Van Horn would be interested in manufacturing this machine. He has stated that the market for Wilcut is between two and three thousand units a year, and that Van Horn could have the business at a unit price of $48. The president has therefore requested that estimates be prepared to show both the incremental and full-cost effects of accepting this order. The full cost is to be that given by the company's regular accounting procedures, with the exception that the sales commission is to be excluded on the grounds that this would be a "house account" handled directly by the sales manager.

The Wilcut, although slightly inferior in quality, is otherwise similar to the Suburban and requires no new equipment for its production. From the specifications given, the following cost estimate has been developed:

Direct material	$25.80
Direct labor	7.00
Variable manufacturing overhead	5.00
Variable selling expense	0.20
Total Variable Cost per Unit	$38.00
Allocated fixed manufacturing overhead	4.35
Allocated fixed selling expense	1.25
Allocated administrative expense	2.90
Average Total Cost per Unit	$46.50

A somewhat lower manufacturing cost (primarily in materials) combined with elimination of the $3 sales commission results in a $38 variable cost per unit as compared with that of $43.20 for the Suburban (see Exhibit 19–2). No fixed cost increase being foreseen as a result of adding this product, the unit fixed charges shown above have been obtained by reallocating present total fixed costs over all products including Wilcut.

From this analysis, it appears that even excluding sales commissions, Wilcut would show a profit of only $48.00 − $46.50 = $1.50 per unit on a full-cost basis. It would, on the other hand, contribute $48 − $38 = $10 a unit to fixed cost and profit. This means $20,000 to $30,000 a year depending on the volume of business.

This is an instance of the application of the concept of *opportunity cost*. Opportunity cost is measured by the amount of net cash inflows that must be sacrificed in order to divert an input factor from one use to another. It is the value of an opportunity foregone. In this case, it is assumed that the facilities would be idle if the Wilcut order were to be rejected; the opportunity cost of these facilities is thus zero because nothing must be foregone to make these facilities available to the Wilcut model.

Although this incremental return will loom large in the final decision, due consideration must also be given to the reactions of certain members of the Van Horn management to the proposal. The sales manager points out that the company's present business is primarily with small independent dealers and that their goodwill may be lost by selling a comparable product to a chain at a substantially lower price. He is reinforced in his opposition by the controller who suggests that such price cutting to Wilde might result in retaliation by competitors in the markets regularly served by Van Horn. If taking on the Wilcut at $48 were to lead to a reduction of as much as $3 in the Suburban price, the overall result would be unprofitable.

Against these adverse considerations, the production manager argues the potential dynamic advantages of the move. He feels that the increased output would, in ways so far unrecognized, lead to improved methods of manufacture and lower costs on all mowers produced. Van Horn's share of the market, he asserts, has declined during the past decade largely because the company has not participated in the rapidly growing portion of total mower sales handled by mail-order houses and other large retail distributors. He is most eager to gain a foothold in this area in order to acquire some experience in producing for and selling to such firms.

These divergent points of view serve to illustrate not only the limitations of purely quantitative analysis in decision-making situations involving major policy issues but also the typical range of management reactions to the use of incremental cost data for pricing purposes. While a comprehensive discussion of price policy is beyond the scope of this text, some consideration of the subject is needed to understand the continuing debate as to the relative merits of incremental and full costs as the basis for pricing and, particularly, the position of the accountant with respect to this issue.

Catalog Pricing: Variable versus Full Cost

A second major category of pricing decisions is the establishment of what might be called "catalog prices"—prices that are to be quoted on the company's regular products for a substantial period of time. In other words, unlike the price for a special order, a catalog price is to be the basis of many price quotations to many customers during a period of many months.

The need for cost data for this kind of pricing decision has been an important reason in the past for the installation of cost accounting systems. Without adequate cost records, the businessman prices on the basis of off-the-cuff estimates of labor and material costs, commonly adding some percentage of either or both to cover overhead and profit. The direct cost figures are subject to some margin of error in the first instance, and it is most unlikely that the overhead loading factor employed adequately reflects real product cost differences. This is no great problem so long as sales volume is high and overall profits satisfactory. However, given a business depression or overexpansion in the industry, an excess of productive capacity develops, and additional business at any price in excess of direct cost may be looked on as immediately profitable. Under such conditions, competition has been seen to reduce prices to levels but little above the costs of the most efficient producers in the industry and substantially below those of many other firms.

In this situation, better cost information is looked upon as one of the requirements for restoring a healthy state of industry affairs. Trade associations urge their members to find out what their costs really are, and even develop uniform accounting systems for this purpose. The members of the industry are persuaded that the proposed cost collection and allocation methods result in "scientifically" determined product costs and, most important, that selling below the figures thus established is unprofitable. If the effort is successful, the system is widely installed, it becomes general policy to use the resultant data in pricing, and emphasis is gradually shifted from price to other forms of competition such as quality and service. Since the cost system proves to be of some assistance in curing the industry's ills, the accountant becomes identified with the development of the "full-cost" approach to pricing.

Some accountants are devoted to full cost for more general reasons. Production and sales people often have a tendency to be highly volume conscious, sometimes to the extent of indiscriminately sacrificing price for volume. To counteract this bias, some accountants maintain that the full cost of a product is the only figure which should be admitted for management consideration. These accountants fear that acknowledging to operating people the validity of variable cost as a basis for pricing is to invite their cutting prices to this level in the quest for volume. They argue further that costs which are fixed in the short run have a remarkable tendency to become variable with the passage of time. While a plant manager's salary is not a function of production, it may nevertheless be raised as the scale of plant operations increases.

Perhaps the most telling argument on the other side—that is, against full-cost-plus formula pricing—is that it is apparently inconsistent with a profit maximization decision rule. Not even the most hardened advocate of full cost as a basis for pricing would claim that full-cost measures the increment in factory cost that will result from producing an additional unit of the product. Full unit cost, in other words, cannot be used in conjunction with price/volume estimates to pick the most profitable price.

For this reason, and because full cost provides little assistance in pricing incremental business and in solving similar short-run problems, an increasing number of accountants feel that factory accounting systems should not produce full-cost figures. Instead, they prefer the *variable costing* systems mentioned in Chapter 18. Under variable costing, it will be recalled, only variable costs are included in product unit cost, all fixed costs being regarded as a lump-sum charge against the aggregate variable profits of the time period to which they relate. The use of variable costing (or *direct costing*, as it is more popularly called) is likely to lead to a product-line income statement like that of Exhibit 19–4. Fixed costs are completely separated from variable costs, and the only fixed costs deducted from product-line revenues are those directly traceable to that product line, such as product advertising or the salaries of specialized salesmen or customer engi-

Exhibit 19–4

VAN HORN COMPANY

Product Profit Contribution Report, 1968

Item	Manual Mowers			Power Mowers			Total
	16″ Economy	16″ De Luxe	18″ De Luxe	Clipper	Sub-urban	Estate	
Sales (units)...............	30,000	65,000	15,000	20,000	10,000	5,000	
Sales revenue..............	$300,000	$910,000	$240,000	$900,000	$600,000	$350,000	$3,300,000
Direct material............	$150,000	$377,000	$ 96,450	$480,000	$275,000	$160,000	$1,538,450
Direct labor...............	75,000	169,000	45,000	120,000	75,000	60,000	544,000
Variable factory overhead....	45,000	100,750	26,250	70,000	50,000	30,000	322,000
Variable cost to manufacture..	$270,000	$646,750	$167,700	$670,000	$400,000	$250,000	$2,404,450
Other variable costs.........	21,000	58,500	15,000	49,000	32,000	18,500	194,000
Total Variable Cost......	$291,000	$705,250	$182,700	$719,000	$432,000	$268,500	$2,598,450
Variable Profit.............	$ 9,000	$204,750	$ 57,300	$181,000	$168,000	$ 81,500	$ 701,550
Traceable fixed marketing costs....................	.....	.....	.....	20,000	15,000	12,000	47,000
Profit contribution..........	$ 9,000	$204,750	$ 57,300	$161,000	$153,000	$ 69,500	$ 654,550
Other fixed costs:..........							
Factory overhead........							$ 310,650
Selling costs.............							23,000
Administrative costs.......							165,000
Total Other Fixed Costs.							$ 498,650
Net Income before Tax......							$ 155,900

neers. The residual left after subtracting traceable costs from variable profit is usually called *profit contribution*. The nontraceable fixed costs are then subtracted from the total of the profit contribution figures, without any attempt to divide them among the various products. With such figures, it is argued, the risk of an incorrect decision based on full cost is eliminated.

Variable costing advocates have no fears that management will price on the assumption that a product selling at any amount above variable cost is profitable. They do not, however, necessarily maintain that a variable costing system automatically grinds out the best information for each price, product line, or other such decision. The argument for variable costing as the preferred basis for management information rests upon the proposition that relatively few alternative choice situations exist in which full product cost is pertinent, and that in most it is likely to be only confusing.

The problem is that both camps may be in the right to some extent.

Variable cost figures are likely to be useful in short-term utilization-of-capacity decisions, including pricing decisions in which direct application of the profit maximization decision rule is possible. Full cost, on the other hand, or something like it that indicates the cost that could be avoided if the company did not produce the product at all, may help management identify a price that will not be unduly attractive to potential customers. In other words, it may help management forecast what sacrifices competitors are making or would have to make to manufacture a similar product, and thereby provide management with a means of estimating a competitive price level. The fact that the manufacture of a particular product requires large quantities of expensive equipment and fixed costs may not be relevant to all pricing situations, but it cannot fail to be relevant to some. The viewpoint that an item selling at any price in excess of variable cost may be considered profitable is frequently a rationalization of the status quo and a means of deferring the fundamental changes needed to deal with the situation. In general, *full cost* should reflect an attempt to measure the *long-run cost* of manufacturing a product.[1]

Fortunately, a middle ground on this issue can be found. The system can be designed to produce "full-cost" figures that represent the average cost required for each particular product, including both variable cost and an allowance for the fixed costs attributable to that product. These full-cost figures can be subcoded into fixed and variable components, so that variable cost figures can be used when they seem more relevant.

In numerous situations failure to develop incremental cost data suppresses valuable information which should be made available to management regardless of any danger that it may be misused. Quite often, the price reduction based on an incremental cost and revenue analysis results in a volume increase which, in turn, either generates production efficiencies and consequent cost reductions or creates a consumer preference for the company's products. When either of these results materialize, the increased output may be both permanent and profitable. Also, taking special business on an incremental cost basis is normally justified when regular markets will not be spoiled and when because the decline in regular business is seen as temporary it is deemed unwise to cut fixed costs by curtailing productive capac-

---

[1] Methods used to derive full cost do not necessarily reflect this concept. Full cost, therefore, should be interpreted as a *first approximation* to long-run incremental cost, subject to redefinition in any given case.

ity. In general, it appears that *variable cost* is most pertinent to *short-run* pricing decisions, but the long run is the outcome of a series of short-run decisions and fixed costs cannot always be ignored.

BREAK-EVEN CHARTS

The relationships among costs, volume, and profit are often described graphically by *break-even charts* or *profit graphs*.

The Basic Chart

The profit graph is simply a diagram showing the amount of profit to be expected at various sales volumes under specified operating conditions. The profit graph developed by Seaton Chemicals, Inc., for its new X-250 plastic is typical. The new product has been brought to the point of being commercially useful, and a study has been undertaken to determine whether it would be profitable to put it on the market at the present time. The sales department reports that X-250 is closest in physical characteristics to Thor, a product of another chemical company, currently selling at $1.30 per pound. It is further estimated that the annual sales of Thor are about five million pounds.

On the basis of data obtained in part from the engineering department, a cost analyst on the controller's staff has estimated the costs of producing and selling X-250, and a summarized statement of his findings is presented below:

Item	Total Fixed Cost	Variable Cost per Pound
Direct material	$	$0.34
Direct labor	......	0.27
Manufacturing overhead	800,000	0.21
Selling and administrative costs	400,000	0.08
Total	$1,200,000	$0.90

The proposed plant would cost $5 million, and its capacity would be 10 million pounds.

The above information may be stated mathematically as follows. If X-250 is sold at the same price as Thor, $1.30 per pound, the total revenue, R, at a level of output, V, is

$$R = \$1.30V .$$

The total cost, C, at an output of V is

$$C = \$1,200,000 + \$0.90V .$$

The level of output at which the firm will *break even* is where $R = C$, and is obtained by equating the above two expressions and solving for V:

$$1.30V = 1,200,000 + 0.90V$$
$$V = 3,000,000 \text{ pounds}$$

This analysis appears in graph form in Exhibit 19–5, where output is on the horizontal axis and revenue or cost on the vertical axis. The utility of this device as a means for *presenting* the relevant informa-

Exhibit 19–5

SEATON CHEMICALS, INC.

Break-even Analysis—Product X-250

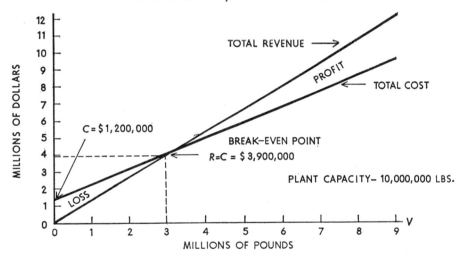

tion is apparent. Here are seen at a glance the fixed costs at zero output, the break-even volume, and the spread between total revenue and total cost at any level of output above or below the break-even point.

Using the Chart

As this chart shows, the indicated break-even volume for the X-250 at a price of $1.30 a pound is about 3 million pounds a year, or 60 percent of the present market for the competitor's Thor. At lower volumes the total cost line is higher than the total revenue line, signaling an expected operating loss. At higher volumes, total revenue would exceed total cost and a profit would be recorded.

The company is not in business to break even, however. It wishes to earn a return on investment of at least 20 percent before taxes. Description of the method used to compute return on investment must be deferred to the next chapter, but the break-even chart can be used to give a rough idea of the product's ability to meet a return on investment test. In this case, the controller estimates that total investment in plant and working capital would be approximately as follows:

$$\text{Investment } (I) = \$6,500,000 + 0.12R.$$

A 20 percent return (r) on this investment would be:

$$rI = 0.20 \times \$6,500,000 + 0.20 \times 0.12R$$
$$= \$1,300,000 + 0.024R.$$

This can be regarded as an added amount that must be covered before the product can "break even" in a real sense. In other words, if the investment is to be profitable, then revenue must equal or exceed the total cost plus the required return on investment:

$$R \geq C + rI.$$

Substituting the formulas above in this equation gives:

$$\$1.30V = \$1,200,000 + \$0.90V + \$1,300,000 + 0.024 \times \$1.30V.$$

This reduces to:

$$\$0.3688V = \$2,500,000$$

$$V = 6,779,000 \text{ pounds}.$$

That is, Seaton Chemicals would have to sell more of this new product than the market is now buying from its competitor.

This analysis is presented graphically in Exhibit 19–6. The required return on investment is added to the cost figures to get a new "total requirements" line. The adjusted break-even point is the volume at which this line and the total revenue line intersect. At volumes greater than this, profit is in excess of the required amount; at lower volumes it is less than the amount required.

In this case, management feels that a volume of 6,779,000 pounds a year is too far out of reach to justify introducing product X-250. Consequently, the sales manager is asked to investigate cheaper products for which X-250 might be a substitute, and to estimate the increase in volume that might be obtained by reducing the price to $1.15 per pound. At the same time, the chief engineer is requested to explore the possibility of moving to a smaller plant with lower fixed

Exhibit 19–6

SEATON CHEMICALS, INC.

Profit Required to Produce 20 Percent
Return on Investment from Product X-250

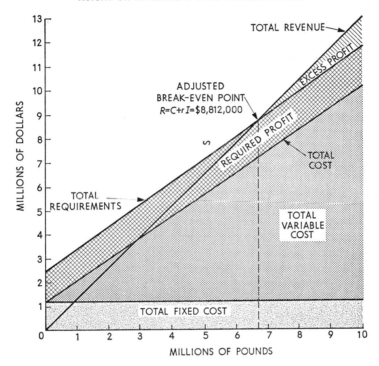

costs and little or no increase in variable unit costs. Decision as to whether the item should be sold at a lower price, produced in a smaller plant, or kept in the laboratory for a few more years is deferred until further information can be obtained.

Problems in Break-Even Chart Construction

By the addition of other revenue and cost lines, the break-even chart can be used to diagram the anticipated results of alternative pricing policies or production methods. It can also be used for rough profit forecasting in multiproduct situations.

To illustrate the multiproduct break-even chart, let us assume (1) that the same plant could be used to produce both X-250 and another new chemical, Y-78; (2) that total fixed costs would be, as before, $1,200,000 a year; and (3) that the estimated volume, revenue, and variable cost data for the two products are as follows:

| Item | Sales Volume | Per Unit | | Total | |
		Price	Variable Cost	Revenue	Variable Cost
X-250..........	2,000,000 lbs.	$1.30	$0.90	$2,600,000	$1,800,000
Y-78...........	3,000,000 lbs.	1.80	1.50	5,400,000	4,500,000
Total......				$8,000,000	$6,300,000

The $6,300,000 total variable cost is 78.75 percent of the $8 million total revenue for the stated sales volumes. Therefore, as sales volume varies in total *with the product mix unchanged,* cost will increase or decrease by $0.7875 per dollar of sales revenue. This information is presented graphically in Exhibit 19–7. Output is measured on the horizontal axis by sales revenue,[2] and the total cost line is

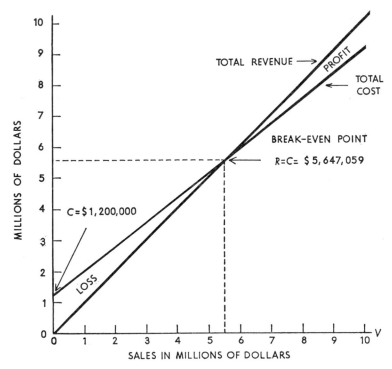

Exhibit 19–7

BREAK-EVEN CHART FOR TWO PRODUCTS

------

[2] Sales revenue is ordinarily used because physical output measures for the various products are not easily added together.

$C = \$1,200,000 + \$0.7875\,V$. The total revenue line is $R = V$, and the break-even point is found to be at a sales volume of \$5,647,059 [i.e., where $C = \$1,200,000 + (0.7875)\,(\$5,647,059) = \$5,647,059$].

Break-even charts may be used to describe a wide variety of situations, but care must always be taken to bear in mind the assumptions on which such charts are based. In the present case, the conditions under which the plant will earn the indicated profit at any given level of volume are (1) that the costs and prices for each product are as estimated, and (2) that the mix in which the two products sell is in the ratio of two pounds of X-250 to three pounds of Y-78.

JOINT PRODUCT COST

In Chapter 18, it was noted that overhead costs that are common to two or more organizations and/or products pose difficult problems in establishing overhead costs per unit of product. Another form of common costs usually called *joint product cost* arises when the processing of a raw material gives rise to two or more products. The classic illustration is meat packing where, for instance, a pig yields bacon, chops, ham, loins, skin, lard, and so forth in unalterable proportions. What portion of the pig's cost is the cost of each of these products?

Measuring the Cost of Joint Product Inventories

Here as elsewhere, the problem of cost measurement for inventory valuation and cost of goods sold determination may be distinguished from the problem of cost measurement for pricing and other decisions. The former problem is the easier one, and it will be examined first. If a meat-packer's inventory always contained the joint products of an animal in the same proportion as the animal yields, no problem of inventory valuation would exist. The cost of the aggregate inventory would be the cost of the equivalent number of pigs or steers. However, the relative quantities of the joint products typically change from one period to the next, and the solution to the problem is allocation of the joint cost among the products.

The practice commonly used is to allocate joint cost according to the market value of each product. To illustrate, assume that a barrel of crude oil costs \$2, that it yields 15 gallons of gasoline with a price of \$0.105 per gallon and 25 gallons of fuel oil with a price of \$0.04 per gallon, and that the refining cost is \$0.25 per barrel of input. The allocated cost per gallon of each product is calculated in Exhibit 19–8.

Exhibit 19-8

MARKET VALUE ALLOCATION OF JOINT COST

Product	(1) Output per Barrel (gallons)	(2) Price per Gallon	(3) Total Value per Barrel (1) × (2)	(4) Cost/ Price Ratio	(5) Total Cost (3) × (4)	(6) Cost per Gallon (5) ÷ (1)
Gasoline..........	15	$0.105	$1.575	$0.874	$1.376	$0.0917
Fuel Oil..........	25	0.040	1.000	0.874	0.874	0.0350
Total.........			$2.575	0.874	$2.250	

The ratio of the total cost of the joint products to their total value, $2.25/$2.575 = 0.874, is multiplied by the total value of each product to determine its total cost. This figure is then divided by the output of the product to arrive at its cost per unit.

Relevance to Business Decisions

The above procedures are eminently reasonable for the purposes of inventory valuation and cost of goods sold determination. At the same time, they illustrate quite vividly how costing methods appropriate for this purpose may be irrelevant for pricing and related decisions. Since the price of each product was used to determine its cost, one clearly cannot turn around and use the cost to arrive at each product's price. In fact, the great virtue of market value cost allocation for pricing purposes is that it is neutral. Each product is made to appear just as profitable as every other product, and the analyst must look elsewhere for information on the profitability of each product.

On occasion, the actual profit percentage of market price may vary among the joint products, because the market prices or the relative amounts of the joint products used in the Exhibit 19-8 type of calculation are obsolete, or because of differences in the profitability of further processing operations on the various joint products. When product cost is determined as described above, however, the resultant data are meaningless as indications of the profitability of each product. The reason is quite simple. In the above case, for example, the refiner cannot obtain an additional gallon of gasoline at a cost of $0.0917. For every gallon of gasoline he obtains at a cost of $0.0917, he also gets one and two-thirds gallons of fuel oil, and spends another $0.058, assuming that the process yields the products only in the indicated proportions.

An illustration may help to indicate the pitfalls to be avoided in joint cost analysis and how they can be avoided. Suppose that the oil refiner has an opportunity to sell an additional 250,000 gallons of fuel oil at $0.04 a gallon. Suppose further that in deciding whether to process enough additional crude oil to produce the extra fuel oil, he has used the unit cost figures from the right-hand column of Exhibit 19–8. The profitability calculation might show the following:

Sales: 250,000 gals. at $0.04...............................		$10,000
Materials and processing costs: 250,000 gals. at $0.035*......$8,750		
Selling and other costs....................................	300	9,050
Contribution to overhead and profit.......................		$ 950

    * From Exhibit 19–8, col. (6).

This shows that the margin on the added business is adequate to justify the expansion.

What this overlooks is that in processing crude oil to get 250,000 extra gallons of fuel oil, the refiner would also get 150,000 gallons of gasoline. This could not be sold at the regular price but would have to be "dumped" in the unbranded gasoline market at $0.085 a gallon. In other words, the refiner should have made the following calculation:

Sales:	250,000 gals. of fuel oil at $0.04...................		$10,000
	150,000 gals. of gasoline at $0.085................		12,750
	Total sales..............................		$22,750
Costs:	10,000 bbls. of crude oil at $2....................$20,000		
	Processing......................................	2,500	
	Selling and other costs: fuel oil...................	300	
	Selling and other costs: gasoline..................	450	23,250
	Net Loss...............................		$ 500

It is evident from this illustration that the cost per unit of a joint product depends on the decision under consideration. If the refiner were considering the advisability of selling more gasoline at a known price, the cost of fuel oil and gasoline would have been different from the values calculated above. In fact, the cost of a joint product depends on the joint material cost and the prices at which *additional quantities* of each of the other joint products can be sold.

The Variable Proportions Case

The previous illustration has made the often unrealistic assumption that the quantities of each final product is always the same percentage of the total physical output of all products combined. If the refiner could modify his operations and thereby increase his output of fuel oil without increasing his output of gasoline, the proposal might be more profitable.

For example, assume that by purchasing another type of crude at $1.72 per barrel and processing it at $0.25 the refiner can obtain 13 gallons of gasoline and 28 gallons of fuel oil. By cutting back on the high gasoline yield crude by 100 barrels and raising production on the high fuel yield crude by 115.4 barrels, the same amount of gasoline is produced plus an extra 731 gallons of crude oil. The cost comparison, therefore, is:

100 bbls. of crude (15 and 25) at $2.25	$2,250.00
115.4 bbls. of crude (13 and 28) at $1.97	2,273.38
Cost of 731 additional gallons of fuel oil	$ 23.38
Cost per additional gallon	$ 0.0320
Additional selling and other costs per additional gallon	0.0012
Total Cost per Gallon of Fuel Oil	$ 0.0332

Under this alternative, the cost of fuel oil is less than its sale value, and the additional business is profitable as long as the cheaper crude can be substituted for the more expensive crude oil.

The above illustrations make clear that the cost of a joint product depends on the production alternatives under consideration, the production possibilities allowed by alternative processes and types of raw material, and the variability of the joint costs. Further exploration of this question, however, must be left to more advanced texts.[3]

By-Product Costing

Joint products are sometimes classified as main products and by-products. When this is done, the by-product is costed at market value less the further costs needed to make the sale. The remainder of the joint cost is charged against the main product. If the oil refiner in the earlier example had treated the extra gasoline as a by-product, the fuel oil would have been costed at $0.0408 a gallon, calculated as follows:

	Total	Per Gallon of Fuel Oil
Cost of buying and processing crude oil	$22,500	$0.0900
Less value of gasoline:		
Sale price at $0.085 a gallon $12,750		
Selling costs 450		
Net value of gasoline	12,300	0.0492
Net Cost of Fuel Oil	$10,200	$0.0408

This is $0.008 a gallon greater than the price of the fuel oil. The company would thus incur a loss of $0.008 × 250,000 plus the $300

[3] For a rigorous statement of the theory of joint costs, see Henderson and Quandt, *Microeconomic Theory: A Mathematical Approach* (New York: McGraw-Hill Book Co., Inc., 1958), pp. 67–72.

selling and other costs if it were to process the additional crude oil. This comes out to about $500, the same figure derived by the method of calculation used originally.

A joint product is usually accounted for as a by-product if the value of the product is small in relation to the main product, or if the product has a market in which the firm can sell all it wants at the prevailing market price. In the latter case, it is legitimate to measure the inventory of the product at adjusted market price. In the former case, doing so is permissible because the amounts involved are not material in amount.

SUMMARY

The basic approach to quantitative analysis for management decisions is to estimate the incremental costs and revenues, the *differences* between a proposed course of action and the action the company would take if the proposal were rejected.

This *incremental analysis* is a simple and powerful concept, but one which is by no means easily applied in all cases. In simple situations, for example, a product's variable cost may be a good estimate of the cost of increasing product output, but revenue effects may be extremely difficult to forecast. In other cases, many fixed costs will also be affected, particularly if large amounts of business are affected by the decision.

This chapter has attempted to indicate briefly how accounting data often need to be modified to make them more relevant to specific decisions. Brief mention has been made of new product introduction, special-order and catalog pricing, and output expansion decisions, followed by an introduction to the use of break-even charts for presenting the results of analyses in pictorial form. A short discussion of joint-product costing rounded out the chapter.

All mention of one very large class of decisions, the choice among alternative investment opportunities, has been studiously avoided in this chapter. For this kind of decision, the essential principles of incremental analysis must be applied within the framework of the present value concept. The next chapter deals with this class of problems.

QUESTIONS AND PROBLEMS

1. What is meant by the "incremental approach" to decision making? Define the terms *incremental cost* and *incremental profit*. Are they the same as *variable cost* and *variable profit*?

2. What problems are encountered in using conventionally developed accounting data in decision making?

3. "We've already spent $100,000 to make this product a success and we can't let that kind of money be wasted. We have to keep on until we succeed." Would you be inclined to agree with this statement? To what extent is the $100,000 relevant to the decision to persist in the effort to market the new product?

4. What are the advantages of using a break-even chart in the analysis of business problems?

5. What are the special situations under which you would consider it sound to sell a product at a price less than its full cost?

6. How does a by-product differ from a joint product? How does by-product costing differ from joint product costing?

7. Why is the product cost information obtained by allocating joint product costs according to the relative market values of the joint products irrelevant for pricing decisions? Is it relevant for other decisions?

8. Discuss the arguments that may be advanced in favor of using full-cost data for pricing.

9. How does variable-cost-based formula pricing differ from full-cost-based formula pricing? Which approach is likely to lead to higher average selling prices?

10. "We sell everything below cost, and the only way we manage to make a profit is because our volume is so big." Can this statement be true?

*11. The Robin Company manufactures a single product for which the price is $6.20. The variable cost per unit is $4.50, and the annual fixed cost is $38,000. What sales volume is needed to break even? To earn a 20 percent return on an investment of $160,000?

*12. The Rise Company makes bumper jacks, and last year it sold 50,000 at a price of $3 and produced them at an average cost of $2.25. The sales manager states that at a price of $2.50 he could sell 75,000 units. The plant manager estimates that 75,000 could be produced at a cost of $2 each. What is the incremental revenue, the incremental cost, and the incremental profit on reducing the price to $2.50 each?

---

* Solutions to problems marked with an asterisk (*) are found in Appendix B.

13. The Walter Company management believes that the company should earn a 20 percent return on investment before taxes at a sales volume equal to 80 percent of capacity. The company's annual capacity is 150,000 units, and the annual fixed costs are $180,000. The variable cost per unit is $8.50, and the investment is $1,300,000.

Assuming that the required sales volume can be achieved, at what unit price will the company realize its return on investment objective?

*14. The Cranby Company sells a single product for which the following data are available:

Current selling price	$4.90 a unit
Expected sales volume	200,000 units
Expected fixed costs	$1.60 a unit
Expected variable costs	$2.20 a unit

The company is contemplating an increase in the selling price of its product to $5.40 a unit.

a) What would be the new break-even point?
b) How many units would have to be sold at the new price to produce a 10 percent increase in total profit before taxes?

15. A sales representative of the Morgan Machinery Company has submitted an offer to the Bragan Products Company to supply Bragan with its requirements of a metal casting at a price of 42 cents each. This metal casting is identical to the X52 casting that the Bragan Products Company now manufactures and uses in several of its products. The following estimate of the cost of making X52 castings has been prepared by the cost accounting department:

UNIT COST OF X52 CASTINGS

Material	$0.18
Labor	0.09
Supplies	0.06
Other variable costs	0.07
Depreciation on casting equipment	0.03
Other fixed costs, including space charges, general factory supervision, etc.	0.05
Total Manufacturing Cost per Unit	$0.48

Prepare a short report analyzing the desirability of accepting the Morgan proposal.

16. During 19x1, the Arapahoe Company sold 300,000 units of product and made a profit after taxes of $70,000. The variable profit per unit was $1 and the selling price was $2.50. Fixed costs were $200,000, and the income tax rate was 30 percent.

For 19x2, variable costs went up $0.10 per unit, fixed costs went up $16,000, and income taxes increased to a rate of 40 percent.

a) What was the break-even sales volume for 19x1, in dollars?

b) What will be the break-even sales dollars for 19x2 if the selling price is not changed?

c) How many units will have to be sold to make a profit after taxes of $60,000 for 19x2 if the selling price is not changed?

d) By how much will the sales price have to be increased to break even at the same sales dollars in 19x2 as in 19x1?

e) What would be the sales price to continue to make $70,000 profit after taxes on sales of 300,000 units?

17. The Meredith Machine Company entered into a contract to manufacture for a foreign concern certain specially designed chemical processing equipment. When the equipment was completed and in the testing stage, currency controls which nullified all import contracts were instituted by the government to which the purchaser was subject. The manufacturing costs incurred by the Meredith Company up to that time were slightly over $700,000. The scrap value of the equipment was estimated to be approximately $80,000.

No purchaser could be found for the equipment in its existing form, but one company was interested if certain major modifications were made. This company offered $500,000; the estimated cost of modification to fit the revised specifications was $200,000.

What course of action should the Meredith Company follow? To what extent is the decision affected by the amount of manufacturing cost that has already been incurred?

18. The Fantasi Corporation is engaged in setting the price to be placed on a new product. It is estimated that sales of 10,000 units would give the company approximately the same share of this particular market as it has been able to maintain in the markets for the company's other products. The sales manager believes that he can obtain this share if the price is not more than 10 percent higher than $13.50, the price at which the most closely competitive product is now being sold. No estimates of sales volume at other prices are available.

The company's policy is to establish prices on new products at factory cost plus 40 percent to cover selling and administrative expenses and provide a profit. Factory cost is defined as direct labor and materials plus overhead. The burden rate for the department in which the new product will be processed is $3.46 per direct labor hour. Direct costs will be $2.50 for materials and 1.5 hours of direct labor at $1.80 an hour.

a) What price should the company establish?

b) Would your answer be affected if competing products were priced at $12.50? If so, quote a new price under these circumstances.

c) Would your answer differ if the competitive price were $10? Explain.

19. The Davis Company produces two products and anticipates, with no changes in prices or programs from the previous year, the following relationships for costs, prices, and volume:

	Product A		Product B
Sales	$3.00 per unit		$5.00 per unit
Variable costs	$1.50 per unit		$2.00 per unit
Fixed costs	$45,000		$60,000
Common fixed costs		$50,000	
Volume	60,000 units		40,000 units

Several changes are being contemplated by management. You are asked to show—arithmetically and graphically—the effect on the break-even point and the effect on anticipated profits of each of the proposed changes. You should consider each proposal independently of the others.

(1) An outlay of $20,000 for advertising which would result in anticipated volume of 50,000 units of A and 50,000 units of B. The individual who proposes this move states that "B is the high margin product—this is what we want."

(2) The installation of a machine which would increase the common fixed costs by $10,000 but would reduce the variable costs of product A by $0.10 per unit and the variable costs of product B by $0.15 per unit. This machine would also expand the capacity of production of A from 70,000 units to 80,000 units, but the sales would not be expected to increase.

(3) A reduction of the price of B to $4.75 which would increase the volume of B to 45,000 units. This would require a $5,000 increase in B's fixed costs. Sales volume of A would be unaffected.

(4) An increase in wage rates for the direct labor is being considered; this increase would raise the variable costs of A by $0.10 a unit and of B by $0.15 a unit.

20. Middleton Enterprises, Inc., owns a baseball team, the Middleton Blue Sox, and a baseball park with a seating capacity of 5,000. Its fixed costs are $15,000 each year, and variable costs are $0.10 per spectator per game. One hundred games are played each year, and the average attendance is 1,000 per game. Therefore fixed costs are $0.15 per spectator per game. The stadium is adequate for all games except a special series of five exhibition games with major league teams. For each of these five games, the estimated demand is as follows:

If the Price Is—	Then Estimated Attendance Is—
$3.00	2,000
2.50	6,000
2.00	9,000
1.75	11,000
1.50	16,000
1.00	20,000

The company can rent a nearby stadium (25,000 capacity) for a fee of $2,000 for each game plus 10 percent of gross receipts. In addition, the company would still have the variable costs of $0.10 per spectator per game.

Asuming that the price charged will be one of the six alternatives above, present a table that will indicate the admission price that will be most profitable for the company and also whether the larger stadium should be rented. Show all calculations.

*21. The total cost of processing 100,000 barrels of crude petroleum—including raw material, labor, and overhead—is $444,000. Expected yields and market values of products are as shown below. Compute unit product costs for inventory costing purposes.

Product	Barrel Yield	Estimated Market Values	
		Per Barrel	Total
Aviation gasoline.............	8,000	$ 6.25	$ 50,000
Motor gasoline.............	42,000	5.00	210,000
Kerosene.................	10,000	4.40	44,000
Distillate fuels.............	20,000	4.00	80,000
Lubricants................	5,000	10.00	50,000
Residual fuels.............	10,000	2.60	26,000
Gases and loss.............	5,000	. . .	. . . . .
Total................	100,000		$460,000

22. The Rancid City Meat Packing Company sells 5,000 pounds of low-grade beef scraps a week, at a price of 10 cents a pound. By the company's method of allocating joint costs, the cost of these meat scraps has been calculated to be 9 cents a pound.

Rancid City's marketing vice president has just made a proposal to mix the beef scraps with grain, cook them, and pack the resulting mixture in cans under the private brand of a large regional chain of supermarkets. The mixture would be sold as dog food. One pound of beef scraps would provide the basic raw materials for two cans of dog food, which would be sold to the chain for 14 cents a can. Additional processing costs, including the costs of grain and other processing materials, would amount to $920 a week.

Prepare an analysis of this proposal, indicating whether the company should accept or reject it. Show how you dealt with the beef scraps' unit cost figure of 9 cents a pound.

23. During the past year the Atom Chemical Company converted certain raw materials into 500,000 pounds of material A and 1,000,000 gallons of liquid B. The total joint cost of production was $388,000. After sepa-

ration, material A was processed further and converted into material C at an additional cost of 3 cents a pound. The selling price of material C was 40 cents a pound and that of liquid B 30 cents a gallon.

On December 31, the inventory showed 20,000 pounds of material A, 50,000 gallons of liquid B, and 35,000 pounds of material C.

a) Allocate the joint costs of production between material A and liquid B. Using these allocations, how much of the joint costs are assigned to each pound of material A? Each gallon of liquid B? What is the total cost of a pound of material C?

b) After computing your answer to (a), you discover that the company's inventories of C have been increasing by about 15,000 pounds a year for the past two years because customers have been abandoning the process for which it was an essential raw material. This trend is likely to continue, and price reductions would not be an effective means of increasing the sales volume of material C. Sales volume of B is relatively constant from year to year. The purchasing agent of Molecule, Inc., has just offered to sign a contract to buy 25,000 pounds of A during each of the next three years. The price for the first year would be 26 cents a pound; prices for later years would be negotiated later. Prepare a short statement indicating whether the offer should be accepted. Be sure to indicate how you used the unit cost figure you obtained in (a) above.

24. A company has four large presses of approximately the same capacity. Each was run at close to its full capacity during 19x8. Each machine is depreciated separately; a declining-charge method is used. Data for each press are:

	No. 1	No. 2	No. 3	No. 4
Date acquired.............	1/1/x0	1/1/x4	1/1/x6	1/1/x7
Cost.....................	$100,000	$120,000	$145,000	$175,000
Operating costs—19x8:				
Labor.................	$ 11,000	$ 10,500	$ 10,000	$ 9,500
Maintenance...........	3,800	2,400	2,000	1,000
Repairs...............	600	1,200	800	500
Depreciation...........	3,500	5,400	7,800	10,800
Total...............	$ 18,900	$ 19,500	$ 20,600	$ 21,800

It is expected that activity in 19x9 will be substantially less than in 19x8. As a result, one machine is to be put on a standby basis. It has been proposed that No. 4 should be that machine on the grounds that it has the highest operating cost.

Do you agree with this proposal? Explain, citing figures from the problem.

*25. The XYZ Company, a large textile manufacturing concern producing a number of types of textile products, sold most of its output to jobbers, manufacturers, and other purchasers of large quantities. During a period of slack business, when the plant was not operating at full capacity, the sales manager brought in two possible jobs, either of which in addition to the company's regular orders would keep the plant operating at capacity for about six weeks. Since it was not possible to accept both orders, the president asked for cost estimates on each of the jobs.

One of the two orders was from an institutional buyer for 27,000 dozen 63-inch by 108-inch sheets. The other was from a furniture manufacturer for 900,000 yards of gray goods to be used for linings. The proposed prices were $7.5095 net per dozen for the sheets and $0.225 per yard for the gray goods. Cost estimates were as follows:

ESTIMATED COST OF ORDER

FOR 27,000 DOZEN 63-INCH BY 108-INCH SHEETS

	Cost per Dozen
Labor (including $0.2505 fixed labor costs)	$2.5045
Manufacturing overhead (including $1.0142 fixed costs)	1.6904
Process material	0.4092
Raw material	2.8240
Freight	0.0895
Total Factory Cost	$7.5176
Selling and administrative expense (5.6% of total factory cost)*	0.4210
Total Cost	$7.9386
Selling price	7.5095
Loss	$0.4291
	X 27,000 dozen
Total Loss	$11,586

* Assigned by type of product on basis of past experience.

ESTIMATED COST OF ORDER

FOR 900,000 YARDS OF GRAY GOODS

	Cost per Yard
Labor (including $0.0067 fixed labor costs)	$0.0681
Manufacturing overhead (including $0.0232 fixed costs)	0.0386
Process material	0.0018
Raw material	0.1131
Total Factory Cost	$0.2216
Selling and administrative expense (6.3% of total factory cost)*	0.0140
Total Cost	$0.2356
Selling price	0.2250
Loss	$0.0106
	X900,000 yards
Total Loss	$ 9,540

* Assigned by type of product on basis of past experience.

Which order, if either, would you advise the company to accept? Why?

26. The manager of the university print shop is trying to decide whether to meet the prices and delivery-time performance of local commercial printing shops on small printing jobs. The commercial shops quote prices that are 10 percent lower than the university shop's schedule and also offer faster delivery at no extra charge. Until now, university departments were required to use the university shop for this sort of work, but a mounting volume of complaints has led the university controller to authorize the use of off-campus print shops. The university shop will continue to do large-volume jobs and confidential work, such as examinations and research reports. The university shop would require the same amount of equipment it now has, even if it were to let the business go outside.

At its present operating volume of 2,000 labor hours per month, the operating costs of the university print shop are:

> Paper stock......................Varies with nature of work
> Labor............................$4 per labor hour
> Other processing costs.............$3 per labor hour

All labor is regarded as wholly variable with volume; other processing costs include $4,000 of fixed costs, the remainder being wholly and proportionally variable with volume, volume being measured in terms of labor hours.

Approximately 600 labor hours per month are now being spent on the work affected by the decision. Materials cost on this work is approximately $3,000 a month, and the amount now being charged by the university shop to other university departments for this work is $7,500 a month.

The shop manager is convinced that he will lose the work unless he meets both the competitive price and the competitive delivery time. To permit faster deliveries, an additional 80 hours of labor a month would be required in excess of the 600 labor hours now devoted to this work. Fixed costs would not be affected by this choice between these two alternatives.

Which alternative should the manager choose? Show your calculations.

27. The Toledo Paint and Glass Company manufactured glass jars. One of the firm's large customers was considering the advisability of substituting another type of container for glass jars. The customer's primary consideration was cost, and Toledo's sales department was certain that a reduction from the present price of $2.90 per hundred jars to a price no higher than $2.45 was necessary to keep the account.

The cost data provided by the accounting department on the item are given below:

Material...	$0.45
Labor...	0.55
Fuel and furnace relining............................	0.40
Factory indirect costs*.............................	0.60
Selling, general, and administrative costs†..............	0.80
Total Cost...................................	$2.80

* Allocated to products on the basis of furnace hours.
† Allocated to products on the basis of total factory costs.

The production manager was anxious to maintain the operations of this plant, and he advocated quoting the lower price. He reasoned that the direct costs (the first three items) amounted to only $1.40 and that a profit could be made on the account at a price of $2.45. The controller took the opposite view and countered as follows: "If we consider each item that covers its direct costs profitable, we can end up with each item showing a profit and the company showing a loss."

State the factors you would consider and the reasoning you would follow in reaching a decision in arriving at a price for the customer.

28. The Albegata Company produces four products, Alpha, Beta, Gamma, and Delta. Its profit and loss statement for the past year is as follows:

ALBEGATA COMPANY
Profit and Loss Statement
For the Past Year
(In Thousands of Dollars)

	Products				Total
	Alpha	Beta	Gamma	Delta	
Sales................................	$4,000	$3,000	$2,000	$1,000	$10,000
Cost of sales:					
Direct material.....................	$1,500	$1,000	$ 500	$ 500	$ 3,500
Direct labor.......................	1,000	1,000	300	200	2,500
Factory overhead (allocated on direct labor cost basis)...........	400	400	120	80	1,000
Total.........................	$2,900	$2,400	$ 920	$ 780	$ 7,000
Gross margin......................	$1,100	$ 600	$1,080	$ 220	$ 3,000
Distribution expense:					
Direct—variable....................	$ 150	$ 50	$ 40	$ 60	$ 300
Apportioned (on sales)—fixed	400	300	200	100	1,000
Administrative expense:					
Apportioned (on sales)—fixed........	600	450	300	150	1,500
Total Operating Expense..........	$1,150	$ 800	$ 540	$ 310	$ 2,800
Net Profit (Loss).....................	$ (50)	$(200)	$ 540	$ (90)	$ 200

It is believed that no external force in the foreseeable future will alter the picture. At the board of directors' meeting, it is decided that something must be done in view of the low overall profit rate (2 percent on sales) and the net loss on all except one product line.

Upon your request, the following additional information is furnished by the company:

(1) Analysis of factory overhead and apportioned operating expenses:

	Alpha	Beta	Gamma	Delta
Factory overhead:				
Direct—variable...................	$150	$200	$100	$ 60
Escapable at shutdown of that line....	150	100	10	10
Inescapable......................	100	100	10	10
Apportioned distribution expense:				
Escapable at shutdown.............	200	100	100	90
Inescapable......................	200	200	100	10
Administrative expense:				
Escapable at shutdown.............	200	300	200	120
Inescapable......................	400	150	100	30

(2) Products Beta and Alpha share the same equipment. For every unit of Beta not produced, one unit of Alpha can be made in its place. The unit sales price for each product is:

Alpha	Beta	Gamma	Delta
$10	$10	$10	$0.50

The sales department feels that with some promotional effort the sales of Alpha and Beta can be increased without reducing the price.

(3) Product Delta is looked on as a loss leader, since it is feared that sales of Gamma would fall by as much as 20 percent if Delta were dropped from the company's line. Alpha and Beta, on the other hand, are sold to other types of buyers, and their sales would not be affected.

a) Give recommendations when only the additional information in (1) is known. (All recommendations must be supported by computations showing estimated improvement in profits.)

b) Give recommendations when only the additional information in (1) and (2) is known.

c) Give recommendations when the additional information in (1), (2), and (3) is known.

29.† "You just can't do it," said Mr. Erik Berggren, controller of AB Sundqvist. "Our policy has always been to bill our distributors at cost and that doesn't mean variable cost. We just can't afford to sell below cost."

AB Sundqvist is a medium-sized manufacturer of cough medicines, headache-pills, and similar products. It has three factories and a large sales force, all in Sweden, and a chain of general agents, one in each country in Western Europe. These general agents buy products from Sundqvist "at cost" and sell them to pharmacies for distribution to the ultimate consumer. The general agents, in addition to the cost price of the products themselves, pay Sundqvist a royalty equal to 5 percent of the amounts they bill their customers for Sundqvist products.

Sundqvist had been very fortunate in obtaining large, well-managed, and well-financed companies as its general agents. Its general agent in Britain, Edwards Enterprises, Ltd., was a subsidiary of a large Belgian company engaged in the manufacture and distribution of a wide variety of pharmaceutical and cosmetic products. Although Edwards Enterprises did no manufacturing itself, its parent company had manufacturing plants to supply it with products representing approximately 30 percent of its annual sales volume. Edwards Enterprises regarded itself as a marketing organization and was reluctant to get into manufacturing, although the issue had come up from time to time as the company encountered difficulties in obtaining adequate supplies of a specific kind of product at profitable prices.

Edwards Enterprises, like Sundqvist's other general agents, represented several manufacturers, but did not carry directly competing merchandise. In other words, if it obtained a line of face creams from one manufacturer, it would not handle another line of face creams.

The statement quoted at the beginning of this case was made by Mr. Berggren in the course of a conversation with Mr. Nils Lindstrom, the company's manager for foreign markets. Mr. Lindstrom was anxious to build up sales volume abroad, particularly in view of the recent plant expansion program which for the first time had provided enough capacity to supply all the company's markets. Although some operations were still subcontracted during peak seasons, the company's plant was operating at about 85 percent of its annual capacity.

The Sundqvist Company had just developed a new liquid headache remedy which it had introduced on the Swedish market with considerable initial success. Mr. Frank Keeling, president of Edwards Enterprises, was very interested in marketing this new item in Britain. Although his parent company had a somewhat similar product, Mr. Keeling regarded it as inferior in quality to the Sundqvist product and much more difficult to market. The British public had recently shown a preference for Swedish-

---

† Copyright 1968 by l'Institut pour l'Etude des Méthodes de Direction de l'Entreprise (IMEDE), Lausanne. Switzerland. Reprinted by permission.

made products in this field, at least partly because of an intensive advertising campaign carried out by Edwards Enterprises itself.

Mr. Keeling was anxious to capitalize on this preference by offering the
Sundqvist product. He was not happy, however, with the price quoted
him by Mr. Lindstrom, a price of 10 Swedish crowns for a case of 12
bottles. "Let's face it," he said, "your direct costs of manufacturing this
product are probably about 6 crowns per case. We make approximately
the same product in Belgium and your cost can't be very different from
ours. This means that you're adding four crowns a case to cover your
overhead cost. I think this just isn't warranted here, particularly because
you get a royalty of 5 percent on our gross sales volume anyway. We
would sell this to retailers at about four times the price we pay you. At 6
crowns a case, our price would be 24 crowns and your royalty alone
would be about 1.20 crowns. We'd be willing to pay you a little more
than your direct cost, but this is just too much to ask."

The accounting system used by AB Sundqvist was a "direct costing"
system. In this system, product cost included only labor and material
cost, and was broken down into four categories:

1. The materials required for the manufacture of the product itself.
2. Containers, packages, and packing materials.
3. Direct manufacturing labor.
4. Filling and packaging labor.

The labor charges included a provision for social benefits of 20 percent,
which was almost exactly the cost of these benefits to the Sundqvist
Company. The salaries of the foremen in the direct production departments were not included in direct cost.

For pricing purposes, Mr. Berggren included in product cost an allowance of 175 percent of direct cost to allow for factory, sales, technical,
and administrative overhead costs. This was based on the breakdown
shown in Exhibit 1. The 175 percent rate was computed as follows:

$$\frac{\text{Overhead Cost}}{\text{Direct Cost of Goods Sold}} = \frac{\text{Kr. } 5,700,000}{\text{Kr. } 3,260,000} = 175 \text{ percent.}$$

The company's accounts included no provision for depreciation on
plant and equipment. The original cost of the factory buildings amounted
to Kr. 1,400,000, while factory equipment had cost Kr. 350,000. As far as
the building was concerned, one company official stated that increases in
the market value of the land were expected to exceed any depreciation on
the building itself and that depreciation was therefore unnecessary. Comparable buildings in Sweden were likely to remain in productive use for 50
years or even longer. The equipment was a different matter. On the average, it was likely to last for 5–7 years, but this was such an uncertain
figure that Mr. Berggren was unwilling to reflect it in the accounts.

Exhibit 1

AB SUNDQVIST

Budgeted Income Statement
(Figures in Thousands)

Sales..		Kr. 10,390
Direct cost of goods sold..............................		3,260
Direct margin..		Kr. 7,130
Overheads:		
Top management..Kr.	160	
Staff (finance, tax, purchasing).........................	230	
Routine clerical......................................	1,060	
Selling expense—Sweden.............................	3,080	
Warehousing and shipping............................	550	
Export sales expense..................................	60	
Factory overhead (see Schedule A).....................	430	
Research and testing..................................	130	
Total Overheads.................................		5,700
Net Income before Taxes..............................		Kr. 1,430

Schedule A: Budgeted Factory Overhead Costs

Materials control..	Kr.	100
Engineering...		105
Supervision...		15
Indirect labor..		30
Outside services..		30
Maintenance..		35
Utilities..		20
Work clothes...		15
Other...		80
Total Factory Overhead Costs......................	Kr.	430

Mr. Lindstrom persisted in his argument with Mr. Berggren. "After all," he said, "if we can increase our sales, only the variable costs will increase; the fixed costs will remain constant. Besides, it is a fact that we can make money on the royalties we get on the added sales."

Mr. Berggren was unimpressed. "If your sales expand by as much as you hope they will," he said, "we'll have to add another shift in at least one factory and make some additional investments in mixing machinery. If you're really successful, we'll even have to expand one of the plants earlier than we now plan. Your variable cost figures ignore these facts. I'm perfectly willing to work out some figures on the profitability of the added volume that might come from price reductions, but don't try to get me to support your bid to sell the product at direct cost. Cost is cost, and that's all there is to it."

a) Would you have supported Mr. Lindstrom or Mr. Berggren? Does it appear that a price equal to direct product cost plus a royalty of 5 percent of the agents' billing price would be profitable or unprofitable for the Sundqvist company?

b) What changes in this company's accounting system, if any, would yield data that are more relevant to decisions of this type?

c) Would your answer to (*a*) differ in any way if this were a one-time order for a single shipment of a product made to a customer's specifications?

d) Would you describe Sundqvist's direct cost system as a variable costing system? How different is it?

e) The company's contracts with its general agents call for billing the latter "at cost." Because of the controversy that arose in this case, the company planned to revise its contract forms to provide a more specific definition of cost. What items do you think should be included as "cost"?

Chapter 20

THE CAPITAL INVESTMENT
DECISION

WHEN A DECISION cannot be made on the basis of the cash flows anticipated during a single time period, it is an investment problem. Typical examples are proposals to build, acquire, replace, or expand long-lived productive assets—that is, capital expenditures. Capital expenditure decisions require a slightly different approach from that developed in Chapter 19; the purpose of this chapter is to see why a different approach is needed and how it can be carried out.

THE PRESENT VALUE APPROACH

An investment outlay may be defined as *an expenditure of cash or its equivalent in one time period or periods in order to obtain a net inflow of cash or its equivalent in some other time period or periods.*

For example, suppose that a company has an opportunity to rearrange the layout of one of its factories at an outlay of $50,000. This will permit the company to save $20,000 a year in the manufacture of a product which it expects to produce for the next three years. The cash flows in this example can be arranged in a *timetable* like the following:

Years from Now	Cash Inflow (+) or Outflow (−)
0	−$50,000
0 to 1	+ 20,000
1 to 2	+ 20,000
2 to 3	+ 20,000
Total	+$10,000

One method of rationing the company's scarce capital funds is to calculate for each proposal the present value of the anticipated cash flows, using the technique described in Chapter 9, and accept only those proposals that seem to promise a positive net present value.

This kind of analysis consists of three steps:

1. Estimate the amount and timing of the cash flows that are expected to result from each alternative under consideration.
2. Compute the present value of each of these cash flow streams.
3. Select the alternative promising the greatest present value.

The principal argument for present value is that it is sensitive to differences in the *timing* of the cash flows associated with an investment proposal. To illustrate, let us assume that the company can choose among the following three proposals:

Years from Now	Net Cash Receipts (+) or Cash Outlays (−)		
	Proposal A	Proposal B	Proposal C
0......................	−$13,000	−$13,000	−$13,000
1......................	+ 1,000	+ 5,000	+ 9,000
2......................	+ 5,000	+ 5,000	+ 5,000
3......................	+ 9,000	+ 5,000	+ 1,000
Net Cash Flow...........	+$ 2,000	+$ 2,000	+$ 2,000

The net cash flows for these three proposals are identical, but the projects are far from equally desirable. Proposal C would ordinarily be regarded as the best proposal because cash is received earlier under this proposal than under either of the others.

This difference appears clearly in a present value calculation. Using discount factors from Appendix A, we can see that the present values of the three proposals are:

Years from Now	Present Values of Cash Flows at 8%		
	Proposal A	Proposal B	Proposal C
0......................	−$13,000	−$13,000	−$13,000
1......................	+ 926	+ 4,630	+ 8,333
2......................	+ 4,286	+ 4,286	+ 4,286
3......................	+ 7,144	+ 3,969	+ 794
Net Present Value	−$ 644	−$ 115	+$ 413

If net present value is greater than zero, this means that the future cash receipts are more than adequate to provide a return on capital equal to the rate which was used in discounting. In other words, proposals A and B promise a return on capital of less than 8 percent; only proposal C promises a return in excess of 8 percent and is therefore good enough to meet the company's minimum profitability standard.

The present value measure, in other words, permits management to compare proposals that differ in the timing of their cash flows. Present value is the means by which all cash flows of all proposals can be restated at their equivalent values at a common point in time. These proposals can therefore be compared directly with each other.

ESTIMATES OF PROJECT CASH FLOWS

It is conceptually unnecessary in capital expenditure analysis to distinguish different types of cash flows, because the timetable requires a distinction only between inflows and outflows. For analytical convenience, however, five separate parameters can be recognized:

1. Amount and timing of initial investment outlays.
2. Amount and timing of subsequent investment outlays.
3. Economic life.
4. Amount and timing of operating cash flows.
5. End-of-life salvage value.

Before examining these, however, we must first examine the relevance of one factor that may influence them all to some extent—the incidence of taxes on business income.

Income Tax Adjustments

The main reason for adjusting project profitability estimates for the effect of income taxes is that both the amount and the timing of the tax impact on cash flows are likely to differ among alternatives. For example, suppose that a company is trying to choose between two proposals to invest $100,000. For one of these, the entire $100,000 must be capitalized for tax purposes; for the other, it can be written off immediately as a tax deductible expense. Other things being equal, the second of these is the better proposal because the tax-deductibility feature will reduce the company's current tax bill by $40,000, assuming a 40 percent tax rate, and this amount can be invested productively elsewhere.[1]

It should be noted that an initial tax write-off of this kind only *postpones* tax payments. There is no tax *reduction* unless the effective

---

[1] The effective tax rate varies slightly from state to state and is subject to change. For simplicity, a rate of 40 percent will be used throughout this section. Although actual rates are ordinarily in the neighborhood of 50 percent, for illustrative purposes it is clearer to use the 40 percent rate, which produces different figures for income tax and after-tax net income.

tax rate is lower in later years. For each proposal the total lifetime tax write-off is $100,000; only its timing differs. The same issue is involved in the choice between straight-line depreciation and some form of declining-charge depreciation for tax purposes. Any device such as immediate deductibility or fast write-off which shifts the income deduction to earlier years results in a higher present value to the taxpayer.

Amount and Timing of Initial Investment Outlays

With this as background, the stage is set for an examination of each of the five parameters listed above. Measurement of the first of these —the initial investment outlay—is not always as simple as it might sound. The initial outlay is defined as the net expenditure of cash or its equivalent required by the proposal. This includes all expenditures necessary to carry out the proposal, whether for plant and equipment or for working capital, whether capitalized on the balance sheet or written off immediately as expense for external financial reporting or tax purposes.

For example, a proposal may call for the following expenditures prior to the start of operations:

Equipment	$ 80,000
Installation	10,000
Working capital	5,000
Training and test runs	7,000
Total Expenditures	$102,000

Payment is to be due for all four of these items when the facilities are placed in full company operation. For convenience, this can be designated as the zero date.

In addition to these cash expenditures, this proposal calls for the use of a machine already under company ownership but now idle. This calls for the direct application of the opportunity cost concept first discussed in Chapter 19. Opportunity cost is at least as high as the current market (resale) value of the asset, and in this case this is the measure of opportunity cost. The amount is $12,000. This is regarded as part of the outlay because the company is depriving itself of this amount of cash if it accepts the proposal. A cash receipt foregone is always equivalent to a cash outlay made.

One final element enters into the calculation of the before-tax investment outlay in this example. If the proposal is accepted, a machine now serving a standby purpose can be disposed of. Opportunity cost is once again the measure of the resources released, in this case equal to the scrap value of the machine, which is $6,000. The displaced resources, in other words, can finance $6,000 of the gross before-tax outlays required by the proposal.

The net initial investment outlay before taxes can now be computed from the above figures:

Equipment..	$ 80,000
Installation..	10,000
Working capital......................................	5,000
Training and test runs................................	7,000
Presently owned surplus equipment to be used (resale value)..........	12,000
Gross outlay..	$114,000
Less: Presently owned operating equipment to be replaced if proposal is accepted (resale value).................................	6,000
Net Investment Outlay before Income Taxes....................	$108,000

The tax adjustment will depend on the tax status of the specific facilities. The equipment and its installation are both capitalized, and the after-tax cash flow on these two items is the same as the before-tax cash flow, $90,000. The working capital outlays have no special tax treatment so that the after-tax and before-tax outlays are again identical.[2] The training and test-run costs are fully deductible from current revenues, however; and thus the after-tax cash flow is only 60 percent of the before-tax outlay:

Gross outlay...	$7,000
Less: Tax reduction at 40 percent.........................	2,800
After-Tax Outlay.....................................	$4,200

The tax effect of retention of the surplus equipment is probably the most difficult to understand. If the company does not accept this proposal, it will be able to dispose of this equipment at a price of $12,000. The book value of this equipment for tax purposes (or, to use technical language, its "adjusted basis") is $20,000. Thus if it is sold, an $8,000 loss will be reported on the income tax return, and this will reduce the company's taxes by $3,200. In other words, the company can realize a total of $15,200. By accepting the proposal, the company must forego this cash receipt—thus $15,200 must be charged against the proposal as a cash outlay. The calculations can be summarized briefly:

(1)	Before-tax cash flow................................	$12,000
(2)	Book value for tax purposes.........................	20,000
(3)	Taxable gain or (loss): (1) − (2).....................	$(8,000)
(4)	Tax or (credit): (3) × 40%.........................	(3,200)
(5)	After-Tax Cash Flow: (1) − (4)	$15,200

[2] This is not always the case. Some countries have special income tax provisions to encourage the investment in inventories, and these would have to be allowed for.

The tax effect of the disposal of the replaced facilities is similar, but probably easier to understand. Assuming a book value for tax purposes of $1,000, the calculations are:

(1) Before-tax cash flow.................................$6,000
(2) Book value for tax purposes............................ 1,000
(3) Taxable gain or (loss): (1) — (2)......................$5,000
(4) Tax or (credit): (3) × 40%............................ 2,000
(5) After-Tax Cash Flow: (1) — (4)......................$4,000

These adjustments are all summarized in Exhibit 20–1. In this case the net difference between the before-tax and the after-tax amounts is relatively small, less than 3 percent; in other cases it will be much higher. Some analysts would prefer to recognize a difference in timing between the outlay and the tax adjustment, taking the outlay into the

Exhibit 20–1

CALCULATION OF AFTER-TAX INVESTMENT OUTLAY

Item	Outlay before Tax	Tax Effect	Outlay after Tax
Equipment, installed............	$ 90,000	$ 0	$ 90,000
Working capital................	5,000	0	5,000
Training and test runs..........	7,000	(2,800)	4,200
Surplus equipment used........	12,000	3,200	15,200
Equipment replaced............	(6,000)	2,000	(4,000)
Total....................	$108,000	$2,400	$110,400

timetable at the zero date and the tax adjustment with the first year's operating cash flows. This is ordinarily an unnecessary complication, first because the time lag before tax payment is relatively short and getting shorter as time goes by, and also because an increase in tax liability ordinarily has approximately the same effect on corporate liquidity as a decrease in cash and thus can be regarded as equivalent to a cash flow.

Amount and Timing of Subsequent Investment Outlays

It is often possible to anticipate special outlays in later time periods that are more like investment outlays than operating expenditures. These, too, may be for equipment or working capital, treated as expense or capitalized, and should be adjusted for their tax effects. The only reason for assigning these outlays to a separate category is that they are the easiest cash flows to overlook, and separate recognition at least serves as a partial reminder to look for them. Their conceptual basis is no different from that of the initial outlays.

Economic Life

Economic life of any particular asset may be defined as *the time interval that is expected to elapse between the time of acquisition and the time at which the combined forces of obsolescence and deterioration will justify retirement of the asset.* Economic life is the *shortest* of the following three figures:

1. Physical life of the tangible assets.
2. Technological life of the tangible assets.
3. Market life of the assets' output.

Although many assets can be repaired and kept in service almost indefinitely, physical life generally comes to an end when replacing it is cheaper than continuing to repair it. Physical life is seldom the measure of economic life in a rapidly changing economy, however. New processes and new equipment often make existing equipment obsolete long before physical life comes to an end—that is, the spread between the cash flows from operating the asset and the cash flows from operating a new asset may become wide enough to justify replacement even if the old asset's operating costs have not risen at all.

Finally, the product market may change even before this happens, so that the company can no longer sell the asset's output at a profitable price. In other words, if market life is shorter than technological life, it becomes the measure of economic life.

Amount and Timing of Operating Cash Flows

Since the success of a capital expenditure will depend largely on the net operating cash flows that it will generate, the analysis of a project should for the most part be concerned with the accounting, marketing, and production data that may be used to forecast these cash flows. The net flow may be either positive or negative in a particular year, but with the possible exception of the first year or two, the projected net operating cash flows will ordinarily be positive. In many cases, the project analyst will have very little basis on which to predict time patterns of the operating cash flows, and he will use some formulistic approximation such as uniform annual amounts or linearly declining amounts. The reasonableness of these formulas should always be questioned, and if a better basis can be justified it should be used.

In arriving at the net operating cash flows the incremental principles used in the previous pages and in Chapter 19 apply. Accounting expenses and cash flows that are independent of whether or not a project is adopted are to be ignored in projecting a project's cash flows. The major difficulty in applying the principle arises in connection with the tax benefit due to the depreciation allowances generated by the project. These calculations begin with the tax basis and the depreciation rate for tax purposes of the assets subject to depreciation. The relevant data appear below:

Item	Tax Basis	Depreciation Rate for Tax Purposes
Installed equipment cost.....................	$90,000	20% of declining balance
Previously owned equipment incorporated in the project...................................	20,000	
Equipment replaced by the project............	1,000	$500 per year

Notice that for three items the tax basis differs from the incremental after-tax cash flow entered in the timetable. The surplus equipment, for example, has a before-tax cash flow of $12,000, an after-tax cash flow of $15,200, and a tax basis of $20,000.

Incremental tax depreciation for the first three years of the project's life will be as follows:

	Year 1	Year 2	Year 3
If proposal is accepted:			
Depreciation on new equipment..............	$18,000	$14,400	$11,520
Depreciation on old equipment..............	4,000	3,200	2,560
Total depreciation if proposal is accepted.....	$22,000	$17,600	$14,080
If proposal is rejected:			
Depreciation on present standby equipment.....	500	500	.....
Incremental Tax Depreciation (Difference).......	$21,500	$17,100	$14,080

The deduction of depreciation on the replaced equipment may be more easily understood if it is recognized as a simple time shift. If the proposal is accepted, the equipment will be replaced and $1,000 will be deducted immediately from taxable income. This was reflected earlier in our calculation of the after-tax investment outlay. If the proposal is rejected, on the other hand, the equipment will be retained and the $1,000 will be deducted from taxable income during the next two years.

Assume now that the incremental before-tax operating cash flows in the first three years are expected to amount to $20,000 a year. This needs to be converted to an after-tax basis by subtracting the incremental tax from the before-tax cash flow. One possible format for doing this as follows (all figures refer to *incremental* amounts):

Year	(1) Before-Tax Cash Flow	(2) Tax Depreciation	(3) Taxable Income (1) − (2)	(4) Income Tax (3) × 40%	(5) After-Tax Cash Flow (1) − (4)
1...............	$20,000	$21,500	$(1,500)	$ (600)	$20,600
2...............	20,000	17,100	2,900	1,160	18,840
3...............	20,000	14,080	5,920	2,368	17,632

Figures for years beyond the third are omitted here to avoid burying the principles in a mass of numbers. An equivalent alternative is:

Year	(1) Before-Tax Cash Flow	(2) Tax Depreciation	(3) Taxable Income (1) − (2)	(4) Income Tax (3) × 40%	(5) After-Tax Net Income (3) − (4)	(6) After-Tax Cash Flow (2) + (5)
1.......	$20,000	$21,500	$(1,500)	$ (600)	$ (900)	$20,600
2.......	20,000	17,100	2,900	1,160	1,740	18,840
3.......	20,000	14,080	5,920	2,368	3,552	17,632

This depreciation add-back procedure is familiar to anyone who has prepared a statement of the sources and uses of funds. The analyst should use whichever method he finds more convenient. The results will be identical.

End-of-Life Salvage Value

The final element in the incremental cash flow timetable is end-of-life salvage value. This consists of the after-tax amount realizable from liquidation of the working capital and sale of the facilities. Alternatively, it is equal to the internal value of the assets to the company at the end of the project's life, if this is greater than liquidation value.

Once again, it is a differential amount that is needed. If the proposal calls for replacing certain assets now, these will not be available later. In the example, facilities with a realizable value of $6,000 are to be replaced. If the proposal is rejected, the company is, in effect, investing the after-tax equivalent of this $6,000—this was reflected above in the incremental investment outlay. By rejecting the proposal, however, the company does retain title to whatever residual value is left at the end of the project's life. If this is, say, $1,500, then this is a charge against the proposal. This shows up in a table of alternatives:

End-of-Project
Salvage Value

If proposal is rejected.............$1,500
If proposal is accepted.............   0
    Difference..................$1,500

To complete this illustration, suppose that the liquidation value of the working capital is equal to its book value for tax purposes ($5,000) and that the equipment required by the proposal has a before-tax residual value of $13,000 and an end-of-life book value for tax purposes of $7,500. The incremental cash flow is:

	(1) Before-Tax Cash Flow	(2) Tax Basis	(3) Taxable Income (1) − (2)	(4) Income Tax (3) × 40%	(5) After-Tax Cash Flow (1) − (4)
If accept proposal:					
Equipment............	$13,000	$ 7,500	$5,500	$2,200	$10,800
Working capital......	5,000	5,000	0	0	5,000
Total Residual Value.........	$18,000	$12,500	$5,500	$2,200	$15,800
If reject proposal:					
Sale value of standby equipment.........	1,500	0	1,500	600	900
Incremental Salvage Value...	$16,500	$12,500	$4,000	$1,600	$14,900

PRESENT VALUE CALCULATIONS

Once the after-tax cash flows have been estimated, their present values can be determined. Although the mechanics of the calculation are simple, five aspects of the calculation deserve comment:

1. Calculating net present value.
2. Calculating the internal rate of return.
3. Choosing the discounting period.
4. Choosing the discount rate.
5. Dealing with uncertainty.

Calculating Net Present Value

The calculation of the net present value of a series of cash flows is a three-step process:

1. List the cash flows in timetable form.
2. Find the present value of each cash flow in the timetable by mul-

tiplying it by the appropriate present value factor from Table 3 or 4 of Appendix A.

3. Add these present values together, subtracting the negative present values from the positive present values. The end result is the *net present value* of the proposal.

To demonstrate this process, let us suppose that management is trying to choose between two ways of manufacturing a new product. Let us call these two methods project X and project Y. The expected economic life of the facilities is 10 years in each case, and the expected end-of-life salvage value is zero. The minimum acceptable return on investment is 8 percent. The cash flows from each proposal and their present values are summarized in Exhibit 20–2. Although project X

Exhibit 20–2

CALCULATION OF PRESENT VALUE

(Figures in $000)

Time	Project X		Project Y		Difference (X − Y)	
	After-Tax Cash Flow	Present Value at 8%	After-Tax Cash Flow	Present Value at 8%	After-Tax Cash Flow	Present Value at 8%
0.............	−$120	−$120	−$ 70	−$70	−$50	−$50
1.............	− 30	− 28	− 10	− 9	− 20	− 19
2.............	0	0	+ 10	+ 9	− 10	− 9
3.............	+ 20	+ 16	+ 20	+ 16	0	0
4.............	+ 40	+ 29	+ 25	+ 18	+ 15	+ 11
5.............	+ 50	+ 34	+ 30	+ 20	+ 20	+ 14
6.............	+ 50	+ 32	+ 30	+ 19	+ 20	+ 13
7.............	+ 50	+ 29	+ 30	+ 17	+ 20	+ 12
8.............	+ 40	+ 22	+ 25	+ 13	+ 15	+ 9
9.............	+ 30	+ 15	+ 20	+ 10	+ 10	+ 5
10.............	+ 20	+ 9	+ 10	+ 5	+ 10	+ 4
Total Lifetime Cash Flow....	+$150		+$120		+$30	
Net Present Value at 8 percent.....		+$ 38		+$48		−$10

has a slightly more favorable lifetime cash flow (+$150,000 versus +$120,000), the present value of project Y's cash flows is significantly greater than that of project X.

The same idea is reflected in the right-hand pair of columns in Exhibit 20–2. In the comparison between the two projects, X requires

$80,000 more in net cash outlays by the end of year 2. The differential cash inflow in the rest of the 10-year period is $110,000. The present value of the inflows is less than the present value of the outflows, however—thus project X is inferior to Y.

Calculating the Internal Rate of Return

An alternative method of applying the present value principle to capital expenditure problems is to compute the *internal rate of return*, defined as *that rate of discount at which the sum of the positive present values is equal to the sum of the negative present values*. In other words, the *net present value* of the cash flows is zero.

The internal rate of return is found by a process of trial and error. All cash flows are first discounted at some rate, say 10 percent. If the net present value is positive, they are then discounted again at a higher rate, say 15 percent. If the net present value at this rate is negative, then the true rate of return must be somewhere between the two trial rates.

For example, the second column of Exhibit 20–2 indicates that if the choice is between project X and no project at all, project X has a present value of $38,000 at a discount rate of 8 percent. This means that the cash flows are adequate to provide a rate of return on investment in excess of 8 percent. That is, the company could afford to pay someone 8 percent for the use of his money and still have something left over.

Trying again at a rate of 14 percent yields a net present value of minus $8,000—i.e., the cash flows are not large enough to provide a 14 percent return on investment. The true rate of return therefore must be somewhere between 8 and 14 percent. The absolute spread between the present values at these two rates is $38,000 + $8,000 = $46,000. Thus the true rate, at which present value would be zero, is about 38,000/46,000 of the distance between 8 and 14 percent. It can be approximated by the following formula:

$$\text{True Rate} \cong 8\% + \frac{\$38,000}{\$38,000 + \$8,000} \times (14\% - 8\%) \cong 13\% .$$

Choosing the Discounting Period

Comparisons often must be made between alternatives with different economic lives. For example, a manufacturer can purchase either railroad cars or tractor-trailer combinations to move his products to regional distribution centers. Railroad cars would have an economic life of 20 years, the tractor-trailers only six.

One solution to this problem is to define the discounting period in terms of the life of the shorter life alternative—in this case, six years. This requires an estimate of the recoverable value of the longer life facilities at this point in time. Unfortunately, resale values often drop sharply in the early years of ownership and then decline more gradually as the equipment ages. For this reason, the use of intermediate salvage value for long-life equipment is likely to penalize the longer life alternative.

One way around this is to compute the present value of the cash flows under each alternative and convert this into an equivalent annuity. For example, suppose that expected cash flows are as follows:

	Proposal A	Proposal B
Initial outlay................	−$10,000	−$20,000
Annual cash flow............	+ 3,000	+ 3,500
Economic life...............	5 years	10 years
Present value at 10%........	+$ 1,372	+$ 1,506
Equivalent annuity at 10%....	+$ 362	+$ 245

In this case the present value of proposal B is greater than that of proposal A. This extra present value can be obtained only by making an investment commitment for a longer period, however. The 10-year annuity equivalent to the $1,506 present value is $245 a year—that is, $1,506 is the present value of a 10-year annuity of $245 a year. This is considerably less than the annuity equivalent to the $1,372 present value of proposal A. Proposal A should be chosen.

Choosing the Discount Rate

Under both the internal rate of return and the net present value methods for evaluating a capital expenditure proposal, the analyst must have a figure for the discount rate or rate of return that the company requires as a condition for making the investment. While projecting the net operating cash flows is the most difficult practical task in arriving at a capital expenditure decision, selecting the discount rate is the most difficult theoretical decision.

The rate of return that a firm should require on an investment is a difficult problem because the future is uncertain and investors have aversion to risk. An investor is willing to include in his portfolio of securities government bonds which yield, say, a 5 percent rate of return, because the interest and principal payments on the bond are free of risk. An investment in the long-term bonds of a financially strong corporation will yield a slightly higher rate of return because the risk is a little greater. Investment in common stocks, however, typically carries with it a greater degree of uncertainty and of risk, and the average purchaser of common stocks does so in anticipation of dividends and capital gains that will yield a return considerably in excess of that available from the bonds of the same companies. To compensate existing shareowners for the risks they bear and to provide an earnings base adequate to induce additional ownership investment in the business, management must try to *make investments that will produce returns equal to or exceeding the minimum rate acceptable to the company's stockholders.* If management fails in this, stockholders will find the value of their stock declining and management will find it extremely difficult to raise additional funds from the sale of stock.

A corporation can also raise funds by borrowing, and the after-tax interest rate it pays may be as low as 2.5–3.0 percent. Consequently, a debt-financed investment with an after-tax return of as little as 4 percent is expected to raise earnings per share. However, debt financed investment increases shareholder risk, and if the expected rate of return on an investment does not exceed the interest cost of the funds by a considerable margin, the consequence will be a reduction in the price of a company's stock. In fact, it has been argued that apart from tax considerations, the cost of debt capital is the same as the cost of equity capital.[3]

The minimum acceptable rate of return on an investment, often referred to as the *cost of capital,* is the rate that will not depress the price of the company's stock. The cost of capital will vary from company to company, depending on the market's evaluation of the degree of risk. The greater the risk, the less the stockholder will be willing to pay for a dollar of anticipated earnings. Thus, the stock of a metropolitan electric power company would be expected to yield a far smaller return on its market value than the stock of an oil exploration company, and typically the latter requires a considerably higher rate of return on its investments than the former.

It would be most misleading to leave the subject of a corporation's cost of capital with the impression that a corporation simply computes its cost of capital, sets that rate (or structure of rates depending on each proposal's risk) as its required rate of return, and makes every investment that meets the required rate of return requirement. The

---

[3] For further discussion of the subject see F. Modigliani and Merton Miller, "The Cost of Capital, Corporation Finance, and the Theory of Investment," *American Economic Review,* June, 1958, pp. 261–97.

cost of capital as defined above is extremely difficult to measure. While considerable progress is being made on how a corporation should measure its cost of capital, there is still considerable theoretical controversy on the subject and the practical problems of measurement are formidable.[4] For this and other reasons, the following is a more accurate description of common practice in selecting investment opportunities.

The capital budget committee establishes a required rate of return that is believed to approximate the corporation's cost of capital and that operating managers and staff analysts are instructed to use in evaluating capital expenditure proposals. If pressed for a figure, many finance people would respond that an after-tax cost of capital of 10–12 percent is common for an average industrial corporation. High-risk industrial corporations might require 15 percent or more, and low-risk corporations such as utilities might require as little as 7 percent.

The capital budget committee then establishes (1) the funds for investment expected from operations and borrowing to the extent consistent with the corporation's financial policies, and (2) the investment funds required by all proposals which are expected to meet the rate of return requirement or are justified on other grounds. If the supply of funds falls short of the demand, the committee will ration the funds to the more profitable projects or explore alternative ways of raising additional funds. The extent to which each alternative will be followed depends on the corporation's circumstances and the attitudes of its management.

If the supply of funds exceeds the demand, the corporation has a more difficult problem. It may relax the standard of profitability to some extent, use the excess funds to improve its financial position, or raise the dividend. However, if the gap is large and persistent, the management is likely to decide that the corporate environment does not encourage the discovery of profitable investment opportunities in adequate volume. A diversification program taking the corporation into new products, increased expenditures on research and development, and a reorganization of the capital budgeting machinery are among the alternatives that might be explored to raise the profitability of investment.

---

[4] For a comprehensive treatment of the subject see M. J. Gordon, *The Investment, Financing and Valuation of the Corporation* (Homewood, Ill.; Richard D. Irwin, Inc., 1962).

Dealing with Uncertainty

Uncertainty as to the future means that the forecast cash flow for a future period is some average of a range of possible outcomes. This average may be arrived at in a variety of ways. One is to take each possible cash flow for a period, assign a probability to the outcome, and compute the mean or expected value of the cash flow. These probabilities are obtained by some combination of data analysis and subjective judgment. More commonly, the analyst examines the relevant data and proceeds directly to a figure that is considered the mean of the cash flows for a period.

Unfortunately, the development of a probability distribution for the cash flow in each future period on a long life investment project requires so much data estimation as to make the task unmanageable or the resultant data highly questionable. At the same time a project analysis which presents only the expected value of the cash flow in each future period is often looked upon as not containing adequate information for a decision. Some firms, therefore, have found it useful to develop pessimistic and optimistic forecasts of a project's cash flows.

Exhibit 20–3 shows how this approach might be applied to a plant renovation proposal. With both estimates discounted at 10 percent, the pessimistic one involves a loss of $420,000[5] and the optimistic one a gain of $509,000. With the average of the two estimates not far

Exhibit 20–3

SENSITIVITY ANALYSIS OF PLANT RENOVATION PROPOSAL

Years Hence	Pessimistic Estimates		Optimistic Estimates	
	Cash Flow after Tax	Present Value at 10%	Cash Flow after Tax	Present Value at 10%
0........	−$2,200,000	−$2,200,000	−$1,900,000	−$1,900,000
0–15.....	+ 190,000 per yr.	+ 1,445,000	+ 260,000 per yr.	+ 1,978,000
15.......	+ 1,400,000	+ 335,000	+ 1,800,000	+ 431,000
Total.....	+$2,050,000	−$ 420,000	+$3,800,000	+$ 509,000

---

[5] The −$420,000 is a loss from an opportunity cost point of view, since the firm has alternative projects that might be expected to earn 10 percent. The internal rate of return for the project under the pessimistic forecast is about 5 percent.

different from zero, the internal rate of return is about 10 percent if the two estimates are equally probable. Of comparable importance is the fact that under the pessimistic estimates the undiscounted cash flows are positive and at the 10 percent discount rate the loss in relation to the investment is not a catastrophe. The conclusion suggested by the data is that the plant renovation proposal promises about a 10 percent return with comparatively low risk.

This technique does not yield probability estimates in any sense of the term, but it does give management some idea of how critical the potential estimating errors are. Other estimates could also be inserted if desired—e.g., shorter economic life or declining sales volume—but the introduction of more than two or three alternative estimates is likely to be more confusing than helpful.

ADMINISTRATION OF THE CAPITAL EXPENDITURE PROGRAM

No less important than establishing the comparative profitability of alternative investment proposals is the organization of a company for the administration of its capital expenditure program. Although a thorough discussion of the subject is not possible here, the essential elements of corporate practice in administering a capital budget should be noted.[6]

Appropriation Request

Common practice under any formal procedure for capital outlay planning and control is to require that every proposal be covered by an appropriation request such as the one illustrated in Exhibit 20–4. These requests fall in two broad categories: (1) those representing necessary or desirable projects for which it is difficult or impossible to estimate the resultant increase in earnings—improvements in product quality or in working conditions, for example; and (2) those involving cost reduction or capacity expansion proposals bearing more directly upon future profits.

Justification of projects in the first category is necessarily of a qualitative nature. For those in the latter class, it is normally required that the expected rate of return or some other index of profitability be shown, together with the analysis on which this figure is based. In each and every case, the request must show evidence of a systematic

---

[6] For a description of representative practice, see National Industrial Conference Board's report, *Managing Capital Expenditures* (New York, 1963).

Exhibit 20–4

AN APPROPRIATION REQUEST FORM

REQUISITION FOR FACILITIES	Fac. Comm. Mtg. of ITEM	Facilities Requisition No.

	2. Dept.	3. Location	4. Date
1. Initial) Additional) Appropriation Recommended $ Estimated by Date			

	5. Detailed Description of Facility—Include Make and Source
A. Cost—Including Transportation $	
Installation Cost	
Auxiliary or Accessory Equipment	
Spares	
Other	
Recommended Investment (Total)	
Salvage Value, if Any, on Old Equipment	

B. Corollary Investment (if Increased Volume All or Part of Justification)
(1) CAPITAL a) Other Fixed Assets........ $
          b) Working Capital.........

Estimated Physical Life_____Yrs.

(2) EXPENSE—Est. Cost Reduction to Practice...............................
Est. Promotional Costs (New Product)..
Other...........................

6. Original Appropriation: FR # $_____
   Previous Additional Appropriations $_____
   This Request $_____
   Total Appropriation Recommended $_____
   Spent to Date $_____

TOTAL COROLLARY INVESTMENT.............

7. Purpose: ☐ Replacement ☐ Replacement/Expansion ☐ Replacement/Cost Reduction ☐ Cost Reduction ☐ Cost Reduction/Expansion ☐ Cost Reduction/Quality ☐ Expansion ☐ Quality ☐ Delivery ☐ Improve Working Conditions ☐ Other—Specify	8. Present Equipment for Mdse. Class or Function (List No. of Machines of Each Type and Aver. Age) 9. Present Versus Proposed Method or Process (Explain) 10. Alternatives to This Appropriation and This Particular Equipment (Explain)

11. Is a Move of Present ☐ Yes Equipment Required ☐ No Estimate Cost $	

12. If Part of a Program Total Cost $ Over Years	13. Factual Elements Relating to Justification

14. Justification Summary—Detail Attached
Payoff Period   Before Taxes_____   After Taxes_____
Return on Investment   Before Taxes_____   After Taxes_____

☐ Is ☐ Facilities 15. This Request in the Current ☐ Is Not ☐ Expense Budget	16. Requested and Approved by: Factory Date Merchandising Date

17. Budget Committee
☐ Approval Recommended   Signed
☐ Referred Without Recommendation   Date

collection and analysis of all available information pertinent to the issue. Important from the control standpoint is the fact that this analysis takes the form of a *written permanent record.*

Approval Authority

While proposals may originate anywhere in the organization, the management representative who will be ultimately responsible for the results of the project is usually expected to initiate the request. In preparing it, he will call upon other departments for advice—engineering for operating characteristics of equipment, accounting for cost data, and so forth. In larger firms, lower echelons are given some freedom of action by allowing plant or division heads to authorize certain outlays without higher approval. Limitations on such authority are usually defined in terms of (1) the dollar amount of any one project, and (2) the aggregate dollar amount of all projects for a period. For this purpose, projects may be divided into classes with different sets of limits on each class. Minimum profit standards for those projects susceptible to profitability measurement are normally prescribed.

Typically, each proposal must be approved by each person in the requisitioner's chain of command, and all proposals are finally screened by the budget committee. Requisitions are divided into the two broad categories noted above: in the one case, rank is ordered by profitability; in the other, by subjective criteria of desirability. Total expenditures on projects in the latter class are often limited to a somewhat arbitrarily established percentage of total expenditures, and some effort is made to achieve an equitable distribution among the various functional activities. Requisitions are screened to limit outlays on products or activities which do not figure in the firm's long-range plans. In borderline cases, a recognized tendency exists to favor those departments with the better performance records.

Integration with Annual Capital Budget

Major capital expenditure proposals are typically approved in two stages. At the time of annual budget preparation, each division manager or department head is asked to submit a tentative list of the proposals that he plans to make during the coming year, together with a brief justification of each. On this basis, the top-management budget committee draws up a proposed capital expenditure budget for the year and submits it to the board for review and approval. The formal appropriation request is not submitted, however, until it is time to initiate the project. This gives the sponsor more time to plan the project, as well as an opportunity to take into consideration events that have occurred since the budget was prepared. It also gives the firm more flexibility in that it is not committed for the whole year at the start of the year. If an emergency or an extraordinarily profitable project appears during the year, it can be initiated at once without upsetting the overall budget figure. It is only necessary to delay or cancel other projects if additional investment funds cannot be obtained on short notice from other sources.

Many projects initiated in one budget period will not be completed until the next. Some take even longer. For this reason, the appropriation requests approved in any year will rarely equal the expected capital outlays for the coming year. In view of this, corporations usually prepare a capital expenditure schedule which shows, period by period, the planned expenditures on both previously authorized and

Exhibit 20–5

QUARTERLY CAPITAL EXPENDITURE BUDGET
Revised as of April 1, 1969

	Expenditures				
	1st Quarter	2d Quarter	3d Quarter	4th Quarter	Next Year
Authorizations prior to 1969:					
Actual expenditures..............	3,450				
Budgeted expenditures...........	3.800	2,450	1,100	700	1,500
Authorizations in 1st quarter:					
Actual expenditures..............	800				
Budgeted expenditures...........	750	1,300	1,000	800	1,000
Authorizations in rest of year:					
Budgeted expenditures...........		1,000	2,700	3,400	4,000
Total expenditures:					
Actual........................	4,250				
Budgeted......................	4,550	4,750	4,900	4,900	6,500

newly authorized projects. These schedules are often revised monthly or quarterly and may take the form illustrated in Exhibit 20–5. Notice that actual expenditures in prior periods appear along with the budget for each period in the table. Expenditures below budget are no less undesirable than expenditures above budget. Delay in completing capital projects ties up funds in idle capital and delays the time at which the firm starts earning the prospective profits on the investment. The aggregate picture reflected in Exhibit 20–5 is usually supported by a detailed schedule showing the actual and budgeted expenditures to date and the budgeted expenditures in each future period on each project involving an outlay in excess of some predetermined amount.

Post-completion Review

Finally, when a project is completed, the actual and budgeted out-lays are reported to the capital budget committee. On any project for which the actual expenditure exceeded the budget by some percen-tage, say 10 percent, the person in charge of the project is required to submit an explanation in writing.

Some firms have experimented with post-completion audits of capi-tal expenditures for which the justification was profitability. A year, or longer if necessary, after the project is completed, a study is made to ascertain whether the project realized the projected cost savings or earnings increase. These audits have not proven to be very successful. Typically, the assumptions under which the proposal was made no longer hold, and it is hard to ascertain whether the changed conditions were beyond the individual's control. Furthermore, the portion of the company's profit from a specific capital investment is usually very difficult to isolate.

SUMMARY

Capital expenditure proposals need to be tested against company-wide standards of minimum acceptable profitability. These standards are ordinarily related to the cost of capital—the anticipated rate of return that shareholders and other investors demand as the price of providing funds to the company.

The cash flow streams to which profitability tests must be applied should represent the anticipated differential after-tax cash flows asso-ciated with the proposal. Four kinds of cash flows can be distin-guished: initial investment outlays, subsequent investment outlays, operating receipts and expenditures, and end-of-life salvage value. These differentials should be measured from a bench mark that will be acceptable to the company, and opportunity costs must not be neg-lected.

Once the incremental cash flows have been estimated, their present value can be determined. Other things being equal, proposals should be accepted if they offer a positive net present value. If two alterna-tive proposals are being compared, the better one is the proposal promising the greater net present value. The cash flow estimates are always uncertain, however, and management may wish to compute cash flows and present values on optimistic and pessimistic bases to provide a broader measure of project risks and opportunities.

QUESTIONS AND PROBLEMS

1. The present value approach to capital expenditure decisions is based upon certain assumptions. What are these assumptions? Are they likely to be valid in all companies?

2. Define a capital expenditure. Would you classify research and development costs as capital expenditures? Increased inventory requirements?

3. What does a decision to build a new factory have in common with a decision to refund long-term debt at a lower rate of interest?

4. In what ways does the concept of opportunity cost enter into the evaluation of capital expenditure proposals?

5. Why is authority to approve requests for capital expenditures one of the least widely delegated powers of top management?

6. Define the cost of capital. What objections can be raised to measuring the cost of capital by the after-tax yields on the company's debt securities?

7. "Taxes merely take a proportionate share of earnings. Therefore the decision based on a before-tax analysis will be the same as one based on an after-tax analysis." Discuss.

8. What reasons might support the continuation of operations of a division for which a low return on investment is reported?

9. Most large capital expenditure proposals are approved twice—once when they are included in the annual capital budget and again when the sponsor is ready to commit the first funds to it. Is this duplication of effort desirable? Explain.

10. There is no contractual obligation to make interest or dividend payments to the common stockholders. How can common equity capital be said to have a "cost"?

11. Which of the following are likely to be "investment problems" and why?

a) Asset replacement decisions.
b) Rate of output decisions.

c) Decisions to advertise special "sales" in local newspapers.
d) Decisions to rent or buy equipment.
e) Product-discontinuation decisions.

12. On April 24 the X Manufacturing Company completed the installation of a new made-to-order packaging machine at a cost of $50,000. On the following morning an equipment salesman offered the president of the X Company, at an installed price of $35,000, a newly developed standard machine guaranteed to do exactly the same job. The expected economic life, eight years, was the same for both pieces of equipment. But whereas the projected per annum out-of-pocket operating costs were $14,000 on the first machine, A, they were only $8,000 on the second machine, B. Unfortunately, the company could expect to salvage no more than $20,000 from its recent purchase should it decide to replace immediately.

a) Should the X Company seriously consider acquiring the new machine? What factors bear upon the decision?
b) With respect to (*a*) above, would it make any difference if the cost of the original machine had been $70,000? Why or why not?

13. An engineer with the Zimmerman Brothers Company sent a memorandum to the controller which read in part as follows: "An operation in the stamping department now being performed with hand tools could be mechanized by the purchase of the machine described in the attached folder. The machine costs $40,000 installed, and it would probably have an economic life of 20 years.

"The machine would save $5,500 a year in labor costs at the present volume of activity. Space requirements would be reduced by 3,000 square feet which at the current charge of $0.50 per square foot is another $1,500. Maintenance, repairs, and all other operating costs would remain unchanged. The old hand tools have a zero scrap value.

"The return on investment in equipment is the saving in operating cost less the depreciation on the machine divided by one half of the investment. This is:

$$R = (\$7,000 - \$2,000)/\$20,000 = 25 \text{ percent.}$$

Since the company requires a 20 percent return on investment, this machine should be purchased."

Do you agree with the engineer's analysis? Why?

*14. The Arnold Machine Company has been having a neighboring company perform certain operations on a part used in its product at a cost of 50 cents per part. The annual production of this part is expected to average 6,000 pieces.

---

* Solutions to problems marked with an asterisk (*) are found in Appendix B.

The Arnold Machine Company can perform this operation itself by bringing into operation two machines: a spare lathe which has a net book value of $2,000, and a new machine which can be purchased at a price of $7,000. The new machine is expected to last seven years. The old machine has a remaining physical life of at least 10 years and could be sold now for approximately $1,500. The final salvage of both machines is considered negligible. In performing the operation itself, the Arnold Company will incur out-of-pocket costs for direct labor, power, supplies, etc., of 20 cents per part.

Prepare an analysis (including explanatory comments) which would help to determine whether it is profitable for the Arnold Company to perform these operations itself. The company normally expects to earn a rate of return before taxes of about 15 percent on its invested capital. (Ignore income tax effects.)

*15. John Briant and Sons, Inc., has outstanding $500,000 of 5 percent, first-mortgage bonds which were originally sold at par and which mature 10 years hence. The opportunity of replacing these with a 4 percent 10-year promissory note is now available. The call price of the bonds is 107. The general policy of the firm is to avoid committing liquid funds to any use which promises an annual after-tax rate of return of less than 8 percent. The expected income tax rate is 50 percent. Any loss on bond retirement can be deducted immediately in computing taxable income.

Prepare an analysis of the refunding opportunity to show whether the action should be taken.

16. Late in 1952, the Trion Company sold a $1 million issue of 4 percent, 15-year bonds dated January 1, 1953. The net proceeds of this issue were $955,000. In 1962, the board of directors was considering the possibility of refunding the 4 percent bonds as of January 1, 1963, by borrowing $1 million from an insurance company on a five-year, 3 percent promissory note. At that date, the call price of the bonds would be 104.

The directors felt that this should be done only if the annual rate of return on the requisite cash outlay were at least 12 percent after taxes. It was expected that the income taxes paid by the company would continue to be approximately 50 percent of annual net income. Any loss on bond retirement could be deducted immediately in computing taxable income.

Prepare an analysis to show whether or not the bonds should have been refunded, given the criterion established by the board of directors. Amortization of bond discount for tax purposes is by the straight-line method.

17. The initial investment outlay is $40,000, of which $30,000 will be capitalized for tax purposes. Before-tax operating cash receipts will be

$12,000 a year for five years; these amounts will be received at the end of each year. Estimated end-of-life salvage value is zero.

Straight-line depreciation and a five-year life are to be used for tax purposes. The tax rate is 40 percent. Taxes are paid or tax credits are received immediately, as soon as the taxable or tax-deductible transaction takes place.

a) What is the present value of this proposal at an annual interest rate of 8 percent?
b) What is the after-tax internal rate of return?
c) What would be the internal rate of return if end-of-life salvage were to be $5,000 but annual depreciation for tax purposes continued to be based on zero salvage?
d) What would be the rate of return on investment if economic life and tax life were both six years, with zero salvage value?
e) What would be the rate of return if economic life and tax life were five years, salvage was zero, and double-rate, declining-balance depreciation was used for tax purposes?
f) Prepare a short commentary on the relationships indicated by your answers to the previous parts of this question.

18. The Gibbons Tool Company was considering the purchase of a new lathe. The purchase price, delivered, was $23,415. Installation costs would amount to $3,400. Wage, power, and repair costs on the new machine were estimated to amount to $3,000 every three months. Its useful life was estimated at seven years.

The new lathe would replace two existing lathes which would then be given to a junk dealer. They had a remaining physical life of at least seven years. Wage, power, and repair costs on each of these machines was expected to amount to $2,900 every three months if they were not replaced.

a) Assuming that 20 percent per year, compounded quarterly, is an adequate return, would it be worthwhile to purchase the new machine? Show your calculations. (Assume that all savings are realized at the end of each three-month period.)
b) How different would your answer have been if you had assumed that each cash receipt was to be received at the end of the year instead of in quarterly installments, with interest compounded annually instead of quarterly.

19. Company B is currently considering the possibility of replacing one of its machines with a new one which will yield savings in both labor and material spoilage costs because it is equipped with improved automatic controls. The salvage value of the present machine is considerably less

than its book value. If the new machine is purchased, the installation cost will be substantial.

The company is currently in the 50 percent tax bracket and expects to remain there indefinitely. If the new machine is purchased, it will be permissible to depreciate it for tax purchases by either the double-rate, declining-balance method or the sum-of-the-years'-digits method.

a) How, if at all, may the fact of income taxation influence either the company's decision to acquire the machine or its accounting for the outlays if the machine is acquired? Explain.

b) How, if at all, does the freedom of election with respect to depreciation bear upon this decision? Explain.

20. J. T. Long, owner of the Long Office Building, was recently approached by a buyer for that property. The offer consisted of $200,000 down plus yearly installments of $50,000 a year for five years—a total of $450,000.

Mr. Long had bought the land and built the building 15 years earlier. The land had cost $40,000; the building had cost $600,000. Annual depreciation for tax purposes had been charged at a straight-line rate of $20,000 a year. The remaining life of the building seemed to be about 15 years more.

Mr. Long expected future income to be about $30,000 a year for the remaining life, calculated as below:

Yearly revenues from office rental...............		$79,000
Yearly expenses:		
Taxes.....................................	$ 4,000	
Repairs...................................	12,000	
Depreciation..............................	20,000	
Heat and miscellaneous....................	13,000	49,000
Total Income.........................		$30,000

He also expected to be able to invest any cash he would receive at 5 percent, compounded annually.

Disregarding tax considerations, would you advise Mr. Long to keep or sell the building? Present a brief table showing the figures supporting your recommendation.

21. The Griffa Machine Company has been purchasing from a neighboring company a part used in one of its products. The purchase price of this part is 75 cents per part, and the expected average annual production is 6,000 parts.

The methods department of the Griffa Machine Company has submitted a proposal to manufacture this part in the company's own plant. To do this, the company would have to purchase a new machine at a price of $10,000. It would also use a lathe now owned by the company but not in current use. This lathe has an estimated market value now of $1,000, but its book value is $2,000. Depreciation for tax purposes on the old lathe is at a straight-line rate of $400 per year. The new machine would be depreciated for tax purposes at a straight-line rate of $1,000 per year. Both machines would be usable for 10 years, and the final salvage value of both machines is assumed to be negligible.

The incremental costs of operating the two machines, other than depreciation costs, would be as follows:

	Cost per Part
Direct labor, 0.1 hours at $2 per hour	$0.20
Direct materials	$0.10
Power, supplies, etc.	$0.05

All other costs would be unaffected by the decision to manufacture this part. The company uses a burden rate of $3 per direct labor hour to absorb factory overhead costs.

Assuming an income tax rate of 50 percent and a minimum acceptable rate of return on investment of 10 percent after taxes, should this proposal be accepted?

*22. Under a new proposal just submitted by the production manager of the Romano Company, the proposed facilities will cost $100,000, half of which will be capitalized for tax purposes. The rest will be expensed immediately. A government investment incentive device known as an investment credit allows the company an immediate tax rebate of 7 percent of the capitalized portion of the outlay. Depreciation charges for subsequent years will be based on the full amount capitalized, however.

The proposal will also require a $10,000 increase in working capital.

Cash operating savings are expected to amount to $20,000 a year. Expected life for tax purposes is eight years, and the double-rate, declining-balance method is used in computing depreciation. The tax rate is 50 percent.

a) Compute the after-tax initial cash outlay for this proposal.
b) Compute the after-tax cash saving for each of the first two years of the life of the facilities.

*23. The Walpole Cotton Company is currently considering the installation of weaving equipment with a total cost including freight and installation of $40,000. If this proposal is accepted, this equipment will replace equipment which three years before cost $50,000 and is still in good running order. Because of the greater efficiency of the new equipment, the present equipment now has a resale value of only $5,000. The cost of removing the old equipment and revamping the machine service facilities will be $15,000, of which $5,000 is considered a part of the installation cost and is included in the $40,000 to be capitalized, while the remaining $10,000 is to be charged to expense.

The manufacturing cost tabulation shows a substantial reduction in annual operating cost, as follows:

	At Present	After New Installation
Annual costs:		
Labor...................................	$ 12,500	$ 3,000
Depreciation (10% of cost, straight-line)........	5,000	4,000
Supplies, repairs, and power..................	4,000	3,400
Taxes, insurance, and miscellaneous............	900	1,000
Total..................................	$ 22,400	$ 11,400
Annual Production—Units....................	500,000	500,000

a) If a 16 percent return on investment before taxes is required, would you recommend the expenditure?

b) If a 10 percent return on investment after taxes is required, would you recommend the expenditure? Assume a tax rate of 50 percent.

24. A second investment proposal at the Walpole Cotton Company (see Question 23 above) is the acquisition of new spinning machinery, partially to replace certain less efficient equipment and partially to increase total productive capacity. Market surveys indicate that the anticipated increase in productive capacity can be disposed of only by additional sales effort coupled with a price reduction. Pertinent data are as indicated below:

Cost of new equipment, including freight and installation..............$60,000
Cost of removal of equipment replaced, rearrangement and re-
  vamping, etc., to be charged to expense......................... 15,000
Net book value of equipment replaced (original cost: $40,000)......... 8,000
Amount to be realized from sale of equipment replaced............... 5,000

Annual Processing Costs	Present		Proposed	
	Dollars	Per Lb.	Dollars	Per Lb.
Labor.....................................	$120,000	$0.0600	$135,000	$0.0540
Supplies, repairs, and power...............	80,000	0.0400	93,000	0.0372
Taxes, insurance, and miscellaneous........	20,000	0.0100	22,000	0.0088
Depreciation (10% of cost, straight-line)....	4,000	0.0020	6,000	0.0024
Total............................	$224,000	$0.1120	$256,000	$0.1024

Annual production:

Present...2,000,000 lbs.	
Proposed..2,500,000 lbs.	

Estimated manufacturing margin (estimated selling price minus estimated material cost):

Present...$ 0.150	
Proposed (allowing for reduction of ½¢ in selling price)............	0.145

Estimated additional selling and administrative expenses:

Commissions...$ 5,000	
Branch office sales expense (including advertising).................	11,000
Billing and miscellaneous administrative...........................	1,500
Total...$17,500	

a) Would you recommend this expenditure if a 16 percent return before taxes is required?

b) Would you recommend the expenditure if a 10 percent return after taxes is required? Assume a tax rate of 50 percent.

*25. The expected life of a facility proposal is 10 years, the installed cost will be $50,000, and the expected end-of-life salvage value is zero. The equipment will replace facilities now in use that have a book value of $30,000 and a market value of $10,000. The remaining tax life of the old facilities is eight years.

Double-rate, declining-balance depreciation will be used on the new facilities. No "investment credit" or other tax rebate is available. The present facilities are being depreciated by the straight-line method down to an end-of-life salvage value of zero.

Estimated before-tax, before-depreciation cash savings amount to $20,000 a year. The tax rate is 50 percent, and all savings are assumed to take place at the end of each year.

a) Compute the incremental after-tax present value of this proposal at 10 percent, compounded annually.

b) Compute the incremental after-tax discounted cash-flow rate of return on this proposal.

26. Company Z has contracted to supply a governmental agency with 50,000 units of a product each year for the next five years. A certain component of this product can be either manufactured by Company Z, or purchased from the X Corporation, which has indicated a willingness to enter into a subcontract for 50,000 units of the component each year for five years if the price offered is satisfactory. These alternative methods of procurement are regarded as equally dependable.

If Company Z decides to manufacture the component, it expects the following to occur:

(1) A special-purpose machine costing $110,000 will have to be purchased. No other equipment will be required.

(2) For tax purposes, this machine will be assumed to have a 10-year life, but management does not expect the machine to be useful beyond the contract period. Estimated salvage value at the end of five years is $10,000.

(3) Depreciation for tax purposes will be by the double-rate, declining-balance method. The item method of depreciation will be used. There will be no "investment credit."

(4) The manufacturing operation will require 1,000 feet of productive floor space. This space is available in a building owned by Company Z and will not be needed for any other purpose in the foreseeable future. The costs of maintaining this building (including repairs, utilities, taxes, and depreciation) amount to $2 per square foot of productive floor space per year.

(5) Variable manufacturing costs—materials, direct labor, etc.—are estimated to be $0.50 a unit.

(6) Fixed manufacturing costs other than those mentioned in (1) through (4) above—e.g., supervision, etc.—are estimated at $20,000 per year.

(7) Income taxes are computed at the rate of 50 percent of taxable income or taxable savings.

(8) The policy of Company Z is to subcontract if and only if the costs saved by manufacturing instead of subcontracting provide less than a 10 percent annual return on investment. For this purpose, return on investment is defined as the relationship between cost saving, after provision for income taxes, and the capital investment that will have to be made to permit Company Z to manufacture the component in its own plant.

What is the maximum price per unit which Company Z should be willing to offer to the X Corporation? Make explicit any assumptions which you believe to be necessary in solving the problem.

27. Mr. Adams burst into the office of his superior, the works manager, one day to announce that a new machine which had just come out should be bought to replace the one used in the manufacture of product W. To support his argument, Adams presented the following evidence.

	Old Machine	New Machine
Expected life........................	Not applicable	10 years (new)
Original cost.........................	$ 53,000	$105,000
Amount already depreciated.............	15,000	0
Present trade-in value...................	10,000	Not applicable
Expected trade-in value after 7 years......	3,000	$ 35,000
Expected trade-in value after 10 years.....	0	5,000
Capacity in units per year...............	60,000	80,000
Expected output (units per year).........	50,000	50,000
Value of output per year................	200,000	200,000
Cost of production per year:		
Direct materials and supplies...........	50,000	50,000
Direct labor........................	40,000	30,000
Depreciation.......................	5,000	10,000
Departmental overhead:		
$10,000 + 0.5 × labor cost........	30,000	25,000
Other: Fixed plant overhead distributed		
on the basis of $2 per labor dollar..	80,000	60,000
Net Profit (Loss) before Tax....	(5,000)	25,000
Net Profit (Loss) after 50% Tax........	(2,500)	12,500

"No matter how you look at it," Mr. Adams said, "this investment can very easily bring the 8 percent annual return on investment after taxes that we want. We are losing money by using the old machine now anyhow and we should stop producing product W unless we buy the new machine.

a) Based on the above information, present and support a recommendation as to the desirability of purchasing the new machine. Be sure to show your calculations of investment required and annual savings expected. (Assume that the company will continue to produce product W, whether or not the new machine is bought. Assume also that any savings from machine replacement occur at the end of each year and that any capital losses are treated as current expense for tax purposes. Tax and book depreciation schedules are by the straight-line method and are identical. There is no "investment credit.")

b) Assume that the new machine is not purchased and that the company decides to discontinue any product that does not yield an 8 percent return on investment. Should production of product W be discontinued now? Should it be discontinued later? Explain. (If you find it necessary to make any assumptions to reach a conclusion, state any such assumptions.)

28. The Caldwell Manufacturing Company is using a special-purpose A-16 machine in the manufacture of a certain product. Because of expected increases in sales volume, additional capacity will have to be acquired. Two possibilities are under review:

A. Purchase an additional A-16 machine identical to the present one, and operate the two machines; or

B. Purchase a new high-speed B-32 machine with double the capacity of the present machine and keep the present A-16 machine as standby equipment.

The following information is available:

(1) Production requirements are expected to average 70,000 units a year.

(2) All machines are assumed to have a 10-year life from date of installation, with zero salvage value at the end of that time. Straight-line depreciation is used for tax purposes.

(3) The present A-16 machine had a cost of $9,000 four years ago. Its present market value is $4,800.

(4) The price of the new A-16 machine is $10,000. Unless the B-32 machine is bought now, the present A-16 will have to be replaced six years from now at a cost of $11,000. The market value of this replacement machine will be about $5,000 when it is four years old.

(5) The price of a new B-32 machine is $40,000.

(6) Repair and maintenance costs for an A-16 machine used regularly during the year are $2,800 a year.

(7) Repair and maintenance costs for the B-32 machine and an A-16 machine used for standby purposes would total $4,000 a year.

(8) Comparative variable costs per unit of output are:

	A-16	B-32
Materials....................	$0.136	$0.208
Supplies....................	0.052	0.024
Labor........................	0.212	0.088
Total....................	$0.400	$0.320

(9) The minimum acceptable rate of return is 8 percent after taxes. Income tax rate is 50 percent.

a) Which alternative would you choose? Show your calculations.

b) Indicate for *each* of the following whether the purchase of the B-32 machine would become more or less desirable. Explain your answer.

(1) New labor contract raises wage rates.

(2) After-tax minimum acceptable rate of return increases.

(3) Demand for product increases, so machine usage is increased to 80,000 units a year.

(4) Materials prices increase.

29. Early in 1969, the Nonon Company was considering whether to begin the manufacture and sale of a new product. Information on the new product is summarized below:

(1) Development costs through the end of 1968 were $80,000. Further development costs of $100,000 in 1969 and $200,000 in 1970 would be required.

(2) A manufacturing facility would be built in 1970. The plant would cost $1,200,000 and have a life of 25 years. The equipment would cost $2,000,000 and have an average life of 15 years.

(3) The estimated price and cost data developed on the new product were:

Sales price per pound.................................$	0.90
Variable manufacturing cost per pound....................	0.40
Variable selling and administrative cost per pound..........	0.10
Fixed manufacturing cost per year exclusive of depreciation..	225,000
Fixed selling and administrative cost per year..............	150,000

(4) The sales forecast for the product was:

1971......................	500,000 lbs.
1972......................	1,500,000
1973......................	2,000,000
1974......................	2,700,000
1975......................	3,000,000

(5) The plant had a capacity of 3.5 million pounds, but it could readily be increased if the demand should go above that level. It was expected that sales would continue to grow after 1975 at a modest rate. However, a forecast of sales for the first five years was difficult, and forecasting beyond that year was largely guess work. It was therefore decided to make the analyses on the assumption that sales of 3,000,000 units would be maintained through 1995.

(6) The company is subject to a 50 percent tax rate and has been quite profitable. It uses double-rate, declining-balance depreciation for book and tax purposes.

(7) From 1971 to 1975, the expenditures on plant and equipment not included in the above costs were expected to be negligible. From 1976 to 1995, they were expected to be about equal to the depreciation expense which would be maintained at about the 1976 level by these expenditures.

(8) Introduction of the new product would require additional working capital totaling $700,000, but not all of this would be necessary immediately. The working capital would be built up according to the following schedule (increments would be required as of the *beginning* of each year):

1971.........................	$200,000
1972.........................	300,000
1973.........................	150,000
1974.........................	50,000
1975.........................	...

(9) In 1995, the plant was expected to be worth $300,000, the equipment $1,400,000, and the working capital the amount invested.

(10) The corporation requires a 10 percent return on investment after taxes.

Should the Nonon Company have begun the manufacture and sale of the new product?

30.† Mr. Walter Weber, general manager of Sovad, S.A., looked across his desk at Mr. Karl Huber, the company's sales manager. Mr. Huber had just suggested that Sovad increase its capacity to manufacture automatic timing devices.

"All right," said Mr. Weber, "let's see if the profits from the increased sales will give us a big enough return on investment. As soon as you're ready, give Mr. Berner (the company's controller) your estimates of sales and what you'll need for advertising and sales promotion. He can work with purchasing and manufacturing to get the rest of the data he needs. I'll ask him to give me a recommendation on your proposal sometime next week."

Sovad, S.A. was a manufacturer of industrial controls and precision instruments, with headquarters and manufacturing facilities in Winterthur, Switzerland. Its manufacturing operations in 1967 were conducted entirely in Winterthur, but more than half of its 1967 sales were made in other countries.

First introduced in 1964, the company's automatic timers had been well received by Sovad's customers both at home and abroad. By 1967 Sovad was selling all that it could manufacture. Mr. Huber was convinced that he could expand his sales in Switzerland by large amounts if adequate factory capacity could be provided.

Before coming to Mr. Weber with his suggestion, Mr. Huber had discussed the idea of expansion with Mr. Gluck, the company's director of manufacturing. "Our Winterthur factory is already crowded," Mr. Gluck told him. "The authorities won't give us a building permit to expand it, but I know of some vacant space that we can rent in Zurich for Fr. 50,000 a year. We could put all the timer operations in there." Zurich is only 20 kilometers from Winterthur and Mr. Gluck was confident that he could supervise manufacturing operations in both places without difficulty.

Working with Mr. Gluck, Mr. Huber prepared the preliminary estimates shown in Exhibit 1.

As he gave this exhibit to Mr. Berner, Mr. Huber remarked that an eight-month payback period was hard to beat. He hoped that Mr. Berner wouldn't take too long to pass the proposal on to Mr. Weber for approval.

In the course of his examination of these figures, Mr. Berner discovered

---

† Copyright 1968 by l'Institut pour l'Etude des Méthodes de Direction de l'Entreprise (IMEDE), Lausanne, Switzerland. Reprinted by permission.

Exhibit 1

ZURICH TIMER FACTORY

Preliminary Profitability Estimate

Sales (30,000 units at Fr. 50)...................		Fr. 1,500,000
Out of pocket expenses:		
Factory labor and materials (30,000 units		
at Fr. 28.40)............................Fr.	852,000	
Rent.....................................	50,000	
Other factory costs (not including depreciation)..	70,000	
Marketing expenses.........................	160,000	
Total Expenses.........................		1,132,000
Profit Contribution............................		Fr. 368,000
Equipment required:		
New equipment to be purchased...............Fr.	250,000	
Old equipment, to be moved from Winterthur....	1	
Cost of moving old equipment from Winterthur		
and installing it at Zurich...................	5,000	
Total.................................		Fr. 255,000

$$\text{Payback Period} = \frac{\text{Fr. } 255,000}{\text{Fr. } 368,000} = 0.69 \text{ Years} = 8.3 \text{ Months.}$$

two things. First, the sales and expense figures given in Exhibit 1 were not expected to be achieved until the third year of the new factory's operation. Second, they represented the *total* sales and expenses of the timers. Since the company was already selling 10,000 timers a year, Mr. Berner did not believe that the profit on these units should be used to justify the opening of the new factory. As he put it, "The data that we need are differential or incremental figures, the differences between having the new factory and not having it." Mr. Huber estimated that he would be able to sell 30,000 timers a year after a two-year introductory period. His detailed estimates of annual sales and marketing expenses are summarized in Exhibit 2.

Mr. Berner knew that these volumes of sales would require sizable investments in working capital which Mr. Huber had omitted from Exhibit 1. On the basis of the company's past experience, he estimated that working capital requirements would be as follows:

	Cumulative Balance Required at Beginning of Year
If timers are manufactured in Zurich:	
Year 1..Fr.	700,000
Year 2..	750,000
Year 3..	800,000
If timers are not manufactured in Zurich.............Fr.	300,000

Exhibit 2

ZURICH TIMER FACTORY

Estimated Annual Timer Sales
and Marketing Expenses

	Annual Sales		Annual Marketing Costs
	Units	Value	
If all timers are manufactured in Zurich:			
Year 1	20,000	Fr. 1,000,000	Fr. 260,000
Year 2	25,000	1,250,000	260,000
Year 3 and after	30,000	1,500,000	160,000
If timers are not manufactured in Zurich	10,000	Fr. 500,000	Fr. 60,000

When questioned about the manufacturing cost estimates in Exhibit 1, Mr. Gluck gave Mr. Berner the figures shown in Exhibit 3. Mr. Gluck explained that if the Zurich factory were opened, all automatic timer production would be shifted to Zurich. If the expansion proposal were to be rejected, however, the cost of producing 10,000 timers a year at Winterthur would be Fr. 31 per unit plus Fr. 20,000 a year. All of these costs could be eliminated if operations were transferred to Zurich.

Mr. Berner also questioned Mr. Gluck about the equipment that would be moved from Winterthur to Zurich. "That is the old test equipment that we are now replacing here in Winterthur," he replied. "It's perfectly adequate for the timers, and it saves us from buying new equipment for the new location. It's fully depreciated on our books, but it's in perfect condition and I see no reason why it wouldn't last for years.

"If we don't open up in Zurich, we'll sell this old equipment locally for about Fr. 10,000. If we keep it, our only cost will be about Fr. 5,000 to get it from Winterthur to Zurich. We can subtract this Fr. 5,000 from

Exhibit 3

ZURICH TIMER FACTORY

Estimated Factory Costs

	Variable Costs per Unit	Fixed Costs per Year		
		Rental	Depreciation	Other
Year 1	Fr. 29.60	Fr. 50,000	Fr. 25,000	Fr. 70,000
Year 2	28.80	50,000	25,000	70,000
Year 3 and after	28.40	50,000	25,000	70,000

the taxable income from our other operations right away, even before we start operating at Zurich."

For purposes of analysis, Mr. Berner and Mr. Huber agreed that the new Zurich plant should be able to operate for at least 10 years and that the company's investment in working capital would be a reasonable measure of the value of the Zurich assets at the end of that time.

In evaluating capital expenditure proposals, Mr. Berner used an income tax rate of 30 percent of ordinary taxable income. Gains on the sale of equipment were also taxed at a 30 percent rate. Depreciation for tax purposes on the new equipment to be purchased for the Zurich plant would be Fr. 50,000 a year for five years.

a) Prepare a time table of the before-tax cash flows that are relevant to the evaluation of this expansion proposal. Do you agree with Mr. Berner that these should be differential figures?

b) If Sovad required at least a 20 percent return on investment, before income taxes, should Sovad have opened the Zurich factory?

c) How would your analysis differ if you were to use after-tax cash flows and a minimum acceptable rate of return of 14 percent?

Chapter 21

STANDARD COSTING FOR FACTORY COST CONTROL

ACCOUNTING DATA enter the control process in the first instance as inputs to management planning. This was the focus of the last four chapters. Now it is time to consider a second managerial use of accounting data—their use in routine control reporting. Routine reports on operating performance are used in the process referred to in Chapter 17 as *responsive control*—the adaptation of methods or plans on the basis of analyses of results achieved.

SHORTCOMINGS OF ACTUAL COST SYSTEMS

The striking characteristic of a job cost system using actual costs is its conceptual simplicity. When given the problem of product costing in a manufacturing company, almost anyone with no exposure to accounting other than the first four chapters of this book might come up with something pretty close to the system described in Chapter 17. The structure of the system is clear, the bookkeeping necessary to implement it is straightforward, and to interpret the information which it provides one need only say that these are the *actual* costs.

This conceptual simplicity is offset, however, by some serious disadvantages. First, the bookkeeping work required by a job cost system is relatively heavy, and hence relatively expensive. Second, even with predetermined burden rates, a considerable lag may occur between the time of a transaction and the time it is recorded in the accounts, with a corresponding delay in the presentation of reports to management. Third, the actual unit cost incurred in producing a product does not necessarily represent the best information the accountant can produce for management use in alternative choice decisions. Finally, and perhaps most important, actual costs classified by *jobs* or *products* are of practically no use to a management con-

673

fronted with the problem of *controlling* a large decentralized organization.

This chapter will demonstrate how a standard cost system may be used to provide responsive control of direct labor and direct material cost. Overhead costs will be excluded from the presentation by assuming that all manufacturing costs are direct. This is permissible because the methods employed to account for direct labor and material costs are independent of the treatment of overhead.

STANDARD PRODUCT COSTS

A necessary condition for the employment of a standard cost system is the development of a standard cost for each product the firm manufactures.

The Standard Cost Sheet

Exhibit 21–1 presents the Landau Company's standard cost sheet for one of its products, No. 6948. The first column lists all the items of

Exhibit 21–1

A STANDARD COST SHEET

Department	Stamping					
Description	Door Front No. 6948			Quantity	1,000	
Standard Cost	$457.00			Standard Cost per Unit	$0.457	

Operation or Item	Materials			Labor		
	Quantity	Price	Total	Hours	Rate	Total
Steel Sheet	3,600	$0.08	$288.00			
Cut				4.8	$3.50	$ 16.80
Drill				16.0	3.75	60.00
Stamp				7.3	4.00	29.20
Finish				18.0	3.50	63.00
Total			$288.00			$169.00

direct material and all the direct labor operations required in the manufacture of the product. The next three columns contain the standard quantity of material required per 1,000 units of the product, the standard price per unit of the material item, and the standard cost of the standard material quantity. The next three columns contain the analogous information for direct labor.

The development of a standard cost sheet for each product is facilitated by the prior development of standard cost files for materials and labor. The materials cost file contains the standard price for each item of direct material purchased by the company, and the labor cost file contains the standard wage rate for each class of labor. The standard materials prices and wage rates are set by the Landau Company prior to the start of each year, and they represent the expected materials prices and wage rates that will prevail for the coming year.

Standard Usage Rates

An efficient manufacturing operation requires that a company establish a *bill of materials* and an *operations routing sheet* on each product it manufactures. These are vital ingredients in the establishment of standard product cost. The bill of materials specifies each kind of material that is required to manufacture the product and the *expected usage* of the material per unit of the product. ("Materials" in this context includes component parts that are obtained either from stock or from outside vendors.) The operations routing sheet specifies each operation required to manufacture the product and the *expected labor time* per operation on the product.

Departmentalization of Standard Costs

Each product that a company sells to its customers may go through two or more manufacturing departments prior to its completion. For instance, in the manufacture of automobile fenders, one department may cut the steel into fender blanks, another department may stamp the blanks into fenders, while a third may attach the fenders to the auto body.

The fender blank in this case is an *intermediate product* with a standard labor and material cost. The standard labor and material cost of this intermediate product in the cutting department is regarded by the stamping department as its standard *material* cost. The fender in turn is an intermediate product with a standard labor and material cost that becomes standard material cost in the assembly department. In a standard cost system, a standard cost is required for each intermediate product as well as for each end product.

A STANDARD COST SYSTEM

The type of standard cost system employed by the Landau Company is referred to as a *basic plan* standard cost system. Various modifications of this plan are likely to be encountered in practice, as each company adapts its system to the character of its own operations and to its objectives in employing standard costs, but the basic plan is the least expensive standard costing plan, as well as the simplest.

The Concept of Standard Costing

The central idea of standard costing is to charge each department with the standard cost of all the direct labor and direct materials used (inputs) and credit the department with the standard cost of all of the products it manufactures (outputs). The output of a given period consists of the amount of products completed during the period plus the increase (or minus the decrease) in the quantity of work in

Exhibit 21–2

LANDAU COMPANY

Factory Ledger Account Balances
As of September 1, 19—

	Dr.	Cr.
Raw material	$ 32,800	$
Material in process—machining	23,240	
Labor in process—machining	8,500	
Material in process—assembly	31,300	
Labor in process—assembly	10,100	
Finished goods	51,000	
Control		156,940
Total	$156,940	$156,940

process between the beginning and the end of the period. The difference between input and output, measured in this way, is one measure of departmental efficiency during the period.

The mechanism by which this is accomplished begins with the departmentalization of costs. Exhibit 21–2 shows the balances in the Landau Company's inventory accounts on September 1, 19—. The dollar amount of each balance is the inventory costed at standard cost, and each department has its own work in process accounts. Under an actual cost system, in contrast, one work in process account or two— one for labor and one for material—may cover the labor and materials content of all work in process in the entire factory.

As the ledger indicates, the Landau Company has only two manufacturing departments, machining and assembly, whereas a typical standard cost installation must deal with many more. The accounts required for a hundred producing departments, however, present no conceptual problems beyond those to be encountered in two, and therefore no useful purpose would be served by burdening this illustration with the additional detail.

Purchases of Materials

When material is purchased, the goods acquired are charged by the Landau Company to the Raw Material account at standard cost. To accomplish this, each item on the vendor's invoice is repriced at its standard cost, obtained from the standard cost file mentioned earlier. Of course, the supplier must be paid the actual cost or invoice prices of the material, and the difference is charged to a *material price* variance account. In accounting terms, a "variance" is any deviation between a standard cost and an actual cost, or any subdivision of such a deviation.

During September the actual cost of the material purchased by the Landau Company was $63,800, while the same material priced at standard was $60,250. The summary entry covering all these purchases is:[1]

(1)

Raw Material	60,250	
Material Price Variance	3,550	
Control (Accounts Payable)		63,800

The balance in this variance account is to be interpreted like under- or overabsorbed overhead. A debit balance in the account is "unfavorable" in that the actual cost is greater than the standard or "absorbed" cost, while a credit variance is a type of gain because the work was accomplished at less than standard cost.

Issues of Materials

When material is requisitioned by one of the manufacturing departments, the standard cost of that material is credited to the Raw Material account and charged to the department's material in process account. The summary entry for all materials issued during the month of September is:

(2)

Material in Process—Machining	53,200	
Material in Process—Assembly	15,800	
Raw Material		69,000

---

[1] The control account represents the head office's investment in factory inventories and is used to permit a separate factory ledger to balance. In the entries in this illustration, the account title shown in parentheses (Accounts Payable) is the account that would be credited in the general ledger at the time this entry is recorded in the factory ledger.

Notice that no reference is made here to entries on job cost sheets. Although standard cost systems can be designed to provide for this added feature, the basic plan used by the Landau Company makes no such provision. Instead, the *department* is the basic unit to which actual costs are assigned. Furthermore, when all materials inventories are priced at standard prices, the materials ledger can be kept in physical quantities only—dollar amounts can be computed at any time by multiplying the quantities on hand by their standard prices.

Accounting for Labor Costs

Direct labor costs, like direct materials costs, are charged to departments and not to jobs. Each department is charged with the direct labor hours it uses, multiplied by the standard wage rates for each class of labor employed. On this basis, the summary entry for the actual direct labor hours used in the Landau Company's two departments during September is:

(3)

Labor in Process—Machining	21,400	
Labor in Process—Assembly	20,000	
Accrued Labor		41,400

The periodic payrolls are calculated on the basis of the actual hours and the actual wage rate for each worker. The payrolls for September give rise to the following entry:

(4)

Accrued Labor	39,220	
Control (Wages Payable)		39,220

If the September payrolls cover only the September labor, the balance in the Accrued Labor account is the *labor rate variance*, the difference between the actual labor hours at standard wage rates and the same number of hours at actual wage rates. This account can be closed out by entry (5):

(5)

Accrued Labor	2,180	
Labor Rate Variance		2,180

In this case the labor rate variance was favorable (credit balance), indicating that the average actual wage rate was less than the standard wage rates for the work done during the period.

Completion of Intermediate and End Products

When a department completes a production order, the output is transferred to another department or to the finished goods storeroom.

If the output is an intermediate product that is stored with the raw material, such as a batch of component parts, the transfer of the output is to the raw material stock room. These transfers are all recorded at standard cost, obtained in this case from the file of standard product costs developed from the standard cost sheets illustrated in Exhibit 21–1.

In terms of procedure, the completion of a production order by a department is evidenced in the Landau Company by a *transfer slip* which identifies the item, the quantity transferred, the department that produced the item, and the department or inventory location to which the item was transferred. The accounting department refers to the standard product cost file to establish the standard labor and material cost per unit. The quantity transferred is then costed at these unit figures to establish the relevant totals.

To illustrate, assume that the machining department has completed and transferred to the assembly department 200 units of item 6948, referred to in Exhibit 21–1. With the standard material, labor, and total cost per unit at $0.288, $0.169, and $0.457, respectively, the journal entry would be:

Material in Process—Assembly............................91.40
    Material in Process—Machining.......................   57.60
    Labor in Process—Machining.........................   33.80

Returning to the Landau Company's transactions for the month of September, the standard costs of the products completed by the machining and assembly departments during the month were as follows:

	Transferred to Assembly Department	Transferred to Finished Goods Storeroom	Total Transfers
Machining department:			
Materials...............	$52,050	$ 5,200	$ 57,250
Labor.................	18,850	4,100	22,950
Total..............	$70,900	$ 9,300	$ 80,200
Assembly department:			
Materials...............	x	$ 98,400	$ 98,400
Labor.................	x	26,300	26,300
Total..............	x	$124,700	$124,700

The transfers from the machining department require the following entry:

(6)

Material in Process—Assembly..........................70,900
Finished Goods....................................... 9,300
    Material in Process—Machining.......................   57,250
    Labor in Process—Machining........................   22,950

Notice how the standard labor cost in the machining department becomes part of the standard material cost in assembly. This is the cost invested in the materials by the time they reach the assembly stage, and the breakdown of this cost into its constituent elements has no significance to the manager of the assembly department.

Finally, the entry to record the transfer of finished products from assembly to the finished goods storeroom is recorded in entry (7):

(7)

Finished Goods......................................124,700
    Material in Process—Assembly......................   98,400
    Labor in Process—Assembly.........................   26,300

DEVELOPMENT OF USAGE VARIANCES

The departmental labor and materials cost accounts are of central importance in the use of a standard cost system for cost control purposes. Recall that each account is charged with the actual labor or material at standard prices and is credited with the actual output at standard cost. The two will differ insofar as the labor or material used per unit of output was above or below standard.

The Basic Calculation

To illustrate this point, assume that 3 pounds of material are required per unit of output and that the standard cost per pound of material is $0.50, so that the standard material cost per unit of output is $1.50. Assume also that the department received 3,600 pounds of material, delivered 1,100 units of finished product, and had no material in process either at the start or at the end of the period. The material in process account would read as follows:

Material in Process—Department X

⟶3,600 lbs. at $0.50 1,800	1,100 units at $1.50 1,650⟶

It is evident that the department used more material than the standard quantity to produce the output, because it had an unfavorable usage variance (debit balance) of $150, or 300 pounds at $0.50 a pound.

Derivation of Usage Variances

The above illustration is very much oversimplified. Typically, a department will produce many products rather than one, and it will have work in process both at the start and at the end of the period. To see the consequences of these additional complications, let us return to the departmental accounts of the Landau Company, shown in Exhibit 21–3.

Looking first at the machining department's material in process account, we see that the department started the period with $23,240 worth of material at standard prices and received another $53,200 of

Exhibit 21–3

LANDAU COMPANY

Unadjusted Department Cost Accounts
As of September 30, 19—

Material in Process—Machining				Material in Process—Assembly			
Bal. 9/1	23,240	(6)	57,250	Bal. 9/1	31,300	(7)	98,400
(2)	53,200			(2)	15,800		
				(6)	70,900		
Bal. 19,190				Bal. 19,600			

Labor in Process—Machining				Labor in Process—Assembly			
Bal. 9/1	8,500	(6)	22,950	Bal. 9/1	10,100	(7)	26,300
(3)	21,400			(3)	20,000		
Bal. 6,950				Bal. 3,800			

material at standard prices during the month. If the department had no material in process at the end of the month, this would indicate that the department had used $19,190 more material (at standard prices) than the standard material cost of the month's output.

The department manager would be quick to point out, however, that this calculation did not consider the material remaining in the department at the end of September. The extent to which the department's usage of material was above or below standard depends on the amount of material in process at the end of the month. This may be determined by taking an inventory of the material in process and pricing it at standard or by totaling the materials requisitions on production orders that have not yet been finished.

For the Landau Company, the standard cost of the material in process in the machinery department at the end of September was $24,000. Therefore, the end-of-month material in process plus the material content of the goods finished is $24,000 + $57,250 = $81,250. Comparing this with the total standard cost of the materials issued to the department during the month plus the materials in process in the department at the beginning of the month reveals a favorable materials usage variance of $4,810. This calculation can be summarized as follows:

```
Output at standard cost:
  Products completed...................................$57,250
  Increase in materials in process
    ($24,000 − $23,240)................................     760
      Total Output at Standard Cost....................$58,010
Input at standard cost...................................  53,200
  Material Usage Variance (Favorable)..................$ 4,810²
```

Entry (8) serves to isolate this variance and restore the account to its correct end-of-month balance:

(8)
```
Material in Process—Machining...........................4,810
  Material Usage Variance—Machining...................        4,810
```

The standard costs of the other elements of the work in process on September 30 were found to be:

```
Labor in process—machining..............................$ 8,400
Material in process—assembly............................ 18,800
Labor in process—assembly..............................  7,900
```

With these figures, it is a simple matter to compute the other usage variances for the month:

	Machining Labor	Assembly Material	Assembly Labor
Output at standard cost:			
Completed production.......	$22,950	$98,400	$26,300
Increase (decrease) in work			
in process...............	(100)	(12,500)	(2,200)
Total Output at Standard	$22,850	$85,900	$24,100
Input at standard cost........	21,400	86,700	20,000
Favorable (Unfavorable)			
Usage Variance...........	$ 1,450	$ (800)	$ 4,100

---

² The material usage variance can also be found more simply by subtracting the correct account balance ($24,000) from the balance shown in the material in process account before adjustment ($19,190). The explanation above is intended to demonstrate why this is so.

The entries which pick up the variances and restore the work in process accounts to their correct end-of-month balances are:

(9)

Labor in Process—Machining..................................1,450
    Labor Usage Variance—Machining.....................   1,450

(10)

Material Usage Variance—Assembly........................ 800
    Material in Process—Assembly.........................   800

(11)

Labor in Process—Assembly..............................4,100
    Labor Usage Variance—Assembly.....................   4,100

In other words, the assembly department used slightly more materials in the aggregate than the standards called for, while both departments were able to process their outputs with less than the standard quantities of labor.

Cost of Goods Sold under Standard Costing

Finally, the goods sold are credited to finished goods and debited to cost of goods sold at standard cost. The entry is:

(12)

Cost of Goods Sold...................................119,300
    Finished Goods....................................   119,300

This entry requires only a tabulation of the quantities of each item sold, taken from some source such as the file of customer invoices for the period, multiplied in each case by standard cost. Thus here again the only cost information that is needed is the file of standard product costs.

Transactions Summary

The cost flows in a basic plan standard costing system are summarized in Exhibit 21–4. Raw material is purchased and then issued to departments. Labor is used and charged to departments. Products are finished and eventually sold. Finally, variances are computed and transferred to variance accounts.

The entries summarizing the factory cost transactions of the Landau Company for the month of September are shown in work sheet form in Exhibit 21–5. The liabilities arising from the acquisition of material and labor have been credited to the control account. The income statement accounts in this exhibit are the Cost of Goods Sold account and all the variance accounts. After the information provided by these accounts has been established, they are properly closed out to the control account. After this has been done, only the inventory

Exhibit 21–4

DIRECT LABOR AND DIRECT MATERIALS COST FLOWS
IN A BASIC PLAN STANDARD COSTING SYSTEM
(Departmental Detail and Overhead Costs Omitted)

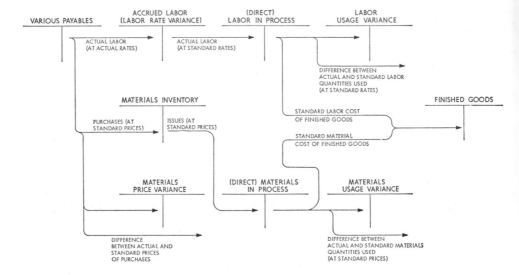

accounts and the control account will have balances, as in Exhibit 21–2 above.

The variances in Exhibit 21–5 appear in report form in Exhibit 21–6. We see there that the excess of actual over standard cost of material purchased during September resulted in an unfavorable variance of $3,550. On the other hand, actual wage rates were below standard by $2,180, and all of the usage variances were favorable with the exception of the material usage in assembly. Actual material usage in machining and labor usage in assembly were impressively less than the standard usage.

These variances can all be shown in the monthly income statements as adjustments to the cost of goods sold, as follows:

Cost of goods sold at standard..................		$119,300
Less: Favorable variances......................$12,540		
Plus: Unfavorable variances.................... 4,350		(8,190)
Cost of Goods Sold at Actual...................		$111,110

COMPARATIVE INCOME STATEMENTS

Under a standard cost system the periodic income statements submitted to management typically contain two cost of goods sold fig-

Exhibit 21–5

LANDAU COMPANY

Trial Balance, September 30, 19—

	Trial Balance September 1, 19—		September Transactions		Trial Balance September 30, 19—	
	Debit	Credit	Debit	Credit	Debit	Credit
Raw material........	32,800		(1) 60,250	(2) 69,000	24,050	
Material in process— machining.........	23,240		(2) 53,200 (8) 4,810	(6) 57,250	24,000	
Material in process— assembly..........	31,300		(2) 15,800 (6) 70,900	(7) 98,400 (10) 800	18,800	
Labor in process— machining.........	8,500		(3) 21,400 (9) 1,450	(6) 22,950	8,400	
Labor in process— assembly..........	10,100		(3) 20,000 (11) 4,100	(7) 26,300	7,900	
Finished goods.......	51,000		(6) 9,300 (7)124,700	(12)119,300	65,700	
Accrued labor........			(4) 39,220 (5) 2,180	(3) 41,400		
Control.............		156,940		(1) 63,800 (4) 39,220		259,960
Cost of goods sold....			(12)119,300		119,300	
Material price variance..........			(1) 3,550		3,550	
Labor rate variance...				(5) 2,180		2,180
Material usage variance—machining				(8) 4,810		4,810
Material usage variance—assembly....			(10) 800		800	
Labor usage variance —machining.......				(9) 1,450		1,450
Labor usage variance —assembly........				(11) 4,100		4,100
Total..........	156,940	156,940	550,960	550,960	272,500	272,500

Exhibit 21–6

LANDAU COMPANY

Variance Report
For the Month of September, 19—

Item	Unfavorable	Favorable
Material price variance.................	$3,550	$
Wage rate variance.....................		2,180
Material usage—machining.............		4,810
Material usage—assembly..............	800	
Labor usage—machining...............		1,450
Labor usage—assembly................		4,100
Total......................	4,350	12,540

ures. One figure is the standard cost of the goods sold, which was $119,300 for the Landau Company. The other figure is the standard cost of goods sold plus or minus the variances carried to the income statement. Although the latter figure is often called cost of goods sold at actual, it differs from the cost of goods sold under an actual cost system. In evaluating the desirability of adopting a standard cost system and in using the periodic statements generated by the system to evaluate performance, it is useful to understand how the "actual" cost of goods sold under a standard cost system differs from the "actual" cost of goods sold under an actual historical cost system. The term actual is being bandied about so, because a standard cost system no less than an actual cost system incorporates actual costs in the accounts.

The cost of goods sold under an actual cost system may be described as the standard cost of the goods sold plus the variances on the goods sold. The material in the goods sold during a month may have been purchased six months earlier, and the production may have taken place two months earlier. Regardless of when the purchases and production took place, the variances appear on the income statement in the month in which the goods are *sold*. The only exception is that variances in factory *overhead* costs appear on the income statement at the time of *production*.

Under the basic plan standard cost system, in contrast, the cost of goods sold for a month is the standard cost of goods sold, plus or minus: (1) the price variances on the material and labor *purchased* during the month; and (2) the usage variances on the *production* during the month.

Cost of goods sold, in other words, differs only because variances are recognized at different times. In one case, they are recognized when the goods are sold, and in the other case they are recognized when the variances take place. Which is preferred? Clearly if the cost of goods sold should be the actual cost of the actual goods sold, the actual cost system is correct and preferred. However, if the purpose of monthly income statements is to provide management with useful information, the standard cost system yields the preferred figure. Variances represent differences between actual and standard or expected costs. To take corrective action, management wants to be informed of the variances as soon after they take place as possible. For instance, if material prices have gone up, management should be advised of their consequences for operations currently and not a few months later when the month's purchases are sold.

ADVANTAGES OF STANDARD COSTING SYSTEMS

Standard costing can produce many benefits for management. Its main advantages are:

1. Better control information.
2. Better data for decisions.
3. Clerical economy.
4. Faster reporting.

Better Control Information

Actual cost systems lack one important ingredient of good control information, a bench mark for comparison. In job order costing, furthermore, even when some form of bench mark is available, it is available by product and not by department. Costs classified by product are useless for control, because a product cannot be held responsible for or asked to explain a deviation from standard.

These defects are corrected by standard costing. The difference between actual and standard cost of goods manufactured is classified according to major areas of responsibility—materials price variance, wage rate variance, and labor and material usage variances. The last, in turn, are broken down to correspond to the department or individual immediately responsible for controlling the difference between actual and standard cost.

As long as variances are small, costs are deemed to be under control, *by definition*, and higher management need not concern itself with the subject. When substantial differences between actual and expected costs appear, however, they are automatically called to the attention of higher management, and that attention is directed to the place in the organization where the search for causes and corrective action should begin. This is known as *management by exception.*

Better Data for Decisions

It may be wondered how a standard cost system can be considered superior to an actual cost system in providing cost information for pricing and similar decisions. An actual cost system is continuously developing information on *actual* product costs. By contrast, the standard cost accounts can be said to provide no information on product costs, since actual costs are classified only by organization unit. The only product cost information in the accounts is standard product cost, and that is known before the production for the period is undertaken.[3]

The advantages of an actual cost system in this area are more apparent than real, however. Product cost analyses are useful only for pricing and other alternative choice decisions, and the information desired is what the cost *will be*, not what it *has been* during some prior period. The record of the actual cost the last time the item was produced may or may not provide this information.

In the first place, actual wage rates and material prices prevailing at that time may differ from those appropriate to the problem at hand. Consequently, unless the historical data are unusually detailed as regards quantity and price per unit of each class of labor and material used, it will be difficult, if not impossible, to translate them into current or expected prices. Second, because of the special conditions under which the job was produced, the actual quantities of labor and material used may be above or below what one might expect at present or in the future. If an attempt is made to correct any such unique conditions by averaging costs over a number of prior jobs, the difficulty then encountered is that the data become less and less relevant as one goes back in time, and comprehensive adjustments for both price differences and technological change become necessary.

A further limitation on the usefulness of job cost information varies in importance from one firm to another but should in no case be underestimated. A department head regards his job as one of employing his men and material as efficiently as possible. Recording on each

---

[3] This comment applies to the kind of standard costing system described in this chapter. Other, more complex systems can provide actual cost data by product as well as by department.

time slip and material requisition the job to be charged often appears a burdensome and senseless bookkeeping task which interferes with his primary responsibilities. He may therefore become lax in this regard, being careful only to charge each cost to *some* job, thereby keeping the bookkeepers from bothering him. The accuracy of usage data derived from job cost sheets is therefore always open to some question.

In short, the development of expected costs for decision problems from historical cost records may involve difficult and time-consuming analysis, and limitations in the organization and detail of the cost records may even then result in estimates that are far from satisfactory.

Standard cost systems, on the other hand, yield product cost information which may well be more useful than historical data. The standard cost sheet provides an estimate of what the product will cost broken down into the quantity and price for each factor: labor, material, and overhead. Insofar as current or expected labor and material prices differ from the standard prices, it is an easy task to substitute the expected values. The standard usages of labor and material are not distorted by abnormal conditions on some particular run, and therefore represent best estimates of expected usage.

Clerical Economy

The previous description of a basic plan standard cost system indicates the main sources of clerical savings by comparison with an actual job cost system. First, an actual cost system requires raw material and finished goods ledgers with price and quantity information for each item of inventory. This information is required to cost material issues and goods sold. Because successive lots of a given item are likely to have different unit costs, the ledgers will have to keep track of separate lots (e.g., FIFO) or recompute average unit costs after each acquisition.

Under a standard cost system, no supporting ledgers are required for the raw material and finished goods accounts, since the debits and credits to these accounts are made at standard. Item inventory records can be kept in physical units only, to meet the needs of purchasing, production scheduling, and other staff departments. Debits and credits to the raw materials and finished goods accounts can be made simply by multiplying quantities in and quantities out by standard unit prices. This is simpler than maintaining an actual cost ledger, whether bookkeeping is done manually or by computer.

The second major savings in clerical cost arises from the elimination of the job cost sheets. To record actual material costs on job cost sheets, the material requisitions must be priced as described above, and then charged to individual jobs. For direct labor, the hours worked must be identified by job and the actual wage rates paid must be established and posted to the job cost sheets. This last set of operations is such a nuisance that many actual cost systems in fact charge jobs with actual hours at predetermined rates. A standard cost system just carries this to its logical conclusion. The actual material and labor used are costed at the more easily obtained standard prices, and the costs thus obtained are charged to departmental accounts only. The requisitions and time slips may or may not identify the job worked on, but the costs are not as a matter of routine classified by job.

These same features of standard costing can promote clerical cost savings in still another direction. Purchasing and production scheduling departments need up-to-date physical inventory records, as well as data on units on order or in production. The accounting department, on the other hand, needs inventory figures in monetary units to prepare external financial statements or to provide means of detecting loss and pilferage of materials and products. Actual-cost inventory ledgers, however, either cannot be updated rapidly enough to meet the needs of purchasing and production planners or are not readily accessible to nonaccounting personnel. Furthermore, they may be difficult to integrate with physical data on units on order or in production.

As a consequence of all this, purchasing and production planning often keep their own perpetual inventory records in physical terms, a costly duplication of clerical effort. Because standard costing eliminates the need for dollar figures in the ledgers used for routine financial reporting, one set of physical-unit ledgers can serve both purposes. The clerical savings from this kind of integration can be substantial.

Faster Reporting

Standard costing can make another kind of contribution by enabling the accounting department to issue reports to management more promptly after the end of a reporting period. For example, when a job is finished, this fact can be recorded immediately, without waiting for the complete posting of data from the requisitions and time tickets to the job cost sheet. Furthermore, with fewer clerical operations to be performed, the accounts themselves can be brought up-to-date more rapidly. If management can be more effective with a prompter feedback on the results of operations, the payoff from this feature can be extremely great.

PROBLEMS WITH STANDARD COSTING

Many, perhaps most, standard costing systems are more elaborate than the system description in this chapter would imply. Daily reporting of quantity or usage variances, classified by machine center (group of similar machines), by individual machines, or by individual operators is a common practice. Such systems are certainly more costly than simple basic plan systems and may even be more costly than the actual cost systems they replaced. They also provide more information. Management's job is to decide whether the added information is worth the added cost.

A second problem arising under standard costing is that the installation of such a system is often time-consuming and expensive. If the installation is not carried out carefully, the vital ingredient of employee cooperation may be lost and the system may fail to achieve its objectives.

Furthermore, management may expect too much from its standard cost system. It may try to use it as a motivating device to induce employees to *reduce* costs, which generally requires methods changes, rather than to control costs. The adoption of standards may lead to cost reduction if it is accompanied by or incidental to work standardization and simplification and if proper attention is paid to the effects on employee compensation and job satisfaction. Cost reduction and cost control are two separate objectives, however, and management should be very clear as to why it wants standard costing and what has to be done to make it accomplish these desired results.

SUMMARY

Historical product costs ordinarily come too late for many planning purposes and fail to provide an adequate basis for cost control reporting. To remedy these defects, many companies have adopted standard cost systems. The primary feature of such systems is that they accumulate in the accounts differences or "variances" between actual and standard costs for the volume of operations achieved during a given time period. These variances are classified between rate or price variances and quantity or usage variances. The usage variances, in turn, are accumulated departmentally and are reported periodically to the executives responsible for departmental operations.

The system described here has the added advantage of low clerical cost, but at the sacrifice of some of the information that is provided by more complex systems that are often found in practice. The description has also been simplified by the omission of any reference to factory overhead costs. This departure from realism will be remedied in the next chapter.

QUESTIONS AND PROBLEMS

1. Some observers have maintained that a standard cost should represent the best possible performance under ideal conditions. Discuss the merits of this point of view.

2. In adopting a standard cost system, a firm typically hopes to achieve a reduction in its clerical costs and an improvement in management control. Describe how each of these objectives is expected to be realized.

3. What is the primary purpose of the bill of materials? The operations routing sheet? What other purposes do they serve?

4. Why is it ordinarily regarded as unnecessary to classify materials price and labor rate variances by department?

5. What information should the standard cost card for a product contain?

6. Does classification of factory costs by job contribute to their control? Explain.

7. What are the advantages of recognizing materials price variances at the time of purchase?

8. Why is a job cost sheet for each production order unnecessary under a standard cost system? For what purposes and under what circumstances would maintenance of the job cost sheet be desirable?

9. Assuming that standard costs can be prepared for each job entering a job shop, what additional control information can be obtained by incorporating these standard costs into the formal accounting records instead of merely listing them on the job order cost sheets and accounting for actual costs by job order costing procedures?

10. Much of the bookkeeping economy achieved with a standard cost system is accomplished by giving up information obtained with an actual cost system. State three types of information lost under a basic plan standard costing system; indicate how giving up this information reduces bookkeeping costs; and discuss the problems connected with giving up the information.

11. "We don't use accounting reports for cost control. By the time a variance shows up in an accounting report, it is too late to control costs." Comment on this point of view.

*12. Materials can be purchased for $1 a pound. Under normal conditions, 10 percent by weight of the materials placed in production will be recovered as scrap, with a scrap value of $0.10 a pound. The remaining 90 percent of the materials shrinks to half its weight in processing. The final product weighs 6.3 pounds. What is the standard net materials cost per pound of finished product?

*13. Products A and B have standard labor requirements of two hours and three hours per unit, respectively. The standard wage rate is $3 an hour. During April, 1,500 units of product A and 4,000 units of product B were manufactured. Labor for the period totaled 14,500 hours and cost $44,000. Compute the labor variances.

14. The Hillman Company manufactures a single product known as Quik-Tite. Material A is the only raw material used in the manufacture of Quik-Tite. Transactions in material A for the month of June are as follows:

	Standard	Actual
Units of Quik-Tite produced..................		61,000
Pounds of material A required to produce one unit of Quik-Tite..........................	1.6 lbs.	1.5 lbs.
Cost of material A purchases during June........	$2.00/lb.	$2.05/lb.
Inventory of material A on June 1, costed at $2 a pound..................................	4,000 lbs.	4,000 lbs.

Compute the materials usage variance for the month.

15. The standard bill of materials for 100 units of product A is as follows:

	Standard Quantity	Standard Unit Price	Standard Cost of Materials
Material X................	105 lbs.	$0.70	$ 73.50
Material Y................	560 feet	0.40	224.00
Part Z...................	102 units	1.20	122.40
Standard Materials Cost..			$419.90

* Solutions to problems marked with an asterisk (*) are found in Appendix B.

The purchases and consumption of materials were as follows:

Item	Purchases	Price	Units Consumed
X........	40,000 lbs.	$0.65/lb.	33,000 lbs.
Y........	150,000 feet	0.45/ft.	161,000 feet
Z........	32,000 units	1.30/unit	31,200 units

The output was 30,000 units of product.

Determine and identify the various materials variances for the month.

16. The Mongol Company's factory contains 17 production departments. Products typically require processing in five or more of these departments. All products are subjected to final inspection before they are either placed in inventory or shipped to customers. Units rejected by the inspectors are sold immediately as seconds.

The company's industrial engineers have studied past experience with production rejects and have established the following standards: for products A, B, D, G, and H, rejects of 10 percent of the number of units placed in process; for all other products, rejects of 5 percent are regarded as normal.

During May, the production record was as follows:

Product	No. of Good Units	No. of Re-jected Units
A..............	470	50
B..............	820	60
C..............	1,460	110
D..............	320	40
F..............	540	40
G..............	990	60
H..............	80	20
K..............	3,400	300
M..............	650	70

a) Prepare a report that will provide management with information on the effectiveness of quality control in the plant.

b) What additional data would you regard as essential to good management information on this aspect of performance?

c) If the company were to manufacture 1,000 different products each month, would you find it necessary to make changes in the report structure? Explain.

*17. The factory uses a standard costing system. The following facts were recorded for one department for November:

(1) Materials purchased and placed in storeroom:
   At actual prices, $106.
   At standard prices, $100.
(2) Materials received from storeroom (at standard prices), $105.
(3) Labor used:
   At actual wage rates, $70.
   At standard wage rates, $68.
(4) Products finished (at standard cost):
   Standard materials cost, $85.
   Standard labor cost, $63.
(5) Work in process, November 1—none.
(6) Work in process, November 30 (at standard):
   Standard materials cost, $15.
   Standard labor cost, $8.

a) Compute the variances.
b) Enter the month's transactions in T-accounts, including any entries necessary to prepare the accounts to accumulate December transactions.

18.† Follow the instructions given for each of the four exercises presented below:

EXERCISE A

Luceri, Inc., reports factory materials and labor quantity variances to management monthly. It has two products, for which the following data are available:

	Materials Required per Unit	Labor Required per Unit	Units Produced during March
Product A...........	4 lbs.	1.5 hrs.	1,000
Product B...........	5	4.0	2,000

Usage of materials and labor during March was as follows:

Materials: 13,000 pounds.
Labor: 10,000 hours.

a) Compute materials and labor quantity variances for the month in terms of pounds of materials and labor hours. Indicate whether each variance is favorable or unfavorable.
b) The standard materials price is $4 a pound. The standard wage rate is $3 an hour.

† Copyright 1968 by l'Institut pour l'Etude des Méthodes de Direction de l'Entreprise (IMEDE), Lausanne, Switzerland. Adapted and reprinted by permission.

(1) Compute standard unit cost for each product in dollars.

(2) Restate your quantity variances (from *a*) in monetary terms.

EXERCISE B

A. B. See, Inc., uses a standard cost system. It had no inventory of materials on December 1 and no work in process either on December 1 or on December 31. The following information was collected for the month of December:

(1) Materials:

　　　　Standard price: $12 a pound.

　　　　Purchased 10,000 pounds at a cost of $115,000.

　　　　Used during December: 8,000 pounds.

(2) Labor:

　　　　Standard wage rate: $2.50 an hour.

　　　　Used during December: 2,700 hours at a cost of $7,000.

(3) Product output:

　　　　Standard cost per unit of product:

　　　　　　Materials: 3.9 pounds.

　　　　　　Labor: 1.5 hours.

　　　　Products manufactured during December: 1,900 units.

a) Compute labor and materials variances, in dollars, in whatever detail you think is appropriate.

b) Indicate to whom each of your variances should be reported.

EXERCISE C

Herren, Inc., uses a standard cost system. The following information was collected for one department for the month of December:

(1) Inventory of work in process, December 1 (at standard cost):

　　　　Materials cost: $13,000.

　　　　Labor cost: $8,000.

(2) Used during month:

　　　　Materials (at standard prices), $30,000.

　　　　Labor:

　　　　　　At actual wage rates, $15,000.

　　　　　　At standard wage rates, $16,000.

(3) Products finished and transferred out of the department during month (at standard cost):

　　　　Materials cost: $31,200.

　　　　Labor cost: $15,700.

(4) Inventory of work in process, December 31 (at standard cost):

　　　　Materials cost: $9,000.

　　　　Labor cost: $9,000.

a) Compute labor and materials variances in whatever detail you think is appropriate.

b) Using T-accounts, show how these data might appear in the company's ledger accounts.

EXERCISE D

Smythe, Ltd. has a factory with four production departments. Department Baker receives partly processed products from department Able, performs certain operations on them, and then transfers them to department Charlie for further work. A standard cost system is in use. The following data are available for department Baker for the month of February:

(1) Received from department Able during February:
Product units received, 5,000.
Unit cost in department Able:

	Standard Cost	Actual Cost
Materials.........	$1.00	$1.10
Labor...........	6.00	6.90

(2) Received materials from stock room during month, at standard prices, $2,100; standard cost of these materials, 40 cents per product unit.

(3) Used 2,200 labor hours during February, $4,200 at standard wage rates; standard cost of department Baker labor was 90 cents per product unit.

(4) Transferred to department Charlie during February, 4,800 product units.

(5) Work in process inventories in department Baker were negligible both on February 1 and on February 28.

(6) Damaged 200 product units in processing operations; these units were not usable and had no salvage value.

a) Compute labor and materials quantity variances for department Baker for the month of February.

b) Standard cost per product unit includes no allowances for losses of products during processing. How much of the variances computed in (*a*) were attributable to product losses? What do the remaining portions of the variances mean?

c) Using T-accounts, indicate how these events could be recorded in the company's ledger accounts.

19. The Neptune Company operates a small factory which makes only one product. Four production operations are necessary, one in each of the factory's four departments. The company's engineers have determined that these operations should require the following labor-hour allowances under normal conditions:

	Labor Hours per Unit of Product			
	Operation No. 1	Operation No. 2	Operation No. 3	Operation No. 4
Operators........	1.0	3.0	1.5	0.5
Helpers..........	0.5	2.5	2.0	0.1
Handlers.........	0.2	0.5	1.0	0.3

Operators are paid $3 per hour, helpers earn $2 per hour, and handlers are paid $1.50 per hour.

During August, the factory's operations were:

	Operation No. 1	Operation No. 2	Operation No. 3	Operation No. 4
Units produced........	2,000	1,800	2,100	2,000
Labor hours:				
Operators..........	1,100	5,200	3,400	980
Helpers............	550	4,600	4,600	190
Handlers...........	210	1,000	2,200	610

a) Prepare a report for management, summarizing labor operations for the month in terms of both hours and dollars, and write a brief paragraph commenting on the effectiveness of labor control during the month.

b) What advantages, if any, do you see in including dollar figures on this report? Explain.

*20. The Durabilt Company, manufacturer of men's work clothes, employs a standard cost system similar to that discussed in this chapter. You are given the following information concerning the month of September (overhead costs are omitted for simplicity):

(1) Inventory September 1:
    Raw material.....................................$58,500
    Material in process............................... 6,700
    Labor in process.................................. 2,400
    Finished goods.................................... 32,100
(2) Material purchases:
    Actual cost....................................... 42,380
    Standard cost..................................... 44,620
(3) Deliveries to finished goods:
    Standard material cost............................ 40,350
    Standard labor cost............................... 22,300
(4) Direct labor employed (at standard rates)......... 23,600
(5) Material put in process........................... 46,650

(6) Inventory October 1:
    Raw material.....................................   ?
    Material in process.............................. 12,300
    Labor in process.................................   4,700
    Finished goods...................................   ?
(7) Shipments to customers, at standard labor and materials cost 63,500
(8) Direct labor payroll.............................. 24,400

a) Prepare a list of the labor and materials variances for the month, and state briefly the meaning of each. Indicate in each case whether the variance is favorable or unfavorable.

b) Prepare a set of T-accounts and enter the opening balances and the effects of the month's transactions, using the basic plan system described in this chapter. State briefly the meaning of the end-of-month balance in each account.

21. The following material and labor cost variance report was prepared for a factory during July:

	—Material—	—Labor—
Raw material inventory, July 1...........$10,000		$ ....
Work in process inventory, July 1........ 4,000		4,500
Materials purchased during July.......... 24,000		....
Labor used during July....................		45,000
Total Cost to Be Accounted For......	$38,000	$49,500
Raw material inventory, July 31..........$ 8,000		$ ....
Work in process inventory, July 31....... 3,000		3,750
Goods completed during July............ 29,000		44,700
Total Cost Accounted For..........	40,000	48,450
Variance......................	$ 2,000	$ (1,050)

Additional data were as follows:

Materials purchased during July:
    At actual cost....................$24,000
    At standard cost................. 26,400
Materials used during July:
    At standard cost................. 28,400
Labor used during July:
    At actual cost................... 45,000
    At standard cost................. 44,250

a) Compute the price and usage variances for materials and labor.

b) What action would you recommend as a result of the information revealed by your analysis of variance? The action might be to acquire certain additional information; in that case assume the necessary facts and then state what action should be taken on the basis of these facts.

22. The Continental Company employs a standard cost system under which purchases are taken into inventory at standard cost and labor and material are charged to work in process at standard prices. (The company's overhead costs and its method of accounting for them are not covered in this problem.)

The company has only one producing department and transfers to finished goods are priced at standard product cost. A trial balance of the factory ledger on May 1 is given below:

```
Raw material............................... $29,460
Material in process..........................  18,400
Labor in process.............................   9,650
Finished goods...............................  35,000
Accrued wages...............................              $ 1,620
Control.....................................               90,890
        Total...............................  $92,510   $92,510
```

The transactions for the month were:

(1) Material costing $36,500 and with a standard cost of $37,900 was purchased.

(2) Material with a standard cost of $41,300 and an actual cost of $40,500 was put into process.

(3) Labor employed during the month at standard rates came to $28,400.

(4) The output transferred out of the department had the following standard costs:

```
Material.................................... $42,600
Labor......................................   28,300
```

(5) Finished goods with a standard cost of $79,200 were sold.

(6) The standard cost of the work in process at the end of the month was found by physical inventory to be:

```
Material.................................... $15,200
Labor......................................   11,000
```

(7) The payrolls paid during the month came to $32,180, and there were no unpaid wages as of the end of the month.

Open T-accounts for the balances at the start of the month, account for the month's transactions, and transfer all variances to a Variance Summary account. Indicate the nature of each variance and state whether it is favorable or unfavorable.

23. Eiseman, Inc., manufactures a line of children's sleds. It has a basic plan standard costing system in its factory. Materials price variances are separated at the time of purchase, and all materials inventories are costed at standard prices.

Factory overheads are regarded as wholly fixed and are charged to expense as incurred, without passing through the product inventory accounts Factory overhead is expected to total $69,000 a month.

Standard costs and production and inventory data for the four models manufactured in the sled department during September were:

	Model 3	Model 5	Model 22	Model 30
Standard cost per unit:				
Materials..............	$0.80	$1.20	$1.50	$2.00
Labor................	1.00	2.00	3.00	5.00
Total.............	$1.80	$3.20	$4.50	$7.00
Units completed...........	5,000	10,000	4,000	2,000
Units in process, Sept.1	None	1,000	None	200
Units in process, Sept. 30....	None	1,000	None	None

Units in process on any given date are assumed to be 100 percent complete as to materials and 50 percent complete as to labor.

The following transactions relate to the sled department during the month of September:

(1) Purchased materials on account (standard cost, $35,000): $35,400.
(2) Issued materials:
   Direct materials, at inventory cost, $24,300.
   Indirect materials, at inventory cost, $3,000.
(3) Payrolls are prepared and employees are paid at the end of each month for their entire month's work. Payroll for September (including indirect labor), $64,200.
(4) Direct labor hours, 23,800; standard wage rate, $2 an hour.
(5) Indirect labor, at standard wage rates: $20,000.
(6) Other factory overhead, paid in cash: $50,000.

a) Record the above information in appropriate T-accounts. Be sure to enter any opening balances.
b) Prepare a list of variances for the month, with titles that are sufficiently descriptive to identify the nature of each variance.

24. The Jiffy Dinner Company manufactures 15 types of frozen dinners. A standard menu priced at predetermined food prices, labor rates, and standard processing times for each operation is the basis for a standard cost system in which the entire plant is treated as one department.

Work in process is small, and subject to little fluctuation from one month to the next. Therefore, to avoid the job of counting and valuing it, the in-process inventory is assumed to be the same and equal to the following amounts at the end of each month:

Food, trays, etc., in process............................$18,000
Labor in process...................................... 3,000

Actual overhead is charged to expense each month and is not included in product cost.

The firm's factory account balances on April 1 were as follows:

Raw food and supplies......................	$ 33,000	
Food, trays, etc., in process.................	18,000	
Labor in process...........................	3,000	
Frozen dinners............................	67,000	
Accrued wages.............................		$ 1,800
Factory control............................		119,200
Total..............................	$121,000	$121,000

The transactions for the month were as follows:

(1) Food and supplies purchased: actual cost $73,000, and standard cost, $70,300.

(2) Direct labor cost: at standard wage rates, $26,400.

(3) Payrolls paid, $25,000; accrued wages as of the end of the month, $1,300.

(4) Actual overhead costs incurred, $42,000, including $4,000 of supplies at standard prices.

(5) Food, trays, and other direct material transferred out of the storeroom: standard cost, $63,000.

(6) Standard cost of frozen dinners produced:

Food, trays, etc................................	$60,200
Direct labor....................................	27,500
Total.....................................	$87,700

(7) Standard cost of dinners sold: $115,000.

a) Open T-accounts for the opening balances, account for the above transactions, and present the cost of goods sold including all variances. Identify the nature of each of your variances.

b) How would the cost of goods sold have been different if the company had measured its inventory on a Fifo actual cost basis?

25. The Glocken Steel Company has a standard cost system for direct labor and materials, the essentials of which as applied to the rolling mill are outlined below:

(1) The rolling mill is charged with:
   a) Ingots consumed at standard unit cost.
   b) Actual direct labor hours at standard rates.

(2) The rolling mill is credited with or "earns":
   a) Good product at standard unit cost.
   b) Scrap at $18 per ton.

(3) The standard labor and material cost per ton of good product for each type (size, thickness, chemistry) of steel rolled is arrived at as follows:
   a) The standard cost per ton of ingots is multiplied by the standard usage rate to obtain the gross material cost per ton of product. The standard scrap production per ton of good

product at $18 per ton is deducted from the gross material cost to obtain the net material cost.

b) The standard rolling time per ton of good product is multiplied by $37, the standard direct labor cost per hour of mill operation, to obtain the standard direct labor cost per ton of product.

c) The standard labor and material cost per ton of good product is the sum of (a) and (b).

(4) The mill's "profit" or "loss" on labor and material in any month is the difference between its earnings and its costs, as defined above.

The operating data for the 8th month (the mill uses a 13-month year of four weeks each) are given below:

(1) Ingots consumed: 13,000 tons; standard cost, $325,000.
(2) Actual direct labor hours at standard rates: $14,720.
(3) Good product at standard cost:

	Quantity	Cost
Material..........................	10,500 tons	$285,360
Labor............................	410 mill hours	15,170
Total.......................		$300,530

(4) Scrap production: 2,500 tons.
(5) Including downtime caused by production interruptions, the mill operated 400 hours. The downtime was 14 hours. The actual direct labor time listed in (2) above included the costs of labor crews made idle by machine downtime.

a) Prepare the transactions (in T-accounts) which show the mill's operations.

b) Prepare whatever reports and analyses you feel would be helpful to management in reviewing the mill's operations.

26. The Prentice Company manufactures two products in its Denver plant. The plant uses a standard cost system for direct labor and direct materials costs. Factory overhead costs are not taken into product costs and are not introduced into this problem in any way.

The factory contains two production departments, X and Y. Production on most products is initiated in department X and completed in department Y. Materials inventories are carried at standard cost. Each department has two work in process accounts—Materials in Process and Labor in Process. The standard cost of materials received by a department from the storeroom is charged to the Materials in Process account of that department. The standard labor and materials costs of the operations performed in department X are charged to the Materials in Process account of department Y at the time the semifinished goods are transferred from X to Y.

The standard costs for the two products are shown below. Note that operations and costs are listed in the order in which the work moves through the plant.

Product A: Standard cost per unit.

Operation	Department	Labor Cost	Materials from Storeroom	Cumulative Cost
14...............	X	$2.00	$5.00	$ 7.00
12...............	X	1.50	0.10	8.60
20...............	X	1.00	0.50	10.10
18...............	Y	3.00	...	13.10
32...............	Y	1.00	0.90	15.00

Product B: Standard cost per unit.

Operation	Department	Labor Cost	Materials from Storeroom	Cumulative Cost
11...............	X	$0.10	$0.30	$0.40
16...............	X	0.25	...	0.65
27...............	X	0.20	0.05	0.90
32...............	Y	0.05	0.05	1.00

The following data describe the financial aspects of the factory's operations during the month of July:

	Actual Prices	Standard Prices
(1) Materials received from suppliers and placed in storeroom..	$31,402	$30,100
(2) Materials issued from storeroom:		
To department X................................	xxx	20,530
To department Y................................	xxx	4,260
(3) Actual direct labor:		
Department X..................................	21,470	21,400
Department Y..................................	15,351	14,620

(4) Goods finished and transferred:

Product	From Dept. X to Dept. Y	From Dept. Y to Finished Goods
A................	3,100 units	3,000 units
B................	14,000 units	15,000 units

(5) Work in process, July 1:
    Department X: 200 units of product A, complete through operation 12.
    Department Y: 1,000 units of product B, complete through operation 27.
(6) Work in process, July 31:
    Department X: none.
    Department Y: 100 units of product A, complete through operation 18.

a) Prepare journal entries to record the month's transactions, including interdepartmental transfers.
b) Prepare a list of variances, indicating for each whether it is favorable or unfavorable and the level of management at which control responsibility is likely to lie.

Chapter 22

CONTROL OF FACTORY
OVERHEAD COSTS

As FACTORIES GROW in size and increase in complexity, direct labor and materials ordinarily account for an ever smaller percentage of total factory costs. The problem of controlling overhead therefore assumes greater and greater significance.

Overhead cost control is most commonly exercised with the aid of budgets—the amount of overhead planned for a given period of time. The objective of this chapter is to indicate how these budgets ought to be designed, how they might be integrated into a standard cost system, and what kinds of behavioral or nonaccounting issues are likely to be encountered along the way.

SEMIVARIABLE OVERHEAD BUDGETS

On a very fundamental level, the methods employed to control overhead are similar to those used to control direct costs. The accounting system is used to generate, for each department each accounting period, the actual overhead costs and what the overhead costs should have been during the period. As we saw in Chapter 18, however, overhead costs in the typical case are neither constant per unit of output nor constant in total. Under these circumstances, no one budget is applicable to all possible operating volumes; instead, a series of alternative budgets must be prepared, one for each possible level of operating volume. This series of budgets is known collectively as the *flexible budget* or *semivariable overhead budget*. The applicable budget in any given period is the specific budget for the level of output achieved during that period.

Structure of the Flexible Budget

An example of a flexible budget is shown in Exhibit 22–1. This shows the semivariable overhead budget for the molding department of the Lester Plastics Company. This department, consisting of 60 injection molding machines and certain auxiliary equipment, has a department head and a general foreman for each of the two shifts it operates. Each shift also has a section foreman who is responsible for supervising the operation of the department's manual machines. Supervision of the automatic machines is performed directly by the general foreman on the shift. In addition, the department has a maintenance foreman to keep the machines in operation and a material control foreman to keep the machines supplied with material and to inspect and move the finished product out of the molding room.

Exhibit 22–1

LESTER PLASTICS COMPANY, MOLDING DEPARTMENT

Manufacturing Overhead Budget

Item	Monthly Fixed Cost	Cost per Machine-Hour
Indirect labor:		
Foremen and section foremen................	$2,941	x
Floormen..................................	x	$0.390
Maintenance...............................	825	0.070
Material control and testing.................	1,000	0.023
Idle time..................................	x	0.043
Overtime premium.........................	x	0.050
Other direct charges:		
Employee benefits..........................	424	0.160
Indirect materials..........................	365	0.280
Machine setup.............................	530	0.025
Power.....................................	x	0.093
Depreciation...............................	695	x
Allocated service department costs.............	1,640	x
Total.................................	$8,420	$1.134

The first column of Exhibit 22–1 lists the categories into which the department's overhead is classified; the second column shows the monthly fixed costs for each of these overhead items; and the third gives the variable cost per hour of machine operation.[1] Machine-hours were selected as being the most accurate measure of production, on the basis of the criterion laid down in Chapter 18.

Notice that a linear cost/volume relationship is assumed in this case

---

[1] This budget is primarily for the use of the department head; to maintain secrecy, his salary is not charged to the department but is included in general factory overhead and allocated to the molding department with the costs of the service departments.

—that is, the cost budget can be represented on a chart by a straight line, fitting a formula in the form:

Budgeted Cost = Fixed Costs + Variable Cost per Unit × Volume.

As Exhibit 22–1 shows, the department's estimated fixed cost is $8,420 a month, while its variable cost is $1.134 per machine-hour. The total budgeted overhead cost at any level of output for any month is found by substituting the number of machine-hours operated during the month for MH in the equation,

Budgeted Cost = $8,420 + $1.134 × MH,

and solving for budgeted cost. For instance, in a month when 12,000 machine-hours are recorded, the budget in total will be:

Budgeted Cost = $8,420 + $1.134 × 12,000 = $22,028.

The budget for any of the individual overhead items may be found in the same way.

Although it is almost always used for simplicity in textbook illustrations, the linear form is not necessarily applicable in all cases. Budgeted overtime premium, for example, could be zero for all volumes up to 10,000 machine-hours a month, 50 cents an hour for the next 4,000 hours, and then $1.50 an hour for all hours in excess of 15,000. The flexible budget allowances should conform to the anticipated facts and need not be squeezed out of shape to conform to some universally applicable formula.

Defining the Cost Center

One of the most difficult problems in the design of a flexible budget system is to decide how finely the company's organization should be subdivided for the purpose of budget preparation and reporting. To illustrate the nature of this problem, let us turn temporarily away from the Lester Plastics Company and look at the organization structure of a more complex organization. Exhibit 22–2 presents a simplified organization chart for a steel plant. The plant is divided into three main production departments—blast furnaces, open-hearth furnaces, and rolling mills—plus four main administrative departments and a number of minor units identified in Exhibit 22–2 simply as "other" departments.

The exhibit shows part of the internal structure of the rolling mills. The rolling mills manager is responsible for three mills and a number of miscellaneous departments. The foreman of each mill, in turn, has overall responsibility for three departments: the soaking pits, the mill machine itself, and the inspection department.

One possibility is to prepare only one flexible budget for the plant as a whole. The plant's operations are so large and so heterogeneous that this solution will ordinarily be ruled out. At the other extreme, each organization unit could be designated a cost center, with a flexible budget and monthly cost reports. If these units are large enough, this will probably be done.

Exhibit 22–2
ILLUSTRATIVE ORGANIZATION CHART FOR A STEEL PLANT

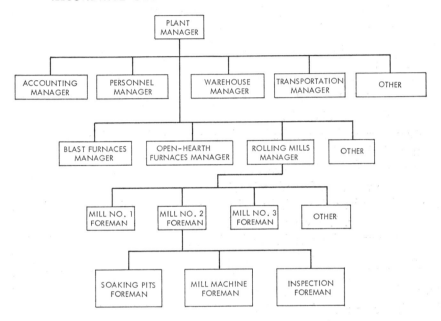

Establishing the soaking pit, mill machine, and inspection departments as cost centers does not eliminate the need for flexible budgets for mill No. 2 as a whole, for the rolling mills division, or for the entire plant. All overhead costs in mill No. 2 for which the three cost center foremen are not immediately responsible are the immediate responsibility of the foreman of mill No. 2. Every cost charged to the plant that is not classified as a direct cost must be classified as the responsibility of the manager or foreman of some cost center.

Sources of Cost Information

A variety of information sources are used to develop the budget amounts appearing in Exhibit 22–1. First, it is most helpful if the actual costs have been classified in the accounts in fine descriptive detail, since mere inspection of such data reveals many of the fixed costs. However, for certain of the variable and semivariable costs, engineering studies or statistical analyses of historical data obtained from the accounts must be used to establish the expected amounts at each level of output. Engineering studies may rely on informal observation or on very careful and extensive time studies. Analyses of historical data may rely on a very fine classification of costs and involve adjustments for changes in prices or production methods. The point at which increased effort ceases to pay off in greater accuracy is not easy to establish, but it cannot be ignored.

Another source of cost information which must be used for a number of reasons is the *cost center head*. Frequently, he is a valuable source of information on the variation of cost with output. In any event, he must feel that he has participated in arriving at the budget figures; he must understand how the figures were developed; and he must be satisfied that they are fair. Otherwise, the budget cannot be an effective control device.

As one goes through the list of departmental costs for the purpose of establishing what they should be at each level of output, one soon encounters costs which are determined by *management policy* and not by the volume of production. These costs, unlike direct labor and material, can be substantially reduced without forcing a reduction in current output. They are not reduced to their minimum, however, because they are incurred to maintain and strengthen the organization rather than to secure the current output. This is particularly true of staff activities such as personnel and industrial engineering; it is also true of line management, but to a lesser degree. Neither analysis of historical cost records nor time studies can establish what these costs should be at any given volume. Rather, it is the task of management to decide the extent to which it wishes to maintain the stability of the organization and the extent to which it wishes to secure variability in costs with output. In short, management sets the budget by *deciding* what these costs shall be at each level of output.

CONTROL REPORTING

Although preparation of the flexible budget has merit for its own sake, the primary payoff comes in periodic cost performance reporting. Some overhead cost reports are issued daily, some weekly, and some at longer intervals. A month is the typical reporting period for the main departmental cost summaries.

Departmental Overhead Cost Summaries

The monthly overhead cost summaries consist of *comparisons* of the actual costs for the month with the budget allowances appropriate to the volume actually achieved during the month. For example, the report shown in Exhibit 22–3 was issued to the head of the molding

Exhibit 22–3

LESTER PLASTICS COMPANY, MOLDING DEPARTMENT

Factory Overhead Cost Report

MONTHLY COST SUMMARY

Department   Molding   Month   October
Volume this month   14,300   machine-hours

Item	Budget	Actual	(Over) Under
Indirect labor:			
Foremen and section foremen...............	$ 2,941	$ 2,985	$ (44)
Floormen................................	5,577	6,442	(865)
Maintenance.............................	1,826	2,306	(480)
Material control and testing................	1,329	1,188	141
Idle time...............................	615	942	(327)
Overtime premium.......................	715	1,293	(578)
Other controllable direct charges:			
Employee benefits.......................	2,712	2,922	(210)
Indirect materials.......................	4,369	4,065	304
Machine setup..........................	887	851	36
Power.................................	1,330	1,283	47
Total Controllable Costs...............	$22,301	$24,277	$(1,976)
Noncontrollable costs:			
Depreciation...........................	695	705	(10)
Allocated service department costs...........	1,640	1,640	..
Total Department Costs...............	$24,636	$26,622	$(1,986)

department, covering his department's operations for the month of October. During this month, the department operated at a volume of 14,300 machine-hours. This figure, applied to the budget formulas of Exhibit 22–2, provides the budget allowances shown in the "budget" column of Exhibit 22–3. Except for the allocated service department costs, the costs in the actual column are those recorded in the departmental accounts on the basis of requisitions, time tickets, and the like.

The differences between actual costs and the flexible budget allowances are most commonly referred to as *spending variances,* although other terms such as *budget variances* and *performance variances* are also used.

The Controllability Criterion

The comparisons in Exhibit 22–3 are with the flexible budget allowances rather than with a budget that is independent of the month's output. The reason is that cost is *expected* to vary with output. The department head is not expected to operate at average normal cost when volume is far in excess of normal. Conversely, a fixed budget is likely to be too "loose" when volume is less than normal.

The department head's interest in this report centers on those items that he can influence. Notice that the costs charged to the molding department in Exhibit 22–3 are classified into controllable and noncontrollable costs. Service department allocations in this case are entirely predetermined, and thereby produce no spending variance. Depreciation, on the other hand, was $10 higher than the budget allowed. Because the department head cannot influence this cost, it is shown "below the line" as a noncontrollable spending variance.

Following Up the Reports

Cost reports of this type are only the first step in effective responsive control. Although the advantage of the flexible budget is that it adjusts the cost standard to current volume conditions, it cannot allow for changes in other factors such as wage rates, purchase prices, or manufacturing methods. Furthermore, management may deliberately incur excessive costs when volume is changing rapidly, to avoid even greater cost penalties in future periods.

The issuance of the report should be followed, therefore, by an attempt to identify the causes of major deviations. Whenever the deviations are unfavorable and the causes are controllable, corrective action should be initiated; other portions of the deviation are likely to call for replanning the future.

Spending Variance versus Total Variance

Even though the costs of every department may be *less* than its flexible budget allowance, the company may be losing money because overhead costs are too *high*. The reason for this seeming contradiction is that the budget is based on actual output, while the prices of the company's products are usually set to cover overhead costs at normal output. Hence, if output is low, overhead costs may be low for that level of output but high in relation to the revenue from the sale of that output.

It will be recalled from Chapter 18 that two overhead cost figures enter the departmental accounts: the actual costs and the amount absorbed by production. The difference between these two figures is the amount of overhead over- or underabsorbed, also known as the total overhead variance. The flexible budget allowance was introduced to divide the total variance into two components: a volume variance and a spending variance. It is this volume variance which can convert favorable cost control performance into unprofitable operations.

Thus, although the volume variance is not within the control of the department head, it cannot be ignored. It must be included in any internal profit reporting at higher levels, where responsibility for volume and profit is lodged. This will be discussed briefly later in the chapter.

Interdepartmental Cost Allocations

Production department burden rates, it will be recalled from Chapter 18, often include allowances for service department costs. Service cost allocations are also made after the fact in many cases, and thus appear on the overhead cost reports of the production departments.

In Exhibit 22–3, for example, the final line item showed allocated service department costs of $1,640 for the month of October. This was shown "below the line," as a noncontrollable item, exactly equal to the budget. In other words, the allocation method adopted by the Lester Plastics Company insures that no variance is ever reported in this item. The method is to charge production departments each month for a fixed amount of service department costs, exactly equal to the amount budgeted at the start of the year.

This should not be interpreted to mean that service cost allocations must always be equal to budget. If a department's use of a service department's services is variable, management may wish the cost records to reflect the history of service usage by each department. Furthermore, a charge for service should be made if the department's consumption is to some extent controllable by the department head. In the latter situation, however, the services should be billed to the department at a predetermined price; the production department manager cannot control the unit cost of operating the service department, and his charge for services should vary only as a result of variations in service quantities.

CONTROL OF OVERHEAD UNDER STANDARD COSTING

A company which uses standard costing for its direct labor and materials is likely to develop standard product costs for its factory overhead, too. Like standard labor and materials costs, the total standard overhead cost for a period is proportional to the amount of physical output. For example, if standard overhead cost is $2 a unit, the total standard overhead cost will be $2,000 if 1,000 units are manufactured and $4,000 if 2,000 units are produced.

Actual overhead costs will not be proportional to output, however, and therefore standard overhead cost cannot be used as an aggregate cost standard for cost control reporting. Instead, departmental flexible budgets must be used, no less than in a factory which does not use standards for its direct costs.

Selection of the Volume Index

The new problem that is introduced by the existence of a standard costing system is whether to base the flexible budget allowances on the actual inputs for the period or on the standard inputs.

For example, suppose that the standard burden rate is $3 per direct labor dollar. During March, the department turns out production with a total standard direct labor cost of $20,000; actual direct labor cost amounts to $21,000. The question is whether overhead cost performance should be judged against a budget appropriate to a volume of $20,000 labor cost or $21,000.

The answer to this question depends on the answer to another: do overhead costs vary with *actual* input or with *standard* input? If overhead costs are governed by actual inputs, then the appraisal standard should be the flexible budget allowances appropriate to the actual inputs. Otherwise, the allowances should be based on standard inputs.

Calculating the Spending Variances

Suppose for a moment that the cost of the Lester Plastics Company's molding department is expected to vary with the number of *standard* machine-hours and that the department's output for the month of October had a standard machine-hour content of 14,000 machine-hours. The budget allowance can be computed by inserting this figure in the formula implicit in Exhibit 22–1:

$$\text{Budgeted Overhead} = \$8,420 + \$1.134 \times 14,000$$
$$= \$24,296 .$$

The spending variance will be as follows:

Actual costs (at 14,000 standard machine-hours, from Exhibit 22–3).......$ 26,622
Overhead costs budgeted at 14,000 standard machine-hours.............   24,296
    Spending Variance...$ (2,326)

Suppose, however, that overhead costs are expected to vary with the number of *actual* machine-hours. Under these circumstances, the spending variance will be computed exactly as if the company had no standard costs at all, using the figures developed in Exhibit 22–3:

Actual overhead costs (at 14,300 actual machine-hours, from
    Exhibit 22–3)..$ 26,622
Overhead costs budgeted at 14,300 machine-hours (from formula and
    Exhibit 22–3)..   24,636
    Spending Variance...$ (1,986)

The difference between these two figures ($2,326 — $1,986) is $340. If overhead costs do in fact vary with *actual* machine-hours, then this measures the effect of inefficient machine usage on overhead cost. It can be called a *machine efficiency variance*. (If volume were measured in terms of labor hours or labor cost, it would be called a *labor efficiency variance*.) In other words, the department used 300 more machine-hours than the standards called for (14,300 — 14,000 = 300). Each machine-hour leads to additional spending of $1.134. The total effect of the excess machine utilization, therefore, was 300 × $1.134 = $340.

Overhead Absorption under Standard Costing

The application of standard product costing to overhead costs changes the basis on which overhead costs are absorbed by production. The total amount of overhead absorbed is computed by multiplying the number of *standard* machine-hours by the burden rate.

For example, suppose that normal volume in the molding department is 20,000 machine-hours a month. The burden rate is:

$$\text{Burden Rate} = \frac{\$8,420 + \$1.134 \times 20,000}{20,000}$$
$$= \$1.555 \text{ per Machine-hour.}$$

The total amount absorbed during October, therefore, was:

Amount Absorbed ("Earned") = 14,000 × $1.555 = $21,770.

The actual number of machine-hours used has no relevance of any kind to this calculation and should be ignored.

The Volume Variance

Calculation of the volume variance under standard costing is simple. It is the difference between the amount *earned* (standard overhead cost of the actual output—specifically, the burden rate times standard machine-hours) and the flexible budget allowances at earned volume. In this example, the calculation is as follows:

Overhead costs earned at 14,000 standard machine-hours	$21,770
Overhead costs budgeted at 14,000 standard machine-hours (from formula above)	24,296
Volume Variance	$(2,526)

The Total Variance

These figures can be put together in a single summary such as the following:

(1)	Actual overhead costs	$26,622	
(2)	Overhead costs budgeted at 14,000 standard machine-hours	24,296	
(3)	Spending variance ([1] − [2])		$(2,326)
(4)	Standard overhead costs earned	21,770	
(5)	Volume variance ([2] − [4])		(2,526)
(6)	Total Variance ([1] − [4])		$(4,852)

The spending variance can then be subdivided into two components—a machine efficiency variance and a residual spending variance—if actual overhead costs are a function of actual machine-hours instead of standard or earned machine-hours.

Accounting Entries

The entries to recognize standard overhead costs add little to the previous discussion of standard costing and can be summarized quickly. Actual costs are recorded in departmental accounts, as before:

Factory Overhead—Molding	26,622	
Various Accounts (Accounts Payable, etc.)		26,622

The amount earned is charged to the departmental overhead in process account:

Overhead in Process—Molding	21,770	
Factory Overhead—Molding		21,770

The balance in the Factory Overhead—Molding account is thus the total overhead variance for the month. No overhead variance enters the overhead in process account. Furthermore, the figure obtained by multiplying actual machine-hours by the burden rate has no meaning in this system and *should not be calculated or recorded in the accounts.*

Some firms consider it desirable to incorporate in the accounts a breakdown of a department's over- or underabsorbed burden into its component variances. In that event, the $4,852 balance in the Factory Overhead—Molding account would be closed out with the following entry.

Spending Variance—Molding.............................2,326
Volume Variance—Molding...............................2,526
    Factory Overhead—Molding........................... 4,852

As discussed earlier, this provides higher levels of management with an analysis of how volume as well as performance have influenced overhead costs.

Finally, the overhead in process account must be credited for the standard overhead cost of any products completed by the molding department during the month and transferred to other departments or to finished goods inventory. For example, suppose that the molding department finished and transferred to the finishing department products with a standard molding department overhead cost of $21,000, standard materials cost of $33,000, and standard direct labor cost of $10,000. The entry would be:

Materials in Process—Finishing.........................64,000
    Materials in Process—Molding...................... 33,000
    Labor in Process—Molding.......................... 10,000
    Overhead in Process—Molding....................... 21,000

These cost flows are represented schematically in Exhibit 22–4. The difference between the actual overhead costs charged to a department during a period and the absorbed cost is the over- or under-

Exhibit 22–4

SIMPLIFIED T-ACCOUNT MODEL OF OVERHEAD COST FLOWS UNDER A STANDARD COST SYSTEM

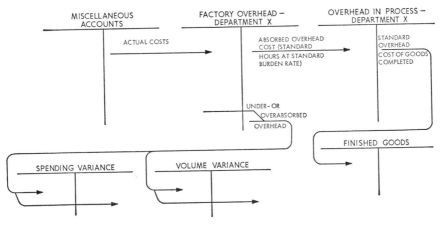

absorbed overhead, and it is closed out to the appropriate variance accounts on the basis of the analysis discussed above. The absorbed cost is the standard hours of the production for the period, costed at the standard overhead rate per hour. Overhead in process is charged with this amount and credited with the standard overhead cost of the goods completed.[2] The balance in the account is the standard overhead cost of the goods in process. These overhead accounts may be related to the other accounts in a standard cost system by referring back to Exhibit 21-4. The Factory Overhead—Department X and Overhead in Process—Department X accounts are analogous to the Accrued Labor and Labor in Process accounts.

BEHAVIORAL ISSUES IN COST CONTROL SYSTEMS

The purely accounting problems involved in the design and use of semivariable budgets for the control of overhead are small in comparison with the behavioral or human relations problems in employing such systems to aid management control of large organizations. Furthermore, it will be seen in the discussion which follows that the behavioral and organization problems that arise with semivariable budgets are also encountered with standard costs.

Organizational Classification of Costs

The most difficult task in the adoption of semivariable overhead budgets is the assignment of each overhead cost to a cost center. The objective is to develop an *organizational classification of costs* in which those costs charged to a cost center and included in the supervisor's budget are in fact the costs for which he may be held responsible. A cardinal rule in management is that a department head cannot be held responsible for personnel not under his supervision or for material or services that he has not requisitioned. For example, if men and material under the supervision of Jones are employed to provide a service used by Smith, Smith cannot be held responsible for the cost of providing the service. He may be held responsible for the usage of the service, but the primary point for control of the cost is Jones.

However, embarking on a classification of overhead costs with this rule in mind, one typically encounters the following situation. An organization chart, such as Exhibit 22-2 and its supporting manual,

---

[2] These two figures will differ by the change in overhead in process during the period. With $22,770 charged to and $21,000 credited to overhead in process, the standard overhead cost of the production during the period was greater than the standard overhead cost of the output transferred to finished goods.

specifies lines of responsibility and authority in a company, but the actual authority and responsibility relations as they are perceived and practiced in the company will typically depart in significant respects from the formal organization structure. Furthermore, the existing classification of overhead costs in the accounts may be motivated by the objective of dealing with the accounting problems of absorbing overhead costs into inventory accounts, and it typically bears little relation to the formal or the effective organization structure.

The circumstances just described cannot be blamed on management incompetence in establishing an organization structure. Rather, organization charts such as Exhibit 22–2 are a gross oversimplification of reality. Even the plant manager has more than one boss, and to represent the connection between a staff worker or a department manager and other personnel in a company one would have to draw a number of lines upward, laterally, and at various angles. Furthermore, it is remarkable how many people in a plant work with everyone and are responsible to no one but the plant manager.

Notwithstanding the complexities of organizational relationships, one must follow the rule stated earlier of assigning each cost to the individual with the day-to-day responsibility for requisitioning the material or supervising the personnel. For instance, maintenance material and personnel under the supervision of the maintenance manager are charged to him notwithstanding the fact that the work is done for the managers of other departments and that they have considerable influence on the level of maintenance costs.

The behavioral problem involved in organizational classification of costs is to insure that all levels of management recognize that (1) a department manager is not *solely* responsible for the costs assigned to him, and (2) he is not *without* responsibility for the costs. At the same time management must recognize that the employment of budgetary control systems is consistent with a middle ground between these two extreme reactions to the dilemma of responsibility in a complex interrelated organization.

Level of Budgetary Control

How far down in the organization should budgets be carried as an instrument of control? Using the molding department of the Lester Plastics Company as an illustration, the department as a whole may be treated as one cost center; alternatively, its two machine groups, each with two shifts, may be made four separate cost centers. The questions at issue are the following: Does the department head's day-to-day contact with the foremen provide adequate control over their areas, or is control and cost consciousness better served by putting each of the four foremen in direct contact with the budget? Can the foremen operate from a budget, or is their ability limited to dealing with men and material, i.e., do budgets confuse and frighten them?

Since the variation in costs with output may differ between the two machine groups, or even between the two shifts of one machine group, budgets on the foreman's level may be more accurate. However, certain manufacturing costs, such as the maintenance men, are common to the whole department. Therefore, the maintenance men would have to be split into four groups, which may not be economical, or they would have to remain the responsibility of the department head. In short, the overhead costs directly chargeable to each foreman and not common to the whole department may not be important enough to warrant the additional bookkeeping and other costs necessary to bring the budget down to the foreman's level.

Quite often the issue is resolved by a form of passing the buck. The manager at each level decides that he will meet the budget his superior gives him by converting it into a set of budgets for his subordinates. The buck-passing ends with the front-line foremen. If they are unable or unwilling to assume the responsibilities thrust upon them, the system collapses. A responsive control system is effective only to the extent that subordinates accept the responsibilities placed on them.

Development of Standards

The discussion of standard cost systems in Chapter 21 said little on the subject of how one goes about arriving at standards for labor and material. As stated there, the expected wage rates and cost price per unit as of the start of the year are used for standard material prices and standard wage rates. However, the problem of standard usage rates is not so easily disposed of. The discussion of this subject is also relevant to the problem of developing semivariable overhead budgets.

On initial installation of a standard cost system, a firm may use its historical job cost data, if these are reasonably well organized, to establish standard allowances for the material and labor content of each product. It is wise to supplement, or at least to check, such figures by consultation with production people in each department. Since the typical firm has developed and used this kind of product cost information for pricing purposes, it is usually readily available, and no great outlay of time and money is therefore needed to formulate workable standards.

However, the functions of a system based on such crude standards should be limited to reducing bookkeeping costs and shortening the time required for producing operating statements. Since many firms are well satisfied with systems which accomplish no more, one should not underestimate the practical importance of these objectives. As evidence of how little by way of accuracy may be required, some firms find it possible to revise standards as infrequently as once in five years. In such cases, top management continues to rely on observation and personal contact with department heads for incentives and control.

Once a standard cost system is installed, however, actual costs may no longer be classified by jobs, and job cost sheets can no longer be used to provide information on the cost of a product. The material and labor usage variances for each department, which are generated by the system in operation, tell management where the standards are unrealistic and require improvement, but they do not identify the products that are out of line.

When the variances in a department are persistently large and in one direction, or when the department head complains about certain of his standards, better figures are probably needed. One means of developing these is to accumulate job costs *for that department*. For the length of time needed to obtain accurate information on labor and material usage for each product, a job cost system is used in the department, and care is taken to insure that the costs are charged to the jobs as accurately as possible. For instance, if variances in the molding department of the Lester Plastics Corporation are found to be large, the *actual labor and material quantities* charged to the department *at standard rates* are classified by jobs and the job cost sheets are then analyzed to establish actual usage rates on each product. The resultant information is more accurate and less expensive than data obtained by collecting job costs at actual prices for all products in all departments. As standards become obsolete because of changes in equipment or production methods or both, new standards may be developed in this manner.

So far, no mention has been made of the use of industrial engineering techniques for the development and maintenance of standards. These methods are generally considered the most accurate, and some firms bring in a battery of engineers to establish standards when they install a system. This is, however, both an expensive and a potentially dangerous approach to the problem. It is dangerous because the large outlay to develop accurate standards tends to generate false expectations with respect to what the system will accomplish for management. Experience indicates that the cost of time studying an operation *for the purpose of developing a standard* is rarely justified by the resultant benefits. Consequently, it is coming to be generally accepted that industrial engineering studies should be undertaken *for the purpose of discovering improved methods of production.* When studies are made for this purpose, accurate usage standards can be obtained as a by-product at little additional cost. Also, the reduction in bookkeeping costs accomplished through the adoption of standard costing can be used to expand the resources available for engineering studies aimed directly at cost reduction.

In other words, it is the authors' opinion that the adoption of a standard cost system will better precede than follow intensive work methods analysis. On installation of the system, existing information can be used to set temporary standards. Subsequently, the variances produced by the system in operation, the complaints of department heads, and the introduction of new operating methods will indicate to management which standards should be reviewed for possible revision. The improvement of usage standards should be a continuous process involving some combination of two methods: (1) accounting analyses of actual labor and material usage on jobs accomplished by taking samples of job costs (actual quantities at standard prices) as described above; and (2) industrial engineering studies undertaken primarily for the purpose of discovering better production methods. It follows, of course, that variances from standard costs must be used cautiously in evaluating performance until the standards have been proved reasonably accurate.

Accuracy Required for Control

The big question now arises. What level of accuracy in standards is necessary to allow a management to use the system to control and evaluate performance? A management sometimes asks this question with another in mind, which is: What must we do in developing standards so that when a variance appears we know that the department head and not the standard is at fault? Unfortunately, standards of such accuracy are practically impossible.

For example, material usage and time standards may be very carefully developed for a steel mill's blast furnace department, which uses iron ore, coal, and limestone to make iron. Nevertheless, if the purchasing department buys ore with a different iron content or coal of a different grade from that assumed in the standard, usage variances will appear which are not due to the department's performance. While it is not likely to be economical to do so, the firm may develop and use standards for every possible combination of grades of ore, coal, and limestone. Even so, the objective, elimination of all variances caused by reasons beyond the department head's control, is still not attained. Shutting down and reheating a blast furnace is very expensive, and iron must be delivered hot to the open-hearth furnaces. Consequently, the former operate continuously, and fluctuations in the demand for iron at the open hearths is adjusted for by tapping the blast furnaces more or less frequently. The costs of production, and hence the blast furnace variances, will therefore depend in part on the stability of operations in later departments and, finally, on the stability of the demand for the mill's end products.

Consider now a rolling mill which receives steel ingots from the open hearths and rolls them into slabs. The standard rolling time and the "yield" (percentage of the ingot tons not scrapped) will depend on the chemistry of the steel, the width and thickness of the slab to be produced, and the efficiency of the mill. Accordingly, a standard is set up for each dimension of the product and for each type of mill on which it may be rolled. The difference between the standard cost under normal conditions and the standard cost under the nonstandard conditions may be charged to a nonstandard methods variance account. However, the rolling time per ton and the yield will also vary with the size of the ingot. Further, the temperature of the ingot when it arrives at the mill (depending in turn on the transit time) and the quality of the ingot will materially influence the yield of good steel. Both of these causes of variance are beyond the control of the rolling mill superintendent, and it is not feasible to set a standard for each possible value of these variables.

In short, variances will appear which are due to (1) incorrect standards, (2) nonstandard conditions which can be allowed for only by making the system unduly complex and costly, (3) nonstandard conditions which arise from poor performance in other departments, as well as to (4) the performance of the department in whose account the variance appears. Variances for reasons other than department performance will depend in part on the resources devoted to obtaining accurate standards and in part on the complexity and interdependence of the manufacturing operations.

A firm may try to establish an allowance for every nonstandard condition with the objective of charging each variance from the basic standard to an appropriately designated account; but the implication of the above discussion is that regardless of the pains taken, it will be impractical in most cases to devise a system which clearly and exactly segregates all performance variances by cause.

It does not, however, follow from this fact that the causes for variance must remain open to question. When the standards are reasonable representations of efficiency under normal conditions, the system is an effective automatic device for advising management when costs are deviating from plan. As long as variances are small, while costs may not be at the absolute minimum, neither are they such as to jeopardize overall objectives, and top management may safely leave the control of production to subordinates. When large variances appear, management itself must find the reasons and decide on the corrective action. As previously noted, however, the account in which the variance appears is a good indication of where to start the investigation.

Here again it should be emphasized that a standard cost system serves control objectives in the broader sense through the incentives it creates for cost reduction. Under actual costing, a department head may be strongly motivated to reduce costs only if he feels that his superior knows enough of his department to recognize when costs are lower than they might otherwise be. Under a standard cost system, improved performance is called to the attention of his superior through favorable variances or reductions in unfavorable variances. Because variances are imperfect measures of performance, relating automatic bonuses and like rewards to their magnitude is usually poor policy. However, variances properly interpreted by management should be given considerable weight in the evaluation of a subordinate's performance, and by this means can serve as a powerful stimulant to cost control and reduction efforts at the lower echelons.

Finally, when evaluation of his performance rests in considerable measure on cost reports, a department head is more likely to become fully aware of all the factors which influence the apparent costs of his operations. Accepting credit for a favorable variance is far more pleasant than explaining away an unfavorable one. Hence, he becomes interested in what goes on outside of his own area with the object of securing the cooperation of other departments in avoiding practices which increase his costs. The department head in a large company may thus become more of a businessman and less of a bureaucrat.

It is seen then that there is no simple answer to the question originally posed: How accurate must standards be to serve as a control device? The accuracy to be sought will depend on what management expects of and needs from the system, how far the company has already gone in developing standards and in understanding how to use the information, and other similar qualitative considerations. It may be concluded, however, that *no standards can be accurate enough to relieve management of the job of managing.*

SUMMARY

This chapter concludes our discussion of the use of accounting data in factory cost control. The main tools for this purpose are standard product costs of materials and labor inputs, and flexible budgets for factory overhead costs. These tools are used widely in connection with manufacturing operations, but also have some application in nonmanufacturing activities.

Although standard costing can be adopted without standard overhead costs, and flexible budgets can be used without a tie-in to product cost absorption, integrating the product-costing and cost-control elements of the accounting system has advantages that are usually deemed adequate to justify the cost. In this chapter, how this integration takes place and what kinds of additional information it provides have been indicated. No attempt has been made to analyze this information in any depth, which is left for more advanced study, but a number of practical problems that are encountered in developing accounting information for control have been discussed.

QUESTIONS AND PROBLEMS

1. Should the overhead volume variance be reported to the department foremen? Explain.

2. The budget director of one company stated: "The front-line foreman is the man who actually incurs costs, and to achieve control we must carry the budget right down to him." Discuss.

3. "Incorporating the semivariable overhead cost budget in the accounts involves complicated and unnecessary bookkeeping." Discuss.

data for the overhead budget may be obtained?
4. What are the sources of information and methods by which the cost

5. How frequently should actual and budgeted costs be reported to management?

6. Does the use of departmental burden rates provide data that will help plant management control factory costs? Explain.

7. "The performance of a department in controlling overhead is measured satisfactorily by the over- or underabsorbed burden account." Discuss.

8. Standard overhead cost per unit of product is not used in departmental cost control. Why is it computed?

9. "Industrial engineering studies are too expensive to be used solely for setting cost standards." Discuss.

10. The volume variance arises because actual volume differs from normal or estimated volume, but it does not equal this volume difference multiplied by the burden rate. Explain why this is the case.

11. Should flexible budget allowances be based on the quantity of departmental output or on some measure of departmental input such as actual labor hours? Discuss.

12. How does the use of semivariable overhead budgets realize the objectives of the "management by exception" principle?

13. What use is a semivariable overhead budget if a department's performance variance is due to factors beyond the department head's control?

14. The Sanders Electronics Company issues monthly cost reports to the head of each department. No detailed breakdown of costs is provided; each department head is merely notified of his total costs for the month, his budget, and the difference between the two. In support of this practice, the company's president stated: "We don't want our people to be pencil pushers. If costs are out of line, we expect them to know enough about their operations to find out what is wrong and to do something about it." Discuss this statement.

15. The foreman of producing department A is concerned about a report on his control of overhead costs. "Look here," he says—

	Allowed	*Actual*
June......................	$15,500	$15,500

"I suppose I should be happy because the report shows no difference from budget, but I remember the original budget for overhead for June showed $12,500 and that would mean I'm over. I sneaked up to the accounting department—a fellow I bowl with works there—and saw the overhead accounts. They show overhead incurred $15,500 but overhead applied $17,500 which is even more confusing to me. I know my department produced 7,000 units of product. Here are the same figures last month—

	Allowed	Actual
May	$12,500	$12,500

"The overhead incurred was $12,500 and the overhead applied was $12,500 and our production was 5,000 units. Maybe that 2,000 units has something to do with it, but I sure can't tell."

a) What is the explanation of the $2,000 overapplied overhead?
b) What is the explanation of the $15,500 allowed for June?

16. "Whadda ya mean, I'm over my budget?" said Bob Dietz, shop foreman. "It says right here in the annual budget that my regular monthly indirect labor allowance is $3,300. You made up the budget, not me. I only spent $3,200, so where do you get off telling me I'm $200 over? Maybe it's those birds up in the accounting department, fouling me up again."

a) As Dietz's boss, how would you explain the situation to him? Was he right? Should he have had an allowance of $3,300?
b) If Dietz is typical of the shop foremen, what do you think should be done to strengthen the factory's overhead cost control system?

17. The Cotton Company uses a standard cost system and develops volume and spending variances on its overhead costs. You are given the following information for one of its departments: (1) the opening balance of Overhead in Process was $6,680; (2) the actual overhead for the month was $17,400; (3) the overhead budget is $4,680 per month plus $1.15 per direct labor hour; (4) the normal level of production is 9,000 direct labor hours; (5) during the month, the department worked 10,800 direct labor hours, but the standard labor content of the materials transferred out of the department was only 10,500 hours; and (6) the standard labor content of the work in process at the start of the month was 4,000 hours and at the end 3,600 hours.

Costs are expected to vary with output rather than with actual direct labor hours.

a) What was the amount of overhead cost earned by this department during the month?
b) What is the correct month-end balance in the Overhead in Process account?

c) Develop the department's overhead cost variances for the month, in as much detail as you deem appropriate.

*18. For each of the following, compute the number of hours on which flexible budget allowances should be based:

a) A job order cost system is used. The department's budget is based on actual machine-hours. The work completed by the department and transferred out of the department during the month had a machine-hour content of 15,000 machine-hours. Job orders in process in the department at the beginning of the month had already accumulated 3,000 machine-hours in previous months. Some 1,400 machine-hours had been accumulated on job orders still in process in the department at the end of the month.

b) A standard cost system is used. The department's budget is based on standard labor hours. Normal volume for the department is 20,000 standard labor hours per month, and the burden rate is $3 per standard labor hour. During the month, 21,300 actual labor hours were worked. The department finished and transferred to other departments during the month products with a standard overhead cost in this department of $69,000. The standard departmental overhead cost of work in process was $16,200 on the first of the month and $18,000 at the end of the month. Overhead cost fluctuations correlate more closely with product output than with direct labor input.

19. The Dearborn Company manufactures product X in standard batches of 100 units. A standard cost system is in use. The standard costs for a batch are as follows:

Direct materials—60 pounds at $0.45 per pound.....$ 27.00
Direct labor—36 hours at $2.15 per hour........... 77.40
Overhead—36 direct labor hrs. at $2.75 per hour.... 99.00
Total Standard Cost per Batch................$203.40

Dearborn's normal monthly output is 240 batches (24,000 units). Factory fixed costs are budgeted at $4,752 a month.

The Dearborn Company's new president is worried by the size of the factory overhead costs, which make up almost half of the standard costs of product X. Accordingly, when he found that the actual overhead cost for April was down to $2.60 per actual direct labor hour, he felt somewhat encouraged.

Actual production in April amounted to 210 batches. Actual overhead cost totaled $20,592. Variable overhead costs vary with the actual number of direct labor hours.

a) Should Dearborn's president be encouraged by the reduction in aver-

---

* Solutions to problems marked with an asterisk (*) are found in Appendix B.

age overhead cost? Prepare an analysis of the overhead costs in April
that will help him understand the causes of the reduction.

b) Would average overhead cost per direct labor hour be a useful index
of production efficiency for the factory manager? For the president?
Comment.

20. Department X is a factory service department. It provides labor
services, on request, to all other factory departments.

Department X's flexible budget for overhead costs is $5,000 a month
plus $4 per man-hour of service provided to other departments. Its normal
volume is 5,000 man-hours a month.

Department A is a factory production department. Its normal monthly
volume is 20,000 machine-hours. Its flexible budget includes a provision
for department X services: 100 service man-hours a month plus one man-
hour for every 50 department A machine-hours.

Each month, the factory accountants find department X's actual cost
per service man-hour. Department A is then charged for its use of department X by multiplying this actual unit cost by the number of department
X man-hours used in department A during the month.

During the month of June, department X recorded 4,500 man-hours, of
which 500 were charged to department A. Operating costs in department
X for the month totaled $24,300. Department A recorded 20,500 machine-
hours during the month.

a) What purpose, if any, is served by allocating service department costs
to other departments? Is this likely to be a valid purpose in this case?

b) Develop a department A budget formula from which flexible budget
allowances, in dollars, can be derived for department A's consumption
of department X services.

c) Compute the amount of department X cost charged to department A
for the month of June and compare this with the flexible budget
allowance for department A derived from (b) above.

d) Analyze the costs of department X and explain the reasons for the
deviation between the allocated and budgeted cost.

e) Suggest a way or ways by which the company's interdepartmental
service cost allocation method could be improved.

21. A standard costing system is in use and standard factory overhead
cost is $2 per direct labor hour. Overhead costs vary with the number of
actual direct labor hours, according to the following formula:

Budgeted Costs = $11,000 per Month + $0.90 per Direct Labor Hour.

Actual overhead costs for October totaled $22,140, at an operating
volume of 11,200 direct labor hours. Product standard cost and actual
production volumes for October were:

Product	Standard Overhead Cost per Unit	Units Produced, October
A..............	$ 5	100
B..............	6	500
C..............	10	1,000
D..............	3	1,200
E..............	2	2,000

a) Compute the total overhead variance, an overhead spending variance, a labor efficiency variance, and an overhead volume variance for the month. Indicate in each case whether the variance is favorable or unfavorable.

b) How, if at all, should the labor efficiency variance and volume variance be reported to management? To what management level would you report them?

22. The Kwikbilt Company manufactures portable screened enclosures for use by summer campers. It has two models, with the following standard costs:

	Model 14	Model 22
Materials...............	$12	$16
Labor..................	18	20

Factory overhead is not charged to individual products on a monthly basis; instead, actual factory overhead is compared with flexible budget allowances each month. The flexible budget allowance is determined from the formula:

Budget = $6,500 + $1 per Standard Labor Dollar Earned.

Factory output during the month of May consisted of 400 units of model 14 and 250 units of model 22. There was no work in process at either the beginning or the end of the month.

The following transactions took place during the month of May:

```
Materials purchased:
    Standard price.......................$ 9,000
    Actual price.........................  9,700
Materials issued (at standard)............  8,500
Labor cost:
    Standard wage rate...................  13,000
    Actual wage rates....................  13,200
Factory overhead cost...................... 21,000
```

The company's factory cost accounts conform to the system described in the last two chapters.

a) Prepare journal entries to record all of the month's transactions.

b) Prepare a list of factory cost variances, indicating for each whether it is favorable or unfavorable.

*23. The Omega Desk Company manufactures one type of desk for office use. At a production of 50,000 direct labor hours, which is considered normal, the overhead costs are expected to be $20,000.

The standard costs for the desk are:

Material:
    30 square feet of lumber at $0.80.........$24.00
Labor:
    10 hours at $1.75...................... 17.50
Overhead:
    10 hours at $0.40...................... 4.00
        Total Standard Cost................$45.50

The chief accountant has calculated a semivariable budget for overhead. This budget may be represented by the equation.

$$O.H. = \$8,000 + \$2.40 \times A.D.$$

$O.H.$ = overhead, and $A.D.$ = all desks produced. The latter includes firsts, seconds and equivalent complete units of work in process.

Some of the desks manufactured cannot be sold as firsts, and they are accounted for as follows. Work in Process is credited with the standard cost of firsts on all desks, but the offsetting debits for seconds are:

Finished goods—seconds.............$35.00 per desk
Loss on seconds.................... 10.50 per desk

The Loss on Seconds is an overhead account, and the overhead budget includes a standard allowance for this expense.

The transactions for the month of May are:

(1) Material purchased: 200,000 square feet at $0.77 ....$154,000
(2) Material requisitioned: 180,000 square feet.
(3) Labor: 53,500 hours at $1.80 ....$96,300
(4) In addition to the loss on seconds the overhead costs are:

Depreciation....................$ 1,000
Power and light.................. 2,500
Taxes......................... 750
Supplies...................... 8,250
Insurance..................... 500
Salaries...................... 7,500
        Total....................$20,500

(5) Production for the month was: 4,800 firsts, 300 seconds, and 600 units in process with all material applied and two-thirds completed with respect to labor and overhead. There was no beginning inventory of work in process.

a) Journalize the company's transactions for the month. On direct costs pick up the price variances on purchases and the quantity variances on production. On overhead pick up whatever variances you consider useful.

b) Briefly explain the meaning of each of your overhead variance accounts.

*24. M. B. Valence, Inc., uses a standard costing system in one of its manufacturing plants. Materials price variances are isolated at the time of purchase. Each department's work in process accounts are charged with actual quantities of labor and materials used, at standard wage rates and materials prices. These accounts are credited with the standard cost of the department's output. Variances are accumulated and reported monthly, and at the end of each month work in process inventories are restated at standard cost. Standard materials prices include an allowance for freight charges.

On January 1, 1961, selected factory inventory accounts showed the following balances:

> Materials inventory.....................$76,000
> Materials in process—department Y........ 13,000
> Labor in process—department Y........... 8,000
> Overhead in process—department Y....... 12,000

The following transactions relating to department Y took place during the month of January, 1961:

(1) Purchased materials: actual prices, $48,000; standard prices, $50,000; and freight and delivery charges paid, $800.

(2) Accrued direct and indirect labor payrolls for department Y: actual direct labor hours at actual rates, $21,000; actual indirect labor hours at actual wage rates, $8,700.

(3) Actual direct labor hours, department Y, at standard wage rates, $20,000.

(4) Materials issued to department Y, at standard prices; direct materials, $17,000; indirect materials, $4,500.

(5) Overhead costs, other than indirect labor and indirect materials, charged to department Y, $15,000.

(6) Work completed by department Y during the month, at standard cost (assume that all completed work was transferred to the warehouse and its costs debited to Head Office Control).

> Direct materials...............................$25,000
> Direct labor................................... 24,000
> Overhead....................................... 36,000
> Total Standard Cost of Work Completed.......$85,000

(7) Inventories in department Y on January 31 (at standard cost):

> Materials in process—department Y.................$4,100
> Labor in process—department Y.................... 5,400
> Overhead in process—department Y................ 8,100

(8) Overhead is absorbed at a rate of $1.50 per standard direct labor dollar.

(9) Budgeted monthly overhead costs for department Y are:

$17,000 + $0.50 × Standard Direct Labor Cost.

a) Find the normal or budgeted volume of activity for department Y, using standard direct labor cost as the measure of departmental activity.

b) Record the above information in appropriate T-accounts and prepare a list of variances, showing as much detail as possible.

25. The cost accounting department of the Bayou Refinery of the Bipex Petroleum Company prepared the following comparative summary of operating costs, exclusive of the costs of crude oil and other product ingredients, for the month of December:

	This December		Increase (Decrease) Over Last December	
	Amount	Per Barrel	Amount	% Change
Barrels per calendar day............	51,791	...	3,268	6.7
Controllable:				
Salaries and wages:				
Operating....................	$ 224,268	$0.1397	$ 16,419	7.9
Maintenance..................	43,973	0.0273	2,915	7.1
Accounting...................	10,358	0.0065	804	8.4
Administration...............	21,713	0.0135	434	2.0
Total Payrolls..............	$ 300,312	$0.1870	$ 20,572	7.4
Operating material.............	26,947	0.0168	7,229	36.7
Maintenance material...........	39,421	0.0246	5,937	17.7
Catalyst......................	54,839	0.0342	28,138	105.4
Other processing supplies........	52,402	0.0326	3,674	7.5
Employee benefits..............	22,552	0.0140	3,723	19.8
Fuel consumed.................	195,269	0.1216	15,613	8.7
Contract costs.................	37,195	0.0232	8,573	30.0
Coker rental..................	67,073	0.0418	(1,797)	(2.6)
All other controllable...........	44,583	0.0278	2,997	7.2
Total Controllable..........	$ 840,593	$0.5236	$ 94,659	12.7
Noncontrollable:				
Depreciation....................	$ 208,789	$0.1300	$ 13,554	6.9
Taxes........................	37,398	0.0233	14	...
Laboratory....................	15,436	0.0096	2,293	17.4
Process advisory...............	7,390	0.0046	1,053	16.6
Maintenance engineering.........	3,487	0.0022	204	6.2
Head office administration........	10,415	0.0065	496	5.0
Other........................	3,774	0.0023	1,563	70.7
Total Noncontrollable........	$ 286,689	$0.1785	$ 19,177	7.2
Total Operating Cost.......	$1,127,282	$0.7021	$113,836	11.2
Increase (decrease) over cost per barrel last year..............		$0.0284		

Analysis of Major Increases:

Payrolls:

Increased salaries and wage rates	$12,422
Increased work force	5,152
Increased overtime	1,055
Increased vacation and holiday pay	1,078
Increased sickness and accident pay	865
Total Increase in Payrolls	$20,572

Operating supplies:

Low-value items formerly charged to warehouse, now charged to refinery when purchased	$ 5,769
Other increases	1,460
Total Increase in Operating Supplies	$ 7,229

Catalyst:

Reformer unit No. 1—catalyst change	$ 6,213
Reformer unit No. 2—initial batch for start-up	17,888
Desulfurizer—initial batch for start-up	3,418
Increased requirements	619
Total Increase in Catalyst	$28,138

Fuel consumed:

Increased price of fuel gas	$ 5,865
Increased quantity consumed	9,748
Total Increase in Fuel Consumed	$15,613

a) Of what significance are the figures relating to increases or decreases over the comparable month in the previous year?

b) Do you feel that the analysis of major increases provides sufficient information for cost control purposes? What additional information, if any, would you like to have to assist you in evaluating the cost control performance in the refinery?

26. The Tumbler Company uses a system of departmental flexible budgets to provide overhead cost control information for its factory department managers. The machining department of this company's factory assigns overhead to products by means of a burden rate of $0.67 per machine-hour. The monthly flexible budget for the machining department is as follows:

Machine-Hours	10,000	12,000	14,000	16,000	18,000
Supervision	$ 900	$ 900	$ 900	$ 1,200	$ 1,200
Indirect labor	1,000	1,200	1,400	1,600	1,800
Supplies	500	600	700	800	900
Payroll taxes	1,210	1,430	1,660	1,930	2,210
Overtime premiums	50	70	220	400	1,000
Depreciation	800	800	800	800	800
Floor space charges	3,000	3,000	3,000	3,000	3,000
Engineering services	600	650	700	750	800
Total	$8,060	$8,650	$9,380	$10,480	$11,710

During May, this department operated at a rate of 16,000 machine-hours and was charged the following amounts:

Supervision...........................	$ 1,400
Indirect labor........................	1,710
Supplies.............................	720
Payroll taxes........................	2,000
Overtime premium.....................	900
Depreciation.........................	850
Floor space charges...................	2,700
Engineering services..................	820
Total.............................	$11,100

The following additional information is available:

(1) The departmental supervision account is ordinarily charged for the straight-time wages earned by assistant foremen. Although these men are paid on an hourly basis, they usually work a full workweek. When the department head deems it necessary, a senior machinist is given additional supervisory duties and part of his wages are charged to the supervision account.

(2) The plant manager assigned a quality control supervisor to this department for one week during May to assist the department manager in the production of a long run of parts with very tight specifications. The departmental supervision account was charged $230 for the supervisor's services during this period.

(3) The indirect labor account is charged for the wages of departmental materials handlers and helpers, and also for the nonproductive time of machine operators. During May, machine operators were idle for approximately 100 hours due to machine breakdowns and delays in receiving work from other departments. The account was charged $420 for this idle time. The indirect labor budget figure includes an allowance for such costs in the amount of 1 cent per machine-hour.

(4) Departments are charged for payroll taxes on all departmental wages, both direct and indirect. Payroll taxes are charged to the departments at a predetermined rate per labor dollar. This rate is not changed during the year.

(5) Overtime work in each department is scheduled monthly by the production scheduling department, on the basis of scheduled production for the month. The department manager's primary responsibility is to meet the production schedule, and he may use whatever amount of overtime premium is necessary to accomplish this objective.

(6) The depreciation charge is computed monthly on the basis of the original cost of the equipment located in the department as of the first day of the month.

(7) Floor space charges are computed monthly by multiplying the number of square feet of floor space occupied by each department by the average cost of building depreciation, insurance, utilities, and janitorial and maintenance services for that month.

(8) Engineering services are provided to production departments by the factory engineering department. These services consist primarily of methods studies prepared at the request of the plant manager or on the initiative of the chief engineer. The charge for these services is based on a predetermined rate per engineering hour.

a) What is the normal operating volume for this department?

b) Compute the total overhead variance for this department for the month of May.

c) Prepare an analysis of the May overhead variance in as much detail as possible. Indicate what you would report to the department manager and why. Prepare a report for the department manager to show the format that you would use.

d) Would the figures for May seem to warrant any action by the department manager? By anyone else? Explain.

27. The Greystone Manufacturing Company owns one plant which also houses its sales and administrative offices. The company manufactures and distributes two products which are sold to more than a hundred local manufacturers. Product B is in fact simply a deluxe version of product A. The performance characteristics of the two are identical, but B has an improved finish and makes a better appearance. The industrial users purchase B for their higher priced models and A for standard or utility models.

The production process is relatively simple. In department 1, the products are formed and subassembled, and in department 2 they are finished and packed. Product B requires one and one-fourth pounds of material, while A requires only one pound. In department 1, the process is the same for both, and production at the rate of five units per labor hour is expected. In department 2, however, five units of product A are finished per hour as compared to only three units of product B.

On the basis of the operating budgets presented by the controller, the annual fixed costs for the expected range of activity are as follows:

Manufacturing: Department 1	$198,000
Department 2	206,400
Selling	216,000
Administrative	180,000
Total Annual Fixed Costs	$800,400

Planned annual volume was 720,000 units of product A and 600,000 units of product B.

Variable manufacturing overhead costs are budgeted at $1.25 per direct labor hour in department 1 and $1.65 per direct labor hour in department 2. The expected raw material price is $0.40 per pound; the expected direct labor rates are $2 per hour in department 1 and $2.40 per hour in department 2. Finished products are packed in department 2, and the planned cost of packing materials is $0.10 per product unit.

a) Manufacturing overhead is absorbed on the basis of direct labor hours. Compute separate fixed and variable burden rates for each department.

b) Develop standard unit costs for each product at each stage of manufacture.

28. Early in January, it became apparent that some customers of the Greystone Manufacturing Company (see question 27 above) wanted deliveries sooner than had been planned. Although there was as yet no evidence that total sales for the year would exceed the forecast, it seemed advisable to build up inventories against the earlier spring demands. Accordingly, production was stepped up to 110 percent of the monthly average, that is, to 66,000 units of A and 55,000 units of B. Sales for the month were exactly 60,000 units of A and 50,000 units of B, leaving 6,000 of A and 5,000 of B in the finished goods inventory at the month end.

January was not without its production difficulties. In department 1, a considerable amount of material was spoiled as a result of the unfamiliarity of the workers with one aspect of a change in design which had been put into effect January 1. This difficulty was remedied by the second week of the month, but there resulted an excessive use of material, as well as an attendant wastage of labor and variable overhead. Moreover, in order to attain the stepped-up goal of 110 percent of average monthly production after the time lost in the earlier part of the month, some overtime work had to be authorized. As a result, the average earnings for direct labor were $2.05 per hour instead of $2 as planned.

In summary, the following events took place during January.

Department 1:
  (1) 160,000 pounds of raw material were bought at $0.39 a pound.
  (2) 140,000 pounds of raw material were used in production.
  (3) The direct labor payroll was 27,000 hours at an average of $2.05 per hour.
  (4) Variable indirect manufacturing costs were $32,000.
  (5) Actual fixed overhead costs were $16,600.
  (6) 66,000 units of A and 55,000 units of B were completed and transferred to department 2. No units remained in process.

Department 2:
  (7) $13,000 of packing materials were purchased at exactly the estimated price.
  (8) $12,050 of packing materials were used.
  (9) The direct labor payroll was 31,300 hours at an average of $2.40 per hour.
  (10) Variable indirect manufacturing costs were $51,600.
  (11) Actual fixed overhead costs were $17,400.

(12) 66,000 units of product A and 55,000 units of B were finished. No units remained in process.

Trace the flow of costs for the month through appropriately titled T-accounts, and prepare an analysis of variances in as much detail as possible.

29. The Balfour Label Company employs a standard cost system with the following characteristics. Purchases are taken into inventory at standard material prices, and transfers out to the printing department Material in Process account are at these same prices. Direct labor is charged to the departmental labor in process accounts at actual hours and standard wage rates. Overhead is charged to departmental cost accounts at actual cost, and service department overhead is redistributed to the producing departments on the basis of the characteristics of each cost element.

The output of the printing department is transferred to the cutting and packing (C and P) department at standard product cost, and finished labels are carried to finished goods at the standard costs of the labels.

Each department has labor and material usage variances and overhead volume and spending variances. The latter are derived from departmental semivariable budgets. Variances are closed out to profit and loss at the close of each month.

Below are the balances in the accounts as of May 1:

	Debits	Credits
Raw material..........................	$ 36,400	
Printing department:		
Material in process.................	18,200	
Labor in process....................	2,700	
Overhead in process................	7,250	
C and P department:		
Material in process.................	22,600	
Labor in process....................	4,300	
Overhead in process................	5,400	
Finished goods......................	42,800	
Service department overhead..........	...	
Accrued wages......................		$ 980
Control.............................		138,670
Total.......................	$139,650	$139,650

The transactions for the month of May are presented below:

(1) Material purchased during the month: actual cost, $37,492; standard cost, $36,100.

(2) Material issued to the printing department: standard cost, $31,900.

(3) Direct labor employed during the month:
Printing department—actual hours, 2,100, at standard rates $5,500.
C and P department—actual hours, 8,000, at standard rates $11,700.

(4) Actual overhead for the month:

Printing department...................................$9,500
C and P department.................................. 9,300
Service department.................................. 8,600

(5) The distribution of the service department overhead: to printing, $4,900; to C and P, $3,700.

(6) Work completed during the month, transferred out at standard cost:

	Printing Dept.	C and P Dept.
Standard material cost.........	$32,700	$48,300
Standard labor cost...........	5,700	11,750
Standard overhead cost.......	12,600	13,400
Total Standard Cost......	$51,000	$73,450

(7) Work in process at standard cost remaining in each department at the end of the month:

	Printing Dept.	C and P Dept.
Material..................	$17,600	$25,900
Labor...................	3,250	3,900
Overhead................	7,700	4,700

(8) The semivariable overhead budgets for the two producing departments are given by the following equations:

$$\text{Printing} = \$6,000 + 1.10 \times S.L.C.$$

$$\text{C and P} = \$5,000 + 0.72 \times S.L.C.$$

(9) Payrolls paid for the month; $17,100. As of the end of the month, the hours worked but unpaid were:

Printing...300
C and P...550

(10) Standard cost of the goods sold: $76,200.

In the above, "S.L.C." is the standard cost of the production for the month. Production is the work transferred out plus the increase in work in process.

Account for the transactions of the month in appropriate T-accounts and prepare the reports on the month's operations which convey the information you consider of interest to management.

30. The Apex Wire Company manufactures a complete line of plastic and other insulated wires for appliance, building, military, and industrial uses. The company's line includes more than seven hundred types of wire,

but only eighty of them are produced for stock. On the average, about one hundred production orders are processed during a month.

In the manufacture of insulated wire, labor and overhead costs are small in relation to the cost of material. Also, each production order involves a large number of operations with the material going back and forth among departments a number of times before a job is completed.

Because of the nature of the product line and the manufacturing operation, the company operated for a long time without any cost system whatsoever. Every six months the inventory would be counted and priced on the basis of current material prices and wage rates, estimated material and labor content, and the plantwide percentage relationship between labor and overhead costs for the prior period. Cost of goods sold was then determined as the beginning inventory plus material purchased, wages paid, and all overhead costs, less ending inventory.

The management was unhappy about the lack of monthly profit and loss information. It also wanted better cost information for pricing and the control of costs, particularly material usage and overhead costs. Insofar as cost information has been used for pricing, it has been obtained by a cost analyst under the production manager, who maintained a file with a card for each item which showed the estimated labor and material requirements. This information was developed by consultation with the production people. When asked for a cost figure by the sales department, the analyst would extend the labor and material at normal wage rates and material prices and add overhead on the basis of a burden rate provided by the accounting department.

Although the company had a strong aversion to paper work, the growth in its size and in the diversity of its product line forced the adoption of a production and inventory control system. A production control clerk under the plant manager maintained a perpetual inventory in quantities of raw material and finished goods. The plant initiated production only on the authority of a production order, and material moved out of the storeroom only on requisitions initiated on the basis of production orders. A copy of the production order itself covered the movement of the completed order into the finished stock room.

A consultant was called in to advise on the possibility of improving the information that might be obtained from the accounting system without materially increasing the costs of bookkeeping. After a study of the company's operations and cost records, he recommended that the company install a standard cost system. Part of his proposal is quoted below.

(1) "At the start of the period establish a standard cost for each product as follows. Take the estimated material and labor requirements from the cost analyst's file and extend them at current material prices and wage rates. For overhead use a plantwide burden

rate given by the percentage relationship between total manufacturing overhead costs and total direct labor cost.

(2) "Charge material purchases to a raw material control account at standard prices, and charge the difference between the actual and the standard cost of purchases to a material price variance account.

(3) "Credit raw material and charge one plantwide material in process account with the standard cost of all material requisitioned. On these requisitions identify by number the production order on which the material was requisitioned and maintain a file of the requisitions.

(4) "Charge the direct labor payroll to one plantwide labor in process account, and the overhead to one plantwide overhead in process account.

(5) "When a production order is completed, charge a finished goods control account with the standard cost of the product as determined in (1) above, and make the offsetting credits to the material, labor, and overhead in process accounts.

(6) "Obtain the material in process at the end of the month by establishing the production orders which have not been completed and totaling the requisitions which have been issued on those production orders.

(7) "Obtain the labor and overhead in process at the end of the month as follows. First obtain the average percentage relationship between direct labor cost and direct material cost. Financial statements for one or more prior periods may be used for this. Next, take one half of this percentage and apply it to the month-end material in process balance to obtain the month-end labor in process balance. For overhead in process follow the same procedure.

(8) "Charge cost of goods sold at standard and credit finished goods with the standard cost of all shipments."

a) Do you think that the proposed system would meet the objectives of Apex Wire's management? What are those objectives?

b) What are the limitations of the proposed system as a vehicle for factory cost control? How would you go about improving it? What problems would you encounter?

Chapter 23

BUDGETARY PLANNING
AND CONTROL SYSTEMS

MANAGEMENT'S PRIMARY FUNCTION is to plan. Much planning is episodic, concerned with individual situations, individual proposals. Important though it is, this kind of activity needs to be supplemented and reinforced by overall periodic planning. This can then be followed by periodic comparisons of planned progress with the results actually achieved. The purpose of this chapter is to provide a broad sketch of the directions these overall planning and control systems can take.

FINANCIAL PLANNING THROUGH BUDGETS

Budgets are the expression, largely in financial terms, of management's plans for operating and financing the enterprise during specific periods of time. The budget can be defined as *a predetermined, detailed plan of action developed and distributed as a guide to current operations and as a partial basis for the subsequent evaluation of performance.*

Some budgets apply only to a single year or season; others extend farther into the future and are called long-range plans. Both types of budgets represent attempts by management to look ahead and to adapt current actions to the future environment. They differ mainly in the degree of confidence with which they are advanced, in the detail in which they are presented, and consequently in the force of their impact on day-to-day operating decisions.

Purposes of the Budget

Budgets are instruments of management control in three ways: (1) as the means of organizing and directing a large segment of the management planning process; (2) as continuing reminders of current plans and programs for the guidance and motivation of day-to-day management; and (3) as the bench marks against which to measure actual performance (responsive control).

The values of budgeting lie as much in the process as in the resulting documents. Perhaps the greatest advantage of the budgeting process is that it forces periodic *self-examination* as to functions, methods, objectives, and costs. Although a budget can be prepared simply on the basis of what was done last year, adjusted for any changes in conditions or scope of the activity that may be anticipated for the coming year, the soundly conceived budgeting plan should stimulate the executive to take a more critical view of his own operations than he is likely to do in directing day-to-day operations.

The budgeting process also forces executives to *quantify* their plans and to examine the feasibility of these plans in terms of both profitability and consistency with the plans of other segments of the company. The budget gives management a chance to anticipate and in many cases to consider revision of basic policies before the need for this revision might otherwise become apparent.

Components of the Budget

A complete budget system is made up of a number of individual sub-budgets. These components may be classified into four groups, as shown in Exhibit 23–1. These components are of course all interre-

Exhibit 23–1

BUDGET COMPONENTS

Physical Budgets	*Cost Budgets*	*Profit Budgets*	*Finance Budgets*
Unit sales		Dollar sales	Cash
Unit production	Manufacturing costs		Capital outlays
Unit purchases	Selling costs	Cost of goods sold	Financing
Unit inventories	Administrative costs	Expenses	Balance sheet
Manpower	Financing costs		
Facilities	Research costs		

lated. The physical production budget depends on the physical sales budget. Cost budgets are derived from the physical budgets, and the profit and finance budgets represent the consolidation of all the other components of the system.

Most of these components will be further subdivided to show details that are necessary for planning or control. For example, the unit sales and dollar sales budgets will probably be broken down by sales divisions and by product lines. They may also be classified by sales territory, customer category, or any other desired grouping. Each plant will have its own manufacturing cost budget, classified according to organization lines within the factory and also according to the nature of the cost. Finance budgets are more likely to be restricted to the company as a whole, but a certain amount of subdivision is frequently encountered in these as well. A company which has incorporated subsidiaries may even have separate financing budgets for each subsidiary.

The Process of Budgeting

Comprehensive budgetary planning ordinarily begins with the distribution to all executives of a set of forecasts and assumptions as to the future state of the economy and its probable impact on the company's business. This may be drawn up with the aid of the company's own planning staff or acquired from outside economic analysts.

Next, the head of each division or department collects the factual information necessary for an informed analysis of past performance and future possibilities. He solicits suggestions and proposals from his subordinates. After an analysis of all of this information, he arrives at what he conceives to be the best course of action with respect to the operations under his control.

These tentative plans are then submitted to higher management for review and consolidation. The reviewing authority may be either the next level in the management chain or a central planning staff or budget department. The proposed plans need to be examined from three points of view: (1) is it *realistic;* (2) is it *consistent* with company objectives and plans of other parts of the organization; and (3) is it *feasible* in the light of the company's financial, marketing, and production capacities?

This process is more iterative than the above description is likely to imply. That is, tentative budgets are proposed, discussed, and revised again and again as they move upward toward final approval. The process is one of progressive dialogue; an executive seldom receives a budget proposal from a subordinate without having discussed vital aspects of it ahead of time. Through vertical and horizontal communication within the management group, these plans are adjusted and readjusted until they become a set of integrated and realizable objectives consistent with overall company policies.

The Profit Plan and the Profit Center Concept

Probably the most critical focus of the budgeting process is on the profit plan. Each major operating segment of the business—product line or market area—ordinarily has its own profit plan, consisting of a schedule of budgeted sales and expenses for the period. The overall company profit plan is then the consolidation of these various segment profit plans.

Profit plans are drawn up by profit-responsible executives. Although profit responsibility may reside only at the top-management level, many companies have elected to delegate a good deal of profit responsibility for specific business segments to subordinate executives. These segments are usually called departments or divisions, but when the division manager is given authority to operate his segment largely as if it were an independent company his division can be referred to as a *profit center*. A company that is organized around a number of these profit centers is said to be a *decentralized* company.

Ideally, each profit center should be completely independent of its sister divisions. To approach this, the divisional boundaries should be drawn so that each division has its own manufacturing and distributive facilities and relatively few transfers of product to other divisions. In short, decentralization is at its best whenever a division's operations come closest in scope and depth to those of separate independent companies. Under these circumstances, the profit reported by each division is largely independent of operating performance in other divisions of the company, thus facilitating the interpretation of reported profits. Organization units that come closest to meeting these specifications are those that are responsible for the manufacture and sale of a single product line or a group of related product lines, although in some industries divisionalization on a regional basis is feasible.

Reasons for Profit Decentralization

The creation of profit centers and the delegation of profit responsibility has three major objectives:

1. To provide a basis for delegating portions of top management's decision-making responsibility to executives who have closer operating familiarity with individual products or markets.
2. To bring subordinate executives into more direct contact with the ultimate profit objectives of the firm.
3. To provide an integrated training ground for the top managers of the future.

Undoubtedly the most important of these is the first—to over-come the sheer weight of the decision-making responsibility in a large corporation. With operations spread over a vast geographical area and encompassing hundreds of products and thousands of customers, central management cannot hope to be completely and continuously in direct personal contact with every segment of the company's business. To provide flexibility and adaptability to changing conditions, it has become increasingly necessary to delegate substantial powers to executives who can maintain a closer, more detailed familiarity with individual products or markets. In other words, decentralization aims to recreate in the large organization the conditions that give life and flexibility to the small company without sacrificing the advantages of size.

Participation and the Profit Plan

As indicated above, most profit plans are established jointly by profit-responsible executives, their subordinates, and their immediate superiors. The purpose of this multilevel participation is partly to increase the motivational impact of the resulting plan. Participation, the argument runs, will lead the subordinate executive to accept the plan more readily and to commit himself more wholeheartedly to its achievement.

Although behavioral scientists are not entirely agreed on the implications of the various empirical studies that have been made, one interpretation is that if participation in profit planning is to affect performance, it must succeed in increasing the executive's sense of identification with a larger group which accepts profit generation as a desirable goal.[1] Executives of many companies believe that it does just that.

One point that is often misunderstood in this connection is the role of higher management. Some people have interpreted participation to mean a complete abdication of responsibility by managers at higher levels in the organization. This is certainly not the intent. For one thing, one manager's plan is an integral part of his superior's plan, so that the latter cannot abdicate responsibility even if he wants to. Secondly, participation is likely to further company goals only if some leadership force steers it in that direction.

From this brief description, one point should have emerged clearly.

---

[1] Selwyn Becker and David Green, Jr., "Budgeting and Employee Behavior," *The Journal of Business*, October, 1962, pp. 392–402; and George J. Benston, "The Role of the Firm's Accounting System for Motivation," *The Accounting Review*, April, 1963, pp. 347–54.

Budgeting is not simply a matter of forecasting what the future has to offer. It is a highly creative process, in which executives at all levels are expected to evaluate and compare different possible courses of action, selecting those which seem most likely to meet company goals.

The Role of Accounting Management

As the foregoing would imply, the development of operating plans is a responsibility of line management. The task of pulling together all the elements of a profit plan, however, ordinarily falls to the lot of the budget director or controller. The amount of detail and the number of interrelationships among components of the plan in a large corporation can be enormous, and the budget director has no easy task.

The budget director or controller is also responsible for designing and securing support for the procedural aspects of periodic planning, mainly the questions of what is to be budgeted, when, and by whom. This is ordinarily done by the budget staff, working closely with operating executives. The final installation is likely to be summarized in a budget manual, spelling out deadlines for various budget components, assigning responsibilities for budget preparation, prescribing forms, and describing the overall budget pattern. For example, Exhibit 23–2 shows the budget flow chart from the budget manual of a large decentralized company, indicating relationships between local management and the corporate staff. This is followed by a detailed time schedule of due dates for various parts of the plan.

Even if budget components have been reviewed carefully and critically all the way up the line within a given segment of the organization, the corporate controller or budget director often has the authority to subject the proposals to his own tests of feasibility and profitability. He is always free to seek clarification or question whether other alternatives have been investigated, and in some cases he even has the power to ask individual managers to revise their programs.[2] It must be emphasized, however, that in taking any actions of this sort *the controller is acting as the agent of line management* and is applying tests that line executives would apply. The difference is probably not too great because top management often relies heavily on the controller for profitability criteria in any case. When the controller does not exercise this kind of rejection authority, a top-

---

[2] For further discussion of these points, see Neil W. Chamberlain, *The Firm: Micro-Economic Planning and Action* (New York: McGraw-Hill Book Co., Inc., 1962), chap. xi.

management budget committee is often formed for the same purpose, but once again the analytical work itself is still within the province of the controller or budget director.

Exhibit 23–2

PLANNING SEQUENCE AND COORDINATION CHART

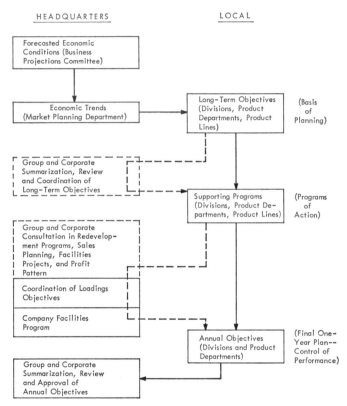

PERIODIC FINANCIAL REPORTING

Preparation of financial budgets is to some extent an end in itself, as indicated earlier. Once prepared, however, the budgets have one more major service to perform: to provide bench marks for responsive control of current operating performance. The vehicle by which financial budgets contribute to the responsive control process is the periodic financial report, and particularly the periodic profit report. The remainder of this chapter will be devoted to a brief examination of periodic profit reporting.

The Profit Reporting Structure

Segmental profit reporting is not restricted to companies that have elected to decentralize on a profit center basis. Product-line and regional profit reports are prepared routinely in highly centralized companies, for the use of executives at the top-management level. The difference is that in decentralized companies a greater number of executives receive profit reports and are expected to be motivated and guided by them.

At lower responsibility levels, the report is likely to show a single set of figures, summarizing all of the activities under the executive's authority. In other words, the reports will cover the activities of an *organizational unit*. At higher levels, the summary profit report will also be a comprehensive, organization-based report. It is likely to be supplemented, however, by detailed reports on individual segments of the activities within the executive's area of responsibility. Some of these will be organizational—for example, each executive is likely to get information copies of the reports issued to his immediate subordinates. Still others will cut across organizational lines and be *program-centered*. For example, suppose that a company's household appliance division is subdivided geographically in a number of market areas. The basic profit reports will thus be geographical in structure. In addition, however, the division manager is very likely to be interested in the amount of profit contributed in total by each product in his line. Thus he will ask for periodic profit reports on a product-line basis.

Basis for Performance Evaluation

An executive's interest in the periodic profit reports focuses on three questions:

1. How successful have his subordinates been in managing the activities entrusted to them?
2. What problems and opportunities seem to have arisen since the preparation of the budgetary plan?
3. Should any of the activities within his control be discontinued?

The last of these is basically an investment/disinvestment question, and the bench mark for performance evaluation is related to the cost of capital figure discussed in Chapter 20. This kind of analysis is highly specialized, and will not be studied here.

For the other two questions, the bench mark is the previously established profit plan. Each organization unit has its own profit plan, representing its part in the overall structure. Profit plans typically can be and are reclassified on a program basis as well. Once top management has accepted these plans, they become the bench mark or standard against which subsequent performance is compared.

The Profit Contribution Approach

Most internal profit reporting schemes emphasize one of two basic profit concepts:

1. *Profit contribution:* revenues, less the variable costs attributable to these revenues, less any fixed costs traceable to this segment of the business.
2. *Net profit:* profit contribution, less a pro rata share of all nontraceable fixed costs.

An example of a profit report based on the profit contribution concept is shown in Exhibit 23–3. This company divides its business into two segments: regular products and custom products. Separate columns are provided in Exhibit 23–3 for each of these. Notice that the product-line columns extend down only to the profit contribution figures—net income is computed only for the company as a whole,

Exhibit 23–3

PRODUCT PROFIT CONTRIBUTION STATEMENT

	All Products	Regular Products		Custom Products	
		Amount	% of Net Sales	Amount	% of Net Sales
Net sales.....................	$2,000,000	$1,640,000	100.0	$360,000	100.0
Variable costs (standard):					
Factory....................	$1,097,600	$ 836,600		$261,000	
Order filling................	65,100	52,600		12,500	
Total Variable Costs........	$1,162,700	$ 889,200	54.2	$273,500	76.0
Variable profit................	$ 837,300	$ 750,800	45.8	$ 86,500	24.0
Product-traceable fixed costs.....	$ 195,400	$ 148,500		$ 46,900	
Labor and materials variances....	7,900	10,600		(2,700)	
Profit contribution.............	$ 634,000	$ 591,700	36.1	$ 42,300	11.8
Common fixed costs:					
Factory....................	$ 137,200				
Selling and administrative......	283,500				
Net Income before Tax..........					
	$ 213,300				

not for individual product lines. Company net income is the sum of the segment profit contributions, less the total of the fixed costs not traceable to individual product-line segments.

The argument for the profit contribution approach is that most allocations of the nontraceable fixed costs are to a large extent arbitrary. How much of the president's salary should be charged to regular products and how much to custom products is a question of metaphysics, not of management. Even when some apparently reasonable basis can be found for allocating nontraceable items, however, these allocations add nothing to the information content of the periodic reports. Profit contribution indicates the amount of profit generated by each individual business segment, the amount available to cover general fixed costs and provide a net profit for the company as a whole.

Comparison Reports

The profit report shown in Exhibit 23–3 is of limited usefulness because it provides no comparison bench mark, but the profit contribution concept can be applied in comparative statements as well. Exhibit 23–4, for instance, shows a report that might be issued to the

Exhibit 23–4

DISTRICT PROFIT PERFORMANCE REPORT

| DISTRICT SALES AND EXPENSE SUMMARY | | | | |
| DISTRICT Boston | | | MONTH January, 1967 | |
	Budget	Actual	Deviation	Actual % of Sales
Net sales billed..................	$500,000	$514,000	$14,000	100.0
Cost of sales.....................	375,000	381,000	(6,000)	74.1
Gross margin....................	$125,000	$133,000	$ 8,000	25.9
District office costs:				
Branch salaries.................	$ 2,500	$ 2,500	. . .	0.5
Sales salaries..................	25,000	25,500	$ (500)	5.0
Travel........................	8,000	6,800	1,200	1.3
Entertainment.................	1,000	1,300	(300)	0.2
Local advertising..............	500	500	. . .	0.1
Storage and delivery...........	7,000	7,300	(300)	1.4
Branch office expense...........	900	1,100	(200)	0.2
Other........................	600	700	(100)	0.1
Total district cost..............	$ 45,500	$ 45,700	$ (200)	8.8
District Profit Contribution.........	$ 79,500	$ 87,300	$ 7,800	17.1

district sales manager as an overall summary of his district's profit contribution. The business segment in this case is the company's sales in this company's Boston district rather than companywide sales of a specific product line as in Exhibit 23–3. The format is the same, however, in that no allocations of head office fixed costs are charged against the individual district's revenues.

Exhibit 23–5

DISTRICT SALESMAN REPORT

Salesman	Net Sales Billed	Cost of Sales	Salary and Expenses	Profit Contribution		
				Amount	Budget Deviation	% of Sales
	SALESMAN PERFORMANCE SUMMARY					
DISTRICT Boston				MONTH January, 1967		
Brown..............	$ 40,000	$ 29,200	$ 2,400	$ 8,400	$ (400)	21.0%
Cannon.............	31,000	24,300	3,200	3,500	(900)	11.3
Evars............ ..	63,000	42,700	4,100	16,200	3,700	25.7
Johnson............	30,000	24,200	2,900	2,900	(1,400)	9.7
Kelly..............	54,000	40,100	4,200	9,700	200	18.0
Lusso..............	47,000	34,400	3,100	9,500	2,100	20.2
McGregor..........	76,000	56,000	3,800	16,200	4,000	21.3
Nelson	55,000	41,900	3,300	9,800	500	17.8
Stern............ ...	68,000	51,600	3,600	12,800	1,200	18.8
Williams..........	50,000	36,600	3,000	10,400	(600)	20.8
Total.........	$514,000	$381,000	$33,600	$99,400	$8,400	19.4%
Other branch expenses..........				12,100	(600)	1.7
District Profit Contribution......				$87,300	$7,800	17.1%

A glance at this report will tell the district manager that his actual sales volume was $514,000, that this gave him a gross margin $8,000 larger than his profit plan called for, and that his district profit contribution for the month was $7,800 greater than his profit objective.

While this kind of report is useful as an overall summary, it does not provide the district manager with any explanation of the *sources* of the main deviations. Another report that he might receive is shown in Exhibit 23–5, to permit him to monitor the performance of his individual salesmen. Although many companies limit such summaries to sales volume alone, the interjection of product costs and traceable fixed expenses can add a significant dimension to the sales figures. Salesman Kelly, for example, sold $4,000 more than Williams during the month but showed a $700 smaller profit contribution. Williams, on the other hand, failed to meet his profit objective for the period, as did three of the other salesmen.

Some companies prefer to show figures for the comparable period of the previous year in addition to the deviations from the profit plan. No serious objection can be raised to this practice as long as it does not lead to *de facto* displacement of the current year's profit plan as the relevant bench mark. Graphic presentations of year-to-date performance against planned performance are also useful supplements to the tabulated figures in most cases.

The district manager might receive another report summarizing the same data but arranged as in Exhibit 23–6, if he is expected to influ-

Exhibit 23–6

DISTRICT PRODUCT SALES REPORT

PRODUCT CONTRIBUTION REPORT						
DISTRICT Boston				MONTH January, 1967		
Product Line	Net Sales Billed		Cost of Sales	Other Product Expenses	Profit Contribution	
	Actual	Variance			Actual	Variance
White Shield.........	$204,000	$26,000	$136,000	$500	$ 67,500	$14,000
Red Label..........	133,000	(50,000)	103,000	. . .	30,000	(11,000)
Commercial........	177,000	38,000	142,000	. . .	35,000	5,000
Total..........	$514,000	$14,000	$381,000	$500	$132,500	$ 8,000
Other branch expenses...........					45,200	(200)
District Profit Contribution.........					$ 87,300	$ 7,800

ence product mix actively. Notice that in this exhibit a much smaller percentage of expenses is assigned to individual segments of the district's business. Salesmen's salaries and expenses are traceable to individual salesmen but not to individual product lines. Local advertising, on the other hand, in this instance is completely product-traceable and thus moves "above the line."

It is unnecessary, of course, to carry all reports down to the same final profit or variance figure. The tie-in has been made here, however, to emphasize that a single set of figures has been combined in several ways to illustrate different facets of the problem.

Reports for Higher Management

Profit reports for higher levels of marketing management are similar in structure to those just illustrated, but the level of aggregation is higher. For line management, the basic segmentation is typically along organizational lines, as in Exhibit 23–7. A product manager would receive a similar type of report, limited to his own product line.

Exhibit 23–7

MARKETING DIVISION PERFORMANCE REPORT

DISTRICT SALES PERFORMANCE SUMMARY (000 Omitted)						
DIVISION Marketing					MONTH January, 1967	
District	Net Sales Billed	Cost of Sales	District Selling Expense	District Profit Contribution	Budget Deviation	Contribution % of Sales
Boston...............	$ 514	$ 381	$ 46	$ 87	$ 8	17.0%
New York...........	946	603	84	259	25	27.4
Baltimore...........	472	365	51	56	(33)	11.9
Atlanta.............	348	260	42	46	5	13.2
Pittsburgh...........	588	434	63	91	3	15.5
Cleveland...........	627	472	58	97	(2)	15.5
Total............	$3,495	$2,515	$344	$636	$ 6	18.2%
Head office expense:						
Management........				$ 40	$ 1	
Market research....				26	(1)	
Advertising.........				103	10	
Other.............				23	(3)	
Total head office expense........				$192	$ 7	5.5
Net Marketing Margin				$444	$13	12.7%

Sales management may also get routine or special profit reports on such bases as customer group or channel of distribution. Such reports are often restricted to gross sales or variable product profit unless the importance of other expenses is great enough to justify some form of distribution cost analysis.

It will be noticed that none of these performance reports has shown any factory cost variances. Manufacturing performance measures become an integral part of routine profit reports only at the level at which manufacturing and marketing responsibility are joined. In a straight line organization, this may be at the divisional or top-management level. When product managers are used, they may see the results of manufacturing as well as marketing operations. The product manager's report, however, should show manufacturing cost variances only if they depend at least partly on characteristics of the product line or methods of distribution. Excessive unfavorable factory cost variances, for example, may signify an ultraliberal product modification policy which may be worthy of the product manager's attention. Alternatively, if it shows that the factory cannot meet cost standards in a particular line, consideration may be given to changing product specifications, raising prices, or something else.

Allocations of Nontraceable Fixed Costs

One final point deserves emphasis. If fixed costs are allocated so that product-line reports show net profit, then the allocated fixed costs that are not traceable to individual product lines should be exactly equal to the amounts implicit in the product-line profit plan for the period. *Profit deviations should never result from changes in the basis on which allocations are made unless the allocations are designed to influence managerial behavior.* By accepting the division's profit plan for the year, top management has also agreed to incur fixed costs at the planned level. If these costs vary from the planned amounts, the variations are the result of head office rather than divisional activities. To put this another way, the place to analyze these variations is in the head office, where they arise, rather than at the various divisional offices. For this reason, the allocation should be a fixed quantity, unchanged from month to month throughout the year.

The Return on Investment Concept

In Chapter 20 we emphasized quite strongly the importance of return on investment criteria in management decisions. The complete absence in this chapter of any reference to using return on investment as a measure of operating performance may therefore have come as a surprise.

Many companies, it is true, include return on investment measurements in their routine periodic profit reports. We have no objection to this practice, but we are skeptical about the value of these measures, for two reasons. First, return on investment requires measurements of net income and total investment. These figures are extremely difficult to measure on a divisional or product-line basis because many costs and many investment elements are centrally determined and centrally administered. The amount of cash devoted to the support of a given product line, for example, is impossible to determine and difficult to approximate. The more important these elements are, the less reliance can be placed on the return on investment figure.

The second reason is even more important. Use of return on investment measurements presumes that the bench mark for comparison is some companywide standard of minimum acceptable profitability. Although such a standard is valid in the planning process, in deciding whether to expand operations or withdraw entirely from a given activity, it has no relevance to the evaluation of current operating performance. Once a company has decided to keep an activity in operation, it makes no difference whether the activity earns 2 percent or 40 percent. What matters is whether it is doing better or worse than the plan anticipated.

This same point can be applied in another sense. Most investment is not currently controllable by profit center management, and return on investment measurement tends to reward the management of profitable profit centers and penalize the management of unprofitable ones. In fact, the manager of the unprofitable profit center may be doing better, considering the conditions he faces, than the manager of the profitable division. Therefore, if top management approves a profit plan for a profit center, calling for a low return on investment, it should be satisfied if division management succeeds in achieving the planned results, no matter how low the absolute return on investment is. The return on investment concept is valid at the planning stage, but not in the short-range responsive control process.

Transfer Pricing Problems

One final measurement problem deserves recognition. Most profit centers are not fully independent of sister divisions within the company. Interdivisional purchases and sales do take place, because they permit the company to capitalize on economies of scale in manufacturing, marketing, research, and other functional activities. When one division buys a product or service from another, however, the market is by-passed and the transfer price is in some sense determined administratively. The measurement problem, therefore, is to select transfer prices that will support rather than conflict with company profit objectives.

Briefly speaking, the transfer price will serve its decision-making objectives satisfactorily only if it will lead division management to make the same decisions that top management would make if it had time to study the problem and full access to the available data. If the transfer price leads to departures from this ideal, it is said to cause *suboptimization.*

Space does not permit further discussion of the transfer pricing problem, but it is undoubtedly the main problem in the measurement of profit center performance. A general rule for solution of this problem is that *an appropriate transfer price for management guidance in decision making is one that approximates opportunity cost.* Opportunity cost for this purpose is defined as the sacrifice that the supplying division must make to provide the buying division with the quantity of products or services that are being tranferred. The difficulty is to find the numbers to put this solution to work.[3]

PROFIT VARIANCE ANALYSIS

Most internal profit statements include some form of analysis or commentary on the deviations between actual and budgeted performance. The commentary may call attention to unusual events that had significant favorable or unfavorable effects on reported income during the period, and it may indicate whether these effects are expected to continue and what actions management is taking to cope with or capitalize on the situation.

These qualitative commentaries are often supported and supplemented by quantitative breakdowns of the aggregate profit variance in each segment of the business. For example, the analysis may identify the difference between actual and planned *selling prices* for the actual volume of business done. It may also measure a *sales volume* variance, measured by the deviation of physical sales volume from the planned volume, multiplied by the planned profit margin per unit.

This kind of analysis is technically complex, but it may help management identify more closely the main deviations from plan. Having identified these deviations, management is then in a better position to plan corrective or adaptive action—that is, either to get operating results back on the planned track or to revise the plan itself.[4]

---

[3] For further discussion of this problem, see Gordon Shillinglaw, *Cost Accounting: Analysis and Control* (rev. ed.; Homewood, Ill.: Richard D. Irwin, Inc., 1967), chap. xxvi, and David Solomons, *Divisional Performance: Measurement and Control* (New York: Financial Executives Institute Research Foundation, 1965).

[4] For one analytical scheme, see Shillinglaw, *op. cit.,* pp. 757–65.

SUMMARY

Budgetary planning is basically a device to force management to lift its sights from immediate day-to-day problems and think creatively about the future. Its primary benefits therefore are achieved by the time the budgetary plan is adopted and approved.

These budgets then serve a further purpose, however, in providing a bench mark against which actual results can be compared. The profit plan, for example, becomes the standard that is used in evaluating the current profit performance of profit centers, product lines, or other business segments.

The profit contribution approach has been developed to serve this latter purpose. Its main strength is that it provides the manager with only those figures that are clearly traceable to his operations, without arbitrary allocations of costs that are incurred for the common benefit of his and other operations.

This chapter has merely scratched the surface of the measurement problems that must be solved in the design of budgetary planning and control systems. Transfer pricing is particularly difficult when transfers take place between two profit centers within a decentralized company. Workable solutions to these problems can be found, however, and they should not be allowed to stand in the way of a budgetary planning and control system, if the benefits of such a system appear to justify the effort of putting it into effect.

QUESTIONS AND PROBLEMS

1. What is a business budget? What are its main purposes?

2. What is a profit center? In what kinds of companies would you expect to find profit centers?

3. What is the role of accounting management in budgeting?

4. What reasons can you suggest for initiating a policy of profit decentralization? Do you believe that these are good reasons?

5. What are the purposes of periodic profit reports? To whom should they be issued?

6. What is meant by "profit contribution?" How does it differ from net profit? From variable profit?

7. To what extent should the return on investment concept be used in routine managerial performance evaluation?

8. How can the transfer price influence performance evaluation? How can it influence managerial decisions?

9. What is the objective of profit variance analysis?

10. Is the concept of a profit plan inconsistent with the flexible budget? How do the two relate to each other?

11. Discuss the benefits to management (*a*) from the development of budgets, and (*b*) from use of the budget data during the course of the year.

12. Assuming that a company has a well-designed system of routine reports, why is it necessary to supplement these from time to time by the preparation of special reports?

*13. From the information below, compute the amount of the profit variance due to variations in (*a*) selling prices, (*b*) sales volume, and (*c*) other factors, in as much detail as you deem appropriate.

	Budget	Actual
Sales..............................	$60,000	$60,500
Cost of goods sold:		
Direct material....................	$10,000	$11,200
Direct labor........................	13,000	14,700
Factory overhead..................	13,000	14,100
Total Cost of Goods Sold.........	$36,000	$40,000
Gross margin.......................	$24,000	$20,500
Selling and administrative expenses......	18,000	18,500
Net Income........................	$ 6,000	$ 2,000
Units sold.........................	10,000	11,000

Additional information:

(1) Materials prices and wage rates were at budgeted levels.
(2) Production volume and sales volume were identical.
(3) Factory overhead is budgeted at $7,800 plus 40 percent of direct labor cost.
(4) Selling and administrative expenses are assumed to be wholly fixed.

14. The management of the Cranmore Manufacturing Company at the beginning of 19x1 anticipated (1) a decrease in sales as compared with 19x0 because of production time lost due to conversion to new products, and (2) a considerably smaller profit margin due to higher material and labor costs. The controller was asked to prepare a cash budget based

---

* Solutions to problems marked with an asterisk (*) are found in Appendix B.

on estimated 19x1 sales of $2,400,000 (a decrease of $300,000) and, in particular, to forecast the cash position at the close of 19x1.

The treasurer's forecast of certain balance sheet and other items was as follows:

Accounts receivable (net)...........................	$ 35,000 decrease
Accounts payable.	20,000 decrease
Inventories..	17,000 increase
Additions to plant (gross)...........................	125,000
Additions to retained earnings appropriated for contingencies.....................................	25,000
Net income for 19x1 (after depreciation and before income taxes).......................................	95,000
Depreciation expense, 19x1...........................	48,000
Income taxes for 19x1 (payable in 19x2)...............	45,000
Dividend payments (at 19x0 rates)....................	30,000

The cash balance on January 1, 19x1, was $54,000, and the accrued tax liability on that date, arising from 19x0 taxable income, amounted to $93,000. The company had no bank loans outstanding as of January 1, 19x1.

a) Assuming that any balance sheet items not listed above would be unchanged, prepare a schedule of forecasted cash receipts and cash disbursements for 19x1 and determine the expected cash balance as of December 31, 19x1.

b) What action would you expect management to take when it sees the cash flow estimates for the year?

15. The Ferris Manufacturing Company produces a home appliance and uses a standard cost system. Materials purchased are charged to materials inventory accounts at standard cost, and any purchase price variance, as well as all other variances, are added to or subtracted from the cost of goods sold in the current period. Inventories are measured at standard cost. The standards for cost and price for each unit of product are:

Material—4 units of "A" at $2.88.................$11.52		
3 units of "B" at $2.16.................. 6.48	$18.00	
Direct labor—5 hours at $2.........................	10.00	
Manufacturing overhead—75% of direct labor........	7.50	
Factory Cost......................................	$35.50	
Selling and administrative expense..................	7.70	
Total Cost.....................................	$43.20	
Net profit......................................	4.80	
Selling Price.....................................	$48.00	

The normal volume for purposes of standard cost determination is 12,000 units of product each month. The month of March was expected to be normal in every respect, with budgeted production and sales of 12,000 units. This target was reached, but instead of a forecast net income of $57,600, the company did little more than break even. You have the following additional information:

(1) A bulk sale of 1,000 finished units had been made at a price of $45.60 each. All other sales were at the standard selling price.
(2) During the month 60,000 units of material "A" had been purchased at $3 each, and 40,000 units of material "B" were purchased at $2.10 each. Material issued was 49,500 units of material "A" and 37,000 units of material "B."
(3) Direct labor cost was $121,056. Hourly wage rates averaged 3 percent less than standard.
(4) Actual manufacturing overhead costs were $112,800.
(5) Selling and administrative expenses totaled $110,880.
(6) Work in process and finished goods inventories were at the same level at the end of the month as at the beginning.

Prepare an income statement for the month and explain the deviation from the forecast net profit in as much detail as possible.

*16. The Dorsey Corporation has prepared the following performance summary for its industrial division for the month of December:

Net sales..............................		$2,000,000
Cost of goods sold:		
Labor..............................	$ 400,000	
Materials.............................	100,000	
Overhead (actual).....................	1,000,000	
Costs incurred......................	$1,500,000	
Overhead overabsorbed.................	100,000	
Product costs........................	$1,600,000	
Decrease in inventory..................	160,000	
Cost of goods sold...................		1,760,000
Gross margin...........................		$ 240,000
Less: Selling expenses....................	$ 300,000	
Administrative expenses..............	50,000	350,000
Profit (loss) on sales......................		$ (110,000)
Add: Factory overhead overabsorbed........		100,000
Net Income (Loss) before Taxes............		$ (10,000)

(1) Manufacturing overhead costs are all traceable to the division.
(2) At normal operating volumes, variable manufacturing overhead costs are approximately 30 percent of total manufacturing overhead costs in the industrial division. Variable overhead cost per labor dollar is not affected by fluctuations in production volume.
(3) The volume variance in manufacturing overhead costs in the industrial division was favorable, amounting to $20,000.
(4) Variable selling expenses amount to 4 percent of industrial sales. All administrative expenses are fixed.
(5) $50,000 of fixed selling expense and $5,000 of administrative expense are traceable to the industrial division; all other fixed selling and administrative expenses come from allocations.
(6) An absorption costing system is in use in the factory. The ratio of the variable cost content of work in process and finished goods

inventories to the total costs of these inventories is the same as the ratio of variable manufacturing cost to total "product costs" for the division for the period. Price level changes may be assumed to be negligible.

a) Compute the following:
  (1) Factory overhead spending variance.
  (2) Budgeted fixed manufacturing cost.
  (3) Variable profit ratio.
b) Prepare a profit contribution statement in good form, summarizing the results of the month's operations.

17. The XYZ Company sells its products through two channels of distribution: through dealers and direct to the ultimate consumer. In addition, it bills its customers for the work performed for those customers by its customer engineering department. The company operates a single factory with three production departments and four small service departments.

The sales manager has been receiving monthly sales reports for each of these three business segments, but no attempt has been made to compute or report profit figures for individual segments.

From the following data, prepare a summary profit report, showing the profits of each division individually and of the company as a whole. Use whatever format you feel is appropriate and be prepared to defend your choice.

  (1) Sales revenues:
        Dealer sales, $28,000.
        Direct sales, $36,000.
        Customer engineering, $15,000.
  (2) Standard cost of goods sold:
        Dealer sales: variable costs, $11,000; fixed costs, $4,000.
        Direct sales: variable costs, $13,000; fixed costs, $5,000.
  (3) Total factory costs:
        Direct materials: earned, $10,000; actual, $10,500.
        Direct labor: earned, $12,000; actual, $13,200.
        Factory overhead: earned, $17,000; actual $20,400.
  (4) Factory overhead volume variances included in (3) above: $3,000 (unfavorable).
  (5) Cost variances in opening inventory, none.
  (6) Commissions on direct sales, $2,700.
  (7) Dealer discounts, $10,500.
  (8) Other direct field expenses (fixed):
        Dealer sales department, $1,000.
        Direct sales department, $4,500.
        Customer engineering department, $15,800.

(9) Product advertising (budgeted at 3 percent of direct and dealer sales), $2,500.

(10) Cost of time spent by customer engineers on work not billable to customers (included in amount given in [8] above):

For dealer sales customers, $600.

For direct sales customers, $150.

(11) General sales division overheads, $1,500.

(12) Administrative expenses, $4,900.

18. Great Circle Airlines, Inc., operates a combined airfreight and passenger service in Alaska. Each of its six planes is equipped to carry both passengers and freight. Some flights are run as straight cargo flights, but for the most part freight is moved on regular passenger flights when passengers and their baggage do not bring the plane up to its weight limit.

In addition to a small headquarters executive and clerical staff, the company's work force consists of pilots, air stewardesses, passenger ticket office personnel, ground crews, and one freight clerk. The number of men required for the ground crews depends on the number of planes and the number of flights per day. It does not vary with the number of people or the amount of cargo carried per flight.

Many of the company's sales are made directly by ticket office personnel or the freight clerk. Travel and freight agents bring in a good deal of additional business, for which they do the paper work and for which they are paid modest commissions.

The executive staff consists of Mr. Irwin Bult, the president, and four vice presidents: a controller, an operations vice president, a vice president for passenger service, and a vice president for cargo service. Mr. Peter Thomas is the passenger vice president; Mr. Donald Singlecot is cargo vice president. Mr. Thomas and Mr. Singlecot are responsible for the amounts of profit generated by their respective parts of the company's business.

Discuss the problems you would encounter in designing a profit planning and reporting system for this company, and indicate how you would proceed to solve them.

19. "This budget is a big nuisance," said Mr. Hiram Baumgartner, president of Colleyford, Inc., the United States subsidiary of a large European manufacturer of electrical and electronic products. "I have to spend most of my time on it for the better part of a month, and I don't know how many man-hours my controller puts in on it. As far as I'm concerned, it's just another report that I have to make to headquarters."

Colleyford operated one small electronics factory in upstate New York, but otherwise imported all of its needs from parent company factories in Europe and Japan. It operated primarily in the northeastern United States and on the West Coast, and had fairly large product distribution warehouses in New York and in San Francisco.

For budgeting purposes, Colleyford used the parent company's product classification scheme. It marketed products in six of the parent's product categories:

1. Lighting products.
2. Electronic tubes and transistors.
3. Components for computers and industrial communications equipment.
4. Radios, television receivers, and phonographs.
5. Industrial equipment and parts.
6. Service and repair.

Some products were marketed through wholesalers, while others were sold directly to industrial consumers by the company's own salesmen. Colleyford had a sales force of approximately 40 men. Although some of these men tended to concentrate on one or two product groups, all of them handled all of the company's lines.

Mr. Baumgartner was allowed to manufacture any product that his plant was equipped to produce. The types and amounts of this production were included in the budget that he submitted to headquarters each November. The parent company headquarters then informed him which factories would supply his remaining requirements. The prices charged for these intergroup transfers were established by the head office in advance of budget preparation.

Two or three staff executives from the parent company's headquarters ordinarily spent a week or so at the Colleyford offices while the budget was being prepared, and were also in frequent communication by telephone. They offered their advice and suggestions, and raised questions about parts of the budget proposal as it was in process. Mr. Baumgartner usually presented his budget to the parent company in person at the end of November; and the final budget received from headquarters in December was ordinarily almost identical to the one submitted by Mr. Baumgartner.

a) What benefits might Mr. Baumgartner reap from the company's system of budgetary planning? Comment on possible reasons for his attitude toward the budget and offer suggestions as to what might be done to give him a more favorable view of the budgetary process.

b) Discuss the problems of data classification in Colleyford, Inc. What kinds of data should the profit plan include, and how should these data be subdivided and classified?

20. At the start of each quarter, the Wickwire Products Company develops a budgeted income statement for *each month* during the coming quarter, a schedule of budgeted cash receipts and cash disbursements for the *entire quarter*, and a balance sheet as of the *end of the quarter*. Income statements and balance sheets are prepared in the form shown below.

From the information provided below, prepare the budget schedules for the second quarter of the year (the months of April, May and June):

BALANCE SHEET

AS OF MARCH 31

ASSETS

Current Assets:

Cash..		$ 65,400
Accounts receivable...........................$110,000		
Less: Allowance for uncollectible accounts....... 2,600		107,400
Inventories..................................		140,800
Total Current Assets......................		$313,600

Fixed Assets:

Equipment....................................$250,200		
Less: Allowance for depreciation.............. 67,000		183,200
Total Assets...........................		$496,800

LIABILITIES AND SHAREOWNERS' EQUITY

Current Liabilities:

Accounts payable.............................	$ 52,000
Sales commissions payable.......................	5,600
Accrued income tax...........................	47,100
Notes payable................................	60,000
Total Current Liabilities....................	$164,700

Shareowners' Equity:

Common stock..............................$125,000		
Premium on common stock..................... 75,000		
Retained earnings............................ 132,100		
Total Shareowners' Equity.................		332,100
Total Liabilities and Shareowners' Equity....		$496,800

INCOME STATEMENT

FOR THE THREE-MONTH PERIOD ENDING MARCH 31

Gross sales...................................		$400,000
Less: Estimated credit losses.......................		4,000
Net sales.....................................		$396,000
Standard cost of goods sold........................		300,000
Standard manufacturing profit......................		$ 96,000

Factory cost variances:

Materials price...............................$ (4,800)		
Materials usage............................... 700		
Labor rate................................... (2,600)		
Labor usage.................................. (500)		
Overhead volume............................ (11,500)		
Overhead spending............................ 300		(18,400)
Manufacturing profit.............................		$ 77,600

Other expenses:

Salesmen's salaries............................$ 7,500		
Sales commissions............................. 16,000		
Administrative salaries........................... 7,500		
Other selling and administrative expenses........... 7,500		
Interest expense.............................. 1,000		39,500
Earnings before tax.............................		$ 38,100
Income tax....................................		15,240
Net Income...................................		$ 22,860

Factory cost information:

(1) The company manufactures one product, and its standard costs are:

Direct materials, 10 lbs. at $0.08........................$0.80
Direct labor, ½ hour at $2.............................. 1.00
Factory overhead at $2.40 per direct labor hour........... 1.20
    Total Standard Cost............................$3.00

(2) No usage variances are expected during the second quarter, but direct materials prices are expected to be 8 percent above standard and direct labor wage rates are expected to be 5 percent above standard.

(3) The factory overhead cost per unit is based on an output of 40,000 units a month. The monthly overhead budget for that level of output is:

	Fixed	Variable
Indirect materials........................	$ 5,000	$10,000
Indirect labor...........................	9,000	12,000
Maintenance labor........................	3,000	3,000
Depreciation.............................	2,000	...
Rent.....................................	4,000	
Total Factory Overhead................	$23,000	$25,000

(4) Spending and price variances in factory overhead costs are expected to be negligible during the second quarter.

(5) No inventories of indirect materials are maintained; instead, all indirect materials are delivered to the factory floor immediately upon purchase and their costs are charged directly to factory overhead accounts at that time.

Operating information:

(6) Actual and forecast unit sales and production, January–September:

	Sales	Production		Sales	Production		Sales	Production
Jan...	35,000*	30,000*	Apr...	40,000	40,000	July...	50,000	50,000
Feb...	30,000*	30,000*	May..	40,000	50,000	Aug...	60,000	50,000
Mar...	35,000*	40,000*	June..	45,000	50,000	Sept...	60,000	50,000

* Actual.

(7) The buildup in inventory in May and June is for the third quarter, when sales are expected to be considerably in excess of production capacity. Work in process inventory will remain at the March 31 level regardless of the level of production, and the production desired for a month can be obtained by putting the equivalent quantities into production. With respect to raw material, however, the policy of the company is to have on hand

at the start of each month 40 percent of the requirements for the production scheduled for the month.

(8) Sales terms are net 30 days, and 30 percent of the sales during a month are usually paid for in the same month, 60 percent in the followng month, 9 percent in the next month following, and the remainder are written off against the Allowance for Uncollectible Accounts at the end of that month. Selling price is expected to remain at $4 a unit throughout the second quarter.

(9) The selling and administrative expenses consist entirely of salaries, purchased services and supplies. Administrative expenses are fixed and are expected to continue in the second quarter at their first quarter levels.

(10) Sales salaries are expected to amount to $2,500 a month, while sales commissions are set at 4 percent of gross sales.

(11) All borrowing is done from one bank, and interest is deducted monthly from the company's bank balance at an interest rate of 6 percent a year. The budget is to be prepared on the assumption that the notes payable to the bank will remain at $60,000 throughout the quarter. The actual short-term borrowing is to be determined after review of the budget figures.

(12) The current income tax rate is 40 percent of earnings before taxes.

Other information:

(13) The March 31 inventory consisted of the following:

```
Raw materials............160,000 lbs. at $0.08......$ 12,800
Work in process.................................    38,000
Finished goods...........30,000 units at $3.00......    90,000
       Total.......................................$140,800
```

(14) The company has contracted to purchase equipment in June at a cost of $24,000.

(15) All purchases, including equipment, indirect materials, and all nonlabor services except factory rent are paid for in the month following the month of purchase.

(16) Sales and administrative salaries for each month are paid at the end of the month. Sales commissions are paid in the month after the month in which they are earned. Factory employees are paid weekly, but the final payroll periods in March and June end on March 31 and June 30, so no wage accruals are necessary on those dates.

(17) Other selling and administrative expenses are paid for in the following month.

(18) Factory rent is paid monthly, on the first day of the month.

(19) A portion of the March 31 balance in the Accrued Income Taxes account represents the final payment of taxes on the previous

year's income. This payment is to be made in June. Taxes on the current year's income will not be paid until next year.

(20) A dividend of $10,000 will be declared in April, to be paid on May 15.

21.† During the first nine months of 1967, Verlies & Winst, N.V. operated its only factory two shifts a day, plus a good deal of overtime work, and expected to continue at this production rate through the end of the year. At this rate, it was unable to meet the growing demand for its products, and inventories of finished products had been reduced during 1967 to amounts that the management felt were inadequate, in view of the company's reputation for delivering its products promptly on the dates promised.

To correct this situation and to satisfy customers' demands, the company's executives in November, 1967 decided to consider the desirability of moving to three-shift operations. To provide data useful for this decision, Mr. J. C. Verlies, the company's controller, was to prepare a profit plan and cash budget for 1968.

The Verlies & Winst product line consisted of two items of unusual design, both invented by the company's president, Mr. H. L. Winst. One product was a desk calendar holder of unusual design called "Dagmat"; the other was a desk-size device in which to list frequently called telephone numbers, sold under the name "Telemat."

In addition to Mr. Winst, the company's management consisted of Mr. Verlies and two product managers, one for each of the two products. Because the company was small, Mr. Winst performed the duties of general sales manager and production manager, in addition to his functions as president.

Using an economic forecast supplied by the company's bank, together with reports of dealer sales and inventories gathered by the company's salesmen, the two product managers gave Mr. Verlies the tentative budgets for 1968 shown in Exhibit 1.

Mr. Winst's estimates of maximum production capacity and "general factory costs" (all factory costs except materials, labor, and depreciation) were:

	Production Capacity (Machine-Hours)	General Factory Costs at Capacity Operating Rates
Two-shift operations........	91,450	Fl. 90,000
Three-shift operations.......	122,900	118,000

† Copyright 1967 by l'Institut pour l'Etude des Méthodes de Direction de l'Entreprise (IMEDE), Lausanne, Switzerland. Reprinted by permission.

These estimates included allowances for labor overtime and also provided for a normal amount of time lost due to machine breakdowns and other kinds of work interruptions. Factory personnel for the third shift could be obtained without difficulty, and new people required almost no training.

Exhibit 1

VERLIES & WINST, N.V.

Product Managers' Budget Proposals
For the Year 1968

	Product	
	Dagmat	Telemat
1968 sales (in units)............	400,000	300,000
Increase over 1967..............	+100,000	+ 90,000
Price per unit (both years).......	Fl. 1.00	Fl. 3.00
1968 production costs:		
Material cost per unit.........	Fl. 0.25	Fl. 0.55
Labor cost per unit...........	Fl. 0.15	Fl. 0.45
Machine-hours required		
per unit.................	0.10	0.30
1968 product promotion expense..	Fl. 50,000	Fl. 60,000
Increase over 1967..............	+Fl. 12,500	+Fl. 18,000
Increase in finished goods inventories required with no increase in sales over 1967.....	5,000 units	4,500 units
Additional increase in assets because of increased sales over 1967:		
Accounts receivable..........	+Fl. 20,000	+Fl. 54,000
Materials inventories.........	+Fl. 2,500	+Fl. 4,950
Finished goods inventories.....	+5,000 units	+3,500 units
Work in process inventories....	Negligible	Negligible
Increase in accounts payable accompanying increased sales	+Fl. 2,500	+Fl. 4,950

All monetary amounts are stated in guilders (Fl.). In 1967 the Dutch Guilder was approximately equivalent to U.S. $0.28.

The increases in sales promotion expenditures in excess of 1967 levels would consist mostly of increases in local newspaper advertising and point-of-sale promotional displays. No increase in the number of salesmen was anticipated.

Other estimates and budget proposals that were submitted to Mr. Verlies were:

General sales and administrative expenses (except depreciation).....Fl. 210,000
Depreciation:
    Factory and factory equipment.............................. 50,000
    Office and sales facilities...................................... 25,000
Interest on long-term debt (maturing in 1975).................... 50,000
Dividends on common stock...................................... 30,000
Research and development expenditures.......................... 100,000
Equipment replacement expenditures............................. 90,000
Plant expansion expenditures (these additional facilities would not
    be completed in 1968)...................................... 300,000
Interest to be paid in 1968 on short-term bank loans was at a rate
    of 5% on the balance of the bank loans outstanding at the
    end of 1967.
Income taxes were computed at a rate of 47% of taxable income and
    were due in the first six months of the year following.
Minimum cash balance... 140,000

Research and development expenditures are charged to expense as incurred. Depreciation for 1968 would not be affected by replacement expenditure decisions for 1968. Taxable income and reported income before taxes are identical in this company.

Mr. Verlies estimated that working capital balances would be as follows on January 1, 1968:

Cash....................................	Fl. 160,000
Accounts receivable.......................	186,000
Inventories..............................	33,350
Total..............................	Fl. 379,350
Less:	
Bank loan payable........................Fl. 30,000	
Accounts and interest payable............ 19,050	
Income taxes payable.................... 54,000	103,050
Working Capital....................	Fl. 276,300

Mr. Verlies was convinced that the company would be unable to obtain any new long-term capital during 1968. Cash had to be paid for all assets and services purchased except that trade credit (i.e., accounts payable) was available to finance increases in raw materials inventories. In addition, bank credit was available up to 50 percent of the sum of the face amount of accounts receivable and the total cost of all inventories. (Finished goods were costed at their materials and labor costs only, general factory costs being considered an expense). Bank credit was available in units of Fl. 10,000. For budgeting purposes, it was assumed that any amounts borrowed during the year would be borrowed on July 1, 1968. Interest on bank loans in force during 1968 would be paid in cash during January, 1969.

a) Did the company have adequate production capacity to service the tentative sales budget? What criteria would you use to allocate productive capacity between the two product lines whenever total capacity is inadequate to meet all demands?

b) Prepare a *factory cost* and *production volume* plan for 1968 that would have been technically feasible. Factory capacity should be assigned to the products in such a way as to maximize company profits, subject to the following restrictions: (1) the sales of each product are to be at least as large as they were the preceding year; and (2) inventories of finished goods must be built up to the minimum established for the level of sales anticipated in your *revised* sales plan for 1968.

c) Prepare a tentative cash budget for 1968, reflecting your factory cost and production volume plan and all the other estimates and budget proposals listed above. Is this budget feasible? In case of a shortage of cash, how should management decide which expenditures to cut back?

d) Prepare a profit plan for the year that is both technically and financially feasible, and which meets the restrictions listed under (*b*) above. Would this plan be accepted automatically, or would management be likely to subject it to further tests?

Appendixes

Appendix A

COMPOUND INTEREST

AND BOND TABLES

THE TABLES in this appendix contain the multipliers or conversion factors necessary to convert cash flows of one or more periods into their equivalent values at some other point in time. The basic explanation of the reasons for conversion is given in Chapter 9. Only the mechanical details of how the numbers in the tables should be used are explained here.

Table 1: Future Value of $1

Once the rate of interest is specified, the future dollar equivalent of a present sum can be determined by solving the formula,

$$F_n = P(1 + r)^n \tag{1}$$

in which F_n is the equivalent future value n periods hence of a present sum P at an interest rate r. Solutions of this formula for various values of n and r, P equal to $1, are given in Table 1. Thus, at an interest rate of 6 percent per annum, $1 now will grow to $1.0600 at the end of one year, $1.1236 at the end of two years, and so on. If P equals $10,000, the corresponding future values are $10,600, $11,236, etc.

In other words, to obtain the future value of any present sum, find the multiplier in the table corresponding to the desired values of n and r and multiply it by the present sum.

In using these tables, care must be taken to insure that the *interest rate* is appropriate to the *period*. Thus, if an amount is compounded *semianually* at r percent *per annum* for n years, the number of interest periods is $2n$, and the interest rate per period is $r/2$. To illustrate, if interest is compounded *annually* at 6 percent, $10,000 now will grow to $32,071 by the end of 20 years. If interest is compounded *semiannually*, however, the future value is $32,620, reflecting interest at 3 percent per 6-month period for 40 periods.

Extending the Table

This table can be extended easily to provide multipliers for any
number of periods. For example, suppose one wants to find the future value of $10,000 compounded annually at 6 percent for 21
periods. No 21-period row is in the table. However, it is known that
at the end of 20 years, the future value will be $32,071. If rein-
vested for one more year at 6 percent, this sum will amount to
1.06 × $32,071 = $33,995. This is the future value of $10,000 21
periods hence at 6 percent per period.

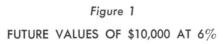

Figure 1

FUTURE VALUES OF $10,000 AT 6%

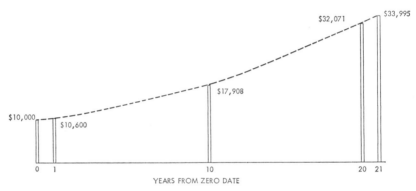

Alternatively, $10,000 will grow to $17,908 in 10 years, and this
sum will grow to $17,908 × 1.8983 = $33,995 in 11 additional years
(the 1.8983 figure comes from the 6 percent column, 11-period row
of Table 1). These relationships are shown in Figure 1.[1]

In other words, the future value of a dollar at any time in the future
can be obtained by multiplying together any two or more multipliers
for which the number of periods adds up to the desired number.
Thus, the multipler for 21 periods can be obtained by multiplying the
factors for 1 and 20 periods, or 3 and 18 periods, or any other
combination of periods totaling 21.

Table 2: Future Value of an Annuity of $1

An annuity was defined in Chapter 9 as a series of equal receipts
(or outlays) of cash. The future value of an annuity is simply the sum
of the future values of each of the individual receipts (or outlays).

---

[1] A similar set of relationships at an interest rate of 5 percent is shown in Exhibit
9–1 in Chapter 9.

For example, $10,000 invested now at 6 percent, compounded annually, will grow to $11,236 at the end of two years (Table 1). If another $10,000 is invested a year from now, it will grow to $10,600 a year later, or two years from now. Thus, a two-year annuity of $10,000 a year will amount to $11,236 + $10,600 = $21,836 at the end of two years.

This is an example of an annuity *in advance*—that is, the cash flow took place at the *beginning* of each period. Suppose, instead, that the payments were made *in arrears*—that is, at the *end* of each period. The first payment would be made a year from now and would thus have only one year to grow before the two-year period ended. Thus, its future value would be only $10,600. The second payment, made at the end of the second year, would have no time at all to grow, and thus its future value would be $10,000. The future value of a two-year, $10,000 annuity in arrears, compounded annually at 6 percent, therefore, is $10,600 + $10,000 = $20,600, or $2.06 for each annuity dollar. This is the factor shown in the 6 percent column, two-year row of Table 2. *The multipliers in Table 2 are for annuities in arrears.*

Converting Table 2 for Annuities in Advance

The relationship between an annuity in arrears and an annuity in advance is shown in Figure 2. Annuity A consists of three annual payments of $100 each, the first payment being made on January 1 of year 2 (an annuity in arrears). Its future value at the end of year 3 is

Figure 2

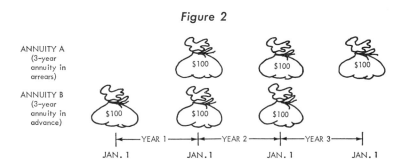

the sum of $100 (the final payment, which earns no interest), $100 plus interest on this amount for one year (the second payment), and $100 plus interest on this amount compounded for two years (the first payment). No interest is earned during year one because no money is placed on deposit until the end of that year.

Annuity B also consists of three annual $100 payments, but the first payment is made on January 1 of year 1 (an annuity in advance). Thus, its future value at the end of year 3 is the sum of $100 plus one year's interest (the final payment), $100 plus two years' compounded interest on this amount (the second payment), and $100 plus three years' compounded interest (the first payment).

Notice that the two annuities are identical for two of the three payments. The difference is that the annuity in arrears substitutes a payment at the end of year three for an initial payment at the beginning of year one. Thus, the difference between the future value of the annuity in arrears and the future value of the annuity in advance is the

Figure 3

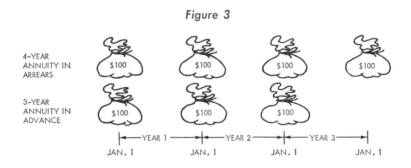

difference between the future value of an initial payment and that of a terminal payment. The future value of a terminal payment is equal to the amount paid (in this case, $100); the future value of the initial payment is the amount paid times $(1 + r)^n$. Therefore, the future value of an annuity in advance can always be computed by calculating the multiplier for an annuity in arrears from Table 3, subtracting 1.0000 and adding the multiplier for n periods from Table 1. For example, a three-year annuity in arrears of $1 at 6 percent has a future value of $3.1836 (Table 3). A three-year annuity in advance has a future value at the same interest rate of $3.1836 — $1.0000 + $1.1910 (Table 1) = $3.3746.

Another way of looking at the same phenomenon is illustrated in Figure 3. From a vantage point at the end of year 3, the only difference between a four-year annuity in arrears and a three-year annuity in advance is a single noninterest-bearing payment at the end of year 4. Hence, the rule stated at the bottom of Table 2 is derived: to convert a table of future values of annuities in arrears to like values of annuities in advance, *take the multiplier for the next period and subtract 1.0000*. For example, for a three-year annuity in advance at 6 percent, take the factor for a four-year annuity in arrears, 4.3746, and subtract 1.0000. The result is 3.3746, the same figure derived by the previous method.

Table 3: Present Value of $1

The present value, P, of any future sum, F_n, is given by the formula:

$$P = F_n(1 + r)^{-n} \qquad (2)$$

and values of P, with F_n equal to $1, are given in Table 3. To obtain the present value of any sum, simply multiply that sum by the factor taken from the appropriate column and row of Table 3.

Once again, if compounding is to be semiannual, the factor should be taken from the column for an interest rate equal to $r/2$ and the row for a number of periods equal to $2n$. If quarterly compounding is used, use $r/4$ and $4n$ (e.g., 2 percent for 40 periods to show present value compounded quarterly at 8 percent a year for 10 years).

Furthermore, any column in the table can be extended by multiplying factors in the manner described earlier. Thus, $0.7473 is the present value of a dollar five years hence at 6 percent compounded annually; the present value of a dollar 10 years hence is 0.7473 times $0.7473 = $0.5585. This differs from the factor shown in the 10-period row of the 6 percent column of Table 3 by a rounding error which is immaterial in amount.

Table 4: Present Value of an Annuity of $1 per Period

The present value of an annuity is the sum of the present values of each of the annuity payments (or receipts). For example, a series of three payments of $100 each, to be paid on December 31 of years 1, 2, and 3 has a present value at 6 percent, compounded annually, as follows:

(1) Time of Payment	(2) Amount of Payment	(3) Multiplier at 6 Percent (from Table 3)	(4) Present Value at 6 Percent (2) × (3)
End of year 1...............	$100	0.9434	$ 94.34
End of year 2...............	100	0.8900	89.00
End of year 3...............	100	0.8396	83.96
Present Value of Annuity.			$267.30

Thus, the multipliers in Table 4 are merely the sum of the multipliers in Table 3 for periods 1 through n.

These conversion factors or multipliers are applicable to an annuity *in arrears*. The difference between an annuity in arrears and an annuity in advance is illustrated in Figure 4. From a vantage point at the beginning of year one, the only difference between a four-year annuity in advance and a three-year annuity in arrears is the initial payment. Since the present value of an immediate payment is equal to the amount of the payment itself (the present value today of a dollar

Figure 4

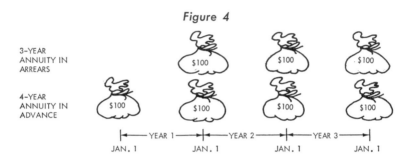

today is a dollar), the rule stated at the foot of Table 4 is derived: to convert a table of present values of annuities in arrears to like values of annuities in advance, *take the multiplier for the next shorter period and add 1.0000*. For example, for a four-year annuity in advance at 6 percent, take the factor for a three-year annuity in arrears, 2.6730 and add 1.0000 to obtain a multiplier of 3.6730.

Annuity Formulas

The equations for the future and present values of a single amount are:

$$F_n = P(1 + r)^n . \tag{1}$$

$$P = F_n(1 + r)^{-n} . \tag{2}$$

A brief derivation of these formulas is given in Chapter 9. The formula for the future value of an annuity in arrears derives from equation (1). If A represents a series of payments occurring at the *end* of each of n periods, the first of such payments (A_1) is compounded for $n - 1$ periods (see Figure 2) and has a future value of

$$F_{n-1} = A_1(1 + r)^{n-1} .$$

The future value of the second payment (A_2) is

$$F_{n-2} = A_2(1 + r)^{n-2} .$$

By induction, the like value of the last, or nth, payment is

$$F_{n-n} = A_n(1 + r)^{n-n} = A_n(1 + r)^0 = A_n(1) = A_n .$$

The sum of the future values (F_A) of all payments is

$$F_A = F_{n-1} + F_{n-2} + \ldots \ldots + F_{n-n} .$$

By substitution,

$$F_A = A_1(1 + r)^{n-1} + A_2(1 + r)^{n-2} + \ldots \ldots + A_n$$

$$= A[(1 + r)^{n-1} + (1 + r)^{n-2} + \ldots \ldots + 1] . \qquad (3)$$

Multiplying equation (3) by $(1 + r)$, results in

$$(1 + r)F_A = A[(1 + r)^n + (1 + r)^{n-1} + \ldots \ldots + (1 + r)] . \qquad (4)$$

By subtracting equation (3) from equation (4), the formula appearing at the head of Table 3 is obtained:

$$rF_A = A[(1 + r)^n - 1]$$

$$F_A = A\left[\frac{(1 + r)^n - 1}{r} \right] . \qquad (5)$$

Formula (5) yields the values given in Table 3 where $A = \$1$.

The formula for the *present value* of an annuity in arrears derives from equation (2) above in a like manner. Thus, the present value of the first payment (A_1), which is discounted for one period, is

$$r = A_1(1 + r)^{-1} = \frac{A_1}{(1 + r)} .$$

The present value of the second payment (A_2) is

$$P = A_n(1 + r)^{-2} = \frac{A_2}{(1 + r)^2} .$$

By induction, the like value of the last, or nth, payment is

$$P = A_n(1 + r)^{-n} = \frac{A_n}{(1 + r)^n} .$$

The sum of the present values (P_A) of all payments is

$$P_A = \frac{A_1}{1 + r} + \frac{A_2}{(1 + r)^2} + \ldots \ldots + \frac{A_n}{(1 + r)^n}$$

$$= A\left[\frac{1}{1 + r} + \frac{1}{(1 + r)^2} + \ldots \ldots + \frac{1}{(1 + r)^n} \right] . \qquad (6)$$

Multiplying equation (6) by $(1 + r)$, results in

$$(1 + r)P_A = A\left[1 + \frac{1}{1 + r} + \ldots \ldots + \frac{1}{(1 + r)^{n-1}} \right] . \qquad (7)$$

Subtracting equation (6) from equation (7) results in the formula appearing at the head of Table 4:

$$rP_A = A\left[1 - \frac{1}{(1+r)^n}\right] = A[1 - (1+r)^{-n}]$$

$$P_A = A\left[\frac{1 - (1+r)^{-n}}{r}\right]. \qquad (8)$$

Formula (8) yields the values given in Table 4 where $A = \$1$.

Bond Value Tables

Tables 5 through 11 give the present values at various yield rates of bonds bearing various coupon rates from 3 percent to 6 percent and of various terms from 6 months to 30 years. Values are stated in dollars per $100 of face value. To find the present value of any other face amount, multiply the face value by one one-hundredth of the factor shown in the table.

These tables are intended only as illustrative samples for use in connection with the problems in this book and are far less complete than the tables used in the investment banking community. Missing values can be derived, using Tables 3 and 4 in the manner prescribed in Chapter 13, but in practice it is more economical to obtain and apply more extensive published tables or work directly with standard computer programs.

Table 1. Future Value of $1

$$F_n = P(1 + r)^n$$

Pe-riods	2%	2½%	3%	4%	5%	6%	8%	10%
1...	1.0200	1.0250	1.0300	1.0400	1.0500	1.0600	1.0800	1.1000
2...	1.0404	1.0506	1.0609	1.0816	1.1025	1.1236	1.1664	1.2100
3...	1.0612	1.0769	1.0927	1.1249	1.1576	1.1910	1.2597	1.3310
4...	1.0824	1.1038	1.1255	1.1699	1.2155	1.2625	1.3605	1.4641
5...	1.1041	1.1314	1.1593	1.2167	1.2763	1.3382	1.4693	1.6105
6...	1.1262	1.1597	1.1941	1.2653	1.3401	1.4185	1.5869	1.7716
7...	1.1487	1.1887	1.2299	1.3159	1.4071	1.5036	1.7138	1.9488
8...	1.1717	1.2184	1.2668	1.3686	1.4775	1.5938	1.8509	2.1436
9...	1.1951	1.2489	1.3048	1.4233	1.5513	1.6895	1.9990	2.3589
10...	1.2190	1.2801	1.3439	1.4802	1.6289	1.7908	2.1589	2.5938
11...	1.2434	1.3121	1.3842	1.5395	1.7103	1.8983	2.3316	2.8532
12...	1.2682	1.3449	1.4258	1.6010	1.7959	2.0122	2.5182	3.1385
13...	1.2936	1.3785	1.4685	1.6651	1.8856	2.1329	2.7196	3.4524
14...	1.3195	1.4130	1.5126	1.7317	1.9799	2.2609	2.9372	3.7976
15...	1.3459	1.4483	1.5580	1.8009	2.0709	2.3966	3.1722	4.1774
16...	1.3728	1.4845	1.6047	1.8730	2.1829	2.5404	3.4259	4.5951
17...	1.4002	1.5216	1.6528	1.9479	2.2920	2.6928	3.7000	5.0545
18...	1.4282	1.5597	1.7024	2.0258	2.4066	2.8543	3.9960	5.5600
19...	1.4568	1.5987	1.7535	2.1068	2.5270	3.0256	4.3157	6.1160
20...	1.4859	1.6386	1.8061	2.1911	2.6533	3.2071	4.6610	6.7276
22...	1.5460	1.7216	1.9161	2.3699	2.9253	3.6035	5.4365	8.1404
24...	1.6084	1.8087	2.0328	2.5633	3.2251	4.0489	6.3412	9.8498
26...	1.6734	1.9003	2.1566	2.7725	3.5557	4.5494	7.3964	11.9183
28...	1.7410	1.9965	2.2879	2.9987	3.9201	5.1117	8.6271	14.4211
30...	1.8114	2.0976	2.4273	3.2434	4.3219	5.7435	10.0627	17.4495
32...	1.8845	2.2038	2.5751	3.5081	4.7649	6.4534	11.7371	21.1140
34...	1.9607	2.3153	2.7319	3.7943	5.2533	7.2510	13.6901	25.5479
36...	2.0399	2.4325	2.8983	4.1039	5.7918	8.1473	15.9682	30.9130
38...	2.1223	2.5557	3.0748	4.4388	6.3855	9.1543	18.6253	37.4047
40...	2.2080	2.6851	3.2620	4.8010	7.0400	10.2857	21.7245	45.2597
42...	2.2972	2.8210	3.4607	5.1928	7.7616	11.5570	25.3395	54.7643
44...	2.3901	2.9638	3.6715	5.6165	8.5572	12.9855	29.5560	66.2648
46...	2.4866	3.1139	3.8950	6.0748	9.4343	14.5905	34.4741	80.1804
48...	2.5871	3.2715	4.1323	6.5705	10.4013	16.3939	40.2106	97.0182
50...	2.6916	3.4371	4.3839	7.1067	11.4674	18.4202	46.9016	117.3920
60...	3.2810	4.3998	5.8916	10.5196	18.6792	32.9877	101.2571	304.4846

Table 2. Future Value of Annuity of $1 in Arrears

$$F = A\left[\frac{(1 + r)^n - 1}{r}\right]$$

Pe-riods	2%	2½%	3%	4%	5%	6%	8%	10%
1..	1.0000	1.0000	1.0000	1.0000	1.0000	1.0000	1.0000	1.0000
2..	2.0200	2.0250	2.0300	2.0400	2.0500	2.0600	2.0800	2.1000
3..	3.0604	3.0756	3.0909	3.1216	3.1525	3.1836	3.2464	3.3100
4..	4.1216	4.1525	4.1836	4.2465	4.3101	4.3746	4.5061	4.6410
5..	5.2040	5.2563	5.3091	5.4163	5.5256	5.6371	5.8666	6.1051
6..	6.3081	6.3877	6.4684	6.6330	6.8019	6.9753	7.3359	7.7156
7..	7.4343	7.5474	7.6625	7.8983	8.1420	8.3938	8.9228	9.4872
8..	8.5830	8.7361	8.8923	9.2142	9.5491	9.8975	10.6366	11.4360
9..	9.7546	9.9545	10.1591	10.5828	11.0266	11.4913	12.4876	13.5796
10..	10.9497	11.2034	11.4639	12.0061	12.5779	13.1808	14.4866	15.9376
11..	12.1687	12.4835	12.8078	13.4864	14.2068	14.9716	16.6455	18.5314
12..	13.4121	13.7956	14.1920	15.0258	15.9171	16.8699	18.9771	21.3846
13..	14.6803	15.1404	15.6178	16.6268	17.7130	18.8821	21.4953	24.5231
14..	15.9739	16.5190	17.0863	18.2919	19.5986	21.0151	24.2149	27.9755
15..	17.2934	17.9319	18.5989	20.0236	21.5786	23.2760	27.1521	31.7731
16..	18.6393	19.3802	20.1569	21.8245	23.6575	25.6725	30.3243	35.9503
17..	20.0121	20.8647	21.7616	23.6975	25.8404	28.2129	33.7502	40.5456
18..	21.4123	22.3863	23.4144	25.6454	28.1324	30.9057	37.4502	45.6001
19..	22.8406	23.9460	25.1169	27.6712	30.5390	33.7600	41.4463	51.1601
20..	24.2974	25.5447	26.8704	29.7781	33.0660	36.7856	45.7620	57.2761
22..	27.2990	28.8629	30.5368	34.2480	38.5052	43.3923	55.4568	71.4041
24..	30.4219	32.3490	34.4265	39.0826	44.5020	50.8156	66.7648	88.4989
26..	33.6709	36.0117	38.5530	44.3117	51.1135	59.1564	79.9544	109.1835
28..	37.0512	39.8598	42.9309	49.9676	58.4026	68.5281	95.3388	134.2119
30..	40.5681	43.9027	47.5754	56.0849	66.4388	79.0582	113.2832	164.4962
32..	44.2270	48.1503	52.5028	62.7015	75.2988	90.8898	134.2135	201.1402
34..	48.0338	52.6129	57.7302	69.8579	85.0670	104.1838	158.6267	245.4796
36..	51.9944	57.3014	63.2759	77.5983	95.8363	119.1209	187.1021	299.1302
38..	56.1149	62.2273	69.1594	85.9703	107.7095	135.9042	220.3159	364.0475
40..	60.4020	67.4026	75.4013	95.0255	120.7998	154.7620	259.0565	442.5974
42..	64.8622	72.8398	82.0232	104.8196	135.2318	175.9505	304.2435	537.6428
44..	69.5027	78.5523	89.0484	115.4129	151.1430	199.7580	356.9496	652.6478
46..	74.3306	84.5540	96.5015	126.8706	168.6852	226.5081	418.4261	791.8039
48..	79.3535	90.8596	104.4084	139.2632	188.0254	256.5645	490.1322	960.1827
50..	84.5794	97.4843	112.7969	152.6671	209.3480	290.3359	573.7702	1163.9209
60..	114.0515	135.9916	163.0534	237.9907	353.5837	533.1282	1253.2133	3034.8470

NOTE: To convert this table to values of an annuity in advance, take one more period and subtract 1.000.

Table 3. Present Value of $1

$$P = F_n(1 + r)^{-n}$$

Periods (n)	1%	1½%	2%	2½%	3%	3½%	4%	4½%	5%	6%	7%	8%	10%
1......	0.9901	0.9852	0.9804	0.9756	0.9709	0.9662	0.9615	0.9569	0.9524	0.9434	0.9346	0.9259	0.9091
2......	0.9803	0.9707	0.9612	0.9518	0.9426	0.9335	0.9246	0.9157	0.9070	0.8900	0.8734	0.8573	0.8264
3......	0.9706	0.9563	0.9423	0.9286	0.9151	0.9019	0.8890	0.8763	0.8638	0.8396	0.8163	0.7938	0.7513
4......	0.9610	0.9422	0.9238	0.9060	0.8885	0.8714	0.8548	0.8386	0.8227	0.7921	0.7629	0.7350	0.6830
5......	0.9515	0.9283	0.9057	0.8839	0.8626	0.8420	0.8219	0.8025	0.7835	0.7473	0.7130	0.6806	0.6209
6......	0.9420	0.9145	0.8880	0.8623	0.8375	0.8135	0.7903	0.7679	0.7462	0.7050	0.6663	0.6302	0.5645
7......	0.9327	0.9010	0.8706	0.8413	0.8131	0.7860	0.7599	0.7348	0.7107	0.6651	0.6227	0.5835	0.5132
8......	0.9235	0.8877	0.8535	0.8207	0.7894	0.7594	0.7307	0.7032	0.6768	0.6274	0.5820	0.5403	0.4665
9......	0.9143	0.8746	0.8368	0.8007	0.7664	0.7337	0.7026	0.6729	0.6446	0.5919	0.5439	0.5002	0.4241
10......	0.9053	0.8617	0.8203	0.7812	0.7441	0.7089	0.6756	0.6439	0.6139	0.5584	0.5083	0.4632	0.3855
11......	0.8963	0.8489	0.8043	0.7621	0.7224	0.6849	0.6496	0.6162	0.5847	0.5268	0.4751	0.4289	0.3505
12......	0.8874	0.8364	0.7885	0.7436	0.7014	0.6618	0.6246	0.5897	0.5568	0.4970	0.4440	0.3971	0.3186
13......	0.8787	0.8240	0.7730	0.7254	0.6810	0.6394	0.6006	0.5643	0.5303	0.4688	0.4150	0.3677	0.2897
14......	0.8700	0.8118	0.7579	0.7077	0.6611	0.6178	0.5775	0.5400	0.5051	0.4423	0.3878	0.3405	0.2633
15......	0.8613	0.7999	0.7430	0.6905	0.6419	0.5969	0.5553	0.5167	0.4810	0.4173	0.3624	0.3153	0.2394
16......	0.8528	0.7880	0.7284	0.6736	0.6232	0.5767	0.5339	0.4945	0.4581	0.3936	0.3387	0.2919	0.2176
17......	0.8444	0.7764	0.7142	0.6572	0.6050	0.5572	0.5134	0.4732	0.4363	0.3714	0.3166	0.2703	0.1978
18......	0.8360	0.7649	0.7002	0.6412	0.5874	0.5384	0.4936	0.4528	0.4155	0.3503	0.2959	0.2502	0.1799
19......	0.8277	0.7536	0.6864	0.6255	0.5703	0.5202	0.4746	0.4333	0.3957	0.3305	0.2765	0.2317	0.1635
20......	0.8195	0.7425	0.6730	0.6103	0.5537	0.5026	0.4564	0.4146	0.3769	0.3118	0.2584	0.2145	0.1486
21......	0.8114	0.7315	0.6598	0.5954	0.5375	0.4856	0.4388	0.3968	0.3589	0.2942	0.2415	0.1987	0.1351
22......	0.8034	0.7207	0.6468	0.5809	0.5219	0.4692	0.4220	0.3797	0.3418	0.2775	0.2257	0.1839	0.1228
23......	0.7954	0.7100	0.6342	0.5667	0.5067	0.4533	0.4057	0.3634	0.3256	0.2618	0.2109	0.1703	0.1117
24......	0.7876	0.6995	0.6217	0.5529	0.4919	0.4380	0.3901	0.3477	0.3101	0.2470	0.1971	0.1577	0.1015
25......	0.7798	0.6892	0.6095	0.5394	0.4776	0.4231	0.3751	0.3327	0.2953	0.2330	0.1842	0.1460	0.0923
26......	0.7720	0.6790	0.5976	0.5262	0.4637	0.4088	0.3607	0.3184	0.2812	0.2198	0.1722	0.1352	0.0839
27......	0.7644	0.6690	0.5859	0.5134	0.4502	0.3950	0.3468	0.3047	0.2678	0.2074	0.1609	0.1252	0.0763
28......	0.7568	0.6591	0.5744	0.5009	0.4371	0.3817	0.3335	0.2916	0.2551	0.1956	0.1504	0.1159	0.0693
29......	0.7493	0.6494	0.5631	0.4887	0.4243	0.3687	0.3207	0.2790	0.2429	0.1846	0.1406	0.1073	0.0630
30......	0.7419	0.6398	0.5521	0.4767	0.4120	0.3563	0.3083	0.2670	0.2314	0.1741	0.1314	0.0994	0.0573
40......	0.6717	0.5513	0.4529	0.3724	0.3066	0.2526	0.2083	0.1719	0.1420	0.0972	0.0668	0.0460	0.0221
50......	0.6080	0.4750	0.3715	0.2909	0.2281	0.1791	0.1407	0.1107	0.0872	0.0543	0.0339	0.0213	0.0085

12%	14%	15%	16%	18%	20%	22%	24%	25%	26%	28%	30%	40%	50%
0.893	0.877	0.870	0.862	0.847	0.833	0.820	0.806	0.800	0.794	0.781	0.769	0.714	0.667
0.797	0.769	0.756	0.743	0.718	0.694	0.672	0.650	0.640	0.630	0.610	0.592	0.510	0.444
0.712	0.675	0.658	0.641	0.609	0.579	0.551	0.524	0.512	0.500	0.477	0.455	0.364	0.296
0.636	0.592	0.572	0.552	0.516	0.482	0.451	0.423	0.410	0.397	0.373	0.350	0.260	0.198
0.567	0.519	0.497	0.476	0.437	0.402	0.370	0.341	0.328	0.315	0.291	0.269	0.186	0.132
0.507	0.456	0.432	0.410	0.370	0.335	0.303	0.275	0.262	0.250	0.227	0.207	0.133	0.088
0.452	0.400	0.376	0.354	0.314	0.279	0.249	0.222	0.210	0.198	0.178	0.159	0.095	0.059
0.404	0.351	0.327	0.305	0.266	0.233	0.204	0.179	0.168	0.157	0.139	0.123	0.068	0.039
0.361	0.308	0.284	0.263	0.225	0.194	0.167	0.144	0.134	0.125	0.108	0.094	0.048	0.026
0.322	0.270	0.247	0.227	0.191	0.162	0.137	0.116	0.107	0.099	0.085	0.073	0.035	0.017
0.287	0.237	0.215	0.195	0.162	0.135	0.112	0.094	0.086	0.079	0.066	0.056	0.025	0.012
0.257	0.208	0.187	0.168	0.137	0.112	0.092	0.076	0.069	0.062	0.052	0.043	0.018	0.008
0.229	0.182	0.163	0.145	0.116	0.093	0.075	0.061	0.055	0.050	0.040	0.033	0.013	0.005
0.205	0.160	0.141	0.125	0.099	0.078	0.062	0.049	0.044	0.039	0.032	0.025	0.009	0.003
0.183	0.140	0.123	0.108	0.084	0.065	0.051	0.040	0.035	0.031	0.025	0.020	0.006	0.002
0.163	0.123	0.107	0.093	0.071	0.054	0.042	0.032	0.028	0.025	0.019	0.015	0.005	0.002
0.146	0.108	0.093	0.080	0.060	0.045	0.034	0.026	0.023	0.020	0.015	0.012	0.003	0.001
0.130	0.095	0.081	0.069	0.051	0.038	0.028	0.021	0.018	0.016	0.012	0.009	0.002	0.001
0.116	0.083	0.070	0.060	0.043	0.031	0.023	0.017	0.014	0.012	0.009	0.007	0.002	
0.104	0.073	0.061	0.051	0.037	0.026	0.019	0.014	0.012	0.010	0.007	0.005	0.001	
0.093	0.064	0.053	0.044	0.031	0.022	0.015	0.011	0.009	0.008	0.006	0.004	0.001	
0.083	0.056	0.046	0.038	0.026	0.018	0.013	0.009	0.007	0.006	0.004	0.003	0.001	
0.074	0.049	0.040	0.033	0.022	0.015	0.010	0.007	0.006	0.005	0.003	0.002		
0.066	0.043	0.035	0.028	0.019	0.013	0.008	0.006	0.005	0.004	0.003	0.002		
0.059	0.038	0.030	0.024	0.016	0.010	0.007	0.005	0.004	0.003	0.002	0.001		
0.053	0.033	0.026	0.021	0.014	0.009	0.006	0.004	0.003	0.002	0.002	0.001		
0.047	0.029	0.023	0.018	0.011	0.007	0.005	0.003	0.002	0.002	0.001	0.001		
0.042	0.026	0.020	0.016	0.010	0.006	0.004	0.002	0.002	0.002	0.001	0.001		
0.037	0.022	0.017	0.014	0.008	0.005	0.003	0.002	0.002	0.001	0.001	0.001		
0.033	0.020	0.015	0.012	0.007	0.004	0.003	0.002	0.001	0.001	0.001			
0.011	0.005	0.004	0.003	0.001	0.001								
0.003	0.001	0.001	0.001										

Table 4. Present Value of Annuity of $1 in Arrears

$$P_A = A\left[\frac{1 - (1 + r)^{-n}}{r}\right]$$

Periods (n)	1%	1½%	2%	2½%	3%	3½%	4%	4½%	5%	6%	7%
1....	0.9901	0.9852	0.9804	0.9756	0.9709	0.9662	0.9615	0.9569	0.9524	0.9434	0.9346
2....	1.9704	1.9559	1.9416	1.9274	1.9135	1.8997	1.8861	1.8727	1.8594	1.8334	1.8080
3....	2.9410	2.9122	2.8839	2.8560	2.8286	2.8016	2.7751	2.7490	2.7232	2.6730	2.6243
4....	3.9020	3.8544	3.8077	3.7620	3.7171	3.6731	3.6299	3.5875	3.5460	3.4651	3.3872
5....	4.8534	4.7826	4.7135	4.6458	4.5797	4.5151	4.4518	4.3900	4.3295	4.2124	4.1002
6....	5.7955	5.6972	5.6014	5.5081	5.4172	5.3286	5.2421	5.1579	5.0757	4.9173	4.7665
7....	6.7282	6.5982	6.4720	6.3494	6.2303	6.1145	6.0021	5.8927	5.7864	5.5824	5.3893
8....	7.6517	7.4859	7.3255	7.1701	7.0197	6.8740	6.7327	6.5959	6.4632	6.2098	5.9713
9....	8.5660	8.3605	8.1622	7.9709	7.7861	7.6077	7.4353	7.2688	7.1078	6.8017	6.5152
10....	9.4713	9.2222	8.9826	8.7521	8.5302	8.3166	8.1109	7.9127	7.7217	7.3601	7.0236
11....	10.3676	10.0711	9.7868	9.5142	9.2526	9.0016	8.7605	8.5289	8.3064	7.8869	7.4987
12....	11.2551	10.9075	10.5753	10.2578	9.9540	9.6633	9.3851	9.1186	8.8633	8.3838	7.9427
13....	12.1337	11.7315	11.3484	10.9832	10.6350	10.3027	9.9856	9.6829	9.3936	8.8527	8.3577
14....	13.0037	12.5434	12.1062	11.6909	11.2961	10.9205	10.5631	10.2228	9.8986	9.2950	8.7455
15....	13.8651	13.3432	12.8493	12.3814	11.9379	11.5174	11.1184	10.7395	10.3797	9.7122	9.1079
16....	14.7179	14.1313	13.5777	13.0550	12.5611	12.0941	11.6523	11.2340	10.8378	10.1059	9.4466
17....	15.5623	14.9076	14.2919	13.7122	13.1661	12.6513	12.1657	11.7072	11.2741	10.4773	9.7632
18....	16.3983	15.6726	14.9920	14.3534	13.7535	13.1897	12.6593	12.1600	11.6896	10.8276	10.0591
19....	17.2260	16.4262	15.6785	14.9789	14.3238	13.7098	13.1339	12.5933	12.0853	11.1581	10.3356
20....	18.0456	17.1686	16.3514	15.5892	14.8775	14.2124	13.5903	13.0079	12.4622	11.4699	10.5940
21....	18.8570	17.9001	17.0112	16.1845	15.4150	14.6980	14.0292	13.4047	12.8212	11.7640	10.8355
22....	19.6604	18.6208	17.6580	16.7654	15.9369	15.1671	14.4511	13.7844	13.1630	12.0416	11.0612
23....	20.4558	19.3309	18.2922	17.3321	16.4436	15.6204	14.8568	14.1478	13.4886	12.3034	11.2722
24....	21.2434	20.0304	18.9139	17.8850	16.9355	16.0584	15.2470	14.4955	13.7986	12.5504	11.4693
25....	22.0232	20.7196	19.5235	18.4244	17.4131	16.4815	15.6221	14.8282	14.0939	12.7834	11.6536
26....	22.7952	21.3986	20.1210	18.9506	17.8768	16.8904	15.9828	15.1466	14.3752	13.0032	11.8258
27....	23.5596	22.0676	20.7069	19.4640	18.3270	17.2854	16.3296	15.4513	14.6430	13.2105	11.9867
28....	24.3164	22.7267	21.2813	19.9649	18.7641	17.6670	16.6631	15.7429	14.8981	13.4062	12.1371
29....	25.0658	23.3761	21.8444	20.4535	19.1885	18.0358	16.9837	16.0219	15.1411	13.5907	12.2777
30....	25.8077	24.0158	22.3965	20.9303	19.6004	18.3920	17.2920	16.2889	15.3725	13.7648	12.4090
40....	32.8347	29.9158	27.3555	25.1028	23.1148	21.3551	19.7928	18.4016	17.1591	15.0463	13.3317
50....	39.1961	34.9997	31.4236	28.3623	25.7298	23.4556	21.4822	19.7620	18.2559	15.7619	13.8007

8%	10%	12%	14%	15%	16%	18%	20%	22%	24%	25%	26%	28%	30%	40%	50%
0.9259	0.9091	0.893	0.877	0.870	0.862	0.847	0.833	0.820	0.806	0.800	0.794	0.781	0.769	0.714	0.667
1.7833	1.7355	1.690	1.647	1.626	1.605	1.566	1.528	1.492	1.457	1.440	1.424	1.392	1.361	1.224	1.111
2.5771	2.4869	2.402	2.322	2.283	2.246	2.174	2.106	2.042	1.981	1.952	1.923	1.868	1.816	1.589	1.407
3.3121	3.1699	3.037	2.914	2.855	2.798	2.690	2.589	2.494	2.404	2.362	2.320	2.241	2.166	1.849	1.605
3.9927	3.7908	3.605	3.433	3.352	3.274	3.127	2.991	2.864	2.745	2.689	2.635	2.532	2.436	2.035	1.737
4.6229	4.3553	4.111	3.889	3.784	3.685	3.498	3.326	3.167	3.020	2.951	2.885	2.759	2.643	2.168	1.824
5.2064	4.8684	4.564	4.288	4.160	4.039	3.812	3.605	3.416	3.242	3.161	3.083	2.937	2.802	2.263	1.883
5.7466	5.3349	4.968	4.639	4.487	4.344	4.078	3.837	3.619	3.421	3.329	3.241	3.076	2.925	2.331	1.922
6.2469	5.7590	5.328	4.946	4.772	4.607	4.303	4.031	3.786	3.566	3.463	3.366	3.184	3.019	2.379	1.948
6.7101	6.1446	5.650	5.216	5.019	4.833	4.494	4.192	3.923	3.682	3.571	3.465	3.269	3.092	2.414	1.965
7.1390	6.4951	5.988	5.453	5.234	5.029	4.656	4.327	4.035	3.776	3.656	3.544	3.335	3.147	2.438	1.977
7.5361	6.8137	6.194	5.660	5.421	5.197	4.793	4.439	4.127	3.851	3.725	3.606	3.387	3.190	2.456	1.985
7.9038	7.1034	6.424	5.842	5.583	5.342	4.910	4.533	4.203	3.912	3.780	3.656	3.427	3.223	2.468	1.990
8.2442	7.3667	6.628	6.002	5.724	5.468	5.008	4.611	4.265	3.962	3.824	3.695	3.459	3.249	2.477	1.993
8.5595	7.6061	6.811	6.142	5.847	5.575	5.092	4.675	4.315	4.001	3.859	3.726	3.483	3.268	2.484	1.995
8.8514	7.8237	6.974	6.265	5.954	5.669	5.162	4.730	4.357	4.033	3.887	3.751	3.503	3.283	2.489	1.997
9.1216	8.0216	7.120	6.373	6.047	5.749	5.222	4.775	4.391	4.059	3.910	3.771	3.518	3.295	2.492	1.998
9.3719	8.2014	7.250	6.467	6.128	5.818	5.273	4.812	4.419	4.080	3.928	3.786	3.529	3.304	2.494	1.999
9.6036	8.3649	7.366	6.550	6.198	5.877	5.316	4.844	4.442	4.097	3.942	3.799	3.539	3.311	2.496	1.999
9.8181	8.5136	7.469	6.623	6.259	5.929	5.353	4.870	4.460	4.110	3.954	3.808	3.546	3.316	2.497	1.999
10.0168	8.6487	7.562	6.687	6.312	5.973	5.384	4.891	4.476	4.121	3.963	3.816	3.551	3.320	2.498	2.000
10.2007	8.7715	7.645	6.743	6.359	6.011	5.410	4.909	4.488	4.130	3.970	3.822	3.556	3.323	2.498	2.000
10.3711	8.8832	7.718	6.792	6.399	6.044	5.432	4.925	4.499	4.137	3.976	3.827	3.559	3.325	2.499	2.000
10.5288	8.9847	7.784	6.835	6.434	6.073	5.451	4.937	4.507	4.143	3.981	3.831	3.562	3.327	2.499	2.000
10.6748	9.0770	7.843	6.873	6.464	6.097	5.467	4.948	4.514	4.147	3.985	3.834	3.564	3.329	2.499	2.000
10.8100	9.1609	7.896	6.906	6.491	6.118	5.480	4.956	4.520	4.151	3.988	3.837	3.566	3.330	2.500	2.000
10.9352	9.2372	7.943	6.935	6.514	6.136	5.492	4.964	4.524	4.154	3.990	3.839	3.567	3.331	2.500	2.000
11.0511	9.3066	7.984	6.961	6.534	6.152	5.502	4.970	4.528	4.157	3.992	3.840	3.568	3.331	2.500	2.000
11.1584	9.3696	8.022	6.983	6.551	6.166	5.510	4.975	4.531	4.159	3.994	3.841	3.569	3.332	2.500	2.000
11.2578	9.4269	8.055	7.003	6.566	6.177	5.517	4.979	4.534	4.160	3.995	3.842	3.569	3.332	2.500	2.000
11.9246	9.7791	8.244	7.105	6.642	6.234	5.548	4.997	4.544	4.166	3.999	3.846	3.571	3.333	2.500	2.000
12.2335	9.9148	8.304	7.133	6.661	6.246	5.554	4.999	4.545	4.167	4.000	3.846	3.571	3.333	2.500	2.000

NOTE: To convert this table to values of an annuity in advance, take one less period and add 1.0000.

Table 5. Bond Values—Coupon Rate of 3 Percent

Percent Yield per Annum	Years to Maturity							
	½	1	5	10	15	19½	20	30
1.5.........	100.74	101.48	107.20	113.88	120.08	125.28	125.84	136.13
1.6.........	100.69	101.38	106.70	112.89	118.60	123.37	123.88	133.25
1.7.........	100.64	101.28	106.21	111.91	117.15	121.50	121.96	130.25
1.8.........	100.59	101.18	105.71	110.94	115.71	119.66	120.08	127.72
1.9.........	100.54	101.08	105.22	109.98	114.30	117.85	118.23	125.07
2.0.........	100.50	100.99	104.74	109.02	112.90	116.08	116.42	122.48
2.1.........	100.45	100.89	104.25	108.08	111.53	114.34	114.64	119.96
2.2.........	100.40	100.79	103.77	107.15	110.17	112.63	112.89	117.50
2.3.........	100.35	100.69	103.29	106.22	108.84	110.95	111.17	115.11
2.4.........	100.30	100.59	102.81	105.31	107.52	109.30	109.49	112.78
2.5.........	100.25	100.49	102.34	104.40	106.22	107.68	107.83	110.51
2.6.........	100.20	100.39	101.86	103.50	104.94	106.09	106.21	108.30
2.7.........	100.15	100.29	101.39	102.61	103.68	104.52	104.61	106.14
2.8.........	100.10	100.20	100.93	101.73	102.44	102.99	103.05	104.04
2.9.........	100.05	100.10	100.46	100.86	101.21	101.48	101.51	101.99
3.0.........	100.00	100.00	100.00	100.00	100.00	100.00	100.00	100.00
3 1.........	99.95	99.90	99.54	99.15	98.81	98.54	98.52	98.06
3.2.........	99.90	99.80	99.08	98.30	97.63	97.12	97.06	96.16
3.3.........	99.85	99.71	98.63	97.46	96.47	95.71	95.63	94.31
3.4.........	99.80	99.61	98.17	96.63	95.33	94.33	94.23	92.51
3.5.........	99.75	99.51	97.72	95.81	94.20	92.98	92.85	90.76
3.6.........	99.71	99.42	97.28	95.00	93.09	91.64	91.50	89.05
3.7.........	99.66	99.32	96.83	94.19	92.00	90.34	90.17	87.38
3.8.........	99.61	99.22	96.39	93.40	90.92	89.05	88.86	85.75
3.9.........	99.56	99.13	95.95	92.61	89.85	87.79	87.58	84.17
4.0.........	99.51	99.03	95.51	91.82	88.80	86.55	86.32	82.62
4.1.........	99.46	98.93	95.07	91.05	87.77	85.33	85.09	81.11
4.2.........	99.41	98.84	94.64	90.28	86.75	84.13	83.87	79.64
4.3.........	99.36	98.74	94.21	89.52	85.74	82.96	82.68	78.20
4.4.........	99.32	98.64	93.78	88.77	84.75	81.80	81.51	76.80
4.5.........	99.27	98.55	93.35	88.03	83.77	80.66	80.35	75.44
4.6.........	99.22	98.45	92.93	87.29	82.80	79.55	79.22	74.11
4.7.........	99.17	98.36	92.50	86.56	81.85	78.45	78.11	72.81
4.8.........	99.12	98.26	92.08	85.84	80.91	77.37	77.02	71.54
4.9.........	99.07	98.17	91.66	85.12	79.98	76.31	75.95	70.30
5.0.........	99.02	98.07	91.25	84.41	79.07	75.27	74.90	69.09
5.1.........	98.98	97.98	90.83	83.71	78.17	74.25	73.86	67.91
5.2.........	98.93	97.88	90.42	83.01	77.28	73.24	72.85	66.76
5.3.........	98.88	97.79	90.01	82.32	76.40	72.25	71.85	65.64
5.4.........	98.83	97.69	89.61	81.64	75.54	71.28	70.87	64.54

Table 6. Bond Values—Coupon Rate of 3½ Percent

Percent Yield per Annum	Years to Maturity							
	½	1	5	10	15	19½	20	30
2.0.........	100.74	101.48	107.10	113.53	119.36	124.12	124.63	133.72
2.1.........	100.69	101.38	106.61	112.57	117.93	122.31	122.77	131.04
2.2.........	100.64	101.28	106.12	111.61	116.53	120.52	120.94	128.44
2.3.........	100.59	101.18	105.64	110.67	115.15	118.77	119.15	125.90
2.4.........	100.54	101.08	105.15	109.73	113.79	117.05	117.39	123.43
2.5.........	100.49	100.98	104.67	108.80	112.44	115.36	115.66	121.02
2.6.........	100.44	100.88	104.19	107.88	111.12	113.70	113.97	118.67
2.7.........	100.39	100.78	103.72	106.97	109.81	112.07	112.30	116.38
2.8.........	100.35	100.69	103.24	106.07	108.53	110.46	110.66	114.14
2.9.........	100.30	100.59	102.77	105.18	107.26	108.89	109.06	111.97
3.0.........	100.25	100.49	102.31	104.29	106.00	107.34	107.48	109.85
3.1.........	100.20	100.39	101.84	103.42	104.77	105.82	105.93	107.78
3.2.........	100.15	100.29	101.38	102.55	103.55	104.33	104.41	105.76
3.3.........	100.10	100.20	100.91	101.69	102.35	102.86	102.91	103.79
3.4.........	100.05	100.10	100.46	100.84	101.17	101.42	101.44	101.87
3.5.........	100.00	100.00	100.00	100.00	100.00	100.00	100.00	100.00
3.6.........	99.95	99.90	99.55	99.17	98.85	98.61	98.58	98.17
3.7.........	99.90	99.81	99.09	98.34	97.71	97.24	97.19	96.39
3.8.........	99.85	99.71	98.65	97.52	96.59	95.89	95.82	94.66
3.9.........	99.80	99.61	98.20	96.71	95.49	94.57	94.48	92.96
4.0.........	99.75	99.51	97.75	95.91	94.40	93.27	93.16	91.31
4.1.........	99.71	99.42	97.31	95.12	93.33	92.00	91.86	89.70
4.2.........	99.66	99.32	96.87	94.33	92.27	90.74	90.59	88.12
4.3.........	99.61	99.23	96.44	93.55	91.22	89.51	89.34	86.59
4.4.........	99.56	99.13	96.00	92.78	90.19	88.30	88.11	85.09
4.5.........	99.51	99.03	95.57	92.02	89.18	87.11	86.90	83.63
4.6.........	99.46	98.94	95.14	91.26	88.18	85.94	85.72	82.20
4.7.........	99.41	98.84	94.71	90.51	87.19	84.79	84.55	80.80
4.8.........	99.37	98.75	94.28	89.77	86.21	83.66	83.40	79.44
4.9.........	99.32	98.65	93.86	89.04	85.25	82.55	82.28	78.12
5.0.........	99.27	98.55	93.44	88.31	84.30	81.45	81.17	76.82
5.1.........	99.22	98.46	93.02	87.59	83.37	80.38	80.09	75.55
5.2.........	99.17	98.36	92.60	86.87	82.44	79.32	79.02	74.32
5.3.........	99.12	98.27	92.18	86.17	81.53	78.28	77.97	73.11
5.4.........	99.07	98.17	91.77	85.47	80.64	77.26	76.94	71.93
5.5.........	99.03	98.08	91.36	84.77	79.75	76.26	75.92	70.78
5.6.........	98.98	97.99	90.95	84.09	78.88	75.27	74.93	69.65
5.7.........	98.93	97.89	90.54	83.41	78.02	74.30	73.95	68.55
5.8.........	98.88	97.80	90.14	82.73	77.17	73.35	72.98	67.48
5.9.........	98.83	97.70	89.74	82.06	76.33	72.41	72.04	66.43

Table 7. Bond Values—Coupon Rate of 4 Percent

Percent Yield per Annum	Years to Maturity							
	½	1	5	10	15	19½	20	30
2.0.........	100.99	101.97	109.47	118.05	125.81	132.16	132.83	144.96
2.1.........	100.94	101.87	108.97	117.06	124.34	130.27	130.90	142.13
2.2.........	100.89	101.77	108.48	116.08	122.89	128.42	129.00	139.38
2.3.........	100.84	101.67	107.99	115.11	121.46	126.59	127.13	136.69
2.4.........	100.79	101.57	107.50	114.15	120.06	124.80	125.30	134.08
2.5.........	100.74	101.47	107.01	113.20	118.67	123.04	123.50	131.53
2.6.........	100.69	101.37	106.52	112.26	117.30	121.31	121.73	129.04
2.7.........	100.64	101.27	106.04	111.33	115.95	119.61	119.99	126.61
2.8.........	100.59	101.18	105.56	110.40	114.62	117.94	118.28	124.25
2.9.........	100.54	101.08	105.09	109.49	113.90	116.30	116.60	121.94
3.0.........	100.49	100.98	104.61	108.58	112.01	114.68	114.96	119.69
3.1.........	100.44	100.88	104.14	107.69	110.73	113.10	113.34	117.50
3.2.........	100.39	100.78	103.67	106.80	109.47	111.54	111.75	115.35
3.3.........	100.34	100.68	103.20	105.92	108.23	110.01	110.19	113.27
3.4.........	100.29	100.59	102.74	105.05	107.00	108.50	108.66	111.23
3.5.........	100.25	100.49	102.28	104.19	105.80	107.02	107.15	109.24
3.6.........	100.20	100.39	101.82	103.33	104.60	105.57	105.67	107.30
3.7.........	100.15	100.29	101.36	102.49	103.43	104.14	104.21	105.41
3.8.........	100.10	100.19	100.90	101.65	102.27	102.74	102.78	103.56
3.9.........	100.05	100.10	100.45	100.82	101.13	101.36	101.38	101.76
4.0.........	100.00	100.00	100.00	100.00	100.00	100.00	100.00	100.00
4.1.........	99.95	99.90	99.55	99.19	98.89	98.67	98.64	98.28
4.2.........	99.90	99.81	99.11	98.38	97.79	97.36	97.31	96.61
4.3.........	99.85	99.71	98.66	97.58	96.71	96.07	96.00	94.97
4.4.........	99.80	99.61	98.22	96.79	95.64	94.80	94.72	93.37
4.5.........	99.76	99.52	97.78	96.01	94.59	93.55	93.45	91.81
4.6.........	99.71	99.42	97.35	95.23	93.55	92.33	92.21	90.29
4.7.........	99.60	99.32	96.91	94.47	92.53	91.13	90.99	88.80
4.8.........	99.61	99.23	96.48	93.71	91.52	89.94	89.79	87.35
4.9.........	99.56	99.13	96.05	92.95	90.52	88.78	88.61	85.93
5.0.........	99.51	99.04	95.62	92.21	89.53	87.63	87.45	84.55
5.1.........	99.46	98.94	95.20	91.47	88.56	86.51	86.31	83.19
5.2.........	99.42	98.85	94.78	90.73	87.61	85.40	85.19	81.87
5.3.........	99.37	98.75	94.35	90.01	86.66	84.32	84.09	80.58
5.4.........	99.32	98.65	93.94	89.29	85.73	83.25	83.01	79.32
5.5.........	99.27	98.56	93.52	88.58	84.81	82.19	81.94	78.08
5.6.........	99.22	98.46	93.11	87.87	83.91	81.16	80.90	76.88
5.7.........	99.17	98.37	92.69	87.18	83.01	80.14	79.87	75.70
5.8.........	99.13	98.28	92.28	86.49	82.13	79.14	78.86	74.55
5.9.........	99.08	98.18	91.88	85.80	81.26	78.16	77.86	73.42

Table 8. Bond Values—Coupon Rate of 4½ Percent

Percent Yield per Annum	Years to Maturity							
	½	1	5	10	15	19½	20	30
2.5	100.99	101.96	109.35	117.60	124.89	130.72	131.33	142.03
2.6	100.94	101.86	108.85	116.64	123.48	128.92	129.49	139.41
2.7	100.89	101.76	108.37	115.68	122.08	127.15	127.68	136.85
2.8	100.84	101.66	107.88	114.74	120.71	125.41	125.90	134.35
2.9	100.79	101.57	107.40	113.80	119.35	123.70	124.15	131.91
3.0	100.74	101.47	106.92	112.88	118.01	122.02	122.44	129.54
3.1	100.69	101.37	106.44	111.96	116.69	120.37	120.75	127.22
3.2	100.64	101.27	105.96	111.05	115.39	118.75	119.09	124.95
3.3	100.59	101.17	105.49	110.15	114.11	117.16	117.47	122.74
3.4	100.54	101.07	105.02	109.26	112.84	115.59	115.87	120.59
3.5	100.49	100.97	104.55	108.38	111.59	114.05	114.30	118.48
3.6	100.44	100.88	104.08	107.50	110.36	112.53	112.75	116.43
3.7	100.39	100.78	103.62	106.64	109.15	111.04	111.24	114.42
3.8	100.34	100.68	103.16	105.78	107.95	109.58	109.74	112.47
3.9	100.29	100.58	102.70	104.93	106.77	108.14	108.28	110.56
4.0	100.25	100.49	102.25	104.09	105.60	106.73	106.84	108.69
4.1	100.20	100.39	101.79	103.25	104.45	105.33	105.42	106.87
4.2	100.15	100.29	101.34	102.43	103.31	103.97	104.03	105.09
4.3	100.10	100.19	100.89	101.61	102.19	102.62	102.66	103.35
4.4	100.05	100.10	100.44	100.80	101.09	101.30	101.32	101.66
4.5	100.00	100.00	100.00	100.00	100.00	100.00	100.00	100.00
4.6	99.95	99.90	99.56	99.21	98.93	98.72	98.70	98.38
4.7	99.90	99.81	99.12	98.42	97.86	97.46	97.43	96.80
4.8	99.85	99.71	98.68	97.64	96.82	96.23	96.17	95.26
4.9	99.80	99.61	98.25	96.87	95.79	95.01	94.94	93.75
5.0	99.76	99.52	97.81	96.10	94.77	93.82	93.72	92.27
5.1	99.71	99.42	97.38	95.35	93.76	92.64	92.53	90.83
5.2	99.66	99.33	96.95	94.59	92.77	91.49	91.36	89.42
5.3	99.61	99.23	96.53	93.85	91.79	90.35	90.21	88.05
5.4	99.56	99.14	96.10	93.12	90.83	89.23	89.07	86.70
5.5	99.51	99.04	95.68	92.39	89.88	88.13	87.96	85.39
5.6	99.46	98.94	95.26	91.66	88.94	87.05	86.87	84.10
5.7	99.42	98.85	94.84	90.95	88.01	85.98	85.79	82.85
5.8	99.37	98.75	94.43	90.24	87.09	84.94	84.73	81.62
5.9	99.32	98.66	94.01	89.54	86.19	83.91	83.69	80.42
6.0	99.27	98.56	93.60	88.84	85.30	82.89	82.66	79.24
6.1	99.22	98.47	93.19	88.15	84.42	81.90	81.66	78.09
6.2	99.18	98.38	92.79	87.47	83.55	80.92	80.67	76.97
6.3	99.13	98.28	92.38	86.79	82.70	79.95	79.69	75.87
6.4	99.08	98.19	91.98	86.12	81.85	79.00	78.73	74.80
6.5	99.03	98.09	91.58	85.46	81.02	78.07	77.79	73.75

Accounting: A Management Approach

Table 9. Bond Values—Coupon Rate of 5 Percent

Percent Yield per Annum	Years to Maturity							
	½	1	5	10	15	19½	20	30
3.0.........	100.99	101.96	109.22	117.17	124.02	129.36	129.92	139.38
3.1.........	100.94	101.86	108.74	116.23	122.65	127.65	128.16	136.93
3.2.........	100.89	101.76	108.26	115.30	121.31	125.96	126.44	134.55
3.3.........	100.84	101.66	107.78	114.38	119.99	124.30	124.75	132.22
3.4.........	100.79	101.56	107.30	113.47	118.68	122.67	123.08	129.94
3.5.........	100.74	101.46	106.83	112.56	117.39	121.07	121.45	127.72
3.6.........	100.69	101.36	106.35	111.67	116.12	119.50	119.84	125.55
3.7.........	100.64	101.26	105.88	110.78	114.86	117.95	118.26	123.44
3.8.........	100.59	101.17	105.42	109.91	113.62	116.42	116.70	121.37
3.9.........	100.54	101.07	104.95	109.04	112.40	114.92	115.18	119.35
4.0.........	100.49	100.97	104.49	108.18	111.20	113.45	113.68	117.38
4.1.........	100.44	100.87	104.03	107.32	110.01	112.00	112.20	115.45
4.2.........	100.39	100.78	103.57	106.48	108.84	110.58	110.75	113.57
4.3.........	100.34	100.68	103.12	105.64	107.68	109.18	109.33	111.74
4.4.........	100.29	100.58	102.67	104.81	106.54	107.80	107.93	109.94
4.5.........	100.24	100.48	102.22	103.99	105.41	106.45	106.55	108.19
4.6.........	100.20	100.39	101.77	103.18	104.30	105.11	105.19	106.47
4.7.........	100.15	100.29	101.32	102.37	103.20	103.80	103.86	104.80
4.8.........	100.10	100.19	100.88	101.57	102.12	102.51	102.55	103.16
4.9.........	100.05	100.10	100.44	100.78	101.05	101.25	101.27	101.56
5.0.........	100.00	100.00	100.00	100.00	100.00	100.00	100.00	100.00
5.1.........	99.95	99.90	99.56	99.22	98.96	98.77	98.76	98.47
5.2.........	99.90	99.81	99.13	98.46	97.93	97.57	97.53	96.98
5.3.........	99.85	99.71	98.70	97.69	96.92	96.38	96.33	95.52
5.4.........	99.81	99.62	98.27	96.94	95.92	95.21	95.14	94.09
5.5.........	99.76	99.52	97.84	96.19	94.94	94.06	93.98	92.69
5.6.........	99.71	99.42	97.41	95.45	93.96	92.94	92.84	91.33
5.7.........	99.66	99.33	96.99	94.72	93.00	91.82	91.71	89.99
5.8.........	99.61	99.23	96.57	93.99	92.06	90.73	90.60	88.69
5.9.........	99.56	99.14	96.15	93.27	91.12	89.65	89.51	87.41
6.0.........	99.51	99.04	95.73	92.56	90.20	88.60	88.44	86.16
6.1.........	99.47	98.95	95.32	91.86	89.29	87.55	87.39	84.94
6.2.........	99.42	98.85	94.91	91.16	88.39	86.53	86.35	83.74
6.3.........	99.37	98.76	94.50	90.46	87.50	85.52	85.33	82.57
6.4.........	99.32	98.66	94.09	89.78	86.63	84.53	84.33	81.43
6.5.........	99.27	98.57	93.68	89.10	85.76	83.55	83.34	80.31
6.6.........	99.23	98.48	93.28	88.42	84.91	82.59	82.37	79.21
6.7.........	99.18	98.38	92.88	87.75	84.07	81.65	81.42	78.14
6.8.........	99.13	98.29	92.48	87.09	83.24	80.72	80.48	77.09
6.9.........	99.08	98.19	92.08	86.44	82.42	79.80	79.55	76.06

Table 10. Bond Values—Coupon Rate of 5½ Percent

Percent Yield per Annum	Years to Maturity							
	½	1	5	10	15	19½	20	30
3.5..........	100.98	101.95	109.10	116.75	123.19	128.09	128.59	136.96
3.6..........	100.93	101.85	108.62	115.84	121.87	126.46	126.92	134.68
3.7..........	100.88	101.75	108.15	114.93	120.58	124.85	125.28	132.45
3.8..........	100.83	101.65	107.68	114.03	119.30	123.26	123.67	130.28
3.9..........	100.78	101.55	107.20	113.14	118.04	121.71	122.08	128.15
4.0..........	100.74	101.46	106.74	112.26	116.80	120.18	120.52	126.07
4.1..........	100.69	101.36	106.27	111.39	115.57	118.67	118.98	124.04
4.2..........	100.64	101.26	105.81	110.53	114.36	117.19	117.47	122.06
4.3..........	100.59	101.16	105.35	109.67	113.16	115.73	115.99	120.12
4.4..........	100.54	101.06	104.89	108.82	111.99	114.30	114.53	118.23
4.5..........	100.49	100.97	104.43	107.98	110.82	112.89	113.10	116.37
4.6..........	100.44	100.87	103.98	107.15	109.67	111.51	111.69	114.57
4.7..........	100.39	100.77	103.53	106.32	108.54	110.14	110.30	112.80
4.8..........	100.34	100.68	103.08	105.51	107.42	108.80	108.94	111.07
4.9..........	100.29	100.58	102.63	104.70	106.32	107.48	107.59	109.38
5.0..........	100.24	100.48	102.19	103.90	105.23	106.18	106.28	107.73
5.1..........	100.20	100.39	101.75	103.10	104.16	104.91	104.98	106.11
5.2..........	100.15	100.29	101.31	102.32	103.10	103.65	103.70	104.53
5.3..........	100.10	100.19	100.87	101.54	102.05	102.41	102.45	102.99
5.4..........	100.05	100.10	100.43	100.76	101.02	101.20	101.21	101.48
5.5..........	100.00	100.00	100.00	100.00	100.00	100.00	100.00	100.00
5.6..........	99.95	99.90	99.57	99.24	98.99	98.82	98.81	98.55
5.7..........	99.90	99.81	99.14	98.49	98.00	97.66	97.63	97.14
5.8..........	99.85	99.71	98.71	97.75	97.02	96.52	96.48	95.76
5.9..........	99.81	99.62	98.29	97.01	96.05	95.40	95.34	94.41
6.0..........	99.76	99.52	97.87	96.28	95.10	94.30	94.22	93.08
6.1..........	99.71	99.43	97.45	95.56	94.16	93.21	93.12	91.79
6.2..........	99.66	99.33	97.03	94.84	93.23	92.14	92.04	90.52
6.3..........	99.61	99.24	96.61	94.13	92.31	91.09	90.97	89.28
6.4..........	99.56	99.14	96.20	93.43	91.40	90.05	89.93	88.06
6.5..........	99.52	99.05	95.75	92.73	90.51	89.03	88.90	86.87
6.6..........	99.47	98.95	95.38	92.04	89.63	88.03	87.88	85.71
6.7..........	99.42	98.86	94.97	91.36	88.75	87.04	86.88	84.57
6.8..........	99.37	98.76	94.57	90.68	87.89	86.07	85.90	83.45
6.9..........	99.32	98.67	94.16	90.01	87.04	85.12	84.93	82.36
7.0..........	99.28	98.58	93.76	89.34	86.21	84.17	83.98	81.29
7.1..........	99.23	98.48	93.36	88.68	85.38	83.25	83.05	80.24
7.2..........	99.18	98.39	92.97	88.03	84.56	82.33	82.13	79.22
7.3..........	99.13	98.29	92.57	87.38	83.75	81.43	81.22	78.21
7.4..........	99.08	98.20	92.18	86.74	82.96	80.55	80.33	77.23

Table 11. Bond Values—Coupon Rate of 6 Percent

Percent Yield per Annum	Years to Maturity							
	½	1	5	10	15	19½	20	30
3.5..........	101.23	102.44	111.38	120.94	128.98	135.12	135.74	146.20
3.6..........	101.18	102.34	110.89	120.01	127.63	133.42	134.01	143.81
3.7..........	101.13	102.24	110.41	119.08	126.30	131.75	132.30	141.47
3.8..........	101.08	102.14	109.93	118.16	124.98	130.11	130.63	139.18
3.9..........	101.03	102.04	109.46	117.25	123.68	128.49	128.98	136.94
4.0..........	100.98	101.94	108.98	116.35	122.40	126.90	127.36	134.76
4.1..........	100.93	101.84	108.51	115.46	121.13	125.34	125.76	132.63
4.2..........	100.88	101.74	108.04	114.58	119.88	123.80	124.19	130.54
4.3..........	100.83	101.65	107.58	113.70	118.65	122.29	122.65	128.50
4.4..........	100.78	101.55	107.11	112.83	117.43	120.80	121.14	126.51
4.5..........	100.73	101.45	106.65	111.97	116.23	119.34	119.65	124.56
4.6..........	100.68	101.35	106.19	111.12	115.05	117.90	118.18	122.66
4.7..........	100.64	101.26	105.73	110.28	113.88	116.48	116.74	120.80
4.8..........	100.59	101.16	105.28	109.44	112.73	115.09	115.32	118.98
4.9..........	100.54	101.06	104.83	108.61	111.59	113.71	113.92	117.20
5.0..........	100.49	100.96	104.38	107.79	110.47	112.37	112.55	115.45
5.1..........	100.44	100.87	103.93	106.98	109.36	111.04	111.20	113.75
5.2..........	100.39	100.77	103.48	106.18	108.26	109.73	109.87	112.09
5.3..........	100.34	100.67	103.04	105.38	107.18	108.45	108.57	110.46
5.4..........	100.29	100.58	102.60	104.59	106.11	107.18	107.28	108.86
5.5..........	100.24	100.48	102.16	103.81	105.06	105.94	106.02	107.31
5.6..........	100.19	100.38	101.72	103.03	104.02	104.71	104.78	105.78
5.7..........	100.15	100.29	101.29	102.26	103.00	103.50	103.55	104.29
5.8..........	100.10	100.19	100.86	101.50	101.99	102.32	102.35	102.83
5.9..........	100.05	100.10	100.43	100.75	100.99	101.15	101.17	101.40
6.0..........	100.00	100.00	100.00	100.00	100.00	100.00	100.00	100.00
6.1..........	99.95	99.90	99.57	99.26	99.03	98.87	98.85	98.63
6.2..........	99.90	99.81	99.15	98.53	98.07	97.75	97.73	97.29
6.3..........	99.85	99.71	98.73	97.80	97.12	96.66	96.62	95.98
6.4..........	99.81	99.62	98.31	97.08	96.18	95.58	95.52	94.69
6.5..........	99.76	99.52	97.89	96.37	95.25	94.52	94.45	93.44
6.6..........	99.71	99.43	97.48	95.66	94.34	93.47	93.39	92.21
6.7..........	99.66	99.33	97.07	94.96	93.44	92.44	92.35	91.00
6.8..........	99.61	99.24	96.66	94.26	92.55	91.43	91.32	89.82
6.9..........	99.57	99.14	96.25	93.58	91.67	90.43	90.32	88.66
7.0..........	99.52	99.05	95.84	92.89	90.80	89.45	89.32	87.53
7.1..........	99.47	98.96	95.44	92.22	89.95	88.48	88.35	86.42
7.2..........	99.42	98.86	95.04	91.55	89.10	87.53	87.38	85.33
7.3..........	99.37	98.77	94.63	90.89	88.27	86.59	86.44	84.26
7.4..........	99.32	98.67	94.24	90.23	87.44	85.67	85.50	83.22

Appendix B

SOLUTIONS TO SELECTED PROBLEMS

Chapter 2

2–18.

BALANCE SHEET

ASSETS		EQUITIES	
Cash on hand and in banks....	$ 9,000	Liabilities:	
Accounts receivable from		Accounts payable to	
customers................	6,900	creditors................	$12,300
Notes receivable from		Notes payable to banks.....	8,000
customers................	3,900	Long-term debt...........	16,500
Inventory of merchandise.....	29,100	Total Liabilities........	$36,800
Furniture and fixtures........	4,200	Owners' equity.............	52,400
Delivery equipment..........	9,600		
Building....................	24,000		
Land.......................	2,500		
Total Assets..........	$89,200	Total Equities........	$89,200

2–19.

INCOME STATEMENT

Revenue from sales..		$1,000
Cost of goods sold..		700
Gross margin...		$ 300
Operating expenses:		
Salaries and wages...................................	$ 120	
Taxes..	20	
Sundry...	60	200
Net Income..		$ 100

BALANCE SHEET

ASSETS		EQUITIES	
Cash.......................	$ 100	Liabilities:	
Accounts receivable..........	300	Accounts payable...........	$ 250
Inventories.................	380	Wages payable.............	50
Prepaid rent................	40	Taxes payable.............	5
Furniture and fixtures........	600	Note payable..............	350
		Total Liabilities........	$ 655
		R. A. Copake, capital........	765
Total Assets..........	$1,420	Total Equities........	$1,420

2–25. *a)*

ASSET ACCOUNTS

	Cash	Prepaid Rent	Equipment	Merchandise Inventory
(1)	$+300			
(2)	− 45	$+45		
(3)	−110		$+110	
(4)	−100			$+305
(5)	+650			−305
(6a)		− 15		
(6b)			− 21	
(7)	−205			
Balance	$ 490	$ 30	$ 89	$ —

LIABILITY AND OWNER'S EQUITY ACCOUNTS

	Accounts Payable	Earl Holt, Proprietor	Sales Revenue (+)	Cost of Goods Sold (−)	Rent Expense (−)	Depreciation Expense (−)
(1)		$+300				
(4)	$+205					
(5)			$650	$305		
(6a)					$15	
(6b)						$21
(7)	−205					
Balance	$ —	$ 300	$650	$305	$15	$21

b)

BALANCE SHEET, AS OF MONDAY NIGHT

ASSETS		LIABILITIES AND OWNER'S EQUITY	
Cash	$490	Liabilities	None
Prepaid Rent	30	Owner's equity	$609
Equipment	89		
		Total Liabilities and	
Total Assets	$609	Owner's Equity	$609

c)

INCOME STATEMENT FOR FIRST GAME

Sales revenue		$650
Less: Cost of goods sold	$305	
Rent	15	
Depreciation	21	341
Net Income		$309

2–26. *a)*

DINGY DIVE BAR

BALANCE SHEET
January 21, 19x4

ASSETS		EQUITIES	
Cash	$ 1,500	*Liabilities*	
Bar equipment	1,000	Note payable	$11,500
Buildings	9,500	*Owners' equity:*	
Improvements to land	2,000	Mr. Robinson	$ 1,500
Land	2,000	Mr. Griffiths	1,500
		Mr. Thorndike	1,500
		Total Owners' Equity	$ 4,500
Total Assets	$16,000	Total Equities	$16,000

b)   DINGY DIVE BAR

BALANCE SHEET
February 21, 19x4

ASSETS		EQUITIES	
Cash	$1,000	*Liabilities:*	
Accounts receivable	150	Wages payable	$ 50
Inventory	300	Accounts payable	200
Bar equipment	1,000	Note payable	11,500
Buildings	9,500	Total Liabilities	$11,750
Improvements to land	2,000	*Owners' Equity:*	
Land	2,000	Mr. Robinson	$1,400
		Mr. Griffiths	1,400
		Mr. Thorndike	1,400
		Total Owners' Equity	4,200
Total Assets	$15,940	Total Equities	$15,950

c) Since the partners have withdrawn a total of $600, it appears that the enterprise earned only $600 − $300 = $300 *before any charges for depreciation or any payments for services rendered by the proprietors.* The effect of the withdrawals has therefore been to reduce each partner's equity in the business.

Chapter 3

3–14.

Merchandise inventory, January 1		$150,000
Purchases		386,000
Merchandise available for sale		$536,000
Less: Cost of merchandise damaged	$ 18,000	
Merchandise inventory, December 31	126,000	144,000
Cost of Goods Sold		$392,000

3–15. *a*)

Truck	4,000	
Cash		4,000
b) Depreciation Expense	640	
Allowance for Depreciation		640
c) Cash	1,100	
Allowance for Depreciation	1,920	
Loss on Retirement	980	
Truck		4,000

3–22.

(1) Merchandise Inventory	5,000	
Notes Payable		5,000
(2) Cash	4,000	
Accounts Receivable		4,000
(3) Accounts Payable	6,000	
Cash		6,000
(4) Salaries Expense	1,000	
Cash		1,000

(5) Cash...50,000
      Note Payable..............................   50,000

(6) Accounts Receivable........................... 8,000
      Revenue from Goods Sold....................   8,000
      Cost of Goods Sold........................... 6,000
      Merchandise Inventory......................   6,000

(7) Land....................................... 7,000
      Cash.....................................   7,000

(8) Retained Earnings (Dividends Declared)............ 3,000
      Cash.....................................   3,000

(9) Office Supplies Expense........................   60
      Accounts Payable..........................   60

(10) Receivable from Insurance Company...............   100
      Cash.....................................   100

3–23. (1) Merchandise Inventory..........................   450
      Accounts Payable..........................   450
    Asset increase; liability increase.

(2) Accounts Payable.............................   884
      Cash.....................................   884
    Liability decrease; asset decrease.

(3) Cash....................................... 8,500
      Capital Stock.............................   8,500
    Asset increase; ownership increase.

(4) Cash.......................................10,000
      Notes Payable.............................   10,000
    Asset increase; liability increase.

(5) Salary Expense................................ 1,000
      Cash.....................................   1,000
    Ownership decrease; asset decrease.

(6) Accounts Receivable........................... 1,200
      Revenue from Sales........................   1,200
    Asset increase; ownership increase.
      Cost of Goods Sold...........................   920
      Merchandise Inventory......................   920
    Ownership decrease; asset decrease.

(7) Wages Expense................................ 2,800
      Wages Payable.............................   2,800
    Ownership decrease; liability increase.

(8) Utilities Expense..............................   87
      Accounts Payable..........................   87
    Ownership decrease; liability increase.

(9) Cash....................................... 1,106
      Accounts Receivable.......................   1,106
    Asset increase; asset decrease.

(10) Rent Expense................................   500
      Prepaid Rent..............................   500
    Ownership decrease; asset decrease.

Amounts in entries (5), (6), (7), (8), and (10) would appear in full on the current income statement.

Chapter 4

4–16. *a*)

Wages paid in February	$4,200
Less: Amounts earned in January but included in wages paid in February	300
	$3,900
Add: Amounts earned in February but not to be paid until March	500
Total wages expense	$4,400

   b) Accrued wages payable, February 28 = $500

4–20.

9/15	Cash	6,000.00	
	Note Payable		6,000.00
11/14	Interest Expense	60.00	
	Cash		60.00
12/14	Interest Expense	30.00	
	Note Payable	6,000.00	
	Cash		4,000.00
	Note Payable		2,030.00
12/31	Interest Expense	5.75	
	Interest Payable		5.75
	$2,030 for 17 days @ 6 percent.		
1/30	Interest Expense	4.40	
	Interest Payable	5.75	
	Note Payable	2,030.00	
	Cash		2,040.15

4–23.

Materials and Supplies	60,000	
Accounts Payable		60,000
Work in Process	80,000	
Wages Payable, etc.		80,000
Work in Process	55,000	
Materials and Supplies		55,000
Work in Process	30,000	
Accounts Payable, etc.		30,000
Finished Goods	175,000	
Work in Process		175,000
Cost of Goods Sold	167,000	
Finished Goods		167,000

4–26.

(1)	Raw Materials Inventory	35,000	
	Accounts Payable		35,000
	To record purchase of raw materials during April.		
(2)	Work in Process	48,400	
	Raw Materials		48,400

To record transfer of raw materials to work in process during April.

(3) Work in Process............................. 26,000
    Wages Payable............................   26,000
To charge labor costs to April production.

(4) Work in Process............................. 15,600
    Accounts Payable, etc......................   15,600
To record other factory costs for April; some of the credits, of course, would be to such accounts as Allowance for Depreciation or Supplies Inventory, but that information is not provided in this problem.

(5) Finished Goods................................109,000
    Work in Process..........................   109,000
To record the cost of goods finished in April.

(6) Cost of Goods Sold........................... 97,000
    Finished Goods...........................   97,000
To record the cost of goods sold during April.

4–30. *a*) (1) Jobs in Process...........................100,000
    Accounts Payable......................   100,000

(2) Jobs in Process............................. 30,000
    Liability for Corrective Work................ 1,000
    Selling and Administrative Expense............ 13,000
        F.I.C.A. Tax Payable....................   1,240
        Income Tax Withheld.....................   5,450
        Salaries Payable..........................   37,310

    Jobs in Process............................ 1,000
    Liability for Corrective Work................   40
    Selling and Administrative Expense............   200
        F.I.C.A. Tax Payable....................   1,240

    Jobs in Process............................   420
    Liability for Corrective Work................   18
    Selling and Administrative Expense............   84
        Unemployment Tax Payable..............   522

(3) Jobs in Process............................ 4,200
    Accounts Payable......................   4,200

(4) Selling and Administrative Expense............ 5,000
    Accounts Payable......................   5,000

(5) Accounts Receivable.........................124,400
    Revenue from Sales.....................   124,400

    Cost of Sales............................. 99,132
    Jobs in Process.........................   95,400
    Liability for Corrective Work............   3,732

(6) Cash.......................................118,300
    Accounts Receivable....................   118,300

(7) Accounts Payable...........................125,000
    Salaries Payable............................ 37,310
    Income Tax Withheld...................... 5,100

F.I.C.A. Tax Payable...................... 2,100
Unemployment Tax Payable.................. 650
Cash.................................   170,160
(8) Cash.................................... 50,000
Notes Payable........................   50,000
Interest Expense........................... 125
Interest Payable.......................   125

b)   MARJORAM, INC.

INCOME STATEMENT

FOR THE MONTH OF JUNE

Revenue from sales............................ $124,400
Less: Cost of sales..........................$99,132
Selling and administrative expense......... 18,284
Interest expense.......................   125   117,541
Net Income................................. $ 6,859

Chapter 5

5–17. *a*) Accounts Receivable..........................100,000
Revenue from Sales.......................   100,000
b) Credit Losses............................... 1,000
Allowance for Uncollectible Accounts..........   1,000
c) Allowance for Uncollectible Accounts..............   400
Accounts Receivable.......................   400
d) Cash..   150
Allowance for Uncollectible Accounts.........   150

5–18.   *Portion Estimated*
Uncollectible

More than 60 days.................$ 511 at 100% $ 511
46–60 days........................   12,552 at   4   502
31–45 days........................   52,110 at   1   521
0–30 days........................ 283,615 at   0.2   567
Total....................... $2,101

If past experience and aging checks have indicated the Allowance
for Uncollectible Accounts to be truly out of line, then an adjustment
could be made:

Loss on Uncollectible Accounts.............................285
Allowance for Uncollectible Accounts...................   285

5–20. *a*) Merchandise Inventory................................162
Accounts Payable...............................   162
b) Accounts Receivable.................................216
Revenue from Sales.............................   216

Cost of Goods Sold. 162
    Merchandise Inventory.   162

c) Sales Returns and Allowances. 18
    Accounts Receivable.   18

d) Accounts Payable. 18
    Purchases Returns and Allowances.   18
    Credit might be made directly to Cost of Goods Sold in this
    case.

5–24. *a*) The profit on a unit is $25 - $12 - $6 = $7.
The inventory would be shown at sale price less future selling costs,
$25 - $6 = $19.
Cash would be decreased by the amount of the manufacturing cost,
$12.
Owners' equity would increase by the amount of the profit, $7, and
this increase would be recognized when the unit is produced.

	First Year	*Second year*
b) Revenue.	$1,500,000	$1,875,000
Cost of goods sold.	$ 720,000	$ 900,000
Selling expense.	360,000	450,000
Administrative expense.	200,000	200,000
Net Income.	$ 220,000	$ 325,000

5–31. *a*)

HYATT COMPANY

Income Statement

For Month of September

Revenues.		$20,100
Less:		
Cost of sales.	$ 8,710	
Loss from customer defaults.	825	
Selling and administrative expense.	10,000	19,535
Net Income.		$ 1,565

The transactions analyses leading up to these figures may be
helpful:

(1) No entry.
(2) Finished Goods Inventory. 12,480
    Work in Process.   12,480
(3) Unamortized Costs of Machines Outstanding*. 11,700
    Finished Goods Inventory.   11,700

      * This account may appropriately be given any title that indicates that the
balance in the account represents costs that are carried forward as assets into
future periods. In practice, the accountant might debit Accounts Receivable and
credit Revenue from Sales for the full sale price and provide contra accounts to
both for the difference between price and merchandise cost. This has the advantage of showing current shipments as an integral part of the income statement.
The use of double contra accounts is likely to be confusing at this stage, however,
and the entries provided in this solution make it clear that receivables are carried
at cost rather than at realizable value, which is one point we are trying to make.

Accounts Receivable.........................27,000
    Uncollected Accounts..................... 27,000

NOTE: This is a *memorandum entry* and may be eliminated; Uncollected Accounts is a contra account to Accounts Receivable; the balances in the two accounts are always equal to each other.

(4) Cash.....................................20,100
    Revenues from Sales..................... 20,100
Uncollected Accounts........................20,100
    Accounts Receivable..................... 20,100

NOTE: This is a *memorandum entry.*

Cost of Sales.............................. 8,710
    Unamortized Costs of Machines Outstanding.. 8,710

(5) Loss from Customer Defaults.................. 825
Cash...................................... 150
    Unamortized Costs of Machines Outstanding†. 975

† There is $78 in unamortized cost for every $180 of unpaid balance.

Uncollected Accounts........................ 2,250
    Accounts Receivable..................... 2,250

NOTE: This is a *memorandum entry.*

(6) Selling and Administrative Expense...............10,000
    Sundry Accounts........................ 10,000

b)
Unamortized Costs of Machines Outstanding

Bal. 9/1	33,410	(4)	8,710
(3)	11,700	(5)	975
		Bal. 9/30	35,425
Bal. 9/30	35,425		

c) We shall leave this discussion to you. You should consider the matter of uncertainty, and should also try to make some kind of a decision as to what is the more important activity to the firm— shipment or collection.

Chapter 6

6–10.

Accounts receivable	(current assets)
Advances to salesman	(current assets)
Sales returns and allowances	(current revenues) contra
Allowance for uncollectible accounts	(current assets) contra
Credit losses	(current revenues) contra
Customers' notes	(current assets) if short term
Depreciation of office equipment	(current expenses)
Fees received in advance	(current liabilities)
Goods in transit	(current assets)
Income taxes withheld	(current liabilities)

Interest received	(none of these) other income
Investment in short-term government securities	(current assets)
Loss on sale of equipment	(none of these) extraordinary item
Office salaries	(current expenses)
Paid-in surplus	(none of these)
Petty cash	(current assets)
Provision for product warranty	(current liabilities) if current
Purchases discounts	(current expenses) contra to cost of goods (possibly in part contra to inventory)
Raw materials	(current assets)
Royalties earned	(current revenues) or other income
Sales equipment	(none of these)

6–11.

JAMES DANDY SALES COMPANY

INCOME STATEMENT

FOR THE YEAR 19x3

Sales...			$700,000
Less: Returns and allowances....................			14,000
Net sales.....................................			$686,000
Less: Cost of goods sold........................			480,000
Gross margin..................................			$206,000
Less: Operating expenses:			
Wages and salaries............................	$100,000		
Rent expense.................................	22,000		
Office supplies used...........................	5,000		
Insurance expired.............................	1,000		
Depreciation.................................	21,000		
Interest expense..............................	4,000		
Other expenses...............................	9,000		
Income tax...................................	3,000	165,000	
Income before special items......................			$ 41,000
Special items:			
Fire loss....................................	$ 34,000		
Refund of prior years' income taxes...............	(8,000)	26,000	
Net income...................................			$ 15,000
Add: Retained earnings as of January 1............			48,000
			$ 63,000
Less: Dividends declared.......................			3,000
Retained Earnings as of December 31..............			$ 60,000

NOTE: Although the instructions in this problem call for an all-inclusive income statement, in practice the refund of prior years' taxes might be taken directly to the Retained Earnings account on the grounds that it represents a correction of prior years' income figures.

JAMES DANDY SALES COMPANY

BALANCE SHEET

AS OF DECEMBER 31, 19x3

ASSETS

Current Assets:

Cash..		$ 20,000
Accounts receivable...........................	$ 50,000	
Less: Allowance for bad debts.................	1,000	49,000
Inventories.......................................		80,000
Prepaid insurance..............................		2,000
Total Current Assets......................		$151,000

Long-Term Assets:

Furniture and fixtures...........................	$200,000	
Less: Allowance for depreciation.................	62,000	
Total Long-Term Assets....................		138,000
Total Assets...........................		$289,000

EQUITIES

Current Liabilities:

Accounts payable..............................		$ 70,000
Accrued wages................................		2,000
Taxes payable.................................		4,000
Notes payable.................................		30,000
Total Current Liabilities...................		$106,000
Mortgage payable................................		50,000
Total Liabilities........................		$156,000

Stockholders' Equity:

Common stock................................	$ 20,000	
Premium on common stock.....................	53,000	
Retained earnings.............................	60,000	
Total Stockholders' Equity.................		133,000
Total Equities..........................		$289,000

6–17. *a*) In the following, BI = beginning inventory and EI = ending inventory.

Year	Reported Profits	Corrections		Actual Profits
19x6..............	$ 60,000	EI understated $3,000		$ 63,000
19x7..............	76,000	BI understated $3,000 EI overstated 2,875 Total $5,875		70,125
19x8..............	68,000	BI overstated $2,875 EI understated 2,200 Total $5,075		73,075
19x9..............	83,000	BI understated $2,200		80,800
Totals...........	$287,000*			$287,000*

* Since the beginning and ending inventories for the entire period (19x6–x9) were correct, all errors "wash out" over that time.

b) The balance sheet errors were as follows:

Year	Inventory	Retained Earnings
19x6	Understated $3,000	Understated $3,000
19x7	Overstated $2,875	Overstated $2,875 ($5,875 over for year less $3,000 under at beginning of year)
19x8	Understated $2,200	Understated $2,200 ($5,075 under for year less $2,875 over at beginning of year)
19x9	Correct	Correct ($2,200 over for year less $2,200 under at beginning of year)

6–24. *a*)

ROBANT HARDWARE COMPANY

WORK SHEET

Accounts	Unadjusted Trial Balance		Adjustments		Income Statement		Balance Sheet	
Cash	56,000						56,000	
Accounts receivable	170,000						170,000	
Inventory	525,000			(5)300,000			225,000	
Furniture and fixtures	200,000						200,000	
Allowance for depreciation, furniture and fixtures		125,000		(3) 2,000				127,000
Prepaid insurance	2,000			(1) 175			1,825	
Prepaid rent	1,000			(2) 1,000				
Accounts payable		100,000		(4) 4,000				104,000
Capital stock		200,000						200,000
Retained earnings		106,000						106,000
Sales		500,000				500,000		
Wage expense	20,000		(4) 4,000		24,000			
Miscellaneous expenses	55,000		(3) 2,000		58,175			
			(2) 1,000					
			(1) 175					
Dividends declared	2,000						2,000	
Cost of goods sold			(5)300,000		300,000			
Total	1,031,000	1,031,000	307,175	307,175	384,175	500,000	652,825	537,000
Net to retained earnings					115,825			115,825
Total					500,000	500,000	652,825	652,825

b)

ROBANT HARDWARE COMPANY

INCOME STATEMENT AND RECONCILIATION OF RETAINED EARNINGS

FOR THE YEAR ENDED DECEMBER 31

Sales		$500,000
Cost of goods sold		300,000
Gross margin		$200,000
Less: Wage expense	$24,000	
Miscellaneous expenses	58,175	82,175
Net income		$117,825
Retained earnings, January 1		106,000
		$223,825
Less: Dividends declared		2,000
Retained Earnings, December 31		$221,825

ROBANT HARDWARE COMPANY

BALANCE SHEET

AS OF DECEMBER 31

ASSETS			EQUITIES		
Current Assets:			*Current Liabilities:*		
Cash........		$ 56,000	Accounts		
Accounts			payable.....		$104,000
receivable...		170,000			
Inventory.....		225,000	*Stockholders' Equity:*		
Prepaid			Capital stock..$200,000		
insurance...		1,825	Retained		
Total		$452,825	earnings.....221,825		
			Total.....		421,825
Long-Lived Assets:					
Furn. & fix-					
tures.......$200,000					
Accum.					
Deprec......(127,000)		73,000			
Total			Total		
Assets..		$525,825	Equities..		$525,825

6–25.

THE GUYTON COMPANY

WORK SHEET

Accounts	Trial Balance Dec. 31, 1963		Adjustments		Report of Earnings		Balance Sheet	
Cash.....................	28,800						28,800	
Temporary investments.....	17,700						17,700	
Accounts receivable........	91,600			(7) 890			90,710	
Inventory of merchandise...	89,000		(5)344,500	(5)347,060			87,415	
			(6) 975					
Prepaid insurance.........	1,900			(2) 175			1,725	
Other prepaid expense......	1,340						1,340	
Land....................	16,000						16,000	
Bldg. and equipment.......	45,800						45,800	
Allowance for depreciation, building and equipment...		8,100		(4) 1,240				9,340
Accounts payable.........		18,800		(6) 975				19,775
Mortgage on real estate.....		45,000						45,000
Capital stock.............		150,000						150,000
Retained earnings.........		53,120						53,120
Sales....................		412,000				412,000		
Sales discounts, returns and allowances...........	12,000		(7) 890		12,890			
Interest income...........		480				480		
Purchases................	344,500			(5)344,500				
Advertising...............	1,200				1,200			
Salaries and wages........	16,400		(3) 240		16,640			
Miscellaneous selling expense.	5,800				5,800			
Property taxes............	3,300				3,300			
Insurance expense.........	525		(2) 175		700			
Miscellaneous general exp....	8,435				8,435			
Interest expense...........	3,200		(1) 400		3,600			
Accrued interest payable....				(1) 400				400
Accrued wages payable.....				(3) 240				240
Depreciation expense......			(4) 1,240		1,240			
Cost of goods sold.........			(5)347,060		347,060			
Total................	687,500	687,500	695,480	695,480	400,865	412,480	289,490	277,875
Net Income..............					11,615			11,615
Total................					412,480	412,480	289,490	289,490

Note use of Purchases account.

THE GUYTON COMPANY
Report of Earnings
For the Year Ended December 31, 19x3

Sales...		$412,000
Less: Discounts, returns, and allowances..............		12,890
Net sales..		$399,110
Cost of goods sold................................		347,060
Gross margin.....................................		$ 52,050
Operating expenses:		
Salaries and wages............................	$16,640	
Advertising...................................	1,200	
Miscellaneous selling expense...................	5,800	
Insurance expense.............................	700	
Depreciation expense..........................	1,240	
Property taxes................................	3,300	
Miscellaneous general expenses.................	8,435	37,315
Net operating income.............................		$ 14,735
Add: Interest income.............................	$ 480	
Less: Interest expense...........................	(3,600)	(3,120)
Net Income......................................		$ 11,615

THE GUYTON COMPANY
Balance Sheet
As of December 31, 19x3
ASSETS

Current Assets:		
Cash...		$ 28,800
Temporary investments.........................		17,700
Accounts receivable...........................		90,710
Inventory of merchandise.......................		87,415
Prepaid insurance.............................		1,725
Other prepaid expenses.........................		1,340
Total Current Assets.......................		$227,690
Fixed Assets:		
Land...		16,000
Building and equipment........................	$ 45,800	
Less: Allowance for depreciation.................	9,340	36,460
Total Assets.............................		$280,150

EQUITIES

Current Liabilities:		
Accounts payable.............................		$ 19,775
Accrued interest payable.......................		400
Accrued wages payable.........................		240
Total Current Liabilities...................		$ 20,415
Mortgage on real estate...........................		45,000
Total Liabilities.........................		$ 65,415

Stockholders' Equity:

Capital stock..................................	$150,000	
Retained earnings.............................	64,735	
Total Stockholders' Equity.................		214,735
Total Equities..........................		$280,150

Chapter 7

7-23. *a*) Amount of sales billed is posted as a credit to Sales *and* as a debit to Accounts Receivable. Individual postings will also be made to the subsidiary customers' accounts. Amount of cost of goods sold is posted as a credit to Inventory *and* as a debit to Cost of Goods Sold.

    b) Accounts Receivable certainly and Inventory probably.

7-26. *a*) The store should keep a petty cash book of some sort and should maintain a petty cash voucher system so that the fund will contain a given amount in some combination of cash and vouchers at all times.

    b)

Petty Cash...	300	
Cash...		300

    c)

Labor Expense (items No. 1 and 6).......................	124	
Miscellaneous General Expense (items No. 2, 3, 4, 5, and 7)..	91	
Cash...		215

    The expenses may actually be accounted for in greater detail.

7-30.

(1) (S) Accounts Receivable (John Jones)................. 1,000

       Revenue from Sales........................... 1,000

    NOTE: If recorded at net price, the amount is $980.

(2) (VR) Delivery Equipment......................... 2,700

       Vouchers Payable (Speedy Motor Co.).......... 2,700

(3) (CR) Cash...................................... 750

       Revenue from Cash Sales...................... 750

    NOTE: If it is desired to have a complete record of sales in the sales register, there would also be an additional entry of:

    (S) Revenue from Cash Sales...................... 750

       Revenue from Sales........................... 750

(4) (CR) Cash...................................... 980

    Sales Discounts............................. 20

       Accounts Receivable (John Jones)........... 1,000

(5) (VR) Advertising Expense......................... 100

    Prepaid Advertising......................... 80

       Payable................................ 180

    (CD) Vouchers Payable (Texas Bugle).............. 180

       Cash.................................... 180

(6) (J) Depreciation Expense......................... 100

       Allowance for Depreciation, Delivery Equipment....................................... 100

(7) (J) Sales Salaries and Wages Expense................. 250

    Office Salaries and Wages Expense............... 200

       Accrued Wages Payable.................... 450

Chapter 8

	19x3	19x4	19x5	19x6
8–20. *a*) Number of shares (000) 50,000		50,000	52,000	52,000
Earnings available for common stock (000)...............		$96,000	$101,300	$99,100
Earnings per share...........		$1.92	$1.95	$1.91
b) Book value per share.........$16.60		$17.52	$18.60	$19.50
c) Average common equity (000) ..		$853,000	$921,650	$990,850
Return on common equity......		11.3%	11.0%	10.0%

8–21.

	Where Got	Where Gone
From operations......................	$ 7,500	
From long-term debt..................	10,000	
From capital stock....................	5,000	
To increase current assets..............		$ 9,000
To acquire buildings and equipment.......		8,500
To acquire land......................		2,000
To reduce current liabilities............		3,000
Total........................	$22,500	$22,500

Chapter 9

9–16. $\dfrac{\$1,000,000}{12.5779} = \$79,505/\text{year}$ for 10 years (Appendix A, Table 2).

9–17. *a*) Present value of outlay...........................−$ 35,000
Present value of receipts: 0.322 × $100,000 =   +   32,200
Net Present Value........................−$ 2,800 Reject

b) Present value of 1/1/64 outlay..................−$ 80,000
Present value of 1/1/69 outlay: 0.567 × $20,000 = −   11,340
Present value of receipt of $10,000 per period for six periods: 4.111 × $10,000 =   +   41,110
Present value of receipt of $20,000 per period for 10 periods starting six periods hence:
(6.974 − 4.111) × $20,000 =   +   57,260
Net Present Value.......................+$ 7,030 Accept

c) Present value of outlay of $20,000 per period for 11 periods: 6.650 × $20,000 =   −$133,000
Present value of receipt of $250,000 at end of 12 periods: 0.257 × $250,000 =   +   64,250
Net Present Value........................−$ 68,750 Reject

9–28. *a*)

Year	Cash Flow	Present Value
1....................	$100,000	$ 94,340
2....................	180,000	160,200
Total..............		$254,540

b)

0....................	$100,000	$100,000
1....................	180,000	169,810
Total..............		$269,810

c) Income = $269,810 − $254,540 = $15,270.
(This can also be obtained by taking 6% of $254,540 = $15,272.)

d)

Present value, end of year 2...................	$180,000
Present value, beginning of year 2..............	169,810
Income, Year 2.......................	$ 10,190

Chapter 10

10–12. These expenditures are basically in the nature of maintenance, designed to secure the previously anticipated economic life. Although unusual and nonrecurring, they should be reported as expense of the current year.

10–13. The cost of the shares was 21,600 × $15 = $324,000. This figure is obviously a very poor measure of the amount of resources sacrificed by Experimental Company to obtain the new building in 1967. Instead, the company should have used either the current market value of the stock or the current market value of the building, whichever could have been measured more accurately.

A market price of $105 a share gives an indicated market value of 21,600 × $105 = $2,268,000. A sale of this magnitude might very well have depressed the market price of the Respirator stock, however, so the true market value of the 21,600 shares was probably lower. If the shares were traded actively, the amount of the price reduction would have been quite small; for small companies the reduction is often substantial.

Appraisal values, too, are often inaccurate, but urban building appraisals are usually quite reliable. Capitalization in the neighborhood of $2,000,000 would seem reasonable here. A gain of $2,000,000 - $324,000 = $1,676,000 should be recognized on this transaction.

10–14. *a*) Machinery......................................97,500
　　　　　　Accounts Payable........................... 　　　97,500
　　　　b) Machinery...................................... 5,200
　　　　　　Cash....................................... 　　　5,200
　　　　c) Machinery...................................... 2,530
　　　　　　Wages Payable............................. 　　　1,920
　　　　　　Materials Inventory.......................... 　　　610

The essence of the question is what costs should be capitalized. A good case can be made for all, but it should also be pointed out that it might be impractical to sort out the labor costs applicable to the installation.

10–22. In practice, all of these costs except the purchase of special dies, jigs, etc., would be expensed. It can be argued, however, that the research expenditures should be capitalized until the project is abandoned or completed successfully. If this is done, the entries might be as follows:

19x5	Development in Progress....................	4,346	
	Wages Payable, etc.....................		4,346
19x6	Development in Progress....................	18,625	
	Wages Payable, etc.....................		18,625
	Intangible Assets—Cost of New Product........	24,298	
	Development in Progress..................		22,971
	Cash, etc..............................		1,327
19x7	Jigs, Dies, and Fixtures....................	2,852	
	Accounts Payable, etc..................		2,852

The two asset balances would then be subject to amortization, the rates depending on the expected useful lives of the product's marketability and of the jigs, dies, etc.

Chapter 11

11–15. *a*) Depreciation per books...........................$80,000
Correct amount to date:
$14\% \times 2 \times \$200,000$.......................... 56,000
Overstatement..............................$24,000

b) Allowance for Depreciation......................24,000
Adjustment for Prior Years' Depreciation........   24,000

11–16. *a*)	19x0	Depreciation Expense......................	9,000	
		Allowance for Depreciation.............		9,000
	19x1	Cash....................................	1,000	
		Allowance for Depreciation.................	4,000	
		Equipment...........................		5,000
		Depreciation.............................	8,550	
		Allowance for Depreciation.............		8,550
	19x2	Cash....................................	3,000	
		Allowance for Depreciation.................	7,000	
		Equipment...........................		10,000
		Depreciation.............................	7,650	
		Allowance for Depreciation.............		7,650

b) 19x0   Depreciation expense........................20,000
           Allowance for Depreciation.............   20,000

     19x1   Cash.................................... 1,000
           Allowance for Depreciation................. 4,000
           Equipment...........................   5,000
           Depreciation Expense......................15,800
           Allowance for Depreciation.............   15,800

     19x2   Cash.................................... 3,000
           Allowance for Depreciation................. 7,000
           Equipment...........................   10,000
           Depreciation Expense......................12,040
           Allowance for Depreciation.............   12,040

11–19. *a*) Paper Machine................................ 6,000
        Cash......................................   6,000

b) Depreciation Expense............................ 2,875
     Allowance for Depreciation—Paper Machine......   2,875

The life of the machine has not been extended, and the $6,000 outlay is depreciated over the remaining 16 years of life.

c) Allowance for Depreciation—Paper Machine..........12,000
     Cash......................................   12,000

This presumes that the overhaul takes the form of renewal or replacement of component parts; thus a debit to the Paper Machine account would be double-counting.

d) Asset account: $50,000 + $6,000 = $56,000
     Allowance account:
       4 × $2,500 = $10,000
       12 × $2,875 =   34,500
                           (12,000)   32,500
       Book Value...................... $23,500

$$\text{Depreciation} = \frac{\$23,500}{9} = \$2,611 \text{ a year.}$$

Chapter 12

12–12. *a*) Fifo inventory:

                  200 @ $11.70 = $ 2,340
                  400 @   11.60 =   4,640
                  300 @   11.60 =   3,480
                  200 @   11.55 =   2,310
                  1,100 $12,770

Lifo inventory (the year is the accounting period):

                1,000 @ $11.00 = $11,000
                  100 @   11.20 =   1,120
                1,100 $12,120

b) Assuming that Lifo was adopted at the start of the year, the opening inventory is the same under both methods, 1,000 @ $11. The Fifo reported earnings therefore are $650 greater than the Lifo earnings, the amount by which the closing Fifo inventory is greater than the closing Lifo inventory.

12–13. *a*)
Beginning inventory: 1,600 @ $10................		$16,000
Plus: Purchases.............................		32,100
Total Available..........................		$48,100
Less: Ending inventory:		
1,400 @ $12...............................	$16,800	
500 @ 13...............................	6,500	23,300
Cost of Goods Sold.......................		$24,800

b) Moving weighted average method:

Date	Receipts	Issues	Balances
1			1,600 at $10.00 = $16,000
3		900 at $10.00 = $ 9,000	700 at 10.00 = 7,000
5	800 at $11.00 = $ 8,800		1,500 at 10.53 = 15,800
10		800 at 10.53 = 8,427	700 at 10.53 = 7,373
20	500 at 13.00 = 6,500		1,200 at 11.56 = 13,873
23		700 at 11.56 = 8,093	500 at 11.56 = 5,780
31	1,400 at 12.00 = 16,800		1,900 at 11.88 = 22,580
	Total Cost of Goods Sold...	..............$25,520	

c) Market price is $12.

Ending inventory: 1,900 @ $12................		$22,800
Cost of goods sold: $48,100 − $22,800.........		$25,300

12–20. *a*)

Date	Inventory		Year	Cost of Goods Sold	
	Fifo	Lifo		Fifo	Lifo
January 1, 1958......	$1,875,000	$1,875,000			
			1958	$12,175,000	$12,350,000
December 31, 1958...	2,700,000	2,525,000			
			1959	14,600,000	14,500,000
December 31, 1959...	700,000	625,000			

b) The involuntary liquidation increased reported profit before taxes by $125,000. The liquidation amounted to 15,000 tons, but only 10,000 tons were liquidated involuntarily. The computation is:

10,000 tons at current price of $140......		$1,400,000
10,000 tons at inventory prices:		
5,000 at $130.......................	$650,000	
5,000 at $125.......................	625,000	1,275,000
Net Effect on Reported Income......		$ 125,000

c) The effect is to increase the cost of the inventory by $200,000 over the level that would have prevailed if there had been no involuntary liquidation:

Base quantity, 5,000 tons	$ 625,000
1960 layer, 10,000 tons	1,450,000
Total	$2,075,000
Inventory value of 15,000 tons, 12/31/58	1,875,000
Net Effect on Inventory Valuation	$ 200,000

Chapter 13

13–13. a)

Cash receipts	$1,200
Coupon receipts (at 90% of face value)	945
	$2,145
Profit	100
Possible Expenses	$2,045

b) The balance sheet as of January 1 would have shown a liability of Coupons Outstanding of $270, while the balance sheet of January 31 would have shown a liability of Coupons Outstanding of $225.

13–14.

Present value of $2.50 per period for 20 periods, discounted at 2%: 16.3514 × $2.50 =	$ 40.88
Present value of $100 at end of 20 periods, discounted at 2%: 0.6730 × $100 =	67.30
Value of Bonds	$108.18

13–16. a)

Total coupon payments from bond: $50 × 10 =	$500.00	
Less: Bond premium to be amortized	39.90	
Total Payments to Beneficiary	$460.10	

b) The yield is 4½% (Appendix A, Table 9).

13–19. a) The maturity value is $1,000,000, the coupon rate 3½%, and the yield, 4%.

b) $913,100—because the price must be below the maturity value to render the yield above the coupon rate.

c)
Cash	913,000	
Bonds Payable		913,000

d)
Interest Expense ($913,100 × 0.02)	18,262	
Cash		17,500
Bonds Payable		762

e)
Interest Expense ($913,762 × 0.02)	18,277	
Cash		17,500
Bonds Payable		777

f) 30 years (Appendix A, Table 6)

13–25. *a*)

	Present	*Borrowing*	*Stock Sale*
Estimated annual earnings:			
Before interest and taxes..............	$1,500,000	$2,500,000	$2,500,000
Less: Bond interest (4½% × $5,000,000)	....	225,000	....
Earnings before taxes...............	$1,500,000	$2,275,000	$2,500,000
Less: Income taxes (50%)...........	750,000	1,137,500	1,250,000
Available for dividends..............	$ 750,000	$1,137,500	$1,250,000
Number of sharesout standing...........	1,000,000	1,000,000	1,666,667
Earnings per share...................	$0.75	$1.14	$0.75

A stock issue would not change earnings per share, while the bond issue would raise earnings per share by more than 50 percent.

b) Other factors to be considered in reaching a decision:
1. Loss of some control of corporation if new voting stock is issued.
2. Effect of the issue of a large block of stock upon the market price of Randolph Corporation stock.
3. Company's future need for credit—and possibilities of getting it if bonds are issued now.
4. Risk associated with a large debt outstanding.

13–27.   Income calculation:

Income before depreciation and taxes....		$6,200,000
Depreciation........................		850,000
Income after depreciation.............		$5,350,000
Income tax: Current.................	$2,475,000	
Deferred.................	200,000	2,675,000
Net Income.....................		$2,675,000

Entries:

Depreciation................................	850,000	
Allowance for Depreciation................		850,000
Income Taxes..................................	2,675,000	
Income Taxes Payable.....................		2,475,000
Provision for Deferred Income Taxes........		200,000

Current taxable income = $4,950,000

Chapter 14

14–14.
Retained Earnings....................................	30,000	
Common Stock.................................		10,000
Premium on Common Stock......................		20,000

14–15.
Jan. 4	Treasury Stock.............................	3,000	
	Cash....................................		3,000
Mar. 18	Cash.......................................	4,000	
	Treasury Stock...........................		3,000
	Premium on Common Stock...............		1,000

14–16. *a*) Sinking Fund for Bond Retirement.............. 800,000
        Cash....................................   800,000

      b) Retained Earnings Unappropriated..............1,000,000
           Retained Earnings Appropriated for Debt
             Retirement..........................   1,000,000

14–17. Cash...3,000,000
        Common Stock............................   2,000,000
        Premium on Common Stock.................   1,000,000

14–18. *First year:*
      Retained Earnings Unappropriated...................10,000
          Retained Earnings Appropriated for Damage Suit...   10,000
     Second year:
      Retained Earnings Appropriated for Damage Suit.......10,000
          Retained Earnings Unappropriated...............   10,000
      Loss on Damage Suit.............................11,500
         Cash.......................................   11,500

Chapter 15

15–17. *a*) The only items to appear would be:
        Goodwill...$10,000
        Retained earnings................................... 15,000

The latter figure would be combined with the retained earnings of Wolfe Corporation, the combined total being shown as a single figure.

      b) Capital Stock—Lamb Company...................100,000
      Consolidation Goodwill*......................... 10,000
         Investment in Lamb Company—
           Wolfe Company..........................   90,000
         Retained Earnings†—Lamb Company...........   20,000

        * Or "Investments in consolidated subsidiaries in excess of equity in tangible assets acquired."
        † Or "Deficit" if that account title were used in the Lamb Company's trial balance. Usually the account title is still Retained Earnings, but the debit balance is listed as Deficit on the balance sheet.

15–18. *a*) Unconsolidated income.............................$ 55,000
      Less: Dividends from Y   8,000
      Plus: Income of Y.................................   15,000
      Consolidated income...............................$ 62,000
      Less: Minority interest in income....................   3,000
      Net income.......................................$ 59,000

      b) Minority interest.................................$ 21,000
      Common stock.................................... 100,000
      Premium on common stock......................... 20,000
      Retained earnings................................. 404,000

The total ownership equity would commonly be reported as $524,000. The minority interest would not be included.

15–23.   SUMNER CORPORATION AND ACME COMPANY

CONSOLIDATED INCOME STATEMENT AND RECONCILIATION OF
RETAINED EARNINGS

For the Year 19x1

Sales.	$80,000
Cost of goods sold.	58,000
Gross margin.	$22,000
General expenses.	10,300
Net operating income.	$11,700
Less: Minority interest in earnings.	825
Consolidated net income.	$10,875
Dividends paid.	5,000
Net addition to retained earnings.	$ 5,875
Retained earnings, December 31, 19x0.	9,000
Retained earnings, December 31, 19x1.	$14,875

SUMNER CORPORATION AND ACME COMPANY

CONSOLIDATED BALANCE SHEET
December 31, 19x1

ASSETS		EQUITIES		
Current Assets:		*Current Liabilities:*		
Cash.	$ 5,850	Accounts payable.		$ 6,200
Accounts receivable.	10,050	Minority equity in		
Inventory.	13,400	subsidiary.		6,575
Total Current Assets.	$29,300	*Stockholders' Equity:*		
Fixed assets (net).	30,350	Common stock.	$35,000	
Consolidation goodwill.	3,000	Retained earnings.	14,875	49,875
Total Assets.	$62,650	Total Equities		$62,650

CONSOLIDATION WORK SHEET

	Independent Statements				Eliminations and Adjustments		Consolidated Statements	
	Sumner Corp.		Acme Company					
Accounts	Debit	Credit	Debit	Credit	Debit	Credit	Debit	Credit
Balance Sheet Items								
Cash.	3,450		2,400				5,850	
Accounts receivable.	6,500		4,250			(5) 700	10,050	
Inventory.	7,100		6,500			(4) 200	13,400	
Investments.	21,000					(3)21,000		
Fixed assets (net).	15,500		14,850				30,350	
Consolidation goodwill.					(3) 3,000		3,000	
Accounts payable.		5,200		1,700	(5) 700			6,200
Minority equity in subsidiary						(6) 6,000		6,575
						(7) 575		
Capital stock.		35,000		20,000	(3)15,000			35,000
					(6) 5,000			
Retained earnings.		9,000		4,000	(3) 3,000			9,000
					(6) 1,000			
Income Statement Items, Etc.								
Sales.		60,000		30,000	(1)10,000			80,000
Cost of goods sold.	48,000		19,800		(4) 200	(1)10,000	58,000	
General expenses.	3,400		6,900				10,300	
Other income.		750			(2) 750			
Dividends paid.	5,000		1,000			(2) 750	5,000	
						(7) 250		
Minority interest in earnings.					(7) 825		825	
Total.	109,950	109,950	55,700	55,700	39,475	39,475	136,775	136,775

Chapter 16

16–12. Funds obtained from sale of investments........................$47,000
Funds used to purchase investments 8,000

16–14.

REVOLVING DOLLAR COMPANY

STATEMENT OF SOURCES AND APPLICATIONS OF CASH
For the Year 19—

Sources of Cash:
  Net profit for the period...............................$16,211,410
  Add: Depreciation expenses.............................. 5,447,120
    Total Funds Available from Operations................$21,658,530
  Decrease in accounts receivable.......................... 2,214,497
    Total Sources of Cash..............................$23,873,027

Applications of Cash:
  Increase of marketable securities...............$ 800,000
  Increase of inventories........................ 6,098,642
  Increase of equipment, land, fixtures, etc........ 9,886,498
  Decrease of accounts, notes, and taxes payable.... 4,125,940
  Payment of dividends........................ 3,000,000
    Total Uses of Cash................................ 23,911,080
  Excess of Applications over Sources of Cash................. $ 38,053

16–17

WOVEN HOSE AND RUBBER COMPANY

STATEMENT OF SOURCES AND USES OF FUNDS
For the Year Ending August 31, 19—

Sources of Funds:
  From operations:
    Net income...........................$510,000
    Add: Depreciation..................... 350,000 $ 860,000
  From sale of plant assets...................   49,000
  From reduction of accounts receivable*.......   53,000
  From decrease of inventories...............   705,000
  From reduction of cash and marketable
    securities...............................   553,000
    Total Sources of Funds............... $2,220,000

Uses of Funds:
  To purchase plant assets................... $ 894,000
  To reduce mortgage.......................   500,000
  To pay dividends.........................   300,000
  To increase prepaid expenses...............   82,000
  To reduce accounts payable................   104,000
  To decrease accrued taxes.................   340,000
    Total Uses of Funds................. $2,220,000

    * This is based on the concept that the amount of receivables is the net book value, not the gross value.

16–20.   STATEMENT OF THE SOURCES AND USES OF WORKING CAPITAL

Sources of Funds:

From operations:

Net income..........................	$8,203,000	
Add: Depreciation and amortization......	5,501,000	$13,704,000
From sale of common stock...............		12,547,000
From borrowing.........................		7,000,000
From sale of plant assets*................		83,000
Total Sources of Funds...............		$33,334,000

Uses of Funds:

To purchase plant assets.................	$18,082,000
To invest in associated companies..........	1,005,000
To retire preferred stock.................	224,000
To pay preferred dividends...............	40,000
To increase working capital...............	13,983,000
Total Uses of Funds.................	$33,334,000

* Original cost of property retired, $400,000; accumulated depreciation on these assets, $317,000, leaving a book value of $83,000 at the time of retirement. In the absence of further information, sale price has been assumed equal to book value. The amount is immaterial.

Chapter 17

17–11. *a*) Unit Cost = $25,632/9,800 = $2.62 per Unit.

b)

(1)	Work in Process—Job No. 103..................	13,860	
	Raw Materials Inventory....................		13,860
(2)	Work in Process—Job No. 103..................	4,300	
	Accrued Wages............................		4,300
(3)	Work in Process—Job No. 103..................	8,000	
	Manufacturing Overhead....................		8,000
(4)	Raw Materials Inventory.......................	528	
	Work in Process—Job No. 103...............		528
(5)	Finished Goods Inventory......................	25,632	
	Work in Process—Job No. 103..............		25,632

17–13. *a*)

(1)	Materials....................................	16,000	
	Accounts Payable........................		16,000
(2)	Direct Material..............................	18,000	
	Materials................................		18,000
(3)	Direct Labor................................	27,000	
	Accrued Wages Payable....................		27,000
(4)	Manufacturing Overhead......................	17,000	
	Accounts Payable, etc......................		17,000
(5)	Work in Process..............................	65,000	
	Direct Materials...........................		18,000
	Direct Labor..............................		27,000
	Manufacturing Overhead...................		20,000

(6) Finished Goods. 60,000
     Work in Process.   60,000
(7) Cost of Goods Sold. 57,000
     Finished Goods.   57,000

b) $57,000.

c) $3,000 overabsorbed.

d) $20,000.

17–16. *a*) Work in process, March 31: $10,000.

(Direct materials, $20,000, direct labor, $30,000, overhead absorbed, $15,000; less cost of goods finished, $60,000, equals $5,000 increase in work in process.)

b) Direct labor, January 1–31: $30,000.
Work in process, January 1: $4,500.

c) Overhead incurred, January 1–December 31: $17,000.

(Cost of sales, $29,000; underabsorbed overhead, $2,000.)

17–19. *a*) (1) Materials Inventory. 50,000
     Accounts Payable.   50,000

(2) Work in Process. 35,000
     Materials Inventory.   35,000

     Manufacturing Overhead. .12,000
     Materials Inventory.   12,000

(3) Work in Process. 20,000
     Wages Payable.   20,000

(4) Manufacturing Overhead.   500
     Wages Payable.   500

(5) Manufacturing Overhead. 30,000
     Liabilities.   30,000

     Work in Process. 40,000
     Manufacturing Overhead.   40,000

(6) Finished Goods. 86,000
     Work in Process.   86,000

b) Total debits to Manufacturing Overhead. $42,500
Credit to Manufacturing Overhead at $4 per direct
   labor hour.   40,000
     Underabsorbed Manufacturing Overhead. . . . .$ 2,500

c) Total debits to Manufacturing Overhead. $42,900
Credit to Manufacturing Overhead ($4 × 10,400) 41,600
     Underabsorbed Manufacturing Overhead. . . . .$ 1,300

Reduction in Underabsorbed Manufacturing Overhead:
   $2,500 − $1,300 = $1,200

Chapter 18

18–14. Normal burden rate per direct labor dollar:
     Fixed costs ($12,450/$15,000) = $0.83
     Variable costs. 1.15
     Total. $1.98

Absorbed cost $17,600 × 1.98...............$34,848
Budgeted cost $12,450 + $17,600 × 1.15...... 32,690
    Volume variance...................... $2,158 favorable
Actual cost................................ 33,150
    Overhead spending variance..............   460 unfavorable
Net Variance (Absorbed Minus Actual)....... $1,698 favorable

Sundry Accounts			Manufacturing Overhead			
(1)	33,150		(1)	33,150	(3)	32,690
					(4)	460

Overhead Absorbed			Overhead in Process	
(3)	32,690	(2) 34,848		
(5)	2,158		(2)	34,848

Volume Variance		Overhead Performance Variance	
(5)	2,158	(4)	460

18–19.

	Melting and Pouring	Molding	Core Making	Cleaning and Grinding
Indirect labor..............	$1,000	$300	$100	$300
Supplies used..............	50	50	200	100
Taxes:				
Machinery and equipment.	4	1	3	4
Building................	3	12	3	6
Compensation insurance.....	20	15	6	24
Power....................	10	x	10	30
Heat and light.............	10	40	10	20
Depreciation:				
Building................	8	32	8	16
Machinery..............	20	5	15	20
Total...................	$1,125	$455	$355	$520

18–20.

Building cost: $60,000 × $\dfrac{120 \text{ sq. ft.}}{75,000 \text{ sq. ft.}}$.....................$ 96

Depreciation on machine cost: $4,000 × 10%................... 400

Power charges: 20 × 2,500 hrs. × $.015...................... 750

Taxes.. 10

Insurance.. 12

Stores and supplies.. 38

Repairs.. 35

Tools and jigs... 169

Planning cost.. 69

Foremen... 131

Indirect labor.. 70

Total...$1,780

Normal machine-hours....................................... 2,500

Normal machine-hour rate (per machine-hour).................$0.712

NOTE: The number of hours worked in the previous year is irrelvant, since all significant factors have been considered in arriving at the normal work load—2,500 hours.

18–22. $10,000 of the underabsorbed overhead came from the misclassification of the machinery cost, and $3,000 from the misclassification of the president's salary. The entry to correct these two errors is:

Plant and Equipment...............................10,000

Administrative Salaries............................ 3,000

Work in Process............................... 1,560

Finished Goods................................ 2,600

Cost of Goods Sold............................ 8,840

No entry is required to correct the third error, although for data bank purposes the job order cost sheets should be corrected.

Chapter 19

19–11. *a)*

$$\text{Break-even Volume} = \frac{\$38,000}{\$6.20 - \$4.50} = 22,353 \text{ Units, or } \$138,589.$$

b)

$$\text{Desired Volume} = \frac{(\$160,000)(20\%) + \$38,000}{\$6.20 - \$4.50}$$

$$= 41,176 \text{ Units, or } \$355,291.$$

19–12.

		Revenue		Cost		Profit
At 75,000 units	at $2.50	$187,500	at $2.00	$150,000		$37,500
At 50,000 units	at $3.00	150,000	at $2.25	112,500		37,500
Incremental Revenue.......$ 37,500						
Incremental Cost..............................$ 37,500						
Incremental Profit...$ 0						

19–14. *a)*

$$\text{Break-even Volume} = \frac{\text{Total Fixed Costs}}{\text{Price} - \text{Variable Cost}}$$

$$= \frac{\$320,000}{\$3.20} = 100,000 \text{ Units.}$$

b) Desired Profit = $220,000 + $22,000 = $242,000.

New Variable Profit Ratio = $3.20 per Unit.

$$\text{Target Sales Volume} = \frac{\$242,000 + \$320,000}{\$3.20} = 175,625 \text{ Units.}$$

19–21.

Aviation gasoline: $\left(\dfrac{\$50,000}{\$460,000} \times \$440,000\right) \div 8,000 \text{ bbl.} = \$5.978$

Motor gasoline: $\left(\dfrac{\$210,000}{\$460,000} \times \$440,000\right) \div 42,000 \text{ bbl.} = \$4.783$

Kerosene: $\left(\dfrac{\$44,000}{\$460,000} \times \$440,000 \right) \div 10,000$ bbl. $= \$4.209$

Distillate fuels: $\left(\dfrac{\$80,000}{\$460,000} \times \$440,000 \right) \div 20,000$ bbl. $= \$3.826$

Lubricants: $\left(\dfrac{\$50,000}{\$460,000} \times \$440,000 \right) \div 5,000$ bbl. $= \$9.565$

Residual fuels: $\left(\dfrac{\$26,000}{\$460,000} \times \$440,000 \right) \div 10,000$ bbl. $= \$2.487$

19–25.

	Sheets (Doz.)	Gray Goods
Labor (excluding fixed labor costs)	$2.2540	$ 0.0614
Expenses of manufacturing (excluding fixed costs)	0.6762	0.0154
Process material	0.4092	0.0018
Raw material	2.8240	0.1131
Freight	0.0895	
Total Marginal Cost*	$6.2529	$ 0.1917
Selling price	7.5095	0.2250
Gain per unit	$1.2566	$ 0.0333
Number of units	× 27,000	900,000
Incremental Profit	$33,928	$ 29,970

* Selling and administrative costs are excluded on the grounds that such portions as are not fixed have already been incurred (sunk) by reason of the fact that the orders have been obtained.

Chapter 20

20–14.

Present acquisition cost of part: 6,000 at $0.50		$3,000
Proposed production cost (excluding depreciation) 6,000 at $0.20		1,200
Annual savings		$1,800
Present value of annuity of $1 in arrears for seven periods at 16%		4,039
Capitalized value of annual savings		$7,489
Cost of new machine		$7,000
Plus: Sale value of old machine		1,500
Investment Required to Produce Part		$8,500

The present value of the savings is less than the present value of the investment required. The part should continue to be purchased.

20–15. Initial outlay required for refunding:

Outlay to call present bond (1.07 × $500,000)	$535,000
Less: Proceeds from promissory note	500,000
Net before-tax outlay	$ 35,000
Less: Tax reduction (50% of loss on refunding)	17,500
After-Tax Cost of Refunding	$ 17,500

Annual savings in interest payments:

Mortgage bond interest	$25,000
Promissory note interest	20,000
Before-tax saving	$ 5,000

Less: Tax at 50%............................... 2,500
Annual After-Tax Savings.................... $ 2,500

Present value of the annual after-tax saving at 8%
for 10 years = $2,500 × 6.7101 = $ 16,775

Since the present value of the annual after-tax saving is less than
the after-tax cost of refunding, the company should not refund.

20–22. *a*) Cost of machine...................................... $100,000
Less: Tax reduction on portion expensed ($50,000)......... (25,000)
7% tax credit on portion capitalized................. (3,500)
Plus: Working capital required.......................... 10,000
Net Present Outlay.............................. $ 81,500

b)

	Year 1	Year 2
(1) Before-tax reduction in operating costs...........	$20,000	$20,000
(2) Cost subject to depreciation for tax purposes, beginning of year........................	$46,500	$34,875
(3) Tax-allowed depreciation [25% of (2)]..........	11,625	8,719
(4) Taxable saving [(1) − (3)]....................	8,375	11,281
(5) Tax [50% of (4)]............................	$ 4,188	$ 5,641
(6) After-tax cash flow [(1) − (5)]...............	$15,812	$14,359

20–23. *a*) Annual expenses (excluding depreciation):
At present............................... $17,400
After new installation....................... 7,400
Annual savings before tax................. $10,000
Present value of annuity of $1 in arrears
for 10 periods at 16%..................   4.833
Capitalized savings....................... $48,330
Net fund outflow required by new installation:
Invoice price of new machine................ $35,000
Incidental charges capitalized................. 5,000
Incidental charges expensed................... 10,000
Total............................... $50,000
Resale value of the old machine.............. 5,000
Net fund requirement......................   45,000
Excess of Capitalized Savings over Required In-
vestment..................................... $ 3,330

Therefore, at a 16 percent rate of return before tax, the new
installation is justified.

b)

	Years 1–7	Years 8–10
Annual cash flow before tax [see (*a*)]...........	$ 10,000	$ 10,000
Change in taxable income due to change in tax depreciation.........................	+ 1,000	−4,000
Total effect on taxable income...........	$ 11,000	$ 6,000
Tax at 50%.....................................	5,500	3,000
Annual cash flow after tax...................	$ 4,500	$ 7,000
Present value at 10%.........................	$21,908	$ 8,933

Net fund outflow required by new
    installation:
Net fund requirement for purchasing
    new machine [see (*a*)].............. $45,000
    Decreased tax burden for capital loss:
        Cost of old machine..................$50,000
        Accumulated depreciation............ 15,000
        Book value of old machine...........$35,000
        Resale value of old machine.......... 5,000
        Capital loss........................$30,000
        Tax rate........................... 50%
        Tax deduction on capital loss.........$15,000
    Decreased tax burden for expensed in-
        stallation charges, $10,000 at 50%... 5,000   20,000
              Net fund outflow................   25,000
Excess of capitalized savings over
    required investment.................. $ 5,841

Therefore the project is also profitable under a 10 percent after-tax rate of return requirement.

20–25. *a*) Present outlay:
    Cost of machine............................. $50,000
    Less: Sale value of old machine................$10,000
        Tax reduction on retirement loss on
            old machine...................... 10,000   20,000
        Net present outlay....................... $30,000
    Present value at 10% of after-tax future cash
        savings (see table below)..................   68,453
        Net Present Value......................   +$38,453

CALCULATION OF DISCOUNTED CASH FLOWS FROM INVESTMENT DECISION

(1) Years Hence	(2) Net Book Value of New Machine	(3) Tax Depreciation	(4) Depreciation on old Machine	(5) Increase in Depreciation	(6) Taxable Income	(7) Income Tax	(8) After Tax Cash Flow	(9) Present Value at 10%
1.......	$50,000	$10,000	$ 3,750	$ 6,250	$ 13,750	$ 6,875	$ 13,125	$11,932
2.......	40,000	8,000	3,750	4,250	15,750	7,875	12,125	10,020
3.......	32,000	6,400	3,750	2,650	17,350	8,675	11,325	8,508
4.......	25,600	5,120	3,750	1,370	18,630	9,315	10,685	7,298
5.......	20,480	4,096	3,750	346	19,654	9,827	10,173	6,316
6.......	16,384	3,277	3,750	− 473	20,473	10,237	9,763	5,511
7.......	13,107	2,621	3,750	− 1,129	21,129	10,564	9,436	4,843
8.......	10,486	2,097	3,750	− 1,653	21,653	10,826	9,174	4,280
9.......	8,389	1,678	....	1,678	18,322	9,161	10,839	4,597
10......	6,711	1,342	....	1,342	} 13,289	6,645	13,355	5,148
10......	5,369	5,369	....	5,369				
Total....		$50,000	$30,000	$20,000	$180,000	$90,000	$110,000	$68,453

Derivation of amounts in columns (3) through (9):
    (3) 20% of (2).
    (4) 12.5% of $30,000 (remaining book value).
    (5) Col. 4–col. 3.
    (6) $20,000 cash flow less increase in depreciation (col. 5).
    (7) 50% of col. 6.
    (8) $20,000 less col. 7.
    (9) Col. 8 × Table 3, Appendix A.

b) To find the internal rate of return, discount the cash flows in column 8 above, first at 40% and then at 50%:

Year	Cash Flow	Present Value	
		at 40%	at 50%
0	−30,000	−30,000	−30,000
1	+13,125	+ 9,371	+ 8,754
2	+12,125	+ 8,657	+ 5,384
3	+11,325	+ 4,122	+ 3,352
4	+10,685	+ 2,778	+ 2,116
5	+10,173	+ 1,892	+ 1,343
6	+ 9,763	+ 1,298	+ 859
7	+ 9,436	+ 896	+ 557
8	+ 9,174	+ 624	+ 358
9	+10,839	+ 520	+ 282
10	+13,355	+ 467	+ 227
Total		+ 625	− 6,768

The internal rate of return is thus approximately 40.8%.

Chapter 21

21–12. Let x be the quantity of material required to produce 6.3 lbs. of product:

$$(x - 0.1x)\ (0.5) = 6.3 \qquad x = 6.3/0.45 = 14 \text{ lbs. of material}$$

Input: 14 lbs. at $1	$14.00
Less scrap: 1.4 lbs. at $0.10	0.14
Net cost of 6.3 lbs. of product	$13.86
Cost per pound	$2.20

21–13. Labor usage variance:

1500 units of A @ 2 hours = 3,000 hours @ $3	$ 9,000
4000 units of B @ 3 hours = 12,000 hours @ $3	36,000
Standard usage of labor	$45,000
Actual usage of labor 14,500 hours @ $3	43,500
Favorable usage variance	$1,500

Labor rate variance:

Standard cost of labor worked: 14,500 hours @ $3	$43,500
Actual payroll	44,000
Unfavorable rate variance	(500)
Net Labor Variance	$1,000

21–17. *a*)

	Unfavorable	Favorable
Material price variance	$6	
Labor rate variance	2	
Material usage variance	5	
Labor usage variance		$3

b)

Misc. Credits			Raw Material				Material in Process			
	(1)	106	(1)	100	(2)	105	(2)	105	(4)	85
	(3*b*)	70							(6*a*)	5
									Bal.	15
					Bal.	15				

Payroll Costs					Labor in Process			
(3*b*)	70	(3*a*)	68	(3*a*)	68	(4)	63
		(3*c*)	2	(6*b*)	3	Bal.	8
				Bal.	8		

Variances				Finished Goods	
(1) MPV	6	(6*b*) LUV	3	(4)	148
(3*c*) LRV	2				
(6*a*) MUV	5				

21–20. *a*)
Material price variance.........................$2,240 favorable
Wage rate variance........................... (800) unfavorable
Material usage variance....................... (700) unfavorable
Labor usage variance......................... 1,000 favorable
Net Variance.............................$1,740 favorable

Raw Material and Supplies					Material in Process			
Bal. 9/1	58,500	(5)	46,650	Bal. 9/1	6,700	(3)	40,350
(2)	44,620	Bal. 10/1	56,470	(5)	46,650	(6)	700
						Bal. 10/1	12,300
Bal. 10/1	56,470						
				Bal. 10/1	12,300		

Labor in Process					Accrued Wages			
Bal. 9/1	2,400	(3)	22,300	(8)	23,600	(4)	23,600
(4)	23,600						
(6)	1,000	Bal. 10/1	4,700				
Bal. 10/1	4,700						

Control		
	Bal. 9/1	102,700
	(2)	42,380
Bal. 10/1 169,480	(8)	24,400
	Bal. 10/1	169,480

Finished Goods			
Bal. 9/1	32,100	(7)	63,500
(3)	62,650	Bal. 10/1	31,250
Bal. 10/1	31,250		

Cost of Goods Sold	
(7)	63,500

Material Price Variance

		(2)	2,240

Labor Usage Variance

		(6)	1,000

Material Usage Variance

(6)	700		

Wage Rate Variance

(8)	800		

21–22.

Raw Materials and Supplies

Bal. 5/1	29,460	(2)	41,300
(1)	37,900	Bal. 6/1	26,060
Bal. 6/1	26,060		

Material in Process

Bal. 5/1	18,400	(4)	42,600
(2)	41,300	(6a)	1,900
		Bal. 6/1	15,200
Bal. 6/1	15,200		

Labor in Process

Bal. 5/1	9,650	(4)	28,300
(3)	28,400		
(6b)	1,250	Bal. 6/1	11,000
Bal. 6/1	11,000		

Accrued Wages

(7)	32,180	Bal. 5/1	1,620
		(3)	28,400
		(8)	2,160

Finished Goods

Bal. 5/1	35,000	(5)	79,200
(4)	70,900	Bal. 6/1	26,700
Bal. 6/1	26,700		

Control

		Bal. 5/1	90,890
		(1)	36,500
Bal. 6/1	159,570	(7)	32,180
		Bal. 6/1	159,570

Cost of Goods Sold

(5)	79,200		

Material Price Variance

(9a)	1,400	(1)	1,400

Variance Summary

(9b)MUV	1,900	(9a)MPV	1,400
(9d)WRV	2,160	(9c)LUV	1,250
(unfavorable)		(favorable)	

Material Usage Variance

(6a)	1,900	(9b)	1,900

Labor Usage Variance

(9c)	1,250	(6b)	1,250

Wage Rate Variance

(8)	2,160	(9d)	2,160

Chapter 22

22–18. *a*) Machine-hours transferred out.........................15,000 hours
Add: Hours in process, end of month................... 1,400
Less: Hours in process, start of month................. (3,000)
Machine-Hours Worked during Month.............13,400 hours

b) Standard hours transferred out: $69,000/$3..............23,000 hours
Add: Standard hours in process, end of month: $18,000/$3.. 6,000
Less: Standard hours in process, start of month: $16,200/$3 . (5,400)
Standard Labor Hours Worked during Month........23,600 hours

22–23. *a*) (1) Raw Materials Inventory....................160,000
Accounts Payable......................   154,000
Materials Price Variance................   6,000
(2) Work in Process—Materials.................144,000
Raw Materials Inventory................   144,000
(3) Work in Process—Labor.................... 93,625
Labor Rate Variance........................ 2,675
Wages Payable.........................   96,300
(4) Manufacturing Overhead..................... 20,500
Vouchers Payable.....................   20,500
(5) Finished goods—firsts.......................218,400
Finished goods—seconds................... 10,500
Loss on seconds........................... 3,150
Work in Process—Material..............   122,400
Work in Process—Labor...............   89,250
Work in Process—Overhead.............   20,400
(5*a*) Manufacturing Overhead.................... 3,150
Loss on Seconds......................   3,150
(6) Material Usage Variance................... 7,200
Work in Process—Materials............   7,200
(7) Work in Process—Labor................... 2,625
Labor Usage Variance.................   2,625

	Material in Process	Labor in Process
Input during the month.....	$144,000	$93,625
Output during the month...	$122,400	$89,250
In process inventory at standard............	14,400	7,000
Total...................	$136,800	$96,250
Variance—debit (credit) ...	$ 7,200	$(2,625)

(8) Work in Process—Overhead................ 22,000*
      Manufacturing Overhead...............   22.000

      * Standard cost of work completed: 5,100 at $4 + ⅔ of 600 at $4 = $22,000.

(9) Overhead Performance Variance.............. 2,450
      Overhead Volume Variance.............   800
      Manufacturing Overhead...............   1,650

Overhead, actual....................... $23,650 ⎫ Spending
Overhead, budgeted $2.40 × 5,500†   ⎬ Variance $2,450
    + $8,000 = ... 21,200 ⎭

          Output   *Ending Inv.*   ⎫ Volume
          ───────   ─────────   ⎬ Variance (800)
Overhead, absorbed $20,400 + $1,600 = $22,000 ⎭

      Net Variance... $1,650

      † 4,800 Firsts + 300 seconds + 400 ending inventory (⅔ of 600) = 5,500.

b) Variances:

Direct costs:
      Material price variance........................ $6,000 favorable
      Labor rate variance........................... 2,675 unfavorable
      Material usage variance....................... 7,200 unfavorable
      Labor usage variance.......................... 2,625 favorable
Overhead:
      Spending variance............................. 2,450 unfavorable
      Volume variance.............................. 800 favorable

22–24. *a)* Direct labor cost transferred out........................... $24,000
      Plus: End of month balance............................... 5,400
      Less: Start of month balance............................. 8,000
      Standard labor cost of work done...................... $21,400

b)

Materials Inventory

Bal. 1/1	76,000	(4)	21,500
(1)	50,000	Bal. 2/1	104,500
Bal. 2/1	104,500		

Materials in Process—Dept. Y

Bal. 1/1	13,000	(6)	25,000
(4)	17,000	(7a)	900
		Bal. 2/1	4,100
Bal. 2/1	4,100		

Labor in Process—Dept. Y

Bal. 1/1	8,000	(6)	24,000
(3a)	20,000		
(7b)	1,400	Bal. 2/1	5,400
Bal. 2/1	5,400		

Overhead in Process—Dept. Y

Bal. 1/1	12,000	(6)	36,000
(8)	32,100	Bal. 2/1	8,100
Bal. 2/1	8,100		

Head Office Control				Overhead—Dept. Y				

(6)	85,000	Bal. 1/1	109,000	(3b)	8,700	(8)	32,100
		(1)	48,800	(4)	4,500		
		(2)	29,700	(5)	15,000		
Bal. 2/1	117,500	(5)	15,000	(9)	3,900		

		Bal. 2/1	117,500

Variances

Accrued Wages

(7a)MUV	900	(1)MPV	1,200
(10)LRV	1,000	(7b)LUV	1,400
(9)OHSV	500	(9)OHVV	4,400

(2)	29,700	(3a)	20,000
		(3b)	8,700
		(10)	1,000

SCHEDULE OF VARIANCES

	Unfavorable	*Favorable*
Material price variance......................		$1,200
Material usage variance......................	$ 900	
Labor rate variance.........................	1,000	
Labor usage variance........................		1,400
Overhead spending variance..................	500	
Overhead volume variance....................		4,400

Derivation of overhead variances:

Actual overhead..........................	$28,200	
Budget: $17,000 + $0.50 × 21,400 standard direct labor cost of output...........	27,700	
Unfavorable spending variance..........		$ 500
Absorbed: Transferred out.....$36,000		
Plus end of month balance..... 8,100		
Less start of month balance.... (12,000)	32,100	
Favorable volume variance.............		4,400

Chapter 23

23–13. Budgeted profit margin per unit:

Sales..	$6.00
Direct materials.....................................	$1.00
Direct labor..	1.30
Variable overhead...................................	0.52
Fixed overhead......................................	0.78
Profit Margin.......................................	$2.40

Variance analysis:

Increased sales volume: 1,000 × $2.40* =	$ 2,400	favorable
Factory overhead volume variance*..............	780	favorable
Reduced price: 11,000 × $0.50 =	(5,500)	unfavorable
Materials usage variance......................	(200)	unfavorable
Labor usage variance.........................	(400)	unfavorable
Overhead spending variance....................	(580)	unfavorable
Selling and administrative expense variance........	(500)	unfavorable
Total Variance..........................	$(4,000)	

* Can be combined in a single figure.

23–16. *a*) (1) Actual...$1,000
        Total variance................................   100 favorable
            Absorbed..................................$1,100
        Volume variance.............................   20 favorable
            Budget....................................$1,080
        Spending variance............................   80 favorable
    (2) Budgeted fixed cost: $1,080 − 30% of $1,100 = $750
    (3) Variable cost:
            Labor......................$400
            Materials.................. 100
            Overhead (30%)............. 330
                Total....................$830 = 830/1,600 of product cost

            830/1,600 × $1,760 = $913
            Selling expense (4%)........   80
                Total Variable.............$993

        Variable profit = $2,000 − $993 = $1,007 = 50.35%.

  b) Sales.. $2,000
    Variable costs:
        Manufacturing.................................$913
        Selling.......................................   80   993
    Variable profit.................................... $1,007
    Traceable fixed costs:
        Manufacturing.................................$750
        Selling and administrative.......................   55   805
    Spending variance (favorable).......................   (80)
        Profit Contribution............................ $ 282

Index

INDEX

839

This book has been set in 11 and 10 point Janson, leaded 2 points. Part numbers are in 30 and 42 point Weiss Series I, roman and italic; part titles are in 30 point Weiss Series I italic. Chapter numbers are in 24 and 42 Weiss Series I, roman and italic; chapter titles are in 18 point Spartan Medium. The size of the type page is 27 × 46 picas.